AF836187

The Baron and the Marquis

Also by John D. Bessler

Death in the Dark:
Midnight Executions in America

Kiss of Death:
America's Love Affair with the Death Penalty

Legacy of Violence:
Lynch Mobs and Executions in Minnesota

Writing for Life:
The Craft of Writing for Everyday Living

Cruel and Unusual:
The American Death Penalty and the Founders' Eighth Amendment

The Birth of American Law:
An Italian Philosopher and the American Revolution

Against the Death Penalty (editor)

The Death Penalty as Torture:
From the Dark Ages to Abolition

The Celebrated Marquis:
An Italian Noble and the Making of the Modern World

The Baron and the Marquis:

LIBERTY, TYRANNY, AND THE ENLIGHTENMENT MAXIM THAT CAN REMAKE AMERICAN CRIMINAL JUSTICE

John D. Bessler

Associate Professor of Law
University of Baltimore School of Law

Adjunct Professor
Georgetown University Law Center

Carolina Academic Press
Durham, North Carolina

ISBN 978-1-5310-1305-9
e-ISBN 978-1-5310-1306-6

Library of Congress Cataloging-in-Publication Data
Names: Bessler, John D., author.
Title: The baron and the marquis : liberty, tyranny, and the enlightenment maxim that can remake American criminal justice / by John D. Bessler.
Description: Durham, North Carolina : Carolina Academic Press, LLC, [2018]
Identifiers: LCCN 2018044706 | ISBN 9781531013059 (alk. paper)
Subjects: LCSH: Punishment—United States—History. | Legal maxims—United States—History. | Criminal justice, Administration of—United States. | United States. Constitution. 8th Amendment | Enlightenment—United States—History. | Civil rights—France—History. | Despotism—History. | Liberty.
Classification: LCC KF9225 .B49 2018 | DDC 345.73/0773--dc23

Carolina Academic Press, LLC
700 Kent Street
Durham, North Carolina 27701
Telephone (919) 489-7486
Fax (919) 493-5668
www.cap-press.com

Printed in the United States of America

From the past, for the present, about the future—

To a new American Enlightenment . . .

Baron de Montesquieu

Marquis of Beccaria

Every punishment, which does not arise from absolute necessity, says the great *Montesquieu*, is tyrannical. A proposition which may be made more general, thus. "Every act of authority of one man over another, for which there is not an absolute necessity, is tyrannical." It is upon this then, that the sovereign's right to punish crimes is founded; that is, upon the necessity of defending the public liberty, entrusted to his care, from the usurpation of individuals; and punishments are just in proportion, as the liberty, preserved by the sovereign, is sacred and valuable.

—Cesare Beccaria, *An Essay on Crimes and Punishments**

If men were angels, no government would be necessary. If angels were to govern men, neither external nor internal controls on government would be necessary. In framing a government which is to be administered by men over men, the great difficulty lies in this: you must first enable the government to control the governed; and in the next place oblige it to control itself. A dependence on the people is, no doubt, the primary control on the government; but experience has taught mankind the necessity of auxiliary precautions.

—"Publius," *The Federalist No. 51* (1788)**

If Montesquieu had not written, the distinction between the three powers of government would be yet unknown, and their limits undefined. If Beccaria had not written, the torture and its horrid concomitants would not have disappeared from the face of Europe, and sanguinary codes would not almost every where have given way to mild punishments.

—Peter Stephen Du Ponceau, Provost of the Law Academy of Philadelphia (1824)***

* An Essay on Crimes and Punishments, Translated from the Italian, with a Commentary Attributed to Mons. De Voltaire, Translated from the French (4th ed. 1775). The above excerpt is reprinted from Chapter 2, "*Of the Right to punish*," of the 1775 London edition of the Italian *philosophe* Cesare Beccaria's *An Essay on Crimes and Punishments*, a book owned by John Adams. That book, now in the Boston Public Library's rare book collection, was gifted by John Adams to his son, Thomas, as reflected in the handwritten notation, "Thomas B. Adams, From his Father, 1800," on the book's title page. Catalogue of the John Adams Library in the Public Library of the City of Boston 23 (1917). The underlining in the above excerpt is found in that book, which bears the Coat of Arms of John Adams. That Coat of Arms bears the Latin inscription "*Libertatem / Amicitiam / Retinebis / Et Fidem*," which translates as "You will retain liberty, friendship, and faith." Adolph Caso, We, the People . . . : Formative Documents of America's Democracy (2011).

** *The Federalist No. 51*, "To the People of the State of New York" (Feb. 6, 1788), *reprinted in* James Q. Wilson, John J. DiIulio, Jr. & Meena Bose, American Government: Institutions and Policies: The Essentials A27 (13th ed. 2013). *The Federalist No. 51* has been attributed to either James Madison or Alexander Hamilton, though "[t]he internal evidence presented by Edward G. Bourne ('The Authorship of the Federalist,' *The American Historical Review*, II [April, 1897], 449-51), strongly indicates Madison's authorship. Bourne printed in parallel columns sentences from essay 51 which correspond very closely, sometimes exactly, to earlier writings by Madison." 4 Harold C. Syrett & Jacob E. Cooke, eds., The Papers of Alexander Hamilton 497 (1962).

*** Peter S. Du Ponceau, A Dissertation on the Nature and Extent of the Jurisdiction of the Courts of the United States, Being a Valedictory Address Delivered to the Students of the Law Academy of Philadelphia, at the Close of the Academic Year, on 22d April, 1824, at 131 (1824).

Contents

About the Author

John D. Bessler teaches at the University of Baltimore School of Law and the Georgetown University Law Center. He is also of counsel at the Minneapolis law firm of Berens & Miller, P.A., which handles complex, commercial litigation. A two-time Minnesota Book Award finalist and the winner of an *Independent Publisher* Book Award, he is the author of multiple books on the subject of capital punishment. His 2014 book about Cesare Beccaria's influence on America's founders, *The Birth of American Law: An Italian Philosopher and the American Revolution*, was the gold winner of the IndieFab Book of the Year Award for history and received the first prize in the 2015 American Association for Italian Studies Book Award contest for a work focused on the eighteenth and nineteenth centuries. *The Birth of American Law* also won the prestigious Scribes Book Award, an annual award given out by The American Society of Legal Writers since 1961 for "the best work of legal scholarship published during the previous year." His new biography of Beccaria, *The Celebrated Marquis: An Italian Noble and the Making of the Modern World*, won the 2018 Next Generation Indie Book Award for biography and was a National Indie Excellence Awards finalist in that genre. He has also taught at the University of Minnesota Law School, The George Washington University Law School, Rutgers School of Law, and the University of Aberdeen in Scotland. In 2018, he was a visiting scholar at the Human Rights Center of the University of Minnesota Law School and received the University System of Maryland Regents' Faculty Award for Excellence in Scholarship, Research, or Creative Activity.

Acknowledgments

I live within walking distance of Open Book, a quiet, brick-and-mortar sanctuary in the City of Minneapolis for writers, editors, book artists, and the general public. The Open Book's building on Washington Avenue, on the edge of downtown Minneapolis not far from the Mississippi River, houses The Loft Literary Center, the Minnesota Center for Book Arts ("MCBA"), and a tiny new bookstore, Milkweed Books, part of a vibrant and extraordinary collection of local organizations and community gathering places that cultivate the literary arts. The coffee shop at Open Book, wedged between The Shop at MCBA and Milkweed's delightful, 750-square-foot bookshop, is the perfect spot for inspiration, daydreaming and contemplation, and, of course, writing.

After a recent, weekend stroll across the Mississippi River's iconic Stone Arch Bridge to Open Book for a little quality time with my laptop, I picked up a copy of a lovely book, Ella Frances Sanders' *The Illustrated Book of Sayings: Curious Expressions from Around the World*, at The Shop at MCBA. That fantastic, eye-pleasing shop bills itself as "a haven for the unabashedly bookish," and it is filled with products of wordsmiths and creativity: authors' broadsides, limited-edition poetry collections, fine art prints, greeting cards, zines, art supplies and marbled papers, colored pens and pencils, and hand-stitched artists' books. *The Illustrated Book of Sayings* is a wonderful, whimsically illustrated collection of more than fifty expressions from around the globe. And some of those sayings, it turns out, are actually quite well suited to the creation of a book and to the ebb and flow—to the inevitable trial-and-error and put-a-comma-in-one-day-take-a-comma-out-the-next—of the writing and revision processes.

From the looks of it, *The Illustrated Book of Sayings* was clearly a labor of love for its creator. It is a coffee-table-worthy book that imparts little, bite-size nuggets of wisdom. The Japanese "even monkeys fall from trees," Sanders writes of one of the sayings, is a pointed way "of pointing out that everybody gets it wrong sometimes." That's a good, healthy, and humbling reminder for anyone, especially a writer struggling—and earnestly trying and toiling away—to craft, appropriately structure, and put together a readable book. And the fabulous French idiom *pédaler dans la choucroute* ("To pedal in the sauerkraut"), she explains in another short description, "means to be at a complete loss or to have lost the train of one's thoughts." It can mean, she says of the feeling that is, sadly, all too familiar to writers, "that something is no longer progressing," "that the wheels are spinning." That quirky French idiom's origins, Sanders relays, "comes from the early Tour de France races" in which "[t]he broom wagons—the vehicles that follow cyclists and pick up stragglers or those who are unable to finish the race within the allotted time—often featured billboards advertising sauerkraut."

One of my personal favorites from *The Illustrated Book of Sayings*: the Bulgarian "drop by drop, a whole lake becomes." That expression is, frankly, extremely *apropos* to an always-try-to-be-a-glass-half-full writer like me. "Little by little, humans can accomplish almost anything," Sanders observes of that powerful proverb's not-so-subtle meaning, providing excellent and sage advice for how to be patient as one goes about writing and editing a book. Other favorites of mine from Sanders' 2016 compilation, published by Ten Speed Press, for the "logophiles" and "linguists" she aims to reach: the Italian *avere grilli per la testa* ("To have a head full of crickets"), about having whimsical daydreams and flights of fancy amid big, high-leaping ambitions; the Turkish *üzüm üzüme baka baka kararir* ("grapes darken by looking at each other"), reflecting the idea that we mature by learning from those around us; the English "Mind your P's and Q's," a reminder to proofread carefully; and the delightful Spanish saying *tu eres mi media naranja* ("you are my orange half"), said to be "an informal, affectionate way" of referring to someone "as your soul mate or the love of your life."

Every writer needs encouragement, support, and good cheer over the course of writing a book, so the Spanish phrase of endearment goes to Amy, my beautiful, quick-witted wife, and to Abigail, our lovely, generous, and equally funny, whip-smart daughter. While I plodded along on my own on a daily basis to create *The Baron and the Marquis*, trying to connect one idea to another as they raced through my head at Mach 5 speed, often all at once, I got lots of help and guidance, some solicited and some not. That material assistance came from a host of fellow scholars and colleagues, from close friends, and even from total strangers in faraway lands via e-mail. These acts of human kindness, both big and small, made it possible—and at times, downright enjoyable—for me to finish the book you are now holding in your hands. At one lovely dinner in Minneapolis with Vivian Mason, the widow of Jack Mason, the late U.S. Magistrate Judge I had the honor to clerk for in the mid-1990s, I tapped the experience—and picked up some terrific leads—from Jack's son, Peter, and his wife, Melinda, as well as from Lane Ayers, a former prosecutor and public defender and—in his retirement—the Director of Books for Africa's Jack Mason Law & Democracy Initiative.

While many fiction writers pick a universal theme (love, good vs. evil, etc.) and aim to write what they hope will become the Great American Novel or an international or *New York Times* bestseller, this non-fiction book is intentionally built around (as strange as it sounds) a now obscure eighteenth-century *legal maxim*: that any punishment that does not arise from necessity is tyrannical. That maxim originated with the Baron de Montesquieu in France in the late 1740s; it then got popularized in the decades that followed, including in the 1760s by an Italian aristocrat, the Marquis of Beccaria. Although the maxim has largely been forgotten in modern American life, it articulates a principle that is eminently worthy of study and examination. The dividing line between tyranny and liberty is one that was of great concern to America's founders and framers, and that dividing line—set forth in the maxim in memorable language—should be of equal concern to modern-day American citizens.

This is especially so since Americans are now living in the Age of Mass Incarceration—the terminology used by sociologists, criminologists, and others to describe the marked increase in people serving time in American prisons. That verbiage, for example, shows up in the subtitle of an actual *New York Times* bestseller: Michelle Alexander's *The New Jim Crow: Mass Incarceration in the Age of Colorblindness.* It also shows up in John Pfaff's *Locked In: The True Causes of Mass Incarceration and How to Achieve Real Reform* (2017), a book that points out—rounding up a bit—that "the United States is home to 5 percent of the world's population but 25 percent of its prisoners." An April 2015 fact check done by the *Washington Post* of that widely cited statistic (I, myself, have heard TV talking heads use it) pointed out that, as of July 4, 2014, per U.S. Census data, the U.S. population was 319 million, accounting for roughly 4.4 percent of the world's approximately 7.1 billion people. As regards the second half of the statistic, the *Washington Post* observed that the U.K.-based International Centre for Prison Studies—reportedly "the go-to source for the breakdown of global prison populations"—had, in the 10th edition of its World Prison Population List, analyzed global data from September 2011 through September 2013. That data revealed that there were 2.24 million prisoners in the U.S. as of December 31, 2011, accounting for approximately 22 percent of the global prison population (10.2 million). The *Washington Post* further noted in its April 2015 fact check that "[a]bout half of the prisoners in the world were in the United States, Russia or China."

These days, criminal justice reform is—perhaps not surprisingly given those very stark and startling figures—an extremely hot topic in the United States. And that is true across the political spectrum, with groups and individuals as diverse as the American Civil Liberties Union and the Koch brothers weighing in on penal reform. "It makes a lot more sense for us to be investing in jobs and education rather than jails and incarceration," former Democratic presidential candidate and U.S. Senator Bernie Sanders, of Vermont, has argued. Senator Cory Booker, the Democrat of New Jersey, has also decried mass incarceration, sentencing disparities between crack and powder cocaine, and practices such as juvenile solitary confinement. One of his Republican colleagues, the junior U.S. Senator from Kentucky, Rand Paul, has likewise observed, if somewhat less stridently: "The United States has the highest incarceration rate in the world. Many of those people deserve to be in prison; however, some of them do not." While another Republican senator, Rob Portman, has called for more money for prevention and education to combat drug use (and for less money to be spent on prosecution and incarceration in that arena), journalist Nicholas Kristof—a progressive commentator who has won two Pulitzer Prizes—has framed the criminal justice crisis this way: "Since the end of the 1970s, something has gone profoundly wrong in America. Inequality has soared. Educational progress slowed. Incarceration rates quintupled. Family breakdown accelerated. Median household income stagnated."

Given all of the facts, and everything that has been said about American criminal justice, it is certainly worth exploring whether a bit of eighteenth-century wisdom might suggest a better way forward for American law, culture, and society. *The Baron and the Marquis*, a study of the necessity-for-punishment principle developed by a famous Frenchman and then promoted by a now much less well-known Italian aristocrat, does just that. Because the book focuses on criminal justice reform efforts during the Enlightenment *and* at present, it was particularly pleasing to encounter so many legal scholars, historians, and practicing lawyers who were passionate about both as I researched and wrote the book. At a recent conference of the Southeastern Association of Law Schools ("SEALS"), I got a chance to participate on panels on the U.S. Constitution's Eighth Amendment and about the death penalty—two topics that are of considerable importance to the debate over criminal justice reform.

Good ideas get better when you engage in dialogue with other experts, and bad ideas—at least that's the hope—get jettisoned through rigorous debate and intellectual exchange. To regularly meet people who share a passion for history and the principal subject of this book—*American* criminal justice reform—was, in fact, a very gratifying and reassuring experience as I toiled away on the book project week after week. For all those who, through their time or their own advocacy, writings, or scholarship, have made a difference or smoothed my own path in some way, shape, or form, I am very thankful, for it made the journey all the more pleasant and worthwhile. Plenty of books, articles, and op-eds have already argued persuasively for the need for criminal justice reform, and these should certainly be sought out and consulted by anyone interested more in this topic. *The Baron and the Marquis*, on the other hand, seeks to lay the underlying intellectual foundation for such reform efforts even as it attempts to make its own modest suggestions for change.

Every writer—to paraphrase Isaac Newton—sees a little further by standing on the shoulders of giants. For such criminal justice pioneers and prior penal reformers, I am, of course, extremely grateful. This book simply could not have been written without the benefit of all that talent, energy, and scholarship, and all of the studies and reports that have been published in the past few decades. And it most definitely could not have been written without the prior digitization of rare books and old newspaper articles, thus making those sources more easily accessible. All of the data, information, and analysis I located, whether from recent articles or old, searchable databases, informs *The Baron and the Marquis*, an exposé of days gone by but also of the present-day criminal justice system (with an ever-present eye on the future, of course). As the twentieth-century American writer William Arthur Ward, a columnist for the *Fort Worth Star-Telegram*, once offered in his own show of indebtedness: "Gratitude can transform common days into thanksgivings, turn routine jobs into joy, and change ordinary opportunities into blessings." Or as Voltaire, who opposed superstition, barbaric punishments, and religious intolerance, and who became famous for works such as *Candide* (1759) and *Dictionnaire philosophique* (1764), put it: "Appreciation is a wonderful thing. It makes what is excellent in others belong to us as well."

Intellectual and academic endeavors, like most things in life, are reliant on building upon the perceptive, sometimes transformative, ideas of others, so there are always plenty of people to thank and acknowledge by the time a book is finished. In this case, I am particularly grateful to a group of fantastic students I taught during the summer of 2017 at the University of Aberdeen in Scotland, an institution of higher learning that dates back to 1495, the year of its founding. I had a chance to teach a comparative criminal law course that summer, and the nearly twenty students I co-taught with Dr. Susan Stokeld, of the University of Aberdeen, wrote on a wide array of topics. That class, which looked at differences in American and European sentencing policies and approaches to criminality, opened my eyes to the problem of unnecessary punishments and the possibilities for American criminal justice reform. The study of other countries' legal systems—in particular, the big differences in approaches to crime-and-justice issues (say, for example, between Scandinavia and the United States)—makes it clear that no one path is inevitable.

The summer class in Aberdeen—the Granite City—allowed me to explore how U.S. sentencing policy has, over time, diverged quite dramatically from the practices of other Western representative democracies. One of the guest lecturers that particularly impressed me: Scotland's dynamic Karyn McCluskey. She has devoted her adult life to focusing on criminal justice reform, taking on street crime and Glasgow's gangs, and she forthrightly sees violence as a public health issue. She gave our class a particularly inspiring presentation on the interconnectivity of social problems and crime. Recently tapped to lead Community Justice Scotland, that organization—under her leadership—has a simple, clearly stated, and very focused and admirable goal: "WE WANT SCOTLAND TO BE THE SAFEST COUNTRY IN THE WORLD." That goal—which might be reframed as making one's own country the safest in the world—is one that *every* nation in the world, including the U.S., should earnestly work toward and strive to achieve. Crime is undesirable and destructive, and every country's leaders should want to do whatever they can to combat it.

At the outset, I also need to extend a special thank you to two prominent Eighth Amendment scholars, Professor William Berry at the University of Mississippi School of Law and Professor Meghan Ryan at the Southern Methodist University Dedman School of Law. Their invitation for me to participate in the SEALS conference and to contribute a book chapter on the Eighth Amendment's history, a subject I'd explored extensively in a prior book, got me thinking again in earnest about the U.S. Constitution's Eighth Amendment, especially in light of all the writing I'd been doing since finishing that earlier book, *Cruel and Unusual: The American Death Penalty and the Founders' Eighth Amendment* (2012). I'd been writing more recently about capital punishment, about all the psychological torture associated with death sentences and executions, and about the Italian philosopher and criminal-law theorist Cesare Beccaria, though the subjects are, in reality, all connected.

In 1764, in addition to denouncing torture, Beccaria became the first Enlightenment thinker to make a comprehensive case against the death penalty. And it was Beccaria who, inspired by Montesquieu, the French jurist, had popularized the necessity-for-punishment maxim that I'd frequently run across in writing about the Eighth Amendment and in preparing a new biography of Beccaria. That maxim (one of many from that era) forms the core of—is, it could be said, at the very heart and soul of—*The Baron and the Marquis*. It was, in effect, through the thoughtful generosity of two colleagues at other institutions, that the concept for this new book began to percolate in my mind along with what began as the kernel of an idea for a promised new book chapter. One project frequently builds upon another, and that certainly proved to be the case here. The fact that Professor Berry and Professor Ryan brought together such an extraordinary group of scholars for the discussion of the Eighth Amendment at the SEALS conference was, frankly, icing on the cake.

Another academic conference—one held in Indianapolis and hosted by the Liberty Fund and attended by Terry Anker, one of my law school classmates from Indiana University—also gave me the opportunity to reflect anew on the principle of liberty as I read the well-assembled packet of readings, ranging from Thucydides to Machiavelli's *The Prince* to Montaigne. That 2018 conference, titled "Moral Ideals, Political Necessities, and Liberty," allowed me to look with new eyes at the draft book manuscript that, in time, became this printed book. To Professor John Kekes for assembling the readings and moderating the conference, and to my long-time friend, Terry, and his friend (and my new friend), Emilio Pacheco, the President and CEO of Liberty Fund, many thanks for hosting a wonderful conference. Dialogue is extremely important in a representative democracy, and I went away from the conference thankful for having experienced a series of very engaging, enlightening, and highly respectful conversations.

There are, in truth, always a lot of people to thank by the time a book winds its way from inception to publication. I am especially grateful to Dean Ron Weich at the University of Baltimore School of Law and to all of my fantastic colleagues there. General exchanges with fellow attorneys and scholars about crime and punishment—about criminal justice issues, the concept of proportionality, and American sentencing policies—were very enlightening, as were very specific discussions with former Hennepin County Attorney Tom Johnson, lawyers Angela Bailey, Carrie Zochert and Lee Sheehy, Judge Mark Kappelhoff, University of St. Thomas law professor Mark Osler, and Professors Richard Frase and Susanna Blumenthal at the University of Minnesota Law School. The out-of-the-blue e-mail I got in October 2017 from Rob Warden, the Executive Director, Emeritus, of Northwestern's Center on Wrongful Convictions, also came at a particularly fortuitous and opportune time. The offered chance (quickly accepted) to contribute an article to a death penalty-themed symposium issue of the *Northwestern Journal of Law and Social Policy*—a journal I'd published in previously—led to the creation of yet another new article on the Eighth Amendment. Part of that 2018 article, which focuses on the difference between "usual" and "unusual punishments," and which thus intersects with the principal subject matter of this book, found its way, ultimately, into *The Baron and the Marquis*.

That lengthy law review article, titled "The Concept of 'Unusual Punishments' in Anglo-American Law: The Death Penalty as Arbitrary, Discriminatory, and Cruel and Unusual," was first published in Volume 13, Issue 4, of the *Northwestern Journal of Law and Social Policy* and is available online. Most importantly, the journal's invitation to write that article kept me thinking about the role of the Eighth Amendment's Cruel and Unusual Punishments Clause in modern American life as I simultaneously researched Montesquieu and Beccaria's eighteenth-century legal maxim and wrote *The Baron and the Marquis*. A special thank you to Emilie O'Toole, the editor-in-chief of that journal, and to all of the journal's staff, for shepherding my lengthy law review article through the rigorous cite-checking and publication process. My retrospective apologies for all the student work that had to go into cite-checking all *608 footnotes*! Another much-shorter article, one published in the *Montana Law*

Review in 2018, also kept me thinking about Beccaria's contributions to the penal reform movement. That article, deftly guided to publication by Emily Gutierrez Caton and other staff members in Missoula, is titled "The Abolitionist Movement Comes of Age: From Capital Punishment as a Lawful Sanction to a Peremptory, International Law Norm Barring Executions." It, too, is available online.

To Carolina Academic Press, the publisher of *this* book, and to all of its hard-working, always diligent staff, another special thank you is in order. If writing, as E. B. White once aptly offered, is hard work, publishing books is too. A successful publisher needs great people with lots of organizational skills, smarts, and energy. To bring a new book into the world, it requires not only typesetting and the painstaking creation of proofs, but entering scores of corrections to those proofs, then spotting pesky typographical errors through careful proofreading. It also requires attention to detail when it comes to all the marketing and publicity efforts. Carolina Academic Press is a successful publisher because it has great people. Indeed, I do not want to neglect to extend a general thank you to *everyone* who helped me *at any time* and *in any way*—you know who you are and how you helped! As William Arthur Ward, who had a particular penchant for writing quotable aphorisms, once warned of the risk of leaving someone out, if only unintentionally: "Feeling gratitude and not expressing it is like wrapping a present and not giving it." To cover my bases (and because one's memory, I'm told, can fade a bit after fifty), I thus offer a blanket thank you.

Nonetheless, very specific shout outs are in order to various law librarians who were extremely helpful to me. Adeen Postar, the Director of the University of Baltimore's law library, is always incredibly responsive as regards any inquiry, no matter how large or small, I make. And I also want to thank Ryan Greenwood, the Curator of Rare Books & Special Collections at the University of Minnesota Law School's Riesenfeld Rare Books Research Center, and Loren Turner, the Law School's Foreign, Comparative & International Law Librarian. Both Ryan and Loren were equally responsive in answering my queries, and they provided me with a lot of useful information and important leads for this book project. "When in doubt go to the library," bestselling writer J. K. Rowling, of *Harry Potter* fame, once wisely observed, with the American Library Association offering this equally sage bit of advice (which I carefully followed): "When you absolutely positively have to know, ask a librarian." (As a side note, there is a *real* Harry Potter, a former prison chaplain who penned a book called *Hanging in Judgment: Religion and the Death Penalty in England from the Bloody Code to Abolition*, published in London in 1993. It discusses topics that will be taken up later in *The Baron and the Marquis.*)

It was especially gratifying when Ryan Greenwood—in looking through the editions of Montesquieu's and Cesare Beccaria's books in the Law School's extensive collections—discovered a 1778 edition of Beccaria's *An Essay on Crimes and Punishments*. That book was printed in Philadelphia in 1778 by the Scottish émigré, Robert Bell, the same printer who, just two years earlier, much more famously brought out Thomas Paine's *Common Sense*. On the title page of the book, one of the earliest American editions of *On Crimes and Punishments*, is the handwritten signature of one "Frans. L. Lee," almost certainly a reference to Francis Lightfoot Lee. There are, Ryan informed me, actually *two* men named Francis Lightfoot Lee—one a signer of the

Declaration of Independence and the other his nephew, the son of Richard Henry Lee. It was Richard Henry Lee who, in June 1776, made the motion for America's independence in the Second Continental Congress. While Richard Henry Lee and his brother, Francis Lightfoot Lee, are special because they were the only *brothers* to sign the Declaration of Independence, the other Francis Lightfoot Lee—the nephew—was himself a part of the highly influential Lee family. No matter who first owned the book, to find a Revolutionary War era copy of Beccaria's book in the University of Minnesota's rare book collection was a great find, and highlights just how much early Americans valued Beccaria's book (and Montesquieu's work, which is cited in it).

Legal historians and enterprising policymakers must be detectives, and researching and writing a book such as this is a little like putting together a 1,000-piece puzzle, only it takes far, far longer to complete. When assembling a puzzle of that size (as I've done with my daughter, Abigail, on a few occasions during the interlude between Christmas and New Year's Day), or when crafting a book of this magnitude (as I've done in years past), it helps—and is, I recognize, a whole lot more fun—to have some pleasurable company. During my 2018 stint as a visiting scholar at the University of Minnesota Law School, Ryan continually directed me to useful sources, and the sources provided by both Ryan and Loren set me on the path to further discoveries as I drafted and revised the manuscript for *The Baron and the Marquis*. Bottom line: I am extremely thankful for all of the amazing assistance I received from incredibly smart and highly professional law librarians. There is, in fact, great sagacity in the signs I've seen in libraries describing librarians as the first search engines.

Though this book's acknowledgments come first, these acknowledgments—as you might've guessed—were actually written last. As one writer, Judith McCormack, wrote in her book, *The Rule of Last Clear Chance*, of her own musings on an author's innermost thoughts on book acknowledgments: "I have been daydreaming about writing acknowledgments since I started writing this book. Of course, this was largely to avoid doing any work on the book itself." That was—and remains—a good reminder: that before any acknowledgments could be written, the *book itself* had to be written. The actual writing of a book of this size and scope requires hundreds (if not thousands) of hours, plenty of cups of coffee (no decaf, please), lots of fits and starts (hopefully no computer crashes), and, inevitably, lots of planned and unplanned interruptions (many good, some bad) for life itself. In Judith McCormack's case, she playfully admitted in her own book's acknowledgments that her own daydreams "didn't produce any actual acknowledgments" because—in her words—"when my mind started to wander from the book, the next step was to lie down on the floor with my eyes closed, hoping fervently for a bolt of creative energy to strike." (Sounds eerily familiar!)

Periodic bouts of procrastination aside, I was especially blessed during the writing of this book for, of late, I've developed a fairly dependable, more-or-less daily rhythm to my writing. Plus (and this is a big plus), I had a one-semester sabbatical from teaching, and sabbaticals and writing go hand in hand like ice cream and cake or ice dancers at the winter Olympics (okay, that was just one of many, many distractions I faced during a multi-day stretch—actually, *binge* might be the better word choice—of watching NBC's coverage of the 2018 Pyeongchang games). As I researched, wrote and revised *The Baron and the Marquis*, often leading to more research angles to explore, there were, to be sure, plenty of early mornings, long afternoons, and late nights, as well as a fair amount of pedaling in the sauerkraut. But day by day, sentence by sentence, paragraph by paragraph, and chapter by chapter, the book manuscript got written with a little grit and determination.

A special, now *post*-sabbatical thanks is owed to Fionnuala Ní Aoláin, a University Regents Professor at the University of Minnesota Law School and the faculty director of the Law School's Human Rights Center. Fionnuala's generous offer of a visiting scholar position and an office to work out of during my sabbatical made all the difference to a productive spring semester. Founded in 1988 by Professor David Weissbrodt, an expert on torture and corporate responsibility, and a pioneering human rights scholar, the Human Rights Center promotes vital research on real-world challenges. Amanda Lyons, the Executive Director of Walter F. Mondale Hall's Human Rights Center and herself a specialist in international human rights law and advocacy, was, like Fionnuala, an incredibly gracious host, as were Robyn Skrebes, the Outreach Director, and Sarah Thune, the Administrative Coordinator. To David Weissbrodt and Barb Frey, the Director of the University of Minnesota's Human Rights Program, and to everyone else at the university, my alma mater, who made my academic visit an intellectually stimulating one, I offer my heartiest thanks.

I have spent more than twenty-five years now advocating against the death penalty, but *The Baron and the Marquis*—making the argument that only necessary punishments should be authorized or imposed—has a much broader scope and broader implications for America's criminal justice system. That system, without question one of the most punitive and costly in the world, is badly in need of serious reform, with the goal of the death penalty's abolition being, in my judgment, simply the low-hanging fruit to be plucked. Tens of billions of dollars are spent annually on America's correctional system, yet all too often there is too little corrections being done as lives are irrevocably destroyed, shattered, or adversely affected by overly punitive measures. Bail bonding and private prison companies, to use just two examples, are often far more interested in profit taking and filling up their coffers and their prisons than with helping or rehabilitating offenders. Issues of poverty and race—as well as issues pertaining to education and a lack of job skills and suitable employment opportunities—are entangled in the debate, though the reforms suggested in this book, hard as they will be to accomplish, would clearly help to address those issues and bring greater equity, justice, and equality.

I believe strongly, and long have, that the American death penalty is just the tip of an overly vindictive criminal justice iceberg that, in my view, must go the way of floppy disks and dot matrix printers. The death penalty, abandoned in most of the rest of the world, is, certainly, emblematic of the country's long-standing problem with revenge- and retaliation-driven punishments that are incredibly costly and that all too often only exacerbate, not solve, the underlying social ills that lead to crime. Crime victims are entitled to justice, but it is unjust to resort to cruel or torturous practices. The RMS *Titanic* sank in 1912, at a time when the vast majority of the world's countries still made use of the death penalty. But times have changed, just as our understanding of ship design, correctional practices, and human rights principles have through the ensuring decades. Other countries abolished the death penalty long ago, in many cases *decades* ago, putting the United States in an increasingly isolated position in the world community. If countries such as Albania, Moldova, South Africa and Rwanda can see fit to rid themselves of capital punishment (as they have), I believe Americans can and will—at least in time—take that progressive step. *Killing people* in an effort to convince others *to stop killing people* is a misguided endeavor that only sets a bad example—and that inflicts needless and gratuitous, indeed torturous, suffering.

Indeed, I believe (as do many others) that the infliction of *any* unnecessary punishments is, more broadly speaking, extremely degrading, inhumane, and wasteful (both financially and in terms of human capital). Punishing people too severely or when it is not necessary to do so is not only bad policy, it is morally wrong, unconscionable, and ultimately corrosive to any criminal justice system in which it takes place. The infliction of unnecessary punishments, I would argue after examining the history and the current state of affairs, should be found to run afoul of the Eighth Amendment prohibition against "cruel and unusual punishments." That prohibition, derived by the seventeenth-century English Bill of Rights (1689), was adopted and ratified at a time when America's founders well understood that the concept of necessity was the dividing line between liberty, on the one hand, and tyranny, on the other. America's founders despised tyranny and arbitrary governmental actions, and unnecessary punishments are not only cruel and unusual, they are—almost by definition, really—disproportionate and excessive. Along with judges and prosecutors, lawmakers and those who sit on sentencing commissions also have important roles to play in reforming American law and ensuring that only necessary punishments are authorized and imposed.

The history explored in *The Baron and the Marquis*, whether related to the death penalty, prolonged periods of solitary confinement, the pillory, the whipping post, or the bizarre, once-extant punishment for *scolds* known as *ducking*, gives credence to the idea that unnecessary punishments should be abandoned. This book, as noted, is about the history and present-day implications of a now largely obscure eighteenth-century legal maxim—one that originated with Montesquieu in France, and that then found a loyal Italian friend and follower in Beccaria in Milan. That maxim, quickly translated into English, was embraced by the likes of English penal reformer Jeremy Bentham and leading American revolutionaries such as John Adams and Thomas Jefferson. The idea of only meting out those punishments seen as "absolutely necessary" actually shows up in a draft constitution that Jefferson himself wrote for Virginians in the 1770s. But the prohibition against unnecessary punishments, through the French Revolution, also became the law of the land in France, with the idea of jettisoning unnecessary punishments embraced in other societies, too. Because of its multi-cultural, multi-lingual origins and development, I choose here to express my own gratitude in three ways to everyone—past and present, dead or alive—who, in helping me or in pointing the way, conferred some tidbit, or tidal wave, of wisdom: *Merci beaucoup. Molte grazie. Thank you.*

I hope you enjoy and find enlightening this mostly Made-in-Minnesota book, a project facilitated by my sabbatical and largely written during my time as a visiting scholar at the University of Minnesota Law School. Most importantly, I hope the ideas in it stay with you as much as the Enlightenment vision of a French baron and an Italian marquis have stayed with me. Eighteenth-century thinkers, if I may generalize, did not mince words or like to prevaricate, and the straightforward maxim they popularized about unnecessary punishments being "tyrannical" captured a powerful idea pertaining to human liberty using powerful prose. The simple logic of that maxim, which made perfect sense then, is still right on target, and the maxim's implications are broad in scope and continue to resonate and reverberate—and should be given currency today as they were immediately after they first appeared. As the great French novelist, poet, and anti-death penalty campaigner Victor Hugo once emphasized: "There is one thing stronger than all the armies in the world, and that is an idea whose time has come."

Although members of modern societies must always confront the problem of crime and punishment, the foundational idea—that unnecessary punishments are cruel and unjust, indeed tyrannical—has long existed, and that idea has been percolating in plain sight for more than 250 years, if only we care to listen. That basic notion, to safeguard liberty, I contend, was a lucid one at the time of its germination in Europe and should now be given a chance for a major comeback on American soil. While the notion of barring unnecessary punishments can actually be found in an *existing* provision of the U.S. Code, that idea must be given greater attention and traction—and be treated much more seriously—in the twenty-first century. It will never be possible to get everyone to agree on exactly *what* is necessary when it comes to bail determinations or punishments in individual cases, but that doesn't mean it isn't worth arguing about. I am reminded of American economist Edgar Fiedler's quip: "Ask five economists and you'll get five different answers—six if one went to Harvard." In fact, in a liberty-loving country, such as the United States of America, everyone *should* be able to agree (as America's founders appear to have in their time) with the maxim that any punishment that goes beyond what is necessary is tyrannical and, thus, an infringement on liberty. "Your right to swing your fist stops short of my nose," is a common adage on the subject of liberty, but the well-articulated maxim developed by Montesquieu and fostered by Beccaria—one created to apply in the context of punishment—should not be forgotten either.

There is a lot of material presented in *The Baron and the Marquis*, and that, naturally, creates a risk of error (just as juries sometimes make mistakes, even in death penalty cases, as people now know all too well because of the outstanding work of organizations such as the Innocence Project and all of the DNA testing that has led to death-row exonerations). Of course, any mistakes (any of those monkeys falling from trees) in the actual execution of *The Baron and the Marquis* are all mine and mine alone, as are the ideas expressed herein. But if this book—a look at early American law and how, since the 1970s, American law and policy have badly gone awry—can contribute at least in some small way to the in-progress movement for long-overdue criminal justice reform, it will have served its intended purpose. Criminal justice reform, centuries of history proves, is hard to achieve and hard to sustain; it can take a lot of time and effort to change hearts and minds, and since people are, by nature, creatures of habit, making meaningful change is sure to encounter many obstacles and much opposition. Progress is hardly inevitable, and setbacks can be expected.

However, good ideas have great power, and if good ideas—whether from the Enlightenment or modern-day thinkers—can be translated into action by highly committed individuals, those ideas can bring about positive and lasting change. *The Baron and the Marquis*, by compiling some of those ideas, and then contextualizing them through the frame of the Enlightenment, seeks to make its own contributions—to the understanding of the U.S. Constitution's Eighth Amendment and to the broader public discourse over American criminal justice reform. "A pile of rocks," a famous French poet, the pioneering aviator Antoine de Saint-Exupéry, once declared, "ceases to be a rock pile when somebody contemplates it with the idea of a cathedral in mind." In the United States, given the current state of affairs, we clearly need to build *more* cathedrals, to embrace rationality and best practices, and to imprison *fewer* people as we seek to promote liberty and to reject tyranny.

Introduction

In the mid-eighteenth century, the Enlightenment produced scores of revolutionary ideas—in science, medicine, economics, political philosophy and law.[1] It was a time of great debate about slavery,[2] serfdom,[3] and torture,[4] yet when the English "Bloody Code"—a set of laws heavily laden with capital offenses—was, simultaneously, in full force.[5] The iron-fisted reign of European monarchs and royal dynasties, replete with gruesome executions, torturous corporal punishments, and talk of the "divine right of kings,"[6] was gradually giving way to intense discourse on the natural rights of man[7]—and of women.[8] "Man is born free, and everywhere he is in chains," the Genevan philosopher Jean-Jacques Rousseau memorably wrote at the outset of his bestselling book, *The Social Contract* (1762).[9] "Women have the right to mount the scaffold; they should likewise have the right to mount the rostrum," the French playwright and outspoken feminist activist Olympe de Gouges later famously proclaimed in 1791.[10]

From Rousseau's pioneering work, to Voltaire's influential 1763 writings on religious tolerance,[11] to the American Declaration of Independence (1776), America's Revolutionary War (1775–1783), and the French Revolution (1789–1799), the eighteenth century was a time of tremendous social upheaval. It was a time when European monarchs and aristocrats still controlled the levers of power, though "We the People"—the first words of the U.S. Constitution's preamble—would ultimately take control of the reins of government in the newly forged United States of America.[12] By then, the varied titles of European aristocrats, many of whom has vast land holdings and fortunes, had centuries-old origins. As one source notes: "Words designating English titles of nobility except for *king*, *queen*, *earl*, *lord*, and *lady*—namely, *prince*, *duke*, *marquess*, *viscount*, *baron*, and their feminine equivalents—date from the period when England was in the hands of a Norman French ruling class."[13] "In France," another source observes, "the titles were almost the same: *duc*, *marquis*, *comte*, *vicomte* and *baron*."[14] And in southern Europe, on Italian soil, the titles of nobility—*e.g.*, *Duca* (Duke), *Conte* (Count), *Visconte* (Viscount), *Marchese* (Marquess), along with their feminine counterparts (*Duchessa*, *Contessa*, *Viscontessa*, and *Marchesa*)—had likewise long conferred considerable status within Italian society.[15]

The Enlightenment, pulsing with new ideas and ideologies, produced entirely new forms of government, ones never before seen in human history. The U.S. Constitution, marking a distinct break from the past, when people spoke of lords and commoners and when coats of arms and hereditary titles were, like property, bequeathed from father to son, itself guaranteed that "[n]o title of nobility shall be granted by the United States."[16] Not only did the American Declaration of Independence declare that "all men are created equal,"[17] but in the liberty- and rights-focused eighteenth century, the U.S. Constitution and the U.S. Bill of Rights audaciously guaranteed—as they still do today—a number of individual rights, including for those accused of crimes or facing punishment. The right to trial by jury, the right to assistance of counsel, and the right to a grand jury in certain cases, for example, are all enshrined in the U.S. Bill of Rights. The Constitution's Eighth Amendment, one of those important checks on abusive governmental power, contains just sixteen words, though because it is phrased in such general terms, it has spawned much litigation over its proper interpretation. "Excessive bail shall not be required, nor excessive fines imposed, nor cruel and unusual punishments inflicted," the Eighth Amendment reads.[18] In fact, the Eighth Amendment's three specific clauses—the Excessive Bail, Excessive Fines, and Cruel and Unusual Punishments Clauses—have generated almost endless scholarly debate, with a long line of legal commentators weighing in on their meaning, whether in treatises, monographs, or law review articles.[19]

American jurists have, themselves, fiercely argued about what the sixteen words of the Eighth Amendment mean, with some U.S. Supreme Court Justices looking primarily to the eighteenth century to understand their import.[20] Others, meanwhile, finding it extremely troubling that many gruesome punishments were still in existence when the Bill of Rights was ratified in 1791, look to more contemporary approaches or evidence.[21] The debate over the Eighth Amendment's meaning has been intense, especially in death penalty cases and in disputes dealing with the treatment of prisoners. For example, during his nearly thirty years on the U.S. Supreme Court, Justice Antonin Scalia continually upheld the death penalty's constitutionality, with Scalia once writing: "It is entirely clear that capital punishment, which was widely in use in 1791, does not violate the abstract moral principle of the Eighth Amendment."[22] In support of that view, the late Justice Scalia frequently pointed to the U.S. Constitution's Fifth Amendment and a 1790 act of Congress. The Fifth Amendment, adopted at a time when the *mandatory* death penalty was still in use, provides: "No person shall be held to answer for a capital, or otherwise infamous crime, unless on a presentment or indictment of a grand jury ... ; nor shall any person be subject for the same offense to be twice put in jeopardy of life or limb; ... nor be deprived of life, liberty, or property, without due process of law." The Crimes Act of 1790, formally titled "An Act for the Punishment of certain Crimes against the United States," provided that treason, murder, piracy and other felonies "shall" be punished with death. That federal statute was typical of other state laws at the time providing for the mandatory death penalty.[23]

In sharp contrast, Justice William Brennan, during his time on the U.S. Supreme Court, took a far different approach than Justice Scalia. Justice Brennan—like his colleague, Justice Thurgood Marshall—repeatedly called the death penalty a *per se* violation of the Eighth Amendment. "The Framers," Justice Brennan emphasized, "surely understood that judging would not be easy or straightforward: no doubt that is why they took such great pains to ensure the independence of judges by providing life tenure and protecting against diminution of judges' compensation." What is "cruel and unusual," Brennan observed, should not be "frozen in time" because that would violate "the Framers' vision—which was to leave to future judges and future generations the right to decide for themselves what constitutes 'cruel and unusual' punishment."[24] That view, obviously, contrasts quite dramatically—diametrically even—with Justice Scalia's approach. As Scalia once offered: "For me, the constitutionality of the death penalty is not a difficult, soul-wrenching question. It was clearly permitted when the Eighth Amendment was adopted. And so it is clearly permitted today." Although Justice Scalia, in 1988, memorably called himself a "faint-hearted originalist" because of his unwillingness to return to the days of public lashing and branding, he later retracted that statement in 2013, choosing to take a down-the-line-originalist stance. With both lashing and branding in use in the founding period, Scalia decided in 2013 to embrace a purist originalist view of the Constitution, saying of flogging at that time: "And what I would say now is, yes, if a state enacted a law permitting flogging, it is immensely stupid, but it is not unconstitutional."[25]

The Supreme Court's Eighth Amendment cases—as well as the shifting history of punishment practices—thus raise an important series of questions: What punishments are truly necessary? How should non-violent offenders be handled? What kind of bail or parole practices should be used? Is prolonged solitary confinement necessary, or even advisable? How should prisoners be treated? When do punishments that were once thought to be *necessary* become *unnecessary*? When do once accepted punishments become obsolete? And in the Eighth Amendment context in particular, at what point do once *usual* punishments become *unusual* ones? Other related questions also present themselves. What should the criteria or factors be for gauging whether a punishment is necessary or unnecessary? When should a punishment be adjudged to be unusual? And what consequences, if any, do such criteria or factors have for American courts evaluating the constitutionality of punishments such as the death penalty or, say, long-term sentences for non-violent offenders?

These are particularly important questions given what we know now about the effects of solitary confinement and long-term incarceration,[26] as well as about the American death penalty's sordid and error-prone administration since its inception.[27] "On any given day in the United States," one 2016 book notes, "supermax prisons and solitary confinement units hold at least eighty thousand men, women, and children in conditions of extreme isolation and sensory deprivation, without work, rehabilitative programming, or meaningful human contact of any kind."[28] Whether the routine or frequent use of solitary confinement makes American prisons less safe—and opposed to more safe—is also a subject worth taking up, especially since one judge in British Columbia, in 2018, declared the prolonged use of solitary confinement in Canada—America's northern neighbor—to be unconstitutional.[29] In June 2012, the U.S. Senate Judiciary Committee's Subcommittee on the Constitution, Civil Rights and Human Rights held its own, first-ever congressional hearing on solitary confinement. Chaired by Senator Dick Durbin of Illinois, it was noted at the outset of the hearing that there has been a rise in the use of solitary confinement for vulnerable groups, including juveniles, those with mental health issues, and immigrants.[30]

The routine use of harsh prison sentences—some the result of "three strikes" laws or mandatory minimums—itself raises important questions about the best way to protect the public and whether all-important recidivism rates actually fall—or stay the same or rise—with the use of more draconian sentences.[31] Harsh drug sentences have become a particular flashpoint in the criminal justice reform debate. Whereas those inmates released from American prisons in 1986 after serving time for a federal drug offense had spent an average of 22 months behind bars, by 2004 people convicted of a federal drug offense were expected to serve nearly three times that amount: an average of 62 months in prison.[32] On the death penalty front, a clear majority of the world's nations have already abandoned the state's ultimate sanction, turning away from death sentences and executions entirely.[33] The continent of Europe (with the notable exception of Belarus, which still carries out executions in secret) is now essentially a death penalty-free zone, with two protocols to the European Convention on Human Rights—Protocols No. 6 and No. 13—absolutely barring the death penalty's use in both peacetime and wartime, respectively.[34]

History shows that punishments change over time, sometimes dramatically, so it should not be too surprising that what were once seen as usual and necessary punishments were later understood to have been, or to have become, unusual and unnecessary. Punishments that were once usual can even be reclassified as torturous acts. Punishments that are absolutely necessary to protect society, I would argue, cannot be properly described as Eighth Amendment violations, because members of society have a legitimate right to expect, as part of the social compact, that truly necessary measures will be taken to protect them. Punishment, in fact, is part and parcel of justice; a person who transgresses society's norms must be held accountable. But no society should be permitted to torture people or to inflict *unnecessary* human suffering. And that is especially so in a country such as the United States, which explicitly outlaws cruel and unusual punishments and which has ratified the U.N. Convention Against Torture and Other Cruel, Inhuman or Degrading Treatment or Punishment, which bars such conduct.[35] Indeed, it seems crystal clear from examining the arc of history that once usual punishments can clearly become unusual and unnecessary over time, whether through disuse, technological developments, or a greater awareness of the ill-effects, or torturous or cruel nature, of certain punishments.

With that backdrop in mind, *The Baron and the Marquis* explores the necessity-for-punishment principle as well as the difference between "unusual" and "usual" punishments. The infliction of unnecessary, unduly severe punishments, *The Baron and the Marquis* argues, not only infringes on *liberty* (a concept at the very core of America's creed as articulated in the Declaration of Independence), but can be counterproductive to fighting or reducing crime and runs counter to human rights principles. In the case of the Eighth Amendment, its language can be traced all the way back to the English Declaration of Rights and its statutory counterpart, the English Bill of Rights (1689). That seventeenth-century enactment proclaimed in these hortatory words, ones crafted as part of the Glorious Revolution of 1688 that saw a new king and queen, William and Mary, rise to power: "That excessive baile ought not to be required nor excessive fines imposed nor cruell and unusuall punishments inflicted."[36] Those words, a condemnation of the abuses of the Stuart dynasty, including those of King James II and his judges, help to explain why James II was driven from power and forced to abdicate his throne.[37]

The necessity or lack of necessity for a particular punishment, of course, may be dependent on time, place and context. In the Eighth Amendment arena, to better understand what "cruel and unusual punishments" are, it may be helpful—and, in truth, actually seems rather intuitive—to try to better understand the history of that designation and to figure out *what they are not.* By examining and thinking about the concept of necessity, as well as the difference between "unusual" and "usual" punishments, perhaps lawmakers and twenty-first century American judges will gain some insight—whether profound or not—into their own duties, which, for judges, includes Eighth Amendment decision-making. The natural, binary opposite of "unusual punishments" is "usual punishments." While at least a few scholars have written about "unusual punishments,"[38] very little has been written about "usual punishments" or the dividing line between the two.[39] *The Baron and the Marquis* seeks to fill that scholarly void by examining, from an historical perspective, not only "unusual punishments," but the flip side of the "unusual punishments" coin. The book thus surveys historical developments, showing the use and abandonment of particular penal practices through the centuries, exploring, in particular, early English and American sources referencing either "unusual" or "usual" punishments. By gaining insight into the difference between the two, *The Baron and the Marquis* seeks to shed new light on what punishments are truly necessary in twenty-first century America.

Constitutional interpretation is—and perhaps always will be—a contentious subject. But in the modern era and in litigation before the nation's highest court, America's living constitutionalists have, in fact, largely won the broader debate over the Eighth Amendment's interpretation in spite of the fact that the death penalty—a common eighteenth-century punishment—continues to survive in twenty-first century America. "Current justices read the Constitution in the only way we can: as twentieth-century Americans," Justice William Brennan observed in his own time, reflecting the long-prevailing view that rejects a rigid, Justice Scalia-style originalism.[40] From the seventeenth century to the present, each generation has had to grapple with whether particular punishments crossed the line and constituted "excessive" or "cruel and unusual" ones. Though used extensively in America's founding era, capital punishment itself has gradually fallen into disrepute, decline, and—in many places—disuse, and, more and more, appears to be on life support. Already, mandatory death sentences of the kind embraced by the First Congress and early American lawmakers have been replaced by discretionary ones, and the number of death-eligible offenses has been greatly curtailed at the state level.

In terms of the U.S. Supreme Court's Eighth Amendment interpretive methodology, though, originalism—at least in practice, as reflected by the Court's own decisions interpreting the Cruel and Unusual Punishments Clause—has long been a dead letter. The early American constitutions and declaration of rights that outlawed excessive penalties and cruel and unusual punishments borrowed from the text of the English Bill of Rights, but those provisions were informed by the Enlightenment and its focus on progress. America's Founding Fathers, were they still alive today, would, I would venture to say, be horrified by the mere prospect that modern-day thinkers would blindly embrace centuries-old practices without questioning the underlying justification for them. Indeed, since 1958, the Supreme Court—rebuffing an originalist approach—has consistently held that the Eighth Amendment "must draw its meaning from the evolving standards of decency that mark the progress of a maturing society."[41] That test reflects a clear rejection of originalism and a decisive victory for living constitutionalism.

That oft-invoked "evolving standards of decency" test shows up in countless American judicial decisions, though it, like the meaning of the Eighth Amendment's sixteen-word text, is still subject to much modern commentary, controversy, and debate. In any event, the "evolving standards" test is the one that the Supreme Court has consistently employed for decades even as it resorts to other interpretive tools, such as looking for evidence of a "national consensus" (or examining trends) against a particular practice. In an effort to identify a consensus, or a lack thereof, the Court frequently does a nose count of states that use—or that have abandoned—the practice.[42] For example, in 2005, in *Roper v. Simmons*, the Court—in a five-to-four-decision—specifically used that test in declaring unconstitutional the death penalty for juvenile offenders. In overruling *Stanford v. Kentucky* (1989), which had previously upheld death sentences for offenders aged sixteen or higher, Justice Anthony Kennedy—writing for the majority in *Roper*—referred to history but found that the Court was not bound by eighteenth-century practice or, for that matter, the late twentieth-century precedent it overruled. "The prohibition against 'cruel and unusual punishments,' like other expansive language in the Constitution," Justice Kennedy wrote in outlawing the death penalty's use for those younger than eighteen, "must be interpreted according to its text, by considering history, tradition, and precedent, and with due regard for its purpose and function in the constitutional design." "To implement this framework," he continued, though, setting forth the long-standing majority view, "we have established the propriety and affirmed the necessity of referring to 'the evolving standards of decency that mark the progress of a maturing society' to determine which punishments are so disproportionate as to be cruel and unusual."[43]

The Baron and the Marquis encourages Americans, in their roles as citizens, policymakers, lawmakers, prosecutors and judges, to pay close attention to the lessons of history without being trapped by the cruelty and torturous barbarity that one finds so often in history books. In thinking about the Eighth Amendment, the book highlights the importance of reading the U.S. Constitution *as a whole* and in its context, much as lawyers and judges do with contracts.[44] The Constitution is itself a social contract or compact that has survived for many generations,[45] though its interpretation—because it governs the lives of people not yet born at its creation—naturally presents unique, and much more complicated, challenges than the interpretation of a run-of-the-mill commercial contract.[46] The *text* of the U.S. Constitution and its amendments—as well as the *principles* and *values* undergirding those textual provisions—should be of primary importance in deciding how modern judges should read it. Thus, a proper understanding of the foundational, Enlightenment-era necessity-for-punishment principle is of critical importance, as is a proper understanding of the meaning of the words *cruel* and *unusual*. The Constitution, as legal scholars such as Ronald Dworkin have pointed out, conspicuously guarantees various individual rights, often employing broad and general language (*e.g.*, "due process," "equal protection," etc.).[47] Such rights, central to the protection of liberty, frequently protect those accused of crimes and, in the case of the Eighth Amendment's Excessive Fines and Cruel and Unusual Punishments Clauses, safeguard convicted offenders themselves.[48] It is, of course, now *twenty-first century* judges who must decide how to interpret the Constitution, and nothing less than individual liberty and the Rule of Law—and, in death penalty cases, life or death—are at stake.[49]

While the English "Bloody Code" and a wide assortment of draconian punishments (both lethal and non-lethal) are an indelible part of Anglo-American history,[50] *The Baron and the Marquis* specifically discusses the special relevance of Enlightenment thought to America's twenty-first century criminal justice debate. It was, after all, the Enlightenment that gave birth to the American Revolution and America's representative democracy, not to mention early criminal law reforms and subsequent revolutions that occurred elsewhere throughout the world. The U.S. Constitution's Due Process Clauses,[51] as well as the Fourteenth Amendment's Equal Protection Clause,[52] must also be carefully considered in assessing whether a punishment is—or has become—*unnecessary*, *cruel and unusual*, or *torturous*. *The Baron and the Marquis* thus argues that the language of the Constitution's Due Process and Equal Protection Clauses should be fully taken into account as part of the Eighth Amendment analysis and calculus. For example, the arbitrary, discriminatory, error-prone, and torturous nature of death sentences and executions should be fully considered in evaluating whether capital punishment is unnecessary or—in the words of the Eighth Amendment itself—"cruel and unusual." After exploring the history and specific language of the U.S. Constitution, *The Baron and the Marquis* concludes that the American death penalty is arbitrarily applied, unequally and unfairly administered, and is—if fairly judged—not only incredibly "cruel," but unnecessary, torturous, and highly "unusual." The book's analysis also calls into question other penal practices, such as the routine use of extended periods of solitary confinement and the current treatment of various juvenile offenders. A society's approach to crime and punishment is a mirror that reflects that society's beliefs and values, so how a society treats its offenders—whether violent or non-violent, and whether young or old—is of no small consequence.

Often overlooked by American lawmakers and judges, including in the jurisprudential debate over the Eighth Amendment, is the Enlightenment-era *context* in which the protections for individual criminal suspects and defendants were included in the U.S. Bill of Rights.[53] The Eighth Amendment's actual words may have been derived from the English Bill of Rights (1689) and its first American counterpart, the Virginia Declaration of Rights (1776), but how those words were understood in the eighteenth century was materially shaped by the Enlightenment and its leading writers, including French, Italian, English and Scottish *philosophes*. For example, in 1748, decades after the Glorious Revolution of 1688 and the promulgation of the English Bill of Rights, but decades before the start of America's Revolutionary War and the Eighth Amendment's adoption and ratification, a French baron, Charles Louis de Secondat, better known as Montesquieu, published a landscape-changing treatise. That book, published in French as *De l'esprit des loix* (1748) or *De l'esprit des lois*, was later translated into English as *The Spirit of the Laws*.[54] In that extremely popular book, Montesquieu specifically declared: "Every penalty that does not derive from necessity is tyrannical."[55] That particular sentence appeared in Book 19, chapter 14 of *The Spirit of the Laws*. While Book 19 is titled "On the laws in their relation with the principles forming the general spirit, the mores, and the manners of a nation,"[56] chapter 14 is titled "What are the natural means of changing the mores and manners of a nation."[57] In Book 19, chapter 3, "On tyranny," Montesquieu further explained: "There are two sorts of tyranny: a real one, which consists in the violence of the government, and one of opinion, which is felt when those who govern establish things that run counter to a nation's way of thinking."[58]

The concept of liberty, at the center of the extended argument in *The Baron and the Marquis*, is itself discussed at length in *The Spirit of the Laws*. For example, in Book 11, chapter 2, Montesquieu stressed: "No word has received more different significations and has struck minds in so many ways as has *liberty*." As Montesquieu wrote of liberty—and the many varied views of its proper usage—in that section of his book: "Some have taken it for the ease of removing the one to whom they had given tyrannical power; some, for the faculty of electing the one whom they were to obey; others, for the right to be armed and to be able to use violence; yet others, for the privilege of being governed only by a man of their own nation, or by their own laws." "For a certain people," Montesquieu continued, "liberty has long been the usage of wearing a long beard." In Book 11, chapter 3, titled "*What liberty is*," Montesquieu further observed: "In a state, that is, in a society where there are laws, liberty can consist only in having the power to do what one should want to do and in no way being constrained to do what one should not want to do." He then gave this definition, one tied to the rule of law: "Liberty is the right to do everything the laws permit; and if one citizen could do what they forbid, he would no longer have liberty because the others would likewise have this same power."

In the following chapter of Book 11, Montesquieu went on to emphasize that "[p]olitical liberty is found only in moderate governments." "It is present," he said, "only when power is not abused," with Montesquieu quick to point out that "it has eternally been observed that any man who has power is led to abuse it; he continues until he finds limits." "So that one cannot abuse power, power must check power by the arrangement of things," Montesquieu wrote there, aware that the structure of government and the laws thereof could make a difference in checking human nature. "A constitution," Montesquieu added, "can be such that no one will be constrained to do the things the law does not oblige him to do or be kept from doing the things the law permits him to do." Turning his attention, in particular, to "*the constitution of England*," what Montesquieu called the only constitution which "has political liberty for its direct purpose" and which was very much on the minds of America's eighteenth-century founders and framers, Montesquieu wrote, among other things, in a lengthy chapter on that subject:

> Political liberty in a citizen is that tranquillity of spirit which comes from the opinion each one has of his security, and in order for him to have this

> liberty the government must be such that one citizen cannot fear another citizen.
>
> When legislative power is united with executive power in a single person or in a single body of the magistracy, there is no liberty, because one can fear that the same monarch or senate that makes tyrannical laws will execute them tyrannically.
>
> Nor is there liberty if the power of judging is not separate from legislative power and from executive power. If it were joined to legislative power, the power over the life and liberty of the citizens would be arbitrary, for the judge would be the legislator. If it were joined to executive power, the judge could have the force of an oppressor.[59]

Just as America's Founding Fathers had in mind the Glorious Revolution of 1688 and the English Bill of Rights when they decided to foment their own rebellion, Montesquieu's ideas, especially those on checking and preventing abuses of power, played a pivotal role in American constitution-making. North Carolina's 1776 constitution provided that "the legislative, executive, and supreme judicial powers of government, ought to be forever separate and distinct from each other"; Virginia's 1776 constitution stated that "the legislative and executive powers of the State should be separate and distinct from the judiciary"; and Georgia's 1777 constitution made clear that "[t]he legislative, executive, and judiciary departments shall be separate and distinct, so that neither exercise the powers properly belonging to the other." In the Massachusetts Constitution of 1780, John Adams—its principal drafter—set out the separation of powers principle this way, making it crystal clear where he stood and what he was worried about: "In the government of this Commonwealth, the legislative department shall never exercise the executive and judicial powers, or either of them; the executive shall never exercise the legislative and judicial powers, or either of them; the judicial shall never exercise the legislative and executive powers, or either of them; to the end it may be a government of laws and not of men."[60]

Just as Montesquieu's ideas clearly shaped state constitutions, including the Massachusetts Constitution of 1780 (the oldest continuously functioning written constitution in the world), they shaped the U.S. Constitution, too.[61] In *The Federalist No. 47*, James Madison, writing as "Publius," explicitly declared that "the celebrated Montesquieu" is "[t]he oracle who is always consulted and cited" on the subject of separation of powers. As Madison added in *The Federalist No. 47*: "The accumulation of all powers legislative, executive and judiciary in the same hands, whether of one, a few or many, and whether hereditary, self appointed, or elective, may justly be pronounced the very definition of tyranny."[62] "Montesquieu," one source notes, "is the most quoted authority in the *Federalist Papers*." As that source observes of Montesquieu: "He is appealed to by Alexander Hamilton, in #9 and #78, and James Madison, in #43 and #47, with his name being mentioned twelve times."[63] In *The Political Theory of Montesquieu*, Melvin Richter, the book's author, tellingly observes of the famed French thinker's broad scope of influence in revolutionary times: "At the time of the American Revolution, few other theorists could rival Montesquieu's prestige in the English-speaking world. In England, the most widely accepted interpretation of its law and constitution was that of Blackstone, of whom it has been said that his plagiarism of Montesquieu 'would be nauseating if it were not comic.'" "During the debate about adopting the American Constitution," Richter adds, "both federalists and anti-federalists argued their cases on the basis of their respective interpretations of Montesquieu."[64]

But Montesquieu was not alone in shaping American views of tyranny and liberty. Thomas Hobbes could not conceive "that there is any liberty greater than for a man to do what he will, and to forbear what he will," and John Locke wrote that liberty "is the power a man has to do or forbear doing any particular action, according as the doing or forbearance has the actual preference in the mind, which is the same thing as to say, according as he himself wills it."[65] And less than two decades after the appearance of Montesquieu's language on tyrannical punishments in *The Spirit of the Laws*, the once much-celebrated Italian aristocrat, Cesare Beccaria, often commonly referred to by his title, the "Marquis Beccaria" or the "Marquis of Beccaria," very similarly proclaimed in *Dei delitti e delle pene* (1764) that "every punishment that does not derive from absolute necessity is tyrannical."[66] Beccaria's book, translated into English three years later, in 1767, as *An Essay on Crimes and Punishments*, built upon the French baron's keen observation. In *A Defence of the Constitutions of the Government of the United States*, John Adams himself rails against "tyrannical laws" and "tyrannical measures" and cites the works of both Montesquieu and Beccaria, so those political theorists were plainly very much on his mind.[67] In *On Crimes and Punishments*, Beccaria—giving attribution to the late Frenchman he so admired—specifically wrote of his intellectual muse and gave his own take-away from that observation: "As the great Montesquieu says, every punishment that does not derive from absolute necessity is tyrannical. This proposition can be stated more generally in the following manner: every act of authority of one man over another that does not derive from absolute necessity is tyrannical."[68]

Those perceptive words, appearing in "The Right to Punish" section of Beccaria's popular, much-translated book, were followed by these, setting out Beccaria's philosophy of liberty and law: "This is the foundation, therefore, upon which the sovereign's right to punish crimes is based: the necessity to defend the depository of the public welfare from individual usurpations; and the more just the punishments, the more sacred and inviolable the security and the greater the liberty the sovereign preserves for his subjects."[69] Beccaria, a Milanese philosopher, legal theorist, and economist whose *On Crimes and Punishments* became a bestseller, forthrightly opposed the death penalty and torture, with his book seeking proportionality between crimes and punishments and a scale of crimes and a corresponding scale of punishments.[70] For Beccaria, the dividing line between tyranny and liberty, between justice and cruelty, was whether the governmental act was truly necessary. "The masterly Beccaria observes that mankind, when influenced by first impressions, love cruel laws, although, being subject to them themselves, it is the interest of every person that they should be as mild as possible," one barrister, James Paterson, summarized the Italian philosopher's views, writing in 1877 in his own book, *Commentaries on the Liberty of the Subject and the Laws of England Relating to the Security of the Person.*

"Voltaire and Montesquieu," Paterson wrote in the century after both of those men had died, "exposed" the severity of draconian sentences, with Paterson then emphasizing: "Beccaria at length grappled closely with the subject, and succeeded in shaking the faith of those, who had so long blindly believed in them."[71]

Historical context matters, even if history, with all its indignities, warts, and sheer barbarities, cannot be allowed to dictate the future. It cannot be forgotten that the second half of the eighteenth century brought enormous social, political and legal change, and that penal reform was part of that change. The French and Indian War (1754–1763), North America's fragment of Europe's broader Seven Years' War (1756–1763), was fought between the French and the English and their respective allies. After George III ascended to the British throne in 1760, the Stamp Act was passed by the British Parliament in 1765, infuriating North American colonists, just as the revenue-raising Townshend Acts, named after Charles Townshend, the Chancellor of the Exchequer, did, leading to American cries of "No taxation without representation." After the Boston Massacre on March 5, 1770, the Sons of Liberty—originally formed to protest the Stamp Act—fomented and carried out the Boston Tea Party on December 16, 1773. The Declaration of Independence (1776) itself resembled the English Declaration of Rights in that both declarations laid out the causes for revolution and took aim at abusive monarchs—in the American case, at George III, and in the English case, at James II. The Enlightenment period in which America's founders lived shaped institutions and societies, and just as Beccaria had an intellectual debt to the "immortal Montesquieu," John Adams owed one to political theorists such as Montesquieu and Beccaria. The American revolutionaries writ large were indebted to both Montesquieu and Beccaria as regards reshaping of their thinking in the criminal-law arena.

John Adams himself memorably quoted Beccaria in the opening line of his courtroom oration on December 3, 1770, at the historic Boston Massacre trial itself. John Adams' son, John Quincy Adams, later reported that he had "often heard, from individuals, who had been present among the crowd of spectators at the trial, the electrical effect produced upon the immense and excited auditory, by the first sentence with which he opened his defense." John Adam's well-chosen opening line: "I am for the prisoners at the bar, and shall apologize for it only in the words of the Marquis Beccaria: 'If I can but be the instrument of preserving one life, his blessings and tears of transport, shall be a sufficient consolation to me, for the contempt of all mankind.'" With liberty as the watchword of American revolutionaries, it wasn't long, in the wake of the Boston Massacre and the Boston Tea Party, before America's Revolutionary War (1775–1783) began transforming the whole world. The onset of the Revolutionary War quickly led to the issuance of the Declaration of Independence (1776), then the Articles of Confederation (1781–1789). When those Articles of Confederation failed to do the job, the ratification of the U.S. Constitution (1788) and its Bill of Rights (1791) followed. The ratification of the U.S. Constitution also led to the election and administration of the oath of office of George Washington—the revered military man—as the first President of the United States. The French Revolution (1789–1799) and the Haitian Revolution (1791–1804) capped off the eighteenth century's turbulent end, with other revolutions throughout the world soon to follow.[72]

In the eighteenth century, a battle of ideas—between monarchical power and tyranny and individual liberty and freedom—was waged in books, periodicals, and newspapers, even as real battles, on battlefields such as Bunker Hill and at places like Quebec, Trenton, and Saratoga, took place. Looking back at the law's development, James Paterson—writing in his two-volume treatise on liberty and security of persons—contrasted the ideas of John Locke and Cesare Beccaria, explaining: "Locke says that the end of law is not to abolish or restrain, but to preserve and enlarge freedom, and where there is no law there is no freedom." "Beccaria, in his masterly way," Paterson wrote in the first volume of his treatise, "explains his notion of liberty thus: 'The opinion, that every member of society has a right to do anything, that is not contrary to the laws, without fearing any other inconveniences than those which are the natural consequences of the action itself, is a political dogma which should be defended by the laws, inculcated by the magistrates, and believed by the people—a sacred dogma, without which there can be no lawful society—a just recompense for our sacrifice of that universal liberty of action common to all sensible beings, and only limited by our natural powers.'" "Locke and Beccaria," Paterson observed, "are the writers, who seem to look with the steadiest eyes at the central idea involved" in discussing the concept of liberty. "Beccaria," Paterson added, "also says it is better to prevent crimes than to punish them; that this is the fundamental principle of good legislation, which is the art of conducting men to the maximum of happiness and to the minimum of misery."[73]

Like Montesquieu's ideas, Beccaria's ideas thus profoundly shaped the Enlightenment and America's founding, as well as the post-Revolutionary War period. In the wake of the writings of Enlightenment authors, *virtue* and *happiness* were in and *cruelty* and *misery* were to be on their way out. The American Revolution—something few twenty-first century Americans know—was itself closely tied up with penal reform in addition to political liberty, self-determination, the pursuit of happiness, economic justice, and freedom from oppression. Indeed, the need for penal reform was seen then not as a separate subject, but as an important adjunct to maximizing individual liberty, freedom, and happiness. "While the War for Independence from Britain looms large in its impact on late eighteenth-century American politics and culture," Jen Manion writes in *Liberty's Prisoners: Carceral Culture in Early America*, "older forces, including the Enlightenment and the Great Awakening, inspired a great deal of social transformation as well." As Manion relays: "The Enlightenment was characterized as 'the age of reason,' in which human progress would be measured through advances in science, medicine, technology, culture, and politics. Enlightenment writers from Cesare Beccaria to Montesquieu produced progressive theories of criminal justice that rejected the legacy of European brutality and aimed to put logic, predictability, and fairness at the heart of punishment." "In part because of the tremendous importance of these writings," Manion continues, "the revolutionary generation relished the opportunity to craft laws fit for democracy" and the ideas in those writings "inspired many people to question long-standing practices of violent, corporal, and excessive punishment."[74] The emergence of American penitentiaries—the subject that Alexis de Tocqueville and his traveling companion, Gustave de Beaumont, came to America from France to carefully study and analyze—came only *after* the appearance of Beccaria's famous treatise and after Beccaria's many followers, from John Howard to Thomas Eddy, had inspired their construction.[75]

Consequently, it is apparent that Cesare Beccaria's *On Crimes and Punishments*, like Montesquieu's *The Spirit of the Laws*, was nothing short of transformative.[76] For his part, Beccaria broke with prevailing societal custom and sought the death penalty's complete abolition, in part on utilitarian grounds and in part on the basis that it was simply not necessary—an application of the general necessity-for-punishment maxim that he and Montesquieu espoused. "[I]f I can demonstrate that the death penalty is neither useful nor necessary," Beccaria wrote, "I will have won the cause of humanity."[77] Indeed, Beccaria's short and pithy summation of his views on crimes and punishments in *Dei delitti e delle pene* made direct reference to the necessity-for-punishment principle, with Beccaria drawing the following "general and very useful theorem" in his *On Crimes and Punishments* after addressing a number of topics in separate chapters: "*In order that punishment should not be an act of violence committed by one or many against a private citizen, it is essential that it be public, prompt, necessary, the minimum possible in the given circumstances, proportionate to the crime, and established by the law*."[78] His conclusion that punishments be "the minimum possible in the given circumstances" reinforced his assertion that punishments must be absolutely necessary in order not to be tyrannical.

More than twenty-five years after penning *On Crimes and Punishments*, Beccaria was still emphasizing his emphatically made point on the absolute necessity for punishment, reiterating that view in a 1790s report on capital punishment written to encourage criminal justice reform—and the death penalty's abolition—in Austrian Lombardy.[79] As Beccaria and two of his colleagues, Francesco Gallarati Scotti and Paolo Risi, stressed in that minority report: "The three of us were of the same opinion that the death penalty should not be prescribed except in the case of absolute necessity, and in the peaceful circumstances of our society, and with the regular administration of justice, we could not think of any case of absolute necessity other than the situation in which the accused, in plotting the subversion of the state, was capable, either through his external or internal relationships, of disturbing and endangering society even while imprisoned and closely watched."[80] In other words, unless the very overthrow of the government was seen to be at stake, Beccaria and his two colleagues could conceive of no need for capital punishment. As law professor David Luban, of the Georgetown University Law Center, encapsulates Cesare Beccaria's Enlightenment-era views: "Beccaria condemns punishments that are more cruel than is absolutely necessary to deter crime, arguing on classical-liberal grounds that people in the state of nature will surrender only the smallest quantum of liberty necessary to secure society: 'The aggregate of these smallest possible portions of individual liberty constitutes the right to punish; everything beyond that is abuse and not justice, a fact but scarcely a right.'"[81]

When the U.S. Constitution and its Bill of Rights were ratified by the American people, Montesquieu and Beccaria—thanks to their own books and the writings of their many, many fervent disciples[82]—were celebrities in Europe and throughout the Americas.[83] Montesquieu was regularly hailed as "celebrated" and "immortal," and Beccaria—his Italian successor-in-spirit who rose to fame after Montesquieu's death—was similarly praised as the "celebrated" marquis, a "benevolent" and "sublime" philosopher, and as "immortal" and a man of "genius."[84] Montesquieu's name appears multiple times in *The Federalist Papers*[85] and his famous book, *The Spirit of the Laws*, was purchased, owned, and frequently cited and quoted by America's founders and framers.[86] Benjamin Franklin, an early reader of Montesquieu, bought a copy of *The Spirit of the Laws* in 1750.[87] America's first commander-in-chief, George Washington, ordered it from Mount Vernon,[88] John Adams read it as early as 1759,[89] and Alexander Hamilton and Thomas Jefferson quoted and recommended it to others.[90] James Madison, Jefferson's fellow Virginian, had access to the book as a young man and, in his work, made extensive use of it,[91] with Madison also specifically recommending Cesare Beccaria's works for the Library of Congress in 1783.[92] Madison once called Beccaria "a Philosophical Legislator."[93]

In many ways, the American Revolution would not have been the revolution it was *but for* Montesquieu's and Beccaria's writings. Thomas Jefferson, the American lawyer and deft politician, was clearly drawn to Montesquieu's and Cesare Beccaria's ideas—something evident from his own writings. In a draft constitution he wrote for the Commonwealth of Virginia in 1776, Jefferson fully embraced the absolute-necessity-for-punishment principle, though his application of the principle differed somewhat from Beccaria's ideal. As Jefferson wrote in his draft constitution: "The General assembly shall have no power to pass any law inflicting death for any crime, excepting murder, & those offences in the military service for which they shall think punishment by death absolutely necessary: and all capital punishments in other cases are hereby abolished. Nor shall they have power to prescribe torture in any case whatever."[94] In an 1820s autobiographical sketch, Jefferson—in a telling acknowledgment—specifically wrote that Beccaria and other writers had "satisfied the reasonable world of the unrightfulness and inefficacy of the punishment of crimes by death."[95] Elsewhere, Jefferson, who recommended in writing that others read both Montesquieu's and Beccaria's writings,[96] singled out and praised Beccaria's *On Crimes and Punishments* for "the demonstrative manner in which he has treated that branch of the subject."[97]

Not surprisingly given their wide circulation, the ideas of Montesquieu and Beccaria, those megastars of the transatlantic Enlightenment, helped to catalyze and inspire the American and French Revolutions and the other revolutions that ensued, if not as a cascading waterfall then at least as a rapidly flowing river. In October 1774, the Continental Congress—as an entire body—explicitly invoked the names of both men on the very cusp of the Revolutionary War (1775–1783).[98] In the Continental Congress's 1774 address to the inhabitants of Quebec, drafted by a committee composed of Richard Henry Lee, Thomas Cushing, and John Dickinson, one finds reference to "the immortal *Montesquieu*." One also finds these stirring words:

> "In every human society," says the celebrated marquis *Beccaria*, "there is an effort continually tending to confer on one part the heighth of power and happiness, and to reduce the other to the extreme of weakness and misery.

> The intent of good laws is to oppose this effort, and to diffuse their influence universally and equally."[99]

In *The Causes of the War of Independence*, it is noted that American revolutionaries such as John Adams, Samuel Adams, Benjamin Franklin, and Alexander Hamilton read Montesquieu, and that John Hancock owned "Beccaria on Crimes." While Richard Henry Lee of Virginia made the formal motion for independence at the Second Continental Congress on June 7, 1776, John Dickinson—a prominent lawyer—referred to "[t]he genius" and "the masterly hand of a Beccaria."[100]

The writings of Montesquieu and Beccaria were, in fact, extremely well-known—and often quoted and cited in speeches, newspapers, periodicals, and books—before, during, and after the American and French Revolutions.[101] Montesquieu and Beccaria's ideas were, in fact, frequently discussed side by side,[102] with Zephaniah Swift, in *A System of the Laws of the State of Connecticut* (1795), saying that Montesquieu and Beccaria "had immortalized their names in pleading the cause of humanity."[103] One source notes that while Montesquieu was "the father of the philosophy of institutions," Beccaria was "the father of the philosophy of law."[104] In pursuit of the proper historical and modern understanding of the U.S. Constitution's Eighth Amendment, *The Baron and the Marquis* thus endeavors to trace the origin, importance, and impact, in both Europe and America, of the eighteenth-century legal maxim—the one laid down so forcefully by Montesquieu and Beccaria—that unnecessary punishments are tyrannical. After discussing the history of that maxim, as well as examining the evidence pertaining to its many adherents and promotors and its transmission over geography and time from one thinker to another, *The Baron and the Marquis* turns its attention to ongoing American criminal justice reform efforts and the U.S. Supreme Court's modern Eighth Amendment jurisprudence.

In recounting the necessity-for-punishment maxim's eighteenth-century history, *The Baron and the Marquis* specifically recalls the interwoven natures of the American and French Revolutions. The American Revolution, which had its origins in 1763 and which culminated in the Treaty of Paris (1783) after the American Declaration of Independence (1776) and the hard-fought Revolutionary War, arose out of extreme discontentment with British authorities and policies.[105] American revolutionaries, like those in France who fomented the decade-long French Revolution, were extremely well read and versed in Enlightenment writers, including, of course, Baron de Montesquieu and the Marquis Beccaria.[106] While the Declaration of Independence was drafted by a Committee of Five, with Thomas Jefferson, with his felicity with words, taking on the primary role, the French Declaration of the Rights of Man and Citizen (1789) was the work of a committee of more than twenty members of France's National Assembly. The latter declaration was adopted in very close proximity to the U.S. Bill of Rights and, like the Eighth Amendment itself, specifically addresses the issue of punishments.[107] The French Declaration—inspired by both Enlightenment writers and the American Revolution itself—was written into the French Constitution, and it states in no uncertain terms that "[t]he law ought to establish only penalties that are strictly and obviously necessary."[108] This history should not be lost on modern thinkers, just as the influence of the text of the English Bill of Rights (which sought liberty for British subjects) on the drafting of the U.S. Bill of Rights (which sought to secure liberty for American citizens) should not be lost on historians.

The second half of *The Baron and the Marquis* sketches out the implications of reintroducing and incorporating Montesquieu and Beccaria's necessity-for-punishment maxim into the lexicon of American lawmakers and into the U.S. Supreme Court's Eighth Amendment jurisprudence in particular. In opposing tyranny, both Montesquieu and Beccaria were promoting liberty—the concept that, more than any other, drove eighteenth-century revolutionary fervor. The book concludes that American citizens, prosecutors and lawmakers, as well as the U.S. Supreme Court, state supreme courts, and lower courts, should return to first principles. Only necessary punishments should be put in place, and lawmakers, prosecutors and judges should use the necessity-for-punishment principle as a beacon or guiding light—and as a gut check—as they legislate, prosecute and adjudicate. Though it raises some complex and thorny separation-of-powers issues, *The Baron and the Marquis* concludes that Eighth Amendment jurisprudence should pay greater homage to the necessity-for-punishment principle. "In general terms, the principle of necessity," one source observes, "imposes a clear limitation on the intervention of public powers linked to a democratic State living under the rule of law: the attacks on the legal positions of individuals should not go any further than whatever the object that they serve might require."[109] The Eighth Amendment—as part of the foundational law of the U.S. Constitution—clearly establishes a *counter-majoritarian* check on power, and it should be respected and given life and vitality by modern American judges in the pursuit of safeguarding individual liberty.

Already, one provision of the U.S. Code—18 U.S.C. § 3553(a)—states that federal courts shall only impose sentences "sufficient, but not greater than necessary," to serve the goals of punishment.[110] That the necessity-for-punishment principle is already enshrined in federal law is a start. But given the current state of affairs in the United States, more must be done to ensure that the fundamental right to liberty is better protected. Punishments are necessary and can be very just, to be sure. And sometimes long sentences, even life-without-parole sentences, are warranted and necessitated by the facts of a particular case. But reflexively sentencing offenders, even non-violent offenders, to long terms of incarceration may not always be the best way to keep the public safe, and such a strategy should not be seen as the be-all-and-end-all for judges—jurists who, while carrying out their roles to interpret the law and keep the public safe from criminality, must also safeguard individual rights and liberties. A one-size-fits-all approach is not the right answer, and just as the often overly harsh United States Sentencing Guidelines are no longer mandatory but are discretionary, more nuance, fairness, equity, and humanity must be injected into America's criminal justice system. Americans may, in fact, be able to both save taxpayer money and make society safer by being smarter about crime and punishment and about how legislation is crafted and the laws are administered. The bottom line: if a punishment is not serving a legitimate purpose, or if a punishment is actually counterproductive and serves no valid penological objective, it is unnecessary and unjustifiable and should not be inflicted.

Judges, like lawmakers and law enforcement officials, have an important role to play in America's constitutional democracy. The language of the Eighth Amendment is short and simple, but Eighth Amendment jurisprudence, sadly, has grown increasingly complex—and, it must be said, noticeably unprincipled—over the last few decades. Existing Eighth Amendment precedents articulate a wide variety of legal standards—one ("deliberate indifference") for prisoners challenging prison conditions[111] or a lack of medical attention,[112] another ("maliciously and sadistically" using force) for inmates bringing excessive force claims,[113] and still others (gauging the proportionality of punishments or deciding whether sentences are "grossly disproportionate") to evaluate the constitutionality of capital or non-capital offenses.[114] In a number of judicial decisions, the U.S. Supreme Court has explicitly held that punishments must not be "excessive"[115] or "incompatible with 'the evolving standards of decency that mark the progress of a maturing society.'"[116] Though the "excessive" language comes from the Eighth Amendment itself and the "evolving standards of decency" phraseology is, as worded, a lofty sounding legal standard that originates in the 1950s, the actual outcome of Eighth Amendment cases has often not been very decent and has not reflected the kind of well-informed, reasoned decision-making that one should expect from a forward-thinking, liberty-loving republic.

To date, American lawmakers have all too often viewed the criminal system as a one-way ratchet: regularly *increasing* penalties, but hardly ever *decreasing* penalties; regularly *building* prisons, but hardly ever *decommissioning* them. When is the last time you heard about, or read about, a prison being demolished? (Occasionally, it actually does happen, with the Riverfront State Prison, which opened in 1985 in Camden, New Jersey, for example, torn down in 2009 and then redeveloped into a waterfront park because of its prime location. The inmates at the prison, however, were simply transferred to facilities elsewhere in the state.)[117] The State of California, under pressure from the U.S. Supreme Court itself, has taken some concrete steps recently to deal with the problem of overcrowded prisons, but American society, as a whole, needs to grapple much more forthrightly with the problem of mass incarceration.[118] Modern American judges, in fact, have been overly deferential to legislative and executive-branch judgments when it comes to draconian punishments such as the death penalty or prolonged solitary confinement, as well as in their evaluation of the constitutionality of punishments for various non-violent offenders. The *unprincipled* nature of existing Eighth Amendment case law is itself clear. Under existing law, while *lethal* punishments (think executions) are still permitted, *non-lethal* punishments (think whipping or the lash) are no longer tolerated within prisons. Instead, only punishments found to violate the Supreme Court's nebulous, highly deferential "evolving standards" test, to involve the "unnecessary and wanton infliction of pain,"[119] or to be disproportionate (or, in some cases, "grossly disproportionate") to the severity of the crimes,[120] have been declared to be "cruel and unusual punishments."[121]

Despite the growing complexity of Eighth Amendment case law, part of that ever-expanding jurisprudence is, the evidence shows, actually not well-grounded in Enlightenment principles and values. At least some of the Justices of the Supreme

Court have misread the Enlightenment and what it wrought by way of criminal justice reform. In a concurring opinion in *Glossip v. Gross*, Justice Scalia—joined by Justice Clarence Thomas—wrote: "Capital punishment presents moral questions that philosophers, theologians, and statesmen have grappled with for millennia. The Framers of our Constitution disagreed bitterly on the matter." (That's true. The founders, inspired by Montesquieu and Beccaria's writings, were deeply ambivalent about the use of capital punishment.) "For that reason," Justice Scalia then concluded, "they handled it the same way they handled many other controversial issues: they left it to the People to decide." (Not exactly, as various provisions of the U.S. Bill of Rights obviously *restrain* majority action in particular contexts.) Then taking aim at Justice Stephen Breyer's dissent in that case, in which Justices Breyer and Ginsburg jointly concluded that it is highly likely that capital punishment constitutes a cruel and unusual punishment, Justice Scalia wrote in his concurring opinion in *Glossip*: "By arrogating to himself the power to overturn that decision, JUSTICE BREYER does not just reject the death penalty, he rejects the Enlightenment."[122] (That's simply wrong.) That statement by Justice Scalia oversimplifies—indeed, grossly misconstrues—the history of the Enlightenment, part of which focused on core principles of liberty and punishment developed by Montesquieu, Beccaria, and many others.

While a big part of the Enlightenment was, certainly, about *legislative* primacy and obtaining the consent of the governed,[123] the *necessity-for-punishment principle* was also a major focus of Enlightenment thought.[124] That principle has come to be known as "the minimal severity principle" or the "parsimony" or "minimum necessary punishment" principle, with the idea being that societies should inflict "the least possible punishment necessary" under the applicable circumstances.[125] Indeed, the American Revolution—itself driven by the Enlightenment—produced state constitutions and, ultimately, the U.S. Constitution and its Bill of Rights. All of those legal instruments set forth *written* constitutional rights that are, by their very character, *anti*-majoritarian in nature. That is, they guarantee *individual* rights in the face of potentially *tyrannous* majorities—and those individual rights are *not* tied to majority rule or any particular legislative action. To use the oft-quoted words of U.S. Supreme Court Justice Robert Jackson, known, like Thomas Jefferson, for his felicity for words: "The very purpose of a Bill of Rights was to withdraw certain subjects from the vicissitudes of political controversy, to place them beyond the reach of majorities and officials, and to establish them as legal principles to be applied by the courts."[126]

The enforcement of individual rights is, of course, highly dependent on the bench and bar and on impartial and independent judges in particular. The creation of an independent judiciary—a pillar of the Rule of Law, and one that Montesquieu and America's framers cared so deeply about—was itself a product of the Enlightenment and was reflected in the U.S. Constitution, namely, in Article III, which set up America's judicial branch.[127] Article III states that "[t]he judicial power of the United States, shall be vested in one Supreme Court, and in such inferior courts as the Congress may from time to time ordain and establish."[128] Just as Montesquieu understood that there would be no liberty if the power of judging were not separate from legislative and executive power, it is equally clear that if the judiciary's "evolving standards of decency" test degenerates into a stick-one's-finger-in-the-air-and-see-which-way-the-wind-is-blowing test—one that blindly or excessively defers to executive or legislative power—abuses of power, and arbitrariness and overreaching, are sure (indeed, certain) to occur. That kind of unthinking veneration for legislative or executive power is not what America's framers had in mind at all. Indeed, American courts would become totally impotent—and the power of judicial review, explicitly recognized in *Marbury v. Madison* (1803), would be a total farce or a nullity—if those courts constantly, and without questioning, deferred to legislative or executive judgments.[129]

In a real sense, Montesquieu and Beccaria *were* the Enlightenment, or at least a major part of it, with their names continually invoked by American revolutionaries. Moreover, the Enlightenment itself was all about human progress, so the notion that America's founders would have wanted *twenty-first century* jurists to focus on figuring out what punishment practices were prevalent in the *eighteenth century*—and then to reflexively defer to such antiquated practices—is totally absurd and illogical. Thomas Jefferson—one of those founders—himself famously wrote to James Madison from Paris in September 1789, analyzing whether past generations should, through their actions, tie the hands of future ones: "The question Whether one generation of men has a right to bind another, seems never to have been started either on this or our side of the water. Yet it is a question of such consequences as not only to merit decision, but place also, among the fundamental principles of every government." Jefferson's answer: "I set out on this ground, which I suppose to be self evident, '*that the earth belongs in usufruct to the living*': that the dead have neither powers nor rights over it. The portion occupied by any individual ceases to be his when himself ceases to be, and reverts to the society." As Jefferson added later in that 1789 letter: "On similar ground it may be proved that no society can make a perpetual constitution, or even a perpetual law. The earth belongs always to the living generation." "This principle that the earth belongs to the living, and not to the dead, is of very extensive application and consequences, in every country," Jefferson continued, laying out his views.[130] No less a figure than Richard Posner—the famous American jurist, legal scholar, and law-and-economics-driven thinker who sees Beccaria as a foundational figure—has argued that to be "ruled by the dead hand of the past is not self-government in any sense."[131]

The U.S. Constitution, of course, has endured since the 1780s, and it has only been amended infrequently despite Jefferson's desire for what, today, we might call more regular tune-ups. Article V of the Constitution requires Congress to "call a Convention for proposing Amendments" only if "two thirds of both Houses shall deem it necessary" or "two thirds of the several States" submit an "Application" to that effect. And even then, a proposed amendment must be "ratified by the Legislatures of three fourths of the several States, or by Conventions in three fourths thereof" in order to take effect.[132] Because it is so hard to amend, the Constitution, with the exception of its first ten amendments, adopted rather quickly (and ratified in 1791), has been amended only sporadically. Indeed, constitutional amendments have often come about only as a result of large-scale social movements (e.g., the suffrage movement produced the Nineteenth Amendment guaranteeing women the right to vote) or tragic events, such as the Civil War (which produced the Reconstruction Amendments).[133] The difficulty of amending the U.S. Constitution, however, does not mean modern-day judges should not do their level best to protect the individual rights *already protected by* that Constitution, including the rights enshrined in the Eighth and Fourteenth Amendments. Judges are duty-bound to uphold and defend the Constitution, the provisions of which require the safeguarding of liberty, the equal protection of the laws, and the prohibitions of excessive bail, excessive fines, and cruel and unusual punishments.

Initially, Thomas Jefferson's compatriot, James Madison, was actually skeptical—essentially lukewarm—about how efficacious the U.S. Constitution's initial ten amendments, now known as the U.S. Bill of Rights, would be. "My own opinion," he told Jefferson, "has always been in favor of a bill of rights; provided that it be so framed as not to imply powers not meant to be included in the enumeration." (The U.S. Constitution's Ninth Amendment states that "[t]he enumeration in the Constitution, of certain rights, shall not be construed to deny or disparage others retained by the people." And the Tenth Amendment provides that "[t]he powers not delegated to the United States by the Constitution, nor prohibited by it to the states, are reserved to the states respectively, or to the people.") "At the same time," Madison wrote, "I have never thought the omission a material defect, nor been anxious to supply it by *subsequent* amendment, for any other reason than that it is anxiously desired by others. I have favored it because I supposed it might be of use, and if properly executed could not be of disservice." Madison pointed out that, in every state, "[r]epeated violations of these parchment barriers have been committed by overbearing majorities in every State." In his home state of Virginia, Madison confessed that he had witnessed the state's bill of rights "violated in every instance where it has been opposed to a popular current." But America's founders were optimistic about the country's future, a country in which they wanted liberty, not tyranny, to reign supreme, and it was felt that a Bill of Rights was necessary and that, over time, the Bill of Rights would engender greater and greater respect.

Indeed, James Madison knew that the future would bring changes, and—in examining the past—he himself expressed a self-awareness of the shortcomings of the seventeenth- and eighteenth-century thinkers who had preceded him. As he wrote in 1793, after the ratification of the U.S. Bill of Rights and the start of the French Revolution: "Writers, such as Locke, and Montesquieu, who have discussed more the principles of liberty and the structure of government, lie under the same disadvantage, of having written before these subjects were illuminated by the events and discussions which distinguish a very recent period. Both of them, too, are evidently warped by a regard to the particular government of England, to which one of them owed allegiance; and the other professed an admiration bordering on idolatry." "Montesquieu, however," Madison lavishly praised the French jurist while recognizing his particular foibles, "has rather distinguished himself by enforcing the reasons and the importance of avoiding a confusion of the several powers of government, than by enumerating and defining the powers which belong to each particular class."[134] By the time the U.S. Constitution was proposed and ratified by the American people (or at least *a portion* of them) in the 1780s, and by the time the U.S. Bill of Rights was proposed and then ratified on December 15, 1791, the writings of Montesquieu and Beccaria, not to mention those of Voltaire, Locke and Blackstone, had been around for quite some time. And they clearly had been put to good use, including by America's Founding Fathers, though systemic racism and massive gender inequality remained disturbing eighteenth-century facts of life.

The U.S. Bill of Rights, like the English Bill of Rights before it, represented an important step forward for the protection of individual rights. Notably, because America's founders believed in God-given or *natural* rights, rights that one was born with and that one had, simply, as a result of one's birth, some founders had initially seen no need at all for a bill of rights. "As we enjoy all our natural rights from a pre-occupancy, antecedent to the social state," Dr. Benjamin Rush, the Pennsylvania patriot, declared, it would be "absurd to frame a formal declaration that our natural rights are acquired from ourselves." But Thomas Jefferson, James Madison, and many other American leaders wanted—and wisely insisted upon—a bill of rights, one that would, among other things, condemn excessive bail and fines and cruel and unusual punishments. "A bill of rights," Jefferson asserted, "is what the people are entitled to against every government on earth, general or particular, & what no just government should refuse or rest on inference." In commenting on Virginia's declaration of rights, the predecessor of the U.S. Bill of Rights, Edmund Randolph saw "the formation of" that state's bill of rights as serving "two objectives": first, "that the legislature should not in their acts violate" any of its canons; and second, "that in all the revolutions of time, of human opinion, and of government, a perpetual standard should be erected around which the people might rally, and by a notorious record be forever admonished to be watchful, firm and virtuous." In other words, society should always be vigilant about the abuse of power and a bill of rights, if properly framed, could accrue its own force and power over time.

Seeing a U.S. Bill of Rights as a practical necessity and as something that might be of lasting value to the country, Madison took on the task of putting a federal bill of rights in place, one that would include the prohibitions against excessive bail and fines and against cruel and unusual punishments. "The political truths declared in that solemn manner," Madison once observed, "acquire by degrees the character of fundamental maxims of free government, and as they become incorporated with the national sentiment, counteract the impulses of interest and passion." "[A]mendments, if pursued with a proper moderation and in a proper mode," Madison argued, "will be not only safe, but may serve the double purpose of satisfying the minds of well meaning opponents, and of providing additional guards in favour of liberty." "It is my sincere opinion," Madison wrote to a Baptist minister after much thought and consideration, "that the Constitution ought to be revised, and that the first Congress ... ought to prepare and recommend to the States ... the most satisfactory provisions for all essential rights." Madison—who personally pushed for the adoption of the U.S. Bill of Rights in that First Congress—himself spoke of "independent tribunals of justice" serving as the "guardians" of constitutional rights and being "an impenetrable bulwark against every assumption of power" by the legislative or executive branches. His Virginia colleague, Richard Henry Lee, best known for making the motion in the Second Continental Congress calling for the colonies' independence from Great Britain, likewise specifically saw the prohibitions against excessive bail, excessive fines, and cruel and unusual punishments as necessary and indispensable "to prevent oppression" and to restrain "the wicked & tyrannic."[135]

The Baron and the Marquis—a detailed examination of the past and present, with watchful eyes on the future—is, fundamentally, about the promise of American criminal justice reform. It argues that amidst ongoing, high-profile efforts to reform the country's existing criminal justice system (*systems*, actually, is the proper word as different practices exist at the federal level and in each of the states and U.S. territories), policymakers and lawmakers—and yes, prosecutors and courts—would be wise to keep in mind a principle developed centuries ago: that only necessary (or, as Beccaria put it, only *absolutely* necessary) punishments are just and intellectually defensible. Many present-day criminal justice policies throughout the country, from pre-trial detention and bail practices to sentencing and the conditions of confinement for inmates, are in need of reform, and that is what this book aims to shed light on and to help address. In trying to illuminate a path forward, *The Baron and the Marquis* contends that criminal justice practices should be driven by the concept of necessity and guided by the values of proportionality, empathy, compassion, non-discrimination, and human dignity.

As part of the modern application of the now centuries-old necessity-for-punishment maxim, the American death penalty, for starters, should finally meet its end and be declared unconstitutional by the U.S. Supreme Court.[136] The death penalty, though it affects only a tiny percentage of the U.S. prison population,[137] epitomizes an overly vindictive approach to American criminal justice. Capital punishment has an incredibly corrosive effect on the law itself, and it has certainly badly corrupted American law—and America's Eighth Amendment jurisprudence in particular—for far too long. In addition to bidding good riddance to capital punishment,[138] prolonged solitary confinement and the unduly severe punishment of nonviolent offenders (to give a couple of additional examples) should be much more carefully scrutinized by legislators, prosecutors, and the courts in light of viable alternatives to long-term isolation in cells and long-term incarceration. The use of lengthy terms of incarceration—as necessary as that is for certain violent offenders, such as murderers and rapists—should be seen as a last resort to solving America's most pressing social problems, from alcoholism, drug abuse, and poverty, to chronic unemployment or underemployment, the need for more job training, and the opioid crisis. Putting in place sensible, long-overdue gun legislation, including universal background checks, would, all by itself, prevent some criminals and people with severe mental illnesses from getting access to lethal weapons (e.g., AR-15s), and thus potentially prevent some very heinous crimes (e.g., mass shootings at schools or workplaces) from happening in the first place.

Tackling social ills on the front end, instead of merely reactively dealing with their extreme adverse consequences on the back end, would, certainly, be a major step forward. With the advent of technology and a greater awareness of the pitfalls and costs and risks of incarcerating non-violent offenders for long periods of time, greater consideration should be given to more effective, and frankly more cost-effective, measures, such as substance abuse treatment, electronic home monitoring, job and apprenticeship and skills training, and education. The United States, one scholar, Travis Pratt, has lamented, "has become 'addicted to incarceration'"—an addiction "fueled by policies legitimized by faulty information about the crime problem in the United States, American citizens' opinions about crime and punishment, and the efficacy of incarceration as a means of social control."[139] Breaking addictions is hard, as any alcoholic or recovering drug addict would readily admit. But trying to break bad habits—and trying to fix the ills in America's criminal justice system—is worth the fight.

In June 2016, a Gallup poll showed that only 23% of Americans had "a great deal" or "quite a lot" of confidence in the criminal justice system.[140] That poll, and others like it, should be a wake-up call to twenty-first century Americans as they think about the country's institutions and how best to reform them. *The Baron and the Marquis* discusses the best way forward in light of where we stand now and what we know now, though more criminal justice research must be done to fully understand the issues we face. The concept of necessity, however, should be front and center throughout the reform debate. In fact, the consideration of Cesare Beccaria's corollary to the necessity-for-punishment principle—that is, the imposition of the minimum sanction warranted by the given circumstances—has implications for existing systems of bail throughout the country and for efforts to reduce criminal justice costs while keeping the American public equally safe or even safer. Efforts to reform America's bail system and to recalibrate sentencing policies are now underway from coast to coast in the United States, and the necessity-for-punishment principle should not be lost in those important public debates.

The Baron and the Marquis

CHAPTER 1

Enlightened Minds:

Baron de Montesquieu and the Marquis Beccaria

The *Ancien Régime* and the Way It Was

During the *Ancien Régime*, draconian punishments, which get their name from the notorious Greek lawgiver, Draco, were the norm. While the earliest Greek laws were passed down through word of mouth from one generation to the next, Draco of Athens, in about 624 B.C., had the laws carved onto wooden plaques and stone pillars and placed in markets and other public places, with everything from murder to the smallest thefts punishable by death.[1] "As Draco's laws were chiefly a collection of the old customs of the land," another source observes, "they seemed to the later Athenians exceedingly severe and were said to have been 'written in blood.' "[2] The kinds of severe and torturous punishments that were regularly inflicted during medieval times and in the centuries that followed included breaking on the wheel, burning at the stake, drawing and quartering, hanging, and beheading by swords, hatchets, or axes.[3] And executions were frequently done in public. "The ritual of execution," Julius Ruff writes in *Violence in Early Modern Europe, 1500–1800*, "usually began with a procession from the place of confinement to the execution site."[4] English felons were brought to the gallows at Tyburn in open ox carts, often sitting on their own coffins with ropes dangling around their necks. Sometimes, as many as 24 criminals were dispatched at one time. "The 'bells of Old Bailey,'" one source notes, "refer to the St. Sepulchre bell which tolled when condemned prisoners made their way from Newgate Prison towards the gallows at Tyburn or when, after 1783, they were executed outside Newgate."[5]

Throughout human history, societies and their leaders—from monarchs and religious figures to lawmakers—have debated how best to combat crime. "Medieval punishments were often barbarous in their severity," one history observes, pointing out that King Stephen I in early 11th-century Hungary ordered the death penalty for any person found guilty of theft for the third time. In the latter part that century, Hungary's King Ladislas also ordered that men stealing objects worth more than a chicken be hanged and that their children then be enslaved.[6] As another source notes of the Middle Ages: "Punishment for crimes was usually quite severe. In the later Middle Ages, the death penalty was often used, especially for crimes against property. People were hanged for stealing eggs, for instance." As that source continues: "Thieves had their arms and legs amputated. Those conspiring to commit crimes would have their ears cut off and their eyes put out. Accused and condemned criminals could be racked, burned, flayed, flogged, or drawn-and-quartered."[7] One scholar, Douglas

Hay, wrote that "the rulers of eighteenth-century England cherished the death penalty,"[8] with Edmund Burke declaring at the end of the eighteenth century "that he could obtain the consent of the House of Commons to any Bill imposing the punishment of death."[9] The English "Bloody Code," *A Companion to the History of Crime and Criminal Justice* emphasizes, "refers to the body of laws that was established by a substantial increase in the number of capital statutes passed between 1688 and 1815, which together prescribed the death penalty for over 200 separate offences."[10]

The idea that severe punishments were necessary to keep order in a society—and for a monarch to maintain power—was one popularized by the Italian diplomat Niccolò Machiavelli (1469–1527). In *The Prince*, Machiavelli gave this advice in a chapter titled "Cruelty and mercifulness; and whether it is better to be loved or feared": "I maintain that every ruler should want to be thought merciful, not cruel; nevertheless, one should take care not to be merciful in an inappropriate way." On the matter of whether it was better for a ruler to be loved or feared, Machiavelli had this to say: "My view is that it is desirable to be both loved and feared; but it is difficult to achieve both and, if one of them has to be lacking, it is much safer to be feared than loved." For Machiavelli, the key for a ruler was thus to be feared but not loathed or despised. As Machiavelli wrote:

> Men are less hesitant about offending or harming a ruler who makes himself loved than one who inspires fear. For love is sustained by a bond of gratitude which, because men are excessively self-interested, is broken whenever they see a chance to benefit themselves. But fear is sustained by a dread of punishment that is always effective. Nevertheless, a ruler must make himself feared in such a way that, even if he does not become loved, he does not become hated. For it is perfectly possible to be feared without incurring hatred. And this can always be achieved if he refrains from laying hands on the property of his citizens and subjects, and on their womenfolk. If it is necessary to execute anyone, this should be done only if there is a proper justification and obvious reason.[11]

In *Discourses on Livy*, Machiavelli wrote of various prominent Roman executions, writing that "[b]ecause they were excessive and notable, such things made men draw back toward the mark whenever one of them arose." "[W]hen they began to be more rare," he continued, "they also began to give more space to men to corrupt themselves and to behave with greater danger and more tumult." Just as Machiavelli believed that emergencies would inevitably arise in states that would require rulers to resort to extreme measures of cruelty and violence, he believed—in line with that view—that periodic executions would be warranted. As Machiavelli emphasized, giving his opinion as to how often rulers should resort to such spectacles: "For one should not wish ten years at most to pass from one to another of such executions; for when this time is past, men begin to vary in their customs and to transgress the laws. Unless something arises by which punishment is brought back to their memory and fear is renewed in their spirits, soon so many delinquents join together that they can no longer be punished without danger." The councilor who spawned his own adjective, *Machiavellian*, was nothing if not self-assured. "Those who governed the state of Florence from 1434 up to 1494 used to say, to this purpose," Machiavelli added, "that it was necessary to regain the state every five years; otherwise, it was difficult to maintain it."[12] For Machiavelli, periodically inspiring terror and fear was simply what an archetypal ruler should do.

Before the separation of church and state, law and religion were intertwined in prior times in Western civilizations. Criminal laws, including in colonial America in places like Massachusetts, were in fact once framed explicitly by the Bible and the Ten Commandments. In colonial Massachusetts, for example, its "Body of Liberties" (1641) set forth twelve capital offenses, using biblical passages as justification for death sentences.[13] "The Old Testament," one source recounts, "calls for the death penalty on numerous occasions,"[14] though one scholar, the author of *The Biblical Truth about America's Death Penalty*, after taking note of all the capital crimes in colonial times, writes that "the Mosaic law"—the idea of "eye for eye, life for life," also known as *lex talionis*—"was meant to be a limitation that reduced violence," something that would limit "the retaliatory violence of the law of the clan, limiting escalating retaliatory violence to only proportional retaliatory violence." As that scholar, Dale Recinella, writes, quoting another source, in his book about capital punishment and religion: " 'Old Testament scholars have long recognized that the Mosaic Law was meant to be a limitation on violence rather than an endorsement of it.' " But if the *lex talionis* was meant as a *limiting* principle, the way colonial laws were written often gave little evidence of that. Recinella notes that "in 1665 New York, striking one's parents was a capital crime," and that, "in 1647 Massachusetts, the death penalty covered witchcraft, adultery, cursing one's parents, and being a rebellious son."[15]

Early Anglo-American religious figures played a big role in the debate over capital punishment, frequently attending executions and making sermons in close proximity to them, even at the gallows. As one book emphasized of what occurred on execution day: "Public executions in seventeenth- and eighteenth-century America were seen as occasions for making moral statements about the righteousness of punishment and the grim fate that awaited those who broke the law. Often these moral statements appeared in the form of poems, usually anonymous, that were spread about on broadsides, or printed sheets." "Broadsides," that book notes, "might be handed out (or sold) at the execution, or distributed before or after the fatal event."[16] In another book, *In the Shadow of the Gallows: Race, Crime, and American Civic Identity*, it is noted that gallows literature became more popular over the course of the eighteenth century. "Before the sun closes upon us this evening," one sermon admonished the condemned, "you will launch into an awful eternity, and go to appear at the tremendous bar of God, to give up an account of your conduct in the body." As Jeannine Marie DeLombard writes in *In the Shadow of the Gallows*: "On Execution Day, the condemned person stood not merely as a negative exemplar whose gruesome end expiated collective guilt and offered a warning to the surrounding community. Ideally he or she stood as a 'dramatic embodiment of the fundamental Christian paradigm of the penitent sinner confronting death.' "[17]

In England and colonial America, the broadsides printed memorialized the public executions. In 1717, for example, New England preacher Cotton Mather—a Puritan minister and pamphleteer—claimed that a local bookseller had, in just five days, sold almost one thousand copies of his latest execution sermon.[18] One 1754 English sermon—invoking a biblical verse—stressed "*that the Law is not made for a Righteous Man, but for the Lawless and Disobedient, for the Ungodly and for Sinners, for Unholy and Prophane, for Murderers of Fathers and Murderers of Mothers, for Man-Slayers.*"[19] That sermon, preached by Thomas Alcock of Oxford, stressed that "*the Law is good,*" observing in that vein: "As we cannot live in this World, without forming ourselves into Societies, so neither can Societies subsist without Laws to regulate the Conduct of the Members."[20] "Laws," Alcock emphasized, "are absolutely necessary to the good of Society, and Government itself may be considered only as a Power, lodged either in a single Person, or in several Persons, for the due Execution of the Laws." "Kings themselves," he preached, "are always at the Head of the Law, and in all Places of their Government fit in Judgment either in their own Persons, or by their Deputies and Judges."[21]

In *The Doctrine of Philosophical Necessity Illustrated*, a theologian and scientist, Joseph Priestley, writing in the eighteenth century, explicitly discussed punishment in the context of sin. "[I]t is only where the necessity of sinning arises from some *other cause* than a *man's own disposition of mind,*" Priestley wrote, "that we ever say, there is any impropriety in punishing a man for his conduct." "If the impossibility of acting well, has arisen from a *bad disposition*, or *habit*, its having been impossible, *with that disposition*, or *habit*, to act virtuously," he recorded, "is never any reason for our forbearing punishment: because he know, that punishment is proper to correct that disposition, and that habit; and that we thereby both reform the sinner, and warn others, which are all the just ends of punishment; every thing else deserving no other name than *vengeance*, and being manifestly absurd, because answering no good purpose." "At the same time," Priestley continued, "punishment, used with this view, will be administered with the utmost tenderness and compassion." In that book, Priestley also had this to say on "[t]he doctrine of necessity": "We are, therefore, naturally led, by the principles of it, to consider all future evils in the same light as the present, i. e. as corrective and salutary, terminating in good, which is also sufficiently agreeable to the language of the scriptures, with respect to all punishment, present or future."[22]

Heinous crimes or the frequency of crimes, along with a powerful ruler's whim or the public's reaction to such crimes, often determined the nature and substance of a state's criminal laws. That is still true today, just as it was centuries ago in early America and in Great Britain, America's mother country. As Thomas Alcock explicitly observed in 1754, noting the history and continual adjustment of punishments in England fifteen years before the 1769 publication[23] of Sir William Blackstone's *Commentaries on the Laws of England*. As Alcock declared:

> In *England* too we may observe, how Laws have been multiplied somewhat in Proportion as Crimes have increased. About the Time of *William* the Conqueror, and earlier, mulch or Fine was commonly the Punishment of a Criminal, if rich; and whipping or burning in the Hand if poor. But Fine or Whipping or other corporal Punishments not being found sufficient to stop the Progress of Wickedness, Death at last became the Penalty.—At first too, when Death was made the Penalty, it was confined to certain great Crimes,

> as Murder, Parricide, Treason. But the State and Society being still disturbed by other Crime, as Theft and Robbery, it was thought necessary to extend the Penalty of Death to Them.—In Theft too, Death at first was annexed to the greater Sorts of it, to Robbing and putting People in fear of their Lives, to Burglary or House-breaking by Night. But for some Years it has been extended even to a Horse stolen out of a Field, nay of late Years to a Creature much less considerable in Value. So that Crimes of such different magnitudes, as those of stealing a Sheep, and murdering a Man are come to have the same Punishment.[24]

Centuries ago, it was an extremely common, widely shared belief that death sentences and executions as well as harsh corporal punishments—in use, we know, since the beginning of recorded human history—were necessary to a society's well-being or preservation.[25] Such physical penalties were seen as everything from part of God's wrath, to being dictated by Machiavellian machinations, to the appropriate punishment for sin, to—as scholars Nicole Marafioti and Jay Paul Gates write—being "designed as a last resort, for offenders who could not be curbed by any other method."[26] In *The Prince*, a work of political, military, and diplomatic advice delivered to His Magnificence Lorenzo de' Medici, the Renaissance ruler of the Florentine Republic, Machiavelli had this warning for princes ruling cities or kingdoms that, before being acquired, had lived under their own laws: "He who becomes the ruler of a city that is used to living under its own laws and does not knock it down, must expect to be knocked down by it. Whenever it rebels, it will find strength in the language of liberty and will seek to restore its ancient constitution. Neither the passage of time nor good treatment will make its citizens forgot their previous liberty." Machiavelli distinguished between "cruelty well used" and "cruelty abused," writing that "[t]hose who use cruelty well" may find "both God and their subjects are prepared to let bygones be bygones" but that "[t]hose who abuse it cannot hope to retain power indefinitely." "[I]t is necessary for a ruler, if he wants to hold on to power, to learn how not to be good, and to know when it is and when it is not necessary to use this knowledge," Machiavelli observed.[27]

The Enlightenment Pivot

But a change of perspective swept the world during the Enlightenment and, in particular, in the aftermath of the publication of Montesquieu's *The Spirit of the Laws* and Beccaria's *On Crimes and Punishments*. "Throughout the Western world during the late eighteenth century, Enlightenment intellectuals challenged the death penalty," writes Lawrence Goodheart in *The Solemn Sentence of Death: Capital Punishment in Connecticut*. As Goodheart explains of the sea change that occurred: "This pivotal period, which culminated in the American, French, and Haitian revolutions, was characterized by what one scholar has called the 'inventing of human rights.' Connecticut too was part of the international ferment in criminal justice." Over seven months in 1786, Goodheart recounts, the *New Haven Gazette* reprinted the entire English-language translation of Cesare Beccaria's *Dei delitti e delle pene*. "An editorial endorsement of the Italian reformer in the *Gazette*," Goodheart observes, "instructed citizens that 'a mild penal system is a political advantage,' a measure of good government."[28] Whereas Machiavelli had advised well-timed ruthlessness, the most enlightened of Enlightenment writers favored moderate governments that would inflict mild punishments.

In Connecticut, the first chapters of Beccaria's *On Crimes and Punishments* were reprinted in the January 12, 1786 edition of *The New-Haven Gazette*, published by Josiah Meigs, Daniel Bowen, and Eleutheros Dana. In the same issue of the paper that Isaac Beers—a New Haven bookseller who imported and sold books, as well as groceries, gin, and brandy, out of his house—advertised for sale as "Just Imported from LONDON" Blackstone's *Commentaries on the Laws of England* and Montesquieu's *Spirit of Laws*, the first four chapters of *On Crimes and Punishments* was reprinted. That reprinting of Beccaria's treatise was introduced by this editorial note: "*The following Essay will, we doubt not, be acceptable to the Friends of Humanity; and such we hope are all our Readers. We particularly wish that our Legislators, the Solons and Lycurgi of this State, may believe, that a mild penal System is a political Advantage.*" The introductory editorial note went on to quote from Cesare Beccaria himself, with the editors of the paper parroting that sentiment:

> *We are "sensible that the Voice of one Philosopher is too weak to be heard amidst the Clamours of a Multitude blindly influenced by Custom; but there is a small number of Sages, scattered on the Face of the Earth, who will echo to him from the bottom of their Hearts; and if these Truths should happily force their way to the Thrones of Princes, be it known to them, that they come attended with the secret wishes of all Mankind; and tell the" Legislator "who deigns them a gracious reception, that his Fame shall outshine the glory of Conquerors, and that equitable Posterity shall exalt his peaceful Trophies above those of a Titus, an Antoninus, or a Trajan."*

Among the reprinted truths put forward by Beccaria at the very beginning of "Chap. II": "Every punishment, which does not arise from absolute necessity, says the great Montesquieu, is tyrannical."[29]

Josiah Meigs (1757–1822)—one of the publishers of *The New-Haven Gazette*—was something of a prodigy. After graduating from Yale College in 1778, Meigs studied law. "In 1781, when only 24 years of age," it was later written in *Life of Josiah Meigs* by his great-grandson, "Meigs was appointed Tutor of Mathematics, Natural Philosophy and Astronomy in Yale College," a position he held for three years. After being admitted to the bar in New Haven, Connecticut, in April 1783, he established a printing office in 1784 and began publishing *The New-Haven Gazette* with his partners, Daniel Bowen and Eleutheros Dana. Their publication—per a biography of Josiah Meigs—contained "mathematical questions to be solved, poems, sonnets, elegies, news from all parts of the world (often or generally in the shape of extracts from private letters), ænigmas for the ladies, and extracts of some length from recently published books—from the Wealth of Nations, then about ten years old, from Jefferson's Notes on Virginia, and from the Marquis of Beccaria's Essay on Crimes and Punishments, among many others." While Adam Smith's *The Wealth of Nations* was published in 1776, Thomas Jefferson's *Notes on the State of Virginia* first appeared in 1785. In college, Meigs—along with the rest of his class—studied Montesquieu's *Spirit of the Laws* as well as other Enlightenment texts. Josiah Meigs went on to be the first acting president of the University of Georgia in Athens—a school where he put in place its first physics curriculum.[30]

In *A History of Philadelphia* (1839), Meigs' business associate, Daniel Bowen (1760–1856), who lived into his nineties, included a whole section on "PUNISHMENTS." In that section, Bowen, reflecting back in time, referenced the influence of Cesare Beccaria and others on American life. After noting the impact of Pennsylvania's founder, William Penn, responsible for 1682 legislation that severely restricted capital punishments, Bowen wrote: "In 1787, Dr. RUSH read a paper, before a Benevolent Society, assembled at the house of Dr. FRANKLIN, entitled, 'An enquiry into the influence of public executions, on criminals and society:' The philanthropic ideas, which he advanced, were considered wild and visionary notions." That paper, published in Philadelphia in 1787, was titled *An Enquiry into the Effects of Public Punishments upon Criminals, and upon Society; Read in the Society for Promoting Political Enquiries, Convened at the House of His Excellency Benjamin Franklin, Esquire, in Philadelphia, March 9th, 1787*. "In 1788," Bowen continued, "Dr. Rush following the suggestion of the celebrated Marquis Beccaria, in a treatise on 'Crimes and Punishments,' again presented the subject to public consideration, in a printed form, and even denied the right of government, to destroy life, as a punishment." "From these early endeavors," Bowen observed, summarizing the relevant history, "have arisen the great improvements made in our Penitentiary systems, and the certainty of regulated punishments seems, so far to promise, much more in the correction of crime, than the sanguinary code, of former times."[31] Not only were Beccaria's ideas openly debated at Yale College's commencement day exercises in 1788, but Beccaria's advocacy and "victory" against torture was still being celebrated at Yale College in 1884. In the latter year, a statue of scientist Benjamin Silliman—a 1796 graduate of Yale for whom one of Yale's residential colleges is now named—was unveiled.[32]

Excerpts from Beccaria's *On Crimes and Punishments*—along with invocations from Montesquieu's *Spirit of Laws*—were frequently reprinted in American newspapers, both large and small, in the decades after its first appearance. For example, *The Telescope* in Leominster, Massachusetts, reprinted Chapter 2 of Beccaria's treatise—the one containing the necessity-for-punishment maxim—on March 13, 1800.[33] In *The Democrat*, published in Boston, Massachusetts, in 1804, an anonymous letter writer, writing "*To the Legislatures of the Respective States*," also emphasized that, on the subject of crimes and punishments, "the opinions of the enlightened and liberal of all nations, coincide in the leading principles which ought to determine the conduct of the legislator." In the letter, which made reference to the work of Beccaria and Pennsylvania's renowned jurist William Bradford, the letter writer stressed: "A few plain axioms, easy of apprehension, have been universally received. These are 1. That the prevention of crimes is the sole end of government; 2. That every punishment, which is not absolutely necessary for that purpose, is a cruel and tyrannical act; 3. That every penalty should be apportioned to the offence." As the writer's letter, titled "LETTER FIFTH," continued:

> From these leading principles, the following inferences have been draw; 1. That the punishment of crimes should be prompt and certain—2. That pardons should be rarely, if ever, interposed. 3. That, in order to insure a certainty of punishment and to avoid the necessity of pardons, punishments should rather be too light than too severe. Facts have shewn that under a code of laws, founded on these principles, crimes have been few; while, under a sanguinary system, they have invariably become more numerous and atrocious. The English code is the most sanguinary of Europe, and in that kingdom by far more crimes are perpetrated than in any equal population in the world.[34]

The writings of Montesquieu or Beccaria were often invoked by early Americans to rail against cruelty or sanguinary laws. In January 1805, the *Pennsylvania Correspondent* in Doylestown, Pennsylvania, went out of its way to reprint a grand jury charge delivered by Judge Cooper in November of 1804 that invoked the Baron de Montesquieu. That grand jury charge, quoting Montesquieu, contained these words:

> [I]t has long ago been remarked, that Life and Liberty, and Character, are regarded and protected by the Laws of a country, in proportion to the degree of freedom that prevails in it, and the accuracy of the ideas entertained among the People, of the respective Rights, of the Governors and the Governed. "In Turkey," says the Baron *de Montesquieu*, "where little regard is shown to the Honor, Lives or Estates of the Subjects, all Causes are, one way or other, quickly decided. The method of determining them is a matter of indifference; provided they be determined. The Bashaw, after a quick hearing, orders which Party he pleases to be Bastinadoed; and sends them about their Business. But, in moderate Governments, where the Life of the meanest Subject is deemed precious, no Man is stripped of his Honor or Property, but after a long Inquiry; and no Man is bereft of his Life, till his Country has attacked him; an Attack that is never made, without leaving him all possible means of Defence."[35]

The abandonment of sanguinary punishments in favor of proportionate ones was an important goal of Enlightenment thinkers.

A political awakening thus took place as a result of Enlightenment ideas. For example, thc *History of Maryland,* written by historian J. Thomas Scharf in the late nineteenth century, specifically discusses the trajectory of America's transition from the most severe of punishments to much milder ones. "Our ancestors," Scharf wrote in the book, tracing through colonial history, "considered that the greater horror they could excite by the severity of their punishment, the greater check it would be to crime." "Thus," Scharf observed, "offenders were publicly exposed in the most frequented thoroughfares, where their ears were nailed to the pillory and cut off, being whipped afterwards through the public thoroughfares, having his tongue bored with a red hot iron, or his nose slit, or being branded with the initial letter of the offence for which he suffered: 'S.L.,' for seditious libeller, on either cheek; 'M.,' for manslaughter, or 'T.,' for thief, on the left hand; 'R.,' for rogue and vagabond, on the shoulder; and 'P.,' for perjury, on the forehead." In his 1879 history, Scharf—looking back at the shift that occurred in the state—wrote that "[t]he pillory was resorted to for the last time in Maryland, in Baltimore, in 1819, and the stocks and whipping-post were entirely abandoned about the same time, but the gibbet and the hanging in chains was kept up later, in the case of a few notorious criminals, such as pirates and highwaymen, who robbed the coaches carrying the United States mail."[36] Old habits were hard to dislodge, but Enlightenment ideas had great force and caused a great awakening to occur.

Over the course of world history, old laws have gradually given way to new ones, with the severity (or mildness) of punishments ebbing and flowing with the times. Due in large part to the writings of Montesquieu and Beccaria, torture, medieval superstition, and draconian punishments gave way to greater rationality in sentencing, as American history—like European history—clearly shows. For example, the late seventeenth-century Salem Witch Trials, dramatized in Arthur Miller's famous play, *The Crucible*, represented the Old Regime. As one source summarized what happened: "Between June 10 and September 22, 1692, 19 people were hanged for witchcraft in Salem, Massachusetts. One man was pressed to death, and over 150 others from 24 towns and villages went to jail, where at least 4 adults and one infant died and some remained until the following May."[37] "By today's standards," another book explains, "the laws of the Massachusetts Bay Colony were very harsh, and witchcraft was just one of many offenses for which citizens could be put to death." "The Puritans," that book, *The Salem Witch Trials*, emphasizes, "sometimes used passages in the Bible to justify the death sentence."[38]

At one time in Western societies, corporal and capital punishments were routinely meted out to offenders, though nobles and elites were often punished in very different ways than commoners or slaves. "Puritans," scholar John Vile writes, "lived in a hierarchical society where certain punishments were considered too degrading to administer to those of higher classes (gentlemen)." For example, in the Massachusetts Body of Liberties (1641), clause 43 read: "No man shall be beaten with above 40 stripes, nor shall any true gentleman, nor any man equall to a gentleman be punished with whipping, unles his crime be very shamefull, and his course of life vitious and profligate." In the pre-*On Crimes and Punishments* era, that colonial legal code even provided for the use of torture in delineated circumstances, though it simultaneously denounced cruel punishments. In the Body of Liberties, clause 45 read: "No man shall be forced by Torture to confesse any Crime against himselfe nor any other unlesse it be in some Capitall case, where he is first fullie convicted by cleare and suffitient evidence to be guilty, After which if the cause be of that nature, That it is very apparent there by other conspiratours, or confederates with him, Then he may be tortured, yet not with such Tortures as be Barbarous and inhumane." Clause 46 somewhat similarly provided: "For bodilie punishments we allow amongst us none that are inhumane Barbarous or cruel."[39]

Montesquieu and Beccaria, the French baron and the Italian marquis, consequently ushered in a new way of thinking—and a New World Order—as their writings spread like wildfire throughout the Western world. Thoughtless barbarity was to be replaced by rationality and much more measured proportionality. As Frederick Rosen writes in *The Cambridge History of Eighteenth-Century Political Thought*: "In suggesting that Montesquieu set the agenda for the reform of the criminal law during the Enlightenment, it should now be clear that he went further than an opposition to severe penalties and to punishment based more on religious enthusiasm than on actual injuries to individuals. He called for a careful definition of offences based on the idea of individual liberty as security; he sought to proportion punishments to the severity of the threat to security...." "The importance of Montesquieu," Rosen adds, "was readily recognized in discussions of criminal law throughout the latter half of the eighteenth century, and no less so than by one of his most important disciples, Cesare Beccaria, whose celebrated *Dei delitti e delle pene* (*Of Crimes and Punishments*) was published in 1764, sixteen years after *The Spirit of the Laws*."[40]

The Spirit of the Laws was first translated into English with Montesquieu's approval by the Irish-born writer Thomas Nugent (1700–1772). That book—as *Thomas Paine's American Ideology* notes—"was widely known and cited throughout America, and the existence of many copies can be documented." Beccaria's *Dei delitti e delle pene*, on the other hand, was first translated into English by an anonymous translator. That edition, first published in London in 1767, was printed by John Almon. One scholar, Rosamaria Loretelli, who has written an excellent article about that first English translation of *Dei delitti e delle pene*, points out that Beccaria's book "galvanized the attention of European intellectuals and sovereigns, quickly becoming a bestseller." There is evidence that Pietro Molini, an Italian publisher living in London, was connected in some way with that first English-language edition of Beccaria's book, but what is very clear is that Beccaria's book, including its English-language translation, was read by many Englishmen and continental Europeans alike. Alessandro Verri, who had travelled from Milan to Paris with Beccaria in late 1766, went to London after his sojourn to Paris and stayed with Molini, who had printed an Italian language edition of *Dei delitti e delle pene*. "Pietro Molini," Loretelli explains, was part of "a milieu which was active in the dissemination of enlightenment ideas, and which in 1765–66 was starting to have contacts with the representatives of the American colonies in Europe." Alessandro Verri frequently wrote letters to his brother, Pietro Verri, in Milan, and Alessandro—writing from London on January 15, 1767—specifically informed him that "Beccaria's book is being translated into English for the first time and my host Molini is involved in this operation." "I will bring a copy of it with me to Paris because it will see the light in a few days," Alessandro wrote to his brother, Pietro.[41]

Although the vast majority of Enlightenment texts may have first been published in Europe, a thriving, transatlantic book trade quickly brought titles such as *The Spirit of the Laws* and *On Crimes and Punishments* to the American colonies.[42] The first editions of *Dei delitti e delle pene* were, not surprisingly, printed anonymously, and often with a false imprint to shield the printer—as well as the author—from persecution. The Inquisition—a group of institutions within the Roman Catholic Church that sought to combat heresy—made the publication of novel or controversial ideas a dangerous proposition. As Morris Cohen of Yale Law School writes in *Bibliography of Early American Law*: "All of the early European, English, and American editions were published anonymously to avoid persecution for Beccaria's liberal views.

The imprint 'A Philade[l]phie' on the French editions was undoubtedly used for the same reason." In time, Americans, eager to spread new ideas, considered printing—and ultimately did print—Beccaria's book closer to home. An early American edition of Beccaria's *On Crimes and Punishments* was advertised as "in press" by James Rivington's *New York Gazetteer* on October 28, 1773; another edition was planned for Philadelphia in 1776; and editions of the book were actually printed and sold in Philadelphia by Robert Bell (1778), William Young (1793), and Philip Nicklin (1819), as well as in New York by Stephen Gould (1809).[43] Though the initial editions in Europe had been published anonymously, Beccaria's name nonetheless quickly became known, and Beccaria and Montesquieu's ideas—along with those of other Enlightenment thinkers—clearly infused and inspired the American Revolution. Even opponents of the American Revolution were forced to take notice of the new ideas flooding the American consciousness. In *Patriots of North-America: A Sketch* (1775), Myles Cooper—an Anglican priest who served as the president of King's College (today's Columbia University) from 1763 to 1775 and who, as a British loyalist, opposed the Revolution—himself, in an extended poem, made reference to both Montesquieu and Beccaria.[44]

The English-language editions of Cesare Beccaria's book made it easily accessible to an Anglo-American audience. In addition to the English-language edition of Beccaria's book printed in London in 1767 by John Almon, other English editions were printed in London in 1769, 1770, and 1775 by Francis Newbery; in Glasgow in 1770 for Robert Urie; in Dublin in 1767 and 1777 for John Exshaw; in Edinburgh in 1778 by Bell & Murray for William Gordon and William Creech and, in another edition published that same year, by Alexander Donaldson (to be sold at his shops in Edinburgh and London); in 1777 in Charleston, South Carolina, by David Bruce; and—perhaps most significantly, given the influential printer and the key location of his printing shop—in 1778 in Philadelphia, Pennsylvania, by Robert Bell, a prominent publisher during the American Revolution who understood the importance of Beccaria's book.[45] "The more BOOKS are sold, the more will be sold," Bell had written in 1774.[46]

Cesare Beccaria's book—and his ideas on proportionality and deterrence—established the basis for the field of criminology. "Cesare Beccaria's seminal *On Crimes and Punishments* (1764)," Michael Widener of Yale Law Library and Mark Weiner of Rutgers Law School tellingly write, "lay the foundation for modern penology and criminal justice." An Italian edition of *Dei delitti e delle pene*, they point out, was printed in London in 1774 for the Società dei Filosofi.[47] "Ideas about crime, criminality and control rapidly developed following the Enlightenment period," another source notes, adding that "[k]ey thinkers such as Cesare Beccaria, the 'father of criminology', considered the relationship dynamics between the offender, victim, state and society when crimes occurred." In *Dei delitti e delle pene*, Beccaria specifically contrasted "liberty" with "punishment," with Beccaria seeking "general laws that are equally applicable to all" and offering this logic-based approach using a major premise, a minor premise, and a conclusion: "In every criminal cause the judge should reason syllogistically. The major should be the general law; the minor, the conformity of the action, or its opposition to the laws; the conclusion, liberty, or punishment."[48]

The English-speaking publishers of Beccaria's book, those who proudly brought his ideas to a wider audience, were prominent men. Francis Newbery (1743–1780) was educated at Oxford and Cambridge, and he was a bookseller who operated out of Paternoster Row and, after the death of his father, John, in 1767, at St. Paul's Churchyard.[49] Robert Urie (1711–1771) was a printer and bookseller in Glasgow from 1744 to 1771, and he published Francis Hutcheson's *Reflections upon Laughter* and translations of the works of Rousseau, Voltaire and D'Alembert, among others.[50] John Exshaw (1741–1776) was a bookseller, printer and publisher, operating in Dublin from 1749 until his death in the year that America declared its independence.[51] Bell & Murray was a partnership between John Murray (1737–1793), a London bookseller, and John Bell (1735–1806), an Edinburgh bookseller.[52] And Alexander Donaldson (1727–1794), the bookseller in Edinburgh and London, "became known for selling cheap reprints of books which were in his opinion out of copyright."[53] In a time when everyone was talking about liberty and freedom, people's freedom of speech and the freedom of the press—two freedoms that got enshrined in the U.S. Constitution's First Amendment—played a major role in transmitting the ideas of the Enlightenment.

Enlightenment texts, such as Beccaria's treatise, certainly got plenty of attention from revolutionaries and conservatives alike. For example, the first Italian-to-English translation of Beccaria's book got reviewed in *The Annual Register* published in London in 1768. By the time of that review, Beccaria's book was already well known, as the reviewer made clear in this opening sentence: "The merit of the essay before us is so generally known and allowed, that it may seem unnecessary to inform our readers, that it has gained the attention of all ranks of people in almost every part of Europe; and that few books on any subject have ever been more generally read, or more universally applauded." As the reviewer continued:

> This work was written in Italian by the Marquis Beccaria of Milan. The translator informs us in his preface, that it was read at different times to a society of learned men in that city, at whose desire it was published. He also tells us, that it passed through six editions in the original language, in eighteen months; that it was translated into French, and that the translation was also re-printed several times.

Among the ideas from Beccaria's book that the reviewer chose to highlight: "Every punishment, which does not arise from absolute necessity, says the great Montesquieu, is tyrannical."[54] It was in a small Milanese salon, known as the Academy of Fists (or Academy of Fisticuffs), an intellectual society that Beccaria had joined, in which the ideas for *Dei delitti e delle pene* were first hatched.[55]

The Age of Voltaire

Born François-Marie Arouet (1694–1778), the author better known by his pen-name, Voltaire, rose to prominence and literary fame in the eighteenth century.[56] The son of a lawyer, he became well known for his literary works, but also for his biting wit, reform-minded ideas, and stints in prison. As one source, describing his "very dramatic life," observes of his early years: "After his classical education at a Jesuit school, he chose literature over law, and his subsequent satires resulted in his banishment from Paris as well as exile to Holland. He spent almost a year imprisoned in the Bastille. All of this happened by the time he was 24." A prolific and accomplished playwright, critic, essayist, novelist, and historian, Voltaire had a dispute in 1726 with a chevalier, leading to another trip to the Bastille, after which he was exiled to England, where he learned the English language and carefully studied Britain's political system. In 1750, he was appointed as a philosopher-poet to Prussia's Frederick the Great, a ruler with whom he had much correspondence. Voltaire, who later bought a château in Geneva, Switzerland, and a French estate, became one of the most widely read and celebrated authors of his time. Voltaire's writings include works such as *Oedipus*, *The History of Charles XII*, *Philosophical Letters*, and *Treatise on Toleration*. As one source notes of Voltaire's work, a substantial chunk of which focused on criminal justice activism and reform and religious tolerance: "In France he defended Jean Calas, a Protestant who in 1762 was tortured on the rack and executed. Voltaire was by then very rich and he devoted himself to causes against the oppression of the Church." He received many visitors at Ferney, the large château he'd purchased, and his personal and dogged advocacy in a series of *cause-célèbres*, including successful efforts to posthumously exonerate Jean Calas, raised Voltaire's profile to new heights.[57]

Voltaire had a personal distaste for Montesquieu, a major literary rival, though certainly not for all of Montesquieu's ideas. Voltaire, one book notes, had been preparing his *Essays on Manners* when Montesquieu's *The Spirit of the Laws* appeared, "and it seems that this masterpiece annoyed him." Although Voltaire outlived Montesquieu, whom he mentioned frequently in his writings, the feeling of personal contempt was mutual, at least while Montesquieu was still alive. "It would be a disgrace to the Academy if Voltaire were a member: and it will one day be his disgrace that he was not one," Montesquieu once wrote, pejoratively adding of Voltaire, "He has too much wit to understand me." Yet Voltaire, clearly conflicted and feeling affinity for some of Montesquieu's ideas, also called Montesquieu "very imaginative" and "a fine wit." Voltaire specifically reported that *The Spirit of the Laws* had "some excellent bits in it" and was to be ranked among "works of genius that make you yearn for perfection." As Voltaire, speaking through one of his characters, "B," reported of *The Spirit of the Laws*: "It appears to me to be a building with poor foundations, and an irregular structure, in which there are a lot of fine, well-polished, gilded apartments."[58]

Voltaire's admiration of Cesare Beccaria's work was more uniformly positive. As Enlightenment expert, David Williams, the editor of Voltaire's political writings, observes of Voltaire: "During the course of 1765 he was studying in the original Italian a work by Cesare Beccaria, a relatively obscure Milanese jurist, entitled *Trattato dei delitti e dell[e] pene* (On crimes and punishments), which had been published in the previous year, and translated into French by Morellet." André Morellet was a French economist and contributor to the *Encyclopédie* who, in his translation of *Dei delitti e delle pene*, had changed and restructured Beccaria's original work for its French audience. "Beccaria's treatise was the first attempt by a modern legal expert to formulate a coherent theory of penal policy, and it made a deep impression on Voltaire," Williams writes.[59] It was a young Scotsman, James Macdonald, who had delivered to Voltaire a copy of Beccaria's *Dei delitti e delle pene* after a trip he'd taken to Italy. After reading

Beccaria's book, Voltaire called Beccaria "a brother" and "a beneficent genius whose excellent book has educated Europe."[60] Voltaire's prior benefactor, Frederick II of Prussia, himself lauded Beccaria, writing: "Beccaria has left nothing to glean after him; we need only to follow what he has so wisely indicated."[61] It was a sentiment shared by many others during the Enlightenment and as the intellectual awakening occurred that led to the American Revolution and then the French Revolution.

Voltaire liked *Dei delitti e delle pene* so much that he decided to write about it. In *Voltaire and the Century of Light*, scholar Alfred Owen Aldridge explains of Voltaire's warm reception for Cesare Beccaria's book on the criminal law: "In the fall of 1765, Voltare had begun reading the Italian version of Beccaria's *De[i] delitti e delle pene* [*On Crimes and Punishments*] (1764) and delightedly hailed the author as a philosophical brother. In the next year, he had as his guest at Ferney the abbé Morellet, who was translating the work into French." Voltaire, collaborating with his friend, Charles Frédéric Gabriel Christin (1741–1799), in fact ended up writing a famous, somewhat lengthy commentary on *Dei delitti e delle pene*, one that was often reprinted with Beccaria's book in the years and decades to come. In that commentary, written in 1766, Voltaire declared: "I was engrossed by a reading of *On Crimes and Punishments*." As Aldridge writes of the opportunity that Voltaire seized in the wake of the publication of *Dei delitti e delle pene*: "Because of the favorable reception accorded to Beccaria in almost every milieu in France, Voltaire used his treatise as a medium for promoting his personal notions of social reform, publishing his own *Commentaire sur le livre des délits et des peines* [*Commentary on the Book Concerning Crimes and Punishments*] (1766)." "Voltaire's early legal training, together with his life of study and universal inquiry," Aldridge adds, "had fully prepared him to write an interpretation of the theories of the Italian jurist." "This work," Voltaire wrote of *Dei delitti e delle pene*, "will mitigate the remnants of barbarism in the jurisprudence of many nations."[62]

Voltaire had more than one reason to praise Beccaria's book. "Voltaire's decision to write a commentary on this work," *The Cambridge Companion to Voltaire* notes, "was motivated in part by his genuine engagement with the issues of political justice which it raised—and in part too by a desire to seize the moment and to exploit, and even share some part of, Beccaria's success." "Voltaire," that source points out, "did not like being in the shade."[63] In *The History of Human Rights: From Ancient Times to the Globalization Era*, scholar Micheline Ishay writes: "In France, where the use of *supplice* (referring specifically to the public torture and execution of criminals) was one of the great evils of judicial procedure up to the time of the French Revolution, Beccaria found in Voltaire a kindred spirit who would condemn torture repeatedly in his writings: 'It is as absurd to inflict torture to seek out truth as it is to order a duel to assess who is the culprit,' Voltaire wrote. '[O]ften the robust and guilty one resists the ordeal, whereas the debilitated innocent succumbs to it.'" "In France," Ishay explains, "Voltaire drew on Beccaria to criticize the French penal system: '[A] Roman citizen could be condemned to death only for crimes that threatened the security of the state. Our masters, our first legislators, respected the blood of their compatriots, while we lavishly waste that of ours.'"[64] Beccaria's *Dei delitti e delle pene* contained a whole chapter arguing against torture. "The torture of a criminal during the course of his trial," that chapter began, "is a cruelty consecrated by custom in most nations."[65]

Voltaire's *Commentary*, which opposed tyranny and questioned the need for the death penalty in certain circumstances, opened by emphasizing that Voltaire had "read, with infinite satisfaction, the little book on Crimes and Punishments."[66] "It was tyranny in particular," Voltaire proclaimed, "that first decreed the death penalty for those who differed with the established Church on some dogmas." During the Inquisition, a number of people had been put to death for their writings or views, though the number of executions had dwindled over the centuries. "It is clear," Voltaire continued, "that twenty robust thieves, sentenced to labour on some public works for all of their lives, serve the state through their suffering, and that their deaths will only benefit the public executioner, who is paid to kill people in public." "The compassionate author of *On Crimes and Punishments*," Voltaire observed in his commentary, "is more than justified to complain that punishment is too often excessive in relation to the crime, and that sometimes it is even detrimental to the state it was intended to benefit." Emphasizing that "a hanged man is good for nothing," Voltaire urged his readers to "read and reread the work of this lover of humanity." "Where charity is wanting," Voltaire wrote, "the law is always cruel." "The sword of justice is in our hands," Voltaire stressed, "but we ought rather to blunt than to sharpen its edge." Voltaire freely acknowledged that "[t]here have been some judges" who had been "passionately fond of spilling blood," but questioned: "is not the disproportioned punishment dangerous to society?" In his commentary on the section of Beccaria's treatise on torture, Voltaire wrote: "mankind may read with attention the work of that friend to humanity."[67]

Voltaire's *Commentary*—what might, in truth, be called a quasi-commentary, because much of it did not focus on Beccaria's book specifically—indicated that Voltaire had decided "to cast my eyes on the criminal code of nations." "The humane author of the Essay on Crimes and Punishments," Voltaire wrote of crimes and punishments in a section of the commentary about Beccaria, "had but too much cause to complain, that the latter frequently exceed the former, and are sometimes detrimental to the state they were intended to serve." "Those ingenious punishments, the *ne plus ultra* of the human mind endeavouring to render death horrible," he wrote, "seem rather the inventions of tyranny than of justice." For Voltaire, as for Montesquieu and Beccaria, the necessity for a punishment and the punishment's proportionality were important considerations, with Voltaire making reference to "Your illustrious *Montesquieu*" and to a man "executed without mercy." As Voltaire wrote in his *Commentary* in discussing what factors a judge should consider in passing judgment in criminal cases: "He should consider the age of the offender, the nature and degree of his offence, and particularly the necessity of a public example." As Voltaire added in his *Commentary*: "If the law does not expressly say that such a crime shall be punished with death, what judge shall think himself authorized to pronounce that sentence? If the law be silent; if nevertheless a punishment be required, the judge ought certainly, without hesitation, to decree the least severe, because he is a man." "Thieves, in England," Voltaire wrote at one point in his commentary, "are seldom punished with death, but are transported to the colonies." As Voltaire also stressed of the death penalty's disuse—and of the alternatives to it—elsewhere: "This is also practiced in Russia, where not one criminal was executed during the whole reign of the autocratical Elizabeth. Catherine II. who hath succeeded her, with much more genius, follows her example: yet crimes are not multiplied by this humanity; and it generally happens that the criminals sent to Siberia, in time become honest people. The same is observed in the English colonies."[68]

Voltaire—the historian who had familiarized himself with practices outside of his own country, and especially in England—looked to the long arc of history in noting how the death penalty was used in the past, before taking note of the then-prevailing practice in France. As Voltaire, as translated into English by another source, wrote: "The Romans never condemned a citizen to death, unless for crimes which concerned the safety of the state. These our masters, our first legislators, were careful of the blood of their fellow citizens; but we are extravagant with the blood of ours." "The question hath been frequently debated, whether a judge ought to have the power to punish with death, when the punishment is undetermined by the law?" Voltaire queried, answering, "This question was solemnly agitated in the presence of the emperor Henry VII, who decreed that no judge should have such a power." Alluding to the idea that the laws ought to prescribe, in statutes, the punishments for crimes before such punishments can be inflicted, Voltaire continued: "There are some criminal cases which are either so new, so complicated, and so unaccountable, as to have escaped the provision of the laws, and which therefore, in some countries, are left to the discretion of the judge. But for one case in which the laws permit the death of a criminal whom they have not condemned, there are a thousand wherein humanity should save whom the laws have condemned to suffer."

Voltaire added that "[n]ature never intended" men like the notorious Lord Chief Justice George Jeffreys—those "passionately fond of spilling human blood"—"for magistrates, but for executioners." Lord Chief Jeffreys became notorious for the "Bloody Assizes," the name given to the trial of followers of the Duke of Monmouth after their unsuccessful Protestant rebellion against the Catholic king, James II. "After the defeat of Monmouth's forces at the Battle of Sedgemoor (1685)," one source notes, "James II sent Lord Chief Justice George Jeffreys to the west country to dispense justice to the defeated rebels." "Jeffreys," that book observes, "was a notoriously harsh judge" who "ordered the execution of over 400 rebels, mostly peasants, many of whom pleaded guilty because they had been promised mercy."[69] The rebels who had risen up with the Duke of Monmouth in an attempt to depose James II were hanged, drawn and quartered, and disemboweled, with others whipped or sent off to the West Indies to perform hard labor.[70]

At the very first assizes, the maniacal George Jeffreys—an alcoholic who presided over the King's Bench—even condemned to death an elderly woman, Lady Alice Lisle, for feeding and sheltering a fugitive rebel; her sentence, to be burned alive, was only converted to a beheading through a desperate plea to King James II. Her prosecution and horrendous treatment, one historian notes, caused "more opprobrium" for Stuart rule than any other treason trial of that period. Jeffreys's cruel treatment of Alice Lisle, who many saw as simply performing charitable acts, was part and parcel of an effort to inspire great terror—and, in the words of the very indictment against her—to put "the fear of God" into James II's subjects so that they would stand by their "most illustrious prince" and pledge "thy allegiance."[71] With that objective in mind, the mutilated bodies of the executed Monmouth rebels were ordered to be displayed until James finally had them removed in 1687. For example, after more than two hundred men were hanged and drawn and quartered in Somersetshire, the seat of the rebellion, one account painted the rebellion's bloody aftermath this way: "At every spot where two roads met, on every market-place, on the green of every large village which had furnished Monmouth with soldiers, ironed corpses clattering in the wind, or heads and quarters stuck on poles, poisoned the air, and made the traveller sick with horror." "The barbarity and breadth of the punishment," a history of the Stuart dynasty notes, "gained Jeffreys and ultimately James reputations as cold-blooded murderers."[72]

Voltaire has been described as "the most famous writer of the age," with Voltaire's château de Ferney serving as a hub of the Enlightenment. As the steady stream of visitors passed through Geneva to pay their respects, the hospitable Voltaire exchanged ideas—and discussed new books—with them. "In countries where a trifling domestic theft, or breach of trust, is punished with death, is not the disproportioned punishment dangerous to society?" the well-connected Voltaire asked in a chapter of his *Commentary* "On Domestic Theft," no doubt with the English Bloody Code and others like it in mind. "If, on the contrary, the punishment be proportioned to the crime; if those who are guilty of a breach of trust be condemned to labour for the public," Voltaire argued, "the matter will not hesitate to bring the offender to justice, and the crime will be less frequent: so true it is, that rigorous laws are often productive of crimes." In other words, unnecessary severity would multiply crimes while proportionate punishments would reduce criminality and better serve the public and the common good.

In a section of his commentary "On Death Warrants," Voltaire continued: "Must we go to the end of the world, must we have recourse to the laws of China, to learn how frugal we ought to be of human blood?" As he wrote in that section, tracing some history before returning to the parsimony, or necessity-for-punishment, idea: "The members of the supreme council are more enlightened, less liable to prejudice, and better qualified than a provincial judge, to determine whether the state require severe punishments. In short, when inferior courts have judged according to the letter of the law, which possibly may be rigorous, the council mitigates the sentence according to the true spirit of all laws, which teaches, never to sacrifice a man, but in evident necessity." And in the section of his *Commentary* "On Torture," Voltaire continued his praise of Beccaria's advocacy against torture, writing: "I am ashamed of having said any thing on this subject, after what hath been already said by the author of the Essay on Crimes and Punishments. I ought to have been satisfied with wishing, that mankind may read with attention the work of that friend to humanity." Voltaire's *Commentary*, in a section "On the Difference between political and natural laws," also discussed "political laws" made "in compliance with present necessity," noting of the law of reprisal—also called the law of retaliation—by which one man is hanged for another in time of war: "These political sanguinary laws exist but for a time; they are temporary, because they are not founded in truth. They resemble the necessity which, in cases of extreme famine, obliges people to eat each other: they cease to eat men as soon as bread is to be had."[73]

In his own *Philosophical Dictionary*, in a section on "Execution," the ever witty and often irreverent Voltaire wrote: "Yes, we here repeat the observation, a man that is hanged is good for nothing; although some executioner, as much addicted to quackery as cruelty, may have persuaded the wretched simpletons in his neighborhood that the fact of a person hanged is a cure for the epilepsy." In discussing a beheading in that age of superstition, Voltaire specifically asked in a Beccarian fashion: "What necessity required this death?" Voltaire also queried whether it was "absolutely necessary" for a "madman" to be hanged for his crime, saying that particular executions were "neither conformable to humanity or reason, and cannot possibly be of the least utility." In discussing a brutal execution of a teenager, the chevalier de La Barre, carried out in Abbeville, France in the 1766, Voltaire further observed: "What necessity could there be that La Barre should have his hand chopped off and his tongue cut out, that he should be put to the question ordinary and extraordinary, and be burned alive?" "Such was the sentence pronounced by the Solons and Lycurguses of Abbeville!" Voltaire wrote, pouring out his wrath and sarcasm. Being put to *the question* was used extensively by the courts in France, including in the Bastille, from the Middle Ages to the seventeenth and eighteenth centuries.

In France, water torture and leg braces were customary forms of torture. While the *ordinary question* involved forcing roughly a gallon of water down the torture victim's throat or using four wedges when leg braces were used, the *extraordinary question* involved the use of approximately two gallons of water or eight wedges when leg braces were employed. As one source describes these two extremely painful methods of torture used in one French locale:

> Leg braces were the customary form of torture in the jurisdiction during the eighteenth century. The defendant was seated on the stool. Two oaken planks were placed on the inside of each leg, extending from the feet to above the knees; a plank of the same length was placed on the outside of each leg. The six planks were secured by ropes passed through holes at their ends, and the ropes were then wound tightly around the planks to form a casing for both legs. Pain was inflicted, and controlled, by means of wooden wedges. The torturer hammered them between the two planks inside each leg, from the vicinity of the knees down to the ankles. Each wedge increased the pressure. The ordinary *question* by leg braces was four wedges; the "extraordinary" was eight. After each wedge was driven in, the judges asked one or two specific questions concerning the crime and the culpability of the defendant.
>
> In torture by stretching and forced ingurgitation of water, the defendant was tied by the wrists to two rings in the wall of the torture chamber and by the ankles to two rings in the floor, so that he was stretched face upward in a diagonal position. A wooden trestle was placed under the ropes binding his ankles to the floor, which increased the stretching. The torturer pinched his

> nostrils shut and slowly poured water into his mouth from a two-pint container. From time to time, he was allowed to breathe. The maximum quantity of water allowed by the Parlement's ruling was eight containers-full, or about 2 gallons—a very large quantity. After each container was poured, the judges questioned the defendant. This was the most dangerous method of torture.[74]

Voltaire's interest in criminal justice had been piqued in October 1761, when Voltaire read in the *Gazette de France* about the Inquisition's execution of around forty people in Portugal, including an elderly Jesuit, Father Malagrida. Malagrida had been condemned to death for heresy, and Voltaire had found his burning to death an excessive punishment. Such fanaticism had inspired Voltaire to pen his *Pocket Philosophical Dictionary*, which Voltaire freely confided to his friend, Damilaville, "reeks horribly of heresy." The first edition of that book contained 73 articles, and later editions contained even more. "God preserve me, my dear brother," Voltaire wrote Damilaville in July 1764, seeking anonymity, "for having anything to do with the *Pocket Philosophical Dictionary*!" A copy of Voltaire's controversial *Pocket Philosophical Dictionary*—an important book of the Enlightenment—had been found in La Barre's room during a search, and La Barre had been executed on July 1, 1776, his body burned along with the copy of Voltaire's then-controversial book. "The trial and punishment," one modern source recounts, "exemplified all too clearly the vices and prejudices laid bare in Voltaire's *Dictionary*: the improper judicial procedure, the disproportionate punishment, the cruelty of religious fanatics, the lack of simple charity shown by some believers." Voltaire's *Pocket Philosophical Dictionary*, published anonymously in Geneva in July 1764 when Voltaire was 70 years old, had quickly been condemned by the Paris *parlement*, placed on the Catholic Church's Index of Forbidden Books, and burned by Geneva's public executions.[75]

Montesquieu's *The Spirit of the Laws*

Charles-Louis de Secondat, Baron de La Brède et de Montesquieu, was born to a noble and wealthy family at La Brède, near Bordeaux, in 1689, just a year after England's Glorious Revolution of 1688. The Glorious Revolution, which led to the English Bill of Rights of 1689, saw the overthrow of King James II of England (James VII of Scotland) by a union of English Parliamentarians headed by William III, a Dutch stadtholder and the Prince of Orange. Educated at Oratorian Collège de Juilly, Montesquieu received his law degree from the University of Bordeaux in 1708, twenty years after the Glorious Revolution. He then went to Paris to continue the study of law. After his father died in 1713, he returned to La Brède to manage the family estates he inherited, and in 1716 he inherited from his uncle the title Baron de La Brède et de Montesquieu as well as the office of *Président à Mortier* in the Parlement of Bordeaux, at that time mainly an administrative and judicial body. "For the next eleven years," one source notes of his time as a magistrate, "he presided over the Tournelle, the Parlement's criminal division, in which capacity he heard legal proceedings, supervised prisons, and administered various punishments including torture." Because of his service in the office of *Président à Mortier*, later writers often referred to him as President Montesquieu.

In 1721, Montesquieu published his enormously successful *Persian Letters*, turning him into a literary celebrity. As one scholar explains: "His first influential work, the 'Lettres Persanes,' published in the year 1721, was a criticism of the religion, politics and morals of Europe, put into the mouth of a philosophical native of Persia who travels in order to acquire knowledge." One passage of that book, as translated into English, reads: "In countries where punishments are moderate, these are feared exactly as they are in countries where penalties are tyrannical and horrifying." After selling his life interest in his office in 1725 and resigning from the Parlement, he was elected to the Académie Française in 1728 and, after touring Italy, Austria, and other countries, went to England where he lived for two years. Like Voltaire, he was fascinated and impressed by the British political system. After returning to France in 1731, he began work on what would become his masterpiece, *L'Esprit des Lois* (1748). That book was placed on the Catholic Church's Index of Forbidden Books in 1751 in spite of the fact that he published a defense of his book in 1750 to answer his critics. Montesquieu died of a fever in Paris a half-decade later, in 1755, "leaving behind"—as one encyclopedia notes—"an unfinished essay on taste for the *Encyclopédie* of Diderot and D'Alembert."

In *Persian Letters*, Montesquieu wrote about proportionality between crimes and punishments, just as Beccaria would decades later. In that epistolary novel, in Letter LXXXI, Montesquieu penned these words: "Whether a government be mild or cruel, punishments ought always to be graduated: a penalty more or less great ought to be inflicted on a crime more or less great." "Our imagination," he wrote, "is influenced by the manners of the country in which we live: eight days' imprisonment, or a light fine, has as much effect on the spirit of a European, brought up in a country where the manners are gentle, as the loss of an arm has upon an Asiatic." "A certain degree of fear," he added, "is proportioned to a certain degree of punishment, and each shares this fear in his own way: the infamy attached to some penalties would drive a Frenchman to despair, while these same penalties would not rob a Turk of a quarter of an hour's sleep." "[Y]et," Montesquieu emphasized in his book, "I do not see that police regulations, justice, and equity are better observed in Turkey, Persia, or the empire of the Mogul than in the republics of Holland, Venice, and even in England; neither do I see that fewer crimes are committed there, or that men, intimidated by the greatness of the penalties, are more submissive to the laws." "On the contrary," he concluded, "I remark a source of injustice and vexation in the midst of these very states."[76]

In *The Spirit of the Laws*, his masterpiece on law, liberty, and separation of powers, Montesquieu openly critiqued then-existing criminal laws.[77] In *L'Esprit des Lois*, Montesquieu discussed both civil and criminal laws and wrote about the establishment of penalties.[78] In Book XIX, chapter 14, Montesquieu—writing in French, his native language—specifically observed: "*Toute peine qui ne dérive pas de la nécessité est tyrannique. La loi n'est pas un pur acte de puissance.*"[79] The translation: "Every penalty that does not derive from necessity is tyrannical. The law is not a pure act of power."[80] After discussing "despotism," Montesquieu wrote, in particular, of "moderate states" in these words: "[I]n moderate states where the head of even the lowest citizen is esteemed, his honor and goods are removed from him only after long examination; he is deprived of his life only when the homeland itself attacks it; and when the homeland attacks his life, it gives him every possible means of defending it." As Montesquieu added in that section, Book 6, chapter 2: "Men are all equal in republican government; they are equal in despotic government; in the former, it is because they are everything; in the latter, it is because they are nothing."[81] The study of political philosophy reached an apex in the eighteenth century, and in America and France, where thoughts of revolution permeated the air, monarchies would soon give way to republics.

A reduction in the severity of punishments was seen as part and parcel of Enlightenment reform—and reform was destined to come. In Book 6, chapter 9 of *The Spirit of the Laws,* Montesquieu explicitly wrote "*On the severity of penalties in the various governments.*" In that section of his book, he observed:

> Severity in penalties suits despotic government, whose principle is terror, better than monarchies and republics, which have honor and virtue for their spring.
>
> In moderate states, love of the homeland, shame, and fear of blame are motives that serve as restraints and so can check many crimes. The greatest penalty for a bad action will be to be convicted of it. Therefore in moderate states civil laws will make corrections more easily and will not need as much force.
>
> In these states a good legislator will insist less on punishing crimes than on preventing them; he will apply himself more to giving mores than to inflicting punishments.[82]

In a subsequent chapter of Book 6, "*On the power of penalties,*" Montesquieu, who knew the difference between virtue and vice, also had this to say:

> If there are countries in which shame is not an effect of punishment, it is a result of tyranny, which has inflicted the same penalties on scoundrels as on good people.
>
> And, if you see other countries in which men are restrained only by cruel punishments, reckon again that this arises largely from the violence of the government, which has employed these punishments for slight transgressions.[83]

Moving away from Machiavellianism, Montesquieu's *Spirit of the Laws* sought milder punishments. In Book 6, chapter 16, Montesquieu offered this personal assessment "*On the just proportion between the penalties and the crime*":

> It is essential for penalties to be harmonious among themselves, because it is essential that the greater crime be avoided rather than the lesser one, the one that attacks society rather than the one that runs less counter to it.
>
> ....
>
> Among ourselves, it is a great ill that the same penalty is inflicted on the highway robber and on the one who robs and murders. For the public safety, it is evident that there must be some difference in the penalties.
>
> In China robbers who are cruel are cut to bits, the others are not; because of this difference, one robs there but does not murder.

> In Moscovy, where the penalty for robbery is the same as for murder, one always murders. Dead men, they say, tell no tales.[84]

And in Book 6, chapter 17, Montesquieu—living in a society that still thought of torture as a lawful tactic available to the judiciary—wrote "*On torture or the question for criminals*," making these observations on that subject:

> Today we see a well-policed nation reject it [the *question* in criminal cases] without meeting drawbacks. The use of the question is, therefore, not necessary by its nature.
>
> So many clever people and so many men of genius have written against this practice that I dare not speak after them. I was going to say that it might be suitable for despotic government, where everything inspiring fear enters more into the springs of the government; I was going to say that slaves among the Greeks and Romans … But I hear the voice of nature crying out against me.[85]

The necessity-for-punishment maxim that Montesquieu formulated in *The Spirit of the Laws* is discussed in Mark Waddicor's book, *Montesquieu and the Philosophy of Natural Law*. In discussing the origins of that pithily stated maxim, Waddicor wrote:

> It is pertinent to ask whether the preservation of society is always best achieved simply by a suitably severe punishment, or whether it is sometimes better to try to amend the criminal. Eighteenth-century French law made no attempt to do the latter, but the philosophers of natural law, such as Grotius, Pufendorf, and even Hobbes, believed that reform of the criminal was one aim of a good penal code. Montesquieu seems to have agreed with their idea, and to have implicitly criticized the practice prevailing in his own country, when he commented on certain violent punishments administered in Japan.…

Montesquieu, Waddicor explains, associated the idea of cruelty with that of despotism, and—as Waddicor writes—"claimed that a direct correlation can be established between the severity of punishments and the degree of political liberty in any country."

Waddicor emphasized that, in crafting his words, Baron de Montesquieu followed a natural law approach—one that was rooted in the tradition of other thinkers. As Waddicor stresses of Montesquieu's language and Montesquieu's general approach to punishment: "Instead of tritely stating that unnecessarily cruel punishments are unjust—a fact that both he and his readers knew already—he implied it, both by his vocabulary ('tyrannie', 'supplices cruels', 'la violence du gouvernement', 'les esprits sont corrompus'), and by the fact that he felt obliged not simply to state that severe punishments are unwise, but also to exhort governments to abandon them." The "true purpose of punishment" from an Enlightenment-era natural law approach, Waddicor notes, is "not revenge" but "the preservation of society," with "unnecessarily cruel punishments," he adds, being "contrary to natural law." Pufendorf—whose approach Waddicor says "Montesquieu neatly summed up" in the maxim he laid down in Book XIV of *Esprit des lois*—put it this way: "Que celui qui a fait du mal, en souffre, il n'y a rien là d'injuste, à ne regarder que l'action en elle-même. Cependant les hommes ne doivent jamais punir, à moins qu'il n'en revienne quelque utilité. […] on doit […] prendre garde de ne pas faire souffrir sans nécessité un homme, coupable à la vérité, mais toujours uni avec nous par les liens de l'humanité commune, pour une action qui ne saurait plus être redressée."[86] In other words, it is not unjust to punish, but there must be a need for the punishment—and for there to be some utility to be achieved from it—so that a man, as part of a society's common humanity, does not endure needless or indiscriminate suffering.

Montesquieu—as well as Grotius—condemned revenge.[87] To prevent the abuse of power, Montesquieu, whose ideas on separation of powers were, decades later, on very prominent display in *The Federalist Papers*, asserted that the same agency of government which enacts laws should not be entrusted with their enforcement. Conversely, he believed that an enforcement agency (i.e., the executive branch) should not have the power of enacting laws. That principle, Montesquieu offered, was necessary to further liberty, lest "the same monarch or senate should enact tyrannical laws, to enforce them in a tyrannical manner."[88] In *The Spirit of the Laws*, Montesquieu had written: "Nor is there liberty if the power of judging is not separate from legislative power.... If it were joined to legislative power, the power over the life and liberty of the citizens would be arbitrary, for the judge would be the legislator."[89] This line of reasoning made a deep and lasting impression on America's founders, including James Madison, who found himself at the center of the Constitutional Convention in Philadelphia. On July 17, 1787, Madison noted that "[i]f it be essential to the preservation of liberty that the Legisl.; Execut: & Judiciary powers be separate, it is essential to a maintenance of the separation, that they should be independent of each other." Citing Montesquieu, Madison explained that a separation is necessary lest "tyrannical laws may be made and may be executed in a tyrannical manner."

The quest for American liberty was highly dependent on checking the abuse of power. James Madison, often called the Father of the Constitution, believed that "ambition must be made to counteract ambition," and that separation of powers was indispensable to preventing tyranny.[90] As Madison, paraphrasing Montesquieu, made clear in *The Federalist No. 47*: "The accumulation of all powers, legislative, executive, and judiciary, in the same hands, whether of one, a few, or many, and whether hereditary, self-appointed, or elective, may justly be pronounced the very definition of tyranny." Alexander Hamilton—America's first Secretary of the Treasury—himself emphasized the importance of courts in America's constitutional design, writing:

> [T]he courts were designed to be an intermediate body between the people and the legislature in order, among other things, to keep the latter within the limits assigned to their authority. The interpretation of the laws is the proper and peculiar province of the courts. A constitution is, in fact, and must be regarded by the judges as, a fundamental law. It therefore belongs to them to ascertain its meaning as well as the meaning of any particular act proceeding from the legislative body. If there should happen to be an irreconcilable variance between the two, that which has the superior obligation and validity ought, of course, to be preferred; or, in other words, the Constitution ought to be preferred to the statute, the intention of the people to the intention of their agents.[91]

The Eighth Amendment, of course, is now part of America's fundamental law, becoming part of the U.S. Constitution through the adoption and ratification of the U.S. Bill of Rights.

In his *Commentaries on the Constitution of the United States* (1833), Joseph Story—the influential American jurist and Harvard professor who served on the U.S. Supreme Court from 1811 to 1845—also emphasized the importance of separation of powers to America's legal system. As Story wrote: "In the establishment of a free government, the division of the three great powers of government, the executive, the legislative, and the judicial, among different functionaries, has been a favorite policy with patriots and statesmen. It has by many been deemed a maxim of vital importance, that these powers should for ever be kept separate and distinct." "Montesquieu," Story emphasized, "seems to have been the first, who, with a truly philosophical eye, surveyed the political truth involved in this maxim, in its full extent, and gave to it a paramount importance and value." As Story wrote: "No remark is better founded in human experience, than that of Montesquieu, that 'there is no liberty, if the judiciary power be not separated from the legislative and executive powers.'" In his three-volume treatise, Story cited Montesquieu's *Spirit of the Laws* repeatedly, and he also cited Beccaria's *On Crimes and Punishments*. For example, Story had this to say about the French jurist: "Montesquieu has remarked, that the Christian religion is a stranger to mere despotic power. The mildness so frequently recommended in the gospel is incompatible with the despotic rage, with which a prince punishes his subjects, and exercises himself in cruelty."[92]

A review of historical sources reveals that Montesquieu's *The Spirit of the Laws* paved the way for Cesare Beccaria's *Dei delitti e delle pene* and also shaped countless penal reformers. In *A History of the English Criminal Law and Its Administration from 1750* (1948), the noted historian, Leon Radzinowicz, in speaking of the Enlightenment, called Montesquieu "the first notable author of the period to point to a number of defects in contemporary systems of criminal law and to lay down certain guiding principles for future legislation." There, Radzinowicz specifically recognized the work of the German scholar G.W. Böhmer, who, in 1816, in his *Handbuch der Litteratur des Kriminalrechts*, had identified Montesquieu as the "Vater der Kriminal-politik." In his own work, a University of Tennessee political scientist, David Carrithers, points out that "[t]he influence of Montesquieu on Beccaria is by no means difficult to detect" and that "Montesquieu was clearly in the forefront of the Enlightenment movement to moderate the severity of punishments." Montesquieu, Carrithers writes, "posited a direct relation between moderation of punishments and liberty." "It would be easy to prove," Montesquieu contended in *The Spirit of the Laws*, "that in all or nearly all of the States of Europe, penalties have decreased or strengthened to the extent that they have drawn closer to or farther from liberty."

Just as there is a notable relationship between liberty and well-designed forms of government and well-proportioned punishments, Cesare Beccaria clearly shaped the law in his own unique way. Beccaria has been characterized as "the disciple of Montesquieu," Carrithers notes, though on a number of important points, he demonstrates, Montesquieu and Beccaria clearly differed in their approach. "Montesquieu, for example," Carrithers explains, "refrained from linking the right to punish to an express social contract; advocated the Crown's use of the pardoning power; recommended the use of infamy and other shaming punishments; refrained from asserting that all phases of a criminal trial must be public; stopped short of calling for jury trials; believed defendants could properly be made to testify; and recommended that punishments rather than being strictly equal for all persons should respect differences of rank and station." (Beccaria, by contrast, had strong views on the social compact, favored jury trials, opposed infamy, and wanted equal punishments for nobles and those without such status.) "Unlike numerous other theorists of crime and punishment, including Pufendorf, Hobbes, Locke, Rousseau and Beccaria, Montesquieu make little use of social contract theory either in justifying punishment or in explaining the origins of government," Carrithers observes before identifying an important commonality in the thinking of Montesquieu and Beccaria. As Carrithers writes: "Lenient punishments, Montesquieu was convinced, in anticipation of Beccaria who repeated the point, can serve as just as effective deterrents as extremely harsh punishments, since it is much more the certainty of punishment rather than its severity that deters."

In his 1998 article, "Montesquieu's Philosophy of Punishment," David Carrithers emphasizes in the journal, *History of Political Thought*, that "Montesquieu combined utilitarian and retributive perspectives in *The Spirit of Laws*." "Montesquieu," Carrithers writes, "discussed the proper scale of graduated punishments in two widely separated portions of *The Spirit of Laws*." As Carrithers explains of Montesquieu and his famous book: "He placed the first of these discussions in Book VI, and he there struck a utilitarian tone. 'It is an essential point that there should be a certain proportion in punishments', he asserted, 'because it is essential that a great crime should be avoided rather than a lesser, and that which is more pernicious to society rather than that which is less.'" As Carrithers puts it of this strain of thought in the book: "Reserving the harshest penalty of death only for the most serious crimes would have the desired effect, Montesquieu concluded, of making individuals stop short of committing those very worst crimes most threatening to life and property." "As a result of his advocacy of a graduated scale of punishments," Carrithers adds, taking note of extremely harsh, then-existing French laws, "Montesquieu lamented that in France 'the same penalty is inflicted on the highway robber and on the one who robs and murders.'" "Like Beccaria," Carrithers notes, "Montesquieu displayed extreme confidence in the ability of properly proportioned, well publicized punishment scales to deter crime."

The second strain in *The Spirit of the Laws* was retributive. As Carrithers explains, Montesquieu's "justice-oriented, retributivist stance toward punishment is particularly apparent in his discussion of the fourth class of offences within his punishment scale." As Carrithers, quoting from Montesquieu's book, emphasizes:

> This fourth category of offences included crimes deserving capital punishment and consisted of actions harmful either to persons or property. Crimes in this fourth and final category under Montesquieu's schematization were those that, in addition to attacking the public tranquillity, "attack at the same time the security of the subject". In discussing such serious offences

> as these, Montesquieu employed the vocabulary associated with the *lex talionis* approach to punishment. Severe punishments for crimes against persons and property, he concluded, are "a kind of retaliation (*une espèce de talion*) by which the society refused security to a member that either has actually, or intentionally deprived another of his security". Such punishments are "derived from the nature of the thing, founded on reason, and drawn from the very source of good and evil".

"However much he adopted liberal and utilitarian perspectives to define appropriate procedures, modes and levels of punishment," Carrithers writes of Montesquieu, "his perspective in justifying punishment for wrongdoing was very much that of a retributivist."

Balancing the need to punish and deter with the virtuous desire to rehabilitate offenders is not always easy, and over time, people can reach—and regularly have—different judgments in trying to strike that balance. While Montesquieu believed that penalties flow "from the particular nature of the crime," Montesquieu also asserted that "[i]t is ... on the goodness (*bonté*) of the criminal laws that the liberty of the citizen principally depends." Montesquieu worried in particular about "arbitrary decisions (*tout l'arbitraire cesse*)," and though he was not willing to jettison the death penalty entirely, his division of offenses into categories was seen as a novel, progressive approach. As David Carrithers writes:

> By dividing offences into four distinct categories running from the least serious religious misconduct, which he believed should be decriminalized, to the most serious crimes threatening lives and property, Montesquieu made an important advance over existing French criminology. There was no such scale in eighteenth-century France. Article 13 of the French Criminal Ordinance of 1670 listed penalties in order of severity but did not link specific punishments to specific crimes. The royal edicts on the subject of punishment, both prior to and after 1670, often mentioned specific punishments for specific crimes, and sometimes even specified mandatory punishments, but these edicts certainly did not constitute, even in the aggregate, a scale of punishment. Moreover, French judges were left with very substantial discretion.

As criminal-law historian Leon Radzinowicz himself noted: "Montesquieu's classification, although somewhat rudimentary, is important, inasmuch as it was one of the first attempts to divide criminal acts into groups in accordance with their gravity and to revise the scale of punishments." "It constituted a valuable point of departure for future legislators," Radzinowicz stressed.

Montesquieu's *The Spirit of the Laws* thus represented an attempt to take the criminal law in a new direction, which is exactly what it helped to do. "[H]istory sufficiently informs us that penal laws have never had any other effect but to destroy," Montesquieu wrote in his book, further emphasizing that "[p]enal laws ought to be avoided, in respect to religion." Montesquieu's approach, Carrithers writes, was informed by experience. As Carrithers explains:

> Owing to his assignment to the criminal chamber of the Parlement of Bordeaux (*La Tournelle*) for ten and a half years, Montesquieu had first-hand

> knowledge of the destructive effects of penal law where religion is concerned. In 1716, for example, the Parlement of Bordeaux had punished with galley service for life one Jean Martin, a beer-maker[,] and one Jean Miller, a merchant, who had organized a meeting of Protestants.

"The existing French law that Montesquieu was attacking," Carrithers continues, "was based on the following proposition: 'the Church and religion are under the protection of kings and consequently of royal justice; nothing is more important to the tranquillity of the state than the maintenance of religion.'" Religious law and civil law should be treated in separate spheres, Montesquieu believed.[93]

Cesare Beccaria's *On Crimes and Punishments*

The Italian *philosophe* Cesare Beccaria was born in Milan in 1738, studied at a Jesuit school in Parma for young nobles, and then got his law degree from the University of Pavia in 1758. Fascinated by mathematics and economics, the French language, and Enlightenment writers, Beccaria joined a small, informal society in Milan, the Academy of Fists, and contributed to an influential publication, *Il Caffè*, produced by its members. One of the products of Beccaria's association with that group—one formed by Pietro Verri and his younger brother, Alessandro—was a short book, *Dei delitti e delle pene*, a work on the topic of the criminal law. That subject had been suggested to Beccaria by his older mentor, Pietro Verri, a fellow noble and economist. In later years, Beccaria would teach political economy at Milan's Palatine School—an appointment he secured from Maria Theresa, the leader of Austria's Habsburg Empire, which then controlled the Duchy of Milan. Beccaria taught for only a short time, though, ultimately securing another position, one on Milan's Supreme Economic Council, where he served as an economic advisor alongside his mentor, Pietro Verri.

Just two years after the publication of *Dei delitti e delle pene* (1764), before either of those appointments, however, Beccaria was toasted in Paris in 1766 for his literary achievement. Invited to the City of Light by the French *philosophes*, Beccaria made the trip with Alessandro Verri, though Beccaria—feeling homesick and missing his wife—only stayed for a few weeks in Paris. Alessandro, who served as Milan's protector of prisons, was around the same age as Beccaria, and he—along with his brother, Pietro Verri—had helped Beccaria to understand the nature of the Italian penal system as Beccaria wrote *Dei delitti e delle pene*. In time, Beccaria's book, which Pietro Verri played a role in editing and securing a publisher for, was translated into all of the major European languages, though it attracted immediate controversy because of its content. Indeed, almost right after its publication, Ferdinando Facchinei—a monk associated with the Venetian Inquisition—had attacked the author of *Dei delitti e delle pene*, making an accusation of sedition. Like Montesquieu's *The Spirit of the Laws*, *Dei delitti e delle pene* was put on the Catholic Church's Index of Forbidden Books.[94]

In *Dei delitti e delle pene* (1764), Cesare Beccaria drew upon Montesquieu's wisdom about the necessity for punishment[95] and expounded upon it. "In his classic work *Dei delitti e delle pene*," one source reports, "Cesare Beccaria argues with reference to Montesquieu: '*Ogni pene che non derivi dall' assoluta necessità, dice il grande Mon-*

tesquieu, è tirannica; proposizione che si può rendere piú generale cosí: ogni atto di authorità di uomo a uomo che non derivi dall'assoluta necessità è tirannico." The translation: "Every punishment that is not derived from absolute necessity is, says the great Montesquieu, tyrannical—an assertion that can be rendered more generally like this: every authoritative action by man against man that is not derived from absolute necessity is tyrannical."[96] This was an expression of Beccaria's worldview—one clearly inspired by Montesquieu—that would make its way around the world in the decades and centuries to come in scores of languages.[97] In his book, *The Mysterious Science of the Law*, scholar Daniel Boorstin stressed that in Beccaria's introduction to *Dei delitti e delle pene*, Beccaria "had called himself the student of Montesquieu, and had explained, 'I shall be happy, if, with him, I can obtain the secret thanks of the obscure, and peaceful disciples of reason, and philosophy, and excite that tender emotion, in which sensible minds sympathize with him, who pleads the cause of humanity.'"[98]

The advice of Montesquieu and Beccaria would, in fact, often be cited side by side on the questions of crime and punishment, opposition to torture, and in future discourses on liberty versus tyranny. For example, in 1782, Manasseh Dawes—in *An Essay on Crimes and Punishments, with a View of, and Commentary upon, Beccaria, Rousseau, Voltaire, Montesquieu, Fielding, and Blackstone*—began his preface with these words: "Of all the subjects that have ever been written upon, there is not one of them of more importance to the welfare of man, as an individual, or to society, as a body, than that of crimes and punishments. Many celebrated writers have chosen it as a theme, on which to exercise their genius and penetration; among whom, some have deservedly obtained the reward due to their lenity, and others have been reprobated for their rigor." A member of the Inner Temple, Dawes—dedicating his work "To the Right Honorable the Earl of Huntingdon"—invoked Montesquieu and Beccaria's names multiple times, with Dawes referring at points in his essay to "[t]he humane BECCARIA" and "the humane, the tender BECCARIA." In that essay, Dawes juxtaposes "tyranny" or "despotism" and "liberty" on multiple occasions, with Dawes asserting at the outset, in his preface: "That system therefore, of criminal legislation, must be the best which is adopted by the best of governments of the best of people; among whom the necessity of punishment is proportioned to the scarcity of crimes, and the opportunities, either from temptation or otherwise, to commit them; hence it is, that according to the frequency of punishment in any community, is the degree of its corruption, and the error of its government."[99]

In the section of *On Crimes and Punishments* titled "The Right to Punish," Beccaria's words—as translated by scholars Aaron Thomas and Jeremy Parzen in a recent University of Toronto Press translation of Beccaria's by far most famous book, *Dei delitti e delle pene*—appear as follows:

> As the great Montesquieu says, every punishment that does not derive from absolute necessity is tyrannical. This proposition can be stated more generally in the following manner: every act of authority of one man over another that does not derive from absolute necessity is tyrannical. This is the foundation, therefore, upon which the sovereign's right to punish crimes is based: the necessity to defend the depository of the public welfare from

> individual usurpations; and the more just the punishments, the more sacred and inviolable the security and the greater the liberty the sovereign preserves for his subjects. Let us consult the human heart, and in it we will find the fundamental principles of the sovereign's true right to punish crimes, for no lasting advantage can be expected from political morality, unless that morality is founded upon the indelible sentiments of mankind. Any law that deviates from these sentiments will always encounter a contrary resistance that will prevail in the end, just as any force, however small, if continuously exerted will prevail over any violent jolt transmitted to a body.[100]

The translation by Aaron Thomas and Jeremy Parzen made use of the last known Italian edition of *Dei delitti e delle pene* that Beccaria himself was known to have edited.

What Montesquieu and Beccaria meant by their necessity-for-punishment principle is illuminated by the long-prevailing definition of the word "necessity." Derived from the Latin *necesse* (needful) and *necessitas* and the Old French *necessite*, the concept of *necessity* is an age-old concept. According to a Latin dictionary, *necesse* is an adjective that means "*unavoidable, inevitable, indispensable, necessary*," while *necessitas* means "*unavoidableness, inevitableness, necessity, compulsion, force, exigency*."[101] The concept of *necessity*, frankly, has not varied much through the ages, and it has long been defined as, *inter alia*, "indispensableness"[102] or the "State of being necessary; indispensable."[103] The word *necessary*, in turn, has been similarly defined, among other things, as "Needful; indispensably requisite,"[104] "needful, indispensable, unavoidable,"[105] or "needful, that cannot be let alone, or done without, unavoidable."[106] In his own book, Beccaria—in words often later repeated by others—specifically asked "whether the punishment of *death* be really just or useful in well governed state?" It was a question that would be repeated by many thinkers in the decades to come.

Though what is deemed *necessary* is, to a certain degree, in the eye of the beholder, Beccaria concluded that capital punishment was neither just nor necessary. As Beccaria wrote in *On Crimes and Punishments*, speaking of his own conception of the social contract and asking a series of questions:

> *What right, I ask, have men to cut the throats of their fellow creatures?* Certainly not that on which the sovereignty and laws are founded. The laws, as I have said before, are only the sum of the smallest portions of the private liberty of each individual, and represent the general will, which is the aggregate of that of each individual. Did any one ever give to others the right of taking away his life? Is it possible, that in the smallest portions of the liberty of each, sacrificed to the good of the public, can be contained the greatest of all good, life? If it were so, how shall it be reconciled to the maxim which tells us, that a man has no right to kill himself? Which he certainly must have, if he could give it away to another.
>
> But the punishment of death is not authorised by any right; for I have demonstrated that no such right exists. It is therefore a war of a whole nation against a citizen, whose destruction they consider as necessary, or useful to the general good. *But if I can further demonstrate, that it is neither necessary nor useful*, I shall have gained the cause of humanity.[107]

"Perpetual slavery," Beccaria concluded, proposing his own eighteenth-century alternative to capital punishment, "has in it all that is necessary to deter the most hardened and determined, as much as the punishment of death."[108]

The concept of necessity actually infused Beccaria's *On Crimes and Punishments*. For example, in a section of his book "On the Promptness of Punishment," Beccaria wrote of pre-trial detention: "The strictness of incarceration should not exceed whatever is necessary to prevent escape or the concealment of evidence."[109] In another location, Beccaria emphasized: "a punishment for a crime cannot be considered exactly just (which is to say, necessary) until the law has put into use the best possible means in a nation's given circumstances for preventing that crime."[110] Beccaria consequently specifically equated the necessity for a punishment with the concept of justice. "Beccaria's views, filtered through the likes of Bradford, Wilson, and Rush," one scholar writes, referencing the influence of American revolutionaries William Bradford, James Wilson, and Benjamin Rush, "found their way into Pennsylvania law." As that scholar, Michael Zydney Mannheimer, emphasizes:

> In 1776, Pennsylvania adopted a new constitution, section 38 of which called for the legislature to reduce the infliction of capital punishment and replace it in some cases with punishments more proportionate to the offense: "'The penal laws, as heretofore used, shall be reformed by the future Legislature of this State, as soon as may be, and punishments made in some cases less sanguinary, and in general more proportionate to the crimes.'" Section 39 continued this theme by calling upon the legislature to create prisons so as to both make capital punishment less necessary and enhance the deterrent value of punishment by placing imprisoned felons in full view of the public for long periods of time.[111]

Those two sections of Pennsylvania's constitution, adopted in the same year that the Continental Congress issued the Declaration of Independence, were plainly inspired by the ideas of Enlightenment thinkers such as Montesquieu and Beccaria. In a paper titled "The Pennsylvania Prison System," prepared in the late nineteenth century and then read before the American Philosophical Society on June 20, 1884, Quaker Richard Vaux observed that "[t]he Pennsylvania Prison System had its origin in an effort to correct the abuses in the place of incarceration of all classes of violators of law." Vaux noted that, in 1776, the Philadelphia Society for Assisting Distressed Prisoners had been formed, and that although its work had been discontinued by the occupation of the British army, its successor, the Philadelphia Society for Alleviating the Misery of Public Prisons, had revived that important work in May 1787. "It may be justly claimed," Vaux added, "that the reforms in prison systems, or their administration, in the United States, as well as in foreign countries, are the outcome of the century of labors, efforts, and experience of the benevolent and philosophic men who in Philadelphia originated and have given to the Pennsylvania system its renown."

Those men, of course, had been greatly influenced by both Montesquieu and Beccaria, with Richard Vaux—in the last paragraph of his paper, noting that advances in penology "will be slow"—specifically emphasizing: "It must be remembered that Beccaria in his essay on 'Crimes and Punishment' in 1764; Filangieri in his 'Science of Legislation' in 1780 and Montesquieu in his 'Spirit of the Laws,' 1748, were among the first to invite attention to penal jurisprudence."[112] In *The Science of Legislation*, Gaetano Filangieri (1752–1788)—a Neapolitan jurist who corresponded with Benjamin Franklin before his death from tuberculosis—quoted Montesquieu repeatedly and worried about "the people" becoming "prey" to "real tyranny" and a loss of liberty. In discussing Montesquieu, Filangieri (a man who dreamed of traveling to America but who died in his thirties) specifically expressed a fear about the opportunity for the abuse of power. "Exorbitant authority, in the hands of a single person in a republic is the worst of evils," Filangieri wrote, quoting Montesquieu in French. Filangieri then praised early Roman laws for allowing "[t]he dictator, to whom the fate of the republic was confided," to exercise his authority "not a moment longer than the circumstances of the republic rendered it absolutely necessary."[113] And Filangieri was indebted to Beccaria, too, with scholar Marcello Maestro writing as follows: "In his second volume on criminal law Filangieri deals with the problems of crimes and punishments. This subject had been discussed by Beccaria twenty years earlier in his famous treatise, and Filangieri follows in the steps of the Milanese writer, endorsing his basic principles and many of his ideas."[114]

In truth, the necessity-for-punishment maxim as articulated by Montesquieu and then Beccaria was at the heart of the American Revolution itself. In an oration delivered in Boston, Massachusetts, on March 5, 1782, to commemorate the events surrounding the Boston Massacre of March 5, 1770, George Richards Minot (1758–1802) began with the following salutation: "*FATHERS, FRIENDS, AND FELLOW CITIZENS*." A lawyer who served as secretary of the Massachusetts Ratifying Convention from January to February 1788, Minot said the "[t]he full display" of Great Britain's "despotic power" came during "the inglorious reign" of King George III—the man who was indicted by the Continental Congress in America's Declaration of Independence. "Turn to the tragedy we commemorate as imprinted by the bloody act of the tyrant, and view the highest outrage his power could commit, or the forbearance of humanity sustain," Minot said in his speech, referencing the "slaughtered citizens" who "were offered at the shrine of cursed ambition." Observing that the British had "violated the greatest law nations or individuals can be held by, to use the language of the ancients," Minot quoted Beccaria in his speech, uttering these words: "If 'every act of authority of one person over another, for which there is not an absolute necessity, is tyrannical,' and if tyranny justifies resistance, to have remained inactive under these injuries, had been a kind of political stoicism, equally inconsistent with the laws of nature and of society. On such principles arose the memorable declaration of July, 1776: a declaration which at once gave life and freedom to a nation; dissolved a monopoly unnatural as unjust; and extended the embraces of our country to the universe...."[115]

Natural Law, Liberty, and Education

The writings of Montesquieu and Beccaria were, in fact, quoted everywhere in early America. For example, in an anonymously written 1783 address "To the People of South-Carolina," the ideas of both men were put forward. In that address, the writer stated that "[v]estiges of natural society are still to be perceived in most villages of civilized nations, and in whole tribes of uncivilized"—and that "*natural law*" provided "the law of the heart and the law of necessity or self-defence." The "monitor in every breast," the writer emphasized, "at once warns and pains us in case of injustice done by ourselves," "prompts and delights us to do good," and "urges us to condemn or applaud the behaviour of others." "The monitor," the writer observed, "instructs us to entertain a charitable construction of the intention of others; to bear patiently with the petulance of others; and to forbear long shewing resentment." "But, when nothing else will do," the writer continued, "the law of self defence, and a common sense of common danger, suggest the necessity, on particular occasions, of the many uniting to restrain the destructive proceedings of a few." "This natural law," the anonymous writer added, "is not yet effaced," while simultaneously making reference to "customs" and "written laws." "Written or oral laws," the writer stressed, "had two different origins: In cases of tyranny, they were intended to restrict; in cases of ... equal government, to extend; the benefits of natural law." "From these contradictory motives," the writer pointed out, "arose the motley appearance of modern jurisprudence."

In the address, Montesquieu was quoted in the sections of the address on "PERSONAL LIBERTY" and "OF PROPERTY," and it was in a discussion of tyranny—one in a section of the address on "POLITICAL CONSEQUENCE"—that the writer cited passages from Cesare Beccaria's treatise. "When tyranny was once established," the writer relayed, "it behoved every other society of men to be on their guard; for there are no bounds to ambition." "Unanimity was necessary for their defence, unanimity concentered their authority somewhere," the writer declared before turning to this oft-invoked aphorism from Beccaria: "In every human society, there is an effort continually tending to confer on one part the height of power and happiness, and to reduce the other to the extream of weakness and misery. The intent of good laws is to oppose this effort, and to diffuse their influence universally and equally." Lamenting that "[r]iches and power" had been "secured" to "monarchs," the writer discussed how men had been made to take part "against what was otherwise their own interest," and that "*this was to be done, only by diminishing the property and liberty of the multitude.*" "Every act of authority of one man over another, for which there is not an absolute necessity, is tyrannical," Beccaria was further quoted as saying in that address. And in yet another passage on the infliction of "shameful punishment," the writer—in a footnote—also recited these words from Beccaria's treatise: "Whatever laws deviate from the principles of justice, will always meet with a resistance, which will frustrate them in the end."

In the course of quoting Blackstone and "CATO's Letters," the writer contended that "the contentions of the prince and magnates" would, occasionally, "serve the interests of the people." "Some partial conveniences," the writer continued, "were necessary to palliate great hardships, and appearances of attention to qualify violent injustice." Meanwhile, "the poor subject (which is a name implying a conquered slave) stript of natural rights," the writer stressed, "is forced to serve the most ignoble purposes; to bear arms and fight in quarrels not his own; to perpetrate murder, and help to desolate provinces; and thus to uphold in his tyranny, the common foe of mankind." "It is the property of prejudice," the writer lamented, "to maintain all causes espoused, right or wrong; and when people are in this mood, if a constitution defends in some, unnecessary riches and power, it is notwithstanding a good one...." As the writer continued sarcastically, if a society's laws "are replete with cruelty, inconsistency, injustice, ambiguity and fiction," the society is deemed "a good one"; if "the people are made to serve the king, and not the king the people, it is a good one still." "[I]t has been the peculiar felicity of America to have been always in a great measure out of reach, or out of the power of arbitrary tyrants; and it is now to be so altogether." "THE RIGHTS of individuals from society by Natural Law, are," the writer concluded, "SAFETY, LIBERTY, KINDNESS, and DUE PORTIONS of COMMON Property, of POLITICAL CONSEQUENCE, and of SOCIAL EMOLUMENTS."

Cesare Beccaria's words are referenced repeatedly in the 1783 address "To the People of South-Carolina." "The punishment of death," Beccaria wrote, and the address reported, repeating the Italian thinker's words, "is the war of a whole nation against an individual." "The countries and times most notorious for severity of punishments," Beccaria's book had stressed, as the address further recounted, "were always those in which the most bloody and inhuman actions and the most atrocious crimes were committed; for the hand of the legislator and the assassin were directed by the same spirit of ferocity." Protection for life and limb, the 1783 address emphasized, were of paramount importance, with the address returning to the theme of necessity as regards the protecting of life and limb. (The U.S. Constitution's Fifth Amendment would later specifically provide: "[N]or shall any person be subject for the same offence to be twice put in jeopardy of life or limb....") "Both humanity and policy dictate that the members of society should be protected in life, limb, organ and feature," the address observed, adding: "These no resentment should affect, no policy invade. Nothing but indispensable necessity in self-defence, can warrant the effusion of another's blood." "To deduce the propriety of capital punishments from the power of individuals," the anonymous author of the address proclaimed, "is to argue from the abuse for the right." The author of the address also pulled out this quote from Beccaria's *On Crimes and Punishments*: "The most certain method of preventing crimes, is to perfect the system of education."

The address writer's Montesquieu- and Beccaria-inspired views—recognizing the need for punishment but calling for rewards for virtue and for humane treatment—were expressed in this way: "A perfect government should not only punish for crimes, but reward for a contrary conduct. Let humanity, public spirit and knowledge, be distinguished by particular honors." "Those," the address writer stressed, "who would govern only by fear, are but shallow politicians." "Law to be just," the address writer wrote, "should be simple, clear, and intelligible," with the author of the address quoting Beccaria's own words as follows: "Would you prevent crimes? Let the laws be clear and simple; and let the laws be feared, and the laws only." "Every member of society should know when he is criminal and when innocent." Calling education "the natural remedy" for societal ills, the address writer—worried about the abuse of power—went on to quote Montesquieu as follows: "Constant experience shews that every man invested with power is apt to abuse it, and to carry his authority as far as it will go." On the importance of separating the legislative and executive powers, the address writer—in line with Montesquieu's view—wrote: "Whenever both powers are united in one, the temptation to ambition is too great for human frailty; and the danger to liberty imminent."

In a section of the address titled "Of the Administration of Justice," the address writer frequently quoted Blackstone, but again came back to Beccaria and Montesquieu, too. The quotes of Beccaria chosen by the address writer: "It is an admirable law which ordains that every man shall be tried by his peers; for when life, liberty, and property are in question, the sentiments which a difference of rank and fortune inspire, should be silent." "The punishment of a crime cannot be just, that is necessary, if the laws have not endeavored to prevent that crime by the best means which times and circumstances would allow." "Utility from the sufferance of criminals is either negative or positive," the address writer asserted, explaining: "Negative, from an incapacitation to do further harm; as in case of exile, which is a species of punishment perhaps best adapted to offenders not satisfactorily convicted. Positive; as in cases of award of damages to individuals, and, in atrocious malpractices, servitude and even hard labor in public service for a term or for life." "From these methods, advantage will accrue to the community, but none from death," the address writer concluded, channeling the much-admired Italian criminal-law theorist.

In colonial and early America, the ideas of Montesquieu and Beccaria permeated the revolutionary air, shaping debates and policies on American soil. As one "T.Q." wrote in *The Boston Gazette and Country Journal* on April 18, 1763: "Political liberty, as it is defined by a great writer [Baron de Montesquieu] is 'a tranquility of mind arising from the opinion each man has of his own safety.' When this liberty is once destroyed it is to very little purpose to enquire how it was brought about; but before that is done, it is wisdom to guard against whatever has a tendency to it, in order to prevent it." While T.Q. called Montesquieu "the admired writer of *The Spirit of the Laws*," another letter writer—writing in *The Boston Evening Post* on May 23, 1763—referred to the "definition of political liberty" offered by "the very justly celebrated author of *The Spirit of the Laws*." The French jurist was referred to elsewhere—almost everywhere, in fact—as "the great Montesquieu," while Dr. Benjamin Rush—the signer of the Declaration of Independence—had this to say in 1786 about the "advantages of learning upon mankind" in writing a plan for the establishment of public schools: "It is favorable to liberty." "It promotes just ideas of laws and government. 'When the clouds of ignorance are dispelled,' says the Marquis of Beccaria, 'by the radiance of knowledge, power trembles but the authority of laws remains immovable.'"[116]

Likewise, as just one of countless examples, Montesquieu and Beccaria's names also came up in 1791 in Robert Coram's *Political Inquiries, to which is Added a Plan for the Establishment of Schools Throughout the United States*. In that essay, Coram wrote: "It is a melancholy reflection that in almost all ages and countries men have been cruelly butchered for crimes occasioned by the laws and which they never would have committed, had they not been deprived of their natural means of subsistence." Taking a swipe at European monarchs who failed to attend to the basic needs of the people, Coram observed: "[I]f the European governments were erected to supply the wants and lessen the fears of individuals, we may venture to assert that the first projectors of them were errant blockheads. The wants of man, instead of having been lessened, have been multiplied, and that in proportion to his boasted civilization; and the fear of poverty alone is more than sufficient to counterbalance all the fears to which he was subject in the rudest stage of natural liberty." "[T]he governors of mankind," Coram wrote, "seem never to have made any allowance for poverty, but like the stupid physician who prescribed bleeding for every disorder, they seem ever to have been distinguished by an insatiable thirst for human blood." "In the dark ages of Gothic barbarity," Coram stressed, quoting Beccaria, "ignorance was some excuse for the framing of absurd systems, but in the age in which Dr. Blackstone lived, he should have known better, he should have known that the unequal distribution of property was the parent of almost all the disorders of government...." Beccaria, Coram noted, had stressed that the crime of robbery "is commonly the effect of misery and despair."

Education was thus seen not only as pivotal to reducing crime but as the key to societal advancement. "Mr. Noah Webster," Coram emphasized, "is the only American author, indeed the only author of any nation, if we except perhaps Montesquieu, who has taken up the subject of education upon that liberal and equitable scale which it justly deserves." In his 1790 essay, "On Education of Youth in America," Noah Webster—a Revolutionary War veteran who had taught students and developed his incredibly popular dictionary—wrote about the importance of educating young people in public schools. "Education, in a great measure," Webster wrote, "forms the moral characters of men, and morals are the basis of government." "Education," Webster declared, "should therefore be the first care of a legislature, not merely the institution of schools but the furnishing of them with the best men for teachers." As Webster stressed: "A good system of education should be the first article in the code of political regulations, for it is much easier to introduce and establish an effectual system for preserving morals than to correct by penal statutes the ill effects of a bad system." "It is observed by the great Montesquieu," Webster recounted, looking back in time, "that 'the laws of education ought to be relative to the principles of the government.'" Whereas Webster wrote that "[i]n despotic governments the people should have little or no education, except what tends to inspire them with a servile fear," he noted that Montesquieu had concluded that "in a republican government," "the whole power of education is required." In a republican form of government, Webster wrote, "every class of people should *know* and *love* the laws." In 1802, in "An Oration on the Anniversary of the Declaration of Independence," Webster added: "'Virtue,' says the learned, but visionary Montesquieu, 'is the foundation of a republic.'"

In the wake of the American Revolution came the French Revolution. Joel Barlow (1754–1812), in critiquing France's constitution of 1791, and in discussing "liberty," "mankind," "the necessity of proscribing royalty from your constitution," "the social compact," the qualities of republicanism, and a "system of equal rights," also brought up Montesquieu and Montesquieu's "maxims about laws and government." As Barlow wrote at one point in "A Letter to the National Convention of France on the Defects in the Constitution of 1791," written from New York in 1792: "I think Montesquieu has said, that virtue must be the foundation of a republican government. His book is not now by me, or I would try to discover what he means by virtue." In the course of that letter, Barlow called "*imprisonment for debt*" a "species of civil cruelty which all modern governments have borrowed from the Roman law." As Barlow observed on that particular topic: "It is a disgrace to the wisdom of a nation, and can never be allowed in a well regulated state. If no citizen could be arrested or deprived of his liberty, for debt, there would be no need of making an exception in favour of the officers of government; and thus you would remove a distinction which must always appear unjust." On the issue of the crime and punishment more broadly, Barlow specifically called upon the French to give "a farther declaration on the subject of criminal law" and had this to say: "All men of reflection are agreed, that punishments in modern times have lost all proportion to the crimes to which they are annexed, even on that scale of barbarous justice by which they were introduced. Few, however, have had the wisdom to discover, or the boldness to declare the true cause of the evil; and while we remain ignorant of the cause, it is no wonder that we fail in finding the remedy." During the Enlightenment and the early nineteenth century, in titles like Walter Baldwin's *Punishment without Crime; or Imprisonment for Debt*, the imprisonment of debtors came under attack as a violation of liberty.[117]

Barlow, wanting his fellow Americans to do whatever they could to prevent crime, staked out a position seeking to minimize punishments whenever possible. "In the glooms of meditation on the miseries of civilized life," Barlow emphasized, "I have been almost led to adopt this conclusion, That society itself is the cause of all crimes; and, as such, it has no right to punish them at all." "But, without indulging the severity of this unqualified assertion," Barlow continued more pragmatically, "we may venture to say, that every punishment is a new crime; though it may not in all cases be so great as would follow from omitting to punish." In other words, punishments were necessary, but they should be meted out very judiciously. Signaling a shift from a criminal justice system built on cruelty, terror, and revenge to one designed around the concepts of prevention, reformation, and rehabilitation, Barlow wrote at length:

> There is a manifest difference between *punishment and correction;* the latter, among rational beings, may always be performed by instruction; or at most by some gentle species of restraint. But punishment, on the part of the public, arises from no other source but a jealously of power. It is a confession of the inability of society, to protect itself against an ignorant or refractory member. When there are factions in a state, contended for the supreme command, the pains inflicted by each party are summary; they often precede the crime; and the factions wreak their vengeance on each other, as a prevention of expected injuries. Something very similar to this is what perpetually takes place in every nation, in what is called a state of tranquillity and order. For government has usually been nothing more than a regulated faction. The party which governs, and the party which reluctantly submits to be governed, maintain a continual conflict; and out of that conflict proceed the crimes and the punishments, or, more properly speaking, the punishments and the crimes. When we see the power of the nation seizing an individual, dragging him to a tribunal, pronouncing him worthy of death, and then going through the solemn formalities of execution, it is natural to ask, what is the meaning of all this? It certainly means, that the nation is in

a state of civil war; and even in that barbarous stage of war, when it is thought necessary to put all prisoners to death. In deciding the question, whether a particular criminal should be put to death, I never would ask what is the nature of his offence; it has nothing to do with the question; I would simply enquire, what is the condition of the society. If it be in a state of internal peace, I would say it was wicked and absurd to think of inflicting such punishment. To plead that there is a necessity for that desperate remedy, proves a want of energy on the government, or of wisdom in the nation.

When men are in a state of war, with the enemy's bayonets pointed at their breasts, or when they are in the heat of a revolution, encompassed by treason, and tormented by corruption, there is an apology for human slaughter; but when you have established a wise and manly government, founded on the moral sense, and invigorated by the enlightened reason of the people, let it not be sullied by that timid vengeance, which belongs only to tyrants and usurpers. I could wish that your constitution might declare, not merely what it has already declared, that the penal code shall be reformed, but, that within a certain period after the return of peace, *the punishment of death shall be abolished*. It ought likewise to enjoin it on the legislative body to soften the rigour of punishments in general, until they shall amount to little more than a tender paternal correction. Whoever will look into the human heart, and examine the order of nature in society, must be convinced, that this is the most likely method of preventing the commission of crimes.

For many early Americans, the abolition or curtailment of capital punishment became a moral imperative. James Wilson—a signer of the Declaration of Independence and the U.S. Constitution—regularly cited Beccaria's work and called "cruel" punishments "dastardly and contemptible." And in the 1820s, Madison spoke of his attraction to "penitentiary discipline" as a substitute for "the cruel inflictions so disgraceful to penal codes." After receiving an anti-death penalty pamphlet from a correspondent that quoted Beccaria, Madison wrote to that correspondent, a Kentucky physician: "I should not regret a fair and full trial of the entire abolition of capital punishments by any State willing to make it." "The marquis of Beccaria," Dr. Benjamin Rush wrote in an early American periodical, *The American Museum*, in 1789, "has established a connexion between the abolition of capital punishments and the order and happiness of society." In March of 1787, just months before delegates assembled in Philadelphia for the Constitutional Convention, Dr. Rush specifically invoked Beccaria's name at the house of America's elder statesman Benjamin Franklin. At that time, Dr. Rush called death "an improper punishment for any crime." Dr. Rush's essay, which argued that experience had proven that public punishments had increased "propensities to crimes," was later published by Joseph James, a printer and bookseller on Philadelphia's Chestnut Street.[118] As America's founders gathered in Philadelphia to create a new system of government, they were also thinking long and hard about forging a new kind of penal system.

Joel Barlow, like so many people of that era, not only was critical of then-existing criminal laws but, in critiquing the French constitution and giving his advice to the

French, emphasized the importance of education. "In order to be consistent with your yourselves in removing those abuses which have laid the foundation of all offences against society, both in crimes and punishments," Barlow, writing in 1792, said in his "*Tenth*" point, "you ought to pay a farther attention to the necessity of *public instruction*." Calling for a better educated citizenry, Barlow urged French lawmakers: "It is your duty, as a constituting assembly, to establish a system of government that shall improve the morals of mankind. In raising a people from slavery to freedom, you have called them to act on a new theatre; and it is a necessary part of your business, to teach them how to perform their parts." "Every Frenchman, born to liberty," Barlow editorialized, "must now claim, among the first of his rights, the right of being instructed in the manner of preserving them." Urging that people be advised of the laws so that they "shall perfectly understand them," Barlow continued: "The barbarous maxim of jurisprudence, *That ignorance of the law is no excuse to the offender*, is an insolent apology for tyranny, and ought never to disgrace the policy of a rational government. I think therefore it would do honor to your constitution, and serve as a stimulus to your legislature and to your magistrates, in the great duty of instruction, to declare, *That knowledge is the foundation of obedience, and that laws shall have no authority but where they are understood.*"[119]

CHAPTER 2

Blackstone, Bentham and Beyond:

Proportionality and the Tyranny of Unnecessary Punishments

The Notion of Proportionality and (Absolute) Necessity

The concept of proportionality is one that dates back many centuries but that is still much discussed in the modern era. In her article, "Proportionality as a Principle of Limited Government," Alice Ristroph writes in the *Duke Law Journal* that "[p]roportionality limitations on the penal power arise not from the purposes of punishment, but from the fact that punishing is not the only purpose that the state must pursue." As the abstract of Ristroph's article explains: "Other considerations, especially the protection of individual interests in liberty and equality, restrict the pursuit of penological goals. Principles of proportionality put the limits into any theory of limited government, and proportionality in the sentencing context is just one instance of these limitations on state power." "This understanding of proportionality," her abstract observes, "gives reason to doubt the assertion that determinations of proportionality are necessarily best left to legislatures." As the abstract of Ristroph's article concludes: "In doctrinal contexts other than criminal sentencing, proportionality is frequently used as a mechanism of judicial review to prevent legislative encroachments on individual rights and other exercises of excessive power. In the criminal sentencing context, a constitutional proportionality requirement should serve as a limit on penal power."[1]

In writing about the principle of proportionality, one that Montesquieu and Beccaria pioneered, Ristroph explains that principle's continued relevance and importance. As Ristroph observes: "Incarceration and capital punishment involve direct exercises of force against the human body that occur almost nowhere else in domestic politics in a liberal state. Because liberal democratic governments trace their legitimacy to something other than superior physical force, and because liberal democratic governments claim to protect the lives and liberties of their subjects, the imposition of these sanctions may be one of the most illiberal practices of a liberal state." "For a variety of reasons," Ristroph emphasizes, "penal sanctions are often practically and perhaps morally necessary." "But," she explains, "punishment's inherent tension with liberal ideals suggests a need for principled restrictions on the scope of the penal power." In practice, she notes, "few such restrictions apply to American sentencing factors." "Nominally," she goes on to explain, "the Supreme Court considers the Eighth Amendment's prohibition of 'cruel and unusual punishments' to require that penalties be proportionate to offenses." "But that proportionality requirement," she writes, "has been attenuated in recent years." In summarizing the current state of affairs, she points out that the U.S. Supreme Court has found "that lengthy prison sentences mandated by California's 'three strikes' law did not violate the proportionality requirement of the Eighth Amendment, even if those sentences were imposed for seemingly minor offenses such as shoplifting three golf clubs or the theft of approximately $150 work of children's videotapes."[2]

There are, in fact, two types of proportionality: *cardinal* and *ordinal.* "Cardinal proportionality," it has been observed, "refers to the issue of whether the absolute severity of any punishment is appropriate"[3] and "sets out the basic level of severity of response, such as minimum and maximum punishments, that a system can give for any crimes."[4] "Ordinal proportionality," another source notes, by way of contrast, "requires that a punishment should reflect the seriousness of the crime, in the sense that its severity should comport with the severity of punishments for other crimes." As that source, *The Ethics of Proportionate Punishment*, notes of ordinal proportionality:

> It is a purely comparative requirement. It implies that persons convicted for crimes of different seriousness should receive punishments correspondingly rated in terms of severity. In so far as theft is considered less serious than burglary, the thief should be punished more leniently than the burglar. It also implies that persons convicted of equally grave cases of criminal conduct are to be allotted equally severe punishments.[5]

Yet another source, summing up the difference, puts it this way: "Ordinal proportionality involves the internal levels of punishment in the sentencing system, while cardinal proportionality fixes the outer limits, the minima and maxima, that will be permitted."[6]

The principle that punishments be proportionate to crimes actually long predates the writings of Montesquieu and Beccaria, though Montesquieu and Beccaria framed the debate in new, eye-opening ways. Both the Code of Hammurabi and Mosaic law articulated the "eye for an eye" principle, said to be "commonly understood as requiring that punishment be commensurate to the offense." Aristotle, the Greek philosopher, asserted that it was the judge's duty to impose punishment equivalent to the crime. And Cicero, the Roman statesman and famed orator, declared—as translated from the Latin—that "the punishment should fit the offense." "[T]here are certain duties that we owe even to those who have wronged us," Cicero proclaimed, adding: "For there is a limit to retribution and to punishment."[7] In John Locke's writings, Locke himself had suggested graduated penalties, advising: "Each transgression may be punished to that degree, and with so much severity as will suffice to make it an ill bargain to the offender, give him cause to repent, and terrify others from doing the like."[8] The concept of proportionality, clearly, has ancient origins that were refined over time.

The English Bill of Rights (1689), from whence originates the prohibitions against excessive fines, excessive bail, and cruel and unusual punishments, was itself about preserving individual liberty through, among other things, aiming for more proportionality between crimes and punishments. Its immediate predecessor, the English Declaration of Rights (which morphed into the duly enacted Bill of Rights), was designed by English parliamentarians to limit the king's power and to secure the liberty of British subjects. It would change England's legal landscape, materially shaping Anglo-American law for decades to come.[9] Indeed, its prohibitions against excessive bail, excessive fines, and cruel and unusual punishments came to the fore very quickly after its promulgation through a review by England's Parliament of notorious actions and punishments of the King's Bench, including ones involving Titus Oates. A Protestant cleric whose tutor at Cambridge had called him "a great dunce," Oates had been put on trial for perjury in 1685 after James II became king. Oates had made false accusations in 1678 about a supposed Jesuit-concocted "Popish Plot" to assassinate King Charles II, James II's brother and predecessor,[10] and Oates—who had a long-standing penchant for telling lies—had implicated scores of Catholics, including the Duke of York (the future king, James II) and other aristocrats, in the invented plot. After Oates accused the royal physician of conspiring to poison Charles II, the king himself had interrogated Oates, revealing falsehoods and inconsistencies and leading to Oates's arrest. But in the anti-Catholic fervor that the manipulative Oates had whipped up, he'd been released a few days later at the instigation of Parliament and been lauded as a hero. He was even given a pension of £1,200 and an apartment in Whitehall.[11]

In the "Popish Plot" affair, Oates's lies had led to the execution of fifteen Catholics. At first, Oates's allegations about the schemes of "Papists" had been believed. It was only after Oates's lies were exposed that Oates was called "*the Blackest of Villains that ever lived upon the face of the Earth*." Before the Duke of York had ascended to the throne, becoming His Majesty James II, Oates had bitterly denounced him as a rouge and a traitor, naturally drawing the ire of the duke himself. In 1684, as all the lies associated with the "Popish Plot" were unravelling, the Duke of York had brought a libel action against Titus Oates grounded upon the statute *de Scandalis Magnatum* for Oates having called the duke "a traitor." That statute provided that "none devise, speak or tell any false news, lies, or other such false things, of prelates, dukes, earls, barons, or other great men, &c. whereof discord of any slander may arise within the realm."[12]

Unable to make bail, Oates was committed to a debtor's prison, and Oates was, ultimately, fined £100,000 for libeling the Duke of York, the future king. Unable to pay such a princely sum, Oates had then been imprisoned in the King's Bench prison for his default. This, one history later observed, "shut him up in a perpetual imprisonment" until the powers that be "saw a fit opportunity to carry matters further against him." The very next year, after the Duke of York was elevated to His Majesty James II after his brother's death, Oates's lies would come back to haunt Oates even further, with Oates brought from the prison to face criminal charges, to wit, two indictments for perjury. At his 1685 trial, Oates was convicted on both counts and the presiding judge, George Jeffreys, James II's loyal servant, personally decried Oates's "Villainy" and called his crime "a very heinous one."[13]

Before Oates was sentenced, Jeffreys said that "the Old Laws of *England*" punished perjury with death but that those laws had been moderated "[s]ince that time" so that the perjurer would be punished "according to the direction of this Court, so far as that the Judgment extend not to Life or Member." In light of "such a foul and malicious Perjury" that had "so many horrid and dreadful Consequences," Jeffreys—the

Lord Chief Justice from 1683 to 1685 and, later, James II's powerful Lord Chancellor—declared that the King's Bench would "inflict an exemplary Punishment upon this villainous Perjur'd wretch, to Terrify others for the future...."[14] Jeffreys had become known as the "hanging judge" for his role in the Bloody Assizes, so his words were especially ominous, even though he'd just conceded in the courtroom that, in Oates's case, the King's Bench didn't possess the power to impose a death sentence. The severity of the sentence that was ultimately imposed upon Oates, an ordained priest of the Church of England, shocked the consciences of many Englishmen—and, at least to those who believed Oates's concocted tale, about a Catholic conspiracy to assassinate their king, it must have remained a sore point throughout the remainder of James II's short, unpopular reign.[15]

Titus Oates's multi-faceted sentence, as announced in 1685 by Francis Wythens, one of the Lord Chief Justice's fellow justices: "First, *The* Court *does Order for a Fine, That you pay a* Thousand Marks *upon each Indictment*." "Secondly, *That you be strip't of all your Canonical Habits*." "Third," it was announced as to Oates's first perjury conviction, "*The* Court *does Award, That you Stand Upon the* Pillory, *and In the* Pillory, *here before* Westminster-Hall-gate, *upon* Monday *next, for an Hours time, between the Hours of Ten and Twelve*; *with a Paper over your Head*, (*which you must first walk with round about to all the* Courts *in* Westminster-Hall) *declaring your Crime*." "Fourthly," as to Oates's second perjury conviction, "*Upon* Tuesday, *you shall Stand Upon, and In the* Pillory, *at the* Royal Exchange *in* London, *for the space of an Hour, between the Hours of Twelve and Two*; *with the same Inscription*." With Titus Oates standing before the bar of justice, Wythens, the Lord Chief Justice's colleague, further intoned: "*You shall upon the next* Wednesday, *be Whipt from* Aldgate *to* Newgate." "*Upon* Fryday, *you shall be Whipt from* Newgate *to* Tyburn, *by the Hands of the Common Hangman*."[16]

But that was not all that the King's Bench, led by George Jeffreys, had in mind for Titus Oates, the notorious perjurer. In speaking to Oates, Wythens also had this to say: "We cannot but remember, there was several particular Times you Swore false about; And therefore, as Annual Commemorations, that it may be known to all People, as long as you live; We have taken special Care of you, for an Annual Punishment." That annual punishment: "*Upon the Twenty fourth of* April, *every Year, as long as you live, you are to Stand Upon the* Pillory, *and In the* Pillory, *at* Tyburn, *just opposite to the Gallows, for the space of an Hour, between the Hours of Ten and Twelve*." "*You are to Stand Upon, and In the* Pillory, *here at* Westminster-Hall-gate, *every Nineth of* August, *in every Year, so long as you live*." "*You are to Stand Upon, and In the* Pillory, *at* Charing-Cross, *on the Tenth of* August, *every Year, during your Life, for an Hour, between Ten and Twelve*." "*The like, over against the* Temple-gate, *upon the Eleventh*." "*And upon the Second of* September ... *you are to Stand Upon, and In the* Pillory, *for the space of one Hour, between Twelve and Two, at the* Royal Exchange: *And all this you are to do every Year, during your Life*; *and to be Committed close Prisoner, as long as you live*." His parting words for Oates: "This I Pronounce to be the *Judgment of the Court* upon you, for your Offences. And I must tell you plainly, if it had been in my Power to have carry'd it further, I should not have been unwilling to have given Judgment of *Death* upon you: For, I am sure, you deserve it."[17]

This draconian sentence, handed down by the King's Bench during King James II's tumultuous reign, and a sentence which, in truth, might well have been crafted to actually take Oates's life given its extreme severity, became the subject of much public controversy, especially after William and Mary, both Protestants, rose to power in the Glorious Revolution of 1688. This was particularly so given that Oates's himself was no commoner. "[T]he literature of the time," one historian notes, "shows that part of the drama in this celebrated case involved Oates's status." Broadsides with woodcuts depicted Oates in full clerical garb in the pillory, with one titled "The Doctor Degraded" containing these lines of doggerel: "And now must *Oates* stand in the *Pillory*?" / "There to be battered so with Rotten *Eggs*," / "Both on the Face, the Body and the Legs."[18] With Parliament, around that time, also carefully scrutinizing the Stuart-era punishments of the Earl of Devonshire, who'd been fined £30,000 for striking a man with a cane,[19] and of Samuel Johnson, a clergyman who'd not only been fined but severely whipped,[20] Titus Oates himself appealed to Parliament for relief from the judgment of the King's Bench, alleging that he'd been unjustly convicted.[21] At the request of the House of Commons, the new king, William III, had granted relief to both the Earl of Devonshire and Mr. Johnson for the notoriously harsh judgments rendered against them in James II's reign,[22] and Oates similarly sought the newly installed king's intervention to remit his sentence.[23] As *The History of England* (1744) puts it: "*Titus Oates* likewise took the opportunity now of the indignation of the Parliament, against the illegal proceedings of the late reign, to apply to the Lords, for a reversal of the two judgments against him on the point of perjury...."[24]

After being confined in Newgate Prison and scourged multiple times on the anniversaries of his own perjuries in accordance with his 1685 sentence, Oates—the defrocked Anglican minister—had been set free in 1688 after James II was deposed in the Glorious Revolution, with Oates later seeking complete vindication—and compensation—from the new king.[25] Oates began by appealing directly to the House of Lords by filing a writ of error, but that legislative body rejected it, finding Oates to be "so ill a Man." But opinion was divided, with thirty-five peers voting to affirm the judgment against Oates, while twenty-three peers voted to reverse it. The peers in the minority called Oates's punishment "barbarous, inhumane, and unchristian" and "contrary to" the English Bill of Rights. "[T]here is," they concluded, "no precedent to warrant the punishments of whipping and committing to prison for life, for the crime of perjury; which yet were but part of the punishments inflicted upon him." "[U]nless this judgment be reversed," they stressed, "like cruel, barbarous, and illegal judgments" would be encouraged, with the dissenters pointing to the newly issued Declaration of Rights "whereby it doth appear, that excessive bail ought not to be required, nor excessive fines imposed, nor cruel nor unusual punishments inflicted." Their position: the punishment of Oates was "contrary to law and ancient practice; and therefore erroneous, and ought to be reversed."

It was a lively, vigorous debate. Elsewhere, the dissenters opined "that the judgments given in the court of *King's-Bench* against *Titus Oates* are altogether illegal and cruel," "illegal and unjust," and "ought plainly to be declared positively against law, justice, and the undoubted right of the subject." The dissenters, in the context of the legislative fisticuffs, further argued that the notion advanced that "it shall not be lawful at any time hereafter to inflict the like excessive punishments again" would not be "strong enough to deter a corrupt or partial Judge from practicing the same, because it is without a penalty upon such Judge." In the Earl of Devonshire's case, it was specifically determined in 1689 that the £30,000 fine that had been imposed upon him during James II's reign was "excessive and exorbitant, against Magna Charta, the common right of the subject, and against the law of the land."[26] In that case, a "committee of privileges" had been appointed by the House of Lords to examine the draconian fine, it being demanded that the judges who'd rendered the judgment "should be required to attend at the bar of this House, to answer for the great offence, which they have committed thereby." The determination that the fine was excessive was rendered after various judicial officers were hauled before Parliament and closely questioned.[27]

There was even more at stake for Titus Oates than in the Earl of Devonshire's case because of the corporal, non-monetary aspects of his particular punishment. Whereas the heavy fine in the Earl of Devonshire's case was about money, Oates's conviction and the nature of his punishment had inflicted great infamy and stripped a man of his honor along with his clerical robes. "[T]here is no doubt," the dissenters declared in Oates's case, "but all Judges will be hereafter cautious of setting great fines, since of late the subject, in that point has been grievously oppressed, as does appear by several exorbitant fines annulled in this present Parliament." After the House of Commons conducted its own review, Oates—after much contentious debate and a fair amount of back and forth between the House of Commons and the House of Lords—received a pardon and a small pension from William III, with the House of Lords having advised William III: "That whereas Titus Oates ... had already received a severe punishment for the perjury whereof he had been formerly convicted, and some of the said punishments would still be continued upon him, unless they should be remitted by his Majesty; his Majesty would be graciously pleased to grant his pardon to the said Oates." The House of Commons, for its part, had specifically invoked the "cruel and unusual" punishments clause to justify the remission of Oates's 1685 sentence, calling it "barbarous," an "ill Example to future Ages," and "unusual" in that "an Englishman should be exposed upon a Pillory, so many times a Year, during his Life."[28]

Perhaps not surprisingly, things did not end well for George Jeffreys, the infamous judge once described as "a willing tool" of James II. He had become a baron in 1685 after the accession of James II to the throne, and after presiding over the Bloody Assizes, and taking substantial bribes in several cases, he had—in the words of one history—returned to London "a far wealthier man than he had been, and, though only thirty-seven, was made Lord Chancellor and in 1686 Head of the Ecclesiastical Commission...." But his fortunes took a dramatic turn for the worse with the onset of the Glorious Revolution and James II's fall from grace. Fearing the revenge of a mob after learning of James II's flight, Jeffreys had, himself, gone into hiding, disguised himself as a sailor, and made his own plans to flee England. Despite his well-laid plans, Jeffreys was thereafter unable to resist drinking "a pot of ale" at The Red Cow pub, where he was recognized by someone he had "formerly grossly ill-treated when on the bench." Having alienated so many and so badly, Jeffreys, after being taken into custody, had to be taken "under a strong guard," to protect him from being lynched by a mob, to the Tower of London. There, he was imprisoned and died later that same year, in 1689, likely due to the adverse conditions of his confinement and, perhaps, his compulsive drinking, with Jeffreys suffering from a long-standing addiction to brandy.[29]

The English Bill of Rights, restraining the king and queen's power and establishing a constitutional monarchy, was enacted in a particular, seventeenth-century historical context, thus explaining its language. In remarks by Sir John Hawles (1645–1716), a lawyer who served in the House of Commons and who, in 1695, was appointed England's solicitor-general, he spoke explicitly of "[t]he strange Revolution which hath of late happen'd in our Nation," which, he added, "naturally leads one into the Considerations of the Cause of it." After Hawles spoke on the subjects of "the Subversion of the Establish'd Religion" and "Taxes in the Nation," he went on to discuss "some other Reasons for the Disaffectation of the Nation to the late Government." Saying those other reasons "may be ranked" under "six Heads," Hawles laid out the very first reason as follows: "Exorbitant Fines; Cruel and Illegal Prosecutions; Outrageous Damages; ... Dispensing with ... Penal Laws; and undue Prosecutions in Criminal, but more especially in Capital Matters." On that particular point, he observed that when the House of Commons in 1680 had looked into the matter of fines in the context of impeachment proceedings, "the highest Fine at that time complain'd of, was but 1000 *l*." "[A]nd yet," he noted, in a few years "they were heightened to 10000 *l*., 20000 *l*., 30000 *l*. and 40000 *l*." The second reason Hawles listed in his remarks: "The punishment of *Oates*, *Dangerfield*, and Mr. *Johnson*; and the close Imprisonment of Mr. *Hamden*, Sir *Samuel Barnardiston*, and of several other Persons, as they were against Law, so they were without Precedent."[30] It was thus a whole series of injustices and excesses during the reign of the Stuarts, including that of James II, that prompted British subjects to demand great protection for their freedoms—privileges and liberties that were seen as dating all the way back to the Magna Carta (1215).

The concepts of proportionality and necessity—or absolute necessity, as it is sometimes expressed—were thus hardly new concepts in the eighteenth century, not in law and not in the realm of punishment. Both concepts were around long before Montesquieu and Beccaria picked up their pens, and those two thinkers would have been familiar with earlier writers who proceeded them. For example, Thomas Aquinas believed that "*man* has a *natural* aptitude for *virtue*," but that "the perfection of *virtue* must be acquired by *man* by means of some kind of training." "Consequently," Aquinas wrote, "a man needs to receive this training from another, whereby to arrive at the perfection of *virtue*." As Aquinas wrote on the subject of promoting virtue and preventing vice:

> [A]s to those young people who are inclined to acts of *virtue*, by their *good natural* disposition, or by custom, or rather by the *gift* of *God*, paternal training suffices, which is by admonitions. But since some are found to be depraved, and prone to *vice*, and not easily amenable to words, it was *necessary* for such to be restrained from *evil* by force and fear, in order that, at least, they might desist from *evil*-doing, and leave others in peace, and that

> they themselves, by being habituated in this way, might be brought to do willingly what hitherto they did from fear, and thus become *virtuous*. Now this kind of training, which compels through fear of punishment, is the discipline of laws. Therefore in order that man might have peace and *virtue*, it was *necessary* for laws to be framed: for, as the *Philosopher* says, "as *man* is the most noble of animals if he be perfect in *virtue*, so is he the lowest of all, if he be severed from *law* and righteousness"; because *man* can use his *reason* to devise means of satisfying his lusts and *evil* passions, which other animals are unable to do.[31]

In England, the concept of proportionality can be expressly found in the Magna Carta, Latin for "Great Charter," a seminal document in the history of rights discourse. "Magna Carta was sealed in 1215 by both England's King John and a bevy of English barons," one source observes,[32] with clause 20, per one modern translation from the Latin, reading:

> For a trivial offence, a free man shall be fined only in proportion to the degree of his offence, and for a serious offence correspondingly, but not so heavily as to deprive him of his livelihood. In the same way, a merchant shall be spared his merchandise, and a husbandman the implements of his husbandry, if they fall upon the mercy of a royal court. None of these fines shall be imposed except by the assessment on oath of reputable men of the neighbourhood.[33]

Clause 21 and 22 of the Magna Carta also dealt with monetary penalties, known at that time as amercements. Clause 21 reads: "Earls and barons shall not be amerced except through their peers, and only in accordance with the degree of the offense." And Clause 22 provides: "A clerk shall not be amerced in respect of his lay holding except after the manner of the others aforesaid; further, he shall not be amerced in accordance with the extent of his ecclesiastical benefice."[34]

A clear theme emerges when one reads Enlightenment texts. "The lack of proportion between crime and punishment," legal historian Aniceto Masferrer writes, "was one of the most consistent criticism made by the Enlightenment thinkers against the Ancién Regime."[35] However, European writers that *pre-date* Montesquieu and Beccaria discussed both proportionality and the concept of necessity. For example, the Dutch jurist Hugo Grotius (1583–1645), the Latinized version of Hugo de Groot or Huig de Groot, as he was known in Holland, rose to prominence for his *De Jure Belli ac Pacis* (*On the Law of War and Peace*, 1625). In that book, Grotius identified the "justifiable causes" for war as self-defense, reparation of injury, and punishment—or, as he put it in one place, "defence, indemnity, and punishment." In Chapter XX of his book, titled "On Punishments," Grotius specifically delved into "the origin and nature of punishment," writing: "Punishment taken in its most general meaning signifies the pain of suffering, which is inflicted for evil actions. For although labour may some times be imposed instead of punishment; still it is considered in that case, as a hardship and a grievous burden, and may therefore properly be classed with sufferings." In that chapter, Grotius specifically emphasized that "among the dictates laid down by nature, as lawful and just, and which the ancient Philosophers call the law of Rhadamanthus, the following maxim may be placed, THAT IT IS RIGHT FOR EVERY ONE TO SUFFER EVIL PROPORTIONED TO THAT WHICH HE HAS DONE."

Saying the "ancients called it the law of Rhadamanthus," a reference to the king of Crete, yet another popular Enlightenment writer, Emer de Vattel, writing in *The Law of Nations*, put the retaliation principle this way: "When a nation cannot obtain justice, whether for a wrong or an injury, she has a right to do herself justice." "Among those methods of obtaining satisfaction," Vattel wrote, "has been reckoned what is called the law of retaliation, according to which we make another suffer precisely as much evil as he has done." But speaking of "the true origin of the right of punishing" and of "the true and just proportion of penalties," Vattel had this to say: "*Retaliation, which is unjust between private persons, would be much more so between nations, because it would, in the latter case, be difficult to make the punishment fall on those who had done the injury.* What right have you to cut off the nose and ears of the ambassador of a barbarian who had treated your ambassador in that manner?" Elsewhere in his treatise, Vattel had offered that "[t]he punishment pre-ordained for an evil action, lays a more effectual restraint on the wicked than a vague fear," and that "[e]very well-governed state" ought to "have its laws for the punishment of criminals." "It belongs to the legislative power, whatever that be," Vattel wrote in the latter respect, "to establish them with justice and wisdom." Saying punishments must be kept "within just bounds," Vattel observed that "[s]ince they are designed to procure the safety of the state and of the citizens, they ought never to be extended beyond what that safety requires."[36]

In his own work, Grotius discussed both punishment and clemency, an executive's setting aside of a punishment. "'[T]o make a punishment just, it must be inflicted for some crime,'" Grotius quoted Augustin as saying, with Grotius adding that "[i]t is undoubtedly one of the first principles of justice to establish an equality between the penalty and the offence." "For it is the business of reason, says Horace, in one of his Satires," Grotius continued, "to apply a rule and measure, by which the penalty may be framed upon a scale with the offence, and in another place, he observes, that it would be contrary to all reason to punish with the rack a slave, who deserved nothing more than the whip."[37] "No Body is to be punished above his Desert," Grotius emphasized. In discussing "Clemency, which exempts from Punishment," Grotius invoked the declaration "That *it becometh the Just to be merciful*." As Grotius went on to observe: "For since all Punishment, especially if it be severe, has something in itself that is repugnant, not indeed to Justice, but Charity, surely our common Reason will easily suffer us to abstain from it, unless a Motive of Charity more strong and more just irresistibly hinder us. Very apposite to which is that of *Sopater*, where he says, that *That Justice, which is conversant about Contracts, admits of no Favour, but that, which is conversant about Offences, puts on sometimes the mild and gentle Countenance of the Graces.*" Writing in the heyday of monarchs, Grotius stressed: "*A Prince,* saith St. *Austin, may revoke a Sentence, and absolve and pardon the Person condemned to die:* And gives this Reason for it, *that he is not subject to Laws; who has Power to make them. Seneca* is for having *Nero* to reflect upon this Sentence: *Any Man can kill contrary to Law; but no Man can save besides my self.*"[38]

In his book, Grotius thus wrote about punishment at considerable length at a date far in advance of the writings of Montesquieu and Beccaria. "There is one sense," Grotius observed, "in which all punishment may be said to be a matter of strict justice." As Grotius explained: "Thus, when we say that punishment is due to any one, we mean nothing more than that it is right he should be punished. Nor can any one inflict this punishment, but the person, who has a right to do so. Now in the eye of the law, every penalty is considered, as a debt arising out of a crime, and which the offender is bound to pay to the aggrieved party." In that section, Grotius then invoked the law of contracts, writing:

> And in this there is something approaching to the nature of contracts. For as a seller, though no EXPRESS stipulation be made, is understood to have bound himself by all the USUAL, and NECESSARY conditions of a sale, so, punishment being a natural consequence of crime, every heinous offender appears to have VOLUNTARILY incurred the penalties of law. In this sense some of the Emperors pronounced sentence upon malefactors in the following manner, "you have brought this punishment upon Yourselves."[39]

Yet, Grotius, following his exploration of punishment as a form of contract, believed that it was not absolutely necessary to inflict punishments in certain circumstances. As Grotius wrote in another section of his book chapter: "Another part of our inquiry respects the end proposed by punishment. For by what has hitherto been said, it was only meant to shew that in punishing the guilty no injury is done to them. Still the absolute necessity of punishment does not follow from thence." As Grotius observed, pointing out that rulers might effectively employ mercy as regards offenders: "For the pardon of the guilty on many occasions has been considered as the most beauteous feature in the divine and human character. Plato is celebrated for his saying that 'justice does not inflict punishment for the evils that are done and cannot be retrieved; but to prevent the same from being done for the time to come.'" "From Thucydides," Grotius continued, "we find that Diodorus in addressing the Athenians on the conduct of the Mitylenaeans, advises them 'to forbear punishing their avowed injustice, unless it was probable that the punishment would be attended with some good effect.'" "These maxims," Grotius concluded, "may be true with regard to human punishments: for one man being so nearly allied to another by blood, no degree of suffering should be inflicted, but for some consequent good." "For the preceding arguments," Grotius observed, "it is plain that punishment cannot justly be inflicted from a spirit of revenge."[40]

In *On Crimes and Punishments*, Beccaria wanted societies to get to a stage where punishments would always be just and pardons therefore unnecessary. As Beccaria wrote: "As punishments become more mild, clemency and pardon are less necessary. Happy the nation in which they will be considered as dangerous!" In particular, Beccaria made these observations in the chapter of his book on pardons: "Clemency, which has often been deemed a sufficient substitute for every other virtue in sovereigns, should be excluded in a perfect legislation, where punishments are mild, and the proceedings in criminal cases regular and expeditious. This truth will seem cruel to those who live in countries where, from the absurdity of the laws and the severity of punishments, pardons and the clemency of the prince are necessary." As Beccaria explained his reasoning for why an ideal system of criminal justice would no longer need executive clemency: "Clemency is a virtue which belongs to the legislator, and not to the executor of the laws; a virtue which ought to shine in the code, and not in private judgment. To shew mankind that crimes are sometimes pardoned, and that punishment is not the necessary consequence, is to nourish the flattering hope of impunity, and is the cause of their considering every punishment inflicted as an act of injustice and oppression." Beccaria favored *certain* punishments over *severe* ones, and he believed that sporadic, *ad hoc* pardons would not only reduce the certainty of the law's enforcement but would cause offenders to harbor hopes of impunity for their transgressions. "Let, then, the executors of the laws be inexorable, but let the legislator be tender, indulgent, and humane," Beccaria concluded.[41]

Thomas Jefferson, who carefully studied Beccaria's book, came to the same end point, at least as an intellectual matter.[42] In a letter dated August 26, 1776, to Edmund Pendleton, Thomas Jefferson recognized that punishments had to be imposed to check criminal behavior, but he expressed his concerns about the severity of punishments to be imposed. As Jefferson wrote in his letter:

> The fantastical idea of virtue and the public good being a sufficient security to the state against the commission of crimes, which you say you have heard insisted on by some, I assure you was never mine. It is only the sanguinary hue of our penal laws which I meant to object to. Punishments I know are necessary, and I would provide them, strict and inflexible, but proportioned to the crime. Death might be inflicted for murther and perhaps for treason if you would take out of the description of treason all crimes which are not such in their nature. Rape, buggery &c. punish by castration. All other crimes by working on high roads, rivers, gallies &c. a certain time proportioned to the offence. But as this would be no punishment or change of condition to slaves (me miserum!) let them be sent to other countries. By these means we should be freed from the wickedness of the latter, and the former would be living monuments of public vengeance. Laws thus proportionate and mild should never be dispensed with. Let mercy be the character of the law-giver, but let the judge be a mere machine. The mercies of the law will be dispensed equally and impartially to every description of men; those of the judge, or of the executive power, will be the eccentric impulses of whimsical, capricious designing man.[43]

Writers in the seventeenth and eighteenth centuries sought to eliminate practices rooted in the Dark Ages and medieval times. Views toward the law were in great flux during the Enlightenment and the American Revolution in particular, and an examination of Thomas Jefferson's writings exemplifies the shift that was taking place. For instance, Jefferson's 1779 Bill for Proportioning Crimes and Punishments in Cases Heretofore Capital—one written for Virginia lawmakers to consider—explicitly cites Montesquieu and Beccaria's writings. Even though the law-trained Jefferson had difficulty shedding some of the barbarous traditions of the English common law, that bill signaled a shift in tone toward crime and punishment. Above all else, the opening paragraphs of the bill reflect the changing societal views brought about by Enlightenment writers:

> Whereas it frequently happens that wicked and dissolute men resigning themselves to the dominion of inordinate passions, commit violations on the lives, liberties and property of others, and, the secure enjoyment of these having principally induced men to enter into society, government would be defective in it's principal purpose were it not to restrain such criminal acts, by inflicting due punishments on those who perpetrate them; but it appears at the same time equally deducible from the purposes of society that a member thereof, committing an inferior injury, does not wholly forfiet the protection of his fellow citizens, but, after suffering a punishment in proportion to his offence is entitled to their protection from all greater pain, so that it becomes a duty in the legislature to arrange in a proper scale the crimes which it may be necessary for them to repress, and to adjust thereto a corresponding gradation of punishments.
>
> And whereas the reformation of offenders, tho' an object worthy the attention of the laws, is not effected at all by capital punishments, which exterminate instead of reforming, and should be the last melancholy resource against those whose existence is become inconsistent with the safety of their fellow citizens, which also weaken the state by cutting off so many who, if reformed, might be restored sound members to society, who, even under a course of correction, might be rendered useful in various labors for the public, and would be living and long continued spectacles to deter others from committing the like offences.
>
> And forasmuch the experience of all ages and countries hath shewn that cruel and sanguinary laws defeat their own purpose by engaging the benevolence of mankind to withold prosecutions, to smother testimony, or to listen to it with bias, when, if the punishment were only proportioned to the injury, men would feel it their inclination as well as their duty to see the laws observed.
>
> For rendering crimes and punishments therefore more proportionate to each other: Be it enacted by the General assembly that no crime shall be henceforth punished by deprivation of life or limb except those hereinafter ordained to be so punished.[44]

America's political and military leaders, some, like George Washington, trained in the strictly regimented British military to use harsh punishments to enforce discipline, explicitly used the language of proportionality in the wake of the publication of *The Spirit of the Laws* and *On Crimes and Punishments*. For example, in a 1779 letter signed by George Washington, but in then-aide James McHenry's handwriting, one finds these words: "That mutinous spirit which some corps have lately discovered, averse from order, and subordination, must be extinguished by every means in our power, and punishments enforced proportionate to the nature and consequences of the crime."[45] And in a 1785 letter to James Madison, Edmund Randolph—the Virginian who became the first Attorney General of the United States—observed: "The executive are at last persuaded of their power to make the Beccarian experiment on the condemned; altho' the public should undergo some expense. They found their opinion on the law concerning the buildings for the use of the state. An overseer, trusty and diligent, will be therefore appointed, with instructions, fitted to the views of government." As the editors of *The Papers of James Madison* observed of the context of that letter: "In a letter to the mayor of Richmond, 13 Jan. 1785, Governor Henry expressed dissatisfaction with the death penalty as disproportionate to crimes committed in certain cases. Since he believed that unconditional pardon was detrimental to society, he preferred the assignment of convicts to public works as an appropriate punishment, and as a deterrent to future offenders."[46] In "Considerations on a Convention with Spain," signed on March 22, 1792, by Thomas Jefferson, one also finds this assessment as Americans contemplated whether to enter into an extradition treaty with Spain: "All Excess of punishment is a *Crime*. To remit a fugitive to Excessive punishment, is to be *accessary* to the crime."[47]

The notion of avoiding excessive bail and fines—of putting restraints on bail, fines, and punishments—shows up explicitly in a long line of statutes and constitutions, from the English Bill of Rights to the Northwest Ordinance to state constitutions and the U.S. Constitution's Eighth Amendment. Whereas the English Bill of Rights (1689) provided that "excessive bail ought not to be required, nor excessive fines imposed, nor cruel and unusual punishments inflicted," the Eighth Amendment (1791) echoed that language, reading in a slight variation: "Excessive bail shall not be required, nor excessive fines imposed, nor cruel and unusual punishments inflicted." Meanwhile, Article 2 of the Northwest Ordinance (1787) provided in part: "All persons shall be bailable unless for capital offences, where the proof shall be evident or the presumption great; all fines shall be moderate; and no cruel or unusual punishments shall be inflicted; no man shall be deprived of his liberty or property but by the judgment of his peers, or the law of the land; and should the public exigencies make it necessary for the common preservation to take any person's property, or to demand his particular services, full compensation shall be made for the same...."[48] Serious offenders would be held without bail, but moderation and legal process were clearly valued by early Americans as reflected in early American constitutions.

The Northwest Ordinance, formally titled "An ordinance for the government of the territory of the United States, northwest of the river Ohio," was enacted on July 13, 1787, by the Confederation Congress. It created the Northwest Territory, and it is considered one of the most important acts of the Confederation Congress because, in Article VI, it outlawed slavery in that newly created territory. The Northwest Ordinance of 1787 was reaffirmed by the U.S. Congress in its Northwest Ordinance of 1789, passed on August 7, 1789, in light of the adoption of the U.S. Constitution, which took the place of the ill-fated Articles of Confederation. As the first whereas clause of the Northwestern Ordinance of 1789 read: "*Whereas* in order that the ordinance of the United States in Congress assembled, for the government of the territory north-west of the river Ohio may continue to have full effect, it is requisite that certain provisions should be made, so as to adapt the same to the present Constitution of the United States." The original Northwest Ordinance had directed the adoption and publication of such laws "as may be necessary, and best suited to the circumstances of the district" and that, "[f]or the prevention of crimes and injuries, the laws to be adopted or made shall have force in all parts of the district."[49]

William Blackstone's *Commentaries on the Laws of England*

William Blackstone (1723–1780), a prominent jurist and professor of law at Oxford University, was a leading authority on the development of the English common law. Born in London, he studied at Oxford and was admitted to the bar in 1746. In 1758, after working as the college's bursar and writing on issues of jurisprudence, Blackstone was appointed Oxford's first professor of common law, thus founding the Vinerian Professorship. His lectures on the law attracted much attention, and he later got elected to Parliament and served as the solicitor general. William Blackstone's most famous work, *Commentaries on the Laws of England*, represented an enlargement of his law lectures, and his treatise became—as one source notes—"a huge publishing success from its first appearance in four volumes between 1765 and 1769." Eight editions were printed in Blackstone's lifetime, and the treatise was regularly quoted and cited in court—not only in England but in its far-flung colonies. Before his death, Blackstone himself became a judge of the Court of Common Pleas in 1770 and was knighted.[50] As the publishing success of Blackstone's landscape-changing treatise in America has been described: "In the thinly settled American colonies, the need for a portable yet definitive guide to the common law made Blackstone's *Commentaries* an essential treatise for colonial lawyers and magistrates. Even after the revolution, Blackstone's work remained a cornerstone of early American jurisprudence, as adapted and edited by the federalist law professor St. George Tucker in 1803."[51] St. George Tucker, a William and Mary law professor, had—like Thomas Jefferson—studied law under George Wythe, a much-respected Virginia lawyer and jurist.[52]

Sir William Blackstone was, himself, greatly influenced by Montesquieu's *The Spirit of the Laws* and Cesare Beccaria's *On Crimes and Punishments*. In the opening chapter of Volume Four of his *Commentaries on the Laws of England*, Blackstone cited "Baron Montesquieu" and "marquis Beccaria" in a footnote in the opening section. Blackstone thought the criminal law ought to attract the "care and attention of the legislature," and he expressed the view that the criminal law "should be founded upon principles that are permanent, uniform, and universal; and always conformable to the dictates of truth and justice, the feelings of humanity, and the indelible rights of mankind: though it sometimes (provided there be no transgression of these eternal boundaries) may be modified, narrowed, or enlarged, according to the local or occasional necessities of the state which it is meant to govern." In the first chapter of Blackstone's *Commentaries*, titled "Of the Nature and Crimes; and Their Punishment," Blackstone lamented the failure to follow such principles, footnoting Montesquieu and Beccaria after the reference to "ingenious writers":

> And yet, either from a want of attention to these principles in the first concoction of the laws, and adopting in their stead the impetuous dictates of avarice, ambition, and revenge; from retaining the discordant political regulations, which successive conquerors or factions have established, in the various revolutions of government; from giving a lasting efficacy to sanctions that were intended to be temporary, and made (as lord Bacon expresses it) merely upon the spur of the occasion; or from, lastly, too hastily employing

> such means as are greatly disproportionate to their end, in order to check the progress of some very prevalent offence; from some, or from all, of these causes it hath happened, that the criminal law is in every country of Europe more rude and imperfect than the civil. I shall not here enter into any minute enquiries concerning the local constitutions of other nations; the inhumanity and mistaken policy of which have been sufficiently pointed out by ingenious writers of their own. But even with us in England, where our crown-law is with justice supposed to be more nearly advanced to perfection; where crimes are more accurately defined, and penalties less uncertain and arbitrary; where all our accusations are public, and our trials in the face of the world; where torture is unknown, and every delinquent is judged by such of his equals, against whom he can form no exception nor even a personal dislike;—even here we shall occasionally find room to remark some particulars, that seem to want revision and amendment. These have chiefly arisen from too scrupulous an adherence to some rules of the antient common law, when the reasons have ceased upon which those rules were founded; from not repealing such of the old penal laws as are either obsolete or absurd; and from too little care and attention in framing and passing new ones.[53]

William Blackstone was a prominent, even towering, figure—one regularly consulted in the eighteenth century but still studied today for insights into that time. In her illuminating introduction to the Oxford edition of Book Four of Blackstone's *Commentaries on the Laws of England*, scholar Ruth Paley writes: "For all its originality in terms of structure, Book IV naturally does rely for much of its content on Coke, Hale, and Hawkins." Sir Edward Coke (1552–1634) was an English barrister whose law reports and four-volume *Institutes of the Laws of England* were highly influential; Sir Matthew Hale (1609–1676) was one of the greatest scholars on the history of the English common law; and William Hawkins (1673–1746) was an English barrister best known for his work on the English criminal law, including *A Treatise of Pleas of the Crown* (1716). But Paley points outs that "Blackstone also made use of influential international texts of his own generation, some of which, such as Montesquieu's *Spirit of the Laws* and Beccaria's *On Crimes and Punishments*, we now regard as seminal, while others were and remain less well known, such as the *Grand Instructions for Framing a New Code of Laws for the Russian Empire* (1768)."[54] The latter had been written by Russian Empress Catherine II, also known as Catherine the Great, but was, itself, almost entirely inspired by the writings of Montesquieu and Beccaria, two of the European *philosophes* she so admired. "In a Word," those Grand Instructions observed in paragraph 63, borrowing from Montesquieu and Beccaria, "every Punishment, which is not inflicted through Necessity, is tyrannical."[55]

In an essay on Blackstone's *Commentaries*, another scholar, Daniel Boorstin, observed that Blackstone articulated a dislike for "sanguinary" criminal statutes. Seeking to have those laws changed, Blackstone—a highly respected legal mind in the British Isles—turned to *continental* European thinkers to help justify law reform. As Boorstin wrote: "The theory of criminal law suggested by Montesquieu, and developed by Beccaria, was wholeheartedly adopted by Blackstone." "[A]lthough Beccaria's *Essay on Crimes and Punishments* did not appear until 1764," Boorstin stressed, "Blackstone referred to it several times and made extensive use of the ideas in it."[56] As another book notes of Beccaria's particular influence on Blackstone, the prominent English jurist: "Blackstone's *Commentaries* are generally read as an attempt to rationalize and justify the common law of England, and this is largely true of the fourth part, which is on criminal law. However, Blackstone had been deeply influenced by Beccaria before he wrote his account, and he expressed some criticism of the legal system reflecting this."[57] Because England's "Bloody Code" was still in force, it is probably not too surprising that Blackstone would've looked to writers outside his home country as he grappled with how to reshape English law.

In his *Commentaries on the Laws of England*, Blackstone repeatedly referenced the writings of Montesquieu and Beccaria. "Baron Montesquieu lays it down, that luxury is necessary in monarchies, as in France; but ruinous to democracies, as in Holland," Blackstone wrote at one point, explaining in another that "the president Montesquieu observes" that "it would be impolitic for the power of judging and of pardoning to center in one and the same person." Blackstone agreed with Beccaria that "*preventive* justice is upon every principle, of reason, of humanity, and of sound policy, preferable in all respects to *punishing* justice." Blackstone cited Beccaria for the proposition "as punishments are chiefly intended for the prevention of future crimes, it is but reasonable that among crimes of different natures those should be most severely punished, which are the most destructive of the public safety and happiness." Shortly thereafter, Blackstone cited both Montesquieu and Beccaria—the latter of whom he again referred to as an "ingenious writer"—in this passage: "It is the sentiment of an ingenious writer, who seems to have well studied the springs of human action, that crimes are more effectually prevented by the *certainty*, than by the *severity*, of punishment. For the excessive severity of laws (says Montesquieu) hinders their execution: when the punishment surpasses all measure, the public will frequently out of humanity prefer impunity to it."

In another section of Book Four, William Blackstone discussed the use of "[t]he rack, or question, to extort a confession from criminals," saying "the trial by rack is utterly unknown to the law of England," though acknowledging its use in prior times "in the tower of London." Taking note of torture's use in France "and other foreign nations," Blackstone at yet another point again referenced "[t]he marquis Beccaria" and quoted language from Beccaria's *On Crimes and Punishments*, what Blackstone called "an exquisite piece of raillery" articulated "with a gravity and precision that are truly mathematical."[58] In a history of the Tower of London, it is noted that Henry VI, the King of England, "kept the Tower warders busy with his numerous State prisoners—a possible reason why John, Duke of Exeter, Constable in this reign, invented and introduced into the dungeons of the White Tower the first rack ever known in England, afterwards notorious as 'the Duke of Exeter's daughter.'"[59] In France, there were two major types of torture, though the severity of torture varied depending on the locality. As Lisa Silverman writes in *Tortured Subjects: Pain, Truth, and the Body in Early Modern France*: "The *question préparatoire* was designed to elicit a confession from the accused before guilt was determined, while the *question préalable* aimed to elicit the names of accomplices after the guilt of the accused had been determined."[60]

The concept of necessity, along with clear evidence of the importance of Beccaria's and Montesquieu's work, shows up in a prominent fashion in William Blackstone's *Commentaries on the Laws of England*. For example, in Volume 4 of his *Commentaries*, Blackstone writes of "justifiable homicide," describing that category of killing in this manner: "Such as is owing to some unavoidable *necessity*, without any will, intention, or desire, and without any inadvertence or negligence, in the party killing, and therefore without any shadow of blame."[61] In his *Commentaries*, Blackstone spoke pejoratively of "cruel punishments" and "severe punishments" and, then, citing Beccaria with respect to an "ingeniously proposed" idea, observed:

> It is moreover absurd and impolitic to apply the same punishment to crimes of different malignity. A multitude of sanguinary laws (besides the doubt that may be entertained concerning the right of making them) do likewise prove a manifest defect either in the wisdom of the legislative, or the strength of the executive power. It is a kind of quackery in government, and argues a want of solid skill, to apply the same universal remedy, the *ultimum supplicium* [ultimate punishment], to every case of difficulty. It is, it must be owned, much *easier* to extirpate than to amend mankind: yet that magistrate must be esteemed both a weak and a cruel surgeon, who cuts off every limb, which through ignorance or indolence he will not attempt to cure. It has been therefore ingeniously proposed, that in every state a scale of crimes should be formed, with a corresponding scale of punishment, descending from the greatest to the least: but, if that be too romantic an idea, yet at least a wise legislator will mark the principal divisions, and not assign penalties of the first degree to offences of an inferior rank.[62]

In Volume 1 of his *Commentaries*, Blackstone had also written of the "rights of man," of "liberty," and of "necessary and expedient" laws. As Blackstone wrote in an extended discussion of those concepts:

> The absolute rights of man, considered as a free agent, endowed with discernment to know good from evil, and with power of choosing those measures which appear to him to be most desirable, are usually summed up in one general appellation, and denominated the natural liberty of mankind. This natural liberty consists properly in a power of acting as one thinks fit, without any restraint or control, unless by the law of nature: being a right inherent in us by birth, and one of the gifts of God to man at his creation, when he endued him with the faculty of free-will. But every man, when he enters into society, gives up a part of his natural liberty, as the price of so valuable a purchase; and, in consideration of receiving the advantages of mutual commerce, obliges himself to conform to those laws, which the community has thought proper to establish. And this species of legal obedience and conformity is infinitely more desirable, than that wild and savage liberty which is sacrificed to obtain it. For no man, that considers a moment, would wish to retain the absolute and uncontroled power of doing whatever he

> pleases; the consequence of which is, that every other man would also have the same power; and then there would be no security to individuals in any of the enjoyments of life. Political therefore, or civil, liberty, which is that of a member of society, is no other than natural liberty so far restrained by human laws (and no farther) as is necessary and expedient for the general advantage of the publick. Hence we may collect that the law, which restrains a man from doing mischief to his fellow citizens, though it diminishes the natural, increases the civil liberty of mankind: but every wanton and causeless restraint of the will of the subject, whether practiced by a monarch, a nobility, or a popular assembly, is a degree of tyranny. Nay, that even laws themselves, whether made with or without our consent, if they regulate and constrain our conduct in matters of mere indifference, without any good end in view, are laws destructive of liberty: whereas if any public advantage can arise from observing such precepts, the control of our private inclinations, in one or two particular points, will conduce to preserve our general freedom in others of more importance; by supporting that state, of society, which alone cansecure our independence. Thus the statute of king Edward IV, which forbad the fine gentlemen of those times (under the degree of a lord) to wear pikes upon their shoes or boots of more than two inches in length, was a law that savoured of oppression; because, however ridiculous the fashion then in use might appear, the restraining it by pecuniary penalties could serve no purpose of common utility. But the statute of king Charles II, which prescribes a thing seemingly as indifferent; viz. a dress for the dead, who are all ordered to be buried in woollen; is a law consistent with public liberty, for it encourages the staple trade, on which in great measure depends the universal good of the nation. So that laws, when prudently framed, are by no means subversive but rather introductive of liberty; for (as Mr Locke has well observed) where there is no law, there is no freedom. But then, on the other hand, that constitution or frame of government, that system of laws, is alone calculated to maintain civil liberty, which leaves the subject entire master of his own conduct, except in those points wherein the public good requires some direction or restraint.[63]

Summing up Cesare Beccaria's influence on Blackstone, Sir William Holdsworth, in *A History of English Law*, writes:

> If Beccaria's book be compared with Blackstone's remarks on the theory of punishment, it is impossible to doubt that Blackstone owes much to Beccaria. Though Blackstone by no means sees eye to eye with Beccaria on all matters, it is I think clear that it was Beccaria's book which helped Blackstone to crystallize his ideas, and that it was Beccaria's influence which helped to give a more critical tone to his treatment of the English criminal law than to his treatment of any other part of English law.[64]

In fact, Beccaria's ideas had a profound influence far beyond the continent of Europe and the British Isles. As a legal bibliography of American, English, Irish and Scottish legal texts, one printed in Philadelphia in 1847, aptly observes: "Beccaria's liberal and philanthropic views upon criminal jurisprudence, have had a most beneficial influence upon the criminal laws of the whole civilized world. His work has been translated into most European languages, and the truths that it contains have commended themselves to the world." "The English translation of Beccaria," that source notes, "was made from the French translation of the Abbé Morellet, to which Voltaire added a comment of the work."[65]

It was, in many cases, through Sir William Blackstone, that American lawyers got exposed to Beccaria's work. As one modern source notes: "Beccaria came to American lawyers filtered through the most influential law book in the colonies, Blackstone's *Commentaries on the Laws of England* (1765–1769)." Blackstone's treatise called "sanguinary laws" a "bad symptom of the distemper of any state," harkening back to early Roman times in these words: "The laws of the Roman kings, and the twelve tables of the *decemviri*, were full of cruel punishments: the Porcian law, which exempted all citizens from sentence of death, silently abrogated them all. In this period the republic flourished: under the emperors severe punishments were revived; and then the empire fell." And just as Beccaria's ideas influenced Blackstone and other English legal commentators, many of Blackstone's and Beccaria's ideas made an impact on American law. In *Democracy in America*, Alexis de Tocqueville, who visited America in the 1830s to study its penal system, specifically wrote: "In no country is criminal justice administered with more mildness than in the United States. While the English seem disposed carefully to retain the bloody traces of the dark ages in their penal legislation, the Americans have almost expunged capital punishment from their codes." "North America is, I think," de Tocqueville added, "the only one country upon earth in which the life of no one citizen has been taken for a political offense in the course of the last fifty years."[66] It was, thanks in no small measure to Montesquieu, Beccaria, and Blackstone, that de Tocqueville was able to write those words in *Democracy in America*.

The Spirit of Laws, first translated from the French into English by Thomas Nugent, was first published in London in 1750 ("Printed for J. Nourse, and P. Vaillant, in the *Strand*") and in Dublin in 1751 ("Printed for G. and A. Ewing, in *Dame-street*, and G. Faulkner in *Essex-street*"). Though Montesquieu's work is often translated into English as *The Spirit of the Laws*, Nugent's translation—as one modern source notes—"omitted the definite article in the French title, no doubt because the definite article is often used in French where it is neither needed nor welcome in English." It was in those editions that Montesquieu's maxim—"All punishment which is not derived from necessity, is tyrannical."—would have first caught the attention of English-language readers.[67] *The Spirit of the Laws* then appeared in additional English language translations in Aberdeen, Scotland, in 1756, again in London in 1758, in Edinburgh in 1762, again in Dublin in 1767, in Berwick in 1770, again in London and Edinburgh in 1773, and yet again in London in 1777, still again in Edinburgh in 1778, and still again in Dublin in 1792, and so on. Needless to say, Montesquieu's widely read masterpiece soon became the topic of much conversation.[68]

The early American publishers of Beccaria's treatise—one in Charleston, South Carolina, and one in Philadelphia—were, themselves, prominent men and community leaders. While David Bruce (1731–1783), a Scotsman, had settled in Charleston, South Carolina in 1759, formed a partnership with the printer Robert Wells, and brought out the first American edition of *On Crimes and Punishments* in 1777,[69] Robert Bell—the Scottish-born printer who had emigrated to Philadelphia—printed *On Crimes and Punishments* in 1778 in Philadelphia. It was Robert Bell who, earlier in the 1770s, had sold subscriptions to allow the reprinting of William Blackstone's multi-volume *Commentaries on the Laws of England* in Philadelphia.[70] As one source, *A History of the Book in America*, notes of Bell's subscription sale practice for producing books and Blackstone's *Commentaries* in particular: "Subscribers did not pay money in advance but were expected to pay for each volume as it was delivered, thus providing the capital for the next. For Blackstone, he promised to put the work to press as soon as he received 200 subscribers; ultimately he got almost 1,600." Bell's editions, that source notes, "were cheaper than the imports and, because they were printed in America on American paper, they encouraged native manufactures and prevent the export of specie." "The London editions of Blackstone, all quartos, sold for as much as $26.00 in Philadelphia, while Bell's octavo edition sold for $8.00," *A History of the Book in America* explains.[71]

Robert Bell's edition of Blackstone's *Commentaries* proudly noted on the title page that it was printed in "*AMERICA*" at "the late UNION LIBRARY, in *Third-street*, PHILADELPHIA," and that it had been "RE-PRINTED FROM THE BRITISH COPY, PAGE FOR PAGE WITH THE LAST EDITION."[72] The first printing of Blackstone's treatise was, in fact, an important moment for American publishing, and one that would not escape later notice. "The Founding Fathers' most important and widely-owed law book," Lisa Gold writes, "was William Blackstone's *Commentaries on the Laws of England*." As Gold explains: "John Adams, Thomas Jefferson, James Madison, Alexander Hamilton, Benjamin Franklin, John Marshall, and John Dickinson all read and owned various editions and frequently cited it in their writings." While the first edition of Blackstone's four-volume *Commentaries* was published by Oxford's Clarendon Press from 1765 to 1769, Bell's first American edition came out in Philadelphia from 1771 to 1772 and attracted many buyers, with copies ending up in John Adams and Thomas Jefferson's libraries.[73] Before his death in 1784, Robert Bell—perhaps most famously—had published the original edition of Thomas Paine's landscape-changing *Common Sense*, the political pamphlet that helped spur on the American Revolution and the quest for independence from Great Britain.[74] "With rare exceptions, such as octavo editions of Beccaria's *Essay on Crimes and Punishments* and *Miscellanies* by M. de Voltaire," Richard Sher writes in *The Enlightenment and the Book* of the Revolutionary War period, "Bell limited his Enlightenment publications during the early years of the war to smaller works."[75]

Through his printing shop, the Scottish-born printer who had settled in Philadelphia directly exposed readers to Beccaria's *On Crimes and Punishments* through his reprinting of that book in an English translation. But through his reprinting of Blackstone's *Commentaries on the Laws of England*, Robert Bell also exposed countless Americans to Montesquieu's and Beccaria's ideas indirectly, as the ideas of Montesquieu and Beccaria appeared in that text, too. Sales from Bell's first reprinting of

Blackstone's *Commentaries* between 1771 to 1772 were brisk enough, in fact, to warrant a second printing, which Bell brought out from 1773 to 1775.[76] In promoting Blackstone's *Commentaries* in advertisements in his own books, Robert Bell included this verbiage: "*SUBSCRIPTIONS* are also received by said ROBERT BELL, and the Booksellers on the Continent, for RE-PRINTING, A SECOND AMERICAN Edition of Judge BLACKSTONE's *Commentaries on the Laws of ENGLAND* in Four Volumes *Quarto*, at *Three Dollars* each Volume." As that notice advised before Bell's printing of the lengthy list of subscribers: "These Gentlemen who were Subscribers to the First Edition in *Octavo*, and now choose to possess the *Quarto* Edition, shall have their *Octavo* (if not abused) exchanged for the *Quarto*, on paying the Difference between the Prices." Whereas a quarto edition is folded to make four leaves, an octavo has eight leaves.[77]

The "Names of the Subscribers" listed in Bell's reprinting of Blackstone's *Commentaries* contains many familiar ones, but also ones now mostly forgotten or unknown to modern readers. Among the more famous listed in the list of subscribers: "His Excellency William Franklin, Esq.; Governor of New-Jersey," the son of Benjamin Franklin; "John Adams, Esq.; Barrister at Law, Boston"; "Elias Boudinot, Esq.; Attorney at Law, Elizabeth-town, New-Jersey"; "John Dickinson, Esq.; Attorney at Law, Philadelphia"; "John Jay, Esq.; Attorney-at-Law, New-York"; "Governeur Morris, Esq.; Attorney at Law, New-York"; "Edmund Pendleton, Esq; Caroline County, Virginia"; "Samuel Quincy, Esq.; Barrister at Law, Boston"; "The Hon. Roger Sherman, Esq; one of the Judges of the Superior Court of Connecticut"; and "Mr. Charles Thomson, Merchant, Philadelphia." While John Jay, for instance, later memorably participated in the preparation of *The Federalists Papers*, John Adams went on to draft the Massachusetts constitution of 1780—the state constitution adopted several years before the Constitutional Convention in Philadelphia produced the U.S. Constitution. John Adams became the second President of the United States, following George Washington's two terms in office, with Adams ultimately being succeeded by Thomas Jefferson. Adams—much to his disappointment, and due to the bitter Election of 1800—served just one term as president.[78]

The list of subscribers for Blackstone's *Commentaries* notes that "Mr. John Dunlap, Printer, Philadelphia"—a man who has become best known to modern historians for printing broadsides of the Declaration of Independence—ordered "23 sets," with "Mr. James Rivington, Bookseller, New-York," ordering "200 sets" and "Mssrs. Edes and Gill," printers in Boston, ordering "60 sets." James Rivington, a prominent New York bookseller, had, in 1773, actually planned to publish an edition of Beccaria's *Essay on Crimes and Punishments* with Voltaire's *Commentary*, though that project—listed in Charles Evans's *American Bibliography*—apparently never came to fruition as no copies have yet to be located. The list of subscribers set forth by Robert Bell for Blackstone's *Commentaries* also noted that many other institutions and individuals had agreed to purchase copies, in many cases multiple copies, presumably for resale. Robert Wells, a bookseller in Charleston, South Carolina, ordered 68 sets; another bookseller in New York, the Irish-born printer Hugh Gaine, wanted 28 sets; bookseller John Sparhawk in Portsmouth, New Hampshire, ordered 14 sets; printer Solomon

Southwick in New-port, Rhode Island, asked for seven sets; The Library Company of Philadelphia, founded by Benjamin Franklin in 1731, ordered two sets; the Newtown Library in Pennsylvania wanted one copy; and others, including Philadelphia attorney Miers Fisher and Philadelphia merchant Jabez Maud Fisher, ordered multiple sets of the work. Among other prominent individuals who signed up as subscribers were eight members of the Livingston family, including "Philip Livingston, Esq.; New York," "William Livingston, Esq.," and "Robert R. Livingston, Esq.; one of the Judges of the Supreme Court, New York."[79]

The subscriptions Robert Bell obtained for the 1770s American reprinting of Blackstone's *Commentaries* included governors and scores of individuals who identified themselves as either "Barrister at Law" or "Attorney at Law." The individuals were scattered throughout the Americas—Connecticut, Delaware, Florida, Georgia, Maryland, Massachusetts, New Hampshire, New Jersey, New York, North Carolina, Pennsylvania, Rhode Island, South Carolina, Virginia, even the Bahamas, Barbadoes, Bermuda, Grenada, Jamaica, the Island of St. Croix, Nova Scotia, and Quebec. And the occupations listed in the subscriptions showed that not only barristers and lawyers were eager to get their hands on Blackstone's *Commentaries*. Other than attorneys and barristers, judges and justices, governors, lieutenant or deputy governors, and various lawmakers, the following occupations appear in the list: "Binder," "Bookseller," "Cabinet-maker," "Clerk," "Collector of the Customs," "Colonel," "Comedian," "Doctor," "Farmer," "Gent.," "Lieutenant," "Mayor," "Merchant," "Miller," "Minister," "Printer," "Professor of History and Languages," "Scrivener," "Sheriff," "student of Law," "Rector," "Reverend," "Ship Chandler," "Shoemaker," "Silversmith," "Surveyor," "Tavern keeper," "Treasurer" and "Under-sheriff." Captains in "his Majesty's Royal Artillery" and a captain "of his Majesty's armed Schooner, Sultana," also desired a copy, as did a "Major Commandant of his Majesty's Royal Artillery in the Southern District of British America."[80]

One of the subscribers, Samuel Livermore, was New Hampshire's attorney general, and would—years later—himself weigh in during legislative debate over the U.S. Bill of Rights at the First Congress. In discussing the U.S. Constitution's proposed Eighth Amendment language, Livermore worried aloud that American judges might one day read it to bar punishments that were then thought to be acceptable. As Livermore, representing New Hampshire at the First Congress, stated: "The clause seems to express a great deal of humanity, on which account I have no objection to it; but as it seems to have no meaning in it, I do not think it necessary. What is meant by the terms excessive bail? What is understood by excessive fines? It lies with the court to determine." Futilely asserting that "we ought not to be restrained from making necessary laws by any declaration of this kind," Livermore unsuccessfully opposed the inclusion of the Eighth Amendment's language, with Livermore uttering these words: "No cruel and unusual punishment is to be inflicted; it is sometimes necessary to hang a man, villains often deserve whipping, and perhaps having their ears cut off; but are we in the future to be prevented from inflicting these punishments because they are cruel?"[81] It was an important question—one that showed what was on the mind of at least one prominent eighteenth-century lawmaker.

Even before Sir William Blackstone wrote his *Commentaries*, and even before Montesquieu and Beccaria wrote their works, serious questions had actually already been raised in England about the needless severity of punishments. "What a lamentable case it is," Sir Edward Coke had written at the beginning of the seventeenth century, "to see so many Christian men and women strangled on that cursed tree of the gallows, insomuch as if in a large field a man might see together all the Christians, that but in one year, throughout England, come to that untimely and ignominious death, if there were any spark of grace, or charity in him, it would make his heart to bleed for pity or compassion."[82] But it was, in the end, largely Cesare Beccaria's treatise—said to have been "an immediate success" by Sir William Holdsworth in *A History of English Law*—that reframed the debate in Britain and that drew attention to the then-existing defects of the criminal law. As Holdsworth wrote in that multi-volume treatise: "Abroad, Beccaria's famous book had awakened the public conscience to the iniquities perpetrated under the continental codes of criminal procedure, and had turned public attention to a consideration of what was in effect a new subject—the theory or theories which should underlie the infliction of different kinds of punishment, and the qualities which an effective punishment should possess." As Holdsworth added of *On Crimes and Punishments*: "In England the book helped forward the tendency, which had already begun, to reflect upon the deficiencies of the criminal law, and more especially upon its punishments." "The reason why the book was so successful," Holdsworth explained of Beccaria's treatise, "was the fact that the author tried to rationalize criminal law and procedure, by the application of the same principle that Bentham later applied in much greater detail to all branches of the law."

Every work has an historical context, and *On Crimes and Punishments* is no exception. "[S]ome of Beccaria's theories," Sir William Holdsworth emphasized, "had been anticipated, or independently arrived at, by English critics." For example, Holdsworth noted that while "Beccaria insists that 'the punishment of a crime cannot be just (that is necessary) if the laws have not endeavoured to prevent that crime by the best means which times and circumstances would allow" and that pardons should not be handed out under a just set of laws, Henry Fielding had made those same points in 1751.[83] In *An Enquiry into the Causes of the Late Increase of Robbers, &c. with Some Proposals for Remedying this Growing Evil* (1751), Henry Fielding—a barrister and a Justice of the Peace for the County of Middlesex and for the City of Westminster—saw a spike in robberies as deserving of attention. Fielding, like many other jurists of that age, grappled with how best to adjust punishments, writing specifically of "[t]he Terror of the Example"—a tradition of English law—and of "one Man" being "sacrificed" so as to ensure "the Preservation of Thousands." "To speak out fairly and honestly, tho' Mercy may appear more amiable in a Magistrate," Fielding wrote, "Severity is a more wholesome Virtue; nay Severity to an Individual may, perhaps, be in the End the greatest Mercy, not only to the Public in general ... but to many Individuals...." In making that argument, Fielding invoked the writings of the Florentine statesman, Niccolò Machiavelli, who became so well known for writing *Il Principe* (*The Prince*) in 1513.

Using the Elizabethan spelling for Machiavelli, Fielding wrote: "'But the Severity,[']' says *Machiavel*, 'was not only profitable but necessary;' and why? Because a single

Pardon granted *ex mera Gratia & Favore*, is a Link broken in the Chain of Justice, and takes away the Concatenation and Strength of the whole." As Fielding added: "The Danger and Certainty of Destruction are very different Objects, and strike the Mind with different Degrees of Force. It is of the very Nature of Hope to be sanguine, and it will derive more Encouragement from one Pardon, then Diffidence from twenty Executions." Fielding's conclusion: "This I am confident may be asserted, that Pardons have brought many more Men to the Gallows than they have saved from it. So true is that Sentiment of *Machiavel*, That Examples of Justice are more merciful than the unbounded Exercise of Pity." Montesquieu, by way of contrast, had rejected Machiavelli's severe, overarching approach to punishment, with Montesquieu advising: "A good legislator takes a middle way; he does not always order pecuniary penalties; he does not always inflict corporal penalties." While John Jay favored replacing the death penalty for imprisonment for various felonies, limiting the death penalty to treason, murder, and stealing from a church,[84] Montesquieu, in *The Spirit of the Laws*, repeatedly worried about "tyranny" and "putting a great power into the hands of a few citizens."

For his part, Fielding himself was clearly conflicted, writing: "How far such an Example is from being an Object of Terror, especially to those for whose Use it is principally intended, I leave to the Consideration of every rational Man; whether such Examples as I have described are proper to be exhibited must be submitted to our Superiors." "The great Cause of this Evil," Fielding explained after taking note of processions to the gallows at Tyburn on appointed execution days, "is the Frequency of Executions." "One Way of preventing the Frequency of Executions is by removing the Evil I am complaining of," Fielding offered, arguing for more solemn—and more private—executions. "Nor, in plain Truth," Fielding emphasized, "will the utmost Severity to Offenders be justifiable, unless we take every possible Method of preventing the Offence." Invoking Seneca, the Roman philosopher and statesman, Fielding then penned these words: "The Subject, as well as the Child, should be left without Excuse before he is punished: for, in that Case alone, the Rod becomes the Hand either of the Parent or the Magistrate." "This Plea of Necessity is never admitted in our Law; but the Reason of that is, says Lord *Hale*, because it is so difficult to discover the Truth." As Fielding wrote, urging reform:

> Upon the whole, something should be, nay must be done, or much worse Consequences than have hitherto happened, are very soon to be apprehended. Nay, as the Matter now stands, not only Care for the Public Safety, but common Humanity, exacts our Concern on this Occasion; for that many Cart-loads of our Fellow-creatures are once in six Weeks carried to Slaughter, is a dreadful Consideration; and this is greatly heightened by reflecting, that, with proper Care and proper Regulations, much the greater Part of these Wretches might have been made not only happy in themselves, but very useful Members of the Society, which they now so greatly dishonor in the Sight of all Christendom.

And Fielding, a student of history, clearly felt that some punishments went too far. In his book, Fielding thus wrote of "a most severe Law" for "the Punishment of Idleness" adopted in "the Reign of *Edward* VI." That statue provided:

> If any Person shall bring to two Justices of Peace any runagate Servant, or any other, which liveth idly and loiteringly by the Space of three Days, the said Justices shall cause the said idle and loitering Servant or Vagabond to be marked with an hot Iron on the Breast with the Letter V, and adjudge him to be Slave to the same Person that brought and presented him, to have to him, his Executors and Assigns for two Years, who shall take the said Slave and given him Bread, Water, or small Drink, and refuse Meat, and cause him to work by beating, chaining, or otherwise, in such Work and Labour as he shall put him, be it never so vile. And if such Slave absent himself from his Master within the Term, by the Space of fourteen Days, he shall be adjudged by two Justices of the Peace to be marked on the Forehead or the Ball of the Cheek, with a hot Iron, with the Sign of an S, and shall be adjudged to be Slave to his said Master for ever; and if the said Slave shall run away a second Time he shall be adjudged a Felon.

"This Statute," Fielding editorialized, "lived no longer than two Years, indeed it deserved no longer a Date; for it was cruel, unconstitutional, and rather resembling the cruel Temper of a *Draco*, than the mild Spirit of the *English* Law."[85]

Jeremy Bentham: Penal Reformer

Jeremy Bentham (1748–1832) was born in London, and both his father and grandfather were lawyers. He studied Latin and Greek from a young age, and he matriculated at Queen's College at Oxford at the tender age of twelve. Three years later, in 1763, Bentham began his studies at Lincoln's Inn, one of the legendary Inns of Court, studying at the Court of King's Bench, the royal court over which William Murray, the 1st Earl of Mansfield, better known simply as Lord Mansfield, presided. Lord Mansfield, a British barrister and judge known for his reform of English law, had been called to the bar by Lincoln's Inn in 1730 and lived until 1793. In 1763, to further his education, Bentham also went back to Oxford and attended William Blackstone's law lectures. His academic studies continued until age eighteen, though his interest in legal theory continued well beyond the conclusion of his university studies in 1766. He became fascinated by Scottish philosopher David Hume's exploration of the utility principle, and in 1776 wrote to his father to explain that he was writing a treatise to be titled "The Critical Elements of Jurisprudence," a book that would appear long thereafter, in 1789, as *An Introduction to the Principles of Morals and Legislation*. In 1776, Bentham also anonymously published "A Fragment on Government," a response to Sir William Blackstone's *Commentaries on the Laws of England*. The essay got a lot of attention, and he ended up corresponding with French *philosophes* and influencing a number of English and other penal reformers.[86]

Jeremy Bentham spent the bulk of his life studying the law, thinking about penal codes, and then attempting to design a model prison, what he called the Panopticon. As one source notes of Bentham's advocacy: "In 1790 he began to advocate the building of a panopticon prison in Dublin, and his explanatory essay on the subject, *Panopticon: or, The Inspection-House*, appeared early in 1791." The British Parliament, in 1794, actually passed a bill to establish a prison modeled after Bentham's design. But Bentham's heady vision, which he felt was within his grasp, was not realized. As F. C. Montague, the editor of Bentham's "A Fragment on Government," writes in a biographical sketch of Bentham, observing of what happened after Parliament had passed its bill: "[A] spacious site was purchased and everything bade fair for the experiment when it was broken off, it is said, by the obstinate opposition of George the Third." George III refused to sign off on the funding for the panopticon-style penitentiary. As Montague notes: "Bentham received a large sum from the Treasury in recompense of his time and trouble spent on the project of the Panopticon, but this could not make amends for the disappointment which he had undergone. He had built extravagant hopes of public good upon the adoption of his plan, and when it had to be abandoned, he could not bear to look at his papers on the subject."[87]

Montesquieu and Beccaria attracted many disciples in Europe and the Americas, and Jeremy Bentham—the pioneer in prison design—was one of them. As Montague writes: "Long before Bentham began to write, the theory of legislation had been actively canvassed on the Continent of Europe. It had been associated with names that are still famous; with the names of Montesquieu and of Beccaria." "A criticism of Bentham," Montague stresses, "would be incomplete without a brief reference to these great writers." As Montague explains of the first of those writers: "Montesquieu modified the course of subsequent legislation not so much by definite proposals as by infusing a new generation with his own spirit of free criticism and large humanity. What he accomplished for the reform of law is to be measured by the achievements of his disciples." "The best known among these disciples, and the next celebrated writer," Montague adds, "was Caesar-Bonesana, Marquis de Beccaria." The success of Beccaria's *Dei delitti e delle pene*, Montague notes, was "extraordinary," pointing out that Beccaria's essay went through six Italian editions in eighteenth months and was translated into all of Europe's languages, including Greek. "Montesquieu and Beccaria," Montague concludes of the French baron and the Italian marquis, "has thus called the attention of thinkers to the reform of law before Bentham had published anything on that subject."[88]

Jeremy Bentham praised both Montesquieu and Beccaria in his own writings, though Bentham focused like a laser light on utilitarianism and, at times, chided Montesquieu for not having taken his ideas further than he did. As one point, Bentham wrote in conservative England, where the English "Bloody Code" still reigned supreme: "The science of legislation, though it has made but little progress, is much more simple than one would be led to believe after reading Montesquieu. The principle of utility directs all reasons to a single centre; the reasons which apply to the detail of arrangements are only subordinate views of utility." "Montesquieu," Bentham lamented of *The Spirit of the Laws*, "sets out upon the censorial plan, but long before the conclusion as if he had forgot his first design, he throws off the censor and puts on the antiquarian." Montesquieu's *Spirit of the Laws* was written over the course of approximately 20 years, but it was written in pre-Revolutionary France. "With Beccaria, Bentham was in fuller sympathy, for Beccaria, like himself, was above all things a reformer," F. C. Montague stressed, noting that Bentham himself described *On Crimes and Punishments* as "the first of any account that is uniformly censorial." In his "Fragment on

Government," Bentham called Beccaria the "single *Censor*" among "the multitude of *Expositors*" on "the Jurisprudence of every nation." Though Montesquieu could not go unmentioned, Bentham gushed in his "Fragment on Government": "When Beccaria came, he was received by the intelligent as an Angel from heaven would be by the faithful. He may be styled the father of Censorial Jurisprudence. Montesquieu's was a work of the mixed kind. Before Montesquieu all was unmixed barbarism."[89]

Whereas Cesare Beccaria was viewed by James Madison as a philosophical legislator, Jeremy Bentham wanted to put his ideas to very practical use. And in that vein, Beccaria had an especially tight hold on Bentham's thought—and on Bentham's utilitarianism in particular. As one modern source relays, putting Beccaria's work and Bentham's embrace of in context:

> [I]t is the Italian jurist Cesare Beccaria who first argues comprehensively in favor of employing a broadly utilitarian approach to reform contemporary practices of criminal punishment. Beccaria holds that all punishments should be evaluated in terms of whether or not they promote "the greatest happiness shared among the greatest number," and indeed the first English translation of Beccaria's *On Crime[s] and Punishment[s]* (which might have been the form in which Bentham first encountered it) contained the phrase "the greatest happiness of the greatest number" (later adopted by Bentham) as the relevant criterion for evaluating his proposed reforms of penal practice. Any punishment beyond what is strictly necessary to promote happiness, Beccaria maintains, "is no longer justice, but an abuse."[90]

After reading Beccaria's book, Bentham wrote in praise of his Italian intellectual muse: "Oh, my master, first evangelist of Reason, you who have made so many useful excursions into the path of utility, what is there left for us to do?"[91]

On the issue of the necessity for punishment, Bentham explicitly followed Beccaria's assessment, even questioning whether executions would be efficacious in the specific situation contemplated by Beccaria. As Bentham wrote of capital punishment in *The Rationale of Punishment*:

> It has been asserted, that in the crime of murder it is absolutely *necessary*; that there is no other means of averting the danger threatened from that class of malefactors. This assertion is, however, extremely exaggerated: its groundlessness may be seen in the case of the most dangerous species of homicide.... Yet it is never thought necessary that madmen should be put to death. They are not put to death: they are only kept in confinement; and that confinement is found effectually to answer the purpose.
>
> In fine, I can see but one case in which it can be necessary, and that only occasionally: in the case alleged for this purpose by M. Beccaria, the case of rebellion or other offence against government of a rebellious tendency, when, by destroying the chief you may destroy the faction, where discontent has spread itself widely through a community, it may happen that imprisonment will not answer the purpose of safe custody. The keepers may be won over to the insurgent party, or if not won over, they may be overpowered. They may be won over by considerations of a conscientious nature, which is a

> danger almost peculiar to this case; or they may be won over by considerations of a lucrative nature, which danger is greater in this case than in any other, since party projects may be carried on by a common purse.
>
> What, however, ought not to be lost sight of in the case of offences of a political nature is, that if by the punishment of death one dangerous enemy is exterminated, the consequence of it may be the making an opening for a more formidable successor. Look, said the executioner, to an aged Irishman, shewing him the bleeding head of a man just executed for rebellion: "Look at the head of your son."—"My son (replied he) has more than one head." It would be well for the legislator before he appoints capital punishment, even in this case, to reflect on this instructive lesson.[92]

In his *Theory of Legislation*, Jeremy Bentham—following Cesare Beccaria—observed: "Punishment should be *economical*—that is, should be marked by such degree of severity only as is absolutely necessary to achieve its purpose. Anything which goes beyond the need of the occasion is not merely superfluous; it actually begets a host of inconveniences which tend to defeat the ends of justice."[93] In other words, unnecessary punishments are unjust and counterproductive. Elsewhere, Bentham distinguished between "an absolute and a temporary necessity," with Bentham emphasizing: "an absolute necessity is founded upon circumstances that cannot change; a temporary necessity is founded upon accidental circumstances, which may change."[94] In *An Introduction to the Principles of Morals and Legislation*, Bentham—in a chapter on "THE PROPORTION BETWEEN PUNISHMENTS AND OFFENCES"—laid down his view of the four objects of punishment, adding that "[s]ubservient to these four objects, or purposes, must be the rules or canons by which the proportion of punishments to offences is to be governed." One of those rules, in the book that explicitly acknowledged the influence of both Montesquieu and Beccaria: "*The punishment ought in no case to be more than what is necessary to bring it into conformity with the rules here given.*"[95]

And Beyond . . .

Anglo-American lawyers and legal commentators, as well as Francophone thinkers, frequently linked the ideas of Montesquieu and Beccaria, making them a dynamic duo of Enlightenment writers. In fact, in colonial and early America, a whole host of Enlightenment thinkers, including penal reformers such as Montesquieu, Voltaire, and Beccaria, were cited again and again and were much revered for their intellectual contributions. In one book, *The Ideological Origins of the American Revolution*, historian Bernard Bailyn sagely explains: "The ideas and writings of the leading secular thinkers of the European Enlightenment—reformers and social critics like Voltaire, Rousseau, and Beccaria as well as conservative analysts like Montesquieu—were quoted everywhere in the colonies, by everyone who claimed a broad awareness." "In pamphlet after pamphlet," Bailyn stresses, "the American writers cited Locke on natural rights and on the social and governmental contract, Montesquieu and later Delolme on the character of British liberty and on the institutional requirements for its attainment, Voltaire on the evils of clerical oppression, Beccaria on the reform of criminal law, Grotius, Pufendorf, Burlamaqui, and Vattel on the laws of nature and of nations, and on the principles of civil government."[96]

Jean-Louis de Lolme (or Delolme), the political theorist born in Geneva who moved to England, himself wrote about liberty, the English constitution, and Montesquieu and Beccaria in his *Constitution de l'Angleterre* (*The Constitution of England*). In a 1776 edition of *The Constitution of England*, Delolme wrote about the rule of law and the rejection of torture in England in the following passage that lauded the work of Cesare Beccaria:

> If the verdict pronounces, *not guilty*, the prisoner is set at liberty, and cannot, on any pretence, be tried again for the same offence. If the verdict declares him *guilty*, then, and not till then, the Judge enters upon his function as a Judge, and pronounces the punishment which the law appoints. But, even in this case, he is not to judge according to his own discretion only; he must strictly adhere to the letter of the law; no constructive extension can be admitted; and however criminal a fact might in itself be, it would pass unpunished if it were found not to be positively comprehended in some one of the cases provided for by the law. The evils that may arise from the impunity of a crime, that is, an evil which a new law may instantly stop, has not by the English laws been considered as of magnitude sufficient to be put in comparison with the danger of breaking through a barrier on which so mightily depends the safety of the individual.
>
> To all these precautions taken by the law for the safety of the Subject, one circumstance must be added, which indeed would alone justify the partiality of the English Lawyers to their laws in preference to the Civil Law; I mean the absolute rejection they have made of the torture. Without repeating here what has been said on that subject by the admirable Author of the Treatise on *Crimes and Punishments*, I shall only observe, that the torture, in itself so horrible an expedient, would, more especially in a free State, be attended with the most fatal consequences. It was absolutely necessary to preclude, by rejecting it, all attempts to make the pursuit of guilt an instrument of vengeance against the innocent. Even the convicted criminal must be spared, and a practice at all rates exploded, which might so easily be made an instrument of endless vexation and persecutions.[97]

In *The State of the Prisons in England and Wales*, first published in 1777 but with additional editions soon to follow, the English penal reformer John Howard—another much-admired thinker—quoted Beccaria on multiple occasions. As Howard wrote, giving the citations so his own readers could easily locate the references in their own copies of *On Crimes and Punishments*, at least if they had the same edition: "The Marquis Beccaria, in his *Essay on Crimes and Punishments*, *page* 75, observes that 'Imprisonment, being only the means of securing the person of the accused, until he be tried—ought—to be attended with as little severity as possible.'" "The Marquis *Beccaria* justly remarks, in his *Essay on Crimes and Punishments*, chap. 29. 'That the punishment of death is pernicious to society, from the example of barbarity it affords.'" "The benevolent Marquis *Beccaria* closes his 31st chapter with this maxim. 'The punishment of crime cannot be just, (that is necessary) if the laws have not endeavored to prevent that crime by the best means which times and circumstances would allow.'" "The Marquis *Beccaria* justly remarks, in Chap. 28, that 'the death of a criminal is a less efficacious method of deterring others, than the continued example of a man deprived of his liberty.'—And that 'the punishment of death is pernicious to society, from the example of barbarity it affords.'" "The judicial Marquis whom I quoted but now asserts, that 'Privation of liberty being a punishment, ought not to be inflicted before condemnation, but for as short a time as possible.'"[98]

Not everyone agreed with everything Montesquieu and Beccaria had to say, but Montesquieu and Beccaria's books were, almost always and everywhere, an indispensable part of the conversation. In *Thoughts on Executive Justice* (1785), Martin Madan (1726–1790)—an English barrister and clergyman—emphasized that "honour and welfare of the kingdom in general, as well as the security and happiness of individuals, must depend on a due administration of the laws." Unlike Beccaria, Madan favored severe laws of the kind the British Empire had long employed, with Madan writing: "As to the *severity* of our laws, I know of none but of the most wholesome kind; for it is this alone which can deter the savage minds of those who are the objects of that *severity*, from the commission of those outrages and mischiefs against which the *severity* of our laws is levelled." After quoting "the great Judge Hale" for the proposition that the purpose of punishment is "[t]o deter men," Madan further observed that Sir Matthew Hale (1609–1676)—a Justice of the Common Pleas and later the Chief Justice of the King's Bench—determined that "death itself is necessary to be annexed to laws." Though Madan cited Thomas Nugent's English translation of Montesquieu's *Spirit of Laws* in four footnotes, and though, in another footnote, he wrote that "[t]he *Marquis* of *Beccaria* observes very truly, that 'a *less* punishment, which is *certain*, will do more good than a *greater*, which is *uncertain*,'" Madan made this observation as to his own views on how judges of assize should handle their duties as they travelled on the circuits: "The real difference between a *severe* Judge (i. e. a *Judge*, who, with a view to prevent evil, suffers the law to take its course—for such a one is very commonly, though very injuriously, called *severe*) and a *merciful* Judge (i. e. one who '*reprieves all before he leaves the town*') is this—the *former* is a terror to thieves, the *latter* to honest men."

In his book, Martin Madan himself referenced the Bible and its "*Eye for eye, tooth for tooth*" verse from the Book of Leviticus as he advocated for the prevention of crimes. "The prevention of crimes," Madan wrote, "is the great end of all legal severity; nay, the exerting that severity, by making examples of the *guilty*, has no other intention but to deter others, and thus pursue the great end of *prevention*." "If this were not the case," Madan contended, "all punishment would be nugatory, and therefore cruel; for the past could not be recalled, nor the least advantage accrue to the injured party, however much the criminal might suffer." "But if, by *severity* exercised on the guilty," he continued in his extended argument, "those who are following the example of their wickedness and outrage, are deterred by the example of their sufferings, the two grand purposes of all criminal law are answered: the *one*, in the prevention of evil; the *other*, in the security of the public." In his book, Madan advocated for legislative primacy, writing: "What laws ought to be made, is the province of the legislative power alone to determine: but when once made, the executive magistrate is not to arrogate to himself an authority over them, so that they shall, or shall not, operate, according to the will and pleasure of an individual."

Though Martin Madan preferred the infliction of severe punishments, he himself was well versed with Enlightenment writers. As he wrote in *Thoughts on Executive Justice*:

> One observation I must conclude with, which is—that all writers on the subject of laws, that I have ever met with—as *Plato*, *Cicero*, &c. among the antients; *Montesquieu*, the *Marquis* of *Beccaria*, &c. among the moderns—all contend for the certainty of punishment, in order to render laws respected and efficacious. The same reason for which a law is enacted, must certainly call for the certainty of its execution; for to enact a law, and not to enforce the execution of it, is against all reason.

If laws "are thought too sanguinary," Madan offered, using a word synonymous with *bloody*, "they had much better be altered into something less severe, than to let those offences, which are the objects of them, go without any punishment at all." "[T]his is a matter wholly for the consideration of the legislature," Madan wrote.[99]

But if Madan attracted his own followers, there were scores of admirers of Montesquieu and Beccaria's works—in fact, *exponentially* more than Madan, especially if one considers all the glowing references to Montesquieu and Beccaria that appear in the historical record. In the story of the life of one prominent penal reformer, Thomas Eddy, it is expressly noted: "In 1801, Mr. Eddy published an account of the State Prison of New York. His mottos were taken from Beccaria and Montesquieu; in fact, his whole theory of crimes and punishments is drawn from those great friends of liberty, Beccaria, Montesquieu, Howard, Penn, and other celebrated reformers of this and a former age." Elsewhere in *The Life of Thomas Eddy*, its author, Samuel L. Knapp, points out that Eddy had referred glowingly to Beccaria in this passage: "It has been observed by BECCARIA, whose opinions have the force of axioms in the science of penal law, that 'as punishments become more mild, clemency and PARDON become less necessary;'—that 'clemency belongs to the legislator, and not to the executor of the laws: a virtue which ought to shine in the code, not in private judgments. To show mankind that crimes may be pardoned, or that punishment is not the necessary consequence, is to nourish the flattering hope of impunity.'"[100] Eddy, a successful insurance broker turned philanthropist and penal reformer, believed that New York's antiquated criminal code represented "barbarous" customs and exemplified "monarchical principles" that were ill suited to "a new country, simple manners, and a popular form of government."[101] It was Thomas Eddy, an early New York prison administrator, who became known as a Beccaria disciple and the "John Howard of America." As one book, *The Development of American Prisons and Prison Customs, 1776–1845*, notes of Eddy: "His own philosophy of criminal treatment was based upon Beccaria, Montesquieu, Penn, Howard and other writers. He sought a system of penal treatment that would be both disciplinary and humane."[102]

In *An Account of State Prison or Penitentiary House, in the City of New York* (1801), Thomas Eddy chose the following quote from Beccaria for the title page of his book: "A punishment to be just, should have only that degree of severity which is sufficient to deter others:—Perpetual labour will have this effect more than the punishment of death." Eddy then emphasized how "[t]he art of printing, by which one man, however private and obscure, is enabled to make himself heard by a whole people prepared the way for reformation." Tellingly, Eddy singled out three European thinkers—Baron de Montesquieu and the Marquis Beccaria naturally among them—in addition to praising the penal reform efforts of Pennsylvania's founder, William Penn. "MONTESQUIEU," Eddy wrote, "exposed the errors of legislators, and unfolded sounder principles of jurisprudence." "The eloquent BECCARIA," Eddy then noted, "roused the attention of civilized Europe, and, by his unanswerable appeal to reason and humanity, produced those successive efforts to meliorate the systems of penal laws, which constitute the greatest glory of the present age." Eddy specifically associated "the spirit of reform" with the American Revolution itself, with Eddy emphasizing that, in Pennsylvania, "the writings of BECCARIA and others, at length produced that system of punishment for crimes, which reflects so much honour on that State." "HOWARD, the active and indefatigable friend of man, by exploring the prisons and dungeons of Europe, and, from their dark and unvisited recesses, bringing to light the enormous abuses and dreadful miseries produced by cruel laws and their corrupt administration," Eddy added, moving forward in time, "more powerfully awakened the feelings of humanity and justice, by which the legislator is enabled to complete the great work of *correction*."[103]

Thomas Eddy's book, like Beccaria's, focused on the prevention of crimes, with Eddy noting just how much work remained to be done in the arena of penal reform. Right before his book's introduction, Eddy provided his readers with this quote from Montesquieu: "In moderate governments, a good legislator is less bent upon punishing than preventing crimes: he is more attentive to inspire good morals, than to inflict punishments." In his introduction, Eddy then framed the subject of his book using these words: "That branch of jurisprudence which treats of crimes and their punishment, is the most interesting and momentous in the whole code of laws. The peace, security and happiness of society depend on the wisdom and justice of the means devised for the *prevention* of crimes." "In no nation," Eddy lamented, "have legislators bestowed that profound attention on this subject which its importance demands." Eddy went on to speak of the "vindictive and sanguinary spirit" of European criminal codes—what he called "the growth of a rude and barbarous age"—and of how states, while focusing on conquest, commerce, and art, "thought not of the unhappy beings who suffered under the numerous oppressions of tyrannical laws." Alluding to Enlightenment philosophers such as Montesquieu and Beccaria, Eddy emphasized: "Benevolent and virtuous men saw and deplored the evils produced and perpetuated by unequal and cruel punishments; but the mild voice of reason and humanity reached not the thrones of princes or the halls of legislators."[104]

Through his *On Crimes and Punishments*, Beccaria became a brightly illuminated star in the Enlightenment's vast constellation of stars. While William Eden (1744–

1814), the author of *Principles of Penal Law* (1771), has been described as "the most important English follower of Beccaria," it has been written that "Beccaria's legal influence extended to the leading American theorist of criminal law through his power over Edward Livingston." In 1821, Edward Livingston (1764–1836), a prominent American lawyer, had been tasked by the General Assembly of Louisiana with drafting a penal code for the State of Louisiana to "be founded on one principle, viz., the prevention of crime," and that was, among other things, meant to ensure "that punishments should be proportioned to offences." In his 1822 report, in which he unsuccessfully attempted to convince Louisiana legislators to adopt his code, Livingston specifically acknowledged the influence of Dr. Benjamin Rush and Jeremy Bentham, as well as the work of Montesquieu and Beccaria. Livingston emphasized that his code was aimed at eliminating "cruel or disproportioned punishments," and in the course of his report he emphasized that "the law punishes, not to avenge, but to prevent crimes." "No punishments, greater than are necessary to effect this work of prevention, let us remember, ought to be inflicted," Livingston cautioned. Elsewhere, in an "Introductory Report to the Code of Reform and Prison Discipline," Livingston put it this way: "In all the provisions of this code the great truth is never lost sight of, that every evil inflicted beyond that which is necessarily included in the sentence, is illegal, is cruel, is tyrannical." In other words, unnecessary punishments were seen as tyrannous and cruel.

Hoping to inspire a break from the past, Edward Livingston—inspired by stars of the Enlightenment—specifically observed in his 1822 report: "It would be disgusting and unnecessary to pass in review all the modes of punishment which have, even in modern times, been used, rather, it would seem, to gratify vengeance, than to lessen the number of offences. A spirit of enlightened legislation, taught by Montesquieu, Beccaria, Eden, and others; names dear to humanity! has banished some of the most atrocious from the codes of Europe." "But," Livingston continued, "it has happened, in this branch of jurisprudence, as it has in most other departments of science, that long after the great principles are generally acknowledged, a diversity of opinion exists on their application to particular subjects." As Livingston explained: "Thus, although the dislocation of the joints is no longer considered as the best mode of ascertaining innocence or discovering guilt; although offences against the deity are no longer expiated by the burning faggot; or those against the majesty of kings avenged by the hot pincers, and the rack, and the wheel; still many other modes of punishment have their advocates, which, if not equally cruel, are quite as inconsistent with the true maxims of penal law...." In advocating against the death penalty's use, Livingston—a man who recognized the difference between theory and application—stressed: "If the argument were to be carried by the authority of names, that of Beccaria, were there no other, would ensure the victory."[105]

The notion that punishment was an evil and that the criminal law needed to be reformed was an incredibly common theme in the eighteenth and nineteenth centuries. "The Quakers of Philadelphia," one historian, Carolyn Strange, writes of the early period in U.S. history, "were not the only Americans who considered the continuing reliance upon corporal and capital punishment out of kilter with the ideals of the new republic." "Along with fellow penal modernizers, notably Thomas Jefferson and Benjamin Rush," she writes, New York politician George Clinton "became an acolyte of Beccaria." In his 1794 address to New York's legislature, Clinton—a Revolutionary War brigadier general, New York's first governor, and the fourth U.S. vice president, serving in that role to Presidents Thomas Jefferson and James Madison—proclaimed: "It is certainly a matter of serious concern, that capital convictions are so frequent, and that so little attention has been hitherto paid to a due proportion between crimes and punishments." "Following Beccaria's theory," Strange writes, "Clinton stated that the certainty of sanctions, rather than their 'sanguinary character,' combined with the prospect of pardons, presented a superior means to fight crime."[106] DeWitt Clinton, New York's sixth governor, a U.S. Senator, and the nephew of George Clinton, himself cited the work of both Beccaria and Montesquieu in seeking reform.[107]

The writings of Montesquieu and Beccaria shaped the views of countless politicians and writers. At the beginning of chapter 2 of *A Treatise on the Police of the Metropolis*, a book that was first published in 1796 in London but that went through more editions, Patrick Colquhoun wrote:

> PUNISHMENT, (says a learned and respectable author) *is an evil which a delinquent suffers, unwillingly, by the order of a Judge or Magistrate; on account of some act done which the Law prohibits, or something omitted which the Law enjoins.*
>
> All Punishment should be proportioned to the nature of the offence committed; and the Legislature, in adjusting Punishment with a view to the public good, ought, according to the dictates of sound reason, to act on a comparison of the Crime under consideration, with other offences injurious to Society; and thus by comparing one offence with another, to form a scale, or gradation, of Punishments, as nearly as possible consistent with the strict rules of distributive justice.[108]
>
> It is the triumph of Liberty, says the great Montesquieu, when the criminal laws proportion punishments to the particular nature of each offense.—It may be further added, that when this is the case, it is also the triumph of Reason.[109]

"That acute Reasoner, the Marquis BECCARIA, who wrote after Montesquieu," Colquhoun further emphasized, held this opinion: "'A punishment, (says this able writer) to be just should have only that degree of severity which is sufficient to deter others: perpetual labour will have this effect more than the punishment of death.'"[110]

The first American edition of Patrick Colquhoun's book, published in Philadelphia in 1798, and rebranded *A Treatise on the Police of London*, likewise referred to the work of both Montesquieu and Beccaria. "Montesquieu, in his *Spirit of Laws*," Colquhoun wrote, "justly and truly observes, that the liberty of the citizen depends on the excellence of the criminal laws." The idea originating with Montesquieu that prompted Colquhoun to drop a footnote to "[t]hat acute Reasoner, the Marquis BECCARIA," was—as Colquhoun put it—this: "Montesquieu seems to be of opinion that as thieves are generally unable to make restitution, it may be just to make theft a capital crime. But would not the offence be expiated in a more rational manner, by compelling the delinquent to labour, first for the benefit of the party aggrieved, till recompence is made, and then for the State." The idea of forming a scale of crimes and a corresponding scale of punishments, Colquhoun observed, making another reference to Beccaria, "has been already suggested by an Author of the highest reputation, and certainly merits attention." "It is by deterring men from the commission of *smaller* crimes (says the Marquis Beccaria) that *greater* ones are prevented," Colquhoun emphasized in his book.[111]

In that American edition of Colquhoun's book, there is an "Abstract of the Criminal Code of the Emperor Joseph II." That abstract described the seventy-one "CRIMES" and their corresponding "PUNISHMENTS" in two separate columns. For example, for the crime of "Laying violent hands on the Sovereign, whether injury results from it or not," the punishment is listed as follows: "Confiscation of property; imprisonment for not less than 30 years; and branding on each cheek with the mark of a gallows if the prisoner is remarkably depraved." With respect to the latter possibility, a footnote in the text observes: "In cases where a criminal appears to be remarkably depraved, and that the apprehension he may excite require such precautions, he shall be branded on each cheek with the mark of a gallows, so visibly and strongly impressed as not to be effaced either by time or in any other manner whatever." Joseph II, one of Europe's more enlightened despots, was a penal reformer, with one source emphasizing: "Joseph II's penal policy, like that of his younger brother Leopold when Grand Duke of Tuscany, echoed some of the proposals of the Italian savant Cesare Beccaria." Beccaria's *Dei delitti e delle pene*, that source notes, "has been considered as heralding a sea-change in attitudes to punishment and fostering a new humanitarian perspective."[112]

After noting that some crimes were punished by fines or imprisonment and others by corporal punishments (i.e., the pillory, whipping, condemnation to the public works "with or without fetters," and chaining, whereby "[t]he criminal suffers severe imprisonment, and is closely chained, that he has no more liberty than serves for the indispensable motion of his body"), Patrick Colquhoun (1745–1820) made some editorial comments. A Scottish merchant and magistrate who spent time in the commercial trade in Virginia, Colquhoun sided with the Americans during the Revolutionary War, and founded the Thames River Police, partnering with Jeremy Bentham in an effort to curb stolen cargo. In his treatise, he had this to say about Joseph II's code:

> In contemplating the various component parts of this Code, it is easy to discover that although some features of it may be worthy of imitation, upon the whole it is not suited either to the constitution of this country, or the genius of the people. It is, however, a curious and interesting document, from which considerable information may be drawn; if ever that period shall arrive when a revision of our own Criminal Code (in many respects more excellent than this) shall become an object of consideration with the Legislature.—At all events it strongly evinces the necessity of adapting the laws to the circumstances and situation of the Government and People whose vices are to be restrained.
>
> The total abolition of the Punishment of death (excepting in military offences cognizable by Courts Martial) is a very prominent feature in this Code,

> which appears to have been founded in a great measure on the principles laid down by the Marquis Beccaria, in his Essay on Crimes and Punishments; That able writer, already so frequently quoted, establishes it as a maxim, which indeed will scarcely be controverted, "That the severity of Punishment should just be sufficient to excite compassion in the spectators, as it is intended more for them than the criminal.—A punishment, to be just, should have only that degree of severity which is sufficient to deter others, and no more."—This author further asserts, "That perpetual labour has in it all that is necessary to deter the most hardened and determined, as much as the punishment of death...."
>
> Doubtless, the fundamental principle of good legislation is, rather to prevent crimes than to punish.—If a mathematical expression may be applied to this good and evil of human life, it is the art of conducting men to the *maximum* of happiness and the *minimum* of misery.
>
> But in spite of all the efforts of human wisdom, aided by the lights of philosophy, and freed from the mist of prejudice or the bigotry of darker ages;—In spite of the best laws, and the most correct system of police which the most enlightened Legislature can form; it will not be altogether possible, amid the various opposite attractions of pleasure and pain, to reduce the tumultuous activity of mankind to absolute regularity:—We can only hope for a considerable reduction of the evils that exist. To conclude this Chapter with the words of our favourite Beccaria,—*Let the laws be clear and simple,—let the entire force of the Nation be united in their defence; let the laws be feared, and the laws only.*[113]

The idea that only necessary punishments were justifiable—or legitimate—made its way around the globe in the wake of the publication of Montesquieu and Beccaria's writings, thanks in large part to the printing press. For example, in *On Punishments and Prisons*, written by "His Royal Highness Oscar, Crown Prince of Sweden and Norway," and translated from the second Swedish edition into English, the Scandinavian king, Oscar I, had this to say in the very first chapter: "Every punishment, which goes beyond the limit of *necessity*, enters the jurisdiction of despotism and revenge." In that chapter, the Scandinavian monarch noted the shifting views of European society on the issue of capital punishment in particular, arguing for penal reform. "As capital-punishment," he wrote, "is still considered by many, nay perhaps by the majority of the inhabitants of Europe, as a necessary, unavoidable evil, for which one can certainly entertain both disgust and horror, but which no one dares to redress; it will perhaps be desirable, in the first place, to examine more closely its real nature." "The justice of capital-punishment," he stressed, "has, especially in later times, been denied by several lawyers and statesmen, and this important question indeed merits serious consideration." As Oscar argued, raising his own question: "It is undoubtedly, both the right and the duty of society, to punish every action which can disturb the public system of justice; it can even, if the offender has, by a relapse, shown himself incorrigible, or his offence is of a nature to endanger the public safety, render him incapable of again injuring the other members of the community. But does this right extend farther than to the loss of liberty, by which the object is gained?" It is found that capital punishment "is least necessary in those states, where most attention is paid to the diffusion of knowledge," Oscar stressed.[114]

In another book, published shortly thereafter, another writer again weighed the issue of the necessity—or lack thereof—for capital punishment (with the concept of necessity, as was so often the case, viewed as the linchpin). In that book, *The Total Abolition of the Death Penalty Defended*, William Newton included references to Montesquieu and Bentham and to "the advice of the enlightened and far-seeing Marquis Beccaria." Such "witnesses," Newton argued, established that "the only plea for the punishment of death is its absolute necessity." The quote Newton chose from Montesquieu highlighted the overuse of severe punishments when lighter punishments could have proven just as effective. "Experience shows," Montesquieu wrote, "that in countries remarkable for the lenity of their laws, the spirit of the inhabitants is as much affected by slight penalties, as in other countries by severe punishments." The sentence Newton picked from Bentham: "All inflicted evil which does not dispose the delinquent (and, by his example, other men) to obey the laws, is not punishment, but an act of hostility." Willian Newton, educated at Edinburgh University and a practicing surgeon, reportedly held "liberal views in political, religious, and social matters" and "made his entrance into the arena of debate by publishing a pamphlet against capital punishment, and by acting as local secretary to an association for the total abolition of the death penalty."[115]

The Grand Duke of Tuscany, Newton also emphasized, had followed Beccaria's advice by abolishing the punishment of death in his dominions. The edict of Peter Leopold, the Grand Duke of Tuscany, which ordered the destruction of gallows and the abandonment of "barbarous and inhuman punishment of the mutilation of limbs," was later translated into English, giving it a wide Anglo-American audience. Newton's own anti-death penalty book also referenced *On Punishments and Prisons*, the work of "his Majesty the present King of Sweden," which—Newton wrote—"states, in a calm and philosophical enquiry into the supposed necessity and effect of death punishments," that " 'capital punishment is least necessary in those states where most attention is paid to the diffusion of knowledge.' " Identified on the book's title page as the Honorary Secretary to the Newcastle and Gateshead Society for the Abolition of the Punishment of Death, Newton pointed out that even Machiavelli, the Italian thinker, "is not altogether diabolical; for we find him thus discoursing in his infamous Prince:—'If the prince find it *absolutely necessary* to inflict the punishment of death, he should avow the reason for it; and above all things, he should abstain from touching the property of the condemned party. For certain it is that men sooner forget the death of their relations than the loss of their patrimony. Besides, when he once begins to live by means of rapine, many occasions offer for seizing the wealth of his subjects; but there will be little or *no necessity* for shedding blood.' "[116]

The idea that punishments needed to be absolutely necessary thus became a persuasive one in enlightened societies and in American life in particular in the Enlightenment and post-Enlightenment period. For example, in 1836, Maine legislators invoked Montesquieu and Beccaria in their Report of the Committee on Capital

Punishment.[117] As that widely circulated legislative report emphasized, citing chapter 2 of Cesare Beccaria's *On Crimes and Punishments*: "What says the great Montesquieu? 'Every punishment which does not arise from *absolute necessity* is tyrannical.' And Beccaria has made this more general by saying 'every act of authority of one man over another, for which there is not an absolute necessity, is tyrannical.'"[118] "Now," that report observed, "if it can be shown that the destruction of life is absolutely necessary to protect the State or the citizens against foreign or domestic aggressions, it is both lawful and right; it is then not a matter of mere choice, or expediency, because the first law of nature, self-preservation, imposes the necessity."[119] "But if, on the other hand," the report continued, "it can be show that in a civilized, intelligent and moral community like our own, no such necessity exists, then it must be conceded that to inflict the punishment of death is not only unlawful and impolitic, but unjust and cruel."[120] A legislative report from Massachusetts issued around the same time said much the same thing, referring at one point to the "maxim" that "every punishment which does not arise from absolute necessity ... is tyrannical."[121]

The writings of both Montesquieu and Beccaria likewise feature prominently in Nathaniel Chipman's *Principles of Government: A Treatise on Free Institutions, including the Constitution of the United States* (1833). Chipman's book quoted Montesquieu's *The Spirit of the Laws* on liberty, human nature, and the principles of government, and Chipman, also referring to the views of "the Marquis Beccaria" on liberty "in his admirable work on crimes and punishments," emphasized that "[t]he world is more indebted to the Marquis Beccaria for his little 'Treatise on Crimes and Punishments' than to all other writers on the subject." Chipman noted that "Locke, Beccaria, Blackstone, and many others" were "political writers of great eminence," and in addition to writing of the necessity for civil government and laws and of "the necessity of penalties," he quoted Beccaria on the basis of the government's right to punish. Chipman wrote of "the necessary punishment of offenders," adding: "The right of punishment ought to be exercised solely for the prevention of crimes, and to be permitted to those only, who are selected by law for that purpose, and who are supposed to be capable of candor and moderation in their proceedings."

Nathaniel Chipman, in discussing the very foundations of government, discussed the issue of punishment at length. "In a state of any considerable degree of social and civil improvements," Chipman wrote, "men endure with reluctance the exercise of the right of punishment by the party injured." "This happens," he stressed, "not because men are more unfit for the exercise in this state, but because they have a nicer sense of right and wrong." As Chipman explained at length of his view for the social contract:

> [I]t becomes the right, interest, and duty of every civil community, to punish by way of caution, all those injuries which disturb, or have a direct tendency to disturb their happiness, or to render it insecure. And it will extend to whatever the common sentiment has connected with the public happiness. It is evident, then, that the right of government, by way of caution, to punish the crimes of its members, is not an arbitrary institution, nor does it originate

in necessity only, but in the sentiments of the human heart, the existing relations of men in society, and has the full sanction of the laws of nature.

. . . .

There is a three-fold division of the right of punishment, or of the exercise of that right, corresponding with the general division of the powers of government. First, the decreeing of penalties for the breach of any law. This involves a consideration of the importance of the law to the interests of the state, and the means of preventing crimes, the true end of all punishments, and corresponds with the right of legislation. To that branch, therefore, it can alone be intrusted. Secondly, the application of the law to particular cases for the purpose of determining whether it has been violated and who is the offender. This is clearly the proper business of the judiciary. Thirdly, the execution of the sentence upon the criminal, which falls to the province of the executive. The right of punishment is, in practice, frequently limited only by the will of the legislature, and the decisions of the judiciary; but the laws of nature have not left it arbitrary. Those laws have assigned certain limits, beyond which the right ceases, and the exercise of the power becomes a crime against society. These limits are not, in every sense, permanent and invariable. It is universally true that the right is limited by the end of preventing crimes and securing obedience to the laws. It is also true, that the penalties, which, in one state of society and manners are adequate to that end may, in a different state, be wholly inadequate.

Not only the state of manners, but the principles of the government, affect the severity of punishment. Where the support of the reigning powers, without any regard to the good of the people, is the sole end of every measure of state, fear, which is inculcated by the severity of punishment, is the sole principle of obedience. Such governments set limits neither to crimes, nor to the severity of punishments. No actions are considered to be criminal because they are injurious to the people, or against the laws of nature; but because they are supposed to be dangerous to the reigning power, and a contempt of its authority. In proportion as governments have ascended to natural principles and made the happiness of the people the end of their institutions, crimes and punishments have admitted of more definite limits. It has been proved and acknowledged, that, in a civil view, those actions only are criminal, which are injurious to the community at large, or to individuals, whose rights and happiness the community are bound to protect, and secure; that the prevention of crimes is the sole end of punishments, and that all beyond this is the spirit of revenge and wanton cruelty.[122]

The necessity-for-punishment principle of Montesquieu and Beccaria, whether their names are mentioned or not, shows up again and again in legal and social commentaries in the eighteenth and nineteenth centuries.[123] That principle—a bedrock of the Enlightenment impulse to reduce needless cruelty and the severity of punishments—appears in numerous books, newspapers, legal commentaries, and speeches.[124] For instance, it appears in *A Legal and Constitutional Argument Against the Alleged Judicial Right of Restraining the Publication of Reports of Judicial Proceedings* (1822) by J. P. Thomas, Esq.[125] It shows up again in *Reports and Addresses of James H. Titus, upon the Subject of Capital Punishment* (1848),[126] and in Thomas Waterman's *A Complete Practical Treatise on Criminal Procedure, Pleading and Evidence, in Indictable Cases* (1853).[127] The necessity-for-punishment maxim also shows up in Judge J. W. Henry's presentation, "Aid to Discharged Prisoners," at the Tenth Annual National Conference of Charities and Corrections, held in Louisville, Kentucky, in September 1883. "An unnecessary punishment, or one which excites for the victim the deep, enduring sympathy of the spectator," Judge Henry said at that time, "accomplishes no good."[128]

And the maxim appears in many other places,[129] including in the writings of Robert Rantoul, Jr., a prominent Massachusetts penal reformer. In his first letter on the subject of the death penalty, written in Boston on February 4, 1846, and directed "To his Excellency the Governor, and to the Honorable members of the Senate and House of Representatives of the Commonwealth of Massachusetts," Rantoul wrote:

> The founder of the modern science of the philosophy of Law, the illustrious Montesquieu, has announced an axiom, which no one in the Nineteenth Century will be hardy enough to gainsay. *Tout chatiment dont la necessite n'est pas absolue, deviant tyranique.*[130] (*Esprit des Lois.* Published in 1748.) Every act of punishment not demanded by absolute necessity, is tyranny.
>
> Is the DEATH PENALTY necessary; is it effectual to prevent crime? If not it cannot be justified.[131]

The governor of Massachusetts at that time was George Nixon Briggs, a Whig.[132]

The Enlightenment writers, including Montesquieu and Beccaria, had tremendous longevity or staying power, and their ideas were still being regularly invoked by authors, letter writers, and essayists well into the nineteenth century.[133] For example, in 1839, an essay in *The New York Review* on the Auburn and Pennsylvania penitentiary systems described the author's perspective of a just criminal justice system this way: "The state is the stronger party, and the right of personal liberty is, with one exception, the most sacred and inviolable which the citizen enjoys. It should never be abridged for a moment but from stern necessity."[134] "The government," that essay by the noted historian and professor, Francis Lieber, observed, "should be above the suspicion of any selfish or sinister end in the punishment of crime."[135] In support of the proposition that only a "stern necessity" could justify punishment, the names of Montesquieu and Beccaria were specifically invoked by Professor Lieber, a well-known historian at South Carolina College.[136] As a footnote in that source began, echoing the familiar Enlightenment refrain: "[']Every punishment which does not arise from absolute necessity,' says Montesquieu, 'is tyrannical,' and Beccaria observes still more comprehensively, 'that every act of authority of one man over another, for which there is not an absolute necessity, is tyrannical.'"[137]

In his anti-death penalty essay, *Capital Punishment Unlawful and Inexpedient* (1853), John Rippon, grappling with scriptural and others arguments, had a whole chapter—Chapter IV—titled "CAPITAL PUNISHMENT INEXPEDIENT;—UNNECESSARY."[138] He began that chapter by quoting the *Eighth Report of the Criminal Law*

Commissioners (1846), which contains this statement: "We apprehend that the right, even of the legislature, to inflict capital punishment, rests on grounds of *strict and cogent necessity*; and that to go beyond that limit involves a transgression *in foro cœli*,[139] which is criminal in the legislator himself."[140] Rippon then proceeded to engage in an extended discussion of whether the death penalty was truly necessary, with Rippon, drawing upon various sources, writing:

> *The Eclectic Reviewer* remarks, "that the political necessity of capital punishment has never yet been *proved*: it has always been taken for granted, ... it has never been shown that a smaller penalty would not answer equally well in repressing the crime of murder." This must, we think, be regarded as an important point in the discussion of the question. It unquestionably lies upon those who defend capital punishment, on the ground of legislative expediency, to demonstrate its absolute necessity,—"the less punishment is inflicted, consistently with the safety of society, the better." "It was on this very plea of necessity," says Lord Nugent, "that 72,000 thieves were hanged during the reign of Henry VIII., the crime steadily increasing all the while." Even so recently as the time of George III., it was believed to be necessary to annex the punishment of death to no less than two hundred offences. Although not equally ridiculous, the plea may turn out equally unfounded in the case of murder. The unspeakable solemnity of cutting short the probationary period of human existence demands, at the least, a fair experiment of total abolition.[141] Multitudes of men, whose Christian conscientiousness cannot be impeached, may be found supporting the exercise of this fearful prerogative; but the indubitable sufficiency of their warrant, and the absolute necessity of its executions, should be made so palpably clear as to leave no misgivings in the mind. The deliberate destruction of human life is not an act to be performed with indolent or reckless insensibility, nor even with an unsteady conscience.[142]

Rippon asserted that "[t]he non-necessity and inefficacy of the death penalty is most satisfactorily demonstrated by the experience of almost every country in the civilized world."[143] As Rippon concluded Chapter IV of his essay after laying out his supporting evidence: "If experience proves that the punishment of death increases the crime, and that a diminution of murders follows the disuse of the gallows—and further, that these results occur in the relation of cause and effect—it is absurd to speak of the *necessity* of criminal executions."[144]

On December 28, 1882, the Hon. M. D. Follett, of Marietta, also delivered a telling address before the Ohio Bar Association. His topic: "The Proper Punishment of Criminals, and the Restoration of Citizenship of those Discharged from Confinement." Near the very outset of his oration, Follett invoked the Enlightenment maxim on the necessity for punishment in these words:

> Montesquieu said, "Every punishment which does not arise from absolute necessity is tyrannical;" and Marquis Beccaria said, "Every act of authority of one man over another, for which there is not an absolute necessity, is tyrannical." If these be true—and who denies their truth?—the greater part

> of punishment in all past time has been tyrannical, and not only enlightened Europe, but our own land, has been, and is, suffering by reason of the innocent made criminals, and of prisoners wronged and tortured through the practical working of unwise criminal laws and prison discipline, and through the cruelty and greed of those who administer the laws and control prisoners, for private ends and gain.[145]

Judge Martin Dewey Follett, a prominent member of the bar, served on the Supreme Court of Ohio from 1883 to 1888.[146]

At a constitutional convention in New York in 1915, a Mr. Betts sought to abolish capital punishment altogether. He, too, invoked the lack of necessity for capital punishment, arguing at the outset: "Mr. Chairman, it is the duty of this Convention, being a Constitutional Convention, to deal with fundamental principles. I know of nothing more fundamental than human life, and I know of nothing more wicked than to take a human life unnecessarily." "Every intelligent man," Betts declared, "will concede that he has not the right to take a human life except in self-defense, and if he has no such right he cannot transfer the right to the State." As Betts argued: "We need not the authority of a Montesquieu or a Becarria [sic], we need only intelligence and common sense to give complete sanction to the wise maxim that every punishment which does not arise from necessity is tyrannical. Therefore, to inflict the cruel penalty of death when it is unnecessary is the very climax of tyranny." As Betts continued: "If it is a crime for the individual to kill, it is just as great a crime for the State to kill as it is for the individual." Betts called the death penalty a "cruel and inhuman practice," and asserted that it could not be justified through "the specious plea of necessity."[147] Again, the lack of necessity for a punishment was seen as clear evidence of its cruelty and inhumanity.

The concept of necessity is one that has frequently driven legal thought. In *A Selection of Legal Maxims*, Herbert Broom translated a Latin maxim—"NECESSITAS INDUCIT PRIVILEGIUM QUOAD JURA PRIVATA"—as follows: "*With respect to private rights, necessity privileges a person acting under its influence.*" In that particular 1874 source, the seventh American edition of the collection of legal maxims compiled by Broom, an English barrister, one finds this recitation of the concept of necessity:

> As a general rule, the law charges no man with default where the act done is compulsory, and not voluntary, and where there is not a consent and election on his part; and, therefore, if either there be an impossibility for a man to do otherwise, or so great a perturbation of the judgment and reason as in presumption of law man's nature cannot overcome, such necessity carries a privilege in itself.
>
> Necessity, as contemplated in the above rule, may be considered under three different heads:—1. Necessity of self-preservation; 2. Of obedience; 3. Necessity resulting from the act of God or of a stranger.

On the first point, Broom—in his compilation of legal maxims—gave these examples and made these observations:

> Where two persons, being shipwrecked, have got on the same plank, but, finding it not able to save them both, one of them thrusts the other from it,

> and he is drowned; this homicide is excusable through unavoidable necessity, and upon the great universal principle of self-preservation, which prompts every man to save his own life in preference to that of another, where one of them must inevitably perish. So, if a ferryman overload his boat with merchandise, a passenger may, in case of necessity, throw overboard the goods to save his own life, and the lives of his fellow-passengers. For the same reason, where one man attacks another, and the latter, without fighting, flies, and, after retreating as far as he safely can, until no other means of escape remain to him, then turns round and kills his assailant, this homicide is excusable as being committed in self-defence; the distinction between this kind of homicide and manslaughter being, that here the slayer could not otherwise escape although he would,—in manslaughter he would not escape if he could....
>
> It should, however, be observed, that, as the excuse of self-defence is founded on necessity, it can in no case extend beyond the actual continuance of that necessity by which alone it is warranted; for, if a person assaulted does not fall upon the aggressor till the affray is over, or until the latter is running away, this is revenge, and not defence.

In his collection of legal maxims, Herbert Broom emphasized in an introductory section to Chapter 1 of his book:

> The Maxims contained in this section are of such universal application, and result so directly and manifestly from motives of public policy or simple principles on which our social relations depend, that it has been thought better to place them first in this selection,—as being, in some measure, introductory to more precise and technical rules which embody the elementary doctrines of English law, and are continually recurring to the notice of practitioners in our courts of justice.

The first maxim in his collection—the one appearing right before the "NECESSITAS INDUCIT PRIVILEGIUM QUOAD JURA PRIVATA" maxim—was given in Latin as "SALUS POPULI SUPREMA LEX" and then translated into English as "*That regard be had to the public welfare, is the highest law.*" In describing that general maxim, Broom had this to say on the subject of punishments and necessity:

> There is an implied assent on the part of every member of society, that his own individual welfare shall, in cases of necessity, yield to that of the community; and that his property, liberty, and life shall, under certain circumstances, be placed in jeopardy or even sacrificed for the public good....
>
> ....
>
> From the principle under consideration, and from the very nature of the social compact on which municipal law is theoretically founded, and under which every man, when he enters into society, gives up a part of his natural freedom, result those laws which, in certain cases, authorize the infliction of penalties, the privation of liberty, and even the destruction of life, with a view to the future prevention of crime, and to insuring the safety and well-being of the public; penal laws, however, should evidently be restrained

> within the narrowest limits which may be deemed by the legislature compatible with the above objects, and should be interpreted by the judges, and administered by the executive, in a mild and liberal spirit.[148]

In truth, because American laws are the product of a social compact and representative democracy, and because the American people and politicians naturally have different opinions on what is necessary, there is not always one easily identifiable point at which a punishment crosses from a *necessary* to an *unnecessary* one. In time, hard evidence can reveal the cruelty or torturous nature of a punishment as well as the lack of necessity for it (something the evidence has revealed for capital punishment, for example). But the interplay of the law and the popular will is a complex one that can shift with the times. In *Punishment and Democracy*, scholars Franklin Zimring, Gordon Hawkins, and Sam Kamin specifically discuss the notion of popular will and the necessity of punishment in thinking about California's "Three Strikes" law. There, they write: "One of the core benefits of punishing criminals is the reassurance to law-abiding members of the community that standards of justice have been served and that criminal offenders have not benefited from their transgressions." "But," Zimring, Hawkins, and Kamin add, "not all punishments that community members would approve are necessary to secure the benefits of imposing a deserved punishment." Referencing an earlier thinker who pioneered the modern parsimony principle, those three scholars emphasize: "As Norval Morris (1974) argues, it is best to see deserved punishments as a range—anything below the lowest punishment will offend the community's sense of justice, and anything above the highest will seem to community members to be excessive. But any punishment between the minimum and maximum will serve the community's need for the imposition of a just penalty."

This does not mean, of course, that policymakers, lawmakers, prosecutors, and judges should not continually look for the sweet spot, or the dividing line, between what is necessary and what is not, because it is, after all, fundamentally unfair and unjust to impose an unnecessary punishment if the decisonmaker knows better. "[I]f the punishment inflicted on offenders is regarded as a social harm unless justified by the benefits it generates," Zimring, Hawkins, and Kamin explain, "the majority's approval of levels of punishment will not foreclose an inquiry about what a particular punishment is excessive."[149] In that regard, judges—armed with the power of the U.S. Constitution or equivalent provisions in state constitutions—are there to police the administration of justice. They should impose and uphold reasonable punishments, and they should strike down cruel, excessive, or unreasonable ones. Indeed, the whole point of the Eighth Amendment, and its clauses prohibiting excessive bail, excessive fines, and cruel and unusual punishments, is *to check* the power of tyrannous majorities. An independent judiciary plays an indispensible role in America's constitutional design, and judges—the guardians of liberty—must never abdicate that role.

CHAPTER 3

America's Founders and Framers:

Disproportionate Punishments and the Necessity-for-Punishment Maxim

The Embrace of Montesquieu and Beccaria's Ideas

America's founders and framers were taken, if not obsessed, by the Baron de Montesquieu's *The Spirit of the Laws.* Early 1775 editions of Philadelphia's *Pennsylvania Journal* solicited subscriptions for the printing of an American edition of "*Spirit of Laws*" by "the great and immortal M. DE SECONDAT, Baron DE MONTESQUIEU, (so honourably mentioned by the Continental Congress.)."[1] It was a book long known to revolutionaries and reformers, and excerpts or quotations from it continued to appear in American newspapers during the Revolutionary War and before the ratification of the U.S. Constitution.[2] Montesquieu's treatise, in fact, took on a special role in the ratification debate over the U.S. Constitution—the legal instrument that remains in force to this day. "When the Founding Fathers of the United States came together to draft a constitution for their new nation," historian Susan Gordon observes, "they came well versed in Enlightenment writings, including those of Montesquieu." As Gordon writes: "Inspired by Montesquieu, James Madison, along with other Founding Fathers, wrote a series of eighty-five essays in defense of the proposed constitution. These essays were published as *The Federalist Papers* (1788), and they heavily cited Montesquieu's *The Spirit of the Laws* throughout their pages."[3]

Like Montesquieu's *The Spirit of the Laws*, America's Founding Fathers also carefully read and studied Cesare Beccaria's *On Crimes and Punishments.* In her essay, "Cesare Beccaria and the Founding Fathers," legal historian Kathryn Preyer noted that, even before America's Revolutionary War, Americans were reading Beccaria's book. As Preyer wrote of Beccaria's *Dei delitti e delle pene*: "After its translation into French in 1766, the brief work speedily spread its gospel throughout other countries. The first English edition, including Voltaire's *Commentary* by an unknown translator, appeared in 1767 in London. That December, Beccaria's essay was quoted by the *Virginia Gazette* of Williamsburg on the best way to prevent the crime of duelling." As Preyer, the legal historian, observed of how Cesare Beccaria's book spread across the American landscape, both geographically and intellectually: "Booksellers in Boston and New York were advertising the volume in 1771, 1772, and 1773. A circulating library in Annapolis and the Harvard College library contained copies by the latter year, American editions of the *Essay* were published in 1773 in New York, in Charleston in 1777, and in Philadelphia in 1778 and 1793." "At some time between 1774 and 1776," Preyer adds, "Thomas Jefferson, using an Italian edition, copied lengthy extracts from the *Essay* in his *Commonplace Book*."

Jefferson's own entries, carefully transcribed, were in Italian to match the original version. Jefferson, in fact, copied substantial portions of multiple chapters of *Dei delitti e delle pene* into his commonplace book, including, among others, portions of the chapters on the interpretation of the laws, on the proportion between crimes and punishments, on estimating the degree of crimes, on the division of crimes, and on the mildness of punishments. An expert on Beccaria's writings, Kathryn Preyer, penned another essay titled "Two Enlightened Reformers of the Criminal Law: Thomas Jefferson of Virginia and Peter Leopold, Grand Duke of Tuscany." That essay also took note of Beccaria's influence on both sides of the Atlantic, with Beccaria's words shaping the views of everyone from revolutionaries to royal figures. As Preyer wrote: "Beccaria's *Essay* with the commentary by Voltaire was known in America immediately after its first appearance in France; it became popular in lending libraries and as a quickly sold item in bookstores."[4]

As noted, *On Crimes and Punishments* was advertised in American newspapers, with the *Pennsylvania Packet*, in 1778, calling it the "much esteemed modern Work."[5] In another newspaper, Baltimore's *Maryland Journal*, Beccaria's treatise was also advertised that same year along with other titles, with the newspaper publisher emphasizing: "Any Persons in Maryland, and its Neighbourhood, desirous of purchasing any of the above-mentioned Books, may be speedily supplied by giving their Orders to the Printer of this Paper."[6] An entire chapter of *On Crimes and Punishments*, "On the punishment of Death," was reprinted in the *Pennsylvania Evening Herald* in February 1786,[7] and in June 1791, shortly before the ratification of the U.S. Bill of Rights, New York's *Daily Advertiser*, Philadelphia's *Pennsylvania Mercury*, and Boston's *Herald of Freedom* all themselves took note of Beccaria's appointment as a member of a commission set up within the Habsburg Empire "for the reform of the criminal code in Austrian Lombardy." It was noted in the latter three newspapers that "the celebrated Marquis Beccaria," by then a global celebrity in Western societies, was "so well known in the literary and political world, by his admirable" treatise, *On Crimes and Punishments*.[8]

Though Cesare Beccaria's impact on continental European and Anglo-American law is now largely forgotten by the vast majority of Americans, Beccaria's contributions were significant. In two prior books, *The Birth of American Law: An Italian Philosopher and the American Revolution* (2014) and *The Celebrated Marquis: An Italian Noble and the Making of the Modern World* (2018), I documented Cesare Beccaria's substantial influence on Enlightenment-era thinkers, with many others also taking note of Beccaria's tremendous influence on the law since his death in the late eighteenth century. For example, in *A History of Continental Criminal Procedure* (1913), the Marquis Beccaria—and his idol, Baron de Montesquieu—are discussed in the same section of that treatise. That source notes that Montesquieu had pointed out that "[p]olitical liberty" is "never more dangerously attacked than in public or private accusations" and that "[i]t is, therefore, on the good quality of criminal laws that the liberty of the subject chiefly depends." "The 'Treatise on Crimes and Penalties' of the Marquis of Beccaria," that source continues, paying tribute, "was published at Milan in the Italian language," with its influence described as "immense" and "even much greater in France than in Italy" after André Morellet first translated *Dei delitti e delle pene* into French. "Beccaria," the Marquis de Condorcet, of France, himself offered, "refuted in Italy the barbarous maxims of French jurisprudence." *A History of Continental Criminal Procedure* describes Montesquieu, Beccaria, and Voltaire as "the three men who, among the philosophers, did the most for the reform of criminal law."[9]

Beccaria's *On Crimes and Punishments* was thus widely read throughout Europe and the Americas and it was, in general, a favorite text among America's founders and framers. For instance, it is very clear that Thomas Jefferson was moved by—and embraced—Beccaria's proportionality and necessity-for-punishment principles, even if he *interpreted* those principles in his own unique way. In fact, Jefferson's own views evolved substantially over time from the 1770s until the time of his death. Jefferson's draft constitution for Virginia, and his bill to proportion crimes and punishments in that state, are certainly reflective of Beccarian principles, though he applied them somewhat differently than Beccaria, in his native Milan, would have.[10] After Gabriel's Rebellion, a slave revolt that took place in Virginia in 1800, Jefferson—then at Monticello—expressed his own reticence about the use of executions. Gabriel's Rebellion had been quickly and brutally suppressed, including with the hanging of multiple slaves, leading Jefferson to write to James Monroe on September 20, 1800, using these words:

> Where to stay the hand of the executioner is an important question. Those who have escaped from the immediate danger, must have feelings which would dispose them to extend the executions. Even here, where every thing has been perfectly tranquil, but where a familiarity with slavery, and a possibility of danger from that quarter prepare the general mind for some severities, there is a strong sentiment that there has been hanging enough. The other states & the world at large will forever condemn us if we indulge a principle of revenge, or go one step beyond absolute necessity.[11]

Necessity and the Government's Right to Punish

Governments and judicial systems have a right to punish, with punishments being crucial to protect society. As the German-American jurist Francis Lieber, who became known, in Abraham Lincoln's time, for authoring the *Code for the Government of Armies in the Field* (1863), also popularly known as the Lieber Code, wrote in the 1830s: "Common sense has long acknowledged that punishments are necessary, and that society has a right to punish; or, in other words, practical life has long produced the most perfect conviction in all men, the criminals by no means excepted, that a political society cannot exist without punishment...." That right—key to promoting law and order and protecting the public safety and property rights—has long been grounded in the concept of necessity.[12] This is true for criminal conduct,[13] though the justification for punishment—and philosophers' understandings of liberty and tyranny—has been expressed in widely different ways and words through the centuries. "Most philosophical discussions of punishment," one source notes, "focus in one way or another on the question, 'When is punishment just?'"[14] John Locke, the English philosopher and physician, choosing his own words carefully, once put it this way: "To justify bringing such evil [i.e., punishment][15] on any man two things are requisite. First, that he who does it has commission and power to do so. Secondly, that it be directly useful for the procuring of some greater good."[16] "Political liberty in a citizen," Montesquieu once wrote in *The Spirit of the Laws*, "is that tranquility of spirit [*tranquillité d'esprit*] which comes from the opinion each one has of his security, and in order for him to have this liberty the government must be such that one citizen cannot fear another citizen." John Locke, on the other hand, defined tyranny as the "exercise of power beyond right."[17]

The common good or the greater good can be elusive concepts, but in the world of criminal justice everyone should have shared objectives: reduce crime and recidivism, keep the peace, assist crime victims, rehabilitate offenders whenever possible, and make society safer. The American revolutionary Thomas Jefferson—as he made clear in 1776 in draft proposals for a Virginia constitution—set forth his own societal vision, including for how to deal with acts of criminality. In that draft constitution, he explicitly expressed the view—very much in line with Beccaria's—that punishments, while required, should only be imposed when "absolutely necessary."[18] It was an idea recognizably grounded in Beccaria's vision, and one that would—as noted earlier—later find expression in the French Declaration of the Rights of Man and Citizen (1789). In Thomas Paine's *Rights of Man*, dedicated to President George Washington and described by Paine as "a small Treatise in defence of those Principles of Freedom which your exemplary Virtue hath so eminently contributed to establish," Paine appended an English translation of the French "Declaration of the Rights of Man and of Citizens." Section 8 of that translated declaration read as follows: "The law ought to impose no other penalties but such as are absolutely and evidently necessary: and no one ought to be punished, but in virtue of a law promulgated before the offence, and legally applied." In that book, Paine described English and French executions as "cruel spectacles" that "destroy tenderness, or excite revenge."[19]

From Montesquieu and Beccaria to Thomas Jefferson and Thomas Paine to French *philosophes* and revolutionaries, one can easily spot a passing of the baton from European philosophers to American lawmakers and then back to Europe in the form of one of France's most important—indeed, foundational—documents. In actuality, the Enlightenment knew no boundaries or national borders, with the exchange of ideas occurring through letters, periodicals, and books, and in conversations in universities and salons between people of different backgrounds. In the United States, the inclusion of the prohibitions against cruel and unusual punishments in the early American constitutions was explained, in part, by what James Iredell wrote in 1788 in his answers to George Mason's objections to the lack of a federal bill of rights in the originally proposed U.S. Constitution. Mason had begun his objections: "There is no declaration of rights: and the laws of the general government being paramount to the laws and constitutions of the several states, the declarations of rights, in the separate states, are no security."

Iredell, who actually *opposed* the inclusion of a prohibition on cruel and unusual punishments in the U.S. Constitution, was, in 1790, appointed by President George Washington to serve as an Associate Justice of the Supreme Court of the United States. In 1788, however, before that happened, Iredell gave this extended explanation for the inclusion of the bars on cruel and unusual punishments in state constitutions (and for why, in his judgment, the original U.S. Constitution did not contain such a prohibition). Writing one hundred years after the Glorious Revolution of 1688, Iredell gave this explanation for the original federal/state divide:

> As to the constituting of new crimes, and inflicting unusual and severe punishment, certainly the cases enumerated wherein the Congress are empowered either to define offences, or prescribe punishments, are such as are proper for the exercise of such authority in the general Legislature of the Union. They only relate to "counterfeiting the securities and current coin of the United States," to "piracies and felonies committed on the high seas, and offences against the law of nations," and to "treason against the United States." These are offences immediately affecting the security, the honor or the interest of the United States at large, and of course must come within the sphere of the Legislative authority which is intrusted with their protection. Beyond these authorities, Congress can exercise no other power of this kind, except in the enacting of penalties to enforce their acts of legislation in the cases where express authority is delegated to them, and if they could not enforce such acts by the enacting of penalties those powers would be altogether useless, since a legislative regulation without some sanction would be an absurd thing indeed. The Congress having, for these reasons, a just right to authority in the above particulars, the question is, whether it is practicable and proper to prescribe limits to its exercise, for fear that they should inflict punishments unusual and severe. It may be observed, in the first place, that a declaration against "cruel and unusual punishments" formed part of an article in the Bill of Rights at the revolution in England in 1688. The prerogative of the Crown having been grossly abused in some preceding reigns, it was thought proper to notice every grievance they had endured, and those declarations went to an abuse of power in the Crown only, but were never intended to limit the authority of Parliament. Many of these articles of the Bill of Rights in England, without a due attention to the difference of the cases, were eagerly adopted when our constitutions were formed, the minds of men then being so warmed with their exertions in the cause of liberty as to lean too much perhaps towards a jealousy of power to repose a proper confidence in their own government. From these articles in the State constitutions many things were attempted to be transplanted into our new Constitution, which would either have been nugatory or improper. This is one of them. The expressions "unusual and severe" or "cruel and unusual" surely would have been too vague to have been of any consequence, since they admit of no clear and precise signification. If to guard against punishments being too severe, the Convention had enumerated a vast variety of cruel punishments, and prohibited the use of any

> of them, let the number have been ever so great, an inexhaustible fund must have been unmentioned, and if our government had been disposed to be cruel their invention would only have been put to a little more trouble. If to avoid this difficulty, they had determined, not negatively what punishments should not be exercised, but positively what punishments should, this must have led them into a labyrinth of detail which in the original constitution of a government would have appeared perfectly ridiculous, and not left a room for such changes, according to circumstances, as must be in the power of every Legislature that is rationally formed. Thus when we enter into particulars, we must be convinced that the proposition of such a restriction would have led to nothing useful, or to something dangerous, and therefore that its omission is not chargeable as a fault in the new Constitution. Let us also remember, that as those who are to make those laws must themselves be subject to them, their own interest and feelings will dictate to them not to make them unnecessarily severe; and that in the case of treason, which usually in every country exposes men most to the avarice and rapacity of government, care is taken that the innocent family of the offender shall not suffer for the treason of their relation. This is the crime with respect to which a jealousy is of the most importance, and accordingly it is defined with great plainness and accuracy, and the temptations to abusive prosecutions guarded against as much as possible.[20]

Historically, courts have long exercised the power to punish—and to find parties in contempt of court for violating judicial directives.[21] The notion of *the necessity for punishment*, as well as the corresponding need for punishments *to be justified by necessity*, transcends borders and legal systems and is a long-standing one.[22] Indeed, in both civil-law countries in continental Europe and in common-law countries such as England and the United States, the notion that punishments should only be inflicted when necessary is one that pervaded eighteenth- and nineteenth-century thought. Those, of course, were the periods of time when the United States of America emerged—and then matured—as a republic. The record thus shows that Anglo-American writers and jurists, America's own founders and framers, and many others carefully considered or expounded upon the idea of grounding punishments in necessity, whether in treatises, commonplace books, or other writings, such as diaries or personal letters.[23] For example, in 1769, in his widely distributed *Commentaries on the Laws of England*, Sir William Blackstone took note of other commentators' views that death sentences for theft "should be cautiously inflicted, and never without the utmost necessity."[24] In that treatise, Blackstone further observed that executioners—paid by the state to perform their grisly work—themselves carried out their duties only out of "necessity."[25]

Through books, legal maxims and ideas about the law were easily transmitted from one society to another, from Europe to the Americas and back again, even making their way, in time, into more distant places, such as Africa and Asia. From reading Montesquieu and Beccaria's works, American lawyers and revolutionaries were, certainly, very familiar with the maxim that any act that exceeded what was necessary (or absolutely necessary, as it was often phrased) constituted an act of tyranny. For instance, on July 20, 1786, just a year before the Constitutional Convention in Philadelphia, John Adams—then in London, and an avid reader of Beccaria and other political philosophers—made this entry in his diary:

> "Every Act of Authority, of one Man over another for which there is not an absolute Necessity, is tyrannical."
>
> "Le Pene che oltre passano la necessita di conservare il deposito della Salute pubblica, sono ingiuste di lor natura."[26] Beccaria.
>
> The Sovereign Power is constituted, to defend Individuals against the Tyranny of others. Crimes are acts of Tyranny of one or more on another or more. A Murderer, a Thief, a Robber, a Burglar, is a Tyrant.
>
> Perjury, Slander, are tyranny too, when they hurt any one.

Montesquieu himself had, in speaking of war and the law of nations, written about the unlawfulness of killing "unless in case of absolute necessity."

According to the editor of John Adams' papers, John Adams—in recording the Italian words of Cesare Beccaria—was "quoting from his own copy of the Italian text (new edn., Haarlem and Paris, 1780, p. 10), which he had acquired in July 1780." The passage in question was "near the end of ch. 2" of *Dei delitti e delle pene*, with "[t]he quotation in English in the preceding paragraph of this entry" taken from "Beccaria, ch. 2 (near the beginning of that chapter)" and from John Adams' "copy of the English translation (*An Essay on Crimes and Punishments*, London, 1775, p. 7)" (the same edition Adams later gave to his son, Thomas, in 1800).[27] That London edition had been printed by "F. Newbery, at the Corner of St. Paul's Church-Yard," with Newbery having done even earlier printings of Beccaria's treatise in 1769 and 1770. In fact, the very first sentence of chapter 2, "Of the Right to punishment," in the 1775 London edition of Beccaria's book, states: "EVERY punishment, which does not arise from absolute necessity, says the great Montesquieu, is tyrannical."[28] "Francis Newbery's premises," writes Beccaria biographer John Hostettler, "were well-known in London at the corner of the St. Paul's Churchyard where he had taken over the publishing business on the death in 1767 of his father, John, who was a friend and publisher of Oliver Goldsmith and Samuel Johnson and the pioneer in publishing books for children."[29]

By the time John Adams made that 1786 entry in his diary, he had been familiar with Cesare Beccaria's work for a long time. At the trial of British soldiers for their conduct in the Boston Massacre, John Adams—as a practicing lawyer—had prominently referenced a passage from Beccaria's *On Crimes and Punishments* in his opening statement. As Adams had said so memorably in open court in 1770, in words that would further propel Beccaria's ideas to prominence, particularly given the high stakes nature of the criminal-law proceedings: "May it please your honors, and you, gentlemen of the jury: I am for the prisoners at the bar, and shall apologize for it only in the words of the Marquis Beccaria: 'If I can but be the instrument of preserving one life, his blessings and tears of transport, shall be a sufficient consolation to me, for the contempt of all mankind.'" At the Boston Massacre trial, John Adams and his co-counsel, Josiah Quincy, defended a British captain, Thomas Preston, and the other eight soldiers accused of murder for their roles in the deadly shooting that led to the trial. With his clients potentially facing death sentences, Adams—in that opening statement—contextualized his invocation of Beccaria's stirring words in this way: "As the prisoners stand before you for their lives, it may be proper, to recollect with what temper the law requires we should proceed to this trial. The form of proceeding at their arraignment, has discovered that the spirit of the law upon such occasions, is conformable to humanity, to common sense and feeling; that it is all benignity and candor."[30] Like Jefferson, Adams was clearly intrigued by the Marquis Beccaria and the necessity-for-punishment maxim, choosing to quote the celebrated Italian marquis in his successful effort to save his clients from the gallows.[31]

The Necessity-for-Punishment Principle in Early America

In early America, the necessity-for-punishment principle of Montesquieu and Beccaria was specifically invoked in both federal and state legislative debates. For example, in 1789, in congressional debate, Representative James Jackson of Georgia[32] emphasized that "[t]he accurate marquis Beccaria points out a danger which it beho[o]ves us to guard against." As Jackson wrote, invoking Beccaria's words: "In every society, says he, there is an effort continually tending to confer on one part the height of power and happiness, and to reduce the other to the extreme of weakness and misery. The intent of good laws, is to oppose this effort, and diffuse their influence universally and equally." "This celebrated writer pursues the principle still further," Jackson continued of Beccaria, noting that he (Beccaria) "asserts with the great Montesquieu, that every punishment which does not arise from absolute necessity, is tyrannical: A proposition which may be made more general, thus, every act of authority of one man over another, for which there is not an absolute necessity, is tyrannical. It is upon this, then, that the sovereign's right to punish crimes is founded; that is, upon the necessity of defending the public liberty intrusted to his care, from the usurpation of individuals; and punishments are just, in proportion as the liberty preserved by the sovereign, is sacred and valuable."[33] In short, good laws—ones that would be applied to all equally—should only punish acts when it was absolutely necessary to do to.

In May 1791, James Wilson—one of just six signers of both the Declaration of Independence and the U.S. Constitution[34]—delivered a grand jury charge in the Circuit Court of the United States for the District of Virginia. "Gentlemen of the Grand Jury," it began, emphasizing in very Beccarian terms in its opening passages:

> To prevent crimes is the noblest end and aim of criminal jurisprudence.
>
> To punish them is one of the means necessary for the accomplishment of this noble end and aim. The impunity of an offender encourages to repeat his offences. The witnesses of his impunity are tempted to become his disciples in his guilt. These considerations form the strongest—some view them as the sole argument for the infliction of punishments by human laws.
>
> There are, in punishments, three qualities, which render them the fit preventives of crimes. The first is their moderation. The second is their speediness. The third is their certainty.[35]

"When," Wilson offered in his grand jury charge, "punishments are moderate and mild, every one will, from a sense of interest and of duty, take his proper part in detecting, in exposing, in trying, and in passing sentence on crimes." But Wilson then cautioned that, in some cases, "emergencies" and "excesses of a temporary nature" had, on occasion, served to "diffuse a hardened insensibility" among citizens; "[t]hus one degree of severity opens and smooths the way for another, till, at length, under the special appearance of necessary justice, a system of cruelty is established by law."[36]

After reciting the laws of the United States, Wilson's 1791 grand jury charge, channeling Cesare Beccaria and others, continued: "It is the opinion of some writers, highly respected for their good sense, as well as for their humanity, that capital punishments are, in no case, necessary. It is an opinion, which I am certainly well warranted in offering—that nothing but the most absolute necessity can authorize them." In a similar vein, Wilson instructed the grand jurors as regards executions, which were authorized by federal law:

> Another opinion I am equally warranted in offering—that they should not be aggravated by any sufferings, except those which are inseparably attached to a violent death. It was worthy only of a tyrant—and of a tyrant it was truly characteristick—to give standing instructions to his executioners, that they should protract the expiring moments of the tortured criminal; and should manage the butchering business with such studied and slow barbarity, as that his powers of painful sensation should continue to the very last—*ut mori se sentiat*.[37]

In a series of law lectures delivered from 1790 to 1792 at the College of Philadelphia, James Wilson—a lawyer who aspired to be the American Blackstone—emphasized that the "science" of criminal law was "as yet, ... in a weak and infantine state."[38]

In his 1791 instructions to grand jurors, James Wilson also included more than a hint of optimism about the then-existing state of American law. "Let us turn our eyes to a more pleasing prospect," he said, delivering these words in his charge: "How few are the crimes—how few are the capital crimes, known to the laws of the United States, compared with those known to the laws of England!" As Wilson gushed:

> "How happy would mankind be," says the eloquent and benevolent Beccaria, "if laws were now to be first formed!" The United States enjoy this singular happiness. Their laws are now first formed. They are formed by the legitimate representatives of free citizens and free states. Among those citizens and those states they now begin to be diffused. To those citizens and those states they are objects of the greatest and most extensive importance. I speak particularly concerning the *criminal laws*. It is on the excellence of the criminal laws, says the celebrated Montesquieu, that the liberty of the citizens principally depends. The knowledge, continues he, which has been already acquired in some countries, and that which may be hereafter acquired in others, with regard to the surest rules which can be observed in criminal judgments, is more interesting to the human kind, than any thing else in the universe. It is only, adds he, on the practice of this knowledge that liberty can be founded.[39]

Again, bad criminal laws deprived individuals of liberty, while good laws furthered liberty.

In a law lecture on "The Necessity and Proportion of Punishments," James Wilson discussed both Montesquieu's and Beccaria's writings, with Wilson concluding: "The end of criminal jurisprudence is the prevention of crimes." As Wilson said:

> Punishments ought unquestionably to be moderate and mild. I know the opinion advanced by some writers, that the number of crimes is diminished by the severity of punishments. I know, that if we inspect the greatest part of the Criminal Codes, their unwieldly size and their ensanguined hue will force us to acknowledge, that the opinion has been general and prevalent. On accurate and unbiassed examination, however, it will appear to be an opinion, unfounded and pernicious, inconsistent with the principles of our nature, and, by a necessary consequence, with those of wise and good government.

A preamble of a Pennsylvania act passed in 1786—one that abolished the death penalty for robbery, burglary and sodomy—would itself specifically allude to Montesquieu's writing. That preamble read:

> And whereas it is the wish of every good government to reclaim rather than to destroy, and it being apprehended that *the cause of human corruptions proceed more from the impunity of crimes than from the moderation of punishments*, and it having been found by experience that the punishments directed by the laws now in force as well for capital as other inferior offenses do not answer the principal ends of society in inflicting them, to wit, to correct and reform the offenders, and to produce such strong impression upon the minds of others as to deter them from committing the like offences, which is conceived may be better effected by continued hard labor, publicly and disgracefully imposed on persons convicted of them, not only the manner pointed out by the convention, but in streets of cities and towns, and upon the highways of the open country and other public works.

The italicized portion was lifted from Montesquieu's *The Spirit of the Laws*, with that Enlightenment text—per one translation—reading: "If we inquire into the cause of all human corruptions; we shall find that they proceed from the impunity of crimes, and not from the moderation of punishments."[40]

Many others in Pennsylvania—indeed, throughout America—looked to Montesquieu's and Beccaria's words and ideas for guidance. In his *Considerations on the Injustice and Impolicy of Punishing Murder by Death* (1792), Dr. Benjamin Rush—like James Wilson, a signer of the Declaration of Independence—declared that "[t]he punishment of murder by death, is contrary to reason, and to the order and happiness of society."[41] After noting that if Indian tribes punished murder by death it "must have originated in *necessity*,"[42] Rush appealed to principles of justice and Christianity—and, in particular, "to posterity" and "the unborn generations of the next century"—in arguing for the death penalty's abolition.[43] As Rush wrote to those as-yet-unborn future citizens: "You will enjoy in point of knowledge, the meridian of a day, of which we only perceive the twilight. You will often review with equal contempt and horror, the indolence, ignorance and cruelty of your ancestors."[44] Beccaria was such a respected authority in Pennsylvania that, in 1807, a town in Clearfield County was named in his honor.[45]

In his essay, Dr. Rush observed that "[t]he punishment of murder by death, has been proved to be contrary to the order and happiness of society by the experiments of some of the wisest legislators in Europe." Rush argued, looking to European reforms to guide American ones: "The Empress of Russia, the King of Sweden, and the Duke of Tuscany, have nearly extirpated murder from their dominions, by converting its punishment into the means of benefiting society, and reforming the criminals who perpetrate it." In another portion of his 1792 essay, Rush noted: "It has been said, that the horrors of a guilty conscience proclaim the justice and necessity of death, as a punishment for murder. I draw an argument of another nature from this fact. Are the horrors of conscience the punishment that God inflicts upon murder? why, then, should we shorten or destroy them by death, especially as we are taught to direct the most atrocious murderers to expect pardon in the future world?" As Rush's essay concluded:

> From the importance and destiny of every human soul, you will acquire new ideas of the dignity of human nature, and of the infinite value of every act of benevolence that has for its object, the bodies, the souls, and the lives of your fellow-creatures. You will love the whole human race, for you will perceive that you have a common Father, and you will learn to imitate him by converting those punishments to which their folly or wickedness have exposed them, into the means of their reformation and happiness.

Dr. Rush also quoted another source for the proposition that the death penalty was "neither *useful* nor *necessary* to society in general" and that "there can be *no necessity* for *taking away the life* of a citizen."[46]

After Dr. Rush's essay was published in the *American Museum*, a reply to it was published under the signature of "Philochoras" in the *Pennsylvania Mercury*. That reply prompted Dr. Rush to take up his pen again, this time writing of the need for "atonement" and "*forgiveness*." "Reason," Dr. Rush asserted, "establishes the necessity of the atonement, for it has lately taught us in the writings of the Marquis of Beccaria, that in a perfect human government there should be *no pardoning power*: and experience has taught us that where *certainty* take the place of *severity* of punishment, crimes have evidently and rapidly diminished in every country." Rush then transcribed an entire passage from Catherine II's "instructions to the commissioners appointed to frame a new code of laws for the Russian Empire," saying he took "great pleasure in transcribing it, as the sentiments it contains do so much honor not only to the female understanding, but to the human mind." The language he transcribed from those instructions, essentially lifted directly from Beccaria's *On Crimes and Punishments*, read in part:

> Proofs from facts demonstrate to us, that the frequent use of capital punishments, never mended the morals of a people. Therefore, if I prove the death of a citizen to be neither *useful* nor *necessary* to society in general, I shall confute those who rise up against humanity. In a reign of peace and tranquility, under a government established with the united wishes of a whole people, in a state well fortified against external enemies, and protected within

> by strong supports; that is, by its own internal strength, and virtuous sentiments, rooted in the minds of the citizens, there can be *no necessity* for *taking away the life* of a citizen. It is not the excess of severity, nor the *destruction* of the human species, that produces a powerful effect upon the hearts of the citizens, but the continued duration of the punishment. The death of a malefactor is not so efficacious a method of deterring from wickedness, as the example continually remaining, of a man who is deprived of his liberty, that he might repair, during a life of labour, the injury he has done to the community.

"The Marquis of Beccaria," Rush added, showing that, in his view, the pursuit of happiness should include penal reform efforts, "has established a connexion between the abolition of capital punishments, and the order and happiness of society."[47]

Dr. Rush—a highly religious man—saw the Enlightenment and Christianity as having worked hand-in-hand to produce tremendous good. As Rush wrote near the end of his reply to Philochoras: "The world has certainly undergone a material change for the better within the last two hundred years. This change has been produced chiefly, by the secret and unacknowledged influence of Christianity upon the hearts of men." Rush took specific note of "the diminution of the number of capital punishments," further noting that "[t]here was a time when torture was part of the punishment of death, and when the number of capital crimes amounted to one hundred and sixty-one." With respect to the latter comment, Rush noted that "Christianity has abolished the former, and reduced the latter to not more than six or seven." And "[i]t has done more," Rush wrote, continuing: "It has confined in some instances capital punishments to the crime of murder only—and in some countries it has abolished it altogether."[48]

In the last paragraph of his reply, Dr. Rush distinguished tyrannical and republican forms of government. "I cannot take leave of this subject," Rush emphasized, "without remarking that capital punishments are the natural offspring of monarchical governments." As Rush observed: "Kings believe that they possess their crowns by a *divine* right: no wonder, therefore, they assume the divine power of taking away human life. Kings consider their subjects as their property: no wonder, therefore, they shed their blood with as little emotion as men shed the blood of their sheep or cattle." "But the principles of republican governments," Rush added, "speak a very different language." As Rush observed of republics: "They teach us the absurdity of the divine origin of kingly power.... They appreciate human life, and increase public and private obligations to preserve it." After noting that "[t]he spirit of Christianity" had "found its way into schools and families, and has abolished, in both, corporal and ignominious punishments," and that he had read "with great pleasure" in "the instructions to the masters and mistresses" of schools "to use corporal punishments as seldom as possible," Rush ended his reply with these words about the course charted on American soil:

> The United States have adopted these peaceful and benevolent forms of government. It becomes them therefore to adopt their mild and benevolent principles. An execution in a republic is like a human sacrifice in religion. It is an offering to monarchy, and to that malignant being, who has been

> styled a murderer from the beginning, and who delights equally in murder, whether it be perpetrated by the cold, but vindictive arm of the law, or by the angry hand of private revenge.[49]

Thomas Paine, the author of *Common Sense* (1776), also focused in a revealing way on how "[p]unishment is the tyrannical and odious part of a government's duty," with Paine seeing criminal punishment as a last resort in very Beccarian terms. As Paine wrote in 1791, wrestling with the underlying causes of crime: "[A]s to that pretended effect of punishment to prevent the commission of crimes, by deterring the surviving criminals through sight or example of those punishments, your long woeful experience has sufficiently proved this self-evident fact, that *punishment*, whether exemplary or personal, never hath, never will, nor ever can, deter or reclaim one single criminal, so long as they shall all continue to be so situated as that they must of necessity either *steal* or *starve*, inasmuch as the dread or even the suffering of punishment, however repeated or severe, cannot subdue the rage of hunger." "Nor," Paine added, "can a momentary death be compared with the long protracted pangs of starving," with Paine writing: "It is indeed a truth notorious, that the frequency of executions serves merely to harden the surviving criminals." "[A] government that employs punishments as the only means to prevent the commission of crimes, is altogether tyrannical," Paine concluded.[50] For Paine, who recognized that desperate people do desperate things, the elimination of poverty and hunger were to be prioritized.

William Bradford's *Enquiry How Far the Punishment of Death Is Necessary in Pennsylvania*

William Bradford, Jr. was one of the sons of Colonel William Bradford, a prominent colonial figure and the publisher of the *Pennsylvania Journal and Weekly Advertiser*. That newspaper has been described as "a paper devoted to the patriot cause from the beginning of trouble with the mother country in 1765." A 1772 graduate of Princeton, William Bradford, Jr. studied law with Edward Shippen (1729–1806) and volunteered in 1776 for the Pennsylvania militia. In 1780, he became Pennsylvania's attorney general, and after eleven years in that position, became a justice on the Pennsylvania Supreme Court. "During this time," one source notes of his role as a prominent jurist, "he prepared a report on capital punishment in the state, which resulted in the elimination there of the death penalty for all crimes except first degree murder." In 1794, he succeeded Edmund Randolph—the first Attorney General of the United States—as the country's Attorney General, though his tenure in that job, the nation's top law enforcement position, was, regrettably, cut short by his untimely death at a time when physicians lacked the modern technology and pharmaceuticals that they have today. During a yellow fever epidemic in Philadelphia, Bradford contracted the disease and, despite the best efforts of his friend, Dr. Benjamin Rush, to save his life, Bradford died on August 23, 1795.[51]

In *An Enquiry How Far the Punishment of Death Is Necessary in Pennsylvania* (1793), William Bradford, Jr., the renowned Pennsylvania lawyer and jurist who had befriended James Madison at the College of New Jersey, now Princeton,[52] specifically referred to the necessity-for-punishment principle articulated by Montesquieu and

Beccaria.[53] In fact, that principle—along with Montesquieu and Beccaria themselves—took center stage in Bradford's essay. The very first three paragraphs of Bradford's legislative report read as follows:

> The general principles upon which penal laws ought to be founded appear to be fully settled. Montesquieu and Beccaria led the way in the discussion, and the philosophy of all Europe, roused by the boldness of their march, has since been deeply engaged on this interesting topic. Independent of the force of their reasoning a remarkable coincidence of opinion, among the enlight[en]ed writers on this subject, seems to announce the justness of their conclusions: and the questions which still exist are rather questions of fact than of principle.
>
> Among these principles some have obtained the force of axioms, and are no longer considered as the subjects either of doubt or demonstration. "*That the prevention [o]f crimes is the sole end of punishment*," is one of these; and it is another, "*That every punishment which is not absolutely necessary for that purpose is a cruel and tyrannical act.*" To these may be added a third, (calculated to limit the first) which is, "*That every penalty should be proportioned to the offence.*"
>
> These principles, which serve to protect the rights of humanity and to prevent the abuses of government, are so important that they deserve a place among the *fundamental* laws of every free country. The enlightened patriots who composed the first National Assembly in France, placed this check on the power of punishment, where it ought to be placed, among "the rights of a man and a citizen."[54] They had long witnessed the ferocity of the criminal law, and they endeavored to guard against it by declaring, in precise and definite terms, "That the law ought to establish such punishments *only* as are *strictly* and evidently *necessary*." Few of the American constitutions are sufficiently express, though they are not silent, on this subject. That of New-Hampshire declares, "That all penalties should be proportioned to the nature of the offence, and that a multitude of sanguinary punishments is impolitic and unjust, the true design of all punishments being to reform, and not to exterminate, mankind."[55] The constitution of Vermont enjoins the introduction of hard labor as a punishment, in order to lessen the necessity for such as are capital;[56] and that of Pennsylvania framed in 1776, directed the future Legislature "to reform the penal laws—to make punishments less sanguinary, and, in some cases, more proportioned to the offences."[57] But it was in Maryland alone that the *general* principle was asserted; and, in the enumeration of their rights, we find it declared, "That sanguinary punishments ought to be avoided as far as is consistent with the safety of the state".[58] The other constitutions which touch on this subject content themselves with generally declaring, "That cruel punishments ought not to be inflicted." But, does not this involve the same principle, and implicitly prohibit every penalty which is not evidently necessary?[59]

Like many others before him, William Bradford thus distinguished between the harsh punishments meted out by corrupt, power-hungry monarchs versus the milder ones he thought should be handed out in liberty-loving republics.[60] "[S]anguinary punishments, contrived in despotic and barbarous ages," Bradford warned, "have been continued when the progress of freedom, science, and morals renders them unnecessary and mischievous: and laws, the offspring of a corrupted monarchy, are fostered in the bosom of a youthful republic."[61] Focusing on capital punishment in particular, Bradford stressed of the reform of Pennsylvania's penal laws[62] since the Revolutionary War: "Capital Punishments have, in several instances, been abolished; and, in other, the penalty has been better proportioned to the offence."[63] "What success has attended the new system of punishments is, therefore," Bradford wrote, "a question interesting to humanity." Laying out the reason for his *Enquiry*, Bradford—the lawyer who dabbled with statistics—observed of Pennsylvania's new approach to punishment: "Some years have elapsed since its first establishment, and we now have data sufficient to calculate its effects. To aid this important enquiry,—to review the crimes which are still capital in Pennsylvania,—and to examine, whether the punishment of death be, in any case, necessary, is the object of the present attempt."[64]

Like Beccaria and Dr. Rush before him, William Bradford forthrightly considered an alternative to capital punishment (*i.e.*, "perpetual imprisonment") in assessing and grappling with whether the death penalty was a legitimate punishment for particular crimes. As Bradford put it:

> IT being established, That the only object of human punishments is the prevention of crimes, it necessarily follows, that when a criminal is put to death, it is not to revenge the wrongs of society, or of any individual—"it is not to recall past time and to undo what is already done:" but merely to prevent the offender from repeating the crime, and to deter others from its commission, by the terror of the punishment. If, therefore, these two objects can be obtained by any penalty short of death, to take away life, in such case, seems to be an authorized act of power.
>
> That the first of these may be accomplished by perpetual imprisonment, unless the unsettled state, the weakness or poverty, of a government prevent it, admits of little dispute. It is not only as effectual as death, but is attended with these advantages, that reparation may sometimes be made to the party injured—that punishment may follow quick upon the heels of the offence, without violating the sentiments of humanity or religion,—and if, in a course of years, the offender becomes humbled and reformed, society, instead of losing, gains a citizen.
>
> It is more difficult to determine what effects are produced on the mind by the *terror* of capital punishments; and, whether it be absolutely necessary to deter the wicked from the commission of atrocious crimes. This is the great problem, to the solution of which, all the facts I have occasion to mention hereafter, will be directed.[65]

Bradford then concluded that the death penalty was not a necessary or legitimate punishment for "the Crime against Nature,"[66] "Robbery and Burglary,"[67] "Counterfeiting the Coin,"[68] or rape.[69]

As to the crime of murder, which had long been punished by death throughout world history, William Bradford began his analysis in his 1790s *Enquiry* this way:

> IT has been a question which has divided the philosophers of Europe, whether it be lawful, in *any* case, to take away the life of a criminal: and the negative has been advanced and ingeniously supported in our own country.[70] Great names are arranged on the different sides of this question: but, waving useless refinement, it seems to resolve itself into that which we are considered, *viz.* whether it be *necessary* to the peace, order, and happiness of society.[71]

Although the Grand Duke of Tuscany had abolished the death penalty in 1786, William Bradford—uncertain of what the evidence might bear out—was not prepared in his lifetime to do away with it for crimes of premeditated murder. "Murder, in its highest degree," Bradford wrote, "has generally been punished with death, and it is for deliberate assassination, if in any case, that this punishment will be justifiable and useful."[72] Circumspect about the death penalty's usefulness but then unprepared to abandon that punishment altogether for first-degree murder, Bradford thus observed: "If we seek a punishment capable of impressing a strong and lasting terror, we shall find it in an execution *rarely* occur[r]ing—*solemnly* conducted—and inflicted in a case, where the feelings of mankind *acquiesce in its justice* and do not revolt at its severity."[73]

Though Bradford was, at that stage, willing to tolerate the rare infliction of capital punishment for first-degree murderers, his words also made crystal clear that he was willing to entertain the distinct possibility that, in time, executions might be shown to be unnecessary even for that particular category of offenders. As Bradford wrote about the death penalty and the potential that a punishment less than death might be found to suffice through the gathering of further evidence:

> But while I contend that this is the most powerful curb of human governments, I do not affirm that it is *absolutely* necessary, or that a milder one will be insufficient. It is possible that the further diffusion of knowledge and melioration of manners, may render capital punishments unnecessary in all cases: but, until we have had more experience, it is safest to tread with caution on such delicate ground, and to proceed step by step in so great a work. A few years experience is often of more real use than all the theory and rhetoric in the world.[74]

It was in March 1787, just a few months before the start of American's all-important Constitutional Convention in Philadelphia, that Dr. Benjamin Rush—Bradford's friend and fellow Pennsylvania penal reformer—had invoked Beccaria's name at Benjamin Franklin's house, announcing that death is "an improper punishment for any crime."[75] Although Dr. Rush's *application* of the necessity-for-punishment principle was not embraced by many of his fellow citizens at that juncture, including William Bradford, the necessity-for-punishment principle was, itself, rather uncontroversial by that time as an *abstract* principle.

In his "Conclusion," Bradford, while embracing the necessity-for-punishment maxim while disagreeing slightly with Dr. Rush on its precise implementation, made this observation in his *Enquiry* before making reference to "[t]he celebrated *Beccaria*":

"A mitigation of punishment ought, therefore, to be accompanied, as far as possible, by a *diffusion of knowledge* and a *strict execution of the laws.* The former not only contributes to enlighten, but to meliorate the manners and improve the happiness of a people."[76] In particular, Bradford called for laws prescribing "hard labor as a punishment" to be "strictly executed,"[77] then wrote in his concluding paragraph:

> The conclusion to which we are led, by this enquiry, seems to be, that in all cases (except those of high treason and murder) the punishment of death may be safely abolished, and milder penalties advantageously introduced—Such a system of punishments, aided and enforced in the manner I have mentioned, will not only have an auspi[ci]ous influence on the character, morals, and happiness of the people, but may hasten the period, when, in the progress of civilization, the punishment of death shall cease to be necessary; and the Legislature of Pennsylvania, putting the key-stone to the arch, may triumph in the completion of their benevolent work.[78]

In America, hard labor among prisoners in fact emerged as a popular alternative to executions and corporal punishments, thus making capital punishment unnecessary in various situations.[79]

The convention for the framing of Pennsylvania's 1776 constitution—the document that, in Beccarian fashion, called for "more proportionate" and "less sanguinary" punishments and for "houses" of detention to facilitate "punishing by hard labour," so as "to make sanguinary punishments less necessary"—first met at Philadelphia's State House on July 15, 1776. After choosing as its president Benjamin Franklin, a man who, himself, was greatly interested in penal reform, James Cannon, David Rittenhouse, and Timothy Matlack were appointed members of the committee to draft the constitution. Cannon, born in Edinburgh and a talented writer, was a thirty-six-year-old mathematics professor at the College of Philadelphia; Rittenhouse was an astronomer; and Matlack, the grandson of an indentured servant and the son of a farmer, was a self-educated beer bottler from Philadelphia who had led a militia battalion during the Revolutionary War. Because there was, as yet, no federal constitution, the drafting of the state constitution was thus of considerable importance. "[I]t seems clear," one source notes, referencing Judge George Bryan, "that Cannon with the advice and help of Judge Bryan, who was not a delegate to the convention, had the most important part in this work." Pennsylvania's first post-Declaration of Independence constitution—the most democratic of early American state constitutions—was signed on September 28, 1776.[80]

The Pennsylvania constitution, like other early state constitutions, was driven by Enlightenment impulses. A few months before the signing of the Declaration of Independence, a small group of liberal-minded patriots in Philadelphia had formed "The Whig Society." Its leaders: the artist Charles Wilson Peale (1741–1827), a painter who felt an affinity for Montesquieu and in fact quoted him on the issue of liberty; the scientist David Rittenhouse (1732–1796); Thomas Paine (1737–1809), the author of *Common Sense* who forthrightly opposed capital punishment; Col. Timothy Matlack (1736–1826), the brewer and bottler known as a "fighting Quaker" and for his good penmanship, leading him to be chosen as the scribe for the Declaration of Independence; Dr. Thomas Young (1731–1777), a radical political activist and organizer of the Boston Tea Party; and James Cannon (1740–1782), the Scottish-born schoolmaster at the University of Pennsylvania who was educated at the University of Edinburgh. The resulting Pennsylvania constitution produced in 1776, Jonathan Israel writes in *Democratic Enlightenment: Philosophy, Revolution, and Human Rights 1750–1790*, "was for several years the chief focus of American revolutionary democratic republicanism."[81]

These well-educated and well-read men, called "The Furious Whigs," were suspicious of political power and wary of its abuse. David Rittenhouse—as just one example—believed, like Dr. Benjamin Rush, that death ought not to be a punishment for any crime. Rittenhouse greatly admired William Bradford's *Enquiry How Far the Punishment of Death Is Necessary in Pennsylvania* (1793), going so far as to recommend it, and he observed that he was thankful to God for never having served on a jury in a case where a life-or-death decision was involved. "Of all murders," he said, "*legal* murders are the most horrid." While Dr. Thomas Young was a friend of Vermont's famed Ethan Allen and became a surgeon in the army, Thomas Paine criticized cruel punishments, observing that "[t]he effect of those cruel spectacles exhibited to the populace, is to destroy tenderness, or excite revenge; and by the base and false idea of governing men by terror, instead of reason, they become precedents." "It is over the lowest class of mankind that government by terror is intended to operate, and it is on them that it operates to the worst effect," Paine observed. "It is in their sanguinary punishments which corrupt mankind," Paine said of governments, believing that one must "[l]ay then the axe to the root, and teach governments humanity."[82]

One source notes that it is "unknown" who wrote section 38 of Pennsylvania's 1776 constitution, the section providing that "the penal laws as heretofore used shall be reformed by the legislature of this state, as soon as may be, and punishments made in some cases less sanguinary, in general more proportionate to the crimes." Another source, however, observes that James Cannon drafted it. In an early twentieth-century biography of Judge George Bryan, the jurist who worked closely with Cannon, Montesquieu's *The Spirit of the Laws* was described as a "classic," and it has been logically surmised by yet another source—a law review article—that "[t]he requirement that punishments be made more proportionate to the crimes was based on a proposition of Montesquieu." In 1785, Benjamin Franklin—their fellow Philadelphian and himself a man of letters—wrote in one of his many letters, following Montesquieu, that it is an "Eternal Principle of Justice and Equity, that Punishments should be proportion'd to Offences." A few years later, in an essay titled "Considerations on the Injustice and Impolicy of Punishing Murder by Death" (1792), it was another Pennsylvanian—the American revolutionary, Dr. Benjamin Rush—who forthrightly announced: "The punishment of murder by death, is contrary to reason, and to the order and happiness of society." "The punishment of murder by death, has been proven to be contrary to the order and happiness of society by the experiments of some of the wisest legislators in Europe," Dr. Rush wrote, contextualizing the world's then nascent quest for the death penalty's abolition through a frame that might easily find a home in Thomas Jefferson's prose. In the Declaration of Independence, Jefferson wrote of the unalienable right to life and the "pursuit of Happiness."[83]

Numerous elected officials got involved in the movement to reform the criminal laws. Thomas Mifflin (1744–1800), Pennsylvania's first governor, serving in that role from 1790 to 1799, was himself convinced of the need for major penal reform—and of the importance of the necessity-for-punishment principle. In his 1792 message to members of Pennsylvania's house and senate, Mifflin, who had asked William Bradford, Jr. to study the matter, had this to say about the state's efforts to modernize the penal system:

> It must be flattering to the judgment, and grateful to the humanity of the legislature, to learn, from satisfactory evidence, that the experiment in rendering the penal laws of Pennsylvania less sanguinary, has been attended with an obvious decrease of the number and atrocity of offences. I shall therefore take an early opportunity of communicating to you a statement of the facts and observations relating to the subject, which a Judge of the Supreme Court (lately the Attorney General) has made, in compliance with my request, and which, as the result of considerable experience and deliberation, merits particular regard. Such, indeed, have already been the wholesome effects of the new system, that, if, while we consider the prevention of crimes to be the sole end of punishment, we also admit, that every punishment, which is not absolutely necessary for that purpose, is an act of tyranny and cruelty, it has now become a duty to prosecute the business of reform; and I am persuaded, you will find, that, without affecting the just distribution of penalties in proportion to the respective transgressions, a mitigation of punishment may be safely, and even beneficially, extended to many, if not to all, of the offences, except high treason and murder, for which the law still denounces the forfeiture of life.[84]

Of course, the idea that any punishment that was not absolutely necessary is tyrannical and cruel is one that came directly from Cesare Beccaria's treatise. And in the years and decades to come, Beccaria would in fact get well-warranted credit in Pennsylvania and elsewhere for the pivotal role his work played in spurring American penal reform. For example, in his *Treatise on Executive Clemency in Pennsylvania* (1909), William Smithers (with statistics and data provided by his collaborator, George Thorn, the Clerk of the Board of Pardons) had this to say about America's founding period:

> Another man exercised a powerful influence upon the same period and served to focus the philosophical and political discussions upon the many defects in the criminal law. In 1764, the Marquis Beccaria, of Italy, a follower of Helvetius, published *Dei delitti e delle pene*. It was a severe arraignment of the inhumanity of criminal procedure both evidential and expiatory. He protested against secret trials, torture, confiscation, infamous penalties, inequality of punishments and the atrocities of capital executions. He clearly separated divine and human justice, crimes and sins, repudiated

the right of vengeance, declared the only reasonable basis for punishment to be public utility, demanded that the penalty should be proportioned to the crime and that the judicial and legislative powers should be separate. It has been said that never had so small a book created so great an effect. The Marquis was approved universally except as to one theory. He proposed that the laws be made so exact and perfect that there would be no necessity or opportunity for pardon. This, however, was but a logical amplification of an earnest admonition for carefully considered and mild laws. His practical thought was thus expressed: "As punishments become more mild, clemency and pardon are less necessary. * * * This truth will seem cruel to those who live in countries where, from the absurdity of the laws and the severity of punishments, pardons and the clemency of the prince are necessary."

The Treatise on Executive Clemency in Pennsylvania, taking particular note of Beccaria's broader influence on the law, also noted:

During the latter part of the eighteenth century the intellectual awakening of the world culminated in a general modification of views in both criminology and penology through the writings of Hobbes, Locke, Hale, Hawkins, Blackstone, Hume, Howard and Bentham in England, and Grotius, Pufendorf, La Bruyére, D'Aguesseau, Montesquieu, Voltaire, Rousseau, Thomasius and Beccaria on the continent. From this period the barbarous treatment of the accused before and after conviction began to abate and a new basis for criminal law grew up in which ferocity was tempered by ethical considerations. Some writers have denominated this the classical school of criminology in which individualism has always been prominent. Equality of punishment for similar crimes and limitation of punishments to social protection by intimidation became special features but the school has been marked by particular attention to the crime, comparative indifference to the criminal and a general assumption of moral responsibility on the part of every offender. It is essentially founded on crime as a juridical abstraction and its teachings have been distinguished by study of the punishment rather than of the culprit. This system is fundamentally that of England and America to-day. It received its greatest impetus from the work of the Marquis Beccaria who summarized the ideas of his own age including even those of Rousseau published two years before. Under his assault the traditional vengeance visited upon a wrongdoer by right of the *lex talionis* wavered before the demand for rational treatment of criminals as human beings. Many protested that the then new doctrines disturbed all moral and social order but the protests were lost in the world-wide influence of the French Revolution. In the Declaration of Rights of 1789 France proclaimed the limitation of punishment by necessity and in the Constitution of 1793 declared that the law should prescribe only unavoidably necessary penalties, proportioned to the crimes for which inflicted and such as should be beneficial to society.[85]

The Division of Murder into Degrees and the Necessity Principle in Practice

In applying the necessity-for-punishment principle, early Americans came to the conclusion that the death penalty was not necessary for certain crimes. For example, in 1794, after the publication of Bradford's report, Pennsylvanians—at the urging of Bradford and Dr. Benjamin Rush—divided murder into degrees, with only first-degree murder punishable by death. As one source puts it: "If the murderer did not exhibit malice or an intent that gave evidence of a 'depraved mind, regardless of human life', then the murder was of the second-degree."[86] The preamble to Pennsylvania's 1794 statute[87] tellingly declared: "[I]t is the duty of every government to endeavor to reform, rather than exterminate offenders, and the punishment of death ought never to be inflicted where it is not absolutely necessary to the public safety"; "[t]herefore, no crime whatsoever, hereafter committed, except murder in the first degree, shall be punished with death in the State of Pennsylvania."[88] This statutory preamble, Edwin Keedy, a former dean of the University of Pennsylvania Law School, wrote in 1949, "was based on Montesquieu and Beccaria."[89]

On the recommendation of William Bradford and Pennsylvania's then governor, Thomas Mifflin, the state's senate had first agreed to these resolutions on February 22, 1793, as part of the effort to curtail the death penalty:

> Resolved, that, for all offenses (except those of high treason and murder of the first degree) which are made capital by the existing laws of Pennsylvania, the punishment shall be changed to imprisonment at hard labor, varying in duration and severity according to the degree of the crime.
>
> Resolved, that the crimes, at the present classed under the general denomination of murder, be divided into murder of the first and murder of the second degree; the latter punishable by imprisonment at hard labor, or in solitude, or in both, for any time not exceeding twenty-one years.
>
> Resolved, that all murder perpetrated by poison or by lying in wait, or by any kind of wilful, premeditated and deliberate killing, shall be deemed murder in the first degree, and all other kinds of murder shall be murder in the second degree; and the jury before whom any person shall be indicted for murder, if they find the party guilty thereof, shall, in their verdict, ascertain whether it be murder in the first or second degree.

Later that year, after Pennsylvania's addressed the issue again on December 6, 1793, a committee of the state senate had been appointed on December 16th to prepare a bill on that subject. William Bradford participated in the drafting of the bill, which was titled "An act for the better preventing of crimes and for abolishing the punishment of death in certain cases." The bill's first section provided that no crime except "murder of the first degree" shall be punished by death, and the bill's second section provided "that all murder which shall be perpetrated by means of poison, or by lying in wait, or by any other kind of wilful, deliberate and premediated killing shall be deemed murder in the first degree." As Edwin Keedy wrote of that legislation, harkening back to the days of William Penn and his Great Act of 1682: "It seems clear that the words 'wilful' and 'premeditated' were taken from the Act of 1682 and the word 'deliberate' from the memoir of Justice Bradford." Section 2 of the bill was later amended over the course of the legislative debate.

On April 22, 1794, the Pennsylvania Assembly approved the amended act, the preamble and first two sections of which read as follows:

> WHEREAS the design of punishment is to prevent the commission of crimes, and to repair the injury that hath been done thereby to society or the individual, and it hath been found by experience, that these objects are better obtained by moderate but certain penalties, than by severe and excessive punishments: And whereas it is the duty of every government to endeavour to reform, rather than exterminate offenders, and the punishment of death ought never to be inflicted, where it is not absolutely necessary to the public safety: Therefore,
>
> Sect. I. Be it enacted by the SENATE and HOUSE OF REPRESENTATIVES of the commonwealth of Pennsylvania, in General Assembly met, and it is hereby enacted by the authority of the same, That no crime whatsoever, hereafter committed (except murder of the first degree) shall be punished with death in the state of Pennsylvania.
>
> Sect. II. And whereas the several offences, which are included under the general denomination of murder, differ so greatly from each other in the degree of their atrociousness that it is unjust to involve them in the same punishment: *Be it further enacted by the Authority aforesaid*, That all murder, which shall be perpetrated by means of poison, or by lying in wait, or by any other kind of wilful, deliberate and premeditated killing, or which shall be committed in the perpetration of attempt to perpetrate any arson, rape, robbery, or burglary, shall be deemed murder of the first degree; and all other kinds of murder shall be deemed murder in the second degree; and the jury, before whom any person indicted for murder shall be tried, shall, if they find such person guilty thereof, ascertain in their verdict, whether it be murder of the first or second degree; but if such person shall be convicted by confession, the court shall proceed, by examination of witnesses, to determine the degree of the crime, and to give sentence accordingly.[90]

Governor Thomas Mifflin, who had earlier asked William Bradford, the jurist described in one source as part of Philadelphia's "Enlightenment literati," to weigh in on the death penalty, then quickly signed the legislation into law.[91]

In this era, anti-death penalty sentiment was growing in America and in Europe, though sentiment varied somewhat from place to place. In England, the Society for the Diffusion of Knowledge upon the Punishment of Death and the Improvement of Prison Discipline was formed in 1808 to communicate to the public that the death penalty should not be imposed unless "all the means" within society's "power" had been tried for the offender's reformation.[92] Sir Samuel Romilly had proposed a bill in May 1808 to abolish the death penalty for pickpockets, and that July—as one source puts it—"with Romilly's approval, the Quakers William Allen, William Forster, and Luke Howard, along with the London sheriff Richard Phillips and the Benthamite barrister Basil Montagu, met 'to converse on the subject of our little society.'" "This,"

V.A.C. Gatrell writes in *The Hanging Tree: Execution and the English People 1770–1868*, "was the Society of the Diffusion of Knowledge upon the Punishment of Death and the Improvement of Prison Discipline." Montagu himself wrote an *Account of the Origin and Object of the Society for the Diffusion of Knowledge upon the Punishment of Death, and the Improvement of Prison Discipline* that was published in 1812. Those who assailed the English "Bloody Code" in the British Parliament between 1770 and 1819, Gatrell pointed out in his book, "argued from Beccaria and Bentham." Anti-gallows societies were later formed in the United States, too.[93]

The Penitentiary System

The American penitentiary system itself was created in response to Enlightenment ideas, including those of Montesquieu, Beccaria, and the English penal reformer John Howard, whose *The State of the Prisons in England and Wales* (1777) became highly influential. For example, Thomas Eddy, the prominent New York penal reformer, was an admirer of Howard's work. In O. F. Lewis's *The Development of American Prisons and Prison Customs, 1776–1845*, a book published by the Prison Association of New York in 1922, Howard is credited for helping to reform early American penal practices. That source notes that Beccaria had previously written that penalties must not be arbitrary, but should be just, precise, and fit the crime. William Bradford's work, it further stresses, was predicated in part on Montesquieu's work. But as Lewis then emphasized: "it will be found that John Howard was in many respects a founder of our American prison system." As Lewis wrote of Howard: "He was not, to be sure, the direct incentive to prison reform in this country, because 'prison reform,' as we have seen, has already organized a charitable society in Philadelphia by 1776. Yet he was unquestionably a substantial influence."[94]

In the American effort to reform penal laws, Pennsylvanians were the first to act. The Walnut Street Prison in Philadelphia opened in 1790, just a year before the ratification of the U.S. Bill of Rights, and it is considered America's first penitentiary. In an article on the history of American prisons, scholar Matthew Meskell writes that Americans were "particularly receptive to emerging Enlightenment thought challenging the premises of the old social order." In his article in the *Stanford Law Review*, Meskell references Montesquieu's *The Spirit of the Laws* and the writings of "[u]tilitarians such as Bentham and Blackstone." "From the American standpoint," Meskell explains, "these arguments reached their most persuasive and influential form in the works of Italian criminologist Cesare Beccaria." Beccaria, Meskell emphasizes, had "recommended that: (1) legislatures strictly define punishments for various crimes and limit the power of judges to arbitrarily modify them, (2) laws be clear and public, (3) punishments be designed solely to specifically deter any given offender from further offense and to generally deter society from criminal acts, and (4) punishments be the 'least necessary' to achieve deterrence."

The reform impulse was transatlantic in nature. "These ideas," Meskell writes, "gathered enormous support in Europe and in fact formed the basis for the French criminal code passed in 1791." "The newfound philosophy," he adds, "found a ready audience in America." "Spurred by Beccaria's essay," Meskell observes, "William Bradford wrote a widely-circulated article entitled *An Enquiry How Far the Punishment of Death Is Necessary in Pennsylvania, With Notes and Illustrations* in 1793 in which he quoted with approval many of Beccaria's arguments." Pointing out that Bradford's essay "was immensely popular" and that "[r]ationalists such as Beccaria had provided a clear recipe for reform of the criminal laws," Meskell's article goes on to describe how the Walnut Street Jail was transformed in 1790 into a space "for confinement of the most hardened criminals." "The total physical area of the refurbished prison was 400 by 200 feet which was bounded by an outer enclosure," Meskell explains, adding: "Convicts used 300 feet at the north end of the enclosure for their exercise, while debtors and witnesses used 100 feet at the south." With each inmate's cell 8 feet long, 6 feet wide, and 10 feet high, those cells had an outer wooden door, an inner iron door, and "one window that was kept blinded and locked to prevent any glimpse of the outside." "This basic design," Meskell recounts, "was to be the model for all the prisons created in America during the next thirty years."

After the construction of Philadelphia's innovative Walnut Street Prison, the New York legislature, in 1796, passed legislation designed to create two prisons to be modeled after Pennsylvania's new penitentiary. Only one of the prisons ever got built, however. As Meskell observes: "Ultimately, the legislature only provided funds for the prison known as Newgate, located in Greenwich Village. The basic layout of the prison was almost exactly that of its predecessor at Walnut Street. It had a workhouse and large night rooms for housing the less serious offenders." Thomas Eddy, the designer of, and chief advocate for, the new New York prison, also became its first warden. "The reformers," Meskell notes, "were quick to trumpet their achievements and a number of states followed with prisons of their own." As Meskell writes, taking note of the cascade of prisons that were built in the aftermath of the construction of the ones in Philadelphia and New York: "New Jersey, Kentucky, Virginia, Massachusetts, Vermont, Maryland, New Hampshire, Ohio, and Georgia all built prisons in the first two decades of the nineteenth century." Overcrowding at the prisons in the years to come, however, soon led to administrative nightmares, pardons, and even riots. At New York's Newgate Prison, for example, 573 convicts were pardoned in 1816 and 1817 alone. In 1816, with its existing penitentiary system under strain, the New York legislature ordered the construction of a new penitentiary at Auburn. By the time its north wing was completed in 1825, it had 550 cells. Pennsylvania legislators also authorized the construction of two new penitentiaries: the Western Penitentiary at Pittsburgh (1818) and the Eastern Penitentiary at Cherry Hill (1821).[95]

In *A Report on the History and Mode of Management of the Kentucky Penitentiary, from Its Origin, in 1798, to March 1, 1860*, its author, Dr. William Sneed, specifically cited the work of Beccaria, Blackstone, Montesquieu and John Howard in his introduction. As soon as the American colonies separated from Great Britain, Dr. Sneed observed in 1860, the reformation of the criminal law "was regarded as one of the first fruits of liberty, and a confirmation of a remark of Montesquieu, 'that, as freedom advances, the severity of the penal law decreases.'" Pointing to historic reforms in Pennsylvania that made that state's penal code milder by abolishing the punishment of death for any crime except first-degree murder, Dr. Sneed emphasized that such laws "were founded" on the principles "[t]hat the prevention of crime is the sole object of punishment; that every punishment that is not absolutely necessary for that purpose is a cruel and tyrannical act, and that every penalty should be proportioned to the offense."[96]

More than thirty years earlier, another physician, G. F. H. Crockett, had sent James Madison a copy of Crockett's extended essay, *An Address to the Legislature of Kentucky on the Abolition of Capital Punishments, in the United States, and the Substitution of Exile for Life.* That essay invoked Beccaria's name, too, with Madison, in 1823, writing back to Crockett, a veteran and an honorary member of the Lexington Medical Society: "I should not regret a fair and full trial of the entire abolition of capital punishments by any State willing to make it: tho' I do not see the injustice of such punishments in one case at least." It was just four years later, in 1827, that Madison wrote to another correspondent on the subject of the criminal law, saying that he was "attracted to what related to the penitentiary discipline as a substitute for the cruel inflictions so disgraceful to penal codes."[97] The transition in the United States from a sanguinary system to the penitentiary system was thus driven by a love of liberty, with early Americans expressing disdain for cruel, out of the ordinary, and tyrannical punishments.

CHAPTER 4

The Parsimony Principle:

The Sentencing Guidelines and the French Connection

The Parsimony Principle and the U.S. Code

The "parsimony" principle, as it is now known, was much discussed in Anglo-American sources even before the U.S. Constitution's ratification. For example, in *Principles of Penal Law* (1771), William Eden (1745–1814)—a British diplomat and politician who served in the House of Commons—took the position that "[c]apital executions are in all states necessary." Yet, Eden—also known as Lord Auckland or 1st Baron Auckland—freely asserted in *Principles of Penal Law*: "Nothing, however, but the evident result of absolute necessity, can authorize the destruction of mankind by the hand of man." "The infliction of Death," Eden wrote, "is not therefore to be considered, in any instance, as a mode of punishment, but *merely* as our last melancholy resource in the extermination of those from society, whose continuance among their fellow-citizens is become inconsistent with the public safety." In speaking of "transportation," that is, sending someone abroad to labor as a punishment (e.g., to America or Australia), with death as the authorized punishment if the person returned home before the term of service was completed, Eden had this to say: "I cannot dismiss this subject without expressing a doubt, relative to the propriety of punishing with death a return from transportation; especially where the original offence was not capital. It certainly is not justified by necessity; for it is easy, if requisite, to send the delinquent abroad again, without any considerable degree either of expence or trouble." Eden's book cited Beccaria and Montesquieu's work, so it is easy to see how Eden would have come upon the parsimony, or necessity-for-punishment, principle.[1]

Beccaria's *On Crimes and Punishments* and Montesquieu's *L'Esprit des Loix* (also referred to as *L'Esprit des Lois*) were cited in many places, including in *Political Disquisitions: Or, An Enquiry into Public Errors, Defects and Abuses*, a book published in London in 1774. In that source, chapter three—titled "*The Colonies, though so valuable to* Britain, *have been greatly oppressed by the Mother Country*"—quoted the following familiar passage from Beccaria's treatise: "'Every act of authority of one man' [or body of men] 'over another, for which there is not an absolutely necessity, is tyrannical.'" In that source, the writer also had this to say after the Boston Massacre trial and on the very cusp of the Revolutionary War:

> We should not think of punishing with military execution, un-convicted and un-heard, our brave *American* children, our surest friends and best customers. We should not insist on bringing them over to be tried *here*, on pretence of no justice to be had in *America*, in direct violation of the constitution, especially when we had so late an experience of their *candor* in *acquitting* an officer of the *army* charged with murdering one of their people, even *since* the commencement of the present unhappy *dissentions*. We should not think of putting them in a state of subjection to an *army* rendered *independent* on the *civil* magistrate, and secured from *punishment* even for the most atrocious offence, by their being to be sent 3000 miles to their mock-trial, across an ocean, where the *persons* and things indispensably *necessary* for their trial, cannot possibly be had.[2]

Likewise, in *An Essay on Parish Work-Houses* (1786), Edmund Gillingwater quoted "[t]he benevolent Marquis Beccaria" as follows: "The punishment of a crime cannot be just, if the laws have not endeavoured to prevent that crime by the best means which times and circumstances will allow." "Now," Gillingwater argued, building off of Beccaria's assertion, "the same mode of reasoning may be applied to the management of our parish work-houses." Gillingwater favored "a strict, but humane discipline," that, he wrote, "must be firmly adhered to, it being the grand preservative of the peace and good order of the house, the happiness of the poor, and the interest of the parish." "Nevertheless," Gillingwater cautioned, "this strict and exact discipline, however necessary both for the paupers and the parish, must never degenerate into rigid and partial severity; and consequently, those inspectors whose office obliges them to correct the misdemeanors of the poor, should never lose sight of humanity; always remembering, that the poor with all their failings, have innumerable claims to our compassion; and that, while we are chastising them as criminals, must never forget that they are fellow-beings and Christians." As Gillingwater advised: "The government therefore, which is established in our English work-houses, like that in similar institutions for the poor in foreign nations, should always be lenient and gentle; never severe but in cases of absolute necessity, such as reclaiming the disorderly, and the support of due order and subordination: evincing thereby, that the happiness of the poor, and not the wanton exercise of authority, is the only object aimed at in inflicting punishments."[3]

In fact, the parsimony principle, as it has come to be commonly referred to by criminologists and modern commentators, still finds expression—albeit in a different form—today. Under American law, federal and state-court judges, in one of their most solemn and weighty responsibilities, are tasked with formulating and imposing appropriate sentences in criminal cases. They must, above all else, decide what punishments are necessary in the given circumstances, looking to various statutory provisions and precedents as they perform their work. Federal judges, for example, are guided by the Sentencing Reform Act, part of the Comprehensive Crime Control Act of 1984 that aimed to increase consistency in federal sentences. That act established the United States Sentencing Commission and abolished federal parole, except for persons convicted under federal law before November 1, 1987, and those convicted under District of Columbia law, among other narrow exceptions.

The Sentencing Reform Act of 1984, Shahid Shahidullah writes in *Crime Policy in America: Laws, Institutions, and Programs*, "developed a comprehensive system of mandatory sentencing for drug related crimes and violence." "From the beginning of the 1980s," that author notes, "the Congress became skeptical about the efficacy of indeterminate sentencing, effectiveness of bail, role of parole and probation, and the overall capacity of prisons to rehabilitate the violent offenders." "Title II of the Comprehensive Crime Control Act of 1984, known as Sentencing Reform Act of 1984," the summary of the legislation in that source emphasizes, "set up a new institution — United States Sentencing Commission — to develop mandatory sentencing guidelines for drug law offenders and violent criminals." But as Lynn Adelman, a federal district court judge in Wisconsin, has recently written, the "misnamed" Sentencing Reform Act ("SRA") only fueled the growth of "harsher" sentences and that "[m]uch of the federal over-punishment problem stems from the SRA." "Nearly all of the guidelines were excessively severe," Adelman writes of the mandatory Sentencing Guidelines that were initially produced, with the Sentencing Commission, over the next 20 years, regularly amending the guidelines "to make them even more severe."[4]

The so-called "parsimony clause" of the Sentencing Reform Act, now codified at 18 U.S.C. § 3553(a), requires that a court "impose a sentence sufficient, but not greater than necessary," in carrying out the purposes of punishment.[5] "[T]he overarching requirement that binds every sentencing court," the U.S. District Court for the Southern District of New York has written, "is the parsimony clause, which commands that '[t]he court shall impose a sentence sufficient, but not greater than necessary, to comply with the purposes' of sentencing."[6] As another court, the U.S. Court of Appeals for the Ninth Circuit, put it in 2015 of that provision's significance: "[T]he 'parsimony principle' or 'parsimony clause,'" "is a guidepost, an overarching principle that directs judges in the appropriate exercise of their sentencing discretion within the sentencing range authorized and consideration of factors prescribed by Congress." "As such," that court emphasized, "challenging a sentence as violating the 'parsimony principle' is simply another way of stating that the sentence is unreasonable."[7]

The language in 18 U.S.C. § 3553(a) has been invoked by a number of defendants seeking to avoid prison terms or lengthy prison sentences.[8] In one defendant's brief, submitted in 2009, the defendant — appearing *pro se* — actually quoted the language of Montesquieu's necessity-for-punishment maxim before noting: "This quote is taken from Montesquieu's *The Spirit of the Laws* (1748). This simple, yet profound idea was the very root of the principle of 'parsimony'. The core congressional command of 18 U.S.C. § 3553(a) is that district courts must 'impose a sentence, sufficient, but not greater than necessary, to comply' with specified purposes of punishment." And that petitioner's brief, part of the regular submissions that occur in criminal cases, continued: "This statutory language distills one of the most long-established and influential maxims of criminology in a humane society: the principle of 'parsimony'. The principle, that any punishment should never exceed the minimum necessary to effect its purpose, has its roots deep in American soil, as it was well known to our founding fathers through their readings of Montesquieu and his *The*

Spirit of the Laws; a foundation work in the 18th century movement for criminal law reform."[9]

The maxim of Montesquieu, in fact, has been cited in briefs multiple times in submissions to federal judges. For example, in *United States v. Ruiz*, a sentencing memorandum prepared by the defendant in 2015 asserted: "Reflecting the historic idea that '[a]ll punishment which is not derived from necessity is tyrannical,' 18 U.S.C. § 3553(a) requires the Court to impose a sentence that is sufficient, but not greater than necessary, to comply with the purposes of punishment. In this case, a non-custodial sentence can satisfy each of the goals of sentencing."[10] Likewise, the defendant's 2014 sentencing memorandum in *United States v. Gardner*, citing both Montesquieu and Beccaria, observed: "The 'sufficient, but not greater than necessary' rule is rooted in the principle of parsimony. 'All punishment which is not derived from necessity,' wrote Montesquieu, 'is tyrannical.'" "Relying on Montesquieu," that memorandum asserted, "Cesare Beccaria made the same point" in *On Crimes and Punishments* "to influence Enlightenment thinkers like the Framers." "Given that pedigree," the latter sentencing memorandum emphasized, "it is not surprising that Congress saw fit to make the principle of parsimony foremost in Section 3553(a)."[11] The parsimony principle—firmly laid down by Montesquieu, Beccaria, Bentham, and others—has been cited in other sentencing submissions, too, so modern-day judges have certainly read about it (and are familiar with it) as cases have been litigated before them.[12]

It was the Sentencing Reform Act of 1984, passed by the U.S. Congress, that ushered in a new era, that of the U.S. Sentencing Guidelines, which took effect in 1987. "Years from now," a journal published by the Administrative Office of the United States Courts observed in 1991 after those Sentencing Guidelines had become effective, "1987—the year sentencing guidelines went into effect—will be remembered as a milestone in Federal criminal justice."[13] It was a milestone that—as told by Kate Stith and José Cabranes in their book, *Fear of Judging: Sentencing Guidelines in the Federal Courts*—came about only after U.S. Senator Edward Kennedy, of Massachusetts, was convinced in 1975 to sponsor a major sentencing reform bill. Moved by the ideas of Judge Marvin Frankel, a study on sentencing disparities, and a Yale Law School reform proposal, Senator Kennedy came to view then-existing federal sentencing as "arbitrary" and "desperately" in need of reform—indeed, as "a national scandal" and "a disgrace." After introducing versions of his bill in four separate Congresses, the Sentencing Reform Act of 1984 finally became the law of the land. Hailed by President Ronald Reagan as a way to "crack down" on criminals, what started out as "an essentially anti-imprisonment, antidiscrimination measure"—to use the words of Stith and Cabranes—became "a conservative, law-and-order measure." "Liberals and conservatives alike," Stith and Cabranes write of the bill's transformation, "evinced a deep suspicion of discretionary judgment by federal judges; Congress was determined to limit it by delegating sentencing authority to an administrative agency that promised to be more responsive to Congress itself."[14]

The motivations for supporting the Sentencing Reform Act no doubt differed from one legislator to another. Senator Kennedy and his allies, in the main, had sought to eliminate "unwarranted sentencing disparity" among offenders "with similar records who have been found guilty of similar conduct" and to promote "honesty in sentencing" by eliminating parole as a mechanism of early release from prison. "The post-prison supervisory function of parole," Stith and Cabranes explain of the legislation in their book, "would be continued instead in the form of a 'term of supervised release' set at the time of the original sentencing." Although Senator Kennedy had initially envisioned an advisory role for the Sentencing Guidelines, explaining that his legislation "would require only that the sentencing judge 'consider' the sentencing range" set forth in them, he later embraced an amendment proposed by U.S. Senator Gary Hart of Colorado. That amendment required the sentencing judge to impose a sentence within the guideline range "unless the court finds that an aggravating or mitigating circumstance exists that was not adequately taken into consideration by the Sentencing Commission in formulating the guidelines and that should result in a different sentence."[15]

It was Senator Charles McCurdy "Mac" Mathias—a lawyer and U.S. Navy veteran, a senior member of the U.S. Senate's Judiciary Committee, and a liberal Maryland Republican—who got the parsimony clause added into the Sentencing Reform Act of 1984. Senator Mathias ultimately voted against the actual crime bill—the one and only Senator to do so—but during the debate over the legislation, he had expressed great frustration about the "profound mistrust of the Federal bench." "The proponents of the bill," he said, "argue in essence that judges cannot be trusted." In truth, Senator Mathias made a valid—and very important—point, one that should not be lost on modern readers. Federal judges, after all, go through—and must clear—the vetting process and the often-rigorous Senate confirmation process before taking up their positions. And once confirmed, federal judges, by virtue of Article III of the U.S. Constitution, have life-time tenure unless impeached, expressed in the U.S. Constitution through the idea that such judges "shall hold their Offices during good Behaviour." Article III, ensuring that federal judges will be insulated from political pressures, specifically guarantees that the compensation for judges "shall not be diminished" during their time in office.[16]

Major legislation, such as the Sentencing Reform Act, almost always comes about after intense debate and compromise. While the bill in the U.S. House of Representatives would have required the sentencing judge to impose the "least severe" sentence that would meet the four general purposes of sentencing (i.e., retribution, deterrence, incapacitation, and rehabilitation), it was the Senate's version of the Comprehensive Crime Control Act (which included Senator Kennedy's Sentencing Reform Act) that got attached to a continuing appropriations resolution. By a vote of 243 to 166, the U.S. House of Representatives had then approved a motion (brought by Representative Dan Lungren, a California Republican) to recommit that funding measure to the Appropriations Committee. With the Senate's crime bill attached to the House funding measure, the omnibus bill then went back to the Senate, where Senator Mathias—with the support of other senators—was able to amend the Sentencing Reform Act to change the number of judges to serve on the seven-member United States Sentencing Commission from two to three, a small, but nonetheless important victory. Senator Mathias, wary of overly punitive sanctions, was also able to add the parsimony clause that ended up in the final version of the bill, that is, the language requiring a sentencing judge to "impose a sentence sufficient, but not greater than necessary, to comply" with the statute's listed purposes for sentencing. President Reagan signed the omnibus funding bill, including the Sentencing Reform Act of 1984, into law on October 12, 1984.[17]

Federal judges have hard, high-pressure jobs. And arriving at a sentence that is not greater than necessary takes judgment, and involves, by statute, the consideration of a number of factors and the proper assessment of appropriately gathered pre-sentencing information. Section 3553(a) of the U.S. Code, which begins with the parsimony clause, states in part:

> The court shall impose a sentence sufficient, but not greater than necessary, to comply with the purposes set forth in paragraph (2) of this subsection. The court, in determining the particular sentence to be imposed, shall consider—
>
> (1) the nature and circumstances of the offense and the history and characteristics of the defendant;
>
> (2) the need for the sentence imposed—
>
> (A) to reflect the seriousness of the offense, to promote respect for the law, and to provide just punishment for the offense;
>
> (B) to afford adequate deterrence to criminal conduct;
>
> (C) to protect the public from further crimes of the defendant; and
>
> (D) to provide the defendant with needed educational or vocational training, medical care, or other correctional treatment in the most effective manner;
>
> (3) the kinds of sentences available;
>
> (4) the kinds of sentence and the sentencing range established for—
>
> (A) the applicable category of offense committed by the applicable category of defendant as set forth in the guidelines—
>
> (i) issued by the Sentencing Commission ... [18]

The four purposes of punishment articulated in 18 U.S.C. § 3553(a)(2) are thus "just punishment," "adequate deterrence," protecting the public "from further crimes of the defendant," and "to provide the defendant with needed educational or vocational training, medical care, or other correctional treatment in the most effective manner." The U.S. Supreme Court, by way of comparison, has identified the following four reasons that can justify punishment: (1) to rehabilitate the offender; (2) to incapacitate an offender from committing offenses in the future; (3) to deter others from committing offenses; or (4) to assuage the victim or community's desire for retribution. By writing into federal law the parsimony principle, members of Congress essentially codified—whether knowingly or not—a variation of the eighteenth-century maxim laid down by Montesquieu, Beccaria and Bentham.[19] Although Montesquieu and Beccaria had laid down their necessity-for-punishment maxim using only a few well-chosen words, Congress—in the tradition of the lengthy U.S. Code—used lettered and numbered subsections. Though less elegantly phrased than in Montesquieu and Beccaria's books, Congress thereby announced its desire that federal judges pay heed to the parsimony principle.

The U.S. Supreme Court and the Federal Courts

The United States Sentencing Guidelines, as originally enacted, were mandatory. As a result of a U.S. Supreme Court decision handed down more than two decades after the passage of the Sentencing Reform Act, however, those Sentencing Guidelines—thanks to the Justices of the U.S. Supreme Court—became *advisory* instead of *mandatory*. Thus, in *United States v. Booker* (2005), the Supreme Court struck down the mandatory aspect of the Sentencing Guidelines, rendering them merely advisory in nature. In that case, the Supreme Court held that the mandatory nature of the guidelines violated a defendant's Sixth Amendment right to a jury trial. "If the Guidelines as currently written could be read as merely advisory provisions that recommended, rather than required, the selection of particular sentences in response to differing sets of facts, their use would not implicate the Sixth Amendment," the Court emphasized in that case, further observing: "The Guidelines as written, however, are not advisory; they are mandatory and binding on all judges. While subsection (a) of §3553 of the sentencing statute lists the Sentencing Guidelines as one factor to be considered in imposing a sentence, subsection (b) directs that the court 'shall impose a sentence of the kind, and within the range' established by the Guidelines, subject to departures in specific, limited cases."

History is often important, if not decisive, to U.S. Supreme Court Justices. "The Framers of the Constitution," the Court held in *Booker*, quoting *The Federalist No. 83*, "understood the threat of 'judicial despotism' that could arise from 'arbitrary punishments upon arbitrary convictions' without the benefit of a jury in criminal cases." "Section 3553(a)," the Court stressed of federal law, "remains in effect, and sets forth numerous factors that guide sentencing."[20] In *Booker*, the Supreme Court, in fashioning its opinion, held that appellate review of sentencing decisions is limited to determining whether they are "reasonable." Federal district court judges, it was emphasized, must consider the "sentencing range" established for the "applicable category of offense committed by the applicable category of defendant" that is set forth in the Guidelines. And those judges must impose sentences that "reflect the seriousness of the offense, promote respect for the law, provide just punishment, afford adequate deterrence, protect the public, and effectively provide the defendant with needed educational or vocational training and medical care." In reviewing sentences, federal appellate courts, by contrast, are tasked with determining whether a particular sentence is "unreasonable." If a sentence is found to be "unreasonable," it is set aside.[21] As the U.S. Court of Appeals for the Second Circuit put it in 2011: "[W]hile the parsimony clause requires a district court to impose 'a sentence sufficient, but not greater than necessary,' to meet statutory objectives, we review the sentence actually imposed only for reasonableness. The question is not whether we 'might reasonably have concluded that a different sentence was appropriate,' but 'whether the sentence imposed falls within the broad range that can be considered reasonable.'"[22]

The year before *Booker*, in *Blakely v. Washington* (2004), the U.S. Supreme Court had held that a state trial court's sentencing of a defendant to more than three years above the 53-month statutory maximum of the standard range for his offense violated the defendant's Sixth Amendment right to trial by jury. In that case, the State of Washington's Sentencing Reform Act specified a "standard range" of 49 to 53 months for the offense, but provided that a judge could impose a sentence above the standard range if the judge found "substantial and compelling reasons justifying an exceptional sentence." Although the prosecution recommended a sentence within the standard range of 49 to 53 months, the judge rejected that recommendation and imposed a sentence of 90 months because the defendant's actions evidenced "deliberate cruelty," a statutorily enumerated ground for a departure from the standard range. In *Blakely*, the Supreme Court applied the rule it had previously laid down in *Apprendi v. New Jersey* (2000): "Other than the fact of a prior conviction, any fact that increases the penalty for a crime beyond the prescribed statutory maximum must be submitted to a jury, and proved beyond a reasonable doubt." That rule, the Court emphasized, "reflects two longstanding tenets of common-law criminal jurisprudence," one of which—as laid down by Sir William Blackstone—is "that the 'truth of every accusation' against a defendant 'should afterwards be confirmed by the unanimous suffrage of twelve of his equals and neighbours.'"

In determining that the facts supporting the finding of "deliberate cruelty" had neither been admitted by the defendant nor found by a jury, the Court in *Blakely* recognized that a Sixth Amendment violation had occurred. "This case," the Court ruled, "is not about whether determinate sentencing is constitutional, only about how it can be implemented in a way that respects the Sixth Amendment." As the Court emphasized: "Several policies prompted Washington's adoption of determinate sentencing, including proportionality to the gravity of the offense and parity among defendants. Nothing we have said impugns those salutary objectives." "Ultimately," the Court stressed, "our decision cannot turn on whether or to what degree trial by jury impairs the efficiency or fairness of criminal justice." As the Court reasoned in determining that a jury, not a single judge, should make the decision about the defendant's fate: "One can certainly argue that both these values would be better served by leaving justice entirely in the hands of professionals; many nations of the world, particularly those following civil-law traditions, take just that course. There is not one shred of doubt, however, about the Framers' paradigm for criminal justice: not the civil-law ideal of administrative perfection, but the common-law ideal of limited state power accomplished by strict division of authority between judge and jury." "The Framers," the Court concluded, "would not have thought it too much to demand that, before depriving a man of three more years of his liberty, the State should suffer the modest inconvenience of submitting its accusation to 'the unanimous suffrage of twelve of his equals and neighbours,' rather than a lone employee of the State."[23]

In *Kimbrough v. United States* (2007), the U.S. Supreme Court reiterated that the Sentencing Guidelines are only "effectively advisory" and "now serve as one factor among several courts must consider in determining an appropriate sentence." In that case, the Supreme Court held that, "under *Booker*, the cocaine Guidelines, like all other Guidelines, are advisory only," and that the lower court "erred in holding the crack/powder disparity effectively mandatory." "Crack and powder cocaine," the Court noted, "are two forms of the same drug," with powder cocaine generally inhaled through the nose but also capable of being mixed with water and then injected. "Crack cocaine, a type of cocaine base," the Court emphasized by way of contrast, "is formed by dissolving powder cocaine and baking soda in boiling water," with the resulting solid "divided into single-dose 'rocks' that users smoke." "The two forms of the drug," while treated very differently for purposes of sentencing, the Court pointed out, "have the same physiological and psychotropic effects, but smoking crack cocaine allows the body to absorb the drug much faster than inhaling powder cocaine, and thus produces a shorter, more intense high." A district judge may determine, the Supreme Court explicitly held in *Kimbrough*, that "a within-Guidelines sentence is 'greater than necessary' to serve the objectives of sentencing." After citing 18 U.S.C. § 3553(a), the section of the U.S. Code that codified the parsimony principle, the Supreme Court in *Kimbrough* emphasized that "[i]n making that determination, the judge may consider the disparity between the Guidelines' treatment of crack and power cocaine offenses."[24]

In *Rita v. United States* (2007), the U.S. Supreme Court held in yet another case that the law permits an appellate court—in particular, a U.S. Court of Appeals—to presume that a sentence imposed within a properly calculated United States Sentencing Guidelines range is a reasonable sentence. That "presumption of reasonableness," the Supreme Court determined in the post-*Booker* era, "is not binding." "Rather," the Court ruled, "the presumption reflects the fact that, by the time an appeals court is considering a within-Guidelines sentence on review, *both* the sentencing judge and the Sentencing Commission will have reached the *same* conclusion as to the proper sentence in the particular case. That double determination significantly increases the likelihood that the sentence is a reasonable one." "Further," the Court emphasized, "the presumption reflects the nature of the Guidelines-writing task that Congress set for the Commission and the manner in which the Commission carried out that task." "In instructing both the *sentencing judge* and the *Commission* what to do," the Supreme Court wrote in *Rita*, "Congress referred to the basic sentencing objectives that the statute sets forth in 18 U.S.C. § 3553(a)."

The website for the Washington, D.C.-based United States Sentencing Commission explains that it is "a bipartisan, independent agency located in the judicial branch of government" and was created by Congress "to reduce sentencing disparities and promote transparency and proportionality in sentencing." The Commission's seven voting members are appointed by the President of the United States and confirmed by the U.S. Senate, with the commissioners serving staggered six-year terms. As the Commission's website notes: "No more than four members of the Commission can be members of the same political party, and at least three must be federal judges. The Attorney General, or the Attorney General's designee, and the Chair of the U.S. Parole Commission serve as *ex officio*, nonvoting members of the Commission. The affirmative vote of at least four members of the Commission is required to promulgate amendments to the sentencing guidelines." The Commission's staff—approximately 100 employees—is divided into the following five offices: General Counsel, Education and Sentencing Practice, Research and Data, Legislative and Public Affairs, and Administration.[25] Of course, the people selected to serve on the Sentencing Commission will have a major impact on the Sentencing Commission's policies.

Both individual federal judges and the U.S. Sentencing Commission—the members of the judicial branch and the government agency tasked with deciding upon and setting sentencing policy—need to consider 18 U.S.C. § 3553(a). That statutory provision, the Supreme Court observed in *Rita*, "tells the *sentencing judge* to consider (1) offense and offender characteristics; (2) the need for a sentence to reflect the basic aims of sentencing, namely, (a) 'just punishment' (retribution), (b) deterrence, (c) incapacitation, (d) rehabilitation; (3) the sentences legally available; (4) the Sentencing Guidelines; (5) Sentencing Commission policy statements; (6) the need to avoid unwarranted disparities; and (7) the need for restitution." "The provision," the Court wrote, highlighting the statutory language, "also tells the sentencing judge to 'impose a sentence sufficient, but not greater than necessary, to comply with' the basic aims of sentencing as set out above." "Congressional statutes," the Court in *Rita* stressed, "then tell the *Commission* to write Guidelines that will carry out these same § 3553(a) objectives." The Commission, the Court noted, "must seek to 'provide certainty and fairness' in sentencing, to 'avoi[d] unwarranted sentencing disparities,' to 'maintai[n] sufficient flexibility to permit individualized sentences when warranted by mitigating or aggravating factors not taken into account in the establishment of general sentencing practices,' and to 'reflect, to the extent practicable, [sentencing-relevant] advancement in [the] knowledge of human behavior.'" "The upshot," the Court in *Rita* observed, "is that the sentencing statutes envision both the sentencing judge and the Commission as carrying out the same basic § 3553(a) objectives, the one, at retail, the other at wholesale."[26]

The United States Sentencing Guidelines, though now only advisory in nature, continue to be of great importance in America's federal criminal justice system. That is because the Sentencing Guidelines—and the calculations performed under them—provide the jumping off point for sentencing decisions, even though an individual judge now remains in the driver's seat, able to deviate from the Guidelines as the judge finds the specific circumstances may dictate. "Although the Guidelines remain 'the starting point and the initial benchmark' for sentencing," the Supreme Court emphasized in 2017, "a sentencing court may no longer rely exclusively on the Guidelines range; rather, the court 'must make an individualized assessment based on the facts presented' and the other statutory factors." "The Guidelines," the Court held in that case, *Beckles v. United States* (2017), "thus continue to guide district courts in exercising their discretion by serving as 'the framework for sentencing,' but they 'do not constrain th[at] discretion.'" "Because they merely guide the district courts' discretion," the Court wrote in *Beckles*, "the Guidelines are not amenable to a vagueness challenge." Writing that "the system of purely discretionary sentencing that predated the Guidelines was constitutionally permissible," the Court added: "If a system of unfettered discretion is not unconstitutionally vague, then it is difficult to see how the present system of guided discretion could be."[27]

A federal district court judge's job, like that of a state court judge, is to gather sufficient information about the crime and the offender so as to arrive at the right sentencing decision. In that role, a judge must balance the need to administer justice and provide for public safety with the clear liberty interest—and the constitutional rights—of the person being sentenced. "[O]ur post-*Booker* decisions make clear," the U.S. Supreme Court wrote in *Pepper v. United States* (2011), "that a district court may in appropriate cases impose a non-Guidelines sentence based on a disagreement with the Commission's views." "That is particularly true where, as here, the Commission's views rest on wholly unconvincing policy rationales not reflected in the sentencing statutes Congress enacted," the Court in *Pepper* emphasized. In *Pepper*, the Supreme Court held that, post-*Booker*, district courts "may consider evidence of a defendant's postsentencing rehabilitation at resentencing and such evidence may, in appropriate cases, support a downward variance from the advisory Guidelines range."[28] While "a district court is still required to consult the Guidelines," the Supreme Court reiterated in yet another case, *Peugh v. United States* (2013), "the Guidelines are no longer binding, and the district court must consider all of the factors set forth in §3553(a) to guide its discretion at sentencing."[29] The whole idea of applying the parsimony principle suggests that, in practice, there must be considerable flexibility on the judge's part in deciding precisely what is necessary. The basic idea: the punishment should fit the crime.

One of the most difficult things for a court to do, of course, is to figure out what the most appropriate sentence is given that the future is unknowable. At a sentencing, it is simply impossible for a judge to know if—and how—an individual will respond to future rehabilitation efforts if such efforts are made. Efforts to predict or forecast criminality have been made since the 1920s, with statisticians looking to factors such as an offender's criminal record and social history to identify individuals likely to become recidivists. But social science research has its limitations, with one source noting of the response that developed in early decades as a result of efforts to predict criminality: "Civil libertarians began to worry about the tendency of forecasts of criminality to overpredict. Although statistical forecasting methods could identify groups of offenders having higher probabilities of recidivism, these methods showed a disturbing incidence of 'false positives.'" "Many of those classified as potential recidivists," as that source emphasizes, "were, in fact, not found to offend again."[30] The bottom line: judges have extremely difficult jobs because they must decide how much punishment to administer while simultaneously considering every person's liberty interest who appears before the bar of justice. And they must make such judgments knowing that sometimes they may prove to be right but sometimes they may prove to be wrong. As judges make these difficult decisions with very human consequences, the necessity-for-punishment maxim, because of its simplicity and its reminder of what exactly is at stake, can be an extremely helpful tool for judges to use as they go about their work.

In *How Do Judges Decide?: The Search for Fairness and Justice in Punishment*, Cassia Spohn observes that "punishment involves infliction by the state of consequences that are considered to be unpleasant on a person who has been convicted of a crime." Taking note of Cesare Beccaria and Jeremy Bentham's pioneering work before exploring the different approaches taken by retributivists and adherents of utilitarianism and rehabilitation, she notes that modern-day "deterrence theorists suggest that potential offenders will refrain from committing a crime if they believe that the odds of getting caught and being severely punished are high and are not outweighed by any anticipated gain from the crime." "If rehabilitation is the justification for punishment," Spohn writes, "the nature and duration of the punishment will depend on what is needed to reform the offender." Observing that "we can't accurately predict how long it will take to reform the offender," Spohn emphasizes, the societal approach taken to crime and punishment—as well as the judicial philosophy employed by individual judges—has significant consequences, with those consequences felt by both individual offenders and the broader society. As Spohn points out: "Although it may be true that judges in the United States 'tend to be eclectic, reasoning sometimes as utilitarians but sometimes, when they are outraged by a crime, as retributivists', their philosophies of punishment do matter."[31]

The U.S. Constitution's Equal Protection Clause speaks of the "equal protection of the laws," with American courts reading that provision as requiring "that all persons who are similarly situated should be treated alike." That very admirable goal, of treating like offenders alike, has nonetheless proven to be an extremely challenging one for judges, as prior studies of racial bias have shown. Because individualized sentencing is also required by law, and because discretion—like it or not—brings with it the risk of racial, gender, or other biases, including unconscious bias, the American judicial system has long, if not always effectively, struggled to root out and eliminate such biases. The United States, which since its founding has grappled not only with slavery and overt misogyny, but also with other, more subtle forms of racial and gender discrimination, is still—it must be said—on the path towards equality of treatment for all, with major issues remaining to be dealt with in both the criminal justice system and outside of it. The persistent prevalence of racial prejudice and other forms of discrimination, as well as the commission of hate crimes in the country, are stark reminders of the problems, inequities, and disparities that continue to face the country. In the punishment context, the legal requirement of treating similar offenders alike, regardless of race, dates back as far as the Civil Rights Act of 1866, the first federal law to require "equal" protection of the laws and which specifically required the "like punishment" of "white citizens" and those of "every race and color." The Fourteenth Amendment, ratified in 1868, is said to have constitutionalized the Civil Rights Act of 1866, thus requiring—as a matter of constitutional law—that the laws, including the criminal laws, be administered equally regardless of race.[32]

Because the parsimony principle is part of federal law, has deep roots in American culture, and is of utmost importance to liberty itself, courts must grapple forthrightly with the application of it, taking care that their decisions, at all times, also adhere to the dictates of the Equal Protection Clause. "Federal sentencing law," the U.S. Supreme Court stated in *Freeman v. United States* (2011), "requires the district judge in every case to impose 'a sentence sufficient, but not greater than necessary, to comply with' the purposes of federal sentencing, in light of the Guidelines and other § 3553(a) factors." "The Guidelines," the Court noted in that case, "provide a framework or starting point—a basis, in the commonsense meaning of the term—for the judge's exercise of discretion." Rule 11(c)(1)(C) of the Federal Rules of Criminal Procedure, the Court emphasized, "permits the defendant and the prosecutor to agree that a specific sentence is appropriate, but that agreement does not discharge the district court's independent obligation to exercise its discretion." As the Court in *Freeman* observed: "In the usual sentencing, whether following trial or plea, the judge's reliance on the Guidelines will be apparent, for the judge will use the Guidelines range as the starting point in the analysis and impose a sentence within the range. Even where the judge varies from the recommended range, if the judge uses the sentencing range as the beginning point to explain the decision to deviate from it, then the Guidelines are in a real sense a basis for the sentence."[33]

The Sentencing Guidelines, as the starting point, are used on a day-to-day basis in the federal courts, with the parsimony principle explicitly brought up by judges in some of their decisions. By way of illustration, in *United States v. Aranda-Diaz*, the U.S. District Court for the District of New Mexico found that a 37-month sentence was sufficient without being greater than necessary. In that case, the district court judge noted that he had "carefully considered" the Sentencing Guidelines and "other sentencing goals." "Specifically," Judge James Browning emphasized, finding that the punishment set forth in the guidelines was appropriate, "the Court has considered the guideline sentencing range established for the applicable category of offense committed by the applicable category of defendant." Judge Browning then discussed the statutory parsimony clause, observing as follows:

> While there are many factors that could counsel for something in the middle of the guideline sentencing range or at the high end of the range, the Court also concludes that a sentence at the low end of the range adequately reflects these factors. The parsimony clause pushes the sentence to the low end of the guideline range. The Court believes that a sentence of 37 months is adequate to reflect the seriousness of the offense, promote respect for the law, provide just punishment, afford adequate deterrence, protect the public, and otherwise fully and actively reflect the factors set forth in 18 U.S.C. § 3553(a).

As the judge's opinion continued, discussing the parsimony clause's role: "And while the Court's task as a trial court is not to come up with a reasonable sentence, but to balance the 18 U.S.C. § 3553(a) factors correctly, the Court believes that this sentence balances the factors in 18 U.S.C. § 3553(a) and is a reasonable sentence. The Court concludes that this sentence is sufficient without being greater than necessary to comply with the purposes set forth in the Sentencing Reform Act."[34]

The U.S. Supreme Court's latest pronouncement on Title 18, Section 3553(a) of the U.S. Code came in *Dean v. United States* (2017). "[T]he parsimony principle," the Supreme Court wrote in that case, is "a broad command that instructs courts to 'impose a sentence sufficient, but not greater than necessary, to comply with' the four identified purposes of sentencing: just punishment, deterrence, protection of the public, and rehabilitation." "A sentencing court," the Supreme Court continued, "is then directed to take into account 'the nature and circumstances of the offense and the history and characteristics of the defendant,' as well as 'the need for the sentence imposed' to serve the four overarching aims of sentencing." "The § 3553(a) factors," the Supreme Court observed, "are used to set both the length of separate prison terms and an aggregate prison term comprising separate sentences for multiple counts of conviction." "Under § 3582," the Court emphasized, citing another section of the U.S. Code, "a court, 'in determining whether to impose a term of imprisonment, and, if a term of imprisonment is to be imposed, in determining the length of the term, shall consider the factors set forth in section 3553(a).'" "'[I]n determining whether the terms imposed are to be ordered to run concurrently or consecutively,'" the Supreme Court added, quoting another U.S. Code section, § 3584, a court "'shall consider, as to each offense for which a term of imprisonment is being imposed, the factors set forth in section 3553(a).'"[35]

The parsimony principle is, admittedly, difficult, but certainly not impossible, to apply, with federal judges compelled to daily exercise their common sense and individual judgment in applying that principle in their cases. "After *Booker*," one source, *Practice under the Federal Sentencing Guidelines*, advises lawyers, "practitioners should stress to a sentencing court the 'parsimony principle' articulated in 18 U.S.C. § 3553(a), as well as the other dynamic considerations spelled out by Congress in § 3553(a)." "*Booker*," that source stresses, "at the very least is unambiguous in holding that while federal judges are no longer bound by the Guidelines, they continue to be bound by the dictates of § 3553(a)." "[T]his parsimony principle," *Practice under the Federal Sentencing Guidelines* notes, "is the *only* statutory mandate that federal judges are now required to follow in crafting their sentencing orders." As that source emphasizes: "After *Booker*, it could be argued that any sentencing decision (or recommendation) that does not acknowledge the statutory parsimony principle and consider every factor listed in § 3553(a) is contrary to Congress's statutory commands and fails to fulfill the rules set forth in *Booker*." "[I]t is difficult to say exactly how to apply the parsimony principle in any particular case," that practice guide nonetheless observes of the subjective exercise, stressing: "Still, judges should not be excused from acknowledging and seeking to comply with the provision merely because its interpretation may be difficult."[36] In carrying out their responsibilities, judges should definitely ask lots of questions before sentencing offenders—questions that would allow for careful consideration of various alternatives as they apply the parsimony principle.

In another case, *Dillon v. United States* (2010), the U.S. Supreme Court addressed one particular (and quite specific) legal issue, holding that its decision in *Booker* did not compel treating § 1B1.10(b) of the United States Sentencing Commission's Guidelines Manual as nonbinding. While 18 U.S.C. § 3582(c) states that a federal court generally "may not modify a term of imprisonment once it has been imposed," there is an exception to that rule "in the case of a defendant who has been sentenced to a term of imprisonment based on a sentencing range that has subsequently been lowered by the Sentencing Commission." In the latter circumstance, 18 U.S.C. § 3582(c)(2) authorizes a court to reduce the term of imprisonment "if such a reduction is consistent with" applicable Commission policy statements. Citing § 1B1.10(b)(2) of the Guidelines Manual, the Supreme Court in *Dillon* emphasized that "[t]he policy statement governing § 3582(c)(2) proceedings instructs courts not to reduce a term of imprisonment below the minimum of an amended sentencing range except to the extent the original term of imprisonment was below the range then applicable."

In *Dillon*, a jury had convicted the petitioner, Percy Dillon, of various drug-related offenses, including conspiracy to distribute and to possess with the intent to distribute powder cocaine and crack cocaine, as well as the use of a firearm during a drug-trafficking offense. "Dillon's convictions," the Supreme Court emphasized, "exposed him to a statutory sentencing range of 10 years to life for the conspiracy, 5 to 40 years for cocaine possession, and a mandatory minimum sentence of 5 years for the firearm offense, to be served consecutively to the sentence for the drug offenses." The district court had sentenced Dillon at the bottom of the Guidelines range on the drug counts, followed by a mandatory 60-month sentence for the firearms count, leading to a total of 322 months' imprisonment. At Dillon's 1993 sentencing, before the Supreme Court in *Booker* determined that the Guidelines were non-mandatory, the trial judge had described the term of imprisonment being imposed as "entirely too high for the crime committed." Nevertheless, the trial court had felt constrained to impose the sentence within the prescribed Guidelines range, and the U.S. Court of Appeals for the Third Circuit had then affirmed Dillon's convictions and his lengthy sentence.

After the United States Sentencing Commission amended the crack-cocaine Guidelines and made the amendment retroactive in 2008, Percy Dillon had filed a *pro se* motion for a sentence reduction pursuant to 18 U.S.C. § 3582(c)(2). As the U.S. Supreme Court described his court filing: "In the motion, Dillon asked the court to grant not just the two-level reduction authorized by the amendment but also a further reduction consistent with the sentencing factors found in § 3553(a). Based largely on his post-sentencing conduct, including his determined pursuit of educational and community-outreach opportunities, Dillon contended that a variance from the amended Guidelines range was warranted in his case. He further urged that, after *Booker*, the court was authorized to grant such a variance because the amended Guidelines range was advisory notwithstanding any contrary statement in § 1B1.10." Although the district court judge reduced Dillon's sentence to 270 months—at the bottom of the revised Guidelines range—the district court declined to deviate below the Guidelines range, finding that it lacked the authority to impose a sentence inconsistent with § 1B1.10. After the Third Circuit affirmed, Dillon took his case all the way to the U.S. Supreme Court. The Supreme Court, however, rejected Dillon's arguments and affirmed the Third Circuit's judgment.[37]

The Supreme Court's decision in *Dillon* drew a sharp dissent from Justice John Paul Stevens, who took up the parsimony principle as he critiqued the majority opinion. As Justice Stevens, who saw Percy Dillon's lengthy sentence as unfair, began that dissent: "When sentencing petitioner Percy Dillon for crack cocaine-related offenses in 1993, the District Court stated that the punishment Dillon received was 'entirely too high for the crime [he] committed.' Bound by a sentencing regime that was mandatory at the time, the judge had no choice but to sentence Dillon to 322 months of imprisonment—nearly 27 years behind bars. The judge later explained that, were it within his discretion, he would have sentenced Dillon to 5 years of imprisonment." "Had Dillon been sentenced after our decision in *United States v. Booker*," Stevens emphasized, "the judge would have had that discretion." "Instead," Stevens pointed out, invoking the well-established parsimony principle now codified in federal law, "the District Court was compelled to mete out a punishment that it believed to be grossly disproportionate to the offense and, therefore, 'greater than necessary' to meet the goals of our criminal justice system, 18 U.S.C. §3553(a)." To Justice Stevens, the 1993 sentence that Dillon spend more than a quarter of a century in prison did not jibe with his sense of justice.

In his dissent, Justice Stevens put Dillon's original sentence in historical context: "The punishment Dillon received was so high, in part, because at the time of his conviction our drug laws punished crack cocaine offenses 100 times more severely than powder cocaine offenses." Stevens noted that it was only in 2007 that the United States Sentencing Commission "proposed a partial fix to this disparity, lowering its Guidelines Manual ranges for crack cocaine offenses to a 20:1 ratio," and that it was only effective in early March 2008 that the Commission made that change retroactive for individuals, such as Dillon, who were still serving time for crack cocaine offenses. In rejecting the reasoning of the majority, Justice Stevens called the result in *Dillon* "manifestly unjust." He pointed out that Dillon was 23 years old when he was sentenced to nearly 27 years' imprisonment for his drug crimes, and that—at Dillon's original sentencing—the trial judge had explicitly stated: "I don't say to you that these penalties are fair. I don't think they are fair." "Dillon's continued imprisonment," Stevens wrote, "is a truly sad example of what I have come to view as an exceptionally, and often mindlessly, harsh federal punishment scheme."[38]

The sentencing disparity between crack and powder cocaine, and the implications that disparity has had on creating racial disparities in America's criminal justice system, are particularly troubling, and Justice Stevens was certainly right to bring that issue up in his dissent. While every gram of crack cocaine had originally been treated as the equivalent of 100 grams of powder cocaine, resulting in the 100-to-1 ratio in disparity of treatment for crack vs. powder offenders, the U.S. Sentencing Commission eventually determined that the sentencing differential "fosters disrespect for and lack of confidence in the criminal justice system" because approximately 85 percent of defendants convicted of crack offenses in federal court were black. Historically, going all the way back to colonial slave codes and what came to be known as "black codes," blacks and whites were treated much differently in the American criminal justice system. Although overt discrimination—in the form of laws that, *on their face*, punished African-Americans more harshly than whites—are no longer permissible under the law, racial discrimination persists in more subtle ways through the application of laws that, while facially race-neutral, are, in reality, anything but because of their discriminatory effect. In 2010, after much public debate, President Barack Obama signed into law federal legislation that reduced the crack-powder cocaine disparity to an 18:1 ratio. Despite the passage of that law, however, a large disparity in treatment, which has clear implications for faith and confidence in the criminal justice system, persists.[39] The American effort to stop racial discrimination in punishment began after the Civil War, with the Civil Rights Act of 1866, but twenty-first-century Americans must redouble their efforts to stamp out such discrimination.

On criminal appeals, although existing trial-court sentences can be very harsh, parsimony clause challenges are frequently rejected, some rather summarily.[40] For example, the U.S. Court of Appeals for the Second Circuit has determined: "A sentencing judge has very wide latitude to decide the proper degree of punishment for an individual offender and a particular crime," and "a district court's substantive determination" will be set aside "only in exceptional cases where the trial court's decision cannot be located within the range of permissible decisions." "Thus," the Second Circuit ruled in 2011, "while the parsimony clause requires a district court to impose 'a sentence sufficient, but not greater than necessary,' to comply with statutory objectives, we review the sentence actually imposed only for reasonableness." "Although the brevity or length of a sentence can exceed the bounds of 'reasonableness,'" the Second Circuit had ruled in an earlier case, "we anticipate encountering such circumstances infrequently." The appellate review of a district court's imposition of a sentence is, consequently, highly deferential, often allowing very draconian sentences to stand. Speaking of its review of the "substantive reasonableness of a sentence," the Second Circuit has specifically opined: "In applying that standard, we must 'take into account the totality of the circumstances, giving due deference to the sentencing judge's exercise of discretion, and bearing in mind the institutional advantages of district courts.' We will not 'substitute our own judgment for the district court's on the question of what is sufficient to meet the § 3553(a) considerations in any particular case,' and will 'set aside a district court's *substantive* determination only in exceptional cases where the trial court's decision cannot be located within the range of permissible decisions.'"[41]

To date, the parsimony principle laid down in federal law has not, for instance, been interpreted to bar mandatory minimum sentences, though mandatory minimums can sometimes be quite long and may not take into account particular facts and circumstances. Thus, in 2011, the U.S. Court of Appeals for the Fourth Circuit emphasized:

> The Sentencing Reform Act, of which § 3553(a) is a part, dictates that a defendant should be sentenced in accordance with its provisions to achieve the purposes of § 3553(a)(2) "[e]xcept as otherwise specifically provided." Courts have opined that mandatory minimum sentences are "otherwise specifically provided" and thus do not conflict with § 3553(a)'s parsimony clause. Other courts, while not directly ruling on the alleged tension, have similarly rejected arguments that § 3553(a) authorizes deviation from statutorily-mandated sentences.[42]

There is a safety valve in place, but certain criteria must be met before a defendant is deemed eligible. As the U.S. Court of Appeals for the Eighth Circuit wrote in 2011:

> Section 3553(f) allows a district court to sentence a defendant below the statutory mandatory minimum if certain conditions are met. To be eligible for safety-valve relief, the defendant must not have more than one criminal history point. Because he concedes that he had more than one criminal history point, Mendoza was ineligible for safety-valve relief, and thus the district court erred in applying § 3553(f) to impose a sentence below the mandatory minimum.[43]

In thinking about the U.S. Code's parsimony clause, it is understandable that federal judges would not, instinctively, want to rely on one provision of federal law (i.e., the parsimony clause) to set aside or upend another legislative enactment (i.e., a duly enacted mandatory minimum). But the parsimony principle has Enlightenment roots, ones that reach deep into European and American soil, and ones that are focused on liberty and rights and that go to the very essence of what it means to live in a free and democratic society (i.e., the right to be free of tyranny and arbitrary or tyrannous punishments). The American Revolution and the French Revolution were fought in the name of liberty, and the association of tyranny with unnecessary punishments—the association made by Montesquieu, Beccaria, and many others—is a foundational one that should be given effect as part of American *constitutional law* (and which should thus trump the passage of mere legislation). The maxim of Montesquieu and Beccaria draws a clear line in the sand: while free societies impose only necessary punishments, despots and tyrants impose unnecessary ones. The U.S. Constitution's Eighth and Fourteenth Amendments should be read to incorporate that maxim, and that maxim should be given life and vitality through U.S. Supreme Court jurisprudence. Just as discriminatory punishments should be held to violate the Fourteenth Amendment's Equal Protection Clause, sentences that veer into the forbidden territory of unnecessary or arbitrary, or cruel and unusual, criminal sanctions should be invalidated, too.

The French Declaration of the Rights of Man of the Citizen

The Eighth Amendment was not adopted in a historical vacuum, just as the U.S. Code's parsimony clause did not appear out of nowhere (but was, in fact, the product of long-standing historical precedents). Instead, the Eighth Amendment was promulgated and ratified in the context of the Enlightenment and revolutionary impulses. While its language was derived from the English Bill of Rights of 1689[44] and the Virginia Declaration of Rights of 1776,[45] the text of the Eighth Amendment was ratified in 1791, shortly after the 1789 promulgation of the French Declaration of the Rights of Man and of the Citizen (*Déclaration des droits de l'Homme et du Citoyen*)—a declaration of rights that had its own historical context across the Atlantic.[46] At the outset of the French Revolution, the *Cahiers de doléances*, or lists of grievances, had been drawn up by each of the three Estates in France in March and April 1789.[47] The *cahiers* of the nobility, for example, sought "an explicit declaration of the rights of man be made, and that that declaration bear witness to the liberty and secure the safety of all men." The *cahiers*, Alexis de Tocqueville later wrote, demanded, among other things, "that penalties be proportioned to offenses, and uniform; that capital punishment be employed more rarely, and all corporal punishments, torture, &c., be abolished."[48] Just as Montesquieu and Beccaria's best-selling books had shaped Anglo-American penal reformers, they also shaped a wide variety of French criminal-law theorists.

Indeed, participants in the American Revolution became players in France as they interacted with French revolutionaries, some of whom had, themselves, played roles in America's Revolutionary War. Thomas Jefferson, in France during the French Revolution, paid close attention to the events unfolding in Paris, and the Marquis de Lafayette, Jefferson's friend and a man who had fought in America's Revolutionary War, played a key role in drafting the French Declaration of the Rights of Man and

Citizen.[49] "Although he said he was a mere spectator of events," Pulitzer Prize-winning author Gordon Wood has written of France and Jefferson, the American diplomat in Paris, "he couldn't resist the requests from his liberal French friends—Lafayette, La Rochefoucauld, du Pont de Nemours, Condorcet, and others—for constitutional advice." Jefferson, Wood recounts, "periodically met in an informal seminar on political theory with these friends, members of what Jefferson called 'the Patriotic party.'" As Wood writes of how Jefferson thought the French Revolution—one clearly inspired by the American Revolution—would unfold:

> When he learned that the Estates-General would convene in May 1789—the assembly of clergy, nobles, and the Third Estate of commoners hadn't met since 1614—he predicted that France in two or three years would probably enjoy "a tolerably free constitution, and that without it's having cost them a drop of blood." He had come to realize, as he told Washington in December 1788, that "the nation has been awakened by our revolution, they are enlightened, their lights are spreading, and they will not retrograde." Instead of a republic, however, he thought France would end up with a constitutional monarchy like that of England.[50]

"Sometimes," Wood concludes, "Jefferson seemed to forget that he was the U.S. minister to a foreign country; instead of maintaining an official detachment from French affairs, he began acting as if he himself were one of the French reformers—in violation of all diplomatic protocol."[51]

The French Declaration of the Rights of Man and of the Citizen was the work of multiple people and the product of much contentious debate. "While in America," one historian writes, "Lafayette had imbibed the principles put forth during the Revolution."[52] As another source observes:

> Although Lafayette was by no means the sole author of the document, both his and Jefferson's contributions were highly significant. Lafayette's admiration for the American Declaration of Independence and his hopes for a similar French Declaration was symbolized by a dramatic gesture. In his library in Paris, it was reported, he hung a copy of the American Declaration in a half-filled frame. To visitors, he explained that the empty part of the frame was reserved for the French Declaration of Rights that he hoped his country would adopt one day.[53]

Called "one of the most important human rights documents of the eighteenth century,"[54] the Declaration of the Rights of Man and of the Citizen preceded the adoption of the French constitution.[55] "On 9 July 1789," one source notes, "General Lafayette—the hero of the American War of Independence—introduced a draft of a French declaration of human rights, and thereby inaugurated a debate that raged for over six weeks and concluded with the Declaration of the Rights of Man and Citizen on 26 August." "[A] declaration of the rights of the citizen is not an elaboration of the law, but an elaboration of principles," Emmanuel Joseph Sieyès, commonly referred to as Abbé Sieyès, said in that debate in his "Reconnaissance et exposition raisonnée des Droits de l'Homme et du Citoyen" (Reasoned Exposition of the Rights of Man and Citizen), delivered before the National Assembly on July 21, 1789.[56]

The French Declaration of the Rights of Man and the Citizen, like other expressions of rights that followed in France, was shaped by Montesquieu's and Beccaria's ideas.[57] For instance, section 8 of the French Declaration, adopted on August 26, 1789, by the National Assembly of France as part of the assembly's final work product, allowed only "strictly and obviously necessary" punishments.[58] As section 8 has been translated: "The law shall provide for such punishments only as are strictly and obviously necessary, and no one shall suffer punishment except it be legally inflicted in virtue of a law passed and promulgated before the commission of the offense."[59] As another translation of section 8, worded in a slightly different way, reads: "The Law must prescribe only the punishments that are strictly and evidently necessary; and no one may be punished except by virtue of a Law drawn up and promulgated before the offense is committed, and legally applied."[60] Those principles—which have been called "[t]he Principles of 1789"—were later repeated by Olympe de Gouges (1748–1793), the French playwright and political activist, in her 1791 Declaration of the Rights of Woman and the Female Citizen.[61] Gouges, the French activist, sought equal rights for women, writing: "[L]a femme a le droit de monter sur l'échafaud; elle doit avoir également celui de monter à la Tribune" ("A Woman with the right to mount the scaffold ought likewise to have that of mounting the Rostrum.").[62] Ironically, she was executed by the guillotine during the French Revolution's Reign of Terror.[63]

Because the French Declaration was adopted in such close proximity to the ratification of the U.S. Bill of Rights, and because American revolutionaries, such as Thomas Jefferson and Thomas Paine, played such important historical roles during the French Revolution, the American and French experiences are closely intertwined—and one informs the other. Just as legitimate questions were being raised in America about the needless severity of punishments, especially in light of Montesquieu well-stated maxim and Beccaria's further publicizing of it, so too, tellingly, were those same concerns being raised in France, England, and elsewhere in Europe. Indeed, the Marquis de Condorcet—in an initial draft of the French *Déclaration des droits de l'homme et du citoyen*—suggested, in line with Beccaria's views, a clause limiting the death penalty to crimes of murder that threatened the safety of the State. Condorcet further proposed that capital punishment not be associated with treatment "qui la rende plus lente ou plus douloureuse" ("making it slower or more painful"). The guillotine, named for Joseph Ignace Guillotin (1738–1814), the French physician who proposed its adoption to prevent unnecessary pain, was introduced in France in 1792. The guillotine was intended to equalize punishments between classes of citizens, and to eliminate the lingering, painful deaths associated with hanging and the gallows.[64]

The Marquis de Condorcet himself voted against the death penalty for Louis XVI, and he believed that the death penalty—what he called an "irreparable punishment"—"can be legitimized only by absolute necessity." "The penalty of death," Condorcet emphasized, "is the only one that makes an injustice absolutely irreparable; from which it follows that the existence of the death penalty implies that one is exposed to committing an irreparable injustice; from which it follows that it is unjust to establish it." In *Condorcet and Modernity*, an Enlightenment expert, David Williams, observes that Condorcet had become "closely involved" in the "controversy, stoked by Voltaire, arising from the case of La Barre," the teenager "tortured and burnt by the Abbeville magistrates for vandalism of a crucifix." As Williams notes of Condorcet's awakening as a result of the La Barre affair:

> The affair turned Condorcet into Voltaire's apostle and *trompette* in Paris, and confirmed his increasingly public identification with the reformist/dissident camp. It was at this time that Cesare Beccaria's influential *Dei delitti e delle pene* (1764) started to make an impact on philosophical circles in Paris. Impressed by Beccaria's argument about proportionality in the matter of judicial punishments, Condorcet's opposition to French medieval court practices, the judicial use of torture, the infamous rules of evidence, and in particular to the profligate use of the death penalty, hardened. Condorcet knew Beccaria personally, having met him in Sophie de Grouchy's circle. His own *Réflexions sur la jurisprudence criminelle* appeared in 1775.[65]

There is, in fact, ample evidence to show that, from an historical perspective, punishments that were not strictly and obviously necessary were to be considered cruel or tyrannous.[66] As William Schabas, an expert on international criminal justice and the death penalty, has written in *The Death Penalty as Cruel Treatment and Torture*:

> The close ties between the revolutionaries in the thirteen colonies and their comrades in France led to considerable synergy in the drafting of the respective bills of rights. One of the important contributors to the French Déclaration des droits de l'homme et du citoyen of 1789 was the Marquis de Lafayette, who had not only participated in the American Revolution but was actually assisted in his work by the United States ambassador to Paris, Thomas Jefferson.[67] Article 8 of the Déclaration ensures protection against penalties that are not "strictement et évidemment nécessaires" ([strictly and obviously necessary]). It was this provision, when applied to the French Code pénal of 1791, which resulted in a generous reduction in the length of sentences and the suppression of a range of grotesque corporal punishments indulged in by the ancien régime.[68] The context of the adoption of article 8 of the Déclaration indicates that there was concern both about the proportionality of sentences, as such, and about the method by which punishment was imposed.[69]

Of course, the French Revolution—as its horrendous Reign of Terror progressed—strayed far afield from the dictates of section 8 of the French Declaration.[70] But the Enlightenment impulses that led to its initial promulgation are significant because those impulses were present in both colonial and early America and in France.

The American and French Revolutions—and the adoption of the U.S. Bill of Rights and the French Declaration of Rights—took place in relatively close proximity to one another.[71] The American Revolution led to the French Revolution, and figures associated with the former were also associated with the latter.[72] In 1785, just two years after the Treaty of Paris (1783) had ended the Revolutionary War, Thomas Jefferson—the principal drafter of the Declaration of Independence—was appointed to be the Minister for the United States of America in France.[73] While in Paris, Jefferson—like his successors, William Short, Gouverneur Morris, James Monroe, and Charles Cotesworth Pinckney—had a front row seat as the French Revolution (1789–1799), with all its chaos and pamphleteering, rhetoric and speeches, arrests and executions, and fulsome heartbreak and tragedy, unfolded. In striving to preserve "the natural and inalienable rights of man," the French Declaration sought to equalize the treatment of offenders and to cull out features and punishments of the "old criminal system" that were seen as discriminatory or inconsistent with the necessity-for-punishment principle.

On September 13, 1789, just two months after the Storming of the Bastille on July 14, 1789, Jefferson wrote to Thomas Paine to explain how the French "have decided here some principal outlines of their constitution."[74] As one legal historian stresses: "The early days of the French and American republics were intertwined, and it would be erroneous to think that the developments which then took place in the two countries can now fully be understood in isolation."[75] On August 26, 1792, the French National Assembly actually conferred the title of citizen on Thomas Paine, who, the following month, acknowledged "the honor which the late National Assembly" had conferred upon him by adopting him as "a citizen of France." "Convinced that the cause of France is the cause of all mankind, and that liberty cannot be purchased by wish," Paine said that he gladly shared with the French people "the dangers and honors necessary to success."[76] As that legal historian, Vincent Robert Johnson, notes: "The enactment of a bill of rights was proposed to the French National Assembly by the Marquis de Lafayette on July 11, 1789."[77]

The American Declaration of Independence, the French Declaration of the Rights of Man and of the Citizen, the U.S. Bill of Rights, and the American and French constitutions were all part of revolutionary, rights-based impulses. They were, at their core, part of an effort to secure "inalienable" individual rights on both sides of the Atlantic. For example, in close proximity to the ratification of the U.S. Constitution, following the appointment of a French committee to consider various drafts, and following discussions in France's National Assembly, is has been noted that the "Declaration of the Rights of Man and of Citizens (Declaration of Rights) was passed on August 26, 1789."[78] In his article, "Reconceptualizing the Eighth Amendment," one scholar, Alexander Reinert, specifically observes that it was, consequently, not just the English Bill of Rights of 1689 that informs the U.S. Bill of Rights, but the broader Anglo-American and European experience. As Reinert writes: "one other document with foreign provenance was likely influential among the founding generation: the *French Declaration of the Rights of Man*, which required that punishments be 'strictly and obviously necessary.' "[79] "[T]he architects of the Declaration of the Rights of Man, Joseph-Emmanuel Sieyès and the Marquis de Lafayette," another legal commentator has emphasized, "were both heavily influenced by the leading political minds" in the United States—minds that had, themselves, been shaped by a wide array of Enlightenment texts, including Beccaria and Montesquieu's books. In drafting the French Declaration of the Rights of Man, the Marquis de Lafayette—a man who himself opposed the death penalty and executions[80] and who revered the changes wrought by the American Revolution—specifically consulted with America's own experienced revolutionary, Thomas Jefferson, among others.[81]

By the mid-eighteenth century, the world had become increasingly interconnected as newspapers and periodicals sprung up to transmit the news of the day. Americans paid close attention to events transpiring in England, France, Italy, and elsewhere in Europe, and the French Declaration of the Rights of Man and of the Citizen, as well as other French legal documents, were reprinted in American newspapers. For example, on September 20, 1793, under the heading "The NEW Constitution of France," a newspaper in New Bedford, Massachusetts, reprinted the French Declaration. An editorial note at the beginning observed: "*The following is an official copy of the* NEW CONSTITUTION of FRANCE—*extracted from a Paris Paper received by way of Newyork*——*This Plan was formed, submitted to the Convention, discussed Article by Article, and passed as the Constitutional Act*—*(waiting only for the sanction of the people) within the space of a fortnight.*" Among the provisions it reprinted in translated form: Article XV, which—as translated from French into English—read, "The law should only declare punishments strictly and evidently necessary; the punishment should be proportioned to the crime and useful to society."[82] That principle, of course, was already an incredibly familiar one to Americans because it was derived from Montesquieu's and Beccaria's widely publicized necessity-for-punishment maxim, a maxim that had been translated long before the French Revolution got underway.

An understanding of the American Revolution consequently informs one's understanding of the French Revolution—and vice versa.[83] "So similar are the guarantees in the Declaration of Rights to those contained in the American Constitution and Bill of Rights," one commentator, Vincent Robert Johnson, explains of the close connection between the French Declaration and the U.S. Constitution, "that it would be astonishing if the two were not related."[84] Noting the connection between the French Declaration of Rights and the U.S. Bill of Rights, Johnson specifically describes how "the roots of *both* the Declaration of Rights and the American Bill of Rights can be traced to provisions in various American *state* constitutions which had been adopted by the former colonies following America's break with Britain." "As early as 1778," Johnson relays, "at least seven American state constitutions had been translated into French and distributed in France." "Some of these documents—the first written constitutions in the world—reached Paris within weeks of their adoption," he writes.[85] Benjamin Franklin, the scientist and inventor turned diplomat, had personally ordered that early American constitutions be translated into French and then be distributed throughout Europe to help publicize them.[86] "The French prohibition of unnecessary penalties echoes American state constitutional provisions condemning excessive fines or bail or cruel and unusual punishment, or directing that a penal sanction should be proportionate to the offense," Johnson emphasizes after comparing the provisions of early American state constitutions with section 8 of the French Declaration. Another source calls the French Declaration "the most famous document of the early stages of the French Revolution," noting that "[w]hile it was probably suggested by the Bills of Rights attached to American state constitutions, it indicates the existing abuses in France at that time."[87]

The French Revolution—at least as initially conceived—focused not only on achieving liberty for French citizens, but on doing away with torture and corporal punishments and on curtailing the use of state-sanctioned executions. Indeed, on May 30, 1791, just months before the ratification of the Eighth Amendment, the French lawyer and politician Maximilien Robespierre (1758–1794) gave an impassioned speech to his fellow lawmakers on the need to abolish capital punishment. As Robespierre pleaded on that date: "I have come to beg the legislators to efface from our penal code the bloody laws that sanction judicial murder, laws which are repugnant to the Frenchman's way of life and to their new constitution."[88] Echoing the sentiments of Beccaria, Robespierre argued: "I wish to prove to them: first, that the penalty of death is fundamentally unjust; second, that it is not the most restraining of penalties, and that it multiples crimes more than it prevents them." "Thus, in the eyes of truth and of justice, these scenes of death that society orders with so much ceremony are nothing else but cowardly assassinations, nothing but solemn crimes, committed, not by some individuals but by entire nations, with due legal formalities."[89] As Robespierre concluded of lawmakers' authorization of state-sanctioned killing in 1791: "Above all, where they offend humanity by an excess of rigor, it is proof that human dignity is there unknown, that the dignity of the citizen does not exist; it is proof that the legislature is only a master commanding its slaves, punishing them pitilessly according to its own whim. I conclude that the penalty of death must be abolished."[90]

In 1791, Robespierre was not alone in seeking major reform of France's penal system, just as he was not alone in linking the use of capital punishment with the stripping of a person's human dignity. As one source puts it:

> On June 12 and 13, 1791, Etienne Michel Le Pelletier de Saint-Fargeau (1760–93), in the name of the committees for criminal legislation and the constitution, presented to the Assembly a penal code that, according to Jacques-Guy Petit, was a "synthesis of Enlightenment thought." Le Pelletier based the new system of punishments on the principles of "humane" punishments, "proportionate" to the crime, "fixed and determined," "durable" and "public" and essentially based on a deprivation of freedom at three different levels: jail, detention, and prison.[91]

"Although Maximilien Robespierre, Jérôme Petion, and Adrien Duport joined him in defending the abolition of capital punishment," that source reports, "this punishment remained in the repressive arsenal."[92] The death penalty was a long-entrenched punishment, and societies are often slow to change. Just as Tyburn had been the site of many executions in England, the death penalty had been frequently used in prerevolutionary France, making change an uphill battle.

Nonetheless, the French Constituent Assembly passed two acts in 1791[93] and adopted the guillotine to equalize punishments and make executions less painful,[94] with France's National Assembly having made some significant penal reforms two years earlier. As Albert Goodwin writes in *The French Revolution* of what had occurred in France in 1789: "The Assembly began its judicial reforms by abolishing torture on 9th October, and hanging as a form of capital punishment on 1st December, 1789."[95] On the latter day, the Assembly had decreed that "all crimes of the same type will be punished by the same penalty, regardless of the culprit's rank and estate."[96] After Dr. Guillotin, a physician intent on preventing unnecessary pain,[97] proposed his bill for reforming the criminal code on December 1, 1789, a report was presented on May 22-23, 1791, by Louis-Michel Lepeletier de Saint-Fargeau, demanding that capital punishment involve no more than the "simple deprivation of life"—a principle adopted on June 1st. Thereafter, the death penalty's administration was to consist of "simple deprivation of life, without any torture ever being added to it."[98] It would, frankly, have been much to Dr. Guillotin's chagrin that he—a vociferous death penalty opponent—would now be known almost exclusively by twenty-first-century societies for his association with the gruesome beheading machine that took so many lives, the lives of purported "enemies of the state."[99]

French and American Revolutionaries

The close association between the American Revolution and the French Revolution, though separated in time, is clear. In August 1792, in line with that close association, the French government conferred honorary French citizenship upon a small number of "foreign philosophers and writers who had courageously maintained the cause of freedom." Among those accorded the honor: Joseph Priestley, Jeremy Bentham, William Wilberforce, and—in America—George Washington, Alexander Hamilton, and James Madison.[100] In that same year, in the course of acknowledging that honorific action of the new French republic, Jeremy Bentham wrote to France's Minister of Interior, writing that "[t]he general good is everywhere the true object of all political action,—of all law." Emphasizing that he considered "all Frenchmen as my brethren," Bentham stressed in the course of his letter that "every punishment that is not needed is really a lawless punishment."[101] Joseph Priestley (1733–1804), a prolific writer and an English theologian, natural philosopher, and chemist, wrote an early work of political philosophy, *An Essay on the First Principles of Government, and on the Nature of Political, Civil, and Religious Liberty* (1768), and later, in 1794, emigrated to America. Bentham himself once wrote of that thinker: "Priestley was the first (unless it was Beccaria) who taught my lips to pronounce this sacred truth: That the greatest happiness of the greatest number is the foundation of morals and legislation."[102]

Joseph Priestley—in reciting "the more important maxims of *criminal law*"—was of the view that "[t]he object of criminal law is to lessen the number of crimes in future, and thereby to give every man a sense of his personal security." In words that later drew the ire of the Scottish lawyer and judge Lord Kames,[103] Priestley—though he himself believed in the necessity of capital punishment and the use of punishment to "inspire terror"—went so far as to make the following claim as to his articulated objective: "[I]f this could be done without the actual punishment of any criminal, so much evil would be prevented as his punishment implies. Consequently, punishment has no reference to the degree of moral turpitude in the criminal." "Crimes committed by violence, and also by night, ought to be punished with more severity than those committed by stealth, or in the day," Priestley offered, adding: "In order to inspire terror, it is of particular consequence that punishment should immediately follow conviction, which was the case with all the ancient nations. Thus, our Saviour, after being condemned, was immediately led to execution." "A wise and prudent legislature will endeavor to *prevent* the commission of crimes, as well as to see to the punishment of them when they are committed," Priestley advised. "Great severity, as well as great lenity, ought to be avoided in the sanction of laws," Priestley lectured, noting how "[t]he severity of laws hinders the execution of them." As Priestley, a man very familiar with the writings of Cesare Beccaria, John Howard, and other Enlightenment thinkers, emphasized in very Beccarian terms: "When punishment bears no proportion to the nature of the crime, men are punished under the idea of their being more wicked than they really are, which is contrary to the spirit of a moderate government."[104]

As for the eminent Americans named honorary French citizens, each of them had been exposed to, and influenced by, the Beccarian concept of proportionality and the idea that only necessary punishments should be inflicted. For example, George Washington—in a 1781 letter to the president of Congress—wrote of "the inconveniences arising from the want of a proper gradation of punishments in our military code." In that letter, Washington wrote: "Congress are sensible of the necessity of punishment in an army, of the justice and policy of a due proportion between the crime and the penalties, and, of course, of the necessity of proper degrees in the latter." "A variety in punishment is of utility, as well as a proportion," Washington added.[105] Likewise, James Madison had attempted in the mid-1780s to pass Jefferson's bill "for proportioning crimes and punishments in cases heretofore capital." As an editorial note to *The Papers of James Madison* notes:

> Age-old fears were aroused by this bill, which Jefferson had written after much research and with a reformer's view.... The impact of the Enlightenment, particularly Beccaria's *Tratto dei Delitti e delle Pene* (1764), with its strictures on the futility of torture and execution, remained as an ideal. Then, as now, there was much disagreement over the possibilities that a drastic change in the treatment of criminals would be effective.

Ultimately, the bill failed to pass the Virginia legislature by a single vote. In a February 15, 1787 letter to Thomas Jefferson, Madison observed that "[t]he rage agst. Horse stealers had a great influence on the fate of the Bill." "Our old bloody code is by this event fully restored," Madison then lamented to Jefferson in his letter.[106]

Alexander Hamilton himself recognized that the public was turning away from capital punishment. In 1799, Hamilton—after receiving and acknowledging receipt of a death warrant, "a warrant for the execution" for Sergeant Richard Hunt—wrote to America's then-Secretary of War, James McHenry, urging "forbearance." McHenry had sent Hamilton "a Warrant, under the signature of the President, and the seal of the War office of the United States, for the execution of Richard Hunt," who "was tried on a charge of desertion, and also of carrying away the money" intended for other soldiers. McHenry noted that, in President John Adams' letter to him, Adams had advised and "if you and General Hamilton" concur, "the execution of Hunt ... may yet be respited." In his reply, then Major General Hamilton—writing back to McHenry—emphasized: "The temper of our country is not a little opposed to the frequency of capital punishment. Public opinion, in this respect, though it must not have too much influence, is not wholly to be disregarded." "There must be," Hamilton wrote, "some caution not to render our military system odious by giving it the appearance of being sanguinary." As Hamilton's letter continued: "The idea of cruelty inspires disgust, and ultimately is not much more favorable to authority than the excess of lenity." "If, for any or all of these reasons, the utility of the measure be doubtful," Hamilton's letter continued, "in favor of life it ought to be forborne." Hamilton's concluding message:

> It is but too certain that it will not be long before other instances will occur in which the same punishment will be decreed for the same offence. To disseminate the examples of executions so far as they shall be indispensable, will serve to render them more efficacious.
>
> Under these impressions, if I hear nothing to the contrary from you by the return of the post, I shall issue an order to the following effect: "That, though the President has fully approved the sentence of Sergeant Hunt, and, from the heinous nature of his conduct, considers him as a very fit subject for punishment; yet, being unwilling to multiply examples of severity, however just, beyond what experience may show to be indispensable, and hoping that the good faith and patriotism of the soldiery will spare him the painful necessity of frequently resorting to them, he has thought fit to authorize a remission of the punishment; directing, nevertheless, that Sergeant Hunt be degraded from his station."[107]

In France itself, the American Revolution attracted considerable attention, just as Americans themselves closely followed the onset and progress of the French Revolution. And the relationships between American and French citizens—and their shared interest in the ideas of the Enlightenment, including those of Montesquieu and Beccaria—made for a vigorous, transatlantic exchange of ideas. For example, in 1811, Thomas Jefferson finished a French-to-English translation of Destutt de Tracy's *Commentary and Review of Montesquieu's Spirit of the Laws.* Printed in 1811 in Philadelphia by William Duane, that book began with two epigraphs, including this quote from Beccaria: "The most certain means of rendering a people free and happy, is to establish a perfect method of education." Its author, a French aristocrat, had been born in Paris, was a friend of the Marquis de Lafayette, and had been arrested and imprisoned during the French Revolution's Reign of Terror. He had originally published his *Commentaire sur l'esprit des lois de Montesquieu* in 1806, and in Jefferson's English translation, Antoine Louis Claude Destutt, also known as comte de Tracy or Count Destutt Tracy, described himself and his background this way: "I am a Frenchman by birth and education. I was an early friend to the revolution of France, and continued to support it, until those entrusted with its helm, had evidently changed its direction. Flying then from the tyrannies of the monster Robespierre, I found, and still enjoy, safety, freedom, and hospitality, among you." Robespierre, despite passionately calling for the death penalty's abolition in 1791, became a powerful figure on the Committee of Public Safety, the principal organ of the revolutionary government during France's Reign of Terror. A lawyer, he had welcomed the Declaration of the Rights of Man and of the Citizen, which formed the preamble of the French constitution of September 3, 1791. But he then notoriously presided over the Reign of Terror, during which approximately 300,000 people were arrested and roughly 17,000 people were executed, before himself being guillotined in Paris on July 28, 1794. He met his own fate on the *Place de la Révolution* in front of a jeering mob.[108]

Describing his motivation for taking up the subject at hand, Destutt de Tracy, in his *Commentaire*, wrote: "Reading and contemplation have been the occupations of my life, and mostly on those subjects which concern the condition of man. Montesquieu's immortal work on the Spirit of Laws, could not fail, of course, to furnish matter for profound consideration." "I have admired his vivid imagination, his extensive reading, and dexterous use of it," Destutt de Tracy wrote of Montesquieu before adding a note of caution: "But I have not been blind to his paradoxes, his inconsistencies, and whimsical combinations. And I have thought the errors of his book, the more important to be corrected, as its truths are numerous, and of powerful influence on the opinions of society." In mid-August 1830, Destutt de Tracy's son, Victor, himself proposed the abolition of capital punishment in the French Chamber of Deputies—an effort supported by the Marquis de Lafayette, the American Revolutionary War hero. In 1826, the Genevan thinker Jean-Jacques de Sellon had likewise offered a prize for essays favoring the death penalty's opposition, and a number of French and Genevan writers—their interest piqued by the prize—entered the competition.[109]

In a letter to Destutt de Tracy, written from Monticello on January 26, 1811, Jefferson had this to say about the work he had translated (and about his own efforts to secure the publication of the translation):

> I cannot express to you the satisfaction which I recieved from it's perusal. I had, with the world, deemed Montesquieu's a work of much merit; but saw in it, with every thinking man, so much of paradox, of false principle, & misapplied fact, as to render it's value equivocal on the whole. Williams and others had nibbled only at it's errors. a radical correction of them therefore was a great desideratum. this want is now supplied, and with a depth of thought, precision of idea, of language & of logic, which will force conviction into every mind. I declare to you, Sir, in the spirit of truth & sincerity, that I consider it the most precious gift the present age has recieved. but what would it have been, had the author, or would the author, take up the whole scheme of Montesquieu's work, & following the correct analysis he has here developed, fill up all it's parts according to his sound views of them. Montesquieu's celebrity would be but a small portion of that which would immortalize the author. and with whom? with the rational and highminded spirits of the present & all future ages. with those whose approbation is both incitement & reward to virtue and ambition. is then the hope desperate? to what object can the occupations of his future life be devoted so usefully to the world, so splendidly to himself? but I must leave to others, who have higher claims on his attention, to press these considerations.
>
> My situation, far in the interior of the country, was not favorable to the object of getting this work translated and printed. Philadelphia is the least distant of the great towns of our states where there exists any enterprize in this way; and it was not till the spring following the reciept of your letter, that I obtained an arrangement for it's execution. the translation is just now com-

> pleated. the sheets came to me by post, from time to time, for revisal; but not being accompanied by the original, I could not judge of verbal accuracies. I think however it is substantially correct, without being an adequate representation of the excellencies of the original; as indeed no translation can be.[110]

Thomas Jefferson also later translated another of Count Destutt Tracy's works as *A Treatise on Political Economy* (1817).[111]

In Jefferson's translation of Count Destutt Tracy's *Commentary and Review of Montesquieu's Spirit of Laws*, Destutt Tracy—as his words were translated into English—made his object clear in a set of preliminary observations:

> My object in undertaking this work, was to examine and reflect on each of the great objects which had been discussed by Montesquieu; to form my own opinions, to commit them to writing, and in short, to accomplish a clear and settled judgment upon them. It was not very long before I perceived, that a collection of these opinions would form a complete treatise on politics or the social science, which would be of some valuc, if the principles were all just and well digested.

After noting that Montesquieu, in his *Spirit of Laws*, had divided the types of civilizations into three forms—(1) "DEMOCRACY ... DESPOTISM"; (2) "ARISTOCRACY under several chiefs"; and (3) "REPRESENTATIVE GOVERNMENT, with one or several chiefs"—Destutt Tracy further noted that Montesquieu had listed the corresponding "Characteristics of the three forms" of government and the "Motives of punishment in the three forms," respectively, as follows: (1) "Ignorance.... force" and "Human vengeance"; (2) "Opinion.... religion" and "Divine vengeance"; and (3) "Reason.... philosophy" and "Prevention of crimes." Destutt Tracy then noted that despite the fact that Montesquieu's "great and interesting views ... excite our curiosity and admiration," that Montesquieu—"the illustrious author"—"has not sufficiently discriminated between civil and criminal justice." "The criminal laws," Destutt Tracy wrote, "should be as simple as possible, and under every form of government, judgments literally enforced."

For Count Destutt Tracy, the purpose of punishment was clear. As he, as translated by Thomas Jefferson, wrote: "To provide such punishments for crimes as will prevent their repetition, should be the true object of corrective justice: but no one should be permitted to employ the public arm to subserve individual passions, for this would not be justice, but private vengeance.... and that is despotism in its essence." And on the subject of capital punishment, Destutt Tracy then offered this extended critique of Montesquieu's work:

> With regard to the severity of punishments, the first question that presents itself is, whether society has the right to take away the life of one of its members. Montesquieu has said nothing pertinent on this question, probably because he conceived his plan was always to state facts, but never to discuss rights. Although disposed to be scrupulously exact in following him, I think it unnecessary here to attempt the vindication of capital punishments against the reproaches of injustice, which have been heaped upon it, by men respectable for their motives and intelligence. This severe and afflicting measure,

ought not to have too odious a character attached to it, so long as circumstances render it necessary. I acknowlege then, that society possesses the right of previously announcing that it will punish with death, any person who shall commit a crime, the consequences of which appear sufficient to endanger the existence of society. Such persons as are unwilling to submit to the consequences of such established laws, should renounce the society which adopts it, before they render themselves liable thereto; they should always have full liberty so to do, on this and on all other occasions, without which right there is no law universally just; since there is not one, which has been freely adopted with the previous knowlege and consent of the interested: with such a condition, the institution of the punishment of death appears to me as just in itself, as that of any other punishment.

This admission does not imply, that the culprit is obliged in conscience to give up his life because the law requires his death, or to renounce self defence, because the law attacks him; those who profess such sentiments, are as extravagant as those who deny society the right of punishing with death are in theirs: both have but an imperfect idea of criminal justice. When the social body announces that it will punish such an action, in such a manner, it thenceforth declares itself in a state of war on such a point, with whoever may commit the action; but the criminal has not on that account, lost the right of personal defence; as no animated being, can be deprived of that, he is only reduced to his individual force; and the social power, which on every other occasion would have protected him, is here arrayed against him.

It remains only to examine, how far this power may be exercised against crimes, so as to effectually prevent them: in this respect, the excellent observation of Montesquieu, cannot be too much admired, that in proportion as the government is animated by the spirit of liberty, the more mild will the punishments be: and what he says on the inefficacy of barbarous, or even of cruel punishments, and the unhappy effects which they have had in multiplying, instead of diminishing crimes, because they render manners atrocious, and sentiments ferocious, are equally deserving of admiration. The necessity of punishment, he properly observes, is in proportion to the magnitude of the crime, or the temptation to commit it; and it should be a particular object of the law, that the guilty should never escape with impunity; for it is the certainty of punishment, which most effectualy deters from the commission of crimes; and it should never be forgotten, that the only reasonable motive for inflicting punishment, and the only justifiable cause, is not because the evil is thereby supposed to be repaired, for that is impossible; nor for the gratification of hatred, for that would be promoting vice, and substituting blind passion for justice, but simply.... the prevention of evil alone.

These reflections, shew the absurdity of the law of retaliation, which gives justice the appearance of savage vengeance: we are therefore astonished, to find in our illustrious author, a particular chapter on this law of savages, and not to find the illustrations which it called for. There are moments, in which the greatest genius appears to doze; Montesquieu furnishes us with an example, in the chapter following, where he approves of dishonoring innocent men, for the crimes of their fathers, or of their children. The same observations would apply to chapter XVIII. where after these words.... "Our forefathers, the Germans, seldom admitted of any but pecuniary punishments:" he adds.... "Warlike and free men, think their blood should never be spilt but with sword in hand:" nor does he perceive, that if the savages of the forest of Hessia, whom he so much extols, no one knows why, had never accepted pecuniary composition for an assassination, he would have said with more reason.... "These fierce and generous men, estimated the blood of their kindred so highly, that the life of an offender only, could atone for the offence: for they would have despised making a shameful traffic of their blood." This profound thinker is often mistaken, and, like Tacitus, appears to be too great an admirer of barbarous nations and their institutions.

Notwithstanding these trivial faults, he cannot be more admired, than he merits: I cannot, however, but reproach him again in this book, for not expressing himself with more indignation against the use of torture and confiscation, though he disapproves of both. It is certain that the power of pardoning is at least necessary, so long as the punishment of death is continued; for while the fallibility of human judges is exposed to imposition, or to be influenced through their passions to violate justice irreparably, there should be some preventative means; and this is the more indispensible, since it is allowed by the common consent of mankind, that laws themselves are at best very imperfect.

I cannot discover upon what principle it is, that Montesquieu says.... "Clemency is the destructive attribute of the monarch." In republics, where *virtue* is the basis of every thing, clemency is less necessary. Nor do his reflections on this subject please me more. In governments where liberty is held in regard, great precautions should be taken, that the power of pardon be not rendered detrimental, and that it shall not become a privilege to certain persons, or classes, for the perpetration of crimes with impunity, as too often happens in monarchies; an exception which Helvetius makes to Montesquieu with great reason.

For Destutt Tracy, Western civilization was on the advance, with societies progressing through the three forms of civilization Montesquieu identified. Men, Destutt Tracy wrote, "can at first imagine no other means than submitting to the will of all, or to the will of one who has obtained their confidence; ignorance and force prevail with democracy and despotism; then it is that men resort to punishments to avenge themselves of the wrongs which they believe they have suffered, and this is the basis of their criminal code." In "aristocracies," he added, there was only "partial" knowledge and "the idea of divine vengeance was subjoined to human vengeance, and became the foundation of the penal code." But then came the Enlightenment and an increase in human knowledge, with Destutt Tracy emphasizing:

> From time to time, the principles of nature, that is the eternal order of the universe in relation to us, has been observed, and some of its laws acknowleged. Controversy has discovered errors, and these errors have been discussed; and it was perceived, that if we do not comprehend every thing that is, we often know that which is not. Some men, more enlightened and enterprizing than others, or excited by some particular incident, have undertaken to regulate their conduct according to the discoveries which they have made; they have attempted, with various degrees of success, to give themselves a manner of being more conformable to nature, truth, and reason: behold the dawn of this last effort of the human mind, it is offences that are combated and not the offenders; if punishment takes place, it is only to prevent future evil. Such is the only principle of criminal laws, in the third epoch, which is now commencing.[112]

The Marquis de Lafayette, Destutt Tracy's friend, was himself very much opposed to capital punishment. "Lafayette," historian Marcello Maestro explains, taking note of Beccaria's influence on him, opposed capital punishment "as a matter of principle and made clear that he would hold that position 'as long as the infallibility of human judgment was not demonstrated.'" "Lafayette was aware," Maestro observes, "that the whole penal legislation was in need of reform, as had been convincingly demonstrated by Montesquieu, Beccaria, and other writers." As Maestro notes of Lafayette's work in France after returning to his native land after fighting in America's Revolutionary War: "Already familiar with the works of the best known writers, Lafayette was now able to discuss legal problems with several American statesmen, then in Paris, with whom he was in close contact—Franklin, Jefferson, Adams, and John Jay—all legal experts or interested in penal legislation." "Their views," Maestro notes, "undoubtedly helped to convince Lafayette that the French laws were in urgent need of reform, and he did, in fact, propose some changes in the penal code at the Assembly of Notables of 1787...." Though no action was taken at that juncture, on July 11, 1789, Lafayette presented to France's National Assembly the Declaration of the Rights of Man—the declaration that so notably restricted punishments to those "as are strictly and obviously necessary." Later, in 1791, the death penalty was debated, with Jacques-Pierre Prugnon, a deputy from Nancy, pleading that it be retained. "He who puts an end to the existence of a fellowman should pay for his crime with his own life," he argued. At that time, Maximilien Robespierre, a deputy from Arras and then still opposed to capital punishment, had responded: "Human life is sacred, and when the public power plays with it, then the dignity of man is diminished; the idea of murder ceases to terrify us if the law itself gives us an example of it."

The penal reform sought by the Marquis de Lafayette did not come at that time; indeed, France did not abolish the death penalty until 1981, almost two full centuries later. "[D]espite Robespierre's plea and the vote cast by Lafayette and other deputies," Marcello Maestro explains of the 1791 debate, "the majority of the Assembly approved a law that upheld the preservation of the death penalty for those guilty of murder." Much later in his public life, though, a still-determined Lafayette repeated his calls for the death penalty's abolition. "After his triumphal tour of the United States in 1824–1825," Maestro writes, "Lafayette was re-elected to the Chamber of Deputies" (in which he had served after Napoleon's fall from power) and, despite his advancing age, "he continued to show his interest in criminal legislation and never failed to intervene in the discussions on penal problems." "When the question of the death penalty was raised again in the Chamber by one of its members, Victor de Tracy," Maestro stresses, "Lafayette strongly supported the proposal to consider its abolition." Harkening back to the Enlightenment and to a more contemporary voice in the United States, Lafayette said in his speech at that time:

> This problem, gentlemen, is not new. The abolition of capital punishment has been demanded by the most respected writers of all time, it was supported in the Constituent Assembly by many deputies, and it has now been brought before the Senate of the United States by that same Edward Livingston who has done so already before the Legislature of Louisiana. What a misfortune, gentlemen, that the abolition of the death penalty was not adopted by the Constituent Assembly! How much suffering would have been avoided! And as to the people who participated in so many condemnations, how many of them would later have paid with their own blood if they could have changed the path they had taken! I must tell you, gentlemen, that after all our political storms I have, more than ever, an invincible horror for the death penalty. My honorable friend, Victor de Tracy, has asked that the problem of capital punishment be taken into consideration by this Chamber, and I will vote in favor of his motion.

When the question of the death penalty's abolition continued being debated by the Chamber of Deputies for several months, Lafayette—aware of Edward Livingston's push to abolish capital punishment in America—spoke out against putting off the question for another day. As a concerned Lafayette urged his fellow deputies:

> France has pledged to herself and to the whole world that she would march forward, without hesitation, on the road of civilization. Now some members of this Chamber are talking of adjourning the question of the death penalty; they certainly have not seen their innocent friends and relatives perish on the scaffold. Gentlemen, I confirm my support for my friend's proposal to abolish the death penalty; I feel very strongly that it should be adopted as soon as possible, especially in regard to political crimes.

"As a result of further debates," Marcello Maestro pointed out in his history, "the bill which was finally approved was rather weak: it stated that the Chamber was in favor of abolishing the death penalty 'in certain cases, especially in political matters.'" "[N]o new law was enacted," Maestro noted, with Maestro—the eminent historian—reporting, however, that "in the end the only result of these debates was to show to the people at large that a good number of legislators were concerned about the death penalty and were in favor of its abolition."[113]

In *Memoirs of General Lafayette*, it is reported—in another English translation—that the following speech against capital punishment was made by the Marquis de Lafayette:

> I look upon the question of capital punishment to have for its ground an isolated principle, or rather sentiment, which is independent of those judicial reforms of which I, as well as the honorable gentleman, see the necessity. I shall continue to support it, until I am convinced of the infallibilty of the human judgment. This question, gentlemen, is not a new one. At all periods has the abolition of capital punishment been advocated by the most eminent statesmen. It was proposed in the Constituent Assembly by several Deputies, the names of three of whom I will mention: Adrian Duport, one of the most enlightened magistrates; M. de Tracy, the father of my honorable friend, the author of the admirable commentary upon Montesquieu; and lastly, the virtuous Larochefoucauld, that true type of a great and excellent citizen, so cruelly and so basely murdered as Gisors, after the 10th of August. The Senate of the United States is at present occupied with the consideration of this question, which has been proposed by Edward Livingston, who is now completing the work he began in the legislature of the state of Louisiana.
>
> "How unfortunate it was, gentlemen, that the Constituent Assembly did not adopt the abolition of capital punishment! What irreparable misery might we then have been spared! and what would not they who concurred in those innumerable and various condemnations which subsequently took place—what would not they shortly after have given, even to the sacrifice of their lives, to recall their own act! I confess, gentlemen, that ever since the period of our political tempests I have felt an invincible horror of the punishment of death. Our present revolution bears a very different character from all preceding revolutions. In it we have beheld a union of patriotism and courage, with the greatest generosity, and we could do nothing more in character with this last revolution than now, at this early period, to illustrate it by the great act of humanity by my honorable friend. I vote for the consideration of the question.[114]

With time came more impassioned calls for penal reform. In 1829 and 1830, Edward Livingston, whom scholar Paul Christian Jones describes as "one of the prominent voices for abolition in the early decades of the nineteenth century," engaged in an intense advocacy campaign, writing to American writers, including Washington Irving and James Fenimore Cooper, to convince them to join the anti-death penalty cause. "[T]he department of literature," Livingston wrote to Cooper, "is one that enables you to impress most forcibly on the mind the truths you may wish to inculcate." In his appeal, Livingston suggested that Cooper take a shot at "exemplifying (in a work written expressly with that view) the evils of capital punishment" and to focus on the death penalty's "irremediable nature." Livingston felt that, in Cooper's capable hands, even "the hardiest advocate for capital punishment" would "pause in his desire to inflict it." In the early 1820s, Livingston had drafted for Louisiana what become known as the Livingston Code despite the fact that the state legislature there failed to adopt it. In Livingston's work, both at the state and federal level, he drew upon a host of ideas, including from the writings of Montesquieu, Beccaria, Voltaire, and Blackstone. Though Livingston later took up the cause of the death penalty's abolition in Washington, D.C. as a congressman, he became the 11th U.S. Secretary of State in 1831, depriving him of the ability to fully and personally advocate for his ideas in Congress—ideas that were, at that time, ahead of his time. As a result, Livingston's proposed measures never became law, though Livingston's advocacy drew praise from many quarters.[115] What had started in France with Montesquieu as a simply stated maxim, had influenced Cesare Beccaria's anti-death penalty advocacy in *Dei delitti e delle pene*, which, in turn, had shaped the thinking of an American lawmaker and statesman.

CHAPTER 5

"Evolving Standards of Decency":

The U.S. Constitution's Eighth Amendment

A Transplant from the Mother Country

The English Bill of Rights of 1689 included a prohibition on the infliction of "cruel and unusual punishments."[1] That provision was a byproduct of the Glorious Revolution of 1688, a revolution that overthrew King James II of England, a Catholic, and installed two Protestants, the Dutch stadtholder William III of Orange-Nassau, and his wife, Mary II, as England's new king and queen.[2] On February 13, 1689, William and Mary, while seated on armchairs "under a Canopy in the Banqueting-House," listened as a clerk read a declaration recounting how King James II had abrogated the throne and violated the rights of the English people.[3] To vindicate "their Ancient Rights and Liberties," the "Lords Spiritual and Temporal, and Commons"—those who had joined forces with William of Orange to put parliamentary limits on monarchical power—publicly declared their rights, the tenth of which read: "That Excessive Bail ought not to be required, nor Excessive Fines imposed, nor cruel and unusual Punishments inflicted."[4] It was this language that would become so widely known in colonial America, and that would end up—in slightly different wording—in the U.S. Constitution's Eighth Amendment.

The history of the Glorious Revolution of 1688 is critical to understanding the impulses behind the Eighth Amendment's prohibitions. James II, whose own father, Charles I of the House of Stuart, had been convicted of high treason and beheaded in 1649 outside the Banqueting House near the end of the English Civil War (1642–1651), was the last Roman Catholic king of England, Scotland, and Ireland. While Charles I, the Protestant king who ruled from 1625 until his death, had quarreled bitterly with Parliament, believed in the "divine right of kings," and was indicted for his "wicked practices" and acting in a tyrannical manner "against the public interest, common right, liberty, justice, and peace of the people," James II—his power-hungry son—had secretly converted to Catholicism in 1668 or 1669 and, through his own actions and abuses, also alienated the British people. James II's policies as well as his dedication to the Catholic faith, reflected in his issuance, in 1687, of a Declaration of Indulgence ordered to be read by Anglican clergymen from their pulpits, led to great unrest amongst his Protestant subjects. When seven bishops, including the Archbishop of Canterbury, refused to comply with the royal order, James had them arrested and taken to the Tower of London, though they were later acquitted on the seditious libel charges.[5]

James II, previously the Duke of York, the heir to the crown in waiting, had ascended to the throne in February 1685 after the death of his brother, Charles II. The leader of the Restoration (1660–1685), Charles II had, decades earlier, gone into exile in France after Oliver Cromwell rose to power following Cromwell's decisive victory at the Battle of Worcester (1651). The Restoration, in which the English, Scottish and Irish monarchies were all restored under King Charles II, had begun in 1660 following Cromwell's rule (and his son Richard Cromwell's brief, 264-day rule) as the Lord Protector of the short-lived Commonwealth of England, Scotland, and Ireland. Later in 1685, James II had put down rebellions led by an English nobleman, James Scott, the Duke of Monmouth, and one of the duke's staunchest allies, Archibald Campbell, the 9th Earl of Argyll, in Scotland. The Duke of Monmouth, the nephew of James II, was known as the "bastard" son of Charles II and sought to depose his uncle.[6] Both the Duke of Monmouth and the Earl of Argyll, the head of a Scottish clan, were put to death for high treason—the duke in the Tower of London, with his executioner, Jack Ketch, clumsily delivering at least five axe blows (and finally resorting to the use of knife) before the duke's head was severed, and the earl at Edinburgh's Market Cross, where he, as the hereditary chief of Clan Campbell, was executed with "the maiden." The iron-bladed maiden was the Scottish forerunner to the guillotine and the same beheading device that had, in 1661, taken the life of the earl's own father.[7]

James II fought off the 1685 rebellions and temporarily held onto power, but it was a tenuous state of affairs—and his subsequent actions, and the ruthless, unpopular judgments of his royal judges, disillusioned large segments of the populace. After the Duke of Monmouth's failed rebellion, hundreds of rebels, including survivors of the Battle of Sedgemoor, were condemned to death by England's notorious Lord Chief Justice George Jeffreys in a series of trials known as the "Bloody Assizes." Scores of rebels were hanged, drawn and quartered, and disemboweled, with others whipped or sent to the West Indies to perform hard, slave labor.[8] The exact number of executions is unknown, but in addition to summary executions that took place after battles, more than 250 or 300 rebels were executed after the "Bloody Assizes." In addition to the severe punishment of Titus Oates, the clergyman stripped of his clerical robes and notorious ordered to be imprisoned and pilloried for life, other judgments of the King's Bench also attracted much attention.

The judgments of the King's Bench in the reign of James II were severe. For example, Thomas Dangerfield, like Titus Oates, had been fined and ordered to be whipped from Aldgate to Newgate and from Newgate to Tyburn for his own role in the fictitious Popish Plot—in his case, for his libels in a published narrative. But after his initial flogging—said to have left him "[h]alf dead"—his life came to an abrupt end on June 22, 1685, after he got into a deadly argument with an English barrister, Robert Francis, on his way back, by coach, to Newgate Prison after surviving the day's horrendous flogging. Dangerfield had been jeered at by Francis, the "hot-headed" Tory barrister, and Dangerfield responded by spitting in his face. An enraged Francis then struck Dangerfield in the face with a cane, hitting him in or near his eye. The walking-stick hit with such force—surgeons later identified the blow as the cause of Thomas Dangerfield's death—that an already weakened Dangerfield died just a few hours later. For his own conduct, Francis himself was later put on trial for murder, convicted of the charge, and sentenced to death. Despite subsequent efforts to secure a pardon for Francis, King James II refused those entreaties and allowed the execution of the barrister, of Gray's Inn, to go forward.[9]

James II's "attempts to impose absolute monarchy" and his support for Catholicism in a largely Protestant nation led—as one history puts it—to a "wave of popular revulsion" and to "the Revolution Settlement of 1688–89."[10] As two writers observe of James II, who sought, like his Stuart father and brother, to reign with absolute power, "[t]his was obnoxious to Parliament, which since the English Civil War saw itself as the senior partner in the division of power between the King and the legislature."[11] Indeed, the heartless cruelty displayed by George Jeffreys of the King's Bench made him—as one source aptly observes—"England's most reviled judge." Jeffreys took perverse pleasure in tormenting those who appeared before him, and he especially liked giving detailed descriptions of the gruesome punishments that would be faced by those he sentenced. To enter Jeffreys's courtroom, historian Thomas Macaulay once emphasized, "was to enter the den of a wild beast, which none could tame, and which was as likely to be roused by caresses as by attacks." His "yell of fury," Macaulay wrote, "sounded like the thunder of judgment day." "[T]here was a fiendish exultation in the way in which he pronounced sentence on offenders," Macaulay stressed, observing that "he loved to scare them into fits by dilating with luxuriant amplification on all the details of what they were to suffer." A heavy drinker, Jeffreys's bombastic behavior and sadistic streak were on full display in Lady Alice Lisle's case. Reportedly "beside himself with fury" when the jury initially hesitated to convict, Jeffreys bullied witnesses and browbeat jurors into issuing the guilty verdict that sealed her fate. "If I had been among you, and she had been my own mother," Jeffreys callously pronounced after the verdict came in, later bragging about the number of traitors he'd sent to their deaths, "I should have found her guilty."[12]

In the Glorious Revolution of 1688, William III, a Dutch stadtholder and the Prince of Orange, had, at the invitation and behest of seven English nobles, including the Earl of Devonshire, brought an army to the British Isles with the pledge of loyalty and support. In the face of that imminent threat and with few remaining allies, James II fled to France, involuntarily abdicating his throne. His hand forced by powerful parliamentary and Protestant forces, the crown—with the consent of assertive members of Parliament—would be put into the hands of William and his younger wife, Mary, James II's own daughter. In 1677, Mary, as the then-heir to the throne, had married William, her cousin, in a private ceremony at St. James's Palace.[13] The English Bill of Rights, installing William and Mary as co-regents, detailed the wrongs committed by James II and those around him and specifically recited, among other things, these three misdeeds and affronts to liberty: "And excessive baile hath beene required of persons committed in criminall cases to elude the benefitt of the lawes made for the liberty of the subjects." "And excessive fines have beene imposed." "And illegall and cruell punishments inflicted."[14] After America's thirteen colonies declared their independence in July 1776, in the following century, it was the similarly worded prohibitions against excessive bail, excessive fines, and cruel and unusual punishments—

the ones explicitly set forth in section 10 of the English Bill of Rights—that would end up in so many of America's revolutionary constitutions and, in due course, in the U.S. Constitution's Eighth Amendment.[15]

It would be George Mason, of Fairfax County, who after being appointed to a committee tasked with preparing "a DECLARATION OF RIGHTS" for Virginia, had drafted that state's Declaration of Rights (1776), section 9 of which—exactly tracking section 10 of the English Bill of Rights—expressly read: "That excessive bail ought not to be required, nor excessive fines imposed, nor cruel and unusual punishments inflicted."[16] It is unclear what prompted Mason to include that particular provision in Virginia's declaration, but Mason was known to be familiar with English history, and it was a provision that had—he well knew—been included in the English Bill of Rights. "The Stuart Kings, Judge Jeffreys, the Bloody Assizes, and Titus Oates," political scientist Joseph Melusky and U.S. Magistrate Judge Keith Alan Pesto have written, "remained in public memory through the eighteenth century." "To many Americans in 1776," they explain, "the reason for independence from England was their perception that the abuses of the Stuart kings were being replicated by King George's ministers." "As a result," they note, American states, conscious of that history, "imitated the English Bill of Rights's guarantee against cruel and unusual punishment as cheap insurance against would-be Jeffreys."[17] In the late eighteenth century, just as Titus Oates was still portrayed as a notorious figure,[18] so too was George Jeffreys.[19]

Like seventeenth-century Englishmen, eighteenth-century Americans vociferously opposed "excessive" bail and fines and "cruel and unusual punishments," though those legal concepts were left undefined in early American constitutions—just as they had been in the English Bill of Rights of 1689. Prior to the Revolutionary War (1775–1783), American colonists, as British subjects living in the Age of the Enlightenment, felt grossly abused and oppressed by George III.[20] After unsuccessfully seeking fair and equitable treatment in comparison to those in the British Isles, the colonists rebelled, declared their independence, promulgated bills of rights and constitutions containing important legal protections, and became American citizens.[21] In light of that history and the fervent desire of the colonists to safeguard their individual rights, privileges, and liberties, it is hardly surprising that the long-standing English prohibitions against "excessive" fines and bail and "cruel and unusual punishments" were widely copied—sometimes verbatim—in American declarations of rights and in constitutions in the newly forged republic, the United States of America.[22] American lawyers and lawmakers were well versed in English law, so it is easy to see why, when they drafted legal protections, they tapped language with which they were so familiar. While the landmark English Declaration of Rights targeted James II, its American counterpart, the Declaration of Independence, which created the United States of America and laid the foundation for early American constitutions, took aim at King George III.

As noted, the legal protections against "excessive" bail and fines and "cruel and unusual punishments" first found their way into American law through the Virginia Declaration of Rights.[23] That declaration of rights was drafted in 1776 by George Mason, the wealthy plantation owner, before the issuance of the American Declaration of Independence in July of that year.[24] When the United States of America came into being in 1776, it was the *state* constitutions—and the *state* declarations of rights—that were of paramount importance. Indeed, the Articles of Confederation, formally known as the Articles of Confederation and Perpetual Union, were not even approved by the Second Continental Congress until the following year, in 1777, and did not actually come into force until 1781. The safeguards against excessive bail and fines, as well as "cruel" and "unusual punishments," also found a home in other bills of rights or state constitutions, ones that variously prohibited "excessive" penalties and "cruel and unusual," "cruel or unusual," or simply "cruel" punishments.[25] "[I]n the late eighteenth century," Yale Law School professor Akhil Amar has written, "every schoolboy in America knew that the English Bill of Rights' 1689 ban on excessive bail, excessive fines, and cruel and unusual punishments—a ban repeated virtually verbatim in the Eighth Amendment—arose as a response to the gross misbehavior of the infamous Judge Jeffreys."[26]

The wording of American prohibitions against "cruel" or "unusual" punishments, or both, was not uniform.[27] Different lawmakers drafted the early American state constitutions, and different legislators were involved in drafting legislation for Congress. For example, the Northwest Ordinance of 1787, governing newly acquired Western lands and famously barring slavery, included an express prohibition against "cruel *or* unusual punishments."[28] Nathan Dane, of Massachusetts, was one of the main drafters of the Northwest Ordinance, and he used the laws of Massachusetts as a model for portions of it. The Massachusetts Constitution of 1780, most notably, prohibited "cruel or unusual punishments."[29] But in the U.S. Constitution's Eighth Amendment, adopted by Congress in 1789[30] and ratified in 1791,[31] the legal bar was expressed as one against "cruel *and* unusual punishments."[32] In drafting the U.S. Bill of Rights, James Madison—a major participant in the Constitutional Convention in Philadelphia and in efforts to secure the U.S. Constitution's ratification, thus earning him his reputation as the Father of the U.S. Constitution[33]—found, like George Mason before him, the prohibition against "cruel and unusual punishments" to be a worthy one.[34] His chosen language—now set forth in the Constitution's Eighth Amendment—came not from Massachusetts, but from the Virginia Declaration of Rights. Madison, however, made his own tweak, jettisoning the hortatory word "ought" in the respective English and Virginia provisions and replacing it with a "shall not" directive, making the bar on the infliction of "cruel and unusual punishments" an absolute prohibition.[35]

Of course, the notions of cruelty and unusualness long pre-date the English Bill of Rights (1689), the predecessor of the U.S. Constitution's Cruel and Unusual Punishments Clause. Before the English safeguard against the infliction of "cruel and unusual punishments" was put in place, British writers frequently used the words "cruel" and "unusual." One seventeenth-century dictionary associated *cruel* with "anger," "wrath," and "[h]atred,"[36] while another defined cruel, a commonly used word, simply as "cruel."[37] (Lexicographers would not approve, but many, no doubt, thought identifying cruelty was relatively easy, self-evident even, and felt that they—and everyone else—knew precisely what the word "cruel" meant.) Other books published before the Glorious Revolution of 1688 also liberally used the words "cruel" and "unusual," with one source speaking, for example, in terms of "unusual cruelty."[38] In addition, the words "cruel" and "unusual"—commonplace terms in English-speaking societies—appear in a number of religious[39] and secular, or non-religious, tracts.[40]

In one history published in London in 1678, the word "cruel" appears literally dozens of times.[41] There are references to "cruel disposition," "cruel severity," "cruel death," "cruel trade," "cruel Prisons," "cruel Creditors," "cruel Persecutor," "cruel Massacres," "cruel sentence," "cruel Father," "cruel wife," "cruel Tyrant," "cruel torments," "cruel tortures," and "cruel execution."[42] In one passage, there is a description of a man condemned to die for writing this rhyme about King Richard III: "*The Cat, the Rat; and* Lovel *our Dog / Rule all* England *under the Hog.*"[43] That man, the history reported, "was put to a most cruel death; for being hang'd and cut down alive, his bowels rip't out and cast into the fire, when the executioner put his hand into the bulk of his body, to pull out his heart."[44] In another passage, there is a reference to the "cruel custom" of another country's king "to put to death every Tenth Stranger, that came into his Dominions."[45] In that history alone, there are also multiple references to "unusual." Among many others, one encounters "unusual Diseases," "unusual means," "unusual manner," "unusual horrors," and "unusual cruelty."[46] Chapter XXXVI is itself titled "Of the different and unusual ways, by which some men have come to their deaths."[47] If something was cruel, or if something was unusual, it was seen as an outlier or something to be condemned or denounced.

The "cruel and unusual punishments" prohibition in the English Bill of Rights was seen from an early date—as Sir William Blackstone pointed out—as restricting the *discretionary* sentencing authority of abusive judges. For example, in *On the Powers and Duties of Juries, and on the Criminal Laws of England*, Sir Richard Phillips—the former sheriff of London and Middlesex—wrote: "The practice of banishing persons convicted of misdemeanors to distant prisons, is evidently contrary to the tenth clause of the Bill of Rights, which prohibits the infliction of cruel and *unusual* punishments."[48] As Phillips explained: "Of course this clause had reference only to *discretional* punishments, and not to those defined by law, and consequently applies particularly to punishments inflicted for misdemeanors, and still more particularly to discretionary punishments in regard to liberty, the only punishments in which a sound discretion would ever be likely to be abused."[49] After reciting that view, Phillips then argued:

> I contend then, that the sending or banishing a man to a prison distant from the place where he committed the crime, is contrary to law, simply because it is *unusual*. In former times, when communication was difficult, it would have been *impracticable*, and therefore could not have been exercised; it is also *unreasonable*, inasmuch as a distant county is mulcted in the expence of maintaining the prisoner; and it is *inexpedient*, because, as punishments are inflicted as a warning to others, such remote punishments serve as no warning either at the place where the crime was committed, or at that where the punishment takes place.—Those who contend, that the King's Bench has a universal jurisdiction, are right—but they forget that this jurisdiction is universal only for lawful purposes: I agree with them that it is universal, for the purpose of correcting the mal-administration of Gaol-

ers and Sheriffs; that it is universal for the purpose of referring a man by sentence back again to his native county for a crime committed there,—but not universal for imposing the novel punishment of banishment for a misdemeanor, which is *unusual*,—therefore contrary to *the Bill of Rights*—therefore contrary to *law*.[50]

The former sheriff then expanded upon his assertions about the "cruel and unusual punishments" prohibition. As Richard Phillips wrote in an extended argument:

On a point in which the feelings of the people of England are at present deeply interested, I beg leave to urge some other considerations which may probably have weight with the Judges. Their Lordships are aware, 1. That they are not empowered to order any punishment, or pass any sentence, except such as are directed or sanctioned by the statute or common law; 2. That there is no law which empowers them in terms to send persons convicted of misdemeanors or libels to distant prisons; 3. That to carry into execution the legal sentences of the Courts of Law, is the province of the Executive Government; 4. That to prescribe the place of imprisonment when it is not prescribed by law, is to assume the powers of the Executive, and to combine the judicial authority with the executive power; 5. That this can only be legally done under those statutes which especially prescribe particular punishments in houses of correction, *or* in common gaols; 6. That where a statute or the common law directs imprisonment generally as a punishment, the Judges have no legal power to prescribe to the Executive Government in regard to the mode, manner, or place of imprisonment; and, 7. That Judges are legally restricted in the sentences they pass, by the very terms of the statutes, and by the ascertainable usage of the ancient common law, and have no liberty to pass sentences which prescribe the particular execution of general punishments to the Executive Government, nor which exceed, vary, or differ from the terms of the penal laws.

In regard to the duty of the Executive, it is bound by the Bill of Rights, in executing the judgments of the Courts, to conform to immemorial *usage*, and to inflict no punishment in a *cruel* or *unusual* manner; and consequently to inflict imprisonment in the common gaol, except in cases in which the law has specially conferred a discretionary power on the Judges, and these have thought it necessary and proper to exercise that discretion.[51]

The mid-1680s punishment of Titus Oates—the man notoriously sentenced by Lord Chief Justice George Jeffreys and his fellow justices to be defrocked, fined, whipped, and then to be pilloried *for every year for life*—was itself described in that era as "cruel" and "unusual."[52] In 1685, Oates—a Protestant cleric—had been tried and convicted of perjury before the King's Bench.[53] He had falsely accused, and caused the execution of, fifteen prominent Catholics for allegedly organizing, in 1679, a "Popish Plot" to overthrow King Charles II.[54] Oates's actual crime, which at one time had been treated as being punishable by death but which was not then a capital offense, was "bearing false witness against another, with an express premeditated design to take away his life, so as the innocent person be condemned and executed."[55]

At Oates's sentencing, Lord Chief Justice Jeffreys had complained that death was not available as a penalty and lamented that "a proportionable punishment of that crime can scarce by our law, as it now stands, be inflicted upon him."[56] According to Jeffreys, the judges who sat in judgment unanimously agreed that "crimes of this nature are left to be punished according to the discretion of this court, so far as that the judgment extend not to life or member."[57] One justice, taunting Oates, told him "we have taken special care of you," with Oates fined "1000 marks upon each indictment," "stript of [his] Canonical Habits," and ordered to be whipped by "the common hangman" "from Aldgate to Newgate" and then "from Newgate to Tyburn." Though not condemned to die, Oates was ordered to be imprisoned for life and to stand in the pillory annually at certain specified times and places.[58]

After the Glorious Revolution of 1688 and the adoption of the English Declaration of Rights,[59] Oates petitioned Parliament for relief from his sentence, pleading that he had received an "inhumane and unparalleled sentence." Oates's decried the "illegal proceedings and barbarous inhumanities" that, he said, were "intended as a revenge upon him," with Oates pleading: "Your Petitioner doth therefore most humbly beseech your Lordships and Honours to take his deplorable case into your generous and tender consideration, and to give him such redress therein as to your Lordships and your Honours' great wisdom, justice and goodness shall seem meet: and your Petitioner shall ever pray, &c."[60] The House of Lords rejected Oates's pleas, but a minority of Lords dissented, asserting that his sentence violated the "cruel and unusual punishments" provision of England's Declaration of Rights.[61] The House of Commons voted to annul Oates's sentence, and it also issued a report detailing its position.[62] One portion of the dissenting statement by the House of Lords, notably, described Oates' sentence as "contrary to the declaration on the twelfth of February last ... that excessive bail ought not to be required, nor excessive fines imposed, nor cruel nor unusual punishments inflicted."[63] The dissenting Lords, writing when whipping was still a lawful punishment in the British Empire, characterized Oates' treatment as "barbarous, inhuman, and unchristian," with the report of the House of Commons emphasizing that "it was illegal, cruel, and of dangerous Example, That a Freeman should be whipped in such a barbarous manner, as, in Probability, would determine in Death."[64] The House of Commons further stressed that "[i]t was of ill Example, and unusual, That an Englishman should be exposed upon a Pillory, so many times a Year, during his Life."[65] The prohibition against cruel and unusual punishments thus became a rallying cry to spare affected persons from barbarous treatment.

Titus Oates was sentenced in the seventeenth century when bodily punishments, such as executions, public whippings, and the pillory were still in widespread use in England. But it was the combination (and extent) of punishments imposed on Oates that, it seems, attracted so much public attention and that drew the ire of British MPs. Sir William Williams, in the House of Commons, specifically protested: "There may be a precedent for whipping, but for all these parts in one Judgment, let any man give us a Precedent to square with that Judgment."[66] In its report on the Titus Oates affair, the House of Commons criticized, in these words, the discretion exercised by Lord Chief Justice Jeffreys and his fellow judges: "That as soon as they had set up this Pretence to a discretionary Power, it was observable how they put it in Practice, not only in this, but in other Cases, and for other Offences, by inflicting such cruel and ignominious Punishments, as will be agreed to be far worse than Death itself to any Man who has a sense of Honour or Shame."[67] In *The History of England*, Thomas Macaulay offered his own telling historical commentary on the high-profile Titus Oates case and its relationship to the history of the English Bill of Rights. Macaulay concluded that Oates' punishment "cannot be justified" and that "the judges exceeded their legal power."[68] Infamous and degrading punishments, especially among royals, nobles, and the elite, were clearly seen by some as a fate worse than expiating one's crimes on the gallows.

Language is, and always has been and will be, subject to varying interpretations. In the decades and centuries after the ratification of the U.S. Constitution's Eighth Amendment, it would, naturally, fall to American judges to decide precisely what legal prohibitions against "excessive" bail and fines and those against cruelty and unusual punishment actually meant. Indeed, over more than 200 years, the concept of "cruel and unusual punishments" has been the subject of much litigation,[69] endless legal scholarship,[70] and tremendous public controversy in the U.S.[71] In the academic world and in the courts, a fierce battle between "originalism" and "living constitutionalism" has played out, for instance, with a University of Florida law professor, John Stinneford, writing—as just one example—about what he describes as the original meaning of both "cruel"[72] and "unusual."[73] He contends that the framers used the term "cruel" to denote "unjustly harsh"[74] and that they used the term "unusual" to mean punishments "contrary to long usage."[75] "In the seventeenth and eighteenth centuries," Stinneford observes in laying out his interpretative arguments, "the term 'unusual' had many of the meanings we currently associate with the term: 'rare,' 'uncommon,' 'out of the ordinary.'" "The word," he asserts, "also had a more specific meaning, however, as a legal term of art: 'contrary to long usage' or 'immemorial usage.'" As Stinneford, looking to history for guidance in constitutional interpretation, contends: "A review of seventeenth- and eighteenth-century legal and political history shows that this last meaning is the only one that may plausibly be attributed to the term 'unusual' in the Eighth Amendment's Cruel and Unusual Punishments Clause."[76]

In sharp contrast, Professor Akhil Amar, in one of his own law review articles, "America's Lived Constitution," writes about the Eighth Amendment through a much different interpretive lens. "In ordinary language," he explains, "the word 'unusual' focuses not merely on laws on the books but also on the law as actually applied."[77] Emphasizing that "the meaning of the Bill of Rights shifted when its words and principles were refracted through the prism of the Fourteenth Amendment," Amar, taking note of how the Eighth Amendment does not stand in isolation, has reflected on the U.S. Supreme Court's decades-old penchant in Cruel and Unusual Punishments Clause challenges for *counting* jurisdictions that either permit or prohibit a practice to assess its constitutionality. "Suppose that the policies of, say, Wyoming and California differ dramatically on a rights-related issue," Amar observes, posing a hypothetical before raising these important questions as regards interpreting the Constitution's Eighth Amendment: "Should the norms and practices of Wyoming's half-million inhabitants be given the same weight, Senate-style, as those of California's thirty-six million residents? Or should a proper tally reflect the population differential, House-style?" "This issue," Amar explains, "has pointedly arisen in cases pondering whether a given form of criminal punishment practiced in some states but not others violated the Eighth Amendment, which prohibits 'cruel and unusual punishment.'"[78]

Modern Eighth Amendment Jurisprudence

Through the decades, the Justices of the U.S. Supreme Court have, themselves, interpreted the Eighth Amendment's Cruel and Unusual Punishments Clause in widely divergent ways.[79] While a majority of Justices have long eschewed an eighteenth-century-centric view of that clause,[80] in a dissent, the late Justice Antonin Scalia—the prominent originalist voice—once wrote: "The Eighth Amendment is addressed to always-and-everywhere 'cruel' punishments, such as the rack and the thumbscrew."[81] And when it comes to what punishments are "unusual," the Justices have articulated differing views, too. While Justice Potter Stewart emphasized in 1972 that "death sentences are cruel and unusual in the same way that being struck by lightning is cruel and unusual,"[82] Justice William O. Douglas concluded that same year that "the death penalty inflicted on one defendant is 'unusual' if it discriminates against him by reason of his race, religion, wealth, social position, or class, or if it is imposed under a procedure that gives room for the play of such prejudices."[83] Justice Scalia, relying on popular dictionary definitions, himself defined "unusual" in *Harmelin v. Michigan*[84] to mean "such as [does not] occu[r] in ordinary practice" and "[s]uch as is [not] in common use."[85]

Though the Justices vehemently disagree on how to read the Eighth Amendment, a test has been crafted to interpret it. Since 1958, the Eighth Amendment has been interpreted in accordance with the "evolving standards of decency that mark the progress of a maturing society."[86] As the U.S. Supreme Court observed in its 1958 decision in *Trop v. Dulles*, where it established that now decades-old legal standard: "The provisions of the Constitution are not time-worn adages or hollow shibboleths. They are vital, living principles that authorize and limit governmental powers in our Nation."[87] In describing its prior holding in *Weems v. United States*, a 1910 decision invalidating a severe Filipino corporal punishment at a time when the U.S. controlled the Philippines,[88] the Court in *Trop*—which essentially, without extended discussion, adopted a layperson's understanding of *unusual*[89]—emphasized: "This Court has had little occasion to give precise content to the Eighth Amendment, and, in an enlightened democracy such as ours, this is not surprising. But when the Court was confronted with a punishment of 12 years in irons at hard and painful labor imposed for the crime of falsifying public records, it did not hesitate to declare that the penalty was cruel in its excessiveness and unusual in its character."[90] The Supreme Court's decision in *Weems* was reportedly "met with little favor, to put it lightly, from the bar of the Philippine Islands," though that decision has—as one professor puts it—"probably the most interesting discussion which the prohibition of cruel and unusual punishments has received by the Supreme Court."[91]

Whereas the Court in *Trop*, in rejecting a rigid, purely historical interpretation of the Eighth Amendment, struck down the punishment of expatriation or denationalization for desertion, the Court in *Weems*[92] declared unconstitutional a draconian practice in the Philippines known as *cadena temporal.* In so doing, the Court in *Weems* found that the Cruel and Unusual Punishments Clause is "progressive" in nature and "may acquire meaning as public opinion becomes enlightened by a humane justice."[93] For more than 100 years, the Supreme Court has thus eschewed a strictly historical interpretation of the Eighth Amendment's text. Notably, the Supreme Court in *Trop*—self-aware of the lack of logic in striking down a *non-lethal* punishment (in that case, stripping a deserter of American citizenship) when capital punishment laws were still in place—felt the need to consider and mention the death penalty even as it invalidated a punishment that would have rendered an American soldier stateless. "At the outset," the Court stressed, "let us put to one side the death penalty as an index of the constitutional limit on punishment."[94] As the Court, in its plurality opinion,[95] then observed: "Whatever the arguments may be against capital punishment, both on moral grounds and in terms of accomplishing the purposes of punishment—and they are forceful—the death penalty has been employed throughout our history, and, *in a day when it is still widely accepted*, it cannot be said to violate the constitutional concept of cruelty."[96] Those words were penned sixty years ago, decades before the United States, in 1994, ratified the U.N. Convention Against Torture and Other Cruel, Inhuman or Degrading Treatment or Punishment,[97] and decades before the Constitutional Court of South Africa, in 1995, declared the death penalty to be unconstitutional under that country's post-apartheid constitution.[98] The "in a day when it is still widely accepted" language in *Trop* itself seems to indicate that the U.S. Supreme Court might one day revisit the issue of the death penalty's constitutionality.

In applying its "evolving standards of decency" test since *Trop*, the U.S. Supreme Court has used "objective" criteria to assess a punishment's constitutionality[99] while reserving its right—as the final arbiter of the U.S. Constitution's meaning[100]—to make an independent judgment about the constitutionality of a law or practice.[101] "The beginning point," the Court ruled in *Roper v. Simmons*,[102] "is a review of objective indicia of consensus, as expressed in particular by the enactments of legislatures that have addressed the question."[103] This is where the counting of jurisdictions has played out—sometimes to strike down a practice as unconstitutional and sometimes to legitimize one as constitutional. "We must then determine, in the exercise of our independent judgment," Justice Anthony Kennedy wrote for the Court in that case, one dealing with the legality of executing juvenile offenders, "whether the death penalty is a disproportionate punishment for juveniles."[104] In addition to reserving its right to exercise its independent judgment and gauging whether a "national consensus" exists against a specific punishment (or against a specific punishment *for a specific class of offender*),[105] the Court has looked to actual state practices, including past usage and jury verdicts,[106] a punishment's frequency,[107] as well as trends[108] and the consistency of the direction of the change.[109] If Eighth Amendment jurisprudence sometimes seems untethered from the Eighth Amendment's text, it is because the Supreme Court itself has developed so many tests or evaluative tools for interpreting its words instead of simply analyzing the meaning of "cruel" and "unusual" head-on.

Through the years, in response to legal challenges, the U.S. Supreme Court has repeatedly wrestled with what constitutes a cruel and unusual punishment. In applying the "evolving standards" test in actual cases and controversies, the Court—to date—has declared unconstitutional various punishment practices, including: (1) the execution of non-homicidal offenders,[110] those who played a less culpable role in the commission of the crime,[111] offenders under age eighteen,[112] the insane,[113] and the intellectually disabled;[114] and (2) life-without-parole sentences for juveniles, whether for homicide or non-homicide offenses.[115] "While the modern Court has splintered on various issues of counting methodology," law professor Akhil Amar stresses, "'unusual' should mean what it says."[116] As he cogently argues in his *Yale Law Journal* article, using a pragmatic approach to reading the word *unusual*: "If 240 million modern Americans live in states that flatly prohibit punishment X while only sixty million live in states that vigorously practice punishment X, then X is 'unusual' in the ordinary everyday meaning of that word."[117] Taking note of the U.S. Supreme Court's death penalty jurisprudence, one that has allowed many executions to take place while simultaneously barring others, Amar has also written of how the Supreme Court has responded to data on state practice (*e.g.*, executions and the enactment of laws) in the Eighth Amendment context since the 1960s.[118]

The Eighth Amendment is not one-dimensional; it prohibits both "excessive" bail and fines and "cruel and unusual punishments."[119] Those prohibitions should be read together as complementary prohibitions, and the purposes behind those prohibitions should be considered, too. The Eighth Amendment not only furthers liberty, but—as the U.S. Supreme Court itself has read the language—it imposes a duty on government "to respect the dignity of all persons."[120] "The basic concept underlying the Eighth Amendment is nothing less than the dignity of man," Chief Justice Earl Warren wrote in *Trop v. Dulles* in 1958.[121] "Even the vilest criminal remains a human being possessed of common human dignity," U.S. Supreme Court Justice William Brennan later declared in his concurring opinion in *Furman v. Georgia* in 1972.[122]

This sentiment dovetails nicely with the notion of universal human rights, with the Universal Declaration of Human Rights (1948) itself referencing "the inherent dignity ... of all members of the human family" and "the dignity and worth of the human person."[123] "Justice Brennan," a recent monograph on human dignity emphasizes, "had a central role in recognizing human dignity as a constitutional value in American law."[124] In his 1972 concurrence in *Furman*, Justice Brennan specifically wrote: "At bottom, then, the Cruel and Unusual Punishments Clause prohibits the infliction of uncivilized and inhuman punishments. The State, even as it punishes, must treat its members with respect for their intrinsic worth as human beings." "A punishment," he continued, "is 'cruel and unusual,' therefore, if it does not comport with human dignity."[125] Justice Anthony Kennedy, that source observes, more recently took up that mantle. In a five-to-four vote on an Eighth Amendment issue, that source explains of Justice Kennedy, he "cast the deciding vote while invoking the constitutional value of human dignity."[126]

Certain punishments and practices are prohibited by the U.S. Supreme Court's existing Eighth Amendment jurisprudence, though this area of law has been fraught with controversy and a battleground for originalists and living constitutionalists.[127] In *Robinson v. California*,[128] the first case to apply the Eighth Amendment against a state to invalidate a state law, the U.S. Supreme Court declared that a statute making it a crime to be addicted to drugs—a status offense—was a cruel and unusual punishment.[129] "Even one day in prison would be a cruel and unusual punishment for the 'crime' of having a common cold," the Court ruled.[130] The modern Supreme Court, in fact, has used the Eighth Amendment to outlaw various cruel and inhuman practices. The Eighth Amendment, for example, has been interpreted to bar horrendous prison conditions and prison overcrowding.[131] "Most of the Eighth Amendment-based rights to certain levels of prison conditions announced by courts during the high tide of prison reform in the 1970s and 1980s were articulated in terms of specific changes in prison conditions, but underlying them all is constitutional protection for human dignity," explains UC Berkeley law professor Jonathan Simon in his book, *Mass Incarceration on Trial*.[132]

With state-sanctioned executions still authorized in certain American states and tolerated by the U.S. Supreme Court, though, Eighth Amendment case law has been variously described as a mess,[133] as incoherent,[134] and as an enigma.[135] The Supreme Court itself, in a 2008 case, freely acknowledged that one aspect of its Eighth Amendment jurisprudence "is still in search of a unifying principle."[136] Because the Eighth Amendment generally *protects* prisoners from various harms but is then simultaneously read to allow the *execution* of inmates, I have elsewhere described the U.S. Supreme Court's existing Eighth Amendment case law as "a kind of Dr. Jekyll-and-Mr. Hyde jurisprudence."[137] In America's founding era, punishments were divided into categories depending on the seriousness of the offense. For example, in 1777, Thomas Jefferson systematically divided crimes into three categories: (1) capital offenses or, to use his words, "Crimes whose punishmt. Extends to *Life*"; (2) "Crimes whose punishment goes to *Limb*," such as castration for rapists; and (3) "Crimes punishable by *Labor* &c." With various *non-lethal* punishments already held by the U.S. Supreme Court and various lower courts to be outlawed by the U.S. Constitution's Eighth Amendment—and with the U.S. legal system having long ago abandoned the amputation of limbs as punishment—modern American Eighth Amendment jurisprudence has become irrational and illogical and, it must said, nonsensible. If it is unconstitutional *to whip* a prisoner (as the U.S. Court of Appeals for the Eighth Circuit very appropriately held back in the 1960s), how can it still be permissible *to execute* prisoners in today's world?[138]

The U.S. Supreme Court's current Eighth Amendment case law is thus not principled, let alone internally consistent, coherent, or intellectually decipherable. For example, while the death penalty—the state's ultimate punishment—lingers on in American life (at least in certain locales) in spite of the Eighth Amendment's ban on cruel and unusual punishments, the law is clear that "[n]o natural-born citizen may be denaturalized" for desertion under the Eighth Amendment's Cruel and Unusual Punishments Clause.[139] In other words, it is unlawful to strip citizens of their citizenship, just as it would be unlawful to inflict stripes through the use of the lash, but it is not currently unlawful to strip them of their lives. How can that possibly be? In addition, while there is not now, in the U.S., a *per se* bar on executions (as there is European countries and places such as South Africa),[140] America's retentionist jurisdictions are not allowed to execute the insane,[141] non-homicidal rapists,[142] juvenile offenders,[143] the intellectually disabled,[144] or those individuals who did not kill or intend to kill.[145] Certain *categories* of offenders, consequently, cannot be executed[146] even as other offenders are allowed to be executed—and even as various *non-lethal* acts, such a denationalization and gratuitous beatings by prison guards, have been found to constitute Eighth Amendment violations.[147] Another movement—to bar the execution of those who are severely mentally ill—is now underway, too, and if that movement succeeds, it will further restrict the death penalty's use.[148]

Under the Supreme Court's long-standing precedents, harms short of death have long been considered violative of the Eighth Amendment. In 1992, in *Hudson v. McMillian*,[149] the U.S. Supreme Court itself found a violation of the Cruel and Unusual Punishments Clause where prison guards beat up a handcuffed inmate at Louisiana's Angola prison even though the inmate did not suffer any permanent injuries.[150] In its existing Eighth Amendment jurisprudence, the Supreme Court has thus already firmly rejected the notion that "significant injury"—let alone death—is even a "threshold" requirement for stating an excessive force claim. "What is necessary to establish an 'unnecessary and wanton infliction of pain,'" the Court has ruled, "varies according to the nature of the alleged constitutional violation." When prison officials fail to attend to an inmate's serious medical needs, the appropriate inquiry is whether officials exhibit "deliberate indifference." "This standard is appropriate," the Court has stated, "because the State's responsibility to provide inmates with medical care ordinarily does not conflict with competing administrative concerns." "Because society does not expect that prisoners will have unqualified access to health care," the Court held in *Hudson*, "deliberate indifference to medical needs amounts to an Eighth Amendment violation only if those needs are 'serious.'"[151]

Even though certain classes of offenders—as noted—are exempt by U.S. Supreme Court decisions from being executed, the Supreme Court regularly denies requests for stays of execution in individual cases. In the 1940s, the Supreme Court actually permitted an electrocution to go forward after an initial attempt to execute the inmate had failed miserably (in that case sending only a non-lethal surge of electricity through the inmate's body on the first attempt).[152] The Supreme Court has also upheld other severe punishments—ones that, on their face, seem to run afoul of the parsimony principle. For instance, in 1991, the Court—in a 5–4 vote—has upheld a life sentence for the possession of cocaine.[153] In that case, *Harmelin v. Michigan*, the Court approved a life without parole sentence for 45-year-old Ronald Harmelin, a man convicted under Michigan law of possessing 672 grams of cocaine.[154] In another closely divided vote, the Supreme Court—as it later described how it ruled in the case—"rejected a challenge to a sentence of 25 years to life for the theft of a few golf clubs under California's so-called three-strikes recidivist sentencing scheme."[155] "The Court," it further emphasized in 2010, writing about two other precedents, "has also upheld a sentence of life with the possibility of parole for a defendant's third nonviolent felony, the crime of obtaining money by false pretenses, and a sentence of 40 years for possession of marijuana with intent to distribute and distribution of marijuana."[156]

The Supreme Court's "Evolving Standards of Decency" Test

The Eighth Amendment is a creature of the eighteenth century, but its meaning must be ascertained by living, breathing twenty-first-century jurists. The proper interpretation of the Eighth Amendment, the U.S. Supreme Court held in the mid-twentieth century, setting the stage for twenty-first-century litigation, "is determined not by the standards that prevailed when the Eighth Amendment was adopted in 1791" but by " 'the evolving standards of decency that mark the progress of a maturing society.' "[157] The Eighth Amendment, the Court in fact held more than a century ago, in 1910, "is not fastened to the obsolete but may acquire meaning as public opinion becomes enlightened by a humane justice."[158] As part of implementing its "evolving standards of decency" test, the Supreme Court regularly examines state practice, trying to assess—as best as it can—whether a national consensus exists against a particular punishment.[159] And it has even examined—along with tallying practices state by state throughout the country, looking at various state statutes—the "consistency and direction of change," which, in effect, looks at more nebulous trends in the law's development.[160] This has led to charges that the U.S. Supreme Court Justices are simply injecting their own personal views into Eighth Amendment decision-making. Each individual Supreme Court Justice, obviously, must cast his or her vote as he or she sees fit.

Of course, the law itself is constantly evolving, as it ever will be. The way the prohibition against "cruel and unusual punishments" was viewed in the late seventeenth century (when the English Bill of Rights was put in place) was different from the way America's founders viewed that prohibition in the late eighteenth century.[161] And, not surprisingly, the way modern jurists view the Eighth Amendment prohibition is much different than the way eighteenth-century jurists viewed it,[162] especially in light of the Fourteenth Amendment's ratification in 1868. The law's modern concern—now a constitutional right—with equal protection and equality of treatment is something with which eighteenth-century jurists did not concern themselves.[163] Whereas slavery and the slave trade were once lawful, the Thirteenth Amendment abolished slavery and involuntary servitude in 1865, and the Fourteenth Amendment then guaranteed the equal protection of the laws.[164] As historical evidence makes clear, the Fourteenth Amendment was itself intended, at least in part,[165] to constitutionalize the substance of the Civil Rights Act of 1866, which required "like punishment, pains, and penalties" for blacks and whites. The Fourteenth Amendment was adopted and ratified in light of doubts at the time, in both the North and the South, about that act's constitutionality.[166] Because of the Fourteenth Amendment's addition to the U.S. Constitution, equality of treatment is now a constitutional right—and discriminatory treatment can no longer be tolerated or ignored, as it was in America's era of slavery. In early America, overtly discriminatory laws regarding punishments were still in place. But from the time of Montesquieu's eighteenth-century book, *The Spirit of the Laws*, the necessity-for-punishment principle has been there (at least if one pays attention to it) as a bedrock principle amidst the ever-shifting landscape of the criminal law.

In a representative democracy, legislatures naturally have the first say about how crimes will be punished. "[J]udgments about the appropriate punishment for an offense belong in the first instance to the legislature," the U.S. Supreme Court has itself aptly observed, further emphasizing that "any judicial determination regarding the gravity of a particular criminal offense will be inherently imprecise."[167] "[T]hese principles," a majority of the Court observed in 1998 in interpreting the Eighth Amendment's Excessive Fines Clause, "counsel against requiring strict proportionality between the amount of a punitive forfeiture and the gravity of a criminal offense, and we therefore adopt the standard of gross disproportionality articulated in our Cruel and Unusual Punishments Clause precedents."[168] It does make sense that legislatures, especially in a system of federalism, are given the ability to make the initial policy judgments about how best to combat crime—whether through fines, imprisonment or other sanctions. The people's representatives, after all, are entitled to have their say. But if the U.S. Constitution is to be given effect, as it must be, there should be—and, in fact, there are—clear limits on legislative as well as executive power. The Constitution itself sets those limits, and the Eighth Amendment must be read to establish certain of those limits in the realms of bail, fines, and punishments lest its language become a moot portion of America's constitutional law protections.[169] And if there is judicial oversight, as there must be, the *standard of review* to be adopted is obviously of considerable consequence. In carrying out their solemn responsibilities, judges need to ensure that the standard of review is not too deferential or else individual liberty will be unduly infringed.

Legislative bodies, in general, have fairly broad discretion to authorize punishments, with legislative bodies able to choose among various punishment options and permissible ranges of penal sanctions.[170] Although deciding what punishments are truly necessary is, admittedly, a rather subjective enterprise, it is (and rightful so) the U.S. Supreme Court that has—and that must have—the final say about the meaning of the U.S. Constitution in general and the Eighth Amendment in particular.[171] And it makes equally good sense that it is state supreme courts that—so long as they respect *federal* constitutional rights—must have the final say about the meaning of their own state constitutions,[172] which generally have equivalent prohibitions against cruel and unusual punishments, albeit with some textual variations.[173] For example, while Virginia's drafters chose to use a verbatim version of the English Bill of Rights prohibiting "cruel and unusual punishments," the Maryland and Delaware drafters chose the "cruel or unusual" construction.[174]

But in their consideration of these varied prohibitions, the U.S. Supreme Court and state supreme courts, in giving life to the Eighth Amendment and its state-law equivalents, should always carefully consider how those provisions should be read in the modern era so as to protect liberty and to avoid tyrannous punishments. In that respect, the "grossly disproportionate" standard adopted by the U.S. Supreme Court in the context of the Excessive Fines Clause and the Cruel and Unusual Punishments

Clause may not be, it turns out, the most appropriate one. That "grossly disproportionate" standard, used in recent decades by the U.S. Supreme Court, seems to set the bar too high in terms of the legal standard for striking down unnecessary or disproportionate punishments. Of course, under existing constitutional law, state supreme courts can read their own prohibitions against cruelty and excessive bail and fines in a more expansive manner than the U.S. Supreme Court itself reads the Eighth Amendment. The Eighth and Fourteenth Amendments set a *constitutional floor* for the country, but individual states can offer *more protection* for their state residents.[175]

Although judicial decisions come out of both the federal and state systems, the U.S. Supreme Court's opinions obviously get the most attention. Just as the U.S. Supreme Court created its "evolving standards of decency test" out of whole cloth back in 1958, it created the "grossly disproportionate" test out of thin air, too. For example, in one landmark case, *Solem v. Helm*,[176] the Supreme Court held in a 5–4 decision that the Eighth Amendment's text "is explicit that bail and fines may not be excessive"[177] and that the Cruel and Unusual Punishments Clause "proscribes grossly disproportionate punishments."[178] In that case, a man, Jerry Helm, had been convicted in South Dakota of uttering a "no account" check for $100 and was sentenced to life imprisonment without the possibility of parole under South Dakota's recidivist statute because of his six prior felony convictions.[179] The Court in *Solem* concluded that disproportionate punishments were impermissible but that courts should give considerable deference to legislative bodies in setting punishments. As the Court ruled in that case:

> In sum, we hold as a matter of principle that a criminal sentence must be proportionate to the crime for which the defendant has been convicted. Reviewing courts, of course, should grant substantial deference to the broad authority that legislatures necessarily possess in sentencing convicted criminals. But no penalty is *per se* constitutional.[180]

The Court in *Solem* specifically observed that "some sentences of imprisonment are so disproportionate that they are unconstitutional under the Cruel and Unusual Punishments Clause" but determined that those would be "admittedly rare cases."[181]

While American courts may only rarely strike down a law or a particular punishment as unconstitutional, concrete evidence showing the lack of necessity for a punishment should be carefully considered by courts in reviewing a punishment's constitutionality. If a punishment is not necessary, it is disproportionate and—as Montesquieu and Beccaria put it—"tyrannical." In *Solem*, the Supreme Court did, ultimately, strike down Mr. Helm's sentence as unconstitutional. "The principle that a punishment should be proportionate to the crime is deeply rooted and frequently repeated in common law jurisprudence," the Court ruled, noting that "three chapters of Magna Carta were devoted to the rule that 'amercements' may not be excessive" and that "the principle was repeated and extended in the First Statute of Westminster." The Court in *Solem* cited *Hodges v. Humkin*, a case from way back in 1615 from the King's Bench, that held that "imprisonment ought always to be according to the quality of the offence." "In sum," the Court ruled in *Solem*, emphasizing that Helm's offense involved neither violence nor a threat of violence, "we hold as a matter of principle that a criminal sentence must be proportionate to the crime for which the defendant has been convicted."

"We conclude that his sentence is significantly disproportionate to his crime, and is therefore prohibited by the Eighth Amendment," the Supreme Court concluded.[182] A punishment seen as "significantly disproportionate" or "grossly disproportionate" is, of course, far worse than one viewed as simply disproportionate. But courts should be genuinely concerned about *disproportionate* punishments as well as those which are "significantly" or "grossly" disproportionate.

The Supreme Court's numerous Eighth Amendment cases address a wide variety of facts and, because of their factual dissimilarities, reach a wide variety of outcomes. In yet another case, *Estelle v. Gamble*,[183] the U.S. Supreme Court established the standard for what a prisoner has to plead in order to assert an Eighth Amendment claim under 42 U.S.C. § 1983, the federal law designed to allow people to vindicate their constitutional rights if the government infringes upon them. In that case, the Court discussed some older Eighth Amendment precedents and held that a prisoner must allege acts or omissions that evidence "deliberate indifference" to serious medical needs.[184] "[D]eliberate indifference to serious medical needs of prisoners constitutes the 'unnecessary and wanton infliction of pain' proscribed by the Eighth Amendment," the Court observed, invoking the lack of necessity concept as regards the infliction of pain.[185] "This," the Court stressed in its opinion, "is true whether the indifference is manifested by prison doctors in their response to the prisoner's needs or by prison guards in intentionally denying or delaying access to medical care or intentionally interfering with the treatment once prescribed."[186] "Regardless of how evidenced," the Court declared in *Estelle*, "deliberate indifference to a prisoner's serious illness or injury states a cause of action under § 1983."[187] While the Supreme Court's decision in *Farmer v. Brennan*[188] held that the Eighth Amendment's proscription against cruel and unusual punishments imposes a duty on prison officials to make reasonable efforts to ensure inmate safety,[189] other decisions articulate an even broader standard of protection. Thus, the Court announced in *DeShaney v. Winnebago County Department of Social Services*,[190] that the Eighth Amendment requires that the government provide for a prisoner's "basic human needs—e.g., food, clothing, shelter, medical care, and reasonable safety."[191]

The Supreme Court in *Estelle* spoke in that opinion of the Eighth Amendment's intended purpose. "It suffices to note," the Court observed of the Eighth Amendment's history, a subject it had delved into before, "that the primary concern of the drafters was to proscribe 'torture[s]' and other 'barbar[ous]' methods of punishment."[192] "Our more recent cases, however," the Court emphasized, acknowledging the importance of human dignity and human decency, "have held that the Amendment proscribes more than physically barbarous punishments."[193] Quoting the landmark Eighth Circuit case of *Jackson v. Bishop*,[194] which barred the use of the lash on prisoners, and the Supreme Court's own prior, landscape-changing decision in *Trop v. Dulles*,[195] the Court in *Estelle* wrote: "The Amendment embodies 'broad and idealistic concepts of dignity, civilized standards, humanity, and decency ...,' against which we must evaluate penal measures. Thus, we have held repugnant to the Eighth Amendment punishments which are incompatible with 'the evolving standards of decency that mark the progress of a maturing society.'"[196] "[D]enial of medical care," the Court in *Estelle* added, "may result in pain and suffering which no one suggests would serve any penological purpose." "The infliction of such unnecessary suffering," the Court concluded, "is inconsistent with contemporary standards of decency as manifested in modern legislation codifying the common law view that 'it is but just that the public be required to care for the prisoner, who cannot, by reason of the deprivation of his liberty, care for himself.'"[197]

To determine what the Eighth Amendment means, the U.S. Supreme Court has, over time, looked to history[198] and the severity of the offense and the punishment as it has crafted its opinions.[199] The Supreme Court, time and time again, has been called upon to make judgment calls, sometimes on close questions or excruciatingly difficult ones, with some of those judgment calls favoring the government while others have favored criminal offenders. In that work, the Court—trying to stay tethered to public opinion while not abdicating its own responsibility to interpret the U.S. Constitution[200]—has specifically stated multiple times that it looks to "objective indicia" of then-current opinion, laws, and practices,[201] including jury verdicts,[202] while simultaneously reserving the right to independently assess the Eighth Amendment's meaning.[203] "[I]t may be helpful to compare the sentences imposed on other criminals in the same jurisdiction," the Court has ruled, emphasizing of the proportionality concept: "If more serious crimes are subject to the same penalty, or to less serious penalties, that is some indication that the punishment at issue may be excessive."[204] "[C]ourts," the Supreme Court has further observed in the proportionality vein, "may find it useful to compare the sentences imposed for commission of the same crime in other jurisdictions."[205] "In sum," the Court has ruled, "a court's proportionality analysis under the Eighth Amendment should be guided by objective criteria, including (i) the gravity of the offense and the harshness of the penalty; (ii) the sentences imposed on other criminals in the same jurisdiction; and (iii) the sentences imposed for commission of the same crime in other jurisdictions."[206]

A Restraining Principle: Disproportionality vs. "Gross" Disproportionality

In interpreting the Cruel and Unusual Punishments Clause, the U.S. Supreme Court has—as noted—expressly found in some of its rulings that a punishment must not be "grossly disproportionate" to the crime or in the light of the justification of punishment offered.[207] The "grossly disproportionate" concept, of course, is not self-defining, just as the concepts of "proportionality" and "necessity" are context-specific and do not lend themselves to easy or precise definition. "Our cases," the Supreme Court stressed in *Lockyer v. Andrade*,[208] "exhibit a lack of clarity regarding what factors may indicate gross disproportionality."[209] "The gross disproportionality principle," the Court emphasized in that case, seeing its role as a limited one, "reserves a constitutional violation for only the extraordinary case."[210] To date, the kinds of punishments struck down as "grossly disproportionate" have varied, with one commentator noting that "[t]here are only a handful of Supreme Court decisions addressing the Eighth Amendment grossly disproportionate test, and, even within this limited field, the decisions are unquestionably inconsistent."[211] While the Eighth Amendment provides the language that is used to assess the constitutionality of punishments, the Fourteenth Amendment applies the Eighth Amendment against the states while simultaneously grafting or overlaying an "equal protection of the laws" enquiry as regards such punishments.

In assessing punishments, the Eighth Amendment clearly *does* impose limits, with one U.S. District Court putting it this way: "Through the Due Process Clause of the Fourteenth Amendment, the Eighth Amendment's prohibition against cruel, and grossly excessive punishments limits the states' discretion to impose criminal sentences."[212] "Factors considered in making the proportionality determination," that court observed, "include: (1) the degree of reprehensibility of defendant's conduct or the extent of his individual culpability, (2) the relationship between the penalty and the harm to the victim; and (3) the sanctions imposed in other cases for comparable misconduct."[213] "Three factors are relevant to this inquiry," the Second Circuit wrote of punishments which are "grossly disproportionate" to crimes, with that appellate court listing these factors: "(1) the inherent gravity of the offense; (2) the sentences imposed for similarly grave offenses in the same jurisdiction; and (3) sentences imposed for the same crime in other jurisdictions."[214] In the adjudication of these cases, the courts would do well to remember that the Eighth Amendment's protections are tied to preventing excessive penalties and cruelty and to safeguarding liberty, which is, itself, a fundamental right. Any punishment that infringes on one's life, property, or liberty should be carefully evaluated by the courts, and it is inevitable that some punishments will not survive constitutional scrutiny. The question of what constitutes a disproportionate or grossly disproportionate punishment, of course, begs the question: disproportionate or grossly disproportionate *in relationship to what*?

While the concept of proportionality is an incredibly important one and dates back even before Montesquieu and Beccaria, the idea of protecting individual liberty from *unnecessary* intrusions upon it seems, somehow, less tethered to such thorny comparisons. American lawmakers and courts should continue to consider if punishments are proportionate in relation to punishments within a jurisdiction and in relation to punishments being imposed throughout the country. Those are important considerations, and such proportionality analyzes will help to ensure that punishments are not being arbitrarily or unequally imposed or inflicted, either within a particular jurisdiction or in a few jurisdictions but not in others. But the necessity-for-punishment maxim developed by Montesquieu and Beccaria should also be moved to the front burner by American lawmakers, prosecutors, and judges. The application of the necessity-for-punishment principle is needed to prevent improper infringements on life, liberty, and property. Although the State of Arkansas still makes use of the death penalty, showing that it does not yet take the parsimony principle seriously, an existing Arkansas statute actually articulates that principle as well as the equality and proportionality principles. That state statute not only provides that "[s]entencing criteria should be neutral with respect to race, gender, social, and economic status" and that "[r]ational and consistent sentencing policy requires a continuum of sanctions which increases in direct proportion to the seriousness of the offense and the extent of the offender's criminal history," but it further provides that "[r]estrictions on an offender's liberty should only be as restrictive as necessary to fulfill the purposes of sentencing...."[215]

The issue of proportionality affects both federal and state proceedings because state constitutional provisions barring "cruel," "excessive," or "unusual" punishments have also been interpreted to bar "grossly disproportionate" sentences.[216] As one court in California wrote in 2016 in interpreting California's constitution: "A prison sentence will violate the prohibition against cruel or unusual punishment under the California Constitution (art. I, § 17) where 'it is so disproportionate to the crime for which it is inflicted that it shocks the conscience and offends fundamental notions of human dignity.'"[217] Finding that the defendant has a "considerable burden" to show a punishment is cruel or unusual under California's constitution, the court in that case, *People v. Reyes*, stated that "[t]o determine whether a particular sentence is disproportionate to the offense for which it is imposed, we first examine 'the nature of the offence and/or the offender, with particular regard to the degree of danger both present to society.'"[218] "We next compare the punishment imposed with punishments prescribed by California law for more serious offenses," the court stressed, adding: "Finally, we compare the punishment imposed with punishments prescribed by other jurisdictions for the same offense."[219] Missing from the analysis: the prescient warning of Montesquieu and Beccaria—one tied to the notion of protecting liberty and preventing tyranny—that any punishment that goes beyond necessity is tyrannical.

In actuality, the texts of the U.S. Constitution and state constitutions, as well as the power of judicial review, grounded in *Marbury v. Madison*,[220] set now centuries-old limits on what punishments legislative bodies or executive officials can mete out. While the text of the U.S. Constitution and equivalent state constitutions provide the limits in easily readable language, the U.S. Supreme Court and other courts must give those provisions their life. The U.S. Supreme Court, for example, has already explicitly held that various *non-lethal* punishments can run afoul of the Eighth Amendment guarantee against "cruel and unusual punishments."[221] Thus, in *Hope v. Pelzer*,[222] the Supreme Court held that it was an "obvious" Eighth Amendment violation for prison guards to handcuff Larry Hope, a shirtless prisoner, to a hitching post for seven hours—leaving him sunburned and dehydrated—as a sanction for disruptive conduct.[223] "'[T]he unnecessary and wanton infliction of pain ... constitutes cruel and unusual punishment forbidden by the Eighth Amendment,'" the Supreme Court held, quoting one of its prior decisions.[224] Among "'unnecessary and wanton' inflictions of pain are those that are 'totally without penological justification,'" the Court in *Hope* stressed, quoting yet another precedent.[225] Referring to "[t]he obvious cruelty inherent in this practice," Justice John Paul Stevens wrote for the Court about the inmate's mistreatment: "Hope was treated in a way antithetical to human dignity—he was hitched to a post for an extended period of time in a position that was painful, and under circumstances that were both degrading and dangerous. This wanton treatment was not done of necessity, but as punishment for prior conduct."[226] Of course, the Eighth Amendment is targeted at cruelty, of which physical pain is just one part. But unnecessary sanctions are also cruel; they violate the principle of human dignity and represent a waste of limited public resources.

The concept of necessity has appeared from time to time in American judicial opinions, though without reference to Montesquieu and Beccaria's eighteenth-century maxim. Even before *Hope v. Pelzer*, the U.S. Supreme Court—in a case involving the consideration of the infliction of corporal punishments within schools—had noted, years earlier, that, under the common law, any punishments beyond those that are "reasonably necessary" are illegitimate. As the Supreme Court observed in *Ingraham v. Wright*,[227] "Public school teachers and administrators are privileged at common law to inflict only such corporal punishment as is reasonably necessary for the proper education and discipline of the child; any punishment going beyond the privilege may result in both civil and criminal liability."[228] The Court in *Wright*, while declining to apply the Eighth Amendment in that educational context, observed in that case of the law's development over time: "Although the early cases viewed the authority of the teacher as deriving from the parents, the concept of parental delegation has been replaced by the view more consonant with compulsory education laws that the State itself may impose such corporal punishment as is reasonably necessary 'for the proper education of the child and for the maintenance of group discipline.' "[229]

Benjamin Rush—the Beccaria disciple[230] and one of the fifty-six signers of the Declaration of Independence—himself wrote an essay in 1790 against the use of corporal punishments in the educational setting. Among his reasons: "Corporal punishments are not only hurtful, but unnecessary, in schools."[231] Dr. Rush's essay, addressed to Pennsylvania lawmaker George Clymer, a man who represented that state at the 1787 Constitutional Convention, was titled "The Amusements and Punishments Which Are Proper for Schools." Through the decades, others also weighed in on the necessity (or lack thereof) for punishments, discussing, for example, whether corporal punishments were necessary. As Sir George Murray said on one occasion in Parliament in the early 1830s: "I am for the abolition, in civil life, of all punishments not necessary for the benefit of society; and, in military life, I am for the abolition of any punishment not necessary to render the army an efficient instrument for the public service." Once expressing doubts about "extirpating corporal punishments" from the British army, Murray offered his own opinion in these words in the House of Commons:

> I know that it was the anxious wish of the amiable and illustrious prince who was so long at the head of the British army, so much to its advantage and to that of the country, to diminish the number of corporal punishments as much as it was possible to do so; but in some regiments vexatious punishments of a minor description were introduced, with a view to supersede the necessity of corporal punishments; and these minor punishments became, sometimes, harassing and vexatious to the soldiers, without being efficient in maintaining discipline.[232]

The "grossly disproportionate" language has now appeared in multiple U.S. Supreme Court opinions.[233] For example, in *Lockyer v. Andrade*,[234] the Supreme Court emphasized: "A gross disproportionality principle is applicable to sentences for terms of years."[235] Likewise, in *Graham v. Florida*,[236] the Court observed: "Even if the punishment has some connection to a valid penological goal, it must be shown that the punishment is not grossly disproportionate in light of the justification offered."[237] But for those interested in history, and that should include *both* originalists and living constitutionalists, it is important to take note of the fact that neither Montesquieu nor Beccaria wrote of punishments that were "grossly disproportionate." Instead, the French baron and the Italian marquis simply insisted on *proportionate* punishments. Insisting on proportionate sentences has, at times, been confused with tolerating sentences that are not *grossly* disproportionate. For example, as one modern source notes of the European philosophers and the revolution in the treatment of crimes and punishments they wrought:

> It was Montesquieu who initiated the intense public discussions in France regarding a proper scale of punishments. No *philosophe* so substantially influenced Cesare Beccaria in his composition of his influential *On Crimes and Punishments* (1764) as Montesquieu, and owing to the enormous influence of both Beccaria and Montesquieu, liberals ever since have argued for reducing the severity of grossly disproportionate, cruel, and arbitrary punishments.[238]

The "grossly" language is, in actuality, judicial gloss that the U.S. Supreme Court has applied to the Enlightenment's insistence on proportionate punishments.

The U.S. Supreme Court's "grossly disproportionate" language is, in fact, of relatively recent vintage[239] and represents a departure from the notions of simple *proportionality* or *disproportionality*—the key concepts during Montesquieu's and Beccaria's time. Although the "grossly disproportionate" language first appeared in the U.S. Supreme Court's Eighth Amendment decisions a few decades ago,[240] and although Eighth Amendment challenges to punishments began before such language first appeared,[241] it is important for American lawyers, prosecutors and jurists to remember that the Enlightenment writers were focused not on *gross* disproportionality. Instead, they were concerned simply with whether punishments were "proportionate" or "disproportionate," "usual" or "unusual," "unnecessary" or "necessary," or—as the linguistic framing sometimes went, as in Beccaria's case—"absolutely necessary."[242] While the addition of the "gross" or "grossly" modifier may seem to factor in a perceived need by the courts to defer to legislative or executive-branch judgments, it can also easily be seen as undue deference to legislative and executive-branch authority and as working an infringement on liberty. After all, if a punishment is not necessary or is disproportionate, it would violate the precept laid down by Montesquieu and Beccaria no matter whether the punishment is characterized as "grossly disproportionate" or simply "disproportionate."

In their book, *Proportionality Principles in American Law: Controlling Excessive Government Action*, scholars Tom Sullivan and Richard Frase lay out the case for "*Means-Proportionality Limits on Sentence Severity*" this way: "Among equally effective means to achieve a given end, those that are less costly or burdensome should be preferred. In the punishment context, Norval Morris calls this the principle of parsimony." "Cesare Beccaria," they emphasize, "argued that punishment must be not only proportionate to the crime but also 'necessary, the least possible in the circumstances.'"[243] In *The Future of Imprisonment* (1974), Norval Morris, the noted Australian-educated scholar who taught at the University of Chicago Law School and was a close friend of Justice Harry Blackmun, described parsimony as the "least restrictive—least punitive—sanction necessary to achieve defined social purposes."[244] As has been aptly noted by Richard

Frase, a law professor at the University of Minnesota Law School: "For Morris, the principle of parsimony 'is both utilitarian and humanitarian'. Parsimony in the use of custodial sentences also permits the preservation of the defendant's social ties and the avoidance of needless suffering and expense." "Parsimony," Frase stresses, "is one of Morris's most important guiding principles—'[t]he least restrictive (punitive) sanction necessary to achieve defined social purposes should be imposed.'"[245]

Bottom line: a *grossly disproportionate* sentence is obviously cruel, but so too is a merely *disproportionate* one. And a punishment classified as disproportionate (no matter what the level of disproportionality) is, almost by definition, an *unnecessary* one, with necessity—in various ways, and not just in Montesquieu's and Beccaria's lifetimes—having long played an important role in the law's administration.[246] For instance, it has been noted in the modern era that the use of restraints on a criminal defendant at trial must be necessary for physical security, to prevent escape, or to maintain court decorum.[247] Trial court judges, as a general matter, have discretion to keep appropriate order in their courtrooms, but as with exercises of discretion generally, there are limits as discretion can be abused. Thus, in *Davidson v. Riley*, a 1995 case, the U.S. Court of Appeals for the Second Circuit emphasized: "The principles consistently applied are that the trial court has discretion to order physical restraints on a party or witness when the court has found those restraints to be necessary to maintain safety or security; but the court must impose no greater restraints than are necessary, and it must take steps to minimize the prejudice resulting from the presence of the restraints." In the same vein, the unjustified use of water hoses or tear gas on prisoners has been condemned by courts and held to be unlawful where a person either poses no risk or has been secured or stopped resisting.[248]

Likewise, it has been held that a defense to the crime of homicide may be grounded in the notion of necessity. Self-defense—a common defense invoked in criminal trials—is itself justified only by the concepts of *reasonableness* and *necessity*.[249] For example, courts have held that a criminal defendant alleging self-defense must demonstrate "a real necessity for taking a life and a situation causing a reasonably prudent person to believe that danger is imminent."[250] The Supreme Court of California has put it this way:

> "Self-defense, when based on a *reasonable* belief that killing is necessary to avert an imminent threat of death or great bodily injury, is a complete justification, and such a killing is not a crime. A killing committed when that belief is *unreasonable* is not justifiable."

As another court put it:

> An assault predicated upon the doctrine of self-defense is justified only where the accused had reasonable grounds to believe, and did believe, that he was in apparent imminent peril of death or serious bodily harm from his actual or potential assailant. It is the task of the trier of facts to determine whether the accused was justified in meeting force with force. Upon finding such justification, the force used against the assailant must not have been unreasonable or excessive, that is, the defender must not have used more force than the exigency reasonably demanded. While under a particular set

> of facts and circumstances a person may defend himself even to the extent of taking an aggressor's life, it is patently clear that he cannot use more force than is necessary without leaving the sanctuary of self-defense.[251]

In other words, "a person may use deadly force in self-defense if" (but only if) "he or she reasonably believes such force is *necessary* to prevent imminent death or great bodily harm."[252] Necessity, then, is the concept that justifies the use of force, just as it is the concept that Montesquieu and Beccaria identified as justifying (and as being necessary to justify) punishment.

CHAPTER 6

The Times They Are A-Changin':

UNUSUAL PUNISHMENTS AND THE SHIFTING NATURE OF NECESSITY

The March of Progress: From Horse-Drawn Carriages to Helicopters

Laws and societies are constantly in motion as the title of Bob Dylan's famous 1960s song, "The Times They Are A-Changin'," points out.[1] If one compares medieval and modern times, it is easy to see just how much societies—and societal attitudes toward crime and punishment—change over time. Times clearly *do* change, with a wide variety of corporal punishments, including whipping and ear cropping, once considered lawful and necessary by lawmakers and members of society. In the First Congress, Representative Samuel Livermore of New Hampshire—in discussing whether the Eighth Amendment's language was itself a desirable addition to the U.S. Constitution—explicitly offered that "it is sometimes necessary to hang a man, villains often deserve whipping, and perhaps having their ears cut off."[2] At that time, Representative Livermore expressed the view that language that became the Eighth Amendment's Cruel and Unusual Punishments Clause "seems to express a great deal of humanity," but he did not think "it necessary" because of his belief that society needed to execute certain criminals or that others deserved to be corporally punished.[3] Although the African slave trade is now a thing of the past, slaves and criminal offenders were once publicly lashed in English and American life, and cities and towns customarily had pillories, stocks, and whipping posts in that bygone era.[4] What history reveals is that corporal punishments slipped from the scene only after they came under relentless attack as disproportionate, unnecessary, and disgraceful.[5]

The Enlightenment clearly brought a new perspective, though the notion that punishments should be no harsher than necessary has roots far deeper than Montesquieu's *Spirit of the Laws* and Beccaria's *On Crimes and Punishments*. As John Scott, the Rector of St. Giles's in the Fields, preached decades before the appearance of either of those books:

> The Law of Mercy also obliges us to inflict *no more* Punishment on Offenders, than what is absolutely *necessary* to the obtaining those good *Ends* we design by it. For he who punishes and [sic] Offender more than is *needful* to the natural End of Punishment, can design no other End by it but what is *cruel* and *barbarous:* and whatsoever is more than *needful* either to the *Vindicating* our own Right, or the *Reforming* the Offender, or the giving fair *Warning* to others, serves to no other Purpose but to gratifie [sic] our own

> *Revenge* and *Fury*. So far as Punishment is needful to these good *Ends*, it is not only *lawful*, but *good*: but all *beyond* what is needful to these, is perfect *Savageness* and *Cruelty*. When therefore for the obtaining these Ends, we are necessitated to punish an offender, the *Law* of *Mercy* obliges us first to try *lighter* and *gentler* Punishments; and if by these we cannot obtain our End, to proceed in our Severities by *Degrees*, and not to fly to extreme Rigour, till we have found all *gentler* Corrections *ineffectual*. For if a *lighter* Punishment will do the Work, it is Cruelty to lay on a *heavier*.... [6]

Scott called punishment "our last remedy," emphasizing that it "ought never to be applied to offenders, till gentle means have been tried and defeated."[7]

Although the Eighth Amendment prohibits "cruel and unusual punishments," the notion of "unusual punishments"—as a standalone category—dates back many centuries.[8] Its converse, "usual punishments," also appears commonly in historical sources.[9] For example, Edward Gibbon's *The History of the Decline and Fall of the Roman Empire*, published in London in 1776, makes reference to "the usual punishments of death, exile, and confiscation" being inflicted in the Roman empire.[10] Robert Bissett's *The History of the Reign of George III*, published in the United States in 1811, and Edward Baines' history of the French Revolution, also make reference "to the usual punishments prescribed by law."[11] An eighteenth-century Roman history observes that "[t]he usual punishments inflicted were fines, banishment, and death,"[12] while in seventeenth-century proceedings against Thomas Earl of Danby for high treason during King James II's reign, one man emphasized that for "ages" after "the conquest," "confiscation of estate and banishment were the usual punishments."[13]

What is *usual*, of course, cannot be *unusual*, though like the concept of proportionality, one must ask an important question: usual *in relationship to what*? Usual or unusual in terms of historical practice? Usual or unusual in terms of any racial or gender disparity in the punishment's infliction? Usual or unusual in one state? In relationship to the entire country as a whole? The word *unusual*, certainly, implies a comparison of some sort, though if a punishment is not necessary, it would seem to be unusual in that sense all by itself. There is also a usual/unusual continuum of sorts, going from *most frequent*, or *most usual*, to *most infrequent*, or *most unusual*, with a sliding scale in-between. Just as a "grossly disproportionate" punishment is worse than a simply "disproportionate" one, a "highly unusual" punishment (that is, one akin, perhaps, to being struck by lightning because it is so rare) seems less fair than a punishment that falls closer on the dividing line between "usual" and "unusual." Still, if a punishment is both "cruel" and "unusual" (not matter how unusual), it should be declared unconstitutional.

The U.S. Constitution's Eighth Amendment was ratified in 1791, enshrining in American law the protection against "cruel and unusual punishments," though America's founders provided no operating instructions for the interpretation of that clause by future generations. But to better understand what that often-elusive language meant at the time (or at least what *certain* people thought it meant, for there is no twenty-first-century mechanism to get in every founder's or ratifier's head), one can look to historical tidbits. For instance, references to "unusual punishment"—quite apart from concerns about "cruel" punishment—show up in America's founding period in the debate over the Constitution itself.[14] In asserting that the Constitution left states no control of their own militias, William Grayson, an Anti-Federalist lawyer from Prince William County, Virginia, worried specifically about the infliction of "unusual punishments."[15] Likewise, George Mason—the principal drafter of the Virginia Declaration of Rights—expressed concern about "punishments of an unusual nature" in discussing the militia.[16] In that debate, no less a figure than Patrick Henry—fearful of the proposed U.S. treaty power, and of legendary "Give me liberty or give me death!" fame—also expressed a specific apprehension about the infliction of "unusual punishments."[17]

History, of course, is informative but not determinative of how modern-day judges should assess a punishment's legitimacy—and that is especially so when one thinks about torturous or cruel punishments or the necessity or lack of necessity for a punishment. A review of sources published before and shortly after the adoption of the U.S. Bill of Rights—a time of revolutions and earthquake-like social and political upheaval—certainly reveals the historical context for the Eighth Amendment's origins.[18] In such sources, one finds multiple references to "usual punishments"[19] and their opposite, "unusual punishments."[20] Thus, in the eighteenth and early nineteenth centuries—prior to the abolition of American slavery—one finds multiple references to the "usual punishment" inflicted upon slaves.[21] In one source, on Roman history, there is a specific reference to what was described as "the usual punishment inflicted on such slaves as attempted to run away from their masters": the marking of slaves on their foreheads "with a red-hot iron."[22] The concepts of "usual" and "unusual" punishments were even used by Biblical commentators and playwrights—or at least by their English translators.[23]

References to "usual" and "unusual" punishments actually pre-date the English Bill of Rights (1689), with many draconian bodily punishments then in widespread use.[24] In a book published in 1661, before the Glorious Revolution of 1688, a chapter titled "Of the Roman Punishments" speaks of "the usual Punishments exercised" for "City Discipline."[25] "Punishments publickly inflicted on malefactors," Thomas Godwyn wrote there, "are either *Pecuniary mulcts*, or *corporal punishments*."[26] "The corporal punishments," he emphasized, "were either such as were *Capital*, depriving a man of his life: or *Castigatory*, such corrections as served for the humbling and reforming of the offender, or for the destroying of him."[27] Those sentenced to prison for "notorious crimes," Godwyn relayed, had "shackles and bolts about their legs" to prevent their escape, were forced to labor by digging or tilling the ground or grinding with a hand-mill, and also had "their foreheads marked or burned with some letters of infamy."[28] "[P]ublishing the cause" of one's punishment "either by Inscription, or by the voice of a common Crier," Godwyn added, "was not unusual in ... capital punishments."[29] Corporal punishments in Medieval times, and for long thereafter, had been used to systematically humiliate or shame offenders. For example, "walking stocks" were "[a] board with a chain and with three holes in it, one for the head and the other two for the wrists." An offender was required to wear the board, and the chain was used to lead the offender to a dungeon or the place of execution. People would throw things at the defenseless offender as he was paraded around in the walking stocks.[30]

A large number of references to "usual" or "unusual" punishments can also be found in relation to English law,[31] including in the seventeenth and eighteenth centuries, not too distant from the all-important Glorious Revolution of 1688.[32] For example, in 1700, a dictionary of Greek and Roman antiquities—translated from French into English—was published in London.[33] One entry notes that condemned criminals "were exposed to Beasts without any Arms to defend themselves and often they were bound, and the People were pleased to see them torn to pieces, and devoured by those hungry creatures."[34] "This was the most usual Punishment, which the Pagan Emperors inflicted upon the first Christians, whom they ordered to be given to the Beasts," that dictionary reported just over a decade after the adoption of the English Bill of Rights.[35] Another source, printed in Edinburgh, notes how, in 1594, the Parliament itself—for an attempt on Henry IV's life—condemned a Jesuit, John Chatel, "to the usual punishment due to such offenders."[36]

The Dichotomy Between "Usual" and "Unusual" Punishments

The number of eighteenth-century English sources referring to "usual punishments" is substantial.[37] Matthew Hale's treatise, *The History of the Pleas of the Crown*, discusses the "usual punishment" of heretics;[38] David Hume's *The History of England* speaks of "the usual punishment for murder";[39] *The Works of Samuel Johnson* contains a reference to "the usual punishment" for felons;[40] Oliver Goldsmith's *The History of England* notes that "the usual punishment" for traitors was for offenders "to be hanged, drawn, and quartered";[41] and other sources contain references to either "the usual Punishment of Law"[42] or "the usual Punishment of the Law."[43] The phrase "usual punishments" is also found in parliamentary debates[44] and pertaining to the French Revolution.[45] In Great Britain's Parliament, the prohibition against "cruel and unusual punishments" was specifically brought up in discussions of the English Bill of Rights, forthrightly described as "that important statute."[46] Likewise, in the parliamentary debates for April 24, 1809, the Petition of Henry White—reprinted as part of those debates—was presented to Parliament by a member of Parliament, a "Mr. Whitbread." Henry White's petition states in part as follows:

> Your Petitioner submits to the consideration of this honourable house, the extreme severity of the sentence passed upon him, as being contrary to the rights and liberties of every British subject in these realms, guaranteed to them by the Bill of Rights, which expressly says, "that excessive fines ought not to be imposed, nor cruel and unusual punishments inflicted," your Petitioner having already suffered, under a state of severe and dangerous illness, upwards of nine months imprisonment and banishment in Dorchester-Gaol, from his home, his business, and the Country where he was tried, and which has already subjected him to a pecuniary expense of upwards of 500*l*., and which, unless mitigated by the interference of this honourable house, it is more than probable will prove fatal to the life of

your Petitioner, and ruinous to his circumstances, and future welfare of his family.[47]

Commentators on English law, in what must be seen as expressions of the times in which they lived, also frequently made use of the "usual" punishments terminology. For example, Guy Miège (1644–*c.*1718), a Swiss writer from Lausanne who taught English as a foreign language,[48] published a book in 1691 titled *The New State of England Under Their Majesties K. William and Q. Mary.*[49] In it, Miège described the "the publick Justice administered at four times of the Year in Westminster" and by "Twelve Judges," of the courts known as Assizes, "twice a Year ... in the Country ... in the several Counties the King is pleased to appoint them for."[50] Noting that England's judicial system was "divided into Six Parts, called Circuits,"[51] Miège wrote in Chapter XVI: "My Business is now to speak of the Punishments inflicted here upon Criminals of what nature soever."[52] In a chapter titled "Of the Punishments inflicted on Malefactors," he took note of "the Manner of Trying Criminals in England; wherein is to be commended our English Humanity towards Prisoners that are upon their Trial."[53] "Hanging," Miège emphasized, "is the usual Punishment of Death in England, either for High Treason, Petty Treason, or Felony."[54] "As to Persons of great Birth and Quality, convicted of High Treason, Petty Treason, or Felony, tho the Judgment be the same with that of common Persons," Miège qualified, "yet by the Kings Favour they are usually *Beheaded*."[55] In other words, in an era when death sentences and executions were commonplace worldwide, a particular method of execution could be considered a "usual" punishment.

In his popular and widely distributed *Commentaries on the Laws of England*, Sir William Blackstone himself used the phrase "usual punishment" in writing about the punishment of "petit treason" committed "by those of the female sex."[56] "Where the wife killeth her husband, it is petit treason," another Englishman, Francis Bacon, wrote of that crime, noting that the woman was burned to death for the offense.[57] In another part of his *Commentaries*, Blackstone specifically referenced the bar on "cruel and unusual punishments." In particular, Blackstone saw the prohibition against cruel and unusual punishments as constraining *arbitrary* and *discretionary* power. As to fines and prison sentences, Blackstone observed that "the duration and quantity" of such fines or terms of incarceration were properly left to judges. "[H]owever unlimited the power of the court may seem," Blackstone emphasized of such judgments, "it is far from being wholly arbitrary," for the judge's "discretion is regulated by law." "For the bill of rights has particularly declared," Blackstone wrote, "that excessive fines ought not to be imposed, nor cruel and unusual punishments inflicted."[58]

That the English prohibition against cruel and unusual punishments[59] was seen as a constraint on disproportionate and unreasonable penalties, arbitrary judicial power, and otherwise boundless common-law judicial discretion is clear.[60] An extended passage, from "Mr. Emlyn's Preface,"[61] one originally written in 1730 and reprinted in *A Complete Collection of State Trials and Proceedings for High Treason and Other Crimes and Misdemeanors from the Earliest Period to the Year 1783* (1816), makes that abundantly apparent. As the preface to that book, published in London, reads:

> As to smaller Crimes and Misdemeanors, they are differenced with such a variety of extenuating or aggravating circumstances, that the law has not,

> nor indeed could affix to each a certain and determinate Penalty, this is left to the discretion and prudence of the Judge, who may punish it either with Fine or Imprisonment, Pillory or Whipping, as he shall think the nature of the crime deserves; but though he be intrusted with so great power, yet he is not at liberty to do as he lists, and inflict what arbitrary punishments he pleases; due regard is to be had to quality and degree, to the estate and circumstances of the offender, and to the greatness or smallness of the offence; that Fine, which would be a mere trifle to one man, may be the utter ruin and undoing of another; and those marks of ignominy and disgrace, which would be shocking and grievous to a person of a liberal education, would be slighted and despised by one of the vulgar sort. A Judge therefore who uses this discretionary power to gratify a private revenge, or the rage of a party, by inflicting indefinite and perpetual Imprisonment, excessive and exorbitant Fines, unusual and cruel Punishments, is equally guilty of perverting justice and acting against law, as he, who in a case, where the law has ascertained the penalty, willfully and knowingly varies from it. If no measures were to be observed in these discretionary Punishments, a man who is guilty of a Misdemeanor might be in a worse condition than if he had committed a capital crime; he might be exposed to an indefinite and perpetual Imprisonment, a punishment not at all favoured by law, as being worse than death itself: nor does an extravagant Fine, which is beyond the power of the offender ever to pay or raise, differ much from it; for if his Imprisonment depend upon a condition, which will never be in his power to perform, it is the same as if it were absolute and unconditional; if the offender be not able to pay such a Fine as his offence deserves, he must then submit to a corporal punishment in lieu of it, according to the old Rule, *Qui non habet in crumena, luat in cute.*[62] It is true, that Clause of Magna Charta which requires the saving every man's contenement, (viz. his means of livelihood)[63] extends only to Amerciaments,[64] which are ascertained by a Jury, and not to Fines, which are imposed by the Court; but nevertheless those Fines ought to be moderate and within bounds; where a court has a power of setting Fines, that must be understood of setting reasonable Fines: "an excessive Fine," says lord Coke, "is against law," and so it is declared to be by the Act "for declaring the Rights and Liberties of the Subject," &c. The same Statute declares the Illegality of unusual and cruel Punishments.[65]

That the prohibition against cruel and unusual punishments was targeted at runaway discretion also showed up in America, including, in one instance, almost a century after the publication of William Blackstone's *Commentaries on the Laws of England*. On May 30, 1864, at a constitutional convention in Maryland, a Mr. Stockbridge proposed combining into a single provision Maryland's separate prohibitions against "cruel and unusual pains and penalties" and "cruel or unusual punishments."[66] Saying that the proposed change "is one rather of form than of substance," Mr. Stockbridge offered an amendment so that the newly consolidated provision would bar the infliction "in any case" of "cruel, unusual or excessive pains, penalties and punishments."[67] In response, a Mr. Miller objected, saying that the first prohibition was "a prohibition on the power of the Legislature to pass any law inflicting cruel and unusual pains and punishments, and penalties" whereas the second prohibition "relates to the administration of justice by the Courts of Law."[68] Mr. Miller then argued:

> It is well known to gentlemen here, to the gentleman from Baltimore city (Mr. Stockbridge) that the common law prevails in this State, in pursuance of an article adopted in the bill of rights. Under that common law, the Courts, when the party is convicted of any offence, for which no penalty is prescribed by statute, have the power, in their discretion, of inflicting fines, penalties or imprisonment; and this 24th article is directed against undue exercise by the courts of the power they thus have entrusted to them by the common law. When the statutes define the penalty and prescribe the punishment for any offence, then no Court of Law can exceed it in according the punishment for the offencc, And the 24th article is designed to prevent the Courts of Justice from inflicting unusual and cruel punishments in cases where the punishment is left entirely to their discretion; and that I think is a good provision. And as these two articles relate to different subjects-matter, I think they should continue as separate and distinct provisions in the bill of rights. The one prohibiting the passage by the Legislature of an act which would warrant a Court of Justice in inflicting cruel and unusual pains and penalties, and the other providing that, in cases where the common law prevails, no such cruel or unusual punishments should be inflicted at the arbitrary will of the Judge, or in the mere discretion of the Court.[69]

The prohibitions against "cruel and unusual pains and penalties" and "cruel or unusual punishment" in Maryland's constitution remained separate. Article XVI of Maryland's 1867 constitution, using language similar to that in Maryland's 1776 Declaration of Rights,[70] Maryland's 1851 Declaration of Rights,[71] and Maryland's 1864 Declaration of Rights,[72] declared: "That sanguinary Laws ought to be avoided as far as it is consistent with the safety of the State; and no Law to inflict cruel and unusual pains and penalties ought to be made in any case, or at any time, hereafter."[73] Meanwhile, Article XXV of Maryland's 1867 constitution, employing language used in Maryland's 1776 Declaration of Rights,[74] Maryland's 1851 Declaration of Rights,[75] and Maryland's 1864 Declaration of Rights,[76] provided: "That excessive bail ought not to be required, nor excessive fines imposed, nor cruel or unusual punishment inflicted by the Courts of Law."[77] The point not to be lost: the prohibition against cruel and unusual punishments had embedded in it a protection against arbitrary government action. And what could be more arbitrary than inflicting an *unnecessary* punishment? The only thing worse would be inflicting an unnecessary punishment in a *discriminatory* fashion based on race, gender, or some other factor that has no bearing on justice or proportionality between crime and punishment. And as a punishment becomes less and less usual, it becomes more and more unusual—and it becomes clear that it has also become less and less necessary and more and more arbitrary.

The Customs and Practices of Nations

There was a fascination in earlier times—as is still the case today—with the social mores, customs, and laws of other nations. Thus, in eighteenth-century sources, numerous references can be found to "usual punishments" or "unusual punishments," particularly in relation to the practices of other countries or locales.[78] For example, in a section on the "Oriental Islands," a 1751 history of the nations of the world noted: "One of their usual Punishments is to strip the Criminal, bind him Hand and Foot, and tie him to a Post, and expose his Face to the Sun from Morning to Night, when the Musketoes or Gnats almost cover his Body, and sting him unmercifully, and he is perfectly blistered by the Sun's scorching Heat."[79] "[S]ometimes," that source reported, "they lay him flat on his Back on the hot Sands, while he is almost devoured by the Musketoes."[80] The ancient Persians notoriously made use of insects as instruments of torture, with *scaphism* being a practice whereby "[t]he victim"—as one source puts it—"initially force-fed milk and honey to induce severe diarrhea," was then "stripped, lashed to a skiff (or hollowed-out tree trunk) so that his head, hands, and feet protruded over the sides, smeared with honey," and "set adrift on a stagnant pond or simply left in the sun." As that source reports of what occurred next:

> Wasps attracted to the honey delivered excruciating stings, but the coup de grâce came with the insects drawn to the feces accumulating in the boat. Flies would breed in the filth and then begin laying eggs in the victim's anus and increasingly gangrenous flesh. Although the misery could be prolonged by providing the victim with continuing allotments of milk and honey, the condemned would eventually succumb to septic shock associated with being infested with maggots.[81]

The idea of *usual punishments* thus reflected those punishments either commonly or traditionally inflicted in particular places, while the term *unusual punishments* presumably referred to punishments that were seen as foreign or unacceptable in a particular locale.

The writer's viewpoint—or the perception of a place's history—could determine the usage of the "usual" or "unusual" terminology. In discussing Roman history, a subject of great and continuing fascination, writers frequently discussed the "usual punishment" of slaves[82] and offenders,[83] including of vestal virgins who violated their vows of chastity.[84] "The breaking of the legs of slaves," one book noted, "was not an unusual punishment among the Romans; which was done by laying the legs on an anvil, and breaking them in two with hammers."[85] The authors of an earlier book, in discussing "an ancient Roman" who learned a "freed-man" had kissed his "marriageable" daughter, reported: "We are not told whether or not he contended himself with the usual punishment inflicted for a kiss"—"which was whipping."[86] Twelve men, "each carrying a bundle of rods bound together with a leathern throng, in the midst of which was an ax," a 1740 book detailing Roman customs reported, "served" the Roman king "in the double capacity of guards and officers to execute justice and his commands; whether it were to cut off an head, or whip a criminal; which were the usual punishments amongst the Romans."[87] In another source, from 1680, there is a reference to "some strange or unusual punishment,"[88] suggesting a punishment that was, in the eye of the beholder, bizarre or out of the ordinary.

Turkish practices, like Roman traditions, also drew considerable attention. As Thomas Salmon's *Modern History* reported: "The usual punishments appropriated to crimes in Turkey are as follow, viz. A murderer is beheaded, a thief strangled, an apostate burnt, a traytor is dragged at a horse's tail, and afterwards impaled; and if one maims or wounds another, the like punishment is inflicted on the offender: an eye for an eye, a limb for a limb, according to the Jewish law." "[T]he usual punishment in Turkey," Salmon said elsewhere, "is the salack; where the offender being obliged to sit down on the ground, and having his legs held up, receives a certain number of blows upon the soles of his feet with a little rattan or cane of the bigness of a man's finger."[89] "The most usual punishments in Turkey for capital offences," one memoir concluded, revealing the context in which the usual terminology was used, "are beheading, drowning, hanging, strangling, burning, impaling, and the strappadoe; the two last as the most cruel, and are appointed only for Turks who renounce the Mahometan faith, or renegadoes who return to the Christian religion."[90] "The usual punishments for slight offences," wrote another historian, "are whipping, or public labour for a length of time proportioned to the nature of the crime."[91]

The "usual" or "unusual" references are found in countless descriptions of many other places or legal systems, too, including Algiers,[92] Carthage,[93] Ceylon,[94] China,[95] Egypt,[96] France,[97] Germany,[98] Greece,[99] India,[100] Ireland,[101] Japan,[102] Java,[103] Persia,[104] Siam,[105] Sumatra,[106] Sweden,[107] and the West Indies.[108] A translation of *Plutarch's Lives* makes a reference to "the usual punishment,"[109] with another book—on royal genealogies—referencing "the usual Punishment of Sacrilege."[110] Yet another history, published in 1726, tellingly emphasized that "the usual Punishment of Heretics, according to the Sentence and Decrees" of "ancient Councils" was for offenders to be "divested both of the Name and Office of Priests."[111] The number of antiquated crimes from Medieval times—witchcraft, sorcery and fortune-telling—is matched only by the number of horrific and grotesque punishments from pre-Enlightenment times. Ancient practices included everything from disemboweling while alive and drawing and quartering to public dissection and crucifixion.[112]

References to "usual" or "unusual" punishments are thus ubiquitous in Anglo-American sources, with those words used in both legal and non-legal sources. In an English dictionary published in Edinburgh in 1816, one finds a reference to "usual punishments" in the entry titled "PUNISHMENT, CAPITAL."[113] That entry reads: "Every mode of taking away life, which the ingenuity of torture could devise, have been used in different cases. We decline the horrid and unnecessary detail. Hanging and beheading are the usual punishments of civilized nations."[114] That source suggests that whereas hanging and beheading were the usual punishments in civilized countries, unusual punishments were, presumably, the ones involving the use of torture.[115] In another book, *The History of the Life and Reign of Alexander the Great*, Chapter IV begins with the following "friendly remonstrance" received by Alexander: "How long, sir, will you gratify your anger, by executions conducted in a foreign manner? Your own soldiers, your fellow-citizens, without being allowed to plead, are hauled to punishment by their captives. If you deem us to merit death, at least change our executioners." "[B]ut," the history reported, "his rage had proceeded to madness" and he thus "ordered those who had charge of the prisoners ... to plunge them into the river, chained as they were." The history noted: "Nor did this *unusual punishment* raise a second mutiny...."[116]

People's use of language reveals that human beings are prone to characterize the punishments they encounter (or read about) in their daily lives. For example, in an 1825 edition of *The New Annual Register*, one finds reprinted a parliamentary debate in which the idea of "unnecessary punishments" came up. Corporal punishments, it was noted there, had been declared to be "unnecessary" by "some of the best and most humane men" in the naval service.[117] The debate over what punishments were necessary was, in fact, one about liberty itself. As Frederick Rosen writes in *The Cambridge History of Eighteenth Century Political Thought*: "The idea of a proportion between crimes and punishments or a scale of punishments was based on the doctrine of liberty adopted by Montesquieu, Beccaria, and Bentham." "For these writers," Rosen observes, "liberty meant individual security, and the establishment of a proportion between crimes and punishments should work towards a condition in society where arbitrary and unnecessary punishments would be abolished."[118]

The Case of the Ducking-Stool

The truly antiquated and barbarous nature of early Anglo-American punishments was on full display in the 1825 Pennsylvania Supreme Court case, *James v. Commonwealth*.[119] In that case, Pennsylvania's highest court specifically considered the legality of the use of the "ducking-stool," a corporal punishment that was once designated as the "usual punishment" for "scolds."[120] In that case, Nancy James had been convicted of being a common scold and, in 1824, was sentenced in Pennsylvania "to be placed in a certain engine of correction, called a cucking or ducking-stool, on Wednesday, the third day of November, then next ensuing, between the hours of ten and twelve o'clock in the morning, and being so placed therein, to be plunged three times into the water."[121] Her counsel asserted the sentence was "illegal" as being violative of both the U.S. Constitution and Pennsylvania's constitution, teeing up a major public controversy.[122] Finding the Eighth Amendment inapplicable to state-based legal challenges,[123] the Pennsylvania court—in an era before the incorporation of the provisions of the U.S. Bill of Rights against American states[124]—first found that state courts "are left at liberty to regulate their own criminal codes as they may deem proper, without reference to the laws or constitution of the United States."[125] That court then moved into the realm of state law and the common law.

As to Pennsylvania's constitution, which prohibited "cruel punishments," James's counsel contended that ducking "was not a common-law punishment," but had been introduced by statute in the reign of Henry III.[126] "[E]ven if it were a common-law" punishment, counsel contended, "yet it was one of those barbarous customs, which did not suit the spirit of the times in which our ancestors migrated to this country."[127] As counsel asserted: "It had become nearly obsolete in England, and therefore, according to the general rules of colonization, was not included in that part of the common law, which the first settlers brought with them."[128] The record reveals a concerted effort by James's counsel to prove, as a factual matter, that ducking—forthrightly described in William Hawkins's *A Treatise of the Pleas of the Crown* as the "usual punishment" for scolds—was no longer in general use.[129] "[D]ucking," counsel asserted, "is one of those '*cruel*,' or barbarous punishments of our British ancestors, the infliction of which is expressly forbidden by the constitution."[130]

In contrast, Pennsylvania authorities sought to preserve their right to resort to the ducking stool. Pennsylvania's deputy attorney general thus tried to show "that ducking was a common-law punishment for scolding, and the statute of Henry III merely applied it to another offence."[131] "Although it was not often carried into execution," he asserted, "it was still in force in England, at the time of the first settlement of Pennsylvania, and therefore, he argued, brought over by the colonists with the rest of the common law."[132] "It is remarkable," the deputy attorney general specifically pointed out, that Pennsylvania's constitution, "many of the articles of which are copied literally from that of the United States, has omitted the word 'unusual,' and prescribes only *cruel* punishments."[133] "He submitted to the court," the record shows, "that the phrase 'cruel punishments,' here means the torture—the *peine forte et dure*, and such others as shock the mind of every man possessed of common feeling."[134] While the rack had long been associated with torture, *peine forte et dure* was an English practice also known as pressing to death.[135] In fact, prominent American founders and framers had concluded, decades earlier, that the constitutional prohibition on "cruel and unusual punishments" was meant to outlaw torture,[136] though the concept of torture was understood to mean something much different in the eighteenth century than it means today.[137]

In attempting to defend the use of the ducking stool before Pennsylvania's judges, Pennsylvania's deputy attorney general argued that it was very difficult to establish that a punishment was cruel—especially since the death penalty, a more severe punishment, was then still explicitly authorized by law.[138] As he asserted before the Pennsylvania court: "In one sense, *death* is a cruel punishment, and yet no one doubts of its constitutionality. It must be a very glaring and extreme case, to justify the court in pronouncing a punishment unconstitutional on account of its cruelty; and this is not such a case."[139] The deputy attorney general—seeking to show state practice, much as modern lawyers do in twenty-first-century Eighth Amendment challenges—also pointed out that "the penalty of ducking has actually been inflicted upon scolds in the state of Pennsylvania."[140] "The Attorney-General," the case report reflects, "produced the records of the court of quarter sessions of Philadelphia county, by which it appeared that there had been at least three instances of conviction of the offence of being 'a common scold,' in two of which the sentence of ducking had been carried into execution."[141]

The case involving Nancy James attracted considerable interest in Pennsylvania's legal community, especially since state residents thought of themselves as decent, enlightened citizens. After counsel for both sides had made their arguments, a "Mr. *Duponceau*"—a prominent local lawyer who, in 1824, had published *A Dissertation on the Nature and Extent of the Jurisdiction of the Courts of the United States*[142]—addressed the court, having obtained leave "to make a few remarks as *amicus curiae*."[143]

According to the report: "He felt interested, he said, in the question before the court, because he thought the execution of this sentence would be a disgrace to the state of Pennsylvania, and therefore, he trusted, the court would not feel themselves obliged to pronounce it law."[144] "Whatever might be the common law on this subject," he argued, urging the court to distance itself from Great Britain, "it was not brought to this country by the colonists."[145] He then referred the court to a state law passed in 1806, "which he thought conclusive."[146] He emphasized "that this punishment"—speaking of ducking, the once-decidedly *usual* English punishment for scolds—"had become obsolete in England," expressing the sincere hope "we would not continue their barbarous customs, after they had themselves disused them."[147]

Pierre Etienne Du Ponceau (1760–1844), also known as Peter Stephen Du Ponceau, was a French-born linguist who learned English as a boy, was educated by Benedictine monks, and who sailed for America in 1777 as a secretary for Prussian Baron von Stueben—a soldier Benjamin Franklin had recruited to help train and organize the American Continental Army.[148] Du Ponceau was later appointed Assistant Secretary to Robert R. Livingston, George Washington's Secretary of Foreign Affairs, and he became a citizen of Pennsylvania and the U.S., anglicizing his forenames to Peter Stephen.[149] Du Ponceau lived in Philadelphia for many years, became a lawyer and a member of the American Philosophical Society, and then became a founding member of the Law Academy of Philadelphia in 1821.[150] Du Ponceau's one-time boss, Robert Livingston, was part of one of America's most powerful and distinguished political families, one "descended"—as one source puts it—"from a younger son of the fourth Lord of Callendar, a noble Scottish family related to Mary Queen of Scots and Isabel Stuart, mistress of James IV." As that source, *America's Political Dynasties*, reports: "When the First Continental Congress convened, in 1774, William Livingston was a representative from New Jersey, and the five-man New York delegation included his brother Philip and two Livingston in-laws, James Duane and John Jay."

The influence of the Livingston family cannot be understated. Robert R. Livingston, Sr. (1718–1775) was a prominent colonial politician who served as a member of New York's provincial assembly and as a judge of the New York Supreme Court of Judicature; Philip Livingston (1716–1778), a merchant, was a delegate to the Continental Congress from 1775 to 1778 and became a signer of the Declaration of Independence; William Livingston (1723–1790), a lawyer, became the first governor of New Jersey and was a signer of the U.S. Constitution; Robert R. Livingston, Jr. (1746–1813) served on the Committee of Five that drafted the Declaration of Independence and served as the 1st Chancellor of New York from 1777 to 1801 and as the 1st United States Secretary of Foreign Affairs (1781–1783) before serving as United States Minister to France from 1801 to 1804; Henry Brockholst Livingston (1757–1823) served as an Associate Justice on the U.S. Supreme Court from 1806 to 1823, receiving his nomination from Thomas Jefferson; and Edward Livingston (1764–1836)—the prominent penal reformer who so admired the work of Montesquieu and Beccaria—served as Mayor of New York, in Congress (representing New York from 1795 to 1801 and Louisiana from 1823 to 1831), and as the 11th U.S. Secretary of State and as U.S. Minister to France. Edward Livingston had a close friendship with Du Ponceau, whom Livingston described as a "learned counsellor and excellent friend," and the two men specifically corresponded on issues pertaining to the criminal law, with Livingston telling Du Ponceau about his reliance on Bentham's work and Du Ponceau lending Livingston an important text, one written by Francis Bacon.[151]

A correspondent of James Madison and Thomas Jefferson, and often retained by French nationals, diplomats and consuls needing legal representation in American courts, Pierre Etienne Du Ponceau was admitted to practice in the Pennsylvania courts and in the U.S. Supreme Court.[152] Du Ponceau published one of his most important works, *A Brief View of the Constitution of the United States*, in 1834. That book gave an historical introduction to the Constitution, setting out the "prominent features of our excellent constitution," and ended with its actual text and that of the Declaration of Independence.[153] Du Ponceau had been elected a member of the American Philosophical Society in 1791, the same year the U.S. Bill of Rights was ratified, and from 1828 until his death served as its President, following in the footsteps of Benjamin Franklin and Thomas Jefferson.[154] He regularly signed his name "Du Ponceau," but apparently tolerated his name appearing in print as "Duponceau." One nineteenth-century source, *History of Philadelphia* (1884), describes the man's reputation and influence this way: "Peter Stephen Du Ponceau was one of the most eminent of the men who came on after the Revolution, and he is specially to be commended for the services he rendered in the matter of putting the standard of law studies and law literature upon a high eminence...."[155]

In *James*, the Pennsylvania Supreme Court began its opinion by acknowledging precisely what was at stake, noting in its decision that Nancy James's sentence "has created much ferment and excitement in the public mind; it is considered as a cruel, unusual, unnatural and ludicrous judgment."[156] "[B]ut whatever prejudices may exist against it," the court noted, having separated the words *cruel* and *unusual* by commas but putting them in a list of very judgmental-sounding words, "still, if it be the law of the land, the court must pronounce judgment for it."[157] "But," it continued, "as it is revolting to humanity, and is of that description that only could have been invented in an age of barbarism, we ought to be well persuaded, either that it is the appropriate judgment of the common law, or is inflicted by some positive law; and that that common law or statutory provision has been adopted here, and is now in force."[158] Associate Justice Thomas Duncan[159]—who delivered the Pennsylvania Supreme Court's opinion—stressed at the very outset just how much time had been spent by the court researching the punishment of ducking: "I have employed some time, not very pleasantly, certainly not very profitably, in tracing the punishment *ad ludibrium*, to its source, and have followed this stream until it has sunk in oblivion, in the general improvement of society, and the reformation of criminal punishment, and been dried up by time, that great innovator."[160] It was, obviously, very difficult—indeed, impossible—to determine who had actually come up with the idea of ducking in the first instance.

In the Pennsylvania Supreme Court's opinion, Justice Duncan reflected on the oddity—and the inherently degrading and discriminatory nature—of the scolding offense. "It must strike all, as a peculiar feature of this offence," he said, "that it is of the feminine gender, that it degraded woman to a mere *thing*, to a *nuisance*, and does not consider her as a person."[161] "But this is not to be wondered at," he added, "when we reflect on the general degraded state of woman, when this punishment was introduced; she was, in some respects, the servant or slave of the husband; so that he might correct her with a stick as thick as his own thumb."[162] "At the common law," Duncan emphasized, "women were denied the benefit of clergy, merely because their sex precluded them from holy orders, however learned they might be, while their more ignorant husbands, who could with difficulty read even the neck-verse, were burnt in the hand with a cold iron, for the offence for which they were doomed to die on the gallows."[163] Duncan pointed out that, under the authority of Blackstone and others, "[t]he right of the husband" is "to beat his wife," with Duncan noting that "if we add the present instance of partiality, that a scolding woman is to be ducked, while the most scandalously abusive and railing man goes unpunished, the iniquity and injustice will be very striking."[164]

At common law, *benefit of clergy* was—as *Black's Law Dictionary* puts it—"the privilege of a cleric not to be tried for a felony in the King's Court." "[I]n the Middle Ages," that popular legal dictionary notes, "any man who could recite the 'neck verse' was granted the benefit of clergy." As that source explains of the doctrine and its ultimate fate:

> Although *clergy* includes monks and nuns as well as priests, only in rare cases did women claim or receive benefit of clergy. Congress outlawed benefit of clergy in federal courts in April 1790. It was abolished in England in 1827 but survived even longer in some American states, such as South Carolina, where it was successfully claimed in 1855.[165]

The neck-verse—the key to accessing benefit of clergy for those eligible for it—was the first verse of Psalm 51. If a criminal claimed on the scaffold "benefit of his clergy," it has been noted, the priest presented him with a Psalter, and the condemned criminal was then given a chance to read his neck-verse. If Psalm 51 could be recited, the condemned criminal's life would be spared.[166]

Before passing on James' sentence, Justice Duncan—grappling with how to rule at the close of the first quarter of the nineteenth century—also gave an extensive history of the punishment under review, gathered after as much research as possible could be done. After focusing on the actual instrumentalities previously used to inflict the punishment,[167] Duncan—writing for the court, and in light of the varied kinds of ducking or cucking stools known to have been employed in the past—noted: "Thus, in our very outset, we are involved in doubt, and who shall decide, where there is such a difference among the learned? The officer would not know what to do, whether to fix Nancy James on a stool, or in a bucket, whether she is to be run into the river on wheels, or to be soused into a pond, from a beam or rafter."[168] Justice Duncan specifically recounted how the punishment of ducking was so antiquated in England that examples of the devices used to inflict it could not be readily located.[169] Duncan referenced the repeal of "two bloody statutes ... by the voice of humanity," saying "that it seems most probable, that hanging of women as witches and gypsies, and ducking them as scolds, ceased about the same time, viz: the time of the restoration, and before the charter to William Penn."[170] "Indeed," he concluded, "it appears, that at the same period, the race of witches and scolds became extinct, when the law ceased to hang the witches and duck the scolds."[171]

In the state supreme court's opinion, Justice Duncan, focusing on the disuse of the scolding punishment in spite of its prior statutory authorization, next explained that "[t]he instances are numerous of statutes being repealed in fact—a kind of silent legislation."[172] After considering the evidence, Duncan explained: "As to the abrogation of statutes by '*non user*,' there may rest some doubt; for myself, I own, my opinion is, that '*non user*' may be such as to render them obsolete, when their objects vanish or their reason ceases."[173] He then turned to the common law, taking it into account as he weighed the facts at issue. "The common law (and this is but a customary punishment), what is it, but common usage?" Duncan offered. "The long disuetude of any law," he concluded, "amounts to its repeal."[174] A "villeinous judgment, by long disuse," he concluded of one species of punishment, "has become obsolete, it not having been pronounced for ages."[175] "The barbarous writ of attaint, which has as strong a foundation as any principle in common law," he added, "has been long banished." Bills of attainder had once been used by legislatures to condemn people to death without trial, but they had been abolished by the U.S. Constitution.[176]

Justice Duncan—writing less than thirty-five years after the ratification of the U.S. Bill of Rights, but several decades before the adoption of the Fourteenth Amendment—ultimately concluded that once-common punishments, even those still on the statute books, could become improper through disuse. "That such crimes and punishments existed at the common law," he acknowledged of certain punishments, "every treatise to the present day states; but this does not prove," he quickly clarified, "that they now exist."[177] In other words, punishments previously authorized by law could fade away into oblivion, with the common law itself—the very foundation of Anglo-American law—plainly expected to evolve over time. "They are nothing more," he emphasized of antiquated punishments, "than the memorials of times that are past, as the usages of our uncivilized ancestors; and in nothing is the gradual change of the common law more apparent, and in nothing does it accommodate itself more to the change of manners and effect of education, than in the silent and gradual disuse of barbarous criminal punishments."[178]

After citing a treatise from 1581 that distinguished between capital and non-capital corporal punishments, Justice Duncan then noted the diminishing use of corporal punishments and that he could find no evidence of the ducking of scolds for many decades.[179] Duncan referenced both English authorities[180] and Pennsylvania lawyer James Wilson—an American Founding Father and an Associate Justice of the U.S. Supreme Court from 1789 to 1798 in the wake of the Constitution's ratification—in support of his conclusion that ducking was an impermissible and antiquated punishment.[181] Wilson himself had taken an interest in penal reform, with his own son, Bird Wilson, in gathering up and reprinted his father's works, actually quoting Beccaria and citing Montesquieu side by side in the opening preface of the compilation of his father's writings as he wrote about liberty.[182] For his own part, Duncan specifically noted that scolds were once "indictable in the sheriff's tourn,"[183] but ultimately concluded that ducking was no longer an authorized punishment for such offenders. "There is no ground, whatever may be the antiquated theory of the law," Duncan explained, "that it now exists, in fact and in practice, as a legal punishment."[184]

Justice Duncan—in delivering the state court's opinion—noted that all of the Pennsylvania Supreme Court's members might not agree on everything, but they were unanimous as to the question before the court. As Duncan stressed: "I do not know that all the members of the court agree with me in the conclusion, as to the abrogation of this punishment in England, by disuse; but in the inquiry most important, there is no difference of opinion." "We all agree in this," Duncan emphasized, "that this customary ancient punishment for ducking scolds, was never adopted, and therefore, is not the common law of Pennsylvania."[185] After writing that "the ducking-stool, cucking-stool, or choking-stool," as well as "the pillory, the *collisstrigium*, or neck-stretch, are punishments *ejusdem generis*, of the same family," Duncan cited authorities for the notion that putting someone "in the pillory" was intended to "disgrace" the offender.[186] "[I]t is very certain," Duncan explained, "that the legislature never considered the ducking-stool a legal punishment, which could be inflicted by the sentence of the law, or when they abolished the pillory and whipping-post, &c., they would have included it."[187]

Pennsylvania had, by statute, actually begun moving away from draconian corporal punishments decades earlier. In 1790, the Pennsylvania legislature had adopted "An Act to reform the Penal Laws of this state."[188] Among other things, that law substituted prison sentences and hard labor for "whipping" and other previously authorized common-law punishments, listed in the act as "burning in the hand," "cutting off the ears," "nailing the ear or ears to the pillory," and "placing in and upon the pillory."[189] "The object of the framers of the act of 1790," Justice Duncan opined in Nancy James's appeal, "was the abolition of all infamous, disgraceful, public punishments—all cruel and unnatural punishments—for all the classes of minor offences and misdemeanors, to which they had been before applied." "This was the object of the author of our humane penal code," Duncan observed, adding, "I need not mention the name of Mr. Bradford, to whom the civilized world is so much indebted."[190] William Bradford—a prominent lawyer and a close friend of James Madison from their days together at the College of New Jersey, now Princeton[191]—had long before published *An Enquiry How Far the Punishment of Death Is Necessary in Pennsylvania* (1793), his influential essay advocating the curtailment of death sentences and executions.[192]

Outdated punishments were, in fact, referred to in many ways in the early nineteenth century, and, by then, many legal commentators had weighed in strongly against them. Along with crediting William Bradford's *Enquiry*, Justice Duncan's opinion also referred to the efforts of Jared Ingersoll, a prominent jurist.[193] "The late Judge INGERSOLL," Duncan noted, "a name respected and honored, when attorney-general, in his report to the legislature, in 1813, stated that by several acts of assembly, 'cruel and unnatural punishments, which tended only to harden and confirm the criminal, had been abolished for all inferior offences.'"[194] "It is apparent," Duncan emphasized, referring to Bradford and Ingersoll, "that those two distinguished men were of opinion that all infamous corporal punishments, and disgraceful public spectacles, *ad ludibrium*, were abolished; and that the legislature so considered it when they passed the several acts reforming the penal laws, I think, we have the most conclusive evidence."[195] The reference to "cruel and unnatural punishments" instead of "cruel and unusual punishments" shows that people at that time referred to archaic, barbaric, inhuman, or cruel punishments in varying ways.[196]

In considering legal disputes, Anglo-American judges, as they always have, almost reflexively look to past practice and precedents by virtue of their legal training. Justice Duncan himself spent a lot of time recounting the history of laws punishing scolding, whether by fine, gagging, or confinement at hard labor.[197] After referencing seventeenth-century laws passed in 1682 and 1683 that punished scolding, Duncan emphasized that those laws "continued in force until 1700, when another act against scolding passed, inflicting the same penalty of imprisonment, five days at hard labor, or to be gagged and stand at some convenient place, at the discretion of the magistrate."[198] "The act of 1700 was repealed by the Queen in council, but I have not been able to find the repeal of the acts of 1682 and 1683," Duncan added long before the days of electronic legal research.[199] "Whatever be the fact," he ruled, "the conclusion is the same—that the common-law punishment of ducking was not received nor embodied by usage so as to become a part of the common law of Pennsylvania."[200] As Duncan emphasized: "It was rejected, as not accommodated to the circumstances of the country, and against all the notions of punishment entertained by this primitive and humane community; and, though they adopted the common-law doctrines as to inferior offences, yet they did not follow their punishment."[201] In sum, the corporal punishment at issue—ducking—was seen as a barbarous and inhumane one.

In the Pennsylvania Supreme Court's ruling, Justice Duncan specifically spoke of the common law and its evolving nature. "I do not find the rule on this subject," he noted, "more satisfactorily laid down than by the Chief Justice."[202] "Every country, he observed," Duncan recounted of Chief Justice William Tilghman's prior decision in *The Guardians of the Poor of Philadelphia v. Greene*,[203] "had its common law—ours is composed partly of the common law of England, and partly of our own usages."[204] Duncan then emphasized how Americans chose not to adopt the English common law in a wholesale fashion:

> Our ancestors, when they emigrated, took with them such of the English principles as were convenient for the situation in which they were about to place themselves. By degrees, as circumstances demanded, we adopted the English usages, or substituted others better suited to our wants; until, before the revolution, we had formed a system of our own, founded, in general, on the English constitution, but not without considerable variation; and in nothing was the variation greater, than in the trial and punishment of crimes.[205]

The English Bill of Rights, with its 1689 prohibition against "cruel and unusual punishments," was, of course, considered part of the "English constitution."[206] Although the British constitution is unwritten, there are several writings that are considered components of it, including the Magna Carta and the English Bill of Rights of 1689.[207] In *The Federalist Papers*, James Madison—in discussing the separation of powers in *The Federalist No. 47*—discussed the British system in these words: "The

British constitution was to Montesquieu, what Homer has been to didactic writers on epic poetry. As the latter have considered the work of the immortal bard, as the perfect model from which the principles and rules of the epic art were to be drawn, and by which all similar works were to be judged: so this great political critic appears to have viewed the constitution of England as the standard, or to use his own expression, as the mirror of political liberty...." "The accumulation of all powers, legislative, executive, and judiciary, in the same hands, whether of one, a few, or many, and whether hereditary, self-appointed, or elective," Madison emphasized, "may justly be pronounced the very definition of tyranny."[208]

In considering the prior practice of ducking scolds, Duncan wrote in the Pennsylvania Supreme Court's opinion that "all our legislation has been opposed to this punishment; judicial decisions there are none."[209] "I cannot give to the two precedents from the quarter sessions of Philadelphia," he observed, distinguishing a couple of examples he viewed as outliers, "the weight of decisions."[210] As Duncan reasoned in rejecting reliance on those precedents: "The two instances in the quarter sessions, which are principally relied upon to sustain the judgment, are too slight a foundation on which to rest a sentence, so hostile to all the policy and humanity of our penal code, and so much opposed to the sense of the community."[211] "Common-law rights," Duncan emphasized, "are to be found in the opinions of lawyers, delivered by axioms; or in judicial decisions, well considered and established; or to be collected from the universal usage through the country."[212] In other words, one could look to respectable legal maxims or the frequency of a practice *throughout America* to help determine a practice's legitimacy or illegitimacy—and to assess whether that practice was a common, or usual, one.

At the end of the first quarter of the nineteenth century, Justice Duncan thus took a pragmatic, non-rigid approach by looking at the facts themselves before writing the court's judicial decision, as any good judge would do. "What is the evidence here?" Duncan asked, looking for facts before announcing the few instances he could locate of women being ordered ducked for the offense of scolding.[213] In one notorious case from the 1781–1782 time period, Duncan wrote, a sentence of ducking was only "most reluctantly" given before being "humanely" suspended.[214] In that case, the court—"doubtful of the sentence to be given"—instead ordered the woman, by agreement and with her consent, to simply leave the neighborhood in which she had engaged in the conduct in question.[215] The decision-makers in that case, Justice Duncan editorialized, "were glad, as well as the neighborhood, to get rid of her."[216] "Mr. Bradford was then attorney-general," Duncan added, saying that "most probably, all was transacted under his advice; we can thus readily account for this unusual judgment."[217]

While he discussed the common law in some detail, Justice Duncan was clearly not willing to blindly follow ideas—or legal customs—laid down decades earlier. "I must confess," he said of the punishment of ducking, "I am not so idolatrous a worshipper, as to tie myself to the tail of this dung-cart of the common law."[218] "I am far from professing the same reverence for all the degrading and ludicrous punishments of the early days of the common law," he wrote, adding of ducking: "I am far from thinking, that this is an unbroken pillar of the common law, or that to remove this rubbish, would impair a structure, which no man can admire more than I do."[219] "In coming to the conclusion, that the ducking-stool is not the punishment of scolds," Duncan wrote, "I do not take into consideration the humane provisions of the constitutions of the United States and of this state, as to cruel and unusual punishments, further than they show the sense of the whole community."[220] The jurists on the Pennsylvania Supreme Court thus made the common law—not the U.S. Constitution or Pennsylvania's constitution—the basis of their decision. The proscriptions against cruel and unusual punishments, however, reinforced the community's shared revulsion for such punishments.

In alluding to, but not expressly relying on, Pennsylvania's constitution or the Eighth Amendment's specific proscription against cruel and unusual punishments, Justice Duncan's opinion instead focused on the barbarous and undignified nature of ducking as a punishment. As Duncan reasoned, "If the reformation of the culprit, and prevention of the crime, be the just foundation and object of all punishments, nothing could be further removed from these salutary ends, than the infliction in question."[221] "It destroys all personal respect," he explained, emphasizing that "the women thus punished would scold on for life, and the exhibition would be far from being beneficial to the spectators."[222] "What a spectacle would it exhibit!" he emphasized, worried about "a congregation of the idle" and the disorderly and the lack of any persuasive penological justification.[223] "[T]he day would produce more *scolding*," he said, "in this polite city, than would otherwise take place in a year."[224]

By ruling that the ducking-stool was an instrument of the past, not the present, Justice Duncan reversed the judgment of the court of quarter sessions.[225] In so doing, he recognized that the change in the law wrought over time was beneficial to society as a whole. "The city is rescued from this ignominious and odious show, and the state from the opprobrium of the continuance of so barbarous an institution," Duncan wrote, noting that his ruling was in line with those of other states.[226] "The courts of our sister states of New York and Massachusetts, governed by the same common law as we are," he emphasized, looking beyond the borders of Pennsylvania, "have declared that this strange and ludicrous punishment no longer exists with them."[227] "[T]he common law punishment of ducking not being received here," Duncan concluded of Pennsylvania law, "I join in the hope of a learned antiquarian and jurist of our own country, 'that we shall hereafter hear nothing of the ducking-stool, or other remains of the customs of barbarous ages.' "[228]

In the wake of the Pennsylvania Supreme Court's decision, another case—that of a sixty-year-old woman in Washington, D.C.—came into the public eye.[229] Anne Royall (also referred to as Ann Royal) was indicted in 1829 as a "common scold" and as a "common slanderer and a disturber of the peace...."[230] She had allegedly "falsely and maliciously" slandered "good citizens," with the grand jury's indictment alleging she had engaged in such conduct "in the open and public streets of the city of Washington."[231] Described as "an evil disposed person," she was accused of being "a common brawler and sower of discord among her quiet and honest neighbors" and of acting "against the peace and government of the United States."[232] In an era when ducking as a punishment was still under debate and consideration,[233] her trial took place before a jury on July 18, 1829, with Judge William Cranch presiding.[234] A local newspaper, the *National Intelligencer*, reported on the trial, noting that "[t]he examination and cross examination of the numerous witnesses occupied nearly five hours." After retiring for just a few minutes, the jury returned a guilty verdict, leaving only her punishment in question.[235]

Although Anne Royall was never actually subjected to the punishment of ducking, it was a punishment that might have been imposed had the judge so ruled. In a motion to arrest the judgment that was argued on July 28th, Royall's counsel, Richard Coxe, reportedly "suggested to the Court that according to the authorities, there was no discretion in the court to adjudge any other punishment to a common scold than the ducking stool." Because Coxe believed that ducking was an impermissible punishment, he thus sought the Court's intervention. "[A] learned English judge," Coxe argued, "respited judgment in a case of this description because he was of the opinion that a ducking would only have the effect of hardening the offender." As a report of counsel's argument emphasized:

> There was another consequence of this punishment to which he called attention of the country, which was the privilege, according to legal writers, that it conferred upon the delinquent of ever afterward scolding with impunity. He begged the court to weigh the matter and not be the first to introduce the ducking stool which had been obsolete in England since the time of Queen Anne, reminding him that the very introduction of such an engine of punishment might have the effect of increasing the crimes of this class.[236]

In the case, Judge William Cranch was thus forced to confront a plea by Anne Royall's counsel, Mr. Coxe, for an arrest of judgment of the "common scold" charge. As Judge Cranch said in summarizing the arguments of counsel: "In support of the motion to arrest the judgment, it is contended, that the law for the punishment of common scolds is quite obsolete in England, and never was in force in this country; that it is a barbarous and unusual punishment, and therefore is prohibited by the bill of rights, annexed to the constitution of Maryland under whose supposed common law this indictment is framed."[237] Cranch's ultimate conclusion was that Coxe's argument—that the scolding "offence was no longer indictable" because the "only punishment which could be inflicted" was "obsolete"—"rests upon the proposition that ducking was the only punishment which could be inflicted for the offence of being a common scold; and that proposition is supported only by uncertain inferences, drawn from a few loose expressions in the books...."[238] Sir William Blackstone, Cranch pointed out, had written:

> [A] common scold ... is a public nuisance to her neighborhood. For which offence she may be indicted; and if convicted, shall be sentenced to be placed in a certain engine of correction called the trebucket, castigatory, or cucking stool which in the Saxon language is said to signify the scolding stool: though now it is frequently corrupted into ducking stool, because the residue of the judgment is, that, when she is placed therein, she shal[l] be plunged into the water for her punishment.[239]

Judge Cranch examined the writings of legal commentators, as had the members of the Pennsylvania Supreme Court before him. "The authorities ... cited by Blackstone," Judge Cranch found, "do not indicate any opinion that ducking is the only punishment, nor even that it is an indispensable part of the punishment."[240] While Cranch, in discussing Blackstone, wrote that "[i]t is true that the court, in its discretion, might sentence the offender to be ducked only,"[241] he went on to rule:

> If a part of the common law punishment of the offence has become obsolete, the only effect is that the discretion of the court is so far limited. The offence is not obsolete, and cannot become obsolete so long as a common scold is a common nuisance. All the elementary writers upon criminal law admit that being a common scold, to the common nuisance of the neighborhood, is an indictable offence at common law.[242]

"The Court is therefore of opinion," Cranch determined, "that although punishment by ducking may have become obsolete, yet, that the offence still remains a common nuisance, and, as such, is punishable by fine and imprisonment like any other misdemeanor at common law; and that therefore the motion in arrest of judgment must be over-ruled."[243] Anne Royall was ultimately ordered to pay a fine of ten dollars, plus costs, and to put up $250 to guarantee her "good behavior for one year."[244]

The Role of the Courts

In the modern era, it falls to the U.S. Supreme Court (and, of course, state supreme courts and lower courts) to enforce limits on the severity of punishments. Before the nation's highest court, in *Graham v. Florida*[245] and *Miller v. Alabama*,[246] for example, the Supreme Court barred the imposition of mandatory life-without-parole sentences for juvenile offenders. In the latter case, the Court considered life-without-parole sentences that had been imposed on petitioners Kuntrell Jackson and Evan Miller, both 14 years old at the time of their crimes. There, Justice Elena Kagan—writing for the Court—determining that "mandatory life without parole for those under the age of 18 at the time of their crimes violates the Eighth Amendment's prohibition on 'cruel and unusual punishments.'"[247] Indeed, the U.S. Supreme Court—in every case—is the final arbiter of what the U.S. Constitution means. It must, therefore, interpret the Excessive Fines, Excessive Bail, and Cruel and Unusual Punishments Clauses and, on a case-by-case basis, decide when those clauses will be applied to invalidate a governmental action. The Court would actually be abdicating its duty were it to decline to review legislative and executive branch actions and simply defer to another branch of government as to what constitutes an "excessive" fine[248] or bail amount[249] or as to what amounts to a "cruel and unusual" punishment.[250]

Just as the U.S. Supreme Court has struck down "excessive" fines[251] as disproportionate,[252] it has—and must continue to—invalidate punishments that are either torturous[253] or—to use the Eighth Amendment's language—simply "excessive" or "cruel and unusual."[254] "The purpose of the Eighth Amendment, putting the Bail Clause to one side," the Supreme Court once declared, "was to limit the government's power to punish." Because history makes clear that unnecessary punishments have long been considered unjust (indeed, tyrannical), and because that principle is well grounded in common sense, logic, and the very impulse behind the American Declaration of Independence (the protection of liberty), that well-stated Enlightenment principle must be given effect in the twenty-first century. As for the Bail Clause, the U.S. Supreme Court emphasized in *United States v. Salerno* (1987) that "[t]his Clause, of course, says nothing about whether bail shall be available at all" and that bail may be refused in certain cases. As the Court ruled in that case: "The only arguable substantive limitation of the Bail Clause is that the Government's proposed conditions of release or detention not be 'excessive' in light of the perceived evil. Of course, to determine whether the Government's response is excessive, we must compare that response against the interest the Government seeks to protect by means of that response." "In our society," the Court was quick to point out, however, "liberty is the norm, and detention prior to trial or without trial is the carefully limited exception."[255]

Modern jurists still sometimes refer to enforcing obligations—or imposing penalties or punishments—only when "necessary" or "absolutely necessary."[256] For example, in *Holland v. Donnelly*,[257] the U.S. District Court for the Southern District of New York spoke of "the benevolent purpose of restricting the death penalty to cases where the jury believes that the ultimate sanction is absolutely necessary."[258] Likewise, in *Mercury Bay Boating Club Inc. v. San Diego Yacht Club*,[259] a New York court emphasized that forfeiture is "an extreme remedy abhorred by equity" and "should be applied only where absolutely necessary."[260] In *State v. Devlin*,[261] a judge on the Superior Court of New Jersey—after weighing aggravating and mitigating factors—also announced in similar terms: "I am satisfied that a custodial sentence is absolutely necessary."[262] Such pronouncements have strong echoes of what others have said through the years[263] or what Justice Stephen Field once wrote in a dissent in *Ex parte Wall* (1883).[264] And such decisions are in line with Montesquieu's and Beccaria's maxim even though the decisions long post-date the maxim's creation and initial promotion.

In *Ex parte Wall*, a majority of U.S. Supreme Court Justices declined to set aside a lower court ruling barring an attorney, J. B. Wall, from practicing law before the bar of the U.S. District Court for the Southern District of Florida. In that case, Wall had advised and encouraged a lynch mob, and he contended that the lower court erred in excluding him from the practice of law. His exclusion, he offered, was "on account of acts for which he may be indicted and tried by a jury," and was said to be "in violation of the Fifth Amendment of the Constitution, which forbids the depriving of any person of life, liberty, or property without due process of law."[265] "But the action of the court in cases within its jurisdiction is due process of law," the U.S. Supreme Court had emphasized in that case, concluding in these words that Wall had gotten sufficient legal process via the lower court's exercise of a summary jurisdiction over its attorneys to compel them to act appropriately: "It is a regular and lawful method of preceding, practised from time immemorial."[266]

Finding himself unable to concur with his colleagues, Justice Field—while denouncing lawlessness and what had occurred—wrote in his *Ex parte Wall* dissent of the power used to deprive Wall of his ability to practice law: "[M]y brethren are careful to express the opinion that it should seldom be exercised, when the offence charged against the attorney is indictable, until after trial and conviction, unless its commission is admitted. But the possession of the power being conceded, and its exercise being discretionary, there is in the hands of an unscrupulous, vindictive, or passionate judge, means of oppression and cruelty which should not be allowed in any free government."[267] As Justice Field stressed: "To disbar an attorney is to inflict upon him a punishment of the severest character. He is admitted to the bar only after years of study. The profession may be to him the source of great emolument."[268] As Field concluded: "To disbar him having such a practice is equivalent to depriving him of this capital. It would often entail poverty upon himself and destitution upon his family. Surely the tremendous power of inflicting such a punishment should never be permitted to be exercised unless absolutely necessary to protect to court and the public from one shown by the clearest legal proof to be unfit to be a member of an honorable profession."[269] Again, as in the Enlightenment itself, it was the absolute necessity concept that provided the pivot point on which the legal argument—and the asserted liberty interest—rested.

Notably, in *Ho Ah Kow v. Nunan* (1879), another case decided after the Fourteenth Amendment's ratification, Justice Field wrote a judicial opinion that voided the "cruel" punishment of Chinese prisoners who, on account of their race, were subjected to deliberate actions designed to disgrace and humiliate them. In April 1876, the California legislature had passed a law "concerning lodging-houses and sleeping apartments within the limits of incorporated cities." Those "found sleeping or lodging in a room or apartment containing less than 500 cubic feet of space for each person occupying it would be guilty of a misdemeanor and be punished by fine or imprisonment, or both." The City and County of San Francisco had thereafter, in June 1876, declared that every male person imprisoned in the county jail shall immediately upon arrival have his hair "cut or clipped" to a "uniform length of one inch from the scalp thereof." The plaintiff in the case, Ho Ah Kow, had been convicted of violating that law in 1878, and the defendant—the sheriff who had charge of the jail and the policy—had cut off the plaintiff's braided hair ("his queue") during his imprisonment. The plaintiff's complaint in the case—as Justice Field described it—specifically alleged as follows:

> [I]t is the custom of Chinamen to shave the hair from the front of the head and to wear the remainder of it braided into a queue; that the deprivation of the queue is regarded by them as a mark of disgrace, and is attended, according to their religious faith, with misfortunate and suffering after death; that the defendant knew of this custom and religious faith of the Chinese, and knew also that the plaintiff venerated the custom and held the faith; yet, in disregard of his rights, inflicted the injury complained of; and that the plaintiff has, in consequence of it, suffered great mental anguish, been disgraced: in the eyes of his friends and relatives, and ostracised, from association with his countrymen; and that hence he has been damaged to the amount of ten thousand dollars.

The lawsuit brought by the plaintiff further alleged—as Justice Field put it—that the ordinance (1) "exceeds the authority of the board of supervisors, the body in which the legislative power of the city and county is vested," and (2) imposed "a degrading and cruel punishment upon a class of persons who are entitled, alike with all other persons within the jurisdiction of the United States, to the equal protection of the laws." Justice Field, writing for the circuit court, agreed with both of those arguments, finding those positions "well taken." "No one," he emphasized, "would pretend that the board could, for any breach of a municipal regulation or any violation of the consolidation act, declare that a man should be deprived of his right to vote, or to testify, or to sit on a jury, or that he should be punished with stripes, or be ducked in a pond, or be paraded through the streets, or be seated in a pillory, or have his ears cropped or his head shaved." "The cutting off the hair of every male person within an inch of his scalp, on his arrival at the jail," Justice Field emphasized, "was not intended and cannot be maintained as a measure of discipline or as a sanitary regulation." After concluding that the board of supervisors had exceeded its authority in passing the ordinance, he also concluded that the ordinance—known in the community as the "Queue Ordinance"—violated "the equal protection of the laws" (as the Fourteenth Amendment reads) because it "was intended only for the Chinese in San Francisco."

After so finding, Justice Field added:

> The reason advanced for its adoption, and now urged for its continuance, is, that only the dread of the loss of his queue will induce a Chinaman to pay his fine. That is to say, in order to enforce the payment of a fine imposed upon him, it is necessary that torture should be superadded to imprisonment. Then, it is said, the Chinaman will not accept the alternative, which the law allows, of working out his fine by his imprisonment, and the state or county will be saved the expense of keeping him during the imprisonment. Probably the bastinado, or the knout, or the thumbscrew, or the rack, would accomplish the same end; and no doubt the Chinaman would prefer either of these modes of torture to that which entails upon him disgrace among his countrymen and carries with it the constant dread of misfortune and suffering after death. It is not creditable to the humanity and civilization of our people, much less to their Christianity, that an ordinance of this character was possible.

Justice Field then further emphasized:

> The complaint in this case shows that the ordinance acts with special severity upon Chinese prisoners, inflicting upon them suffering altogether disproportionate to what would be endured by other prisons if enforced against them. Upon the Chinese prisoners its enforcement operates as "a cruel and unusual punishment."
>
> ....
>
> [I]n our country hostile and discriminating legislation by a state against persons of any class, sect, creed or nation, in whatever form it may be expressed, is forbidden by the fourteenth amendment of the constitution. That amendment in its first section declares who are citizens of the United States, and then enacts that no state shall make or enforce any law which shall abridge their privileges and immunities. It further declares that no state shall deprive any person (dropping the distinctive term citizen) of life, liberty or property, without due process of law, nor deny to any person the equal protection of

> the laws. This inhibition upon the state applies to all the instrumentalities and agencies employed in the administration of its government, to its executive, legislative and judicial departments, and to the subordinate legislative bodies of counties and cities. And the equality of protection thus assured ... implies not only ... the prevention or redress of wrongs ... but that no charges or burdens shall be laid upon him which are not equally borne by others, and that in the administration of criminal justice he shall suffer for his offenses no greater or different punishment.[270]

In more recent decades, whether a punishment is necessary (or absolutely necessary) continues to be a point of demarcation—at least rhetorically, if not always in practice—for some American jurists as regards that punishment's legitimacy or illegitimacy. For instance, in 1985, the Court of Criminal Appeals of Alabama upheld the constitutionality of that state's electric chair, finding that "[t]here has been absolutely no showing that the State's method of enforcing a death sentence inflicts any more pain than is absolutely necessary."[271] Through the centuries, scores of jurists and writers have grappled with—or condemned—state-sanctioned violence or modes of punishment that inflict unnecessary pain or suffering, with the electric chair itself coming under fierce attack as an unconstitutional punishment in the courts.[272] In *State v. Mata*,[273] in fact, the Nebraska Supreme Court explicitly held that the evidence "substantially supports the district court's conclusion that electrocution 'will result in unnecessary pain, suffering, and torture' for some condemned prisoners."[274] In that case, the Nebraska Supreme Court—under the heading "Substantial Risk That Prisoner Will Suffer Unnecessary and Wanton Pain"—ruled:

> The baseline criterion in a challenge to a punishment is whether it imposes torture or a lingering death that is unnecessary to the mere extinguishment of life. "The traditional humanity of modern Anglo-American law forbids the infliction of unnecessary pain in the execution of the death sentence" and cruelty inherent in the execution method itself. "[T]he execution shall be so instantaneous and substantially painless that the punishment shall be reduced, as nearly as possible, to no more than that of death itself." Capital punishment "must not involve the unnecessary and wanton infliction of pain."[275]

Ultimately, the Nebraska Supreme Court in *Mata* concluded "that electrocution will unquestionably inflict intolerable pain unnecessary to cause death in enough executions so as to present a substantial risk that any prisoner will suffer unnecessary and wanton pain in a judicial execution by electrocution."[276] As that state supreme court, in another heading—one titled "Electrocution Is Cruel and Unusual Punishment"—reported:

> Besides presenting a substantial risk of unnecessary pain, we conclude that electrocution is unnecessarily cruel in its purposeless infliction of physical violence and mutilation of the prisoner's body. Electrocution's proven history of burning and charring bodies is inconsistent with both the concepts of evolving standards of decency and the dignity of man. Other states have recognized that early assumptions about an instantaneous and painless death were simply incorrect and that there are more humane methods of carrying

> out the death penalty. Examined under modern scientific knowledge, "[electrocution] has proven itself to be a dinosaur more befitting the laboratory of Baron Frankenstein than the death chamber" of state prisons. We conclude that death by electrocution as provided in § 29-2532 violates the prohibition against cruel and unusual punishment in Neb. Const. art. I, § 9.[277]

The court in *Mata* affirmed the inmate's death sentence but thus specifically declared the state's *method* of execution to be unconstitutional.[278]

What is considered necessary and just in one generation may be considered unnecessary, cruel, and unjust to a subsequent generation. Before the development of penitentiaries, for instance, societies naturally had their own views of how best to deal with criminality and individual offenses or offenders. The use of branding or the scarlet letter as punishments are just two such examples of American punishments no longer in use.[279] After the 1790 opening of America's first penitentiary—the Walnut Street Prison—societal views shifted significantly as to what punishments should be seen as permissive as penitentiaries got built around the country.[280] And the death penalty, thanks in large part to Montesquieu's and Beccaria's writings, was on that list of long-used punishments that began to be questioned more intensely. In his *Enquiry How Far the Punishment of Death Is Necessary in Pennsylvania* (1793), William Bradford—the leading American lawyer—himself wrote that the implementation of a milder system of punishments would not only have an "influence on the character, morals, and happiness of the people," but would "hasten the period, when, *in the progress of civilization*, the punishment of death shall cease to be necessary."[281] Those words, written in the late eighteenth century by a prominent and much-respected figure, anticipated by many decades—indeed, by more than 160 years—the U.S. Supreme Court's creation, in 1958, of the "evolving standards of decency" test.[282]

In fact, in *Trop v. Dulles*, the case that laid down that test in a case that declared unconstitutional denationalization for desertion, the U.S. Supreme Court itself anticipated that the death penalty might one day come under constitutional scrutiny. As the Supreme Court wrote in that case:

> At the outset, let us put to one side the death penalty as an index of the constitutional limit on punishment. Whatever the arguments may be against capital punishment, both on moral grounds and in terms of accomplishing the purposes of punishment—and they are forceful—the death penalty has been employed throughout our history, and, *in a day when it is still widely accepted*, it cannot be said to violate the constitutional concept of cruelty. But it is equally plain that the existence of the death penalty is not a license to the Government to devise any punishment short of death within the limit of its imagination.[283]

"In *Trop v. Dulles*," one source recalls, "the Court stated that U.S. 'citizenship is not a license that expires, but a fundamental right.' "[284]

Western civilization is constantly in motion, something that the U.S. Supreme Court's "evolving standards of decency" test forthrightly recognizes. Change, in fact, is inevitable—a simple fact of life, something that was true in William Bradford's time and that continues to be true in the present day and age. While the policies and practices of the American criminal justice system are bound, like Tectonic plates, to shift over time, sometimes for good and sometimes for ill, the hope at least is that economic and societal progress will be made in time and that punishments will become better calibrated, and more humane, as more evidence-based research is conducted. In the realm of punishment and the treatment of offenders, American society has, certainly, already come a long way—though there is still much to be done. For example, in colonial and early America, grotesque corporal punishments were in use, something that became more and more uncomfortable for Americans with time and that would be, frankly, inconceivable today. As one source notes of the barbaric punishment of slaves that at one time occurred on American soil: "Common penalties took the form of harsh, often brutal physical punishments, including whippings, branding with hot irons, ear cropping, nose slitting, and castration. Punishments were usually conducted in front of other slaves to serve as a deterrent."[285]

Over time, punishments come and go, with the abolition of the whipping post and the pillory praised in Pennsylvania almost two centuries ago. As Michael Meranze writes in *Laboratories of Virtue: Punishment, Revolution, and Authority in Philadelphia, 1760–1835*: "On May 22, 1823, Roberts Vaux—Philadelphia gentleman, merchant, and philanthropist—addressed a crowd assembled to mark the laying of the cornerstone of the Eastern State Penitentiary. Vaux praised his state and its legislators for breaking the fetters of penal tradition and abolishing the pillory, the whipping post, and the chain—'those cruel and vindictive penalties which are in use in the European countries'—and substituting 'milder correctives' for crime." As Meranze wrote of what Vaux had to say: "In the place of public corporal punishments that, he argued, 'were not calculated to prevent crime, but to familiarize the mind with cruelty, and consequently to harden the hearts of those who suffered, and those who witnessed such punishments' would stand the penitentiary."[286] Whereas punishments such as the pillory and the whipping post were once seen as necessary, the time came when those punishments were seen as not only unnecessary, but as sanguinary and cruel, even torturous.

Sometimes, the law and societal views change so substantially that modern lawmakers and jurists hold views about punishments that would have been utterly inconceivable centuries earlier. For example, the concept of mental or psychological torture would have been quite foreign to America's founders, though they were quite familiar with, and abhorred by, civil-law-style judicial torture. "In the late 18th century," a history of torture and human rights stresses, "European legal systems were reformed to eliminate judicial torture, and by 1800 almost no traces were left." "The abolition of torture," that source notes, "coincided with moves to disallow some punishments that involved public humiliation, protracted physical suffering, and bodily disfigurement (e.g. racking, drawing and quartering, burning at the stake, and mutilation)."[287] "The Founding Fathers," a group of twenty former federal judges declared in a U.S. Supreme Court amicus brief, "embraced the English common law's rejection of torture and other impermissible coercion, which they viewed as a tool of royal despotism." In Virginia's ratification debates, they noted, "Patrick Henry observed that the distinguishing feature of America's common-law ancestors was that 'they would not admit of tortures, or cruel and barbarous punishment.'" In summing up the historical evidence, the former federal judges—a group that included Abner Mikva, William Sessions, and Patricia Wald—observed that "the Founders were well acquainted with the descendants of those who had suffered at the hands of the Kings and inquisitors and, without doubt, understood the connection between torture and tyranny."[288]

While the founders abhorred physical or bodily torture, the concept of mental or psychology torture is of much more recent vintage and would have been totally foreign to America's founders and framers.[289] *Torture*, a practice long prohibited but, for centuries, somewhat ill-defined or imprecisely or loosely defined, is now in fact (thanks to twentieth-century legal drafters) expressly defined in—and absolutely prohibited by—international law. Indeed, torture is explicitly prohibited by a whole series of legal prohibitions throughout the globe, with the U.N. Convention Against Torture and Other Cruel, Inhuman and Degrading Treatment or Punishment—ratified by the United States and scores of other countries—defining *torture* as "any act by which severe pain or suffering, whether physical or mental, is intentionally inflicted on a person" for a prohibited purpose, one of which is explicitly stated to be punishment.[290]

In 2010, the U.S. Supreme Court, citing prior precedents, itself broadly proclaimed torture to be outlawed by virtue of the Eighth Amendment. As the Court ruled: "The Cruel and Unusual Punishments Clause prohibits the imposition of inherently barbaric punishments under all circumstances. '[P]unishments of torture,' for example, 'are forbidden.' These cases underscore the essential principle that, under the Eighth Amendment, the State must respect the human attributes even of those who have committed serious crimes."[291] With both physical *and* mental torture absolutely prohibited by law, Americans—indeed, societies around the world—have obviously moved beyond an understanding of torture as bodily torment inflicted by a judicial body to one that encompasses either physical or psychological torture inflicted by any government actor. Neither physical *nor* psychological torture is necessary as the law now so laudably recognizes, with all types of torture absolutely forbidden. The U.N. Convention Against Torture not only obligates countries to *prevent* torture, it also requires them to *criminalize* torturous acts.[292]

CHAPTER 7

American Criminal Justice and Needless Severity:

The Death Penalty, Solitary Confinement, and Non-Violent Offenders

The Need for the "Necessity" Principle

American law and the U.S. Supreme Court's Eighth Amendment jurisprudence would benefit greatly from an infusion, even a major transfusion, of the Enlightenment necessity-for-punishment principle—the one popularized by Montesquieu and Beccaria and their disciples. American lawmakers would do well to pay heed to this principle, especially in considering particularly severe punishments such as the death penalty. The necessity-for-punishment maxim, for example, helps highlight the death penalty's needless inhumanity, as well as the gratuitous and barbaric nature of prolonged solitary confinement within prisons. The necessity-for-punishment maxim also helps in analyzing whether a particular punishment is justifiable or not, and it can guide the way in decision-making about how best to deal with non-violent offenders.

Whereas modern Eighth Amendment jurisprudence still tolerates capital punishment and prolonged solitary confinement and asks whether other punishments are "grossly disproportionate" to crimes,[1] Montesquieu and Beccaria sagely concluded that any punishment that goes beyond necessity—or beyond absolute necessity, as Beccaria put it—is "tyrannical." While federal and state courts must certainly give adequate and appropriate deference to legislative or sentencing commission findings as to the need for (and appropriateness of) particular punishments, judges must be willing to engage in meaningful judicial oversight of punishments to assess their reasonableness. And in reviewing particular punishments, the courts must wield the tool of the Eighth Amendment or its state constitutional equivalents to do so.[2] If a punishment is not necessary, it should be classified by the courts as a "cruel and unusual" punishment in that process of judicial scrutiny.[3]

Just as the gratuitous beating of a defenseless prisoner is already considered an Eighth Amendment violation,[4] the infliction of unnecessary punishments is both cruel and unusual and must be seen as such.[5] To inflict pain or suffering when it is not necessary to do so is an inherently arbitrary and cruel act, and to allow a government to act in such a manner would also seem to be highly unreasonable and inherently unusual. With all their power, American governments should not be allowed to act arbitrarily, and that is especially so given the equality guarantee set forth in the Fourteenth Amendment's Equal Protection Clause. That clause guarantees "equal protection of the laws" and if arbitrary punishments are imposed it should be found to violate that protection.[6] The U.S. Constitution safeguards a number of individual rights, including the right to equal protection, to due process, and not to be subjected to "cruel and unusual punishments." And those rights should be zealously safeguarded to ensure that, in American society, needless cruelty is not inflicted, and that, as far as possible, like offenders are being treated in a like manner and that individuals' liberty interests are honored.[7]

The concepts of *due process* and *equal protection*—found in the Fifth and Fourteenth Amendments and in the Fourteenth Amendment, respectively—are both intended to ensure that people are not arbitrarily or invidiously deprived of their lives, liberty, or property.[8] For example, in *Barbier v. Connolly*,[9] the U.S. Supreme Court wrote way back in 1884:

> The fourteenth amendment, in declaring that no state "shall deprive any person of life, liberty, or property without due process of law, nor deny to any person within its jurisdiction the equal protection of the laws," undoubtedly intended not only that there should be no arbitrary deprivation of life or liberty, or arbitrary spoliation of property, but that equal protection and security should be given to all under like circumstances in the enjoyment of their personal and civil rights; ... and that in the administration of criminal justice no different or higher punishment should be imposed upon one than such as is prescribed to all for like offenses.[10]

Arbitrariness and unequal treatment are thus antithetical to core American values, and that is especially true as regards the post-Fourteenth Amendment U.S. Constitution.[11] While America's Declaration of Independence recited that "all men are created equal," the equality principle was given much greater life through the ratification of the Fourteenth Amendment and the subsequent judicial decisions interpreting it. And the infliction of gratuitous or unnecessary punishments would seem to fall squarely within the rubric of cruel and unusual punishments, especially where such punishments are meted out sporadically or in an arbitrary or discriminatory manner.

The American death penalty, which involves a great deal of discretion from charging decisions all the way to executions, illustrates the need for a renewed application of the necessity-for-punishment principle. In 1971, in *McGautha v. California*,[12] the U.S. Supreme Court explicitly rejected a due process challenge to the death penalty, holding that "committing to the untrammeled discretion of the jury the power to pronounce life or death" is not "offensive to anything in the Constitution." As the Court ruled in *McGautha*: "To identify before the fact those characteristics of criminal homicides and their perpetrators which call for the death penalty, and to express these characteristics in language which can be fairly understood and applied by the sentencing authority, appear to be tasks which are beyond present human ability."[13] Just a year later, though, the Court in *Furman v. Georgia* (1972) struck down then-existing death penalty laws on the basis of the Eighth and Fourteenth Amendments, effectively putting a *de facto* moratorium on executions.[14] But death penalty statutes—ones bifurcating the guilt/innocence and penalty phases and then regularly asking juries to weigh "aggravating" versus "mitigating" factors to determine the sentence—

then got passed in more than thirty states in *Furman*'s wake.[15] That, in turn, led to the U.S. Supreme Court's decision in *Gregg v. Georgia* (1976), a ruling once again giving the judicial green light to executions.[16] Though provisions of law authorizing the death penalty's infliction can now be found in the U.S. Code and in various state statute books, the U.S. Supreme Court has already declared the mandatory death penalty—the version of capital punishment that existed in America's founding era, in Madison and Jefferson's time—to be unconstitutional.[17] What remains of American death penalty laws are the so-called "guided discretion" statutes that leave life-or-death decisions in the hands of juries.[18]

Criminal justice policies have changed dramatically from centuries ago, and the way the criminal justice system is administered is bound to change again—and again and again, and then again and again. In late seventeenth-century England, Titus Oates—the notorious perjurer—was singled out for a set of punishments (a fine, life imprisonment, flogging, and the pillory) that, while each lawful under English law at the time, were not inflicted on others in the particular manner that Oates had been made to suffer. It was the unusual way in which he had been treated by the King's Bench that drew the ire of Parliament. Something quite similar is, in effect, playing out in modern America as regards the death penalty's administration. While the death penalty is still authorized by various American statutes, just as whipping and the pillory were authorized in Titus Oates's time, present-day American executions are now being imposed in a manner that arbitrarily singles out particular individuals, whether at random, in a racially discriminatory fashion, or based on some other factor that runs afoul of the equal protection of the laws. Death row inmates often spend twenty years—or even thirty years or more—on death row before their executions, if they do not die of disease or natural causes first. And these days, it is race, geography, gender, or other factors, such as poverty or the poor quality of legal counsel, that largely determines who lives and who dies—and that determines who gets treated in a grossly disparate or disproportionate manner.

The American death penalty is rife with discrimination and arbitrariness, something that, in truth, has actually long been the case. Racial discrimination—the disparate treatment of people based on the color of their skin—still takes place on a regular basis in America's criminal justice system, with the extreme consequences of that prejudice particularly pronounced in death penalty cases.[19] Most executions take place in the South, where lynchings were once so common,[20] and only a small handful of jurisdictions actively produce death sentences that are later carried out. "Of the 20 executions in the U.S. in 2016," one source notes, "19 of them took place in just four Southern states: Alabama, Florida, Georgia and Texas."[21] And it is overwhelmingly men who are sentenced to death and put to death.[22] As Victor Streib, Sam Kamin, and Justin Marceau summarize the current state of affairs in their book, *Death Penalty in a Nutshell*: "[T]he hapless few who are actually executed tend not to be the 'worst of the worst' of all of killers. Too often those against whom the penalty is imposed are distinguishable only on the basis of race, sex, poverty, or the luck of the draw with regard to the judge, jury, and defense counsel assigned to their case."[23] The death penalty's administration—and the judicial system's *ad hoc* and discriminatory handling of capital punishment cases—is the direct opposite of a model system of justice that aims to rationally and equally protect each individual's human rights.

From "Usual" to "Unusual" Punishments

Many of the "usual" or "unusual" punishment references in texts from past centuries are to bodily or corporal punishments.[24] An early nineteenth-century treatise on the law of evidence, written by an English barrister, refers to "standing in the pillory" and "branding" as "being the usual punishments for the *crimen falsi*."[25] In one English dictionary published in 1706, the entry for "Gantlop, or Gantlope" reads: "*as to run the Gantlope*, an usual Punishment among Soldiers, the Offender being to run with his Back naked thro' the whole Regiment or Company, and to receive a Lash with a Switch from every Soldier: It is deriv'd from *Gant*, a Town of Flanders, where this Punishment was invented, and the *Dutch* Word *Lope*, *i.e.*, Running." "*The Gantelope*," another source reports, "was a common military punishment for theft, and was practised in two ways, one of which was called running the Gantelope or Gantlet; for the latter, the regiment was formed six deep, the ranks opened and faced inwards." "Each man being provided with a switch," that nineteenth-century magazine notes, "the offender, naked to the waist, passed through the ranks, preceded by a serjeant, the point of whose reversed halbert was pointed to his breast, to prevent his running too fast, and as he thus passed, every soldier gave him a stripe."[26] Other sources make reference to the "usual Punishment" of whipping inflicted upon thieves[27] and the "unusual punishment" of manslaughter, that is, being burned in the hand.[28]

References to "usual" and "unusual" punishments were also routinely used to describe methods of execution, including for acts of treason.[29] In one source printed in London in 1674, just a few years before the adoption of the English Bill of Rights, the following passage appears:

> [F]or *Parricides* the old *Romans* had a strange and unusual punishment, *in culeum dejicere*, to put them alive into a great leather Sack, made of an Ox-Hide, with a live *Dog*, a *Cock*, a *Viper*, and an *Ape*, at first it was with *Serpents*, (after the *murtherers of Parents* had been made bloudy with scourging) then sewed up close, and cast into *Tiber*, or the next *River*, that whilst *alive* they might begin to want the use of all the Elements, not having the benefit of the *Heavens* while they liv'd, nor the burial of the *Earth* when dead. This shews how *odious* this crime was in the height of it to meer *Heathen* men also.[30]

A history published in 1744 also recites that in Tonquin—an Asian locale colonized by the Chinese[31]—"[b]eheading is the usual punishment for murder and other capital crimes, and this is usually performed before the offender's own door."[32] It also notes that in the Sunda Islands "the usual punishment for capital crimes" was revealed by the finding of "carcasses of malefactors fixed to crosses."[33] The cultural context—and, again, the writer's own perspective or judgment—thus could be determinative of whether a punishment was classified as "unusual" or "usual."

In early American cases, the death penalty, imprisonment, and fines were each described at various points in U.S. history as a "usual punishment" for particular acts of criminality in specific locales.[34] For example in the late 1800s, in *State v. Warner*,[35] the Supreme Court of Kansas wrote of all three punishments, emphasizing, in the course of its opinion, the procedural protections thought necessary for capital punishment:

> Where the usual punishment for the commission of a felony was death, great strictness in charging the offense, as well as in the mode of trial, was, and ought to have been, maintained; but in this state, and in this country generally, there is no broad distinction between the character of the punishment inflicted for misdemeanors and for felonies other than murder.[36]

"Fines and imprisonment, with or without hard labor," the court further stressed, "are the penalties usually imposed for both felonies and misdemeanors."[37] While fines and imprisonment are, of course, still usual punishments for various offenses, the pillory and whipping—often once inflicted on slaves—were each also referred to in the past as "the usual punishment" for "one convicted of infamous crimes."[38]

Historical sources are revealing. Another reference to "usual punishment" also shows up in antebellum America, in an 1834 case from North Carolina. In that case, *State v. Negro Will, Slave of James S. Battle*,[39] the Supreme Court of North Carolina determined that "[i]f a slave, in defence of his life, and under circumstances strongly calculated to excite his passions of terror and resentment, kills his overseer, the homicide is, by such circumstances, mitigated to manslaughter."[40] In that case, the slave, Will, was described as a "prisoner" and as "the property of James S. Battle."[41] Meanwhile, "the deceased, Richard Baxter," was described as "the overseer of said Battle, and entrusted with the management of the prisoner at the time of the commission of the homicide."[42] The slave's job was said to be "packing cotton with a screw," and the deceased man, the evidence showed, had shot the slave, Will, with a gun, with "the whole load" from the gun's discharge reportedly "lodged in" that slave's back, "covering a space of twelve inches square."[43] In an ensuing fight between the slave and overseer, the overseer was stabbed with a knife and died from loss of blood.[44] The slave then surrendered himself to his master, whereupon Will, the slave, was charged with murder, found to be guilty of murder, and then sentenced to death.[45]

On appeal, the Supreme Court of North Carolina found that Will, the slave, was guilty of manslaughter instead of murder where he was under an impulse of terror and resentment. In the report of that case, which contains the arguments of counsel, there is an explicit reference to "[t]he usual modes of correction" and to the idea that "[p]unishment short of death serves the end of the master, both as a corrective and as an example."[46] The writings of "Baron Montesquieu" were specifically invoked in that legal case. In particular, it was noted that Montesquieu, in his *Spirit of Laws*, "treats of the subject of slavery, and informs us ... that in governments whose policy is warlike, and the citizens ever ready with arms in their hands to quell attempts to regain liberty, slaves *may* be treated with great rigour and severity, without the hazard of servile wars." "[I]n republics, where the policy is essentially pacific, and the citizens devoted to the arts of peace and industry," Montesquieu observed by way of contrast, "the treatment of slaves *should* be mild and humane: that the power of the master should not be absolute, and that the slave should be put within the keeping of the law."[47] In that particular court case, reference was also made to "the usual punishment" being inflicted,[48] with other sources from around that time also making use of the "usual punishment" moniker.[49]

The transition of a punishment from a "usual" to an "unusual" one can take place over a long period of time. It is not always possible to identify the exact point in time at which a "usual" punishment becomes an "unusual" one, but some punishments have clearly disappeared in American society through the years. In one book about interpreting language and making arguments, the authors recall the contention made by U.S. Supreme Court Justice Potter Stewart in his opinion in *Furman v. Georgia*. "In the first place," he wrote in 1972, speaking of the death sentences under review when they were still being imposed for non-homicidal rape, "it is clear that these sentences are 'cruel' in the sense that they excessively go beyond, not in degree but in kind, the punishments that the state legislatures have determined to be necessary." "In the second place," he wrote, "it is equally clear that these sentences are 'unusual' in the sense that the penalty of death is infrequently imposed for murder, and that its imposition for rape is extraordinarily rare." "These death sentences are cruel and unusual in the same way that being struck by lightning is cruel and unusual," Stewart observed, with the authors of the book on argument and rhetoric, after further discussing his opinion, restating Stewart's supporting argument in this way and in these points: "(1) Very few criminals who were found guilty of crimes that are punishable by death are actually sentenced to death." "(2) Among those found guilty of crimes punishable by death, who is sentenced to death depends on caprice or race." "(3) It is unconstitutional for sentencing to depend on caprice or race." "(4) A punishment is unusual if it is imposed infrequently and on an unconstitutional basis." The conclusion: "(5) The death penalty is an unusual punishment. (from 1–4)." An evaluation of facts, coupled with an evaluation of the common-sense, ordinary meaning of *unusual*, thus drove the observation that the death penalty had become an unusual punishment.[50]

Historically speaking, the "cruel and unusual punishments" terminology is not limited exclusively to the U.S. Constitution. In 1835, for instance, Congress passed "An Act in Amendment of the Acts for the Punishment of Offenses against the United States." Section 3 of that law forbid "cruel and unusual punishment," too, providing in pertinent part as follows:

> That if any master or other officer of any American ship or vessel on the high seas, or on any other waters within the admiralty and maritime jurisdiction of the United States, shall, from malice, hatred, or revenge, and without justifiable cause, beat, wound, or imprison any one or more of the crew of such ship or vessel, or withhold from them suitable food and nourishment, or inflict upon them any cruel and unusual punishment, every such person so offending shall, on conviction thereof, be punished by fine, not exceeding one thousand dollars, or by imprisonment not exceeding five years, or by both, according to the nature and aggravation of the offense.[51]

Just as judges were expected to interpret that statutory provision, judges can—and must—interpret the U.S. Constitution's prohibition against "cruel and unusual punishments." It is judges, ultimately, who must decide when a "usual" punishment has become an "unusual" one, and the lack of necessity for a punishment should clearly enter into that calculus.

The Effects of Long-Term Imprisonment and the Horrors of Solitary Confinement

The criminal justice system, which an offender enters after his or her arrest, leading to detention pending trial or release on bail with conditions, involves both sentencing and corrections. "Sentencing," *The Oxford Handbook of Sentencing and Corrections* notes, "is the legal process by which criminal sanctions are authorized and imposed in individual cases following criminal convictions." "Corrections," in contrast, that source emphasizes, "deals with the implementation, administration, and evaluation of criminal sentences after they are handed down." Calling it "a mistake to insist upon myopic distinctions between the two fields," Joan Petersilia and Kevin Reitz, the editors of that volume, observe: "Sentencing judges have reason to hope, if not expect, that the theories and policies behind their sentencing decisions will be pursued during the corrections phase. A judicial sentence is a mere abstraction until given effect in the correctional context." "From a societal perspective," they write of the connection between sentencing and corrections, "the downstream effects of sentences are what matter most to the public, including crime avoidance, victim and community restoration, and public confidence that the justice system acts with fairness, consistency, and proportionality when it punishes individual human beings." In the end, it is all interconnected, with one decision leading to consequences with a ripple effect.

"As a proportion of its population," Petersilia and Reitz point out of the American penchant for overusing prisons as a criminal justice strategy, "the United States incarcerates five times more people than Britain, nine times more than Germany, and 12 times more than Japan." And, they write, taking note of the racial and ethnic disparities associated with incarcerated populations, the "[c]oncern over mass confinement is inextricably bound up in questions of distributive justice." "Since Reconstruction," they observe, "black-white disparities in prison rates have always been pronounced, and they have generally grown over the past 130 years." The statistical evidence they cite:

> In 2009, an estimated 65 percent of all inmates in America's prisons and jails were either African American or Hispanic. Compared with a white male incarceration rate of 487 per 100,000 nationwide, the black male rate was 3,119 and the Hispanic male rate was 1,193 (Bureau of Justice Statistics 2010: app. table 14). This translates into a "disparity ratio" for black and white males of 6.4 to one, and a ratio of 2.4 to one for Hispanic and white males.

"It is evident from these data," they conclude, "that there has never been a meaningful civil rights movement in American prison policy."[52]

Imprisonment, and especially long-term incarceration, are known to have various psychological effects. Prisons were conceived and built as places to reform offenders, to deter, and to provide an alternative to executing offenders (executions would, of course, forever preclude their reformation). From America's first penitentiary, Philadelphia's Walnut Street Prison, to more modern facilities, these prisons—at least as conceived—thus sought to reduce criminality, not to exacerbate it. High hopes for the penitentiary system eventually led to more mundane concerns with the mechanics of day-to-day prison administration, though the reformation of criminals remained a high priority. "During the last half of the nineteenth century and most of the twentieth—a period widely regarded as the 'age of rehabilitation'—many people believed that prisons could be structured to produce effects that were largely positive or 'reformative' in nature," explains Craig Haney, a psychology professor at the University of California, Santa Cruz. "Indeed," Haney observes, "imprisonment itself was justified during these years largely because of its supposed ability to reduce recidivism—in essence, to change prisoners in beneficial ways that would decrease their likelihood of committing crimes in the future."

Over time, however, penal experts have come to see that prisons do not always serve their intended function or the objective of reformation. Experts, in fact, have begun to speak of adverse "prison effects," including the varied "psychological effects of imprisonment." Several developments, Craig Haney explains, led to this focus on prison effects. "For one," he writes, "systemic empirical research that addressed whether and how well rehabilitation programs actually reduced recidivism led to increased skepticism about their utility." "Although the simplistic characterization that 'nothing works' misrepresented the data on prison programming outcomes," Haney observes, "the effectiveness of rehabilitation proved more complicated and mixed than many had thought." "In addition," Haney recounts, "increased sociological and psychological sophistication about the effects of 'total institutions' such as prisons on the human psyche led to a more critical analysis of the consequences of imprisonment." "As a result," Haney summarizes the history, "at least since the abandonment of rehabilitation as the primary goal of imprisonment in the mid-1970s, most scholarly attention has been focused on the negative or potentially harmful effects of prison confinement, rather than its expected benefits." Researchers and policymakers, of course, are right to try to figure out what works and what doesn't, though it can be a complicated business.

Prison effects, Craig Haney explains, "can be conceptualized in two broad, interrelated ways." One addresses "the direct, hurtful, and potentially damaging effects of the pains of imprisonment—the ways in which the deprivations, indignities, and traumas of prison life produce adverse reactions and negative psychological consequences in the prisoners exposed to them." The other includes "the sometimes subtle psychological changes that prisoners undergo in order to adapt to (and survive) the rigors of prison life." "This latter kind of prison effect represents a specialized form of socialization—psychological accommodations that occur when people strive to adhere to the formal and informal demands of the social structures and settings in which they live." "Called 'institutionalization' when it occurs in total institutions in general, it has been termed 'prisonization' when it takes place in correctional institutions," Haney points out. While not all prisons are alike (some are well managed and others are not, some have significant gang problems while others do not), and while prisons range from minimum- to maximum-security, Haney notes that "[m]any prisoners come from social and economically marginalized groups and have experienced trauma and other adverse childhood and adolescent experiences that may have made them more rather than less vulnerable to psychological stressors, and less able than others (with less problematic backgrounds) to cope effectively with the chronic strains of prison life." "[P]rison victimization, in turn," Haney adds, "can lead to higher levels of distress in prison and symptoms of post-traumatic stress disorder and depression following release." A large number of prisoners, he notes, suffer from mental illness or diagnosable psychological disorders, which only exacerbates the problem.[53]

Societal and expert views of solitary confinement have also changed dramatically from America's founding period to the present day. In early America, Pennsylvania's Quakers combined the use of prolonged solitary confinement and hard labor in an attempt to reform inmates. "Solitary confinement, Quakers believed, would encourage inmates to meditate upon their sins, recognize their errors, and seek redemption," the *Encyclopedia of Prisons and Correctional Facilities* notes. As that source observes of its origins: "The roots of solitary confinement may be found in the Pennsylvania prison system of the late 18th century. The Pennsylvania system required that all prisoners were kept in total isolation from one another for the duration of their confinement, in contrast to the Auburn system, in which individuals worked together all day but were not permitted to talk to or to contact one another." "Although the Pennsylvania system was created with good intentions," that encyclopedia emphasizes, "the Quakers' solitary system had many troubling effects." Among them: the onset of insanity and high rates of suicide.[54] The U.S. Supreme Court itself noted the harsh nature of solitary confinement decades ago. In *In re Medley* (1890), the Court wrote about the effect of the passage of a state law that required death row inmates to be held in solitary confinement before execution. "Nor can we withhold our conviction of the proposition that when a prisoner sentenced by a court to death is confined in the penitentiary awaiting the execution of the sentence, one of the most horrible feelings to which he can be subjected during that time is the uncertainty during the whole of it," the U.S. Supreme Court stressed. In that case, the Supreme Court was considering approximately *four weeks* of solitary confinement, not the *decades* of solitary confinement that death row inmates have endured in more recent times.[55]

In January 2018, a judge in Canada, in the Supreme Court of British Columbia, specifically held that indefinite and prolonged solitary confinement is unconstitutional. In that case, one brought by two non-profits, the British Columbia Civil Liberties Association and the John Howard Society of Canada, that judge, Justice Peter Leask, first laid out the history of solitary confinement. Its use, the judge rule, "was originally conceived as an enlightened and humane alternative to the harsh punishments of the time." After describing its use in early penitentiaries in 19th-century America, in Ontario and Europe, Justice Leask noted that "it was not long before concerns about the psychological effects of rigid solitary confinement were raised." Justice Leask, in recounting the history, then summarized what happened next: "As statistical evidence accumulated over the 19th century that solitary confinement produced a disturbing incidence of psychiatric illness, physical disease and death, what had started as an optimistic experiment in social reform fell into disrepute by the early 1900s. Nevertheless, though entire penitentiaries no longer operated on a strict segregation model, solitary confinement continued as a practice within institutions." Noting that the

U.N. Human Rights Committee, the U.N. Committee Against Torture, and the U.N. Special Rapporteur on Torture and Other Cruel, Inhuman or Degrading Treatment or Punishment have declared that prolonged solitary confinement amounts to conduct prohibited by the International Covenant on Civil and Political Rights ("ICCCPR") and the Convention Against Torture and Other Cruel, Inhuman or Degrading Treatment or Punishment ("CAT"), Justice Leask identified "an emerging consensus in international law that under certain circumstances solitary confinement can cross the threshold from a legitimate practice into cruel, inhuman or degrading treatment ('CIDT'), even torture."[56]

In his ruling, Justice Leask specifically relied upon the work of Dr. Haney, who has both a Ph.D. in psychology and a J.D. degree from Stanford University and who has studied, interviewed, and assessed inmates held in solitary confinement (or administrative segregation, as it is also called) since the 1970s. "According to Dr. Haney," Leask wrote, "the central harmful feature of solitary confinement is the reduction of meaningful social contact." "According to Dr. Haney," Leask continued, "the social deprivation imposed by solitary confinement leaves inmates with no choice but to adapt in socially pathological ways." As Leask wrote, summarizing Dr. Haney's views on what happens to inmates held in solitary confinement:

> Over time, they gradually change their patterns of thinking, acting and feeling to cope with the profoundly asocial world in which they are forced to live, adapting to the absence of social support and the routine feedback that comes from normal, meaningful social contact. Not surprisingly, this has problematic consequences. As they become increasingly unfamiliar and uncomfortable with social interaction, some inmates become further alienated from others and made anxious in their presence. Although their adaptations may have been functional in isolation, they are typically acutely dysfunctional in the social world most inmates are expected to re-enter. In extreme cases, these ways of being are not only dysfunctional but have been internalized so deeply that they become disabling, interfering with the capacity to live a remotely normal or fulfilling social life. In this way, long-term isolation can make inmates' adjustment to general population especially painful and challenging.

The experience of prolonged solitary confinement is thus a painful and dehumanizing one, especially since human beings are social creatures. As Justice Leask described the effects of solitary confinement:

> Studies have identified some of the symptoms that appear to be produced by these conditions as including appetite and sleep disturbances, anxiety, panic, rage, loss of control, paranoia, hallucinations, and self-mutilation. Moreover, direct studies of prison isolation have documented an extremely broad range of harmful psychological reactions. These effects include increases in the following potentially damaging symptoms and problematic behaviours: anxiety, withdrawal, hypersensitivity, cognitive dysfunction, hallucinations, loss of control, irritability, aggression, rage, paranoia, hopelessness, a sense of impending emotional breakdown, self-mutilation, and suicidal ideation and behaviour.

> In addition, self-mutilation and suicide are more prevalent in isolated, punitive housing units such as administrative segregation. For example, clinical researchers have attributed higher suicide rates in solitary confinement-type units to the heightened levels of "environmental stress" that are generated by the isolation, punitive sanctions, and severely restricted living conditions that exist there.
>
> The prevalence of the psychological symptoms suffered in solitary confinement is often very high. For example, in an early study, Dr. Haney conducted systematic assessments of a randomly selected sample of 100 inmates housed at the SHU at Pelican Bay State Prison in California. He found that every symptom of psychological distress that he measured but one (fainting spells) was suffered by more than half of the inmates who were interviewed. Many of the symptoms were reported by two-thirds or more of the inmates assessed, and some were suffered by nearly everyone. Well over half of the inmates reported a constellation of symptoms—headaches, trembling, sweaty palms, and heart palpitations—that are known to be stress-related.
>
> Dr. Haney also found that almost all of the inmates whom he evaluated reported ruminations or intrusive thoughts, an oversensitivity to external stimuli, irrational anger and irritability, difficulties with attention and often with memory, and a tendency to socially withdraw. Almost as many inmates reported a constellation of symptoms indicative of mood or emotional disorders—concerns over emotional flatness or losing the ability to feel, swings in emotional responding, and feelings of depression or sadness that did not go away. Finally, sizable minorities of the inmates reported symptoms that are typically only associated with more extreme forms of psychopathology—hallucinations, perceptual distortions, and thoughts of suicide.
>
> In addition to these specific symptoms and reactions of psychological stress, other significant aspects of the psychological pain and dysfunction that prolonged solitary confinement can produce in inmates include damage to or distortion of their social identities, destabilization of their sense of self and, for some, destruction of their ability to function normally in free society.[57]

In his lengthy summary of Dr. Haney's expert opinion, Justice Leask's opinion laid out why so many people had come to oppose the prolonged use of solitary confinement:

> The widespread recognition of the harmful effects of solitary confinement has led to a consensus about three important limits that must be applied to its use: (1) because the risks of psychological and physical harm increase as a function of the increased length of exposure, the use of the practice must be limited to the briefest amount of time possible; (2) solitary confinement must be used only when it is absolutely necessary and as a last resort; and (3) the added risk to vulnerable groups requires that they be exempted entirely from prolonged solitary confinement.
>
> While some organizations call for an outright ban on the use of solitary confinement, many recommend strict time limits on its use, limits that are

> typically measured in days and weeks. Dr. Haney testified that the international standard is a 15-day maximum, which he accepts as defensible. He testified, "what I am sure of is that the longer somebody is there the greater the risks".
>
> As for the exacerbating effects of segregation on mental illness, Dr. Haney states that there are sound theoretical reasons that explain why inmates with serious mental illness have a much more difficult time tolerating the painful experience of segregation. In part, it is because of the greater vulnerability of the mentally ill in general to stressful, traumatic conditions. Social contact and interaction play a critical role in maintaining psychological equilibrium, and thus its absence is very psychologically destabilizing. In addition, some of the conditions of isolation exacerbate the particular symptoms from which mentally ill inmates suffer.[58]

In his own opinion, Justice Leask found that the Canadian practice of administrative segregation "is a form of solitary confinement that places all Canadian federal inmates subject to it at significant risk of serious psychological harm, including mental pain and suffering, and increased incidence of self-harm and suicide." "Some of the specific harms," the judge concluded, "include anxiety, withdrawal, hypersensitivity, cognitive dysfunction, hallucinations, loss of control, irritability, aggression, rage, paranoia, hopelessness, a sense of impending emotional breakdown, self-mutilation, and suicidal ideation and behaviour." "The risks of these harms," the judge's opinion continued, "are intensified in the case of mentally ill inmates," though the finding was made that "all inmates subject to segregation are subject to the risk of harm to some degree." "The indeterminacy of administrative segregation," the opinion stressed, "is a particularly problematic feature that exacerbates its painfulness, increases frustration, and intensifies the depression and hopelessness that is often generated in the restrictive environments that characterize segregation."[59] After reviewing the evidence, and accepting Dr. Haney's expert opinion, Justice Leask observed, referencing the U.N.'s "Mandela Rules" that govern the treatment of prisoners and that restrict the use of prolonged solitary confinement: "Negative health effects can occur after only a few days in segregation, and those harms increase as the duration of the time spent in segregation increases. The 15-day maximum prescribed by the Mandela Rules is a generous standard given the overwhelming evidence that even within that space of time an individual can suffer severe psychological harm. It is, nevertheless, a defensible standard." The Mandela Rules make the use of solitary confinement a last resort, with Rule 45 of those rules providing: "Solitary confinement shall be used only in exceptional cases as a last resort, for as short a time as possible and subject to independent review, and only pursuant to the authorization by a competent authority. It shall not be imposed by virtue of a prisoner's sentence."[60]

The Lack of Necessity for Capital Punishment

The American death penalty has deep roots. It existed in colonial times as an import from Great Britain, just like branding and the punishment of ducking, and it was used during and after the Revolutionary War.[61] "Executions were especially frequent in moments of real or perceived crisis," scholar Gabriele Gottlieb writes in her Ph.D.

thesis, "Theater of Death: Capital Punishment in Early America, 1750–1800," a study of executions in Boston, Philadelphia, and Charleston, South Carolina.[62] Although William Penn, a Quaker, had restricted the death penalty's use in Pennsylvania in the seventeenth century, it was only after the publication of Cesare Beccaria's landscape-changing *On Crimes and Punishments* that a broad swath of American society began, in earnest, to question the death penalty's legitimacy, efficacy, and morality.[63] Scores of public executions took place on American soil from colonial times to the 1930s, when the last public executions took place in the United States.[64] But the gradual end of American public executions, brought about over the course of a full century, did not end American executions—it just pushed them into the private sphere. From the 1830s to the 1930s, widely attended public, midday executions gave way on a state-by-state basis to much more secretive executions, often conducted at night. Of the 313 U.S. executions that took place from 1977 to 1995, more than 82 percent of them took place between 11:00 p.m. and 7:30 a.m., with more than half of them happening between midnight and 1:00 a.m. The Anglo-American habit of public executions thus simply gave way to more private affairs behind thick prison walls.[65]

The anti-death penalty movement, once known as the anti-gallows campaign, has been active ever since the appearance of Cesare Beccaria's book.[66] In fact, a number of eighteenth-century American political leaders articulated their opposition to, or their skepticism of, capital punishment around the time of the ratification of the U.S. Bill of Rights. In 1792, Dr. Benjamin Rush—the Philadelphia physician, the signer of the Declaration of Independence, and the adamant death penalty foe—wrote *Considerations on the Injustice and Impolicy of Punishing Murder by Death*.[67] And in 1793, William Bradford—James Madison's friend and a prominent Pennsylvania attorney—wrote *An Enquiry How Far the Punishment of Death Is Necessary in Pennsylvania*, in which he studied, and then questioned the need for, capital punishment.[68] It was only later, though, that American states did away with capital punishment entirely. The first U.S. states to abolish the death penalty for murder were Michigan (1846), Wisconsin (1852), and Rhode Island (1853),[69] with lots of anti-gallows advocates—from Wisconsin legislator Marvin Bovee to poet Walt Whitman—stepping forward in the nineteenth century to make their views known.[70]

Marvin Bovee, who cited Montesquieu, Beccaria, and many other early penal reformers in his own work, illustrates just how deeply the ideas of European Enlightenment thinkers had penetrated into America's psyche. In his book, *Christ and the Gallows: Or, Reasons for the Abolition of Capital Punishment* (1869), Bovee specifically traced this intellectual history, writing of how Voltaire and Montesquieu (the two prominent French reformers) had shaped the debate. Both Montesquieu and Voltaire had lived in England for a time, with Bovee penning this extensive recitation of how the Baron de Montesquieu and the Italian *philosophe*, the Marquis Beccaria, had shaped societal views:

> The philosophy of penal legislation has in no country been more carefully investigated than in Italy. The Marquis Beccaria, in 1764, published a work entitled, *Dei Delitti e delle Pene*, which produced a marked effect upon the public sentiment of that day. The *judicial* murder of Calas, at Toulouse, which

> caused a European sensation, a short time prior to the publication of Beccaria's work, occasioned, without doubt, the publication of the work referred to. One of the French authors is said to have written to a member of the Milan Literary Society: "Now is the time to rise against religious intolerance and the exaggerated severity of penal legislation." Beccaria, who was a member of this literary club, and a zealous reader of French authors, especially Montesquieu, Helvetius, and Condillac, was thus incited to write the work referred to, and which has made him famous in the history of penal reform. This book, which its author stated he was induced to write through "love of literary fame, love of liberty, and compassion for the unhappy condition of mankind who were enslaved by many errors," exerted a powerful influence upon Italian public sentiment, and was translated into most of the European languages.

"The motto of Beccaria," Bovee emphasized, "is of permanent truth: 'It is the certainty, rather than the severity, of punishment which constitutes its efficiency.'" In *Christ and the Gallows*, Bovee also quoted John Macrae Moir, who wrote this in his own work on capital punishment: "The publication of Beccaria's work encouraged not only in Italy, but throughout the whole of Europe, the advocates of the abolition of the death punishment, or, at least, its limitation to the gravest crimes."[71]

The administration of the modern American death penalty begins—as it always has—with laws authorizing the death penalty. While common law punishments were once in use, today's criminal laws are statutory in nature. At present, the death penalty is authorized by the federal government and the U.S. military, as well as by thirty American states.[72] Although twenty American states and the District of Columbia no longer authorize capital punishment,[73] the death penalty's use is still a reality despite the fact that death sentences and executions—once firmly entrenched throughout the country—are being meted out, and carried out, less and less frequently in the modern age.[74] This raises a question of considerable public importance: Is the death penalty, once a usual punishment, now an unusual one? If one recalls the history of the punishment of ducking, other subsidiary questions also recur: Is capital punishment inherently barbaric? And has the death penalty become obsolete?

The facts show that America's death penalty is now only rarely used and is, in fact, inhumane, barbaric, and completely unnecessary. The number of American death sentences fell from more than 300 per year in 1995 and 1996[75] to less than fifty per year in 2015 and 2016.[76] And in recent years, the number of executions has fallen from a high of 98 in 1999 to 20 in 2016.[77] Even in Harris County, Texas, known as the "Capital of Capital Punishment," the death penalty is dying. Over the years, Harris County has produced scores of death sentences and executions—more than 125 of the latter since the U.S. Supreme Court, in *Jurek v. Texas* (1976),[78] upheld the constitutionality of Texas's death penalty statute. Yet, no one was sentenced to death or executed from Harris County in 2017.[79] And newly elected Harris County District Attorney Kim Ogg, the Houston-area's chief prosecutor, unabashedly views that "as a positive thing."[80] "I don't think that being the death penalty capital of America is a selling point for Harris County," she said.[81] That is in sharp contrast to Johnny B. Holmes, Jr., a former Harris County District Attorney, who became known as "the deadliest prosecutor in America." "The Harris County District Attorney's Office," one source notes, "was also home to the 'Silver Needle Society,' the name given by former District Attorney Johnny B. Holmes, Jr., to the death penalty unit in the office, and purportedly a sign proudly listed all the inmates who were executed from the County."[82]

To understand the true nature of the death penalty's administration in today's America, one must actually look beyond statute books and the national and state-by-state statistics and study local practices and do a county-by-county examination. "The vast majority of counties do not use the death penalty at all," explains law professor Robert J. Smith in the *Boston University Law Review*.[83] After conducting a granular, county-by-county analysis of the distribution of death sentences and executions from 2004 to 2009, Smith found that "[j]ust 10% of counties nationally returned even a single death sentence during this time period," and that "fewer than 1% of counties in the country sentenced anyone to death (at any point since 1976) whom their respective states executed from 2004 to 2009."[84] With death sentences clustered and concentrated in just a few jurisdictions, Smith emphasized that, in 2009, just "five states—Alabama, Arizona, California, Florida, and Texas—accounted for two-thirds of death sentences nationally."[85] The vast majority of executions take place in the so-called Death Belt: Alabama, Florida, Georgia, Louisiana, Mississippi, South Carolina, and Texas.[86] It can, therefore, no longer be argued with a straight face that the death penalty is a punishment that is inflicted nationwide. It is now largely, at best, a regional punishment—and one that is, at that, only sporadically used. In those respects, the death penalty has—to say the least—become a truly unusual punishment.

In fact, only a handful of American counties have produced the bulk of death sentences and executions, with *2%* of U.S. counties accounting for *the majority* of modern-day death row inmates and recent death sentences.[87] In his 2015 dissent in *Glossip v. Gross*,[88] Justice Stephen Breyer pointedly observed of the U.S. Supreme Court's regular approach and its implications for capital punishment: "Often when deciding whether a punishment practice is, constitutionally speaking, 'unusual,' this Court has looked to the number of States engaging in that practice. In this respect, the number of active death penalty States has fallen dramatically."[89] Justice Breyer's dissent stressed that, in addition to the nineteen states that had already abolished capital punishment, in eleven American death penalty states "no execution has taken place for more than eight years," meaning that "30 States have either formally abolished the death penalty or have not conducted an execution in more than eight years."[90] "Of the 20 States that have conducted at least one execution in the past eight years," Breyer pointed out, "9 have conducted fewer than five in that time, making an execution in those States a fairly rare event."[91] Again, the precipitous decline (and in some cases disuse) of executions, not to mention the limited number of jurisdictions that actively use the punishment on the local level, make the death penalty an extremely unusual punishment.

It is thus only a handful of individual prosecutors who aggressively pursue death sentences who are keeping capital punishment alive. Capital charging decisions, which amount, in essence, to pre-trial *threats of death* against the criminal defendant (and which may, themselves, prompt false confessions or lead defense attorneys to behave in unusual ways), begin with the prosecutor's notice of intent to seek the death penalty.

For example, under federal law, if the government's attorney "believes that the circumstances of the offense are such that a sentence of death is justified," the attorney "shall, a reasonable time before the trial or before acceptance by the court of a plea of guilty, sign and file with the court, and serve on the defendant, a notice ... stating that the government believes that the circumstances of the offense are such that, if the defendant is convicted, a sentence of death is justified under this chapter and that the government will seek the sentence of death."[92] At the state level, prosecutors in locales that retain capital punishment may also file notices of intent to seek the death penalty, even though—it turns out—only a fraction of such cases ever receive death sentences or, ultimately, result in actual executions.[93] The highly disparate ways in which local prosecutors charge cases, with many choosing not to seek death in death-eligible cases while just a handful decide to actively seek death sentences, also makes capital punishment a very unusual practice.

For capitally charged cases that do go to trial, the so-called "death-qualification process" thereafter ensures that death penalty opponents—an increasing number, according to public opinion surveys[94]—are systematically excluded from jury service.[95] "In a narrow 5–4 decision," one source observes of the history, "the U.S. Supreme Court upheld the death qualification process in *Lockhart v. McCree* (1986)."[96] In a practice thus explicitly authorized by the U.S. Supreme Court,[97] and that, problematically, results in more conviction-prone juries, a disproportionate number of women, African-Americans, and other demographic groups are purged from jury venires.[98] This striking of minorities and others from capital jury venires occurs even as it is known that overt racial discrimination remains a major problem in the jury selection process, as the U.S. Supreme Court itself has found in recent cases.[99] Most notoriously, in *Foster v. Chatman*,[100] the Supreme Court found that Georgia prosecutors discriminated against black prospective jurors during the defendant's 1987 capital trial. The prosecutors' files included a list of black venire members' names highlighted in green with the letter "B" written next to them, and prosecutors struck all four black prospective jurors, resulting in an all-white jury.[101]

The U.S. Supreme Court, to date, has allowed executions to continue even though the racial bias in the system is clear. In *McCleskey v. Kemp*,[102] the Supreme Court specifically rejected a death row inmate's Fourteenth Amendment equal protection challenge, ultimately leading to the execution of Warren McCleskey.[103] But it is clear from cases such as *Foster v. Chatman* that the American death penalty—long administered in a racially discriminatory fashion[104]—continues to be infected with significant racial prejudice.[105] Multiple studies, in fact, have shown that the race of the victim plays a material, statistically significant role in the outcome of capital cases, with those who kill whites much more likely to receive the punishment of death than those who kill blacks.[106] Not only has the death penalty been administered in a racially discriminatory manner throughout America's history,[107] but because of the gross inequity in its administration,[108] the concurrent geographic disparities associated with death sentences, and the rarity with which executions are carried out, state-sanctioned killing in the U.S. now resembles a state-sponsored lottery system.[109] In the U.S., the nature of an offender's crime has little or no relationship to whether that offender will live or die; instead, it is *the locale of the crime* and *the race of the victim*—along with the defendant's poverty or the effectiveness or ineffectiveness of the defendant's counsel[110]—that largely determines who gets condemned to death.[111]

In his 2015 dissent in *Glossip v. Gross*, Justice Stephen Breyer explicitly emphasized that "use of the death penalty has become increasingly concentrated geographically."[112] As Justice Breyer, in an opinion joined by Justice Ruth Bader Ginsburg, wrote: "County-level sentencing figures show that, between 1973 and 1997, 66 of America's 3,143 counties accounted for approximately 50% of all death sentences imposed."[113] "By the early 2000s," Breyer added, "the death penalty was only actively practiced in a very small number of counties: between 2004 and 2009, only 35 counties imposed 5 or more death sentences, *i.e.*, approximately one per year."[114] In tracking the most recent figures, Breyer also emphasized: "And more recent data show that the practice has diminished yet further: between 2010 and 2015 (as of June 22), only 15 counties imposed five or more death sentences."[115] As Breyer concluded: "In short, the number of active death penalty counties is small and getting smaller. And the overall statistics on county-level executions bear this out. Between 1976 and 2007, there were no executions in 86% of America's counties."[116] It is, in truth, hard to call a punishment put to use in just 14% of America's counties a "usual" punishment. The American death penalty has become "unusual"; that is the reality of the situation.

Not only is capital punishment meted out arbitrarily and sporadically, but the process by which it is administered is error-ridden and particularly unusual. In a recent book, *Deadly Justice: A Statistical Portrait of the Death Penalty*, the authors make the point that "[t]he 'old' death penalty died with *Furman*" while "the new one rose following *Gregg*."[117] *Furman v. Georgia* (1972) had struck down America's then-existing death penalty as unconstitutional on the basis of the Eighth and Fourteenth Amendments. In contrast, in *Gregg v. Georgia* (1976), the U.S. Supreme Court had allowed the death penalty's resumption, even though the Court, in that case, insisted on procedural refinements in an attempt to make America's capital punishment system less capricious. Yet, despite all the efforts to regulate the way in which capital punishment is used, the authors of *Deadly Justice* note that more than 150 people have been exonerated from death row in the modern era—an error rate of approximately 4%.[118] "[I]t is clear," they write, "that the death penalty harbors serious flaws," with the authors emphasizing that "more than 60 percent" of death sentences are overturned and that "only 16 percent of condemned inmates" are actually executed.[119] With all the judicial reversals and recurring miscarriages of justices, it is apparent that, if anything, the arbitrariness and unfairness of America's death penalty has only reached new, unsurpassed heights. The U.S. Supreme Court, through the years, may have insisted on various substantive and procedural protections when it comes to the death penalty's administration. But clearly, the death penalty remains horrifyingly arbitrary and discriminatory—a total affront to the notion of equal protection of the laws.

After highly discretionary capital charges are brought, the penalty phases of capital trials focus the jury's attention[120] on whether those convicted of capital offenses should live or die. The increasingly limited number of death sentences produced by those penalty phase proceedings, however, are nothing more than state-sanctioned threats of death of an even more serious nature than the initial capital charges. (Executions, of course, do not immediately follow the imposition of death sentences, so death sentences are, when imposed, credible death threats as they are, like capital charges, backed by the power of the state.) Not all people who are sentenced to death will be executed (not by a long shot), but it is still the case that at least some (at least in certain locales) will be, so these threats of death must be taken extremely seriously by those sentenced to death and their lawyers.[121] In early America, as in England, offenders were once regularly told by judges that they would be "hanged by the neck" until dead.[122] And in modern American courtrooms, criminal defendants are—at least occasionally—still sentenced to death, though the method of execution has changed dramatically from colonial times and the early days of the republic.[123] Executions in the United States are now carried out by lethal injection instead of hanging, even though the state-issued threats of death that precede executions are plainly designed—as they were in yesteryears—to put individuals on notice that the government plans to intentionally take their lives.

In the lead-up to executions, death row inmates are confined in small cells and often spend twenty-three hours a day in isolation in those cells.[124] Inmates are also subjected to the torment and uncertainty of the capital litigation process, which can go on for years, and frequently multiple decades.[125] Given that wrongful convictions and miscarriages of justice occur with considerable frequency, both the guilty and (until exonerated) the innocent must endure such conditions and adverse psychological effects. Meanwhile, death warrants—the highly credible and specific threats of death that are issued periodically during capital litigation—set very real execution dates for those condemned to death. For example, in his book, *The Wrong Man: A True Story of Innocence on Death Row*, Michael Mello described how execution dates for inmates were "triggered by the governor's signing of death warrants."[126] "Unless a stay is obtained prior to a specific execution date," Mello explained, "the subject of the warrant will be put to death, even though his conviction may rest upon legal or factual error of constitutional magnitude."[127]

In her bestselling memoir, *Dead Man Walking: An Eyewitness Account of the Death Penalty in the United States*, the anti-death penalty activist, Sister Helen Prejean, writes of her own first-hand encounters with America's system of capital punishment.[128] In one telling passage, she describes a conversation with C. Paul Phelps, the head of the Louisiana Department of Corrections, after the electric-chair execution of Patrick Sonnier, a man for whom she served as a spiritual advisor. "Pat Sonnier was tortured, Mr. Phelps," she recounted of her conversation.[129] As Sister Prejean recalled what she'd said to Mr. Phelps, the man who designed the execution process and then supervised the executions: "I'm not sure what he felt physically when the nineteen hundred volts hit him, but certainly he agonized emotionally and psychologically—preparing to die, anticipating it, dreaming about it."[130] "Amnesty International," she pointed out in her conversation, "defines torture as an extreme physical and mental assault on a person who has been rendered defenseless."[131] "That is what happened to Patrick Sonnier, isn't it, Mr. Phelps?" she queried, with Phelps nodding in response.[132] "Dead man walking," the phrase Sister Prejean popularized, refers to someone—in the death penalty context, a condemned inmate—who is walking or heading towards death.[133] The continuous threat of death that hangs over a condemned inmate, like the Sword of Damocles, is simply impossible for the inmate to ignore. Though cases of ineffective assistance of counsel are common, both competent and incompetent defense attorneys alike must also grapple every day with the notion that if they mess up their representation, a client could die at the hands of the state as a result.

Although the U.S. Supreme Court has yet to categorize the death penalty as a torturous act, the U.N. Convention Against Torture and Other Cruel, Inhuman, or Degrading Treatment or Punishment explicitly defines "torture" as "any act by which severe pain or suffering, whether physical or mental, is intentionally inflicted on a person," for, among other things, "punishing him for an act he ... has committed...."[134] That convention, ratified by the United States, provides that torture "does not include pain or suffering arising only from, inherent in or incidental to lawful sanctions."[135] And for centuries, the death penalty has been considered a permissible and lawful sanction—one used by many countries, time and time again, at various points in world history. But today, the death penalty is no longer lawful in the majority of the world's countries and is, by law, explicitly unlawful in nineteen American states,[136] with death sentences and executions—declining in number[137]—only still in use in select locales.[138] Most importantly, death sentences and executions—though long characterized as lawful sanctions—have the *immutable* characteristics of torture,[139] the aggravated form of cruelty.[140] It is thus difficult to see why the death penalty's use should not be labeled, in law, as an act of torture, and thus clearly cruel and unusual.

In fact, as a condemned inmate's execution date approaches, the inmate is fully aware of his or her impending death but is utterly helpless to prevent that death.[141] The classic definition of *psychological torture* is—as even jurists in death penalty states freely acknowledge—an awareness of one's impending death but a helplessness to prevent that death.[142] As a result, death sentences and executions—when fairly considered—should be classified under the rubric of torture as they bear all the characteristics and indicia of torture.[143] Using that classic definition, one already employed in judicial decisions in the non-state actor context, the death penalty—a state action—must be seen to be psychological torture. To aggravate and exacerbate the torment further, the average time inmates spend on death row between sentencing and execution is now more than fifteen years. "The death row phenomenon is caused by prolonged detention on death row, which causes ever-increasing mental anxiety and mounting tension over one's impending death," one source observes, taking note of the recognition of this phenomenon by the European Court of Human Rights.[144] It is, certainly, an extremely cruel and unusual act—indeed, a torturous one—to subject a person to a continuous threat of death by unnatural means for years, even multiple decades, at a time.[145]

When the Eighth Amendment's "cruel and unusual punishments" prohibition is analyzed through a "living constitutionalist" lens, the American death penalty does not fare well. Several Enlightenment thinkers, including Cesare Beccaria and the American revolutionary, Dr. Benjamin Rush, freely spoke of the death penalty's *unnecessary severity* or *cruelty* more than 200 years ago.[146] Still, America's eighteenth-century death penalty could not then have been plausibly described as an "unusual" punishment because, in that century, death was the *customary* or *standard* penalty for multiple felonies[147] and executions were the *mandatory* punishment for their commission.[148] In light of everything that has transpired in the last two centuries, especially since the development of discretionary capital sentencing and the post-World War II recognition of universal human rights,[149] comparing eighteenth-century laws and practices and twenty-first-century laws and practices is like comparing apples and oranges or rotary dial phones and iPhones. Many punishments that were permissible in the eighteenth century are simply no longer authorized today,[150] and the Fourteenth Amendment—put in place after the Civil War and after all of America's founders had died—changed American constitutional law in monumental and fundamental ways.[151]

Not only has American constitutional law changed substantially since America's founding period, especially by virtue of the Fourteenth Amendment, but American penal practices have also changed dramatically since the eighteenth and nineteenth centuries. Already, *non-lethal* corporal punishments such as ear cropping, whipping, and the pillory have fallen out of use in America's penal system.[152] The abandonment of those punishments came about through legislation but also through court decisions. For example, in *Jackson v. Bishop* (1968),[153] Justice Harry Blackmun—then writing as a judge for the U.S. Court of Appeals for the Eighth Circuit—ruled that the Eighth Amendment prohibited the lashing of prisoners (once a common, or *usual*, practice) within Arkansas prisons.[154] Likewise, in *Hope v. Pelzer* (2002),[155] the U.S. Supreme Court bluntly declared that it was an "obvious" Eighth Amendment violation to handcuff a shirtless Alabama inmate to a hitching post for seven hours, thus resulting in the inmate's dehydration and sunburning.[156] "Despite its long tradition," one scholar notes, "corporal punishment (in the form of whipping, caning, flogging, lashing, paddling, etc.) has been outlawed as method of disciplining adult prisoners and military personnel."[157] It is thus clear that once *usual* punishments can become *unusual* ones, and, consequently, once constitutional punishments can become unconstitutional.

Such facts—and such Eighth Amendment cases—make America's continued use of capital punishment particularly problematic and a particular enigma, with U.S. Supreme Court Justices themselves expressing considerable angst and reservations about the punishment of death.[158] In 1972, in *Furman v. Georgia*,[159] the U.S. Supreme Court—as noted—struck down America's death penalty as violative of the Eighth and Fourteenth Amendments,[160] with some Justices observing then—more than forty-five years ago—the rarity and freakish nature of death sentences and executions.[161] The Supreme Court, though, reversed course four years later in 1976 in *Gregg v. Georgia*[162] and two companion cases,[163] thereby allowing executions to resume.[164] It was Justice Anthony Kennedy who, in 2008 in *Kennedy v. Louisiana*,[165] expressed this quite pointed and well-articulated concern about capital punishment in declaring the death penalty unconstitutional for non-homicidal child rape: "When the law punishes by death, it risks its own sudden descent into brutality, transgressing the constitutional commitment to decency and restraint."[166]

American jurists have, themselves, written explicitly of the lack of necessity for severe punishments, such as capital punishment, over the years. For example, Justice

Thurgood Marshall—responding to the once common argument that capital punishment was necessary to prevent acts of extrajudicial lynching—emphasized of the *lack of necessity* for the death penalty decades ago: "It simply defies belief to suggest that the death penalty is necessary to prevent the American people from taking the law into their own hands."[167] In his dissent in *Gregg v. Georgia*,[168] Justice Marshall specifically wrote that the evidence he had reviewed in *Furman* "remains convincing" that, in his judgment, " 'capital punishment is not necessary as a deterrent to crime in our society.' "[169] In other instances, Justices have either expressed the view that particular methods of executions carry a significant risk of unnecessary suffering[170] or articulated the view that such unnecessary suffering would be legally problematic.[171] Justice William Brennan—in a dissent from a denial of certiorari in *Glass v. Louisiana*,[172] one joined by Justice Marshall—himself specifically emphasized: "[I]t is firmly within the 'historic process of constitutional adjudication' for courts to consider, through a 'discriminating evaluation' of all available evidence, whether a particular means of carrying out the death penalty is 'barbaric' and unnecessary in light of currently available alternatives."[173]

The U.S. Supreme Court Justices have, in actuality, never been of one mind about the Eighth Amendment or about the country's use of capital punishment. In *Furman v. Georgia*, which held the death penalty to be unconstitutional and which led to a short, *de facto* moratorium on executions, Chief Justice Warren Burger—joined by Justices Blackmun, Powell, and Rehnquist—dissented, taking the position that the Eighth Amendment "was included in the Bill of Rights to guard against the use of torturous and inhuman punishments, not those of limited efficacy."[174] That dissent took note of language in *Wilkerson v. Utah*[175] that "it is safe to affirm that punishments of torture ... and all others in the same line of unnecessary cruelty, are forbidden" by the Eighth Amendment,[176] and of language in *Louisiana ex rel. Francis v. Resweber*[177] that made reference to the Eighth Amendment's prohibition against the infliction of "unnecessary pain" in carrying out an execution.[178] But Chief Justice Burger did not read those references to avoiding "unnecessary" cruelty or pain "as a mandate for assessing the value of punishments in achieving the aims of penology."[179] "[N]owhere," Burger said, "are such aims even mentioned in the *Wilkerson* opinion,"[180] with Burger's dissent adding of the "unnecessary" reference in *Resweber*: "The context makes abundantly clear that the Court was disapproving the wanton infliction of physical pain, and once again not advising pragmatic analysis of punishments approved by legislatures."[181] "Apart from these isolated uses of the word 'unnecessary,' " Burger argued, "nothing in the cases suggests that it is for the courts to make a determination of the efficacy of punishments."[182]

It was at that point that Chief Justice Burger brought up the Supreme Court's 1910 landmark decision in *Weems v. United States*. "The decision in *Weems v. United States* is not to the contrary," he wrote of his position that the Court's prior precedents in *Wilkerson* and *Resweber* did not suggest it was for courts to make a determination of the efficacy of punishments. As Burger wrote at length in trying to beat back what he called "the necessity approach":

> In *Weems* the Court held that for the crime of falsifying public documents, the punishment imposed under the Philippine Code of 15 years' imprison-

ment at hard labor under shackles, followed by perpetual surveillance, loss of voting rights, loss of the right to hold public office, and loss of right to change domicile freely, was violative of the Eighth Amendment. The case is generally regarded as holding that a punishment may be excessively cruel within the meaning of the Eighth Amendment because it is grossly out of proportion to the severity of the crime; some view the decision of the Court primarily as a reaction to the mode of the punishment itself. Under any characterization of the holding, it is readily apparent that the decision grew out of the Court's overwhelming abhorrence of the imposition of the particular penalty for the particular crime; it was making an essentially moral judgment, not a dispassionate assessment of the need for the penalty. The Court specifically disclaimed "the right to assert a judgment against that of the legislature of the expediency of the laws...." Thus, apart from the fact that the Court in *Weems* concerned itself with the crime committed as well as the punishment imposed, the case marks no departure from the largely unarticulable standard of extreme cruelty. However intractable that standard may be, that is what the Eighth Amendment is all about. The constitutional provision is not addressed to social utility and does not command that enlightened principles of penology always be followed.

By pursuing the necessity approach, it becomes even more apparent that it involves matters outside the purview of the Eighth Amendment. Two of the several aims of punishment are generally associated with capital punishment–retribution and deterrence. It is argued that retribution can be discounted because that, after all, is what the Eighth Amendment seeks to eliminate. There is no authority suggesting that the Eighth Amendment was intended to purge the law of its retributive elements, and the Court has consistently assumed that retribution is a legitimate dimension of the punishment of crimes. Furthermore, responsible legal thinkers of widely varying persuasions have debated the sociological and philosophical aspects of the retribution question for generations, neither side being able to convince the other. It would be reading a great deal into the Eighth Amendment to hold that the punishments authorized by legislatures cannot constitutionally reflect a retributive purpose.

The less esoteric but no less controversial question is whether the death penalty acts as a superior deterrent. Those favoring abolition find no evidence that it does. Those favoring retention start from the intuitive notion that capital punishment should act as the most effective deterrent and note that there is no convincing evidence that it does not. Escape from this empirical stalemate is sought by placing the burden of proof on the States and concluding that they have failed to demonstrate that capital punishment is a more effective deterrent than life imprisonment. Numerous justifications have been advanced for shifting the burden, and they are not without their rhetorical appeal. However, these arguments are not descended from established constitutional principles, but are born of the urge to bypass an unresolved factual question. Comparative deterrence is not a matter that lends itself to precise measurement; to shift the burden to the States is to provide an illusory solution to an enormously complex problem. If it were proper to put the States to the test of demonstrating the deterrent value of capital punishment, we could just as well ask them to prove the need for life imprisonment or any other punishment. Yet I know of no convincing evidence that life imprisonment is a more effective deterrant than 20 years' imprisonment, or even that a $10 parking ticket is a more effective deterrent than a $5 parking ticket. In fact, there are some who go so far as to challenge the notion that any punishments deter crime. If the States are unable to adduce convincing proof rebutting such assertions, does it then follow that all punishments are suspect as being 'cruel and unusual' within the meaning of the Constitution? On the contrary, I submit that the questions raised by the necessity approach are beyond the pale of judicial inquiry under the Eighth Amendment.[183]

But the maxim laid down by Montesquieu and Beccaria makes the necessity for a punishment the critical, defining issue in deciding whether or not the punishment in question is tyrannous in nature. And just as the unusualness concept invites a review of the nature and frequency of use of a particular punishment, the concept of cruelty itself suggests that moral judgments must be made. If a severe punishment is adjudged to be unnecessary because there are alternatives to it (whether because of developments in technology, the law, or otherwise), judges should not hesitate to take that into account in making their Eighth Amendment judgments. After all, the life or liberty of someone is at stake. In the twenty-first century, the use of capital punishment should certainly be rejected as a cruel and unusual punishment on that ground. As Richard Dieter, the former executive director of the Washington, D.C.-based Death Penalty Information Center, has emphasized: "Today, it would be nearly impossible to make the case that the death penalty is absolutely necessary. The main justifications for capital punishment—deterrence and retribution—are utterly unpersuasive with a punishment applied so rarely and so unnecessarily, and that is especially so given the arbitrary factors such as geography, race, and economic status."[184] The abandonment of capital punishments in other nations—and the lack of its use in various American locales—also shows that capital punishment is not necessary. Like the discontinuance of use of non-lethal corporal punishments in civilized societies, the death penalty's time must be adjudged to be past because capital punishment is unnecessary and because, in light of its inherent characteristics, it constitutes a form of torture.[185]

In the case of the death penalty, it is simply not necessary for any government—be it state or federal—to resort to executions. There is no conclusive statistical proof that the death penalty deters homicides more effectively than life-without-parole ("LWOP") sentences,[186] with death penalty states—on average—actually showing *higher* murder rates than non-death penalty states.[187] And once a criminal is behind bars, there is simply no need to kill that person, let alone any legitimate justification for doing so. Indeed, one survey showed that 88 percent of criminologists believe existing research does not support the notion that the death penalty deters crime, with a 2009 survey of police chiefs showing that the vast majority of such law enforcement officials felt that the death penalty was the least effective in deterring crime.[188] The fact that many countries around the world—in Europe, in Africa, in the Americas, and elsewhere—have already stopped executing criminals makes it even more clear that modern, twenty-first century societies do not need to resort to the use of death sentences and executions. The availability of LWOP sentences as an alternative only solidifies and amplifies the notion that capital punishment is not necessary.[189]

The idea that death sentences are not necessary not only finds roots in the Enlightenment, it finds expression in earlier opinions of U.S. Supreme Court Justices. For instance, in a concurring opinion in *Furman v. Georgia*, Justice Thurgood Marshall wrote way back in 1972:

> In order to assess whether or not death is an excessive or unnecessary penalty, it is necessary to consider the reasons why a legislature might select it as punishment for one or more offenses, and examine whether less severe penalties would satisfy the legitimate legislative wants as well as capital punishment. If they would, then the death penalty is unnecessary cruelty, and, therefore, unconstitutional.[190]

In that concurrence, Justice Marshall had this to say on the subject of deterrence at a time when even less was known, from a social science perspective, about the lack of a measurable deterrent effect for capital punishment in comparison to LWOP sentences:

> Despite the fact that abolitionists have not proved non-deterrence beyond a reasonable doubt, they have succeeded in showing by clear and convincing evidence that capital punishment is not necessary as a deterrent to crime in our society. This is all that they must do. We would shirk our judicial responsibilities if we failed to accept the presently existing statistics and demanded more proof. It may be that we now possess all the proof that anyone could ever hope to assemble on the subject. But, even if further proof were to be forthcoming, I believe there is more than enough evidence presently available for a decision in this case.[191]

At one time, the death penalty was a universally accepted punishment for murder. It was the standard or usual—indeed, the mandatory punishment—for a wide variety of felonies.[192] "In the 1950s," death penalty scholar Hugo Adam Bedau once wrote, "death was the mandatory punishment for at least one crime in many capital jurisdictions."[193] "Of all the reforms in America's long-drawn-out affair with the death penalty," Bedau explained elsewhere of American history and the rise of judicial discretion in America's criminal justice system, "none is more significant (or in sharper contrast with English law) than the end of the death penalty as a mandatory punishment."[194] The U.S. Supreme Court declared mandatory death sentences to be unconstitutional back in 1976,[195] and since that time, it has also insisted on individualized sentencing in capital cases.[196] Indeed, one-time expressions of skepticism about whether the Eighth Amendment's prohibition against disproportionate sentences could ever be applied in the context of murder cases[197] have given way to expressions of the death penalty's unconstitutional, barbarous, and torturous nature, albeit by dissenting Justices since the U.S. Supreme Court reauthorized the death penalty's use in *Gregg v. Georgia* (1976).[198]

The death penalty—once a lawful sanction throughout the world but now rejected by a majority of nations—is itself, as the evidence shows, a *torturous* punishment.[199] In that respect, one must take into account that punishments *less severe than death* have already been jettisoned and so categorized. Already, the U.S. Supreme Court, in *Weems v. United States*,[200] struck down a *non-lethal* corporal punishment, finding that "it is a precept of justice that punishment for crime should be graduated and proportioned to offense."[201] Not only is death different in kind and degree from any other punishment,[202] but various categories of offenders (i.e., the insane, the intellectually disabled, juveniles, non-homicide offenders) are—as noted—already exempt from it.[203] In fact, way back in 1983, a majority of U.S. Supreme Court Justices emphasized, citing earlier cases, that "the Court has applied the principle of proportionality to hold capital punishment excessive in certain circumstances."[204] In that case, *Solem v. Helm*, the Court identified a three-part test for proportionality. "In sum," the Court ruled, "a court's proportionality analysis under the Eighth Amendment should be guided by objective criteria, including (i) the gravity of the offense and the harshness of the penalty; (ii) the sentences imposed on other criminals in the same jurisdiction; and (iii) the sentences imposed for commission of the same crime in other jurisdictions."[205] With many non-lethal acts (e.g., rape, pins under fingernails, flogging, suspension by the hands) already appropriately described as torturous, it only makes sense that state-sanctioned killing should be classified as such, too.[206]

The use of death sentences and executions are not only unnecessary because of the ready availability of LWOP sentences, but they are highly disproportionate as applied because of their arbitrariness[207] and all the racial,[208] geographic[209] and gender disparities[210] so closely associated with them. Moreover, any punishment that is torturous does not, by definition, comport with human dignity, and that is, itself, extremely damning for the death penalty when that punishment is analyzed through an Eighth Amendment and human rights lens.[211] The Eighth Amendment has long been interpreted to bar torture as a matter of constitutional law,[212] and the death penalty—in truth—only coarsens societies in which it is used. In addition to the warning of Justice Anthony Kennedy that the death penalty's use risks the law's "sudden descent into brutality," he wrote of the Eighth Amendment's "constitutional commitment to decency and restraint."[213] The Supreme Court's own Eighth Amendment jurisprudence has already taken note of the importance of human dignity to the Court's decision-making process. Because the death penalty de-humanizes offenders, and because the modern definition of torture bars both physical and psychological torture, the death penalty should not be permissible.[214]

Although the U.S. Supreme Court has referred to "physical torture" on multiple occasions,[215] it needs to take up—and take seriously—the issue of mental or psychological torture. For example, although some U.S. Supreme Court Justices have called upon the Court to review the psychological effect of long stays on death row,[216] and although the Court has written of "physical or psychological" torture in the context of self-incrimination and confessions,[217] the U.S. Supreme Court has not yet written anything close to what the California Supreme Court did about the death penalty in 1972. In *People v. Anderson*,[218] the California Supreme Court declared in that year: "[T]he process of carrying out a verdict of death is often so degrading and brutalizing to the human spirit as to constitute psychological torture."[219] Instead, to date, the U.S. Supreme Court has consistently declined to even review cases seeking to challenge what has been termed the "death row phenomenon." The death row phenomenon relates to the unique psychological impact that prisoners experience while living on death row under its harsh conditions of confinement—all the while with the risk of execution hanging over them. "This bleak isolation and years of torturous uncertainty," the highly effective nonprofit, Reprieve, has emphasized, "can result in a sharp deterioration in a prisoner's mental and physical state, often making inmates suicidal."[220]

Nonviolent Offenders

Since the 1970s, American society has witnessed explosive growth in the number of prisons and in its prison population. The number of federal and state prisons jumped from around 600 in the mid-1970s to more than 1,000 by the year 2000.[221] And according to a March 2018 report of The Sentencing Project, a Washington, D.C.-based nonprofit, "[t]he U.S. prison population grew by more than 600% between 1973 and 2009—from 200,000 people to 1.6 million." As that report observes: "Tough-on-crime policies expanded the number of imprisoned people even while crime rates plunged to 40% below their levels in the 1990s." Although the report notes that, by end of 2016, the number of people held in U.S. prisons had declined by six percent since a 2009 peak in the number of people incarcerated, there were still 1.5 million people in prison as of 2016. "By 2016," the report notes, "42 states had at least modestly downsized their prison populations from their peak levels." Only six states—New Jersey, Alaska, New York, Vermont, Connecticut and California—have reduced their prison populations by 25% or more, however. Nevertheless, that report starkly adds, "the prison population remains larger than the total population of 11 states."[222] In a country that prides itself on freedom and liberty, the infringement on individual liberty brought about by the overuse of prisons is not something that should be swept under the rug.

Disturbingly, a disproportionate number of inmates are minorities, and many offenders are serving time for drug offenses. Per the March 2018 report of The Sentencing Project: "277,000 people are still imprisoned nationwide for a drug offense—over half of them (56%) African American or Latino." "People with drug convictions," that report notes, "comprise nearly half of the federal prison population (46%) and 15% of the state prison population."[223] According to an NAACP action alert: "Over the last 30 years, there has been a 500% increase in incarceration; almost 60% of the people in prison or jail right now are racial or ethnic minorities, while we comprise just over 27% of the national population."[224] An NAACP Fact Sheet further notes that "African Americans represent 12.5% of illicit drug users, but 29% of those arrested for drug offenses and 33% of those incarcerated in state facilities for drug offenses." "In 2012 alone," that fact sheet observes, "the United States spent nearly $81 billion on corrections."[225] While the gap between the number of prisoners who are black and white—and between those who are Hispanic and white—has narrowed somewhat from 2009 to 2016, the number of blacks in federal and state prisons still outnumbers the number of white inmates. The Pew Research Center reports that, at the end of 2016, federal and state prisons held about 486,900 black inmates, 439,800 white inmates, and 339,300 Hispanic inmates. In 2009, there were 584,800 black inmates, 490,000 white inmates, and 341,200 Hispanic inmates.[226]

The actual severity of the sentences being imposed by American courts is also noteworthy and should be of concern to anyone who seeks a more just criminal justice system. According to another report of The Sentencing Project, of those serving time in prison, one out of every seven prisoners—more than 206,000 in total—"was serving a sentence of life with parole, life without parole, or a 'virtual life' sentence of 50 years or more." That 2017 report, "Still Life: America's Increasing Use of Life and Long-term Sentences," showed that two-thirds of those prisoners were people of color. And of that number, 17,000 were convicted of non-violent offenses, while 12,000 were under age 18 at the time of their crimes. "As of 2016," the "Still Life" report observed, "there were 161,957 people serving life sentences, or one of every nine people in prison." "An additional 44,311 individuals are serving 'virtual life' sentences, yielding," the report concluded, "a total population of life and virtual life sentences at 206,268—or one of every seven people in prison." Ashley Nellis, the senior research analyst who prepared the report, compiling the data from the Federal Bureau of Prisons and the departments of corrections for every state, told ABC News after the issuance of the report: "A prisoner who starts his or her sentence in their 30s will, on average, cost the state $1 million." And expenses, because of health care costs, only escalate as prisoners age. "Many people enter prison in poor health to begin with," Nellis said, adding of correctional facilities and the inmates they house: "[P]rison itself is hard on a person's health, and they're being cared for into their geriatric years."[227]

In "A Living Death: Life without Parole for Nonviolent Offences," a report issued in 2013, the American Civil Liberties Union calculated that "as of 2012, there were 3,278 prisoners serving LWOP for nonviolent drug and property crimes in the federal system and in nine states that provided such statistics (there may well be more such prisoners in other states)." "About 79 percent of these 3,278 prisoners," the report noted, "are serving LWOP for nonviolent drug crimes," with "[n]early two-thirds of prisoners serving LWOP for nonviolent offense nationwide" in the federal system. "The overwhelming majority (83.4 percent) of the LWOP sentences for nonviolent crimes surveyed by the ACLU," the report added, "were mandatory." "In these cases," the report observed, "the sentencing judges had no choice in sentencing due to laws requiring mandatory minimum periods of imprisonments, habitual offender laws, statutory penalty enhancements, or other sentencing rules that mandated LWOP." The financial cost of keeping all 3,278 of these offenders behind bars per the ACLU's fiscal analysis: $1,784 billion.[228] And the human cost: people punished in ways that the judges themselves often view as unnecessary, meaning that individual liberty suffers even as taxpayers foot the bill.

The American criminal justice system has, over the last few decades, thus grown increasingly and inexplicably punitive, making consideration of the necessity-for-punishment principle of great importance to modern life. Many people are now working for criminal justice reform, with a new non-profit, the Minnesota Justice Research Center, embarking on a quest to bring evidence-based solutions to the issues of crime and punishment. As the website for that non-profit notes: "The gathering and application of research-based evidence is central to re-envisioning and transforming the criminal justice system. Through such evidence-gathering and analysis, we will be able to understand how to eliminate the racially and socio-economically disparate outcomes that even facially neutral procedures can produce." The organization recognizes that although "our justice system is large and complicated," there is a need "as a community" to "get close enough to its workings" in order "to fully understand its impact on the lives of people and to ensure that it operates in a way that is consistent with our ideals." "To achieve this," the new non-profit's website stresses, "we must subject the justice system to rigorous and regular monitoring, research, and analysis."[229]

The need to better understand and then reform America's criminal justice system—as the statistics starkly show—is great. According to the Alabama-based Equal Justice Initiative: "The United States incarcerates more of its citizens than any other nation in the world. The increase in the jail and prison population from less than 200,000 in 1972 to 2.2 million today has led to unprecedented prison overcrowding and put tremendous strain on state budgets." "The United States," the Equal Justice Initiative reports, referring to the much-cited statistic, "has 5 percent of the world's population but nearly 25 percent of its prisoners." Its analysis and summary of what has led to the current state of affairs: "In the 1990s, as lawmakers campaigned to 'get tough on crime,' America built a new prison every two weeks and still could not meet the demand for prison beds." "Today, nearly seven million people in this country are incarcerated, on probation, or on parole."[230] "According to the most recent data," one criminology textbook notes, "for every 100,000 adults in the U.S. population, 623 are incarcerated."[231] So many people are now behind bars that the phrase "mass incarceration" is frequently used to describe the state of America's correctional system.[232] Clearly, consideration of whether punishments are truly necessary would lead to more liberty and to fewer non-violent offenders being incarcerated.

It is well-known that the imprisonment rate in the United States has skyrocketed since the 1970s. As noted, the large prison population in the U.S. entails large financial costs as well as tremendous human costs, with those costs shifting over time but always remaining. As Bryan Stevenson, the founder and head of the Equal Justice Initiative,[233] writes of America in his *New York Times* bestseller, *Just Mercy*: "Today we have the highest rate of incarceration in the world. The prison population has increased from 300,000 people in the early 1970s to 2.3 million people today. There are nearly six million people on probation or on parole."[234] The statistics are in constant flux, but the Bureau of Justice Statistics reports that, at the end of 2016, the number of prisoners under state and federal jurisdiction stood at 1,505,400. And as of year-end 2016, 1,458,2000 of those prisoners had been sentenced to more than one year of imprisonment, with many of those inmates being nonviolent offenders.[235] There are also hundreds of thousands of people being housed in local jails, bringing the number of people locked up to more than two million people. "The United States," as one report puts it, in what should be of major concern to all Americans, "locks up more people, per capita, than any other nation."[236] Since 1980, the price tag that each U.S. resident is paying on corrections has gone up to about $260 per year, a substantial increase from an average expenditure of $77 per person in 1980. Those high costs mean less money for education and fewer resources for employing other methods to fight crime (e.g., paying for more police officers, spending money on programs for at-risk youth, etc.).[237]

Many offenders are in prison for violent crimes or are habitual recidivists and properly belong there. But many inmates are *not* being incarcerated for those reasons. According to a January 2018 bulletin released by the Bureau of Justice Statistics: "More than half (54%) of state prisoners were serving sentences for violent offenses at year-end 2015, the most recent year for which data are available."[238] That, of course, leaves a large number of people who are being incarcerated for *non-violent* offenses. In Heather Ahn-Redding's *The "Million Dollar Inmate": The Financial and Social Burden of Non-violent Offenders*, the following questions are appropriately raised and brought front and center in the ongoing criminal justice debate: "Do we *need* to send nonviolent offenders to prison? Do we *need* to spend billions of dollars to incarcerate individuals who pose very little physical threats to society?"[239] Noting more than a decade ago, in 2007, that "a nonviolent offender who is sentenced to 45 years in prison will cost the state or federal government over one million dollars (in today's dollars)," *The "Million Dollar Inmate"* highlights the high social and financial costs of America's high rate of incarceration of non-violent offenders.[240] The time for a material change is now at hand, just as the Enlightenment brought changes to societies around the world.

Social Ills, Poverty, and Those in Need of Treatment

Prisons are crowded with people who struggle—and, in many cases, have long struggled—with substance abuse. A 2010 report of The National Center on Addiction and Substance Abuse ("CASA") found that 1.5 million of the 2.3 million inmates met the DMS-IV medical criteria for addiction or substance abuse. Another 458,000 inmates, though not meeting those rigorous criteria, had histories of substance abuse. "Combined," a news release observed, "these two groups constitute 85% of the U.S. prison population." In 2006, the 144-page report emphasized, alcohol or drugs were involved in 78% of violent crimes and 83% of property crimes. The report found, however, that only 11% of all inmates with addiction disorders and substance abuse receive any treatment during their incarceration. As the news release summarized the import of the report's findings: "The report found that if all inmates who needed treatment and aftercare received such services, the nation would break even in a year if just over 10% remained substance and crime free and employed. Thereafter, for each inmate who remained sober, employed and crime free the nation would reap an economic benefit of $90,953 per year." As Susan Foster, CASA's Vice President and Director of Policy Research and Analysis, put it at the time: "States complain mightily about their rising prison costs; yet they continue to hemorrhage public funds that could be saved if they provided treatment to inmates with alcohol and other drug problems and stepped up use of drug courts and prosecutorial drug treatment alternative programs."[241]

The clear relationship between drug and alcohol abuse and crime is a well-documented fact. In a 2002 study of the prevalence of substance dependence or abuse among jail inmates, the authors of the study found that 68% of the more than 610,000 jail inmates surveyed satisfied the criteria for alcohol or drug abuse or dependence. A federal data collection program known as the Arrestee Drug Abuse Monitoring ("ADAM II") further confirms the connection. "The protocol for ADAM II," a book titled *Drugs, Crime, and Their Relationship* notes, "requires that all males arrested in 10 U.S. cities be tested for 10 different drugs within 24 hours of arrest." The results for the ten cities—Atlanta, Charlotte, Chicago, Denver, Indianapolis, Minneapolis, New York, Portland, Sacramento, and Washington, D.C.—revealed a consistent pattern. For all ten cites for the period from 2007 to 2010, ADAM II showed a large percentage of arrestees tested positive for drug use. "The results," the author of *Drugs, Crime, and Their Relationship* summarizes, "indicate a strong and consistent relationship between arrest and a positive drug test, with most sites identifying drug use in 60 to 80% of arrestees." "Marijuana (46.8%), cocaine (22.4%), and heroin (14.4%)," that book explains of the results, "were the three most commonly identified substances across the 10 sites, although wide variations were sometimes found between sites." For example, methamphetamine was detected at relative low levels (less than 4%) in eight of the sites but frequently appeared in Portland, Oregon (19.8%) and in Sacramento, California (33.2%).[242]

In the last few years, the opioid epidemic—and the lack of treatment *within* prisons—has actually led to deaths *upon release* from prison. In a 2018 article, "How America's Prisons Are Fueling the Opioid Epidemic," the writer notes that when an inmate addicted to opioids is released from prison, that inmate's chances of a fatal overdose are "massively elevated." "According to a 2007 study published in *The New England Journal of Medicine*," that article points out, "former inmates' risk of a fatal drug overdose is *129 times* as high as it is for the general population during the two weeks after release." "Other studies," the article continues, "have backed this up, putting the increased risk of overdose death in the tens of times or above 100 times." As Traci Green, a Brown University researcher, puts it: "Globally, there is no more high-risk period and no more high-risk population than those leaving incarceration." "It's during those first two weeks and out to four to six weeks that people are at greater risk of overdose death," Green emphasized.[243] Such statistics demonstrate the clear need for a more coordinated approach to combating drug and alcohol addiction.

Many prisoners, already dealing with major addiction issues, also suffer from mental illnesses. In a book chapter titled "Chronic Mental Illness in Prisons," one scholar summarizes the data in this way: "Those with mental disorders have been increasingly incarcerated during the past three decades, probably as a result of the deinstitutionalization of the state mental health system. Correctional institutions have become the *de facto* state hospitals, and there are more seriously and persistently mentally ill in prisons than in all state hospitals in the United States." One 2006 study, for example, found that while more than half of all prison and jail inmates have a mental health problem compared with 11 percent of the general population, only one in three prison inmates—and only one in six jail inmates—receive any form of mental health treatment. "Prisoners," one source stresses, "have high rates of mental illness—including such serious disorders as schizophrenia, bipolar disorder, and major depression—that are two to four times higher than members of the general public." Over a 15-year period, that source relays of the challenge America's criminal justice system faces, the number of mentally ill people in California prisons almost doubled, with 45 percent of California's inmates treated for severe mental illness in a one-year period.[244]

The long-time, close association between prisoners and poverty is also well-known. In one book, *Poverty in the United States*, it is noted that "prisoners are overwhelmingly poor," something most Americans probably already intuitively know. A 1991 survey of state prisoners, that source observes, showed that 53 percent of the prisoners had an income of under $10,000 per year in the year before they entered prison. Yet, that survey found that 67 percent of the state prisoners had been working—55 percent of them full-time—in the month before their arrests.[245] Another book, *Poverty and the Government in America*, concurs, with that source stressing: "Prisoners tend to come from poor backgrounds. In 1986, for example, 31 percent of prisoners in state prisons were unemployed before their arrest, and another 43 percent had only part-time employment." "In 1992," that source adds, "80 percent of people charged with felonies in the seventy-five largest counties in the country could not afford to hire their own lawyer." These indigent prisoners tend to be poorly educated, too. As that source notes: "Sixty-one percent of state prisoners had not completed high school."[246]

More recent statistics reveal the relationship of poverty and poor educational and job opportunities to imprisonment. In their report, "Prisons of Poverty: 'Uncovering the Pre-Incarceration Incomes of the Imprisoned,' Bernadette Rabuy and Daniel Kopf, after utilizing Bureau of Justice Statistics data, wrote in 2015: "We found that, in 2014 dollars, incarcerated people had a median annual income of $19,185 prior to their incarceration, which is 41% less than non-incarcerated people of similar ages." "We found that incarcerated people in all gender, race, and ethnicity groups earned substantially less prior to their incarceration than their non-incarcerated counterparts of similar ages," the report added. "The American prison system," Rabuy and Kopf note, "is bursting at the seams with people who have been shut out of the economy and who had neither a quality education nor access to good jobs." For example, they observe that in Sandtown-Winchester/Harlem Park, the part of Baltimore that sends the most people to prison, more than half of the area's residents aged 16 to 64 are not employed and that 61% of local residents aged 25 or older have less than a high school diploma. "While the typical non-incarcerated person has at least a high school diploma," they explain of American demographics, "the typical incarcerated person does not." As they conclude in their report, taking note of the difficulty of ex-convicts in finding employment due to their criminal records: "Our society has, in the name of being tough on crime, made a series of policy choices that have fueled a cycle of poverty and incarceration. We send large numbers of people with low levels of education and low skills to prison, and then when they leave just as penniless as they were when then went in, we expect them to bear the burden of legally-acceptable employment discrimination." "Permanently ending the era of mass incarceration,"

Rabuy and Kopf emphasize, "will require reversing the decades of neglect that denied our most vulnerable communities access to good jobs, reliable transportation, safe housing, and good schools."[247]

Running secure prisons, of course, is incredibly expensive, and prison wardens and guards—as well as prison doctors and nurses and mental health professionals—face difficult challenges every day. In 2017, the Center on Sentencing and Corrections of the Vera Institute of Justice published a particularly eye-opening report titled "The Price of Prisons." Prepared by Chris Mai and Ram Subramanian, the report examined state spending trends from 2010 to 2015, with corrections departments in 45 states completing and returning the survey. "In 2015," the report noted of the 45 responding states, "the total state expenditure on prisons was just under $43 billion." Observing that prison administration "is an expensive endeavor," the report detailed precisely why. "Prisons," the report emphasized, "must at all times provide: adequate levels of security; program and administrative staff to run facilities and both supervise and provide services for incarcerated persons; food and programming for the people under their care, including sufficient recreational and educational opportunities; infrastructure maintenance and upkeep, including electricity and other operational costs; and, increasingly, higher levels of specialized health care for a growing population with significant levels of physical and mental health concerns."[248]

The punitive treatment of mostly poor, often-unemployed offenders, coupled with the high cost of running prisons, raises serious questions about whether Americans are pursuing the right approach by making such extensive use of incarceration. "The relationship between the length of prison terms and recidivism," a 2013 Pew report observed, "is one of the central points of debate in sentencing and corrections policy." "Several studies, looking at different populations and using varied methodologies," the Pew report explained, "have attempted to find a relationship between the length of prison terms and recidivism but have failed to find a consistent impact, either positive or negative." It is clear that prison time served has increased over the years. "Nationally, from 1990 to 2009," the Pew report noted, "the average amount of time prisoners spent behind bars increased 36 percent, from 2.1 years to 2.9 years." As that report stated after the data was subjected to scrutiny: "An analysis of data from three states—Florida, Maryland, and Michigan—found little or no evidence that longer prison terms for many nonviolent offenders produced either incapacitation or deterrence effects. That is, the extra time behind bars neither prevented crimes during the period of incarceration nor kept offenders from committing crimes once released from prison. "The study," the report concluded, "found that significant proportions of nonviolent inmates released in these states in 2004 could have served three months to as much as two years less without any decline in public safety, dramatically reducing prison populations and costs."[249]

A recent study conducted in The Netherlands only amplifies these concerns. Using longitudinal data and analyzing recidivism outcomes by imprisonment length in a nationwide sample of Dutch offenders, that study examined "to what extent longer imprisonment length is more, or less, effective in controlling recidivism." "From a theoretical perspective," the study's authors wrote at the outset of their paper, "it is difficult to determine the direction of this relationship because different theories result in contrasting expectations." "On one hand," they observed, laying out the various hypothetical outcomes, "based on deterrence theory it should be expected that a longer stay results in *less* recidivism." "Other theoretical arguments, however," they continued, "suggest that longer prison terms may result in *higher* recidivism rates." "Longer imprisonment length," they hypothesized, applying control theories, "removes individuals for a more extended period of time from the law-abiding community, and as a consequence deteriorates social bonds more than shorter prison sentences will do." Noting that "long prison terms may have detrimental effects on family and work relationships," as well as the fact that "human capital, such as work-related skills and experience, goes unused due to longer confinement," they postulated—in one potential outcome—that longer confinement in prison "may negatively affect the chances of a conventional life after release from prison."

Other theories were also considered in the study, which specifically noted that the Dutch prison population was quite small in comparison with that of the United States and that Dutch prison sentences were, on average, much shorter. "[D]ifferential association and learning theories," the study's authors continued, "assume that criminal behavior is learned from deviant others." "From these theories," they wrote, "it can be derived that offenders with longer prison spells are more exposed to deviant values, and as a consequence can become more deeply embedded in criminal networks." "Finally," they observed, "labeling theory suggests that legal sanctions contribute to the development of a criminal career rather than prevent offenders' involvement in crime." As they explained: "According to this theory, individuals are being treated as offenders by others, and subsequently the offender internalizes this label and starts to behave in accordance with this label. Longer prison terms may result in a criminal identity that is more strongly internalized, which in turn leads to increased offending after release." Whereas the prison population rate in The Netherlands "is 84 per 100,000," the study's authors stressed, the United States—"unique in its scale of imprisonment"—has "an imprisonment rate of 612 per 100,000." And whereas, in the U.S., 97% of the prisoners are sentenced to more than one year, with state prisoners, on average, serving two years, the average Dutch prison term is approximately four months. "Other Western European regions, such as Scandinavia and Germany," the study's authors wrote, comparing them to The Netherlands, "have a fairly similar prison population rate; for instance, 72 per 100,000 in Sweden and 87 per 100,000 in Germany."

Obtaining interview data from 1,904 representative prisoners, 1,764 of whom completed an additional written questionnaire, the authors of the study focused on "future engagement in criminal behavior during the first 6 months after release using three indicators: reoffending, reconviction, and reincarceration." "Ex-prisoners," they emphasized, "experience difficulties at various life domains within the first 6 months of release, and important differences in postrelease labor market success are found in this period." "[S]tatistics," they further wrote, laying out why the six-month time frame was chosen, "seem to suggest that the risk of reoffending is highest shortly after release." As the study's authors ultimately concluded after examining the collected data: "Our findings suggest that length of imprisonment does not have a significant effect on recidivism in the first 6 months after release, and that this conclusion holds across various measures and types of recorded recidivism, that is, reoffending, reconviction, and reincarceration." "[O]ur results," they wrote, "show no evidence for a relationship between time served and each recidivism outcome, and therefore seem to suggest that, based on the first high-risk months after release, there are no crime-control benefits in terms of recidivism of imprisoning individuals for a longer period." In finding "that length of imprisonment exerts an overall null effect on future rates of recidivism and that this conclusion holds across the various types of recidivism," the study's authors observed: "From a policy perspective, the results of the current study suggest that—within the context of imprisonment length up to 15 months—investing in longer prison sentences is not likely to yield higher crime-control benefits." "Alternative ways of punishment, such as electronic monitoring and community service," they continued, "could be more promising in terms of spending and of lowering recidivism."[250]

Recidivism, as a modern dictionary defines it, is the "tendency to relapse into a previous condition or mode of behavior." "The prevalence of recidivism is naturally higher for populations with lengthier criminal careers and deeper penetrations into the justice system," a March 2018 report of Harvard's Kennedy School observes, noting that "[t]here is no perfect way to measure recidivism, but it is generally defined as a person's return to crime following some form of intervention." It is, that report suggests, the *nature* of the intervention—and whether or not that intervention is successful—that is the key. "The probability of an individual crime becoming an official instance of recidivism," the March 2018 report emphasizes, "depends on many factors, including the social-cultural and political-economic environment, the resources available to sustain the sequence of organizational actions ending in recidivism, and the perceptions, beliefs, and biases of the human beings responsible for operating the justice system." "[C]rime reduction," that source stresses, should be viewed "as a complicated change process in which individuals learn to be law abiding over time." In asking, "What helps individuals desist from crime?", that report, looking for "positive outcomes" and examining the "research literature" and inadequacies of a singular focus on recidivism measures that can, at times, be misleading, identifies the following nine critical factors: (1) "Getting older and maturing," (2) "Family and relationships," (3) "Sobriety," (4) "Employment," (5) "Hope and motivation," (6) "Having something to give to others," (7) "Having a place within a social group," (8) "Not having a criminal identity," and (9) "Being 'believed in.'" Community corrections agencies, the report concludes, should broaden their focus to address such concerns and to achieve progress.[251]

The Need for Education, Skills Training, and Better Treatment

Both Montesquieu and Beccaria, while articulating what has become known as the parsimony principle, put a special emphasis on education. "It is in republican government that the full power of education is needed," Montesquieu wrote in *The Spirit of the Laws*. "[G]overnment," Montesquieu emphasized, "is like all things in the world; in order to preserve it, one must love it." "One never hears it said that kings do not love monarchy or that despots hate despotism," he wrote, adding: "Therefore, in a republic, everything depends on establishing this love, and education should attend to inspiring it."[252] In an early English-language edition of Beccaria's *On Crimes and Punishments*, one also finds these words in the chapter "*Of Education*": "[T]he most certain method of preventing crimes is, to perfect the system of education." "A great man, who is persecuted by that world he hath enlightened, and to whom we are indebted for many important truths," Beccaria added, making an allusion to Jean-Jacques Rousseau, "hath most amply detailed the principal maxims of useful education."[253] The need for better education within prisons is clear, especially given that so many inmates lack a high-school diploma and valuable employment skills.

The high cost of incarcerating prisoners—estimated in 2010 to be, on average, $31,286 per inmate annually in the United States—warrants the judicious, not the indiscriminate, use of incarceration.[254] Because that is the *average* cost estimated per inmate, there are some places where, of course, the cost is higher, sometimes much higher. In early June 2017, for example, the Associated Press ran a news story with this eye-popping headline: "At $75,560, housing a prisoner in California now costs more than a year at Harvard." The State of New York, the article noted, had the second highest cost per prisoner, with the average annual cost per inmate coming in at $69,000.[255] Whenever it costs more to incarcerate the poor and the disadvantaged than it does to educate some of the nation's top students, it should be a wake-up call for the American public. Education can provide a ladder out of poverty, while prison is often a dead end, the collateral consequences of which often extend far beyond an inmate's actual prison term. A criminal record means it is hard to find a job, and unemployment or underemployed means poverty, which all the studies show is a risk factor for landing back in prison. The inmate's family is also adversely affected.

The annual dollar figures for incarcerating offenders in California and New York both far exceed the average cost for a student to attend a year of college at a private school. While tuition and fees vary substantially from college to college, the average cost for tuition and fees at a four-year, private college for the 2017–2018 school year was approximately $34,700. When the average cost for room and board—approximately $12,200—is added to that amount, the total annual cost of attendance at a four-year, private college totaled approximately almost $47,000. For an out-of-state student to attend a four-year, public college, the average annual total for tuition and fees and room and board combined was $36,410, while the average annual total for tuition and fees and room and board for an in-state student to attend a four-year, public college totaled $20,770.[256] In other words, Americans are spending far more per year on incarcerating an inmate than an in-state student at a typical four-year, public college pays to get educated and to be housed and fed. In high-cost states like California and New York, the cost of incarcerating an inmate actually exceeds the average annual cost of attending an Ivy League school. For the 2018–2019 academic year, the cost of attending Harvard College is estimated to be $67,580.[257]

The rise of privately-run prison facilities is particularly disturbing, especially when juxtaposed against all the missed opportunities to better educate and better train America's citizenry, including America's at-risk youth. The companies that own and operate private prisons have a duty to their shareholders to maximize profits, and that means—for their corporate officers and employees—making sure prison beds are occupied. "In 2010," one source notes, "the two largest private prison companies, Corrections Corporation of America (CCA) and the GEO Group, reported earnings of US$1.7 billion and US$1.27 billion respectively to their shareholders."[258] Yet, from a societal perspective, it is clearly best that prisons *rehabilitate* offenders and not seek out, or hope for, *repeat customers*. "According to the Bureau of Justice Statistics," the ACLU has noted, "for-profit companies were responsible for approximately 7 percent of state prisoners and 18 percent of federal prisoners."[259] And as private prison populations rise, so too do costs and expenses for the general public. An application of the parsimony principle would suggest that steps be taken to *disincentive* incarceration where it is not deemed necessary. And the use of for-profit, private prison companies runs directly counter to that objective by incentivizing incarceration as a profit-making endeavor.

In America, federal and state prisons and local jails are necessary. Violent offenders who pose a danger to society need to be locked up, and judges—each and every day—are faced with the unenviable task of deciding which offenders pose the kind of risk warranting detention or incarceration, whether short-term or long-term in nature. But the use of incarceration should be about furthering the public good and, whenever possible, rehabilitating offenders so that, if and when inmates are released from prison, they have an actual chance to succeed once their terms of imprisonment expire. Prison life should center around reformation, not around private profiteering at the expense of taxpayers' and peoples' lives. One recent study demonstrated just how many government contracts with private prison companies have injected perverse incentives into the whole law-and-order enterprise. That study examined 62 private prison contracts in 21 states, and it found that the majority of these contracts guarantee that the state will supply enough prisoners to keep between 80 and 100 percent of the beds occupied in private prison facilities. If states fail to meet these "bed guarantees," the states are obligated to pay fines to the companies running the prisons. Needless to say, signing contracts that ensure that prisons will be filled is not exactly a formula for trying to reduce prison populations and to reduce the need for incarceration where that can be done.

While the private sector drives the American economy, protecting the public from crime is a *public* responsibility—and it is one that public officials should work to ensure is carried out honorably and ethically. Elected officials and prison administrators must concern themselves with protecting the public and those confined within prisons at the same time that they acknowledge—and try to further—people's liberty interests and the future prospects of those who have violated the law but who, in many cases, will be returning to society after their sentences expire. Policies that guarantee prison beds will be filled are extremely counterproductive. As the Brennan Center for Justice at New York University School of Law has emphasized: "This incentivizes states to send prisoners to private prisons rather than state-run prisons in order to meet the bed guarantee, regardless of the prisons' distance from families, their security level, or health conditions." Taking note of the problem, the non-profit

Brennan Center for Justice has further observed: "Under basic economic principles, firms that compete for and rely on government contracts want to decrease their costs while maximizing their revenue. Private prison companies are no exception—they reduce costs by cutting reentry and educational programs that would help reduce recidivism, and raise revenue by keeping government funding consistent through lockup quotas." "Unsurprisingly," the Brennan Center for Justice continues in its critique, "many private prison companies actually lobby for harsh criminal justice policies—like mandatory minimums and truth-in-sentencing laws—and against efforts to reduce mass incarceration."[260] The business model and financial incentives of private prison companies are thus totally at odds with what should be the goal: impartially and effectively implementing the parsimony principle.

Ideally, the American criminal justice system should earnestly work to reduce, not maximize, the number of people who need to be put behind bars. A sentence of imprisonment clearly stigmatizes and disrupts a person's life, including one's family life, and it obviously may result in the loss of a person's job, however poorly paid that job might be. Incarcerating offenders is oftentimes necessary, but policymakers, prosecutors and judges should be prepared to consider that sometimes prison terms may not be required and that prison may, in many cases, only exacerbate a problem. Resources might better be directed at substance abuse treatment initiatives, work opportunities for youth, and rebuilding communities in which unemployment and poverty are rampant. In cases where incarceration is appropriate, lawmakers, prosecutors and judges should thoughtfully consider the actual term to be imposed and the conditions of parole or supervised release. Congress, in 1984, eliminated parole at the federal level and established a post-confinement monitoring system known as "supervised release," the term of which is imposed at the initial sentencing hearing and then monitored by a federal probation officer. If an offender violates the terms of supervised release, the individual can be required to serve the term of supervised release in prison.[261]

If, throughout America, federal and state-court judges more carefully considered all the available alternatives in setting the terms or conditions of probation, parole, or supervised release, that would go a long way in making the criminal justice system more just. The conditions of confinement—or the conditions of release or parole—should be specifically calibrated with the parsimony principle in mind and to best ensure that offenders are incentivized to receive the treatment or the skills training that will enable them to escape poverty and to turn their lives around and away from criminal activity. Desperate people who have little or nothing to lose because of their poverty are the ones most likely to end up committing crimes. Someone who is hungry is, naturally, more likely to steal food. Someone who has an untreated drug addiction is, naturally, more likely to commit crimes to fuel that addiction. And an untreated alcoholic is, naturally, more likely to use poor judgment—poor judgment that sometimes leads to the commission of crimes. Whereas educational opportunities, jobs that pay living wages, and effective substance abuse treatment programs may disrupt America's cycle of poverty and incarceration, incarceration that is not coupled with educational opportunities or effective skills training programs will mean that once an inmate's prison term ends, the inmate will be no better prepared to face the real world than before the inmate entered prison in the first place.

Hope is the antidote to despair. Although prison sentences are often necessary to deter crime and to protect the public, lawmakers, prosecutors, judges and others should always strive to ensure that prisons are not dead ends for the people sent to them—people who may be capable of redemption and rehabilitation or of being treated or trained for future employment. Just as Cesare Beccaria forthrightly recognized that there needs to be a scale of crimes and punishments, there is already a recognition of the need for prisons with different security levels to house offenders—prisons that should be set up to deal with the particular challenges that the inmates sent to them face. Maximum-security (or so-called Supermax) prisons have been built to house the worst offenders, while medium- and minimum-security prisons now house the prisoners whose offenses and criminal histories are deemed not to warrant commitment to maximum-security institutions. Inmates serving life-without-parole sentences will not be reentering society, but other inmates eventually will, and the principle of human dignity requires that all prisoners be treated with respect and compassion. Prisons should be designed for security, but also with the idea of human dignity in mind.

Just as the punishment should fit the crime, and just as the type of prison should fit the type of offender, there needs to be careful consideration throughout the criminal justice system of whether prison is actually the appropriate, and most effective (and most cost-effective), response for certain types of offenses. The consideration of the parsimony principle suggests that Americans shouldn't reflexively be resorting to prisons and lengthy prison sentences to deal with complex social problems such as mental illness, poverty, and substance abuse. Prisons certainly have a proper role to play, but there are often options short of prison—pre-trial diversion programs, supervised release, or electronic home monitoring, as just three examples—that are available in appropriate cases, especially for juveniles and non-violent offenses, to deal with certain types of offenders. And when offenders are sent to prison, as many still will be, the goal should be to better calibrate the length of the sentence to be imposed and to educate and train those who end up behind bars so that, if and when they are released, they will not be back. The long-standing Enlightenment maxim of avoiding tyrannous punishments demands no less.

CHAPTER 8

With Liberty and Justice for All:

Bail Reform and the Cruelty of Unnecessary Punishments

The Need for Bail Reform

The U.S. Supreme Court has defined excessive bail as "bail set at a figure higher than an amount reasonably calculated to fulfill [its] purpose."[1] "In this respect," one federal district court observed in 2011, "bail and/or conditions of release should not be imposed beyond what is necessary to serve the purpose of ensuring appearance in court or protecting the welfare of the community against future dangerousness."[2] "If liberty is the norm, and the Bail Reform Act mandates that an accused be released on the 'least restrictive' conditions," that court stressed, "then a determination as to what conditions are to be imposed should be meted out in such a way as to satisfy the government's legitimate objectives of protecting the public without trampling upon the protected liberties of the accused."[3] "Therefore," that court observed, citing other precedents, "the relinquishment of constitutionally protected rights, such as the freedom of movement, on conditions that are more than necessary to satisfy legitimate governmental interests would constitute excessive bail in violation of the Eighth Amendment."[4] Phrasing it from the opposite perspective, the Minnesota Court of Appeals put it this way in 1987: "Bail is not excessive unless it is more than the amount reasonable necessary to guarantee the defendant's appearance at trial."[5] "The plain meaning of 'excessive bail,'" the U.S. Court of Appeals for the Ninth Circuit observed in 2007, "does not require that it be beyond one's means, only that it be greater than necessary to achieve the purposes for which bail is imposed."[6]

It is clear under existing constitutional law that dangerous offenders can be held without bail. If someone represents a danger to the community or is a flight risk, that person should not be eligible for bail. But of late, one of the hottest topics in America's criminal justice debate has been bail reform and the *abuse* of the bail system, especially for relatively minor offenses, by those seeking to profit financially from it. A 2018, student-written article in the *Harvard Law Review* put it this way: "Across the country, from New Jersey to Texas to California, bail reform is being debated, implemented, and litigated at the state and local levels. Lawmakers and the public are learning that cash bail is excessive, discriminatory, and costly for taxpayers and communities." The debate, that article observes, has gone high-tech, but not without controversy, of course. As the article notes: "With promises to replace judicial instincts with validated algorithms and to reserve detention for high-risk defendants, risk assessment tools have become a hallmark of contemporary pre-trial reform. Risk assessment tools have proliferated despite substantial criticisms that the tools' accuracy is overblown or unknown." But still, the guarded promise of bail reform remains. As that writer emphasizes of what is at stake: "Technocratic instruments like risk assessments may obscure but cannot answer tough, fundamental questions of system design. But recent pretrial reforms have shown early signs of progress. If risk assessments are paired with adequate safeguards, sustained reductions in incarceration and progress toward equal treatment may be possible."[7]

In an unflattering exposé of America's bail system published in March 2018, the *New York Times* reported: "As commercial bail has grown into a $2 billion industry, bond agents have become the payday lenders of the criminal justice world, offering quick relief to desperate customers at high prices." When, the article emphasized, the clients of bond agents cannot afford to pay the bond company's fee to get them out, "bond agents simply loan them the money, allowing them to go on a payment plan." Unlike normal lenders, however, many bond agents are endowed with what the article characterizes as "extraordinary powers." Not only do bond agents charge high fees, but they are often empowered to arrest their clients. "It's a consumer protection issue," Judge Lee Coffee of Memphis said in a critique, noting that before recent changes in that locale, criminal defendants regularly complained of extortion-like tactics and bondsmen demanding extra payments. "They're living under a constant daily threat," Coffee said, "that 'if you don't bring more money, we're going to put you in jail.'" The pressure to cough up additional cash, Coffee noted, "would actually encourage people to go out and commit more crimes."

In the *New York Times* exposé, "When Bail Feels Less Like Freedom, More Like Extortion," the article reported that "[t]he use of bail bonds has come under attack in recent years because it keeps the poorest, rather than the most dangerous, defendants behind bars." "In 2015," it noted of New Orleans, "63 percent of misdemeanor defendants and 87 percent of felony defendants in the city had to pay bond as a condition of release before trial, according to a study by the Vera Institute of Justice, a nonprofit." In a section of the article titled "Siphoning Millions from Poor," the *New York Times* reporters recounted the state of the ongoing public policy battle: "State after state has taken steps to reduce or eliminate the practice of making that freedom contingent on money. In response, the bond industry has worked to undermine reforms and regulations, arguing that commercial bail is still the most efficient and taxpayer-friendly way to keep the public safe and the courts running smoothly." As the article observed of how the system typically works: "The bond agent takes a fee in exchange for guaranteeing the amount of the bail on the defendant's behalf." But the fee—or premium—is usually about ten percent, and is often too much for poor defendants to afford. Payment plans, to be paid over weeks or months in installment payments, the article stressed, "can outlast the criminal case." "Some defendants," the article reported, "wind up in jail for no offense other than falling behind on their bail payments." Poverty thus leads to imprisonment and—indeed—greater poverty.

The exorbitant fees—and the reliance on cash bail—has worsened over the past few decades. "The use of financial conditions for bail," the article emphasized, "has not always been as widespread as it is today." As the article noted: "In 1990, only 24 percent of those released from jail before trial were required to pay. That number soared to almost 50 percent in 2009, the most recent year for which national figures are available." And the onerous payment plans, which include steep late fees and, oftentimes, the posting of collateral worth many times more than what is owed, can lead to defaults because of their terms. As the article, written by Jessica Silver-Greenburg and Shaila Dewan, observes of what has occurred: "[W]hile defendants, or the family members and friends who often shoulder the costs, typically pay no interest as long as their payments are on time, if they go into default they can trigger annual interest rates as high as 30 percent." "Commercial bail fees, often scraped together by multiple family members," they explain, "siphon millions from poor, predominantly African-American and Hispanic communities." It is a practice that makes the poor poorer, something that happens in other aspects of government policy, too, as law professor Daniel Hatcher explains in *The Poverty Industry: The Exploitation of America's Most Vulnerable Citizens.*

The statistics are sobering, especially when one considers how the system actually operates in practice. "Over a five-year span," Jessica Silver-Greenburg and Shaila Dewan reported for the *New York Times*, citing one example, "Maryland families paid more than $256 million in nonrefundable bail premiums, according to a report by the state's Office of the Public Defender." "More than $75 million of that," they noted, "was paid in cases resolved with no finding of guilt, and the vast majority of it was paid by black families." In 2017, in New York City, bond companies collected between $16 million and $27 million, what Scott Stringer, the city comptroller, called "a sizeable transfer of wealth to the pockets of opportunistic bail bond agents." "The entire premise on which the commercial bail system is built—that when defendants skip bail, someone must either find them or pay, is somewhat illusory," the *Times*' article stressed, adding: "[I]n most cases where defendants miss court, a bond agent may not have to do anything. Many states allow months for a defendant to be found." While in Texas bond agents have nine months before a felony bond is forfeited, Colorado gives agents two years to find the missing defendant. "With so much time," Silver-Greenburg and Dewan write, "many defendants will resurface on their own, or be caught during a traffic stop or other law enforcement interaction, without any effort on the bond agent's part." Government auditors in Utah found that less than two percent of bonds were actually forfeited. "Bail insurers have shaped the entire industry, as well as the laws they operate under, to safeguard their profits at the expense of people's lives," Rashad Robinson, the executive director of Color of Change, a nonprofit focused on racial justice, has observed.[8]

The concept of bail, intended to ensure a defendant's appearance at trial, has a long history. In the eighteenth century, it was agreed by American society (as it had been in seventeenth-century England) that the amount of bail should not be "excessive." That was the standard incorporated into the U.S. Constitution's Eighth Amendment (a standard borrowed from the English Bill of Rights), and that was the standard also inserted into various state constitutions and declarations of rights. In 1776, Maryland's bill of rights and Virginia's bill of rights explicitly stated "[t]hat excessive bail ought not to be required." The Massachusetts Declaration of Rights of 1780 and the Declaration of Rights of New Hampshire of 1784 both similarly stated, using slightly different language, that "[n]o magistrate or court of law shall demand excessive bail or sureties."[9] "Blackstone, writing in the last decade of America's colonial period," one history of bail recounts of the English jurist so widely read in the colonies, "explains the workings of the bail system known to the founders of the United States." As that source relays: "A suspected offender who was arrested was brought before a justice of the peace. After examining the circumstances, unless the suspicion was completely unfounded, the justice could either commit the accused to prison or grant bail." "Requiring excessive bail," that source emphasizes, "was also prohibited by the common law," with Blackstone noting that what constituted excessive bail was left to the courts to decide considering the circumstances.[10]

Modern bail reform efforts have their origins in the 1960s, and they were proposed to remedy discrimination against the poor. As the *Encyclopedia of Crime and Punishment* notes: "Because of the basic inequities inherent in the traditional bail system, which discriminates against poor defendants unable to raise the required bond, a bail reform movement was initiated in the early 1960s. The bail reform movement attempted to diminish the economic discrimination of the traditional system by emphasizing the defendant's character and community ties as significant criteria in determining the defendant's chances for pretrial release." "In 1961," that encyclopedia observes, "the Vera Institute of Justice in New York City established the first bail reform project, the Manhattan Bail Project, which emphasized the use of these new nonmonetary release criteria." "Following the initial success of the Manhattan Bail Project," that source notes, "nearly 200 similar projects began in cities across the country between 1961 and 1965." In 1966, the United States Congress passed its own law, which only catalyzed more bail reform projects. "By 1971," the *Encyclopedia of Crime and Punishment* observes, "thirty-seven states had enacted statutes authorizing the release of defendants on their own recognizance."[11]

But like most criminal justice policies, one trend led to a backlash as the use of release on recognizance increased following the passage of the Federal Bail Reform Act of 1966. As another encyclopedia, one focused on American street crime, describes how rising crime rates and a changing politics led to a focus on crime control—and a much different type of bail reform—in the 1980s: "Consistent with this 'tough on crime' movement, a new bail reform effort was undertaken with the goal of protecting the public from potentially dangerous individuals. The Bail Reform Act of 1984, diametrically opposed to the first Bail Reform Act of 1966, authorized the use of preventative detention to protect the safety of the community." The Bail Reform Act's constitutionality was upheld in *United States v. Salerno* (1987), and since that time, 48 states and the District of Columbia recalibrated their bail laws to put them in line with the federal system so that preventive detention and pretrial release decisions would be based on potential dangerousness. As the *Encyclopedia of Street Crime in America* (2013) lays out the cost implications for America's criminal justice system and the academic engagement the swing of the criminal-justice pendulum wrought: "Research on bail operations and interest in pretrial detention has gained in popularity, which is understandable given that approximately 62 percent of the 748,000 individuals who occupy U.S. jails are being held in pretrial detention. It is estimated that this pretrial population consumes $9 billion in yearly spending by federal and state authorities. This is the total of administrative, security, and related expenses necessary to hold these criminal defendants who cannot afford bail—many of whom are accused of nonviolent crimes."[12] Like any governmental practice, of course, the imposition of bail can be subject to abuse.

The topic of bail, over the past few decades, has thus drawn a lot of attention—some at the federal level, some at the state and municipal levels, and some before the courts. While legislative reform proposals and new city ordinances in places like Atlanta, Georgia, have shaped the legal landscape, the U.S. Supreme Court's decisions—as is so often the case—set the tone. For example, in *Stack v. Boyle* (1951), an excessive bail challenge came before the U.S. Supreme Court in a case involving the arrest of twelve members of the Communist Party who were charged in California with conspiring to violate the Smith Act, formerly known as the Alien Registration Act of 1940. The federal district court had set the bail at a fixed amount of $50,000 for each of the individuals charged, and the defendants then moved to reduce the bail, claiming that it was "excessive" under the Eighth Amendment. The only evidence offered by the government was that four other persons previously convicted under the Smith Act in another judicial district, the Southern District of New York, had forfeited bail, though no evidence was produced to the petitioners relating to those four persons. The petitioners themselves submitted statements as to their financial resources, health, family relationships, and prior criminal records, among other information, with no evidence offered pertaining to the petitioners.

In an opinion delivered by Chief Justice Fred Vinson, the U.S. Supreme Court emphasized: "From the passage of the Judiciary Act of 1789, to the present Federal Rules of Criminal Procedure, federal law has unequivocally provided that a person arrested for a noncapital offense shall be admitted to bail. This traditional right to freedom before conviction permits the unhampered preparation of a defense, and serves to prevent the infliction of punishment prior to conviction." "Unless this right to bail before trial is preserved," Chief Justice Vinson's opinion continued, "the presumption of innocence, secured only after centuries of struggle, would lose its meaning." In a short opinion, the Supreme Court laid out the rules of the road for pre-trial release: "The right to release before trial is conditioned upon the accused's giving adequate assurance that he will stand trial and submit to sentence if found guilty." "Like the ancient practice of securing the oaths of responsible persons to stand as sureties for the accused, the modern practice of requiring a bail bond or the deposit of a sum of money subject to forfeiture serves as additional assurance of the presence of an accused." "Bail set at a figure higher than an amount reasonably calculated to fulfill this purpose," the Supreme Court concluded, "is 'excessive' under the Eighth Amendment."[13]

In applying the latter principles in *Stack*, the U.S. Supreme Court discussed the particular facts of the case before it. "Since the function of bail is limited," the Supreme

Court wrote, "the fixing of bail for any individual defendant must be based upon standards relevant to the purpose of assuring the presence of that defendant." Those "traditional standards, as expressed in the Federal Rules of Criminal Procedure," the Court stressed, "are to be applied in each case to each defendant." "Upon final judgment of conviction," the Court observed, "petitioners face imprisonment of not more than five years and a fine of not more than $10,000," with the Court adding: "It is not denied that bail for each petitioner has been fixed in a sum much higher than that usually imposed for offenses with like penalties, and yet there has been no factual showing to justify such action in this case." "To infer from the fact of indictment alone a need for bail in an unusually high amount is an arbitrary act," the Court held, cautioning that "[s]uch conduct would inject into our own system of government the very principles of totalitarianism which Congress was seeking to guard against in passing the statute under which petitioners have been indicted." "If bail in an amount greater than that usually fixed for serious charges of crimes is required in the case of any of the petitioners," the Court determined, "that is a matter to which evidence should be directed in a hearing so that the constitutional rights of each petitioner may be preserved." "In the absence of such a showing," Chief Justice Vinson wrote for the Court, "we are of the opinion that the fixing of bail before trial in these cases cannot be squared with the statutory and constitutional standards for admission to bail." "The Court concludes that bail has not been fixed by proper methods in this case, and that petitioners' remedy is by motion to reduce bail, with right of appeal to the Court of Appeals," it was held, with the U.S. Supreme Court finding that the petitioners "may move for reduction of bail in the criminal proceeding so that a hearing may be held for the purpose of fixing reasonable bail for each petitioner."[14]

Historically, the idea of "excessive" sanctions was, in law, tied to a person's ability to pay. In a recent law review article, "Livelihood, Ability to Pay, and the Original Meaning of the Excessive Fines Clause," scholar Nicholas McLean writes that a "foundational" but "largely forgotten principle" of English law was "*salvo contenemento suo* (translated as 'saving his contenement,' or livelihood)." "Enshrined in the Magna Carta," McLean explains, "this principle had become firmly established as a fundamental principle at common law by the seventeenth and eighteenth centuries." As McLean explains: "The principle required, among other things, that a defendant not be fined an amount that exceeded his ability to pay. The historical evidence suggests that the English Bill of Rights' outlawing of 'excessive fines' was intended—at least in part—to reaffirm this principle." "[T]o save a man's 'contenement,'" historian William McKechnie has further emphasized, "was to leave him sufficient for the sustenance of himself and those dependent on him." As McKechnie writes of the doctrine's purpose: "In no case could the offender be pushed absolutely to the wall: his means of livelihood must be saved to him. Even if all other effects had to be sold off to pay the amount assessed, he was to retain his 'contenement.'"

To save one's contenement—as one writer, Thomas Maddox, put it in 1711—meant "[s]aving the maintenance of himself, his Wife and Children." In objecting to his punishment, Titus Oates (1649–1705)—the notorious perjurer who shows up in so many histories of the English Bill of Rights, and whose 1685 punishment sparked such intense parliamentary debate over the newly promulgated English Declaration of Rights that arose out of the Glorious Revolution of 1688—himself lodged this "Exception" to his sentence: "Fined 1,000 marks in each judgment, and committed in execution for the fines aforesaid; which fines are excessive, twice as much as the Defendant was worth, and therefore against Magna Charta, by which all fines ought to be with a *salvo contenimento*." In another case, the *Earl of Devonshire's Case* (1689), a fine of 30,000 pounds imposed by the court of King's Bench was also said to be "excessive and exorbitant, against magna charta, the common right of the subject, and against the law of the land." In arguing for the "excessiveness of the fine," it was contended that the Star Chamber, the notorious and long ago vanquished English court of law, "was taken away, because of the unmeasurable Fines which it impos'd," and that "those great Fines, imposed in that Court, were inconsistent with the Law of England, which is a Law of Mercy, and concludes every Fine which is left at discretion, with Salvo Contenimento." As the argument continued:

> [I]f the judges may commit the party to prison till the fine be paid, and withal set so great a fine as is impossible for the party to pay into court, then it will depend upon the judges pleasure, whether he shall ever has his liberty; because the fine may be such as he shall never be able to pay; and thus every man's liberty is wrested out of the dispose of the law, and is stuck under the girdle of the judges.[15]

The criminal justice pendulum, at least for now, seems to be swinging in favor of a new, more scientific approach to bail determinations less reliant on cash payments, though bail reform remains a contentious, hotly contested subject. For example, in Georgia, the Atlanta City Council—at the mayor's urging—passed an ordinance to eliminate cash bonds as a requirement to secure release for violation of municipal ordinances. Mayor Keisha Lance Bottoms signed the new ordinance in early February 2018, with the mayor stating at the time: "I am pleased to sign this ordinance, which eliminates cash bonding at the City of Atlanta Detention Center. With this ordinance, we are affirming that people should not be held in jail because they cannot pay bond. We are also making a commitment that the City of Atlanta will ensure that no one will be jailed because of their inability to pay." As the city's press release recounted the implications of the new ordinance even as it contextualized the new regime:

> Requiring cash for bail before an initial court hearing can result in extended detention for individuals who are accused of only low-level offenses and who cannot afford to pay the bail. This detention can have a significant impact on people's lives, affecting their ability to maintain jobs and their homes, especially for low-income citizens. Across the country, cities, counties and states are moving away from cash bonding as an essential step towards meaningful criminal justice reform.

"The ordinance," the city's press release stressed, "maintains the ability to impose bail and other conditions for certain offenders including violent offenders, repeat offenders, and offenders who fail to appear for their initial hearing."[16]

Just as it can be applied in the punishment context, the parsimony principle can be applied in the bail arena by lawmakers, prosecutors, and judges. In *Smart De-*

carceration: Achieving Criminal Justice Transformation in the 21st Century, a former inmate, Ronald Simpson-Bey, himself argues: "The country needs a criminal justice system built on social justice, parsimony, compassion, citizenship, and proportionality." In that co-edited collection, another person, Marc Mauer, noted of the history—in a 2015 statement—that "the notion that punishment should be no greater than necessary to achieve a legitimate public purpose has been one of the central conceptions of justice shared by Western nations since the Enlightenment" but that "in recent decades, the concept of parsimony in punishment has been lost." If bail is set too high, or if bail conditions are excessive, the effect is very similar to a punishment (only the alleged offense is, as yet, *unadjudicated*).

Prosecutors, as the primary actors responsible for sending people to prison, are in a unique position to help reform the criminal justice system. As John Chisholm and Jeffery Altenburg write in their own piece in *Smart Decarceration*, one titled "The Prosecutor's Role in Promoting Decarceration": "Prosecutors are the gatekeepers of the criminal justice system. As such, they play an integral role in using research and best practices to ensure that those they bring into the system are appropriate for criminal prosecution and conviction." "By focusing on the sentencing principles of proportionality, parsimony, citizenship, and social justice," they stress, "prosecutors can act consistently with their ethical responsibility to be problem solvers who consider diversionary and deferred prosecution alternatives to the traditional charge-and-convict model that has dominated the criminal justice system for too long." One recent proposal called for shifting the costs of incarcerating prisoners from states to local jurisdictions as a way to reign in disproportionate sentences. That proposal discusses the "correctional free lunch" problem whereby extremely aggressive local prosecutors send people to prison in droves but the state, not the county where the prosecutor holds office, foots the entire bill. If prosecutors had to take into account the cost of incarceration, more proportionate sentences might result and local voters and taxpayers would have a greater awareness of the actual costs associated with incarceration, especially long-term incarceration. As Santa Clara University law professor W. David Ball explains: "The average person could more easily spot the linkage between increasing numbers of local prison commitments and, say, a decrease in the frequency of road repairs or a shorter public school year, allowing political checks on criminal justice to operate more effectively."[17]

The criminal justice system's treatment of juveniles, whose brains are not yet fully developed, should be especially scrutinized by policymakers, prosecutors and the courts. The criminal justice system must always strive to keep the public safe. But pretrial diversion programs can, in appropriate circumstances, make good sense. "The idea of diversion," one source notes, "began in the mid-1960s with programs such as Treatment Alternatives to Street Crime (TASC) for drug abusers and the Manhattan Court Employment project for vocationally disadvantaged offenders." "Diversion," that source observes, "attempts to keep offenders from the negative effects of incarceration, while at the same time providing rehabilitation programs in the community that address challenges the offenders may face." "For juveniles," that book, *Community-Based Corrections*, emphasizes, "diversion serves to eliminate the stigmatization effect of the criminal process; labeling theory posits that processing youths further into the system may contribute to future delinquency."[18]

The State of the Union: Mass Incarceration

Over the past few decades, the dramatic increase in prisoners in the United States has occurred at the federal level but also in the states. The federal criminal justice system focuses more heavily on drug offenders, and—in comparison to state systems—represents only a fraction of those being held in prison. Approximately half of all federal prisoners are doing time for drug crimes, while roughly 16 percent of state inmates are in prison for drug-related offenses. But overall, 87 percent of all prisoners in the U.S. are held in *state* prisons, meaning that state lawmakers and state actors—along with members of Congress—have a major role to play in criminal justice reform. In 1972, the number of people in state and federal prisons was just under 200,000; that number grew to 1.56 million in 2014, with another 700,000 people, at any one time, in county jails—approximately two thirds of whom are simply awaiting trial and have yet to be convicted of anything. "A major barrier to reform," John Pfaff writes in *Locked In: The True Causes of Mass Incarceration and How to Achieve Real Reform*, "is the fractured nature of our criminal justice system." As Pfaff observes: "In fact, there is no single 'criminal justice system,' but instead a vast patchwork of systems that vary in almost every conceivable way." For example, while Maine's 2014 incarceration rate was 169 for 100,000 people, Louisiana's incarceration rate for that year was 818 per 100,000 people, showing a wide range of practice throughout the country. As of May 2018, the overall U.S. incarceration rate was 655 prisoners per 100,000 U.S. residents.

If, as a former Speaker of the U.S. House of Representatives, Tip O'Neill, famously said, "all politics is local," much of America's criminal justice system must be said to be localized, too. Local prosecutors have tremendous power to affect incarceration rates through their charging and plea-bargaining decisions (including through their decisions about the eligibility of individuals for diversion programs), and both state actors and county-level actors can either drive growth or decreases in those incarceration rates. In *Locked In*, Pfaff points out that, between 2010 and 2014, there was a respectable decline—of approximately four percent—in state prison populations, from 1.41 million to 1.3 million inmates. But an examination of the details reveals that a large portion of that decline was attributable to California, where its "Realignment" program led to a reduction in the prison population there by more than 35,000 inmates. "There are plenty of other examples," Pfaff explains, "that show how seemingly national criminal justice problems are really local ones." As Pfaff writes:

> For instance, more than 90 percent of all three-strikes sentences are thought to have been handed down in California; five jurisdictions hold 50 percent of the private prisoners in the country; three states were responsible for half of the executions through 2015 (Texas alone has conducted 37 percent of them, and 42 percent of the executions in Texas were conducted in just three of the state's 254 counties); and five counties have been responsible for a quarter of all juveniles sentenced to life without parole (with Philadelphia alone having sentenced nearly one in ten of these children).[19]

As criminal justice reform is debated at the federal, state, and local levels, it is important to remember that punishment practices and policies are *a choice*. Legislatures pass laws, sentencing commissions set guidelines, prosecutors decide what cases to pursue and what offenders to lock up, and judges impose sentences. In the last several decades, Americans, by and large, at least through their chosen representatives, have selected the path of punitiveness when it comes to criminal justice issues. "The United States," as one source observes of modern American history, "has a persistently stubborn history of mass incarceration since the 1960s, when presidential initiatives expanded federal intervention into crime control." Citing "tough on crime" rhetoric and public initiatives such as the War on Crime and the War on Drugs, that source discusses the "extremely punitive" criminal justice policies that—as another study puts it—has resulted in the United States imprisoning "at least five times more of its citizens per capita" than other advanced Western industrialized nations. "Beginning in the 1960s," Linda Mancillas writes in *Presidents and Mass Incarceration*, "presidents and their administrations began using executive power to build the institutional scaffolding that created and will maintain mass imprisonment."[20] If meaningful change is to come, it would help if—along with grassroots efforts in individual communities and by local leaders—leadership came from the top, from the President of the United States and from the governors of states.

It is worth recalling, if not dwelling excessively on, for the past is past, how Americans got to where we are now. In *The Punishment Imperative: The Rise and Failure of Mass Incarceration in America*, Todd Clear and Natasha Frost observe that "[i]n the early 1970s, the United States embarked on a subtle change in the way it punished people for crimes." "The prison population, stable for a half century," they write, "shifted upward"—a shift that, by the end of the decade, "was no longer subtle." "For the next forty years," they write, tracing the growth of incarceration rates, "virtually every aspect of the punishment system, from the way people were processed before trial to the way people were confined after conviction, grew harder." "[N]owhere else in the democratic world, and at no other time in Western history," they emphasize, "has there been the kind of relentless punitive spirit as has been ascendant in the United States for more than a generation."

In calling for an end to mass incarceration, the paperback edition of their book, published in 2015, notes that, since 2013, "the National Research Council's Committee on the Causes and Consequences of High Rates of Incarceration has published its report on mass incarceration." Many others have also weighed in with their own ideas. Their book observes, for example, that, as part of an explanation of how to change the situation going forward, "the journal *Criminology & Public Policy* recently published a special issue devoted to ending mass incarceration, with Michael Tonry offering 'a ten-step blueprint for moving past mass incarceration' and others offering commentary." In 2003, the authors of *The Punishment Imperative* emphasize, two other thinkers, Susan Tucker and Eric Cadora, had themselves likewise argued "for a new way of thinking about crime and justice." Their simple, yet powerful idea: redirecting some of the money spent on mass incarceration to community reinvestment in the most disadvantaged communities to rebuild those communities and thus *prevent* crime—the very theme articulated by Enlightenment writers such as Cesare Beccaria.[21]

Criminal justice systems are complex, just as the concept of *justice* is complex. And reducing criminality and prison populations can be intricate, multi-faceted, and long-term endeavors, with no one holding a monopoly on ideas. Not everyone, certainly, will agree with everything in law professor Michael Tonry's ten-step plan, but its overarching, global aim—to reduce prison populations to create a more just and effective criminal justice system—is a worthy one. The components of Tonry's ten-point plan, which contains a good deal of flexibility for policymakers who may not agree with every point in it: (1) repeal three-strikes, mandatory minimum sentence, and comparable laws; (2) substantially narrow in scope and severity any three-strikes, mandatory minimum sentence, and comparable laws that are not repealed; (3) amend any three-strikes, mandatory minimum sentence, and comparable laws that are not repealed to include provisions authorizing judges to impose some other sentence "in the interest of justice"; (4) repeal or substantially narrow life-without-possibility-of-parole laws; (5) repeal truth-in-sentencing laws, laws aimed at abolishing or curbing parole so that convicts serve the exact amount of time to which they have been sentenced; (6) amend penal codes to set substantially lower maximum sentences scaled to the seriousness of crimes; (7) set up sentencing commissions in any states currently without such bodies and promulgate presumptive sentencing guidelines; (8) set up parole boards and parole guidelines systems in every state without such boards and systems; (9) reduce the combined rate of jail and prison confinement by half at the state and federal level over a multi-year period; and (10) enact legislation in every state making all prisoners serving fixed terms longer than five years, or indeterminate terms, eligible for consideration for release at the expiration of five years, and making all prisoners 35 years of age or older eligible for consideration for release after serving three years. As the summary of Tonry's article observes: "Decreasing rates of imprisonment by half in the United States, a country with comparatively low crime rates, to a level that will remain 3 to 3.5 times those of other developed Western countries, can hardly be considered overly ambitious."[22]

Life-without-parole ("LWOP") sentences are necessary in appropriate circumstances to protect society. But while the criminal laws should aim to punish like offenders alike and to prioritize (consistent with the proportionality principle developed by Montesquieu and Beccaria) the punishment of violent offenders over non-violent offenders, the overuse of LWOP sentences and three-strikes or mandatory minimum sentences have led to numerous overcrowded prisons—ones that now have costly, often large geriatric wards that saddle taxpayers with inordinate costs. "It was the push for mandatory sentences and three strikes you're out," that led in part to America's greying prison population notes Linda Redford, the director of aging and geriatric programs at the University of Kansas Medical Center. Redford, who works with aging prisoners, stresses: "we're seeing people who came to prison in their 30s and 40s and 50s in their 50s and 60s and 70s today."

Others have also expressed their own concerns in that respect. "Prisons weren't designed for patients who are getting older," observes Owen Murray, the chief physician for Correctional Managed Care at the University of Texas Medical Center, which provides health care for many state prisoners in that locale. The prisons were designed for those aged 18 to 55 who are ambulatory, Murray notes. Yet, currently, one in five Texas prisoners is older than 50. Aging inmates end up in assisted living units, created by prisons to service inmates' needs and requiring full-time nursing staffs. Because prisoners have higher rates of high blood pressure, hepatitis C, diabetes, cardiac disease, and other chronic illnesses, correctional officials recognize that prisoners need geriatric services much sooner than those outside the prison context. "The norm in prisons is to use 55-and-older as the metric associated with older prisoners primarily because the consensus is that our population is 10 years ahead, clinically," of those outside prisons, Murray explains, taking note of how prison life prematurely ages inmates. According to a news story on a 2016 report by the Pew Charitable Trusts: "Corrections departments across the country report that health care for older prisoners costs between four and eight times what it does for younger prisoners."[23]

Overly harsh sentences may satiate a desire for revenge, however primordial in nature. But draconian sentences fly in the face of the proportionality and parsimony principles and taxpayers end up footing the bill, with plenty of casualties and innocent bystanders hurt along the way. One Washington, D.C.-based non-profit, Families Against Mandatory Minimums, that is earnestly trying to reform the system, was founded in 1991 by Julie Stewart. That non-profit, in identifying the problem, observes that Americans built a new prison every 10 days between 1990 and 2005 and that 1 in 28 kids has a parent in prison. In advocating for sentencing and prison reform—as well as the creation and expansion of compassionate release programs for sick and elderly prisoners who pose no threat to public safety—Families Against Mandatory Minimums seeks to help end mass incarceration and to reduce the human and financial costs associated with the overuse of long-term incarceration.

When President Donald Trump, in 2018, called for the execution of drug dealers and for tougher sentencing laws at an event in Manchester, New Hampshire, Kevin Ring, the new president of Families Against Mandatory Minimums, aptly called Trump's proposals merely "doubling down on a failed strategy." The opioids crisis is a real and growing problem, with the U.S. Centers for Disease Control and Prevention finding that 42,000 people died from opioid overdoses in 2016. But harsh sentences do not cure drug dependencies. A judge can hand out a criminal sentence in just a few minutes, but addictions are often a life-long struggle—and overcoming additions can be the struggle of lifetime. And whereas a prison sentence can be delivered by the judge in a matter of minutes, a long sentence may mean years—even decades—in prison for the offender. While addictions to heroin and opioids, including prescription painkillers, remain a major and stubborn problem, neither drug addictions nor the opioids epidemic can be solved by reflexively increasing the severity of drug sentences, let alone by resorting to state-sanctioned executions.[24] Thoughtful, well-structured treatment programs, on the other hand, can make a real difference.

The American people need to tackle criminal justice reform, and that means viewing prisons not as private enterprises and profit centers but as places where the hard work of genuine rehabilitation and transformation occurs. The use of private prisons has, in recent years, drawn increasing scrutiny—and rightfully so. The private prison industry is a direct consequence of the growth in incarceration rates since the early 1970s. "Today," Lauren-Brooke Eisen writes in *Inside Private Prisons* (2017), "126,000 inmates are held in private prisons facilities across twenty-nine states and the federal Bureau of Prisons, accounting for 8 percent of all inmates." "Six states," she notes of the concentrations of prisoners in a few locales, "currently house at least 20 percent of their inmate population in private facilities." "Recently," she adds, "private prison corporations have contracted with Immigration and Customs Enforcement to manage more than *half* of the immigrant detainees being civilly held behind bars in immigrant detention centers." There are now 11 private prisons working with the Bureau of Prisons, nine of which are operated by CoreCivic and GEO Group. Although the Obama Administration had decided to phase out the use of private prisons at the federal level, prisons found to have higher rates of assaults, Jeff Sessions—the Attorney General of the United States—regrettably decided to reverse that positive step forward. "You shouldn't have a profit motivation to fill prison cells with young Americans," then-candidate Hillary Clinton said in a presidential debate. But the Trump Administration, with the president himself the beneficiary of the industry's largesse, has embraced private prisons instead of shunning or moving away from them. After Donald Trump's election, GEO Group held its annual leadership conference at a Miami-area golf resort owned by President Trump and gave $250,000 to his inaugural committee. And during the election itself, a company subsidiary gave $225,000 to a pro-Trump super PAC. "It is the opposite of draining the swamp," observed Carl Takei, a senior staff attorney at the ACLU's National Prison Project.[25]

Criminal Justice Reform: From Needless Severity to Smart-on-Crime Approaches

A criminal justice system should be designed to keep the public safe while administering justice, doling out proportionate punishments, and providing fairness to those accused of criminal activity. Individual liberty is at stake when prosecutors file criminal charges, and how a criminal justice system operates will clearly affect public confidence in that system. If a criminal justice system administers equal justice and produces just results, the public will have reason to trust it and the judges, prosecutors, and public defenders who work in that system. But if a criminal justice system produces arbitrary, capricious, or unfair outcomes, not only will it have produced incredibly bad outcomes, but it will have substantially undermined public trust in that system. While there is absolutely nothing praiseworthy about the production of unjust, draconian, or racially biased sentences, earning the public's trust through just, measured, and race-neutral results *is* a worthy goal. As former career federal prosecutor Sally Yates has offered: "It's really important to me that the public have confidence in their criminal justice system. We don't operate very well if the public doesn't trust us." In calling for reform, including a move away from mandatory minimums in drug cases, Yates—the seasoned prosecutor who has, herself, acknowledged that "change is hard"—spoke of the need "to have a fair and proportional sentencing system in place." "I think we've gotten to a point now where there is some distrust in whether the system is operating fairly," Yates, then the U.S. Deputy Attorney General, said in 2015.[26]

Big organizations or bureaucracies can be extremely challenging to manage, oversee and change. No large system run by people, of course, will ever operate without difficulty or without errors, but that doesn't mean citizens shouldn't continually strive to eliminate injustice and errors. The human beings who run America's criminal justice apparatus—from police officers and prosecutors, to parole officers and prison wardens, to defense lawyers, judges and jurors—are fallible, so perfection is not possible. But while attaining a perfect system is not achievable, improvements clearly are possible and can and should be made. Criminal prosecutions and sentences could be more just, and pretrial proceedings could be fairer, too. "The bail system, enshrined in the Bill of Rights," one 2017 NBC News report explains, "is meant to ensure that all defendants, presumed innocent before trial, get a shot at freedom and return to court." Not every criminal defendant should be entitled to bail; there are flight risks and violent offenders, such as accused murderers and rapists, who simply pose too great a risk to public safety to allow for their pre-trial release. "But allowing people to pay for their release has proved unfair to people who don't have much money," the NBC News report aptly observes of the disparity that exists between the rich and the poor in instances where bail is appropriate, adding: "The poor are far more likely to get stuck in jail, which makes them far more likely to get fired from jobs, lose custody of children, plead guilty to something they didn't do, serve time in prison and suffer the lifelong consequences of a criminal conviction." "Those who borrow from a bail bondsman often fall into crippling debt," the report adds of the adverse collateral consequences of the present-day bail system that exists in many places.[27]

The world is an extremely complex place, and the crushing poverty that all-too-many people face is a major part of that complexity. Poverty is often a product of one's birth or geography, but it can also become endemic by a lack of educational or employment opportunities. In *Not a Crime to Be Poor: The Criminalization of Poverty in America* (2017), Peter Edelman describes what, for some, has been or become the American experience: "Beyond mass incarceration, beginning in the 1990s we adopted a new set of criminal justice strategies that further punish poor people for their poverty. Low-income people are arrested for minor violations that are only annoyances for people with means but are disastrous for the poor and near poor because of the high fines and fees we now almost routinely impose." "Poor people," Edelman writes, "are held in jail to await trial when they cannot afford bail, fined excessive amounts, and hit with continuously mounting costs and fees." "Failure to pay," he explains, "begets more jail time, more debts from accumulated interest charges, additional fines and fees, and, in a common penalty with significant consequences for those living below or near the poverty line, repeated driver's license suspensions." "Poor people," Edelman concludes, calling it a system of modern peonage, "lose their liberty and often lose their jobs, are frequently barred from a host of public benefits, may lose custody of their children, and may even lose their right to vote."[28]

In the South's post-Civil War period, convict leasing and prison labor on cotton-field chain gangs were once similarly used to exploit the poor. "Convict leasing," award-winning writer David Oshinsky explains, "was a system that pitted rich people against poor people, whites against blacks, and ex-masters against former slaves." As Oshinsky describes that system and the profit-taking that occurred under it:

> Across the South, leasing added millions in revenue to state and local coffers; it lowered the tax rate for average citizens and generated money for public projects like bridges, schools, and roads. But this was only part of the story—a rather small part—for the real profits of convict leasing went to the firms that hired out these prisoners and to the employers who worked them to exhaustion and beyond. By the 1870s, there was no more talk about leasing as a temporary response to the forces unleashed by emancipation and war. Now the talk had turned to leasing as a long-term asset, providing cheap, pliable labor to a devastated economy in the early stages of industrial growth.

The system itself regularly relied on petty criminal charges, as well as excessive fines, to provide the system's largely African-American labor force—what Oshinsky describes as the "stream of black bodies to the county chain gangs and local plantations." For example, unemployed blacks would be cited for vagrancy, then forced into the convict leasing system. As another source explains, taking note of the maltreatment and whippings endured on southern plantations: "Thousands of blacks were arrested on trumped up charges, assessed court costs and fines they could not afford to pay, and were forced to work off the fees before they could be released." "Convict leasing," that sources notes, "could best be described as slavery by another name."[29]

A recent article in *The Atlantic* specifically highlighted how relatively minor probation violations can also led to serious jail time. In that article, about Philadelphia's jails, it is noted that while approximately 25 percent of those incarcerated in the city's jails are pretrial defendants too poor to make bail, "a much larger share, roughly 50 percent, is held under what is called a detainer." "Not to be confused with an immigration detainer," that source notes, a detainer "is placed by a judge when a person already under court supervision violates their parole or probation by committing an infraction—minor or otherwise." "Once a detainer is lodged," the article notes of the process," "the possibility of bail is revoked." "Sometimes detainer," the news report continues, "are triggered when a person commits what's called a technical violation, like failing to report to a probation officer or missing curfew." As the story characterizes the detainer process and notes of the collateral consequences for those affected by it: "[A] detainer is somewhat of a second-strike penalty, because a person who's already been convicted of a crime is again suspected of wrongdoing. But even the most minor of infractions can still result in defendants behind bars, while the backlogged court system processes their cases." "Virtually the only alternative to waiting, and putting any work or personal obligations on hold," the story notes, "is to take a plea deal." "Detainers are a very serious issue for our clients," Philadelphia's chief public defender, Keir Bradford-Grey, observes. "When someone has an open case," Bradford-Grey notes, "they are often held for months on end, causing significant personal hardships and making it harder for the individual to assist in their own defense."[30]

Though social and upward mobility can and still does regularly occur in the United States, a recent report, "The Decline in Intergenerational Mobility After 1980," found that "mobility declined sharply for cohorts born between 1957 and 1964 compared to those born between 1942 and 1953." The classic American Dream—access to a good education, home ownership, a good-paying job, and, ultimately, entry into the middle class—is still achievable. But income inequality, inadequate or stagnant wages, and the loss of higher-paying manufacturing jobs in various locales, has—especially when coupled with skyrocketing college, health care, and prescription drugs costs—made achieving the American Dream more challenging in the twenty-first century. Indeed, the problems of homelessness and extreme poverty remain stubborn facts of American life, with the problem of crime inextricably tied up with poverty and feelings of despair and hopelessness in communities gripped by gun violence, youth and adult unemployment, and a lack of affordable housing or job opportunities that pay living wages.

The struggle to find reliable transportation—a critical factor in being able to maintain employment and access health care services—is particularly pronounced for minorities. One survey of 593 cancer patients in Texas, published in the medical journal, *Cancer Practice*, in 1997, found that trouble with transportation led many patients to actually forgo their treatments. While 38 percent of white respondents identified transportation as a major barrier to treatment, a much higher percentage—55 percent of African American and 60 percent of Hispanics—emerged for other groups. If the poor cannot access public transportation for doctors' appointments for cancer treatments, that is plainly a major impediment to life and health and can also make it more difficult to escape from poverty.[31] If a person, quite literally, can't afford to go places (be it the doctor's office, a job, or a community college), it will be extremely difficult for that person to get ahead in life.

While abject poverty, serfdom, and slavery were huge problems in Montesquieu's and Beccaria's era, modern-day poverty and homelessness have, through American laws, and whether inadvertently or not, been, in effect, *criminalized*. As a telling example, from January 2012 to November 2015, the Dallas police department issued more than 11,000 citations for sleeping in public. Such citations come with fines, and the failure to pay those fines can led to jail time. In many cities, it's illegal to camp, sleep in public, live in vehicles, or panhandle. For instance, an ordinance in Houston makes it illegal to use "fabric, metal, cardboard, or other materials as a tent or temporary structure for human habitation." Of course, if a person has no home or apartment and no other place to sleep, that person has no choice but to sleep wherever he or she happens to be. On top of all of that, homelessness, which can be a driver of crime, can also put people in incredibly vulnerable situations and at risk for their own lives or safety. "There's homeless-on-homeless crime, there's civilian-on-homeless crime, there's homeless-on-civilian crime," Bob McElroy, a long-time advocate for the homeless, told the *San Diego Union-Tribune* after a spate of three fatal attacks of homeless victims. In that October 2017 news report, the reporter, Karen Kucher, relayed this sobering statistic: "The nonprofit National Coalition for the Homeless documented 1,650 acts of violence against the homeless by 'housed' assailants in the U.S. between 1999 and 2015—beatings, rapes, mutilations and homicides—including 428 cases where victims were killed."[32]

In a recent report of the Southern Center for Human Rights ("SCHR"), it was noted that before bail reform came to Atlanta, Georgia, in February 2018, "homeless people were often denied release only because they were homeless." As that report emphasized:

> One Atlanta man was arrested for standing on a street corner in downtown Atlanta, holding a sign that read "Homeless Please Help." The man was charged with the offence of "pedestrian soliciting." He was held in jail for 72 days on a $500 bond without coming to court and without seeing a public defendant. He remained in jail until SCHR filed a habeas corpus petition.

The report of the SCHR went on to write about the shift in public attitudes that is underway as regards how petty cases are adjudicated. As that report stressed:

> Even ten years ago, mass detention of indigent people contingent on money bail went unquestioned in most places, and the suggestion that money bail should be eliminated might have seemed radical. Now, the opposite is true. Hardly anyone, save bail industry apologists, are prepared to defend wholesale a criminal legal system that so explicitly conditions the length of one's detention on income. There is recognition across the political spectrum that it is unfair to imprison poor people for debts they cannot pay.[33]

When American children go off to kindergarten and elementary school, one of the first things they learn is the Pledge of Allegiance. As they stand at attention facing the flag and put their right hands over their hearts, they recite the Pledge of Allegiance's well-known words, now codified in federal law: "I pledge allegiance to the Flag of the United States of America, and to the Republic for which it stands, one Nation under God, indivisible, with liberty and justice for all."[34] But *outside* the classroom, or outside any public event or ceremony where people gather and recite the Pledge of Allegiance, a tradition that dates back to 1892,[35] the mantra "with liberty and justice for all" must be met with concrete actions (including in American courtrooms) if that liberty and justice is to be realized. It is unjust and an infringement on liberty to incarcerate people for having fallen on hard times, just as it was—and is—unjust to make use of debtor's prisons, something Cesare Beccaria himself recognized in his own lifetime. Congress actually abolished debtors' prisons in 1833 and states followed suit with their own bans, but as a recent editorial in *USA Today* points out, "[c]ourts are still throwing poor people in jail for failing to pay a debt." As that editorial notes:

> Courts in 44 states and the federal system have gotten around those laws using a technicality. When debtors are sued, ordered by a judge to pay, and then fail to show up at a court hearing—sometimes one they knew nothing about—judges find them in contempt, which is a crime, and the debtor can be arrested and jailed.

It is also unjust and a violation of the fundamental right to liberty to impose excessive bail, to impose excessive fines, to impose cruel and unusual punishments, or to penalize or punish someone without the necessity for doing so. "Is that really necessary?" is the question one modern moral philosopher asks, emphasizing that "anything objectionable that is imposed upon those who are being punished is illicit unless it is strictly necessary."[36]

In the eighteenth century, America's founders spoke frequently—indeed, incessantly—of liberty, even though, by allowing the continuance of slavery and by excluding minorities and women from the social compact, they did not live up fully to its ideal. "Liberty, when it begins to take root, is a plan of rapid growth," America's first president, George Washington, observed, calling "the love of liberty" interwoven "with every ligament of our hearts."[37] "I must study politics and war that my sons may have liberty to study mathematics and philosophy," John Adams, the country's second commander-in-chief, emphasized, explaining in "A Dissertation on the Canon and Feudal Law": "liberty cannot be preserved without a general knowledge among the people." "The tree of liberty," his successor, Thomas Jefferson, said in his time, "must be refreshed from time to time with the blood of patriots and tyrants." As Jefferson proclaimed in 1819: "Of liberty I would say that, in the whole plenitude of its extent, it is unobstructed action according to our will. But rightful liberty is unobstructed action according to our will within limits drawn around us by the equal rights of others. I do not add 'within the limits of the law' because law is often but the tyrant's will, and always so when it violates the rights of the individual."

James Madison, Thomas Jefferson's friend and presidential successor in office, had a lot to say on the subject, too. "Liberty may be endangered by the abuse of liberty, but also by the abuse of power," Madison declared. "The advancement and diffusion of knowledge is the only guardian of true liberty," he wrote to Jefferson in 1787, with Madison also writing to Jefferson the following year:

> It is a melancholy reflection that liberty shall be equally exposed to danger whether the government have too much or too little power. Wherever the real power in a government lies, there is the danger of oppression. In our governments, the real power lies in the majority of the community, and the invasion of private rights is chiefly to be apprehended not from the acts of government contrary to the sense of its constituents, but from acts in which the government is the mere instrument of the major number of the constituents.

Thomas Paine, the author of *Common Sense*, offered this nugget of wisdom: "An avidity to punish is always dangerous to liberty. It leads men to stretch, to misinterpret, and to misapply even the best of laws. He that would make his own liberty secure, must guard even his enemy from oppression; for if he violates this duty, he establishes a precedent that will reach to himself." "Tyranny, like hell," Paine wrote in *The Crisis* in 1776, "is not easily conquered; yet we have this consolation with us, that the harder the conflict, the more glorious the triumph." And Patrick Henry, of "Give me liberty, or give me death!" fame, put it this way, summing up the impulse behind the American Revolution: "When the American spirit was in its youth, the language of America was different: Liberty, Sir, was the primary object."[38]

America's penal system, originating in the Enlightenment, developed over time. In the nineteenth century, Francis Lieber, then a history professor at South Carolina College and a corresponding member of the Philadelphia Society for Alleviating the Miseries of Public Prisons, wrote a lengthy letter to that society's president, John

Bacon, about the then-existing state of affairs. That letter, published by order of the society in 1838, sought "to concentrate and digest all that lies before us or has been discovered" on the issues of penal matters and punishment "into a consistent and strict system" to be known as the science of "penology." In that work, Lieber raised a rhetorical question that paid homage to the Enlightenment: "How long is it since Beccaria and Howard dared to represent the criminal as an unfortunate man, who, though criminal, still remains a man, and to tell mankind that their penal codes and punishments were cruel and unwise?" "In some countries, as in England and the United States," Lieber observed near the outset of his essay, "the jurists have but superficially occupied themselves with the true foundation of the right we have to punish, and the real end we have in view in punishing; a necessary consequence of which has been, that no fixed standard of punishment has ever been established, and punishments of excessive cruelty as well as others showing a morbid philanthropy, are found with the same race, and at the same time in curious contraction to each other." "The German, French, and most Italian jurists," Lieber continued, alluding in part, perhaps, to Beccaria's more theoretical framing of crime and punishment, "have, with great zeal, and not unfrequently with much shrewdness and close reasoning, inquired into the origin of all penal right, but they have again greatly neglected the practical operation of the various systems." "[I]n order to know which is the best and most legitimate mode of punishment," Lieber offered, writing of the need to know "what object we have in view when we punish, and whence we derive our right to inflict punishment," Lieber stressed that, "if ascertained," that object "will show us, at the same time, how far we may go in punishing."

Punishments should have limits, and the Enlightenment began the process of setting those limits. Francis Lieber, in exploring the "due limits" of "civil punition," and in taking note of "the great variety of punishments, many of which we cannot explain on the ground that they were called for by the different degree of civilization existing with those to whom the punishment was to be applied," wrote of the past and then-current punishments inflicted upon "soldiers, sailors, serfs, freemen or noblemen." As Lieber, exploring the vast range of punishments, emphasized:

> We meet in history and the present times, with fine, confiscation of property, apology, privation of honor and stamping infamy on the culprit, degradation, ridicule, public exposure on the wooden horse, the drunkard's cloak, the fiddle, whirligig, brand, stocks and pillory, the ducking stool, flogging, singeing the soles, running the gauntlet, the picket, bastinado, banishment, transportation, imprisonment, lying on edges laths, flaying, maiming, branding, boring the tongue, blinding, racking, killing in almost all possible ways, by strangulation, poisoning, beheading, throwing from a precipice, burning, exposure to wild animals, quartering, breaking on the wheel, stoning, crucifying, pressing to death, burying alive, chaining to beasts of the forest, drowning, starvation, sawing in two, walling up, eating alive (as the Battas do to this day), condemning to suicide, with the choice by what means the malefactor shall think fit, selling into slavery, stamping the children and children's children of the culprit with infamy. Every species of

> punishments here mentioned, which admits of any variety at all, has been made use of in almost infinite variation, while this melancholy catalogue is far from being complete.

In his essay, Lieber discussed the purposes that had been offered for punishment and specifically discussed needless suffering and the necessity-for-punishment concept. "Political expiation," Lieber wrote in a section titled "*Expiation*," "would be inflicting of suffering without object—cruelty; for I know of no other definition of cruelty than that it is the infliction of suffering for no end, or for a bad one." Expiation, Lieber stressed, could be thought of as "a suffering for a committed wrong, solely because it is a wrong, an offence against some law—in short an atonement, without any view as to repairing an injury or improving the sufferer...." In the very section on the purposes for punishment, on "*Necessity, Expediency*," Lieber then observed of that offered justification: "The assumption of this ground seeks for the right of punishment in the very opposite to the previous one—in the effect of the punishment alone, entirely passing over the offender, the individual to be punished—in short, it affords no right of punishment, and destroys all marks of distinction between punishment, and acts of bare necessity which produce any degree of suffering in others...." After covering other theories of punishment, including deterrence, what he described as "establishing examples, the prevention of criminal action in some, by exhibiting to them the suffering which it has brought upon others," Lieber went on to write about "[t]he true standard of punishment." That standard—"the standard of the degree how far we are justified in making use of the previously acquired general right of punishment"—consisted, Lieber wrote, of (1) "Danger" to society, and (2) "The effect the punishment has on society, or the punished individual himself." "If it has no effect on either, it is useless," Lieber stressed of the latter justification.

Lieber specifically addressed his conception of disproportionate and unnecessary punishments in the context of his time. "Disproportionate punishments, however—whether disproportionately heavy or light, are unjust," Lieber observed, an indication that any disproportionate punishment—however disproportionate, whether grossly so or not—should be considered unacceptable. Indeed, in discussing the justification for punishments, Lieber found that not every wrongful act should be punished by criminal sanctions if another available remedy would suffice. As Lieber wrote in his essay:

> The necessity of punishment, before we acquire a full right actually to punish, leads us a step farther, and we find that not every illegal act is punishable, for instance, in those cases in which a restitution of the injury done, or a public declaration that no offence against the character of the injured person had been meant by the offensive words of the injurer, are entirely sufficient. Punishment in this case would go beyond what is necessary, and therefore unjust. Punishment takes place when the avowal of wrong is not sufficient, when the protection of the rights of the offended demand it, or when rights have been violated which can never be re-established, (e. g., in case of murder,) and the rights of others demand protection. Disproportion between offence and punishment is at once acknowledged as unjust.

In laying down some "fixed principles," Lieber emphasized that the right to punish "can be actually made use of only so far as it necessary and useful." "Without this," he wrote, "it is useless—cruel." To be "just," Lieber continued, the punishment must be suited "to the offence" and be inflicted "according to the spirit of the age."[39]

The American people still regularly invoke the importance of liberty, but the real-world *application* of the necessity-for-punishment maxim laid down by Montesquieu and Beccaria, and then repeated or alluded to by thinkers such as Francis Lieber, is necessary *to actualize* the concept of liberty. With that in mind, modern-day elected officials and prison officials must do everything they can to make sure that unnecessary cruelty is avoided in America's criminal justice systems and in its penal systems. And along with prosecutors and the members of sentencing commissions, federal and state court judges—both appointed and elected, as the case may be—must themselves rededicate themselves to protecting and defending the U.S. Constitution and the "liberty" principle laid down in the Declaration of Independence and the U.S. Constitution. For without an independent judiciary, and without the check of an impartial bench dedicated to preserving individual liberty and individual rights, encroachments on liberty will occur and those encroachments may slide into tyranny, or at least a tendency to impose tyrannous punishments.

The Unusual Nature of Unnecessary Punishments

The lack of necessity for a punishment is often evidenced—or at least can be—by a punishment's disuse or abandonment altogether. And there was an awareness, even centuries ago, that what might be considered necessary or "usual" at one point in time might later be deemed to be unnecessary or "unusual" later. Through the centuries, as even a quick perusal of the list of punishments recited by Francis Lieber would suggest, many punishments—from executions to fines, and from imprisonment to exile or banishment—have been employed and, at times, specifically described as *usual* punishments. "Fine and Imprisonment," one 1750 law dictionary recited, for example, "is the usual Punishment at this Day on Indictment for *Conspiracy*."[40] "[T]he usual punishment of death inflicted upon deserters," another source reported in 1784, "was changed in 1775 to an order for all future deserters to work as slaves on the public roads."[41] Yet another source reported that "[t]he usual Punishment ... for *Non-Payment*" of monies owed was "chang'd from *Imprisonment*, into *perpetual Banishment*."[42] On occasion, some offenders were said to have avoided "the usual Punishment" through acts of mercy.[43] It was thus not just ducking—the punishment discussed at length in a prior chapter of *The Baron and the Marquis*—that was described as a "usual" punishment.

Yet, the societal abandonment or declining frequency of a punishment—or, perhaps, just a societal recognition of the simple lack of necessity for it—might, as various sources and authorities have recognized, change a "usual" punishment into an "unusual" one.[44] For instance, the stocks, the pillory, and what became known as *peine forte et dure*—or pressing to death—are no longer in use and have long been considered to be cruel and unusual punishments that civilized societies can—and should—do without.[45] Once *usual* punishments, ones with historical precedent, may even be classified later as *torturous* ones, with torture being the most extreme or aggravated form of cruelty. By way of example, in discussing acts of "torture" previously used in England, a 1796 treatise wrote of everything from the punishment of pressing to death, or *peine forte et dure*,[46] to criminals' thumbs being tied together to force them to plead, to the rack.[47] Over time, customary punishments once widely accepted by societies thus become unthinkable acts of cruelty or torture.

In that 1796 treatise, the Hon. Daines Barrington pointed out that Lord Chief Justice Matthew Hale had said that "the punishment of pressing to death ... was anciently inflicted by the common law."[48] But, Barrington wrote, editorializing a bit, "whatever this punishment might have been by the common law," it had been "superseded" by statute.[49] "[H]aving recourse to this severity, when the criminal stands mute and will not plead," he wrote, "is very unnecessary,"[50] with Barrington, taking a measure of historical practice, also noting that the rack—"with all its attendant terrors"—"was formerly not unknown in this country."[51] "It is not pretended by this" that instances of torture "were frequent," Barrington qualified, emphasizing that "fortunately this most horrid practice hath been discontinued, so that there cannot be the least legal pretence ever to revive it."[52] "The usual punishment for refusing to plead was the 'peine forte et dure,' of pressing to death," one history emphasized of the defunct English criminal justice tactic, taking note of the now long-abandoned practice.[53] In a book published in London in 1719 one also finds a reference to "the usual punishment" at the end of an "account of the *Peine forte et dure*, or pressing to death."[54]

This line of enquiry naturally raises the question of what factors, or criteria, American jurists should use in making the judgment of when a *usual* punishment has crossed over into an *unusual* one. One lawyer, Joshua Shapiro, notes the importance of this inquiry in the *University of Memphis Law Review*, taking up the issue of the death penalty and observing at the outset that "capital punishment is—at least arguably—inherently cruel."[55] As he explains: "If one accepts the view that the Cruel and Unusual Punishments Clause is 'a mandate for recognition and protection of human dignity,' then it is hard to find a punishment that is more antithetical to this norm than the death penalty. As Justice William Brennan remarked in *Furman v. Georgia*, '[t]he calculated killing of a human being by the State involves, by its very nature, a denial of the executed person's humanity.'"[56] "If a cruel punishment is one that is an affront to human dignity," Shapiro observes, "then surely a punishment that ends human life—that ultimately denies a person his or her humanity by literally extinguishing it—would be the most cruel punishment possible."[57] The taking of a person's life is, in fact, the most extreme punishment one can conceive, though killing itself can be further aggravated by the manner in which the killing takes place.

In his law review article, Joshua Shapiro—using a much different analysis than Yale Law School professor Akhil Amar, who has focused on the cumulative *population* of states that bar or outlaw a particular practice to judge its unusualness—concludes that "the number of state legislatures that have (or do not have) capital punishment provisions may be indicative of whether a punishment is unusual."[58] Almost needless to say, the very structure of America's republic, with power divided between the federal and state systems, will always mean that some jurisdictions will punish certain crimes differently, and more harshly, than others.[59] That is, after all, the inherent nature, and very character, of a system of federalism. However, Shapiro—aware that the U.S. Supreme Court sometimes sets a constitutional floor, beneath which no government actor or state may go without running afoul of the Eighth and Fourteenth Amendments—goes on in his article to propose a bright-line test. "[T]he appropriate benchmark for determining whether is punishment is unusual," he asserts, "is when three-fourths of states forbid its imposition."[60] "Until no more than one-fourth of the states allow for capital punishment," he claims, "the death penalty cannot, as a constitutional matter, be unusual."[61] In laying out his preferred interpretive approach to the Constitution's Cruel and Unusual Punishments Clause, Shapiro specifically argues that a three-fourths rule—or benchmark—is necessary to avoid results-oriented Eighth Amendment jurisprudence.[62]

But when it comes to the death penalty, the state's ultimate sanction, the creation of a three-fourths-of-the-states rule is far too simplistic and ignores important human rights—and the underlying constitutional values, including the protection of human dignity—at stake. First, the U.S. Constitution absolutely prohibits "cruel and unusual punishments" and, therefore, if a punishment is cruel and unusual, it is unconstitutional, regardless of how many laws are passed that purport to authorize the punishment.[63] Second, the right to life is a fundamental right,[64] and the arbitrary deprivation of that right has long been condemned by international[65] and domestic law.[66] The lottery-like quality of death sentences and executions is, in fact, directly contrary to due process and equal protection values—no small thing in a country committed to liberty, fairness, and equality.[67] Third, Shapiro's proposed three-fourths-of-the-states rule, which focuses exclusively on what *laws* are on the statute books, does not take into an account whether those laws are being actively enforced or are dormant or inactive. In that vein, Shapiro's proposal does not take into consideration the age of the laws (some decades old) or the practices of states, be they jury verdicts, gubernatorial actions, or prosecutorial decisions not to seek the death penalty in the first place. Only by gauging the actual practices of states, juries, and public officials—as well as by considering if a punishment squares with the parsimony principle, human dignity, and other human rights values, such as the right to be free from cruelty and torture—can the U.S. Supreme Court, or any other court, fully gauge whether *the infliction* of a punishment such as the death penalty is or has become truly unusual.[68]

In the twenty-first century, the criteria for gauging the death penalty's unusualness should include (1) an assessment of how widely it is used, and in fact just how sporadically it is used, *throughout the country* (the provisions of the U.S. Constitution, after all, apply throughout the country, with the Fourteenth Amendment specifically intended to constitutionalize the Civil Rights Act of 1866, which was a response to "Black Codes" passed in various states, with the Civil Rights Act of 1866 requiring "like punishment, pains, and penalties" for people of different races); (2) the viability of any suitable alternatives to it (*i.e.*, life without parole or life sentences) and whether it is truly necessary; (3) how arbitrary, discriminatory, and error-prone the punishment has proven to be; (4) whether death sentences and executions bear the indicia or immutable characteristics of acts of cruelty, indeed torture (which they do); and (5) what is actually at stake (*i.e.*, the fundamental right to life), including whether the use of the punishment comports with human dignity (it does not). Punishments falling short of death do not necessarily raise the same considerations as capital punishment, but as noted earlier, even *non-lethal* corporal punishments have, from time to time, already been adjudged—and properly so—to be cruel and unusual in nature. Executions, however, irrevocably deprive people of their fundamental rights and the most basic right of all: the right to life. Those who are executed are stripped of *that right* and, by definition, *all other rights*, including their right to use the privilege of the writ of habeas corpus to prove, if possible, that they are not guilty of the crimes they were convicted of.

When the five criteria set forth above are carefully weighed and examined in light of the evidence and the text and values of the U.S. Constitution, the conclusion is inescapable: death sentences and executions should be declared to be unconstitutional. In fact, the law has, through the centuries, changed dramatically, and a twenty-first century declaration by the U.S. Supreme Court that capital punishment is unconstitutional would be a welcome, long-overdue development—and one that would send an important message about what kind of American criminal justice system is acceptable in this day and age. Language from the U.S. Supreme Court's own decision in *Trop v. Dulles*,[69] the 1958 case that established the "evolving standards of decency" test, itself supports such a change in the law. In that case, which declared the decidedly *non-lethal* punishment of denationalization to be an Eighth Amendment violation, the Supreme Court justified its ruling by emphasizing that the imposition of that punishment would lead to "the total destruction of the individual's status in organized society."[70] "It is," the Court ruled of denationalization, "a form of punishment more primitive than torture, for it destroys for the individual the political existence that was centuries in the development."[71] "In short," the Court concluded, harkening back to the origins of citizenship, "the expatriate has lost the right to have rights."[72] If the Eighth Amendment prohibits striping an offender of the right to have rights (and *Trop* held that it does), the death penalty (which, of course, does just that) should not be permitted by the U.S. Constitution or American society, especially since the death penalty bears all the characteristics of an act of torture.

Whether any punishment is usual or unusual is, in truth, a factual matter that is readily capable of adjudication.[73] Judges, by virtue of their legal training, have special expertise in parsing the meaning of words and in adjudicating cases—a task involving applying the law to the facts. That is, in fact, precisely what Cesare Beccaria envisioned for judges tasked with adjudicating criminal cases—look at the law, examine the facts, and then decide, *guilty* or *not guilty*. Roughly the same thing can and should be done when it comes to sentencing and enforcing the provisions of the U.S. Constitution—the judge should read the applicable statutory provision and the governing constitutional law (i.e., the text of the U.S. Constitution), then decide if a particular punishment is consistent or inconsistent with the law, including the U.S. Constitution.

Notably, in the past, when a punishment or some particular treatment was described as either *usual* or *unusual*, it was frequently a characterization of the writer's or the speaker's view or judgment as to the *severity* or *frequency* of the punishment or treatment—or an expression as to whether the punishment or treatment comported with societal values or was traditionally authorized or not. For example, in 1898, the U.S. Court of Appeals for the Second Circuit emphasized that "three men claimed that they were justified in leaving the ship by the unusual and cruel treatment" to which "they had been subjected."[74] In an even earlier case, one pre-dating the Civil War, the Supreme Court of Alabama noted that the plaintiff had sought to ask the following question: "whether the use of a cowhide in punishing a slave, so as to produce wales on the arms two or three inches long, and as large as his finger, which could be seen on him a year afterwards, was not an unusual and cruel whipping"?[75] Every time a judge confronts a constitutional provision, statute, or common-law rule, that judge is capable of asking whether a particular act comports with, or is inconsistent with, any such legal provision or rule. Of course, the application of good judgment and common sense is required if fair and just rulings are to be made.

In the United States, life sentences are now the common, or *usual*, punishment for particularly heinous crimes, including first-degree murder.[76] According to a 2013 report of Washington, D.C.'s The Sentencing Project, as of 2012, 159,520 people were serving life sentences in the United States, an 11.8 percent rise since 2008. That report further noted that "[t]he population of prisoners serving life without parole (LWOP) has risen more sharply than those with the possibility of parole: there has been a 22.2% increase in LWOP since just 2008, an increase from 40,174 individuals to 49,081."[77] And that number has only increased over time. According to the latest report of The Sentencing Project, titled *Still Life: America's Increasing Use of Life and Long-Term Sentences*, as of 2016, 161,957 people were serving life sentences, or "one of every nine people in prison." An additional 44,311 individuals are serving "virtual life" sentences (i.e., sentences of 50 years or more), bringing the total number of people serving a life or virtual life sentence up to 206,268, or 13.9% of America's prison population (i.e., approximately one of every seven prisoners). As of 2016, 53,290 people were serving LWOP sentences.[78]

In contrast, there are now fewer than 3,000 people on American death rows, many of whom have been languishing there for years or even decades. As of July 1, 2017, per the NAACP Legal Defense Fund's report, "Death Row USA," there were 2,817 inmates then housed on death row.[79] The largest death row in the United States—at 746 inmates—is in the State of California, but California has not actually carried out an execution *in more than a decade*.[80] The majority of death row inmates are, in truth, clustered in a few states, with the next largest populations (by state) as follows: Florida (374 inmates), Texas (243 inmates), Alabama (191 inmates), Pennsylvania (169 inmates), North Carolina (152) inmates, Ohio (144 inmates), and Arizona (125 inmates).[81] While LWOP and life sentences, which have emerged as the standard punishment for heinous offenses, are necessary to protect the public and to prevent dangerous offenders from posing a future risk or danger to society,[82] putting inmates to death cannot be seen as a legitimate or necessary—let alone an *absolutely* necessary—criminal sanction.[83] And the implications of that conclusion is clear. Going back all the way to the eighteenth century, the well-known maxim of the Enlightenment—one publicized and promoted by Montesquieu, Beccaria, and early American political leaders—made clear that any unnecessary punishment is "tyrannical."[84]

Legislatures and the Courts

American legislatures should never put in place a cruel and unusual punishment. But that sometimes happens, and when it does, courts are obliged to act to make sure cruel and unusual punishments are never carried out. In *Robinson v. California* (1962), the first case in which the U.S. Constitution's Eighth Amendment was applied against a state, the U.S. Supreme Court itself struck down a California statute that made it a crime to "be addicted to the use of narcotics." The Supreme Court did not question what it called "[t]he broad power of a State to regulate the narcotic drugs traffic within its borders." As the Supreme Court emphasized in *Robinson*: "Such regulation, it can be assumed, could take a variety of valid forms. A State might impose criminal sanctions, for example, against the unauthorized manufacture, prescription, sale, purchase, or possession of narcotics within its borders." Citing earlier precedents, the Court further proclaimed:

> In the interest of discouraging the violation of such laws, or in the interest of the general health or welfare of its inhabitants, a State might establish a program of compulsory treatment for those addicted to narcotics. Such a program of treatment might require periods of involuntary confinement. And penal sanctions might be imposed for failure to comply with established compulsory treatment procedures.

Ordinarily, legislative prerogative is, quite properly, given due deference by the courts. After noting that "a State might choose to attack the evils of narcotics traffic on broader fronts also—through public health education, for example, or by efforts to ameliorate the economic and social conditions under which those evils might be though to flourish," the U.S. Supreme Court in *Robinson* specifically stressed: "In short, the range of valid choice which a State might make in this area is undoubtedly a wide one, and the wisdom of any particular choice within the allowable spectrum is not for us to decide." An *invalid* choice that a State was not allowed to make, however, was criminalizing the mere status of being addicted to drugs. Under the way the California law at issue in *Robinson* had been construed by the California courts, it was possible for someone to be convicted of a misdemeanor solely on the basis of the individual's "status" or "chronic condition" of being addicted. In finding the statute unconstitutional, the U.S. Supreme Court in *Robinson* emphasized:

> This statute ... is not one which punishes a person for the use of narcotics, for their purchase, sale or possession, or for antisocial or disorderly behavior resulting from their administration. It is not a law which even purports to provide or require medical treatment. Rather, we deal with a statute which makes the "status" of narcotic addiction a criminal offense, for which the offender may be prosecuted "at any time before he reforms." California has said that a person can be continuously guilty of this offense, whether or not

> he has ever used or possessed any narcotics within the State, and whether or not he has been guilty of any antisocial behavior there.
>
> It is unlikely that any State at this moment in history would attempt to make it a criminal offense for a person to be mentally ill, or a leper, or to be afflicted with a venereal disease. A State might determine that the general health and welfare require that the victims of these and other human afflictions be dealt with by compulsory treatment, involving quarantine, confinement, or sequestration. But, in the light of contemporary human knowledge, a law which made a criminal offense of such a disease would doubtless be universally thought to be an infliction of cruel and unusual punishment in violation of the Eighth and Fourteenth Amendments.
>
> We cannot but consider the statute before us as of the same category. In this Court, counsel for the State recognized that narcotic addiction is an illness. Indeed, it is apparently an illness which may be contracted innocently or involuntarily. We hold that a state law which imprisons a person thus afflicted as a criminal, even though he has never touched any narcotic drug within the State or been guilty of any irregular behavior there, inflicts a cruel and unusual punishment in violation of the Fourteenth Amendment. To be sure, imprisonment for ninety days is not, in the abstract, a punishment which is either cruel or unusual. But the question cannot be considered in the abstract. Even one day in prison would be a cruel and unusual punishment for the "crime" of having a common cold.[85]

Through the years, American courts have thus frequently had to grapple with whether a specific sanction constitutes a "cruel and unusual punishment." In making such judgments, the nature of the criminal act—and the nature of the particular punishment at issue—is critical. For example, in *People v. Mire*,[86] the Supreme Court of Michigan held in 1912 that a term of imprisonment between fifteen and thirty years for a burglary accompanied with the use of high explosives was not a cruel and unusual punishment. In the course of so ruling, the state's highest court held: "The punishment prescribed in the act in question is imprisonment, a most common and usual method of punishment the world over."[87] In upholding the punishment provided for by statute, the court stressed: "That class of cruel and now unusual punishments at one time sanctioned and prevalent under the common law of England, such as burning at the stake, drawing and quartering, mutilation, starvation, and lesser forms of physical torture, to which the constitutional prohibitions were primarily directed, is not involved here."[88] "Approaching the dividing line," the court ruled, "the inquiry as to what does in any particular case constitute cruel and unusual punishment under the constitutional provisions, turns, not only upon the facts, circumstances, and kind of punishment itself, but upon the nature of the act which is to be punished."[89] If the punishment should fit the crime (and it should), a court clearly cannot figure out what punishment is appropriate without understanding the nature of the crime itself—and without understanding the background of the offender who committed the crime. The nature of the act—whether it be an act of criminality or an act of punishment—must be judged, whether it be to decide how much to punish it or whether or not the act (in the case of a punishment) is tyrannical or not.

Ordinarily, the impulse of American courts to defer to legislative prerogative is a healthy one.[90] After all, a representative democracy gets its legitimacy from the people, and the people choose their own legislative representatives (and often, their local prosecutors) to express their will.[91] But since *Marbury v. Madison*,[92] American courts have properly claimed the power of judicial review[93]—and the U.S. Supreme Court, in order to ward off tyrannous punishments, must remain the final arbiter of what the U.S. Constitution means and strike down any unconstitutional laws or unnecessary punishments.[94] The tradition of judicial review is a long-standing one, and it helps to protect individual rights and individual liberty.

English subjects were certainly concerned about the infliction of cruel or novel punishments, as reflected in early writings and in the English Bill of Rights itself.[95] And it is certainly true that, in modern America, there can be shades of gray when it comes to evaluating whether a particular punishment runs afoul of the U.S. Constitution's Eighth Amendment prohibition. But the Fourteenth Amendment, it has now long been held, was intended to apply provisions of the U.S. Bill of Rights, including the Eighth Amendment, against the states,[96] and it is crystal clear that the bar on "cruel and unusual punishments" sets forth a moral imperative—one that is not only subject to adjudication, but that is capable of more than just restricting lawless or newly devised punishments or forms of cruelty or torture. Indeed, by its own terms, the Eighth Amendment does not restrict "new and unusual punishments" or "unauthorized and unusual punishments," it restricts "cruel and unusual punishments."[97] And the very idea behind the U.S. Bill of Rights—and in particular, its Eighth Amendment—was to protect individual rights and individual liberty in the face of cruel or tyrannous acts or laws passed by legislative majorities.[98]

In light of the cruelty of imposing disproportionate or unnecessary punishments, modern American lawmakers should strive, as far as possible, to repeal any existing statutes that provide for the imposition of disproportionate or unnecessary punishments. And the U.S. Supreme Court and lower courts should, in line with the Enlightenment's necessity-for-punishment principle, strike down any disproportionate or unnecessary punishments, though the rub will lie in determining exactly when that is the case. While legislative bodies must be allowed to consider, and to decide to impose, *a range of penalties or punishments*, courts should take more seriously their role to independently review such penalties or punishments and to impartially judge whether they are, in truth, excessive or cruel and unusual in nature and outside the range of what is acceptable in a free and democratic society. Disproportionate or unnecessary punishments are inherently excessive and should be considered cruel and unusual and thus violative of the U.S. Constitution's Eighth Amendment.

Right now, too many American courts are simply too reluctant to strike down a legislatively authorized punishment, no matter what it might be. As one commentator puts it: "Some courts are reluctant to even review a sentence that falls within the statutory limits due to such high deference to the sentence's validity. According to the Supreme Court of Montana, for example, 'a sentence that is within the statutory maximum guidelines does not violate the prohibition against cruel and unusual punishment.'" "Such courts," that commentator, Christopher DeClue writes, "conclude that the mere fact that the sentence is legislatively mandated or within the statutory limits renders the sentence valid under the Eighth Amendment."[99] That, however, is clearly an untenable position—and one not justifiable in a constitutional democracy. Both the federal and state constitutions lay down limits for governmental behavior, and just because a law or a sentencing guideline sets forth a punishment does not make that punishment acceptable or consistent with the U.S. Constitution or a state constitution.

The State of Delaware provides an example of the excessive deference courts have typically afforded to legislative enactments in the past. While section 16 of the Delaware Declaration of Rights of 1776 provided "[t]hat excessive bail ought not to be required, nor excessive fines imposed, nor cruel or unusual punishments inflicted," section 11 of that state's current bill of rights states that "[e]xcessive bail shall not be required, nor excessive fines imposed, nor cruel punishments inflicted." "[I]n *DeShields v. State*," one legal commentator has explained of a 1987 decision interpreting section 11, "the Delaware Supreme Court held that the defendant did not have standing to challenge whether a sentence of death by hanging constituted cruel and unusual punishment in violation of this section." "[I]t is unnecessary for this Court to render an opinion on the constitutionality of death by hanging," the court ruled in that case, emphasizing that the state legislature had enacted legislation allowing for death by lethal injection shortly after the initial death sentence providing for death by hanging had been handed down. "Nor can we rule, as a matter of law, that death by hanging is 'cruel' in violation of Article 1, section 11 of the Delaware Constitution," the court further ruled in *DeShields*. "In *DeShields*," that legal commentator wrote, "the Delaware Supreme Court also determined that this section of the Delaware Constitution relates only to the mode of punishment and not to length of a sentence authorized by the General Assembly." "Reviewing courts," the court itself stressed in *DeShields*, "should grant substantial deference to the broad authority that legislatures possess in sentencing convicted criminals."[100]

The State of Delaware, in one particularly glaring example, was actually the last state in the U.S. to utilize the public whipping post. The whipping post, last used in Delaware in 1952, was not formally abolished until 1972. "[L]ong after most other states had turned away from harsh methods of punishment," one source notes, "Delaware seemed content to maintain stringent measures, such as the six combination stocks and whipping posts erected throughout the state." "The most notorious of them, dubbed Red Hannah by African American prisoners who were ordered to 'embrace' the post," that book recounts, "was originally erected at the Kent County Jail in Dover in the eighteenth century." "The whipping post and the pillory date to the early 1700s in Delaware," George Miller writes of the state's history, noting that while the pillory was abolished in Delaware in 1905, "[t]he last public whipping ... was in 1952 of a man convicted of beating a woman." Indeed, before the whipping post was outlawed in 1972, the Delaware Supreme Court, in 1963, had expressly held that whipping was a constitutionally permissible punishment because the practice was in use in 1776 and, in fact, predated the state's origins, with "[t]he first recorded instance" of whipping as a punishment for crime dating back to 1656 under the Dutch.

In rejecting the notion that whipping was an Eighth Amendment violation or a "cruel" punishment prohibited by Delaware's constitution of 1897, the Delaware Supreme Court emphasized in 1963 that "[t]he origin" of the state's prohibition on "cruel punishments" traced back to Section 16 of the state's Declaration of Rights of 1776, which provided "[t]hat excessive bail ought not to be required, nor excessive fines imposed, nor cruel or unusual punishments inflicted." (The phrase "or unusual" had later been omitted in a new 1792 constitution for the State of Delaware, with the Delaware Supreme Court writing dismissively in 1963 of the subsequent change in wording: "we think the omission of the phrase 'or unusual' has little or no significance.") In giving a wide berth of deference to Delaware's legislature, the Delaware Supreme Court explicitly ruled in 1963:

> It is the province of the General Assembly in its wisdom to give expression to the public will. It may either by inaction permit the practice to continue or, by action, condemn it as a cruel punishment. Judicial restraint and a proper recognition of the function of the Legislative and Judicial branches of government compel us to express no opinion upon the propriety of doing either.

"Today," Delaware's highest court declared, rejecting the state-law claim, "there has been no legal and effective expression of the people speaking through the General Assembly that whipping is a cruel punishment in the constitutional sense." "Accordingly," the Delaware Supreme Court concluded in its 1963 opinion after also analyzing the U.S. Constitution's Eighth Amendment and the lack of any applicable U.S. Supreme Court precedent directly on point, "we are of the opinion that the Eighth and Fourteenth Amendments to the Federal Constitution do not invalidate the statutes of the State of Delaware imposing the punishment of whipping for certain crimes."[101]

It is true that, when the U.S. Constitution and its Bill of Rights were framed, the death penalty, along with grotesque acts of public whipping, were still a ubiquitous presence in American life. At that time, every American state still made use of death sentences, and Congress, in its Crimes Act of 1790, specifically authorized capital punishment along with the use of the pillory and "stripes."[102] And it is also true that American courts, through the centuries, have allowed executions (as well as, at least for a time, lesser corporal punishments) to be carried out, finding no constitutional impediment to their infliction. In fact, American jurists have frequently pondered just what exactly the Cruel and Unusual Punishments Clause means, though an understanding of the Enlightenment—and of the writings of Montesquieu and Beccaria in particular, as the extensive evidence laid out in *The Baron and the Marquis* shows—provides important clues.

From the time of the English Declaration of Rights to the present day, lawyers and jurists have argued over the meaning of "cruel and unusual punishments"—and that will likely continue to be the case for as long as that language remains in use. In *State v. Woodward*,[103] for example, the Supreme Court of Appeals of West Virginia raised this fundamental, long-asked question way back in 1910: "What is meant by the provision against cruel and unusual punishment?" "It is hard to say definitely," the court conceded.[104] As that court then wrote of that legal prohibition at that point in time: "Here is something prohibited, and in order to say what this is we must revert to the past to ascertain what is the evil to be remedied. Within the pale of due process, the Legislature has power to define crimes and fix punishments, great though they may be, limited only by the provision that they shall not be cruel or unusual or disproportionate to the character of the offense."[105] Of course, while the American prohibition against "cruel and unusual punishments" was clearly imported from English law, the conception of proportionality and the necessity-for-punishment principle were pioneered by Montesquieu and Beccaria—the French baron and the Italian marquis who made such an impression on Anglo-American lawyers.

At a distance of more than 100 years ago from today's world, the Supreme Court of Appeals of West Virginia, dealing with an issue of the time, found in *Woodward* that a law closing saloons on Sunday—and penalizing those who violated such a law—was not unconstitutional as imposing a cruel and unusual punishment. In the course of that ruling, the court had this to say about legislative prerogative: "This matter falls under the rule that the Legislature is clothed with power well-nigh unlimited to define crimes and fix their punishment. So its enactments do not deprive of life, liberty, or property without due process of law and the judgment of a man's peers its will is absolute. It can take life, it can take liberty, it can take property, for crime."[106] In that particular case, which upheld a jury's guilty verdict and a judgment that the defendant pay a $50 fine for opening a saloon on Sunday and lose his liquor license for one year, the court emphasized: "How can we say that the statute before us inflicts cruel punishment when our statutes have punished with death, lifelong imprisonment, and fines, and forfeiture of instruments of crime through centuries? Nobody can question their validity."[107] "Inflicting death by electricity," the court observed, citing the U.S. Supreme Court's 1890 decision in *In re Kemmler*, which upheld the constitutionality of New York's electric chair,[108] "is unusual, in a sense, a new mode, but held not contrary to the prohibition; not as cruel as hanging, which is surely not prohibited."[109]

But, in must be said, the U.S. Supreme Court's 1910 ruling in *In re Kemmler* and the dicta written in it was penned before modern-day notions of human rights—and our understanding, in particular, of *universal* human rights—matured after the horrors of World War I and World War II. And, it must also be said, the fact that severe punishments such as branding, ear cropping, the pillory, ducking, and hanging were once in use in the young, newly forged republic,[110] vestiges of America's colonial heritage,[111] does not mean that their use is, or would be, legitimate or morally defensible now. The United States is a republic and a representative democracy, so laws are passed by elected representatives at the federal and state levels. But the United States is also a *constitutional* democracy, one with a *written* constitution that sets forth, among other rights, the rights to due process and equal protection and the bar against cruel and unusual punishments. The U.S. Supreme Court and lower courts have the solemn responsibility of enforcing the provisions of the U.S. Constitution, which protects the rights of every American citizen. And in performing their duties, the U.S. Supreme Court and other courts should not allow wholly arbitrary, long discriminatory, and torturous punishments, such as the death penalty or, say, whipping, to endure. The use of prolonged solitary confinement—an inhuman practice—should also be reevaluated by the Supreme Court under the auspices of the Eighth Amendment's Cruel and Unusual Punishments Clause. That practice, like the death penalty and whipping, also runs afoul of the bedrock principle of human dignity.

The fact that a punishment, even one deeply rooted in history, was once a *usual* punishment is thus not a legitimate or morally sufficient justification for continuing that punishment's use. Punishments such as the pillory, the stocks, and the use of the public whipping post were, the record shows, once considered usual punishments, in some cases into the twentieth century. Yet civilized societies now recoil from the knowledge that such punishments were once in use. Historians fittingly lament their prior use, and instruments of torture and cruelty are displayed in museums, where they belong, for a reason. For decades, the Eighth Amendment has wisely been read in a *non-static* manner, and the U.S. Supreme Court and state supreme courts should continue to take that dynamic, flexible approach. That methodology allows the nation's highest court (as well as other courts) to continually assess and re-assess the legality of particular punishments under the U.S. Constitution as societal understandings of human rights evolve—and as people gain a better understanding of the barbarous and true nature of certain punishments. That approach, employed to gauge everything from conditions of confinement[112] to the conduct of prison officials,[113] to methods of execution and the proportionality of punishments, has already been used to restrict the death penalty's use for—among other groups—juveniles,[114] the insane,[115] and the intellectually disabled.[116]

In reading the U.S. Constitution, its Fourteenth Amendment must also be taken into full consideration as the society's "evolving standards" are gauged. When the Eighth Amendment is seen through the lens of the Fourteenth Amendment, it may actually make little difference whether a modern-day court adopts academic John Stinneford's view of the proper interpretation of "unusual" (*i.e.*, punishments not of long or immemorial usage) or continues to use, as it long has, the standard dictionary definition of "unusual" (*i.e.*, punishments that are rare or uncommon). Before the Fourteenth Amendment's ratification, the courts did not have to concern themselves with equality of treatment in interpreting the U.S. Constitution's Cruel and Unusual Punishments Clause.[117] After the Fourteenth Amendment's ratification, though, every American court must—both as a matter of fairness and justice and because the Fourteenth Amendment's text and history require it[118]—ask itself whether a particular punishment is being meted out in a discriminatory fashion.[119] In short, no matter whether a particular punishment is of ancient heritage, of recent vintage, or is now common or uncommon, a punishment (especially one as severe and as arbitrarily and discriminatorily applied as the death penalty) cannot be applied in an *unequal* fashion given the Fourteenth Amendment's equal protection guarantee.[120]

Life-and-Death Matters

A punishment that is administered in a lottery-like or unequal fashion would, almost by definition, seem to be an "unusual" one (as well as a "cruel" one) in the post-Equal Protection Clause era no matter which definition or understanding of that word is applied. And that is especially so given that American law has common-law origins, with the common-law tradition focused on treating societal members alike for like offenses.[121] When one considers that a person's very life is on the line in capital punishment proceedings, the inequality of the death penalty's administration is grotesque, totally unacceptable, and especially appalling. In *The Common Law*, Oliver Wendell Holmes wrote: "The life of the law has not been logic; it has been experience." And experience shows that the law—and people's views—have shifted significantly over time as regards discriminatory conduct, with equality now being a major concern of people and the law even though early Americans lived in the era of slavery and when minorities and women had no right to vote. "The felt necessities of the time, the prevalent moral and political theories, intuitions of public policy, avowed or unconscious, even the prejudices which judges share with their fellow-men," Holmes stressed in *The Common Law*, "have had a good deal more to do than the syllogism in determining the rules by which men should be governed." "The law," Holmes added, "embodies the story of nation's development through many centuries, and it cannot be dealt with as if it contained only the axioms and corollaries of a book of mathematics." "It is commonly known that the early forms of legal procedure were grounded in vengeance," Holmes further observed, warning of the danger of relying too much on history in these words: "The customs, beliefs, or needs of a primitive time establish a rule or a formula. In the course of centuries the custom, belief, or necessity disappears, but the rule remains."[122]

For barbaric practices and customs to cease, the law had to change—and the law must continue to evolve as societies evolve. It is one thing for American courts to generally defer to legislative bodies around the country so long as such bodies act in a reasonable fashion within a constitutionally acceptable range of legislative prerogative. After all, reasonable lawmakers can disagree—sometimes sharply—about how best to fight crime, reduce violence, and reform offenders. And there are, consequently, multiple—indeed, multitudinous—legal and policy approaches that can be pursued or taken for perfectly legitimate purposes when it comes to punishing misdemeanors and felonies. In actuality, in fact, some differences of opinion, or in ideological outlook, are to be expected from lawmakers and citizens, and are healthy even. Debate can inform and sharpen viewpoints or opinions, and those are good and admirable things. "In a number of the Supreme Court proportionality opinions," one book on sentencing notes of how the U.S. Supreme Court has handled the issue thus far in the Eighth Amendment context, "the Justices have emphasized their deference to legislative decisions."[123] Yet, when it comes to the death penalty, such a severe punishment—especially given its inherently torturous characteristics and the more-or-less randomized way it is administered—should no longer be tolerated by the courts. It is tremendously cruel—and highly unusual and uncivilized—to allow the death penalty to be used at all. And it is exponentially more cruel—and even more unusual and uncivilized—given the incredibly disparate fashion in which capital punishment is carried out, not only geographically speaking but in terms of all the racial prejudice associated with the punishment of death.

Already, the U.S. Supreme Court—in laying out its general approach to the law—has interpreted the Fourteenth Amendment to prohibit the "arbitrary deprivation of life." The Court has emphasizing that, "in the administration of justice," the Fourteenth Amendment "requires that no different or higher punishment shall be imposed upon one than is imposed upon all for like offenses."[124] The bar on "cruel and unusual punishments" in the English Bill of Rights, it is worth recalling, was itself intended to reign in arbitrary punishments and judicial discretion—and there is no better example of an arbitrary punishment in modern life than the American death penalty.[125] Although the English Bill of Rights of 1689 was drafted long before English politician William Wilberforce (1759–1833) led the campaign to stop the slave trade and long before the Fourteenth Amendment's ratification in 1868, the concern about arbitrary government action is one that runs through Anglo-American history—and it is a concern that has constitutional implications. The arbitrary, almost random infliction of capital punishment is, simply put, totally at odds with the Fourteenth Amendment and American constitutional values.[126]

Even if the death penalty was once considered to be a "usual" punishment because it has long been used,[127] today's death penalty (actively used in just a small number of American jurisdictions by just a small number of individual prosecutors) does not, as a factual matter, resemble how death sentences were used much more systematically in the past. In America's founding era, criminals and slaves were hanged or even gibbeted in the public square. The way the American death penalty is applied today—by lethal injection and in an increasingly random, discretionary, and arbitrary manner[128]—is not rooted, and certainly cannot be said to be grounded, in some kind of long or immemorial usage. In the five-year period from 2011 to 2015, FBI data show that, in the U.S., there were more than 60,000 murder victims.[129] In contrast, for that same five-year period, there were 188 executions carried out in the United States.[130] In 2016, a small percentage of American jurisdictions—five states—executed inmates, and in 2017, eight states did. "In the death-penalty lottery, only a fraction of murder cases result in death verdicts, and family members of murder victims in those cases can feel little solace from a sideshow centered on the defendant," Mark Earley, Virginia's attorney general from 1998 to 2001, recently wrote.[131]

The modern system of capital punishment began in 1972 with *Furman v. Georgia*, but the attempt to reign in arbitrariness and discrimination in the death penalty's administration since that time has been an utter and abject failure. And American law, for that reason and many others, including because of the torturous nature of state-sanctioned killing, should no longer tolerate the use of death sentences and executions. As I argued in a recent law review article, "The Inequality of America's Death Penalty: A Crossroads for Capital Punishment at the Intersection of the Eighth and Fourteenth Amendments": "When the Eighth and Fourteenth Amendments are read together, punishments cannot be 'cruel and unusual' and, to avoid that nomenclature, they must not be inflicted in an *unequal* manner either. The words that adorn the U.S. Supreme Court building—'EQUAL JUSTICE UNDER LAW'—must be given effect in the context of *punishment* (just as they were, for example, in the context of *public education* in *Brown v. Board of Education*) if the Fourteenth Amendment is to be meaningful and fully implemented."[132] The Eighth Amendment, simply put, cannot be read without considering the implications of the subsequently ratified Fourteenth Amendment, the nineteenth-century amendment that fundamentally changed American constitutional law.

Eighth Amendment jurisprudence, truth be told, is now in a state of disarray. A number of U.S. Supreme Court cases have contributed to that state of affairs, but in the Fourteenth Amendment context, one especially badly decided U.S. Supreme Court case stands out for its particularly pernicious long-range consequences. In 1987, in *McCleskey v. Kemp*,[133] the Supreme Court infamously rejected an Equal Protection Clause challenge to Georgia's death penalty—a punishment long administered in that state in a racially discriminatory fashion. That decision corrupted and marred Eighth Amendment case law by ignoring racial prejudice, allowing the death penalty to linger on in American life in spite of all that well-documented prejudice—and all the invidious racial bias—that has long been associated with it. In that case, the death row inmate, Warren McCleskey, argued that race had infected the administration of the state's death penalty in two ways: first, those who murdered whites were more likely to be sentenced to death than those murdering blacks; and second, that black murderers were more likely to be sentenced to death than white murderers.[134] "*McCleskey*," Cassandra Stubbs, the Director of the ACLU's Capital Punishment Project, has observed, "has been roundly condemned as a 'low point' in the quest for equality, comparable to *Dred Scott v. Sanford* (1857)—which held that people of African ancestry were not entitled to the protections of the Constitution—and *Plessy v. Ferguson* (1896)—which upheld racial segregation of public facilities."[135]

In rejecting the equal protection challenge, the U.S. Supreme Court held that Warren McCleskey had to prove "the existence of purposeful discrimination" and that decision-makers "in *his* case acted with discriminatory purpose."[136] In further turning back McCleskey's Eighth Amendment challenge, the Court observed that "our decisions since *Furman* have identified a constitutionally permissible range of discretion in imposing the death penalty,"[137] and that, "absent a showing that the Georgia capital punishment system operates in an arbitrary and capricious manner, McCleskey cannot prove a constitutional violation by demonstrating that other defendants who may be similarly situated did *not* receive the death penalty."[138] It was a highly controversial, 5–4 decision that swept under the rug clear evidence of racial prejudice where a person's life was at stake. Perhaps most tellingly, the author of the *McCleskey* majority opinion—Justice Lewis Powell—later famously regretted his vote in that case.[139] Justice Powell's acknowledgement of regret, however, only came in a private, later-published interview with his biographer after he had left the nation's highest court.[140]

Most notoriously, Justice Lewis Powell's opinion employed a slippery slope argument in rejecting Warren McCleskey's unrebutted statistical proof of racial discrimination in Georgia's death penalty system. As Justice Powell wrote: "McCleskey's claim, taken to its logical conclusion, throws into serious question the principles that underlie our entire criminal justice system. The Eighth Amendment is not limited in application to capital punishment, but applies to all penalties."[141] "[I]f we accepted McCleskey's claim that racial bias has impermissibly tainted the capital sentencing decision," he wrote in the opinion he came to regret, "we could soon be faced with similar claims as to other types of penalty."[142] "The Constitution," Powell concluded, "does not require that a State eliminate any demonstrable disparity that correlates with a potentially irrelevant factor in order to operate a criminal justice system that includes capital punishment."[143] But the fear of too much justice expressed in *McCleskey* is not only regrettable, it is morally bankrupt, for instead of grappling with how to combat racial prejudice in the context of such a severe punishment, it simply ignored the evidence of prejudice and said it was of no consequence. In fact, the death penalty is unlike *any* other punishment that human societies still use, and its use runs afoul of core constitutional values and basic human rights.

Human Dignity and Human Decency

The concept of human dignity is one that regularly informs—and that certainly should continue to inform—the U.S. Supreme Court's Eighth Amendment jurisprudence. As Justice Anthony Kennedy wrote in *Brown v. Plata*,[144] for example: "[P]risoners may be deprived of rights that are fundamental to liberty. Yet the law and the Constitution demand recognition of certain other rights. Prisoners retain the essence of human dignity inherent in all persons."[145] As Justice Kennedy's majority opinion in *Brown v. Plata*, which dealt with overcrowded California prisons, continued: "Respect for that dignity animates the Eighth Amendment prohibition against cruel and unusual punishment."[146] The Supreme Court's consideration of the concept of dignity, in fact, dates back many decades, finding voice in the very first case that established the lofty sounding "evolving standards of decency" test.[147] For that reason, a punishment that does not comport with human dignity—a concept that lies at the heart of the Eighth Amendment—is one that must be scrutinized as a "cruel and unusual punishment."[148] It is especially cruel and unusual to dehumanize someone—indeed, to take someone's life—in a manner that involves runaway arbitrariness or that is a reflection of racial prejudice. Along with severe punishments like the death penalty and whipping, the use of prolonged solitary confinement, as yet another example, runs afoul of the concept of human dignity as it strips offenders of what makes people human—their desire, ability, and instinct to interact with others.

There are multiple approaches to interpreting the U.S. Constitution, but law professors and legal commentators frequently try to read the tea leaves of history to divine what certain words or phrases should mean. Law professor John Stinneford, as one commentator notes, "has argued that we *do* know exactly what the word 'unusual' in the English Bill of Rights signified to the English: 'the word "unusual" was a term of art that referred to government practices that are contrary to "long usage" or "immemorial usage."' "[149] As that commentator, Michael Perry acknowledges, though, the implications of Stinneford's observation about the historical record are less than clear. As Perry explains:

> Let's assume, for the sake of discussion, that Stinneford is right about what "unusual" meant in the English Bill of Rights of 1689. Stinneford goes on to argue that the framers of the American Bill of Rights knew what "unusual" meant in the English Bill of Rights and that they intended "unusual" in the Eighth Amendment to mean the same thing. There is reason to doubt that the framers of the American Bill of Rights did in fact know what "cruel and unusual" meant in the English Bill of Rights. But even if we grant to Stinneford that the framers of the Eighth Amendment intended "unusual" in the Eighth Amendment to mean what "unusual" meant in the English Bill of Rights, this problem remains: The issue for an originalist is not what those who drafted the Eighth Amendment—"the framers"—meant by "unusual." The issue, rather, is what "We the People" in 1789–91, on whose behalf the Eighth Amendment was made a part of the Constitution, understood "unusual" to mean.[150]

At this point in American history, the present day, it is actually the "evolving standards of decency" test—a legal standard in place and in use for *six* decades—that is of long use. It has thus been clear, *for decades*, that what is considered cruel and unusual can and will change with the times. In fact, if one goes back in time, Michael Perry—an originalist[151] who is, as a scholarly matter, very interested in history—also makes this critique of Stinneford's analysis and approach:

> For an originalist, the question is "not what the Framers or Ratifers meant or understood subjectively, but what their words would have meant objectively—how they would have been understood by an ordinary, reasonably well-informed user of the language, in context, at the time, within the relevant political community that adopted them. The Preamble to the Constitution tells us who the true authors of the constitutional text are: not the drafters (framers) but "We the People." "It is the adoption of the text by the public that renders the text authoritative, not its drafting by particular individuals." And there is nothing in the historical record to suggest that the public (We the People) in 1789–91 would have understood—indeed, it is less than clear that even the framers understood—"unusual" in the Eighth Amendment to be "a term of art" that meant just what is meant in the English Bill of Rights a hundred years earlier.[152]

The inability to get in every ratifier's head makes an historical analysis extremely difficult, and it leaves a lot to speculation about intent or what particular words were meant to convey. "It is much more likely that the public," Michael Perry stresses, would have understood both *cruel* and *unusual* in the U.S. Constitution's Eighth Amendment "to mean what Samuel Johnson's *A Dictionary of the English Language*, first published in 1756, tells us those two words were conventionally understood to mean at the time." As Perry writes of that popular source: "In volume 1, at page 250, 'cruel' is defined as: '1. Pleased with hurting others; inhuman; hard-hearted; barbarous. 2. [Of things.] Bloody; mischievous; destructive.' In volume 2, at page 503, 'unusual' is defined as: 'Not common; not frequent; rare.' "[153] Although Perry, in 2009, asserted that under the Eighth Amendment "a punishment is not unconstitutional unless it is both 'cruel and unusual',"[154] he simultaneously wrote:

> Few would deny that the Eighth Amendment bans any punishment that is intrinsically barbaric: barbaric in and of itself, no matter how heinous the crime, how culpable the criminal, or how effectively the punishment would deter. (Torture is the paradigmatic example of such a punishment.) Intrinsically barbaric punishment is "cruel" within the meaning of the Eighth Amendment; such punishment is also (we may assume) "unusual" in the sense of "not common; not frequent; rare"—not common, that is, as an officially sanctioned punishment.[155]

"Unless it has a deterrent effect," Perry offers, "capital punishment is significantly harsher than necessary to serve the legitimate aims of punishment."[156]

The Supreme Court, to date, has struck down *capital* sentences for certain *categories* of crimes and offenders, and it has also declared at least some *non-capital* sentences to be unconstitutional.[157] But the necessity-for-punishment principle is one that has, by and large, been mostly lost in the shuffle in the originalism vs. living constitutionalism debate, even though it is a principle that should appeal to both crowds. Originalists should like and embrace the maxim because it originated in the eighteenth century before the U.S. Bill of Rights was adopted and ratified, but living constitutionalists should like and embrace the maxim because the modern-day *application* of it can be used to invalidate barbaric, outdated and disproportionate punishments that no longer meet the "necessity" test.

To rectify the current situation and to make clear that any unnecessary punishments are inappropriate, the U.S. Supreme Court should forthrightly articulate the importance of this necessity-for-punishment maxim in its future Eighth and Fourteenth Amendment cases. And the Court should make clear that, as the severity of punishments increases (from petty offenses and misdemeanors, on the low end, to serious felonies, on the upper level), American courts—just as they do in applying strict scrutiny in other contexts[158]—should give heightened scrutiny to the more severe punishments on the punishment scale. In particular, American judges should make more searching inquiries into whether or not a particular punishment is truly necessary or required in relationship to the relative severity of the punishment in question. Such an approach makes logical sense and is fully consistent with the long-standing strict scrutiny framework that governmental actions be narrowly tailored and the least restrictive means be employed to achieve the goal—a goal that must be a legitimate one.[159]

Indeed, in the punishment context, fundamental rights (*e.g.*, the right to life[160] and liberty,[161] and the right to be free from cruelty[162] and torture)[163] are at stake, with the concept of human dignity infusing those constitutional rights.[164] And the necessity-for-punishment approach not only makes good sense, but it is well-grounded in the maxim of Montesquieu and Beccaria that gained so much currency and traction in the eighteenth and nineteenth centuries. That maxim sought to impose the least pain and suffering that was necessary in a given situation, and it is an Enlightenment-era maxim that resonates—it must be said—with notions of human dignity and decency. "'The Greatest Happiness of the Greatest Number' is the utilitarian political formula" articulated by Beccaria and later similarly proclaimed by Bentham, one book on punishment and culture recounts, noting that "[a]n earlier inkling" of the idea of "the minimum necessary suffering" can be "found in Montesquieu's maxim 'all punishment not deriving from necessity is tyranny.'"[165]

Back to the (Future) Enlightenment: The Necessity of (Absolute) Necessity

Normally, legislators are the proper actors to decide upon the best punishments for crime and the need (or lack thereof) for particular punishments. As Emer de Vattel wrote in *The Law of Nations*: "Every well-governed state ought then to have its laws for the punishment of criminals. It belongs to the legislative power, whatever that be, to establish them with justice and wisdom."[166] But in governments governed by constitutions, there are, of course, limits, including those set forth by the U.S. Constitution's Eighth and Fourteenth Amendments, with Montesquieu's separation-of-powers and necessity-for-punishments principles relevant to understanding the protection of liberty and the shunning of tyranny. As Vattel himself emphasized centuries ago on the subject of punishments: "It would be dangerous to leave the punishment of transgressors entirely to the discretion of those who are invested with authority. The passions might interfere in a business which ought to be regulated only by justice and wisdom."[167] As Vattel observed:

> From the foundation even of the right of punishing, and from the lawful end of inflicting penalties, arises the necessity of keeping them within just bounds. Since they are designed to procure the safety of the state and of the citizens, they ought never to be extended beyond what that safety requires. To say that any punishment is just since the transgressor knew beforehand the penalty he was about to incur, is using a barbarous language, repugnant to humanity, and to the law of nature, which forbids our doing any ill to others, unless they lay us under the necessity of inflicting it in our own defence and for our own security.[168]

There are, certainly, textual differences between the U.S. Constitution's Eighth Amendment, the English Bill of Rights, and the provisions of other constitutions or bills of rights, one of which—as explained in an earlier chapter of *The Baron and the Marquis*—is set forth in section 8 of the French Declaration of the Rights of Man.[169] Such textual differences have, not surprisingly, led legal commentators to draw distinctions, as William Stuntz did in *The Collapse of American Criminal Justice*. As Stuntz, articulating one view of the difference between the Eighth Amendment and its French counterpart, wrote:

> Article 8 is the Declaration's counterpart to the Eighth Amendment, which bars both "excessive fines" and "cruel and unusual punishments." But instead of banning only the most extreme criminal sanctions as American law does—the Eighth Amendment grandfathered existing punishments, including branding and whipping, by banning only "unusual" sanctions—Article 8 rejects *all* punishments that are not "strictly and obviously necessary."[170]

But there are multiple ways to read legal texts, and the collective history of the adoption of the Eighth Amendment and the French Declaration should not be forgotten as lawyers and legal commentators parse English and French words. Both the Eighth

Amendment and the French Declaration were, notably, adopted *after* the maxim of Montesquieu and Beccaria gained widespread acceptance. And to say that a punishment is "unusual" (the word Americans borrowed from the English Bill of Rights) could also just be seen as another way of saying that a punishment is not necessary anymore. No explicit instructions were given by America's founders in the Constitution as to how to read the word "unusual," but we do know that the founders despised arbitrary and unnecessary punishments and that they favored liberty over tyranny. It was in that historical context that the Eighth Amendment came into being. The Enlightenment-era maxim of Montesquieu and Beccaria—one recorded and embraced by early American lawyers, including John Adams, Thomas Jefferson, and William Bradford—in fact provided the intellectual foundation for both American and French lawmakers as they thought about crime and punishment. And that Enlightenment maxim, like the impulses that led to the American Revolution, was specifically designed to further liberty and to ensure that societies would not inflict needless suffering or unnecessary punishments. Societies must protect the public from criminal activity, and that means punishing those who offend societal norms. But societies must punish only to the extent necessary (and only in a proportionate manner).

Although the necessity for a law or a particular punishment is a subjective enterprise,[171] and although it has been asserted that what is "necessary" is "for the general will to decide,"[172] the U.S. Constitution and its Bill of Rights sets forth fundamental protections that legislators cannot, by statute, override. The right to life, in fact, is an important constitutional value—one rooted in the American Declaration of Independence[173] and in the U.S. Constitution's Fifth[174] and Fourteenth[175] Amendments.[176] That right has itself been described as a fundamental right by the U.S. Supreme Court.[177] In *Ford v. Wainwright*,[178] for instance, the Supreme Court held that the execution of the insane did not comport with the Eighth Amendment, ruling as follows: "[T]his Court is compelled to conclude that the Eighth Amendment prohibits a State from carrying out a sentence of death upon a prisoner who is insane. Whether its aim be to protect the condemned from fear and pain without comfort of understanding, or to protect the dignity of society itself from the barbarity of exacting mindless vengeance, the restriction finds enforcement in the Eighth Amendment."[179] In the course of its ruling, the Court in *Ford* emphasized:

> Today, no State in the Union permits the execution of the insane. It is clear that the ancient and humane limitation upon the State's ability to execute its sentences has as firm a hold upon the jurisprudence of today as it had centuries ago in England. The various reasons put forth in support of the common-law restriction have no less logical, moral, and practical force than they did when first voiced. For today, no less than before, we may seriously question the retributive value of executing a person who has no comprehension of why he has been singled out and stripped of his fundamental right to life.[180]

There are thus clearly expressed limits on a state's power when it comes to fundamental rights, such as the right to life. In another case, *Yick Wo v. Hopkins*,[181] the U.S. Supreme Court emphasized that "the law is the definition and limitation of power."[182] "[T]he fundamental rights to life, liberty, and the pursuit of happiness, considered as individual possessions," the Court ruled in that 1886 case, "are secured by those maxims of constitutional law which are the monuments showing the victorious progress of the race in securing to men the blessings of civilization under the reign of just and equal laws, so that, in the famous language of the Massachusetts bill of rights, the government of the commonwealth 'may be a government of laws and not of men.'"[183] The Court handed down its decision in *Yick Wo* before the Nineteenth Amendment, in 1920, guaranteed women the right to vote. But in that decision, the Court held for the first time that a law that is race-neutral on its face, but administered in a prejudicial manner, infringes on the Fourteenth Amendment's Equal Protection Clause. As the Court ruled: "Though the law itself be fair on its face, and impartial in appearance, yet, if it is applied and administered by public authority with an evil eye and an unequal hand, so as practically to make unjust and illegal discriminations between persons in similar circumstances, material to their rights, the denial of equal justice is still within the prohibition of the constitution."[184]

The Enlightenment, history reveals, set the stage for the whole debate over human rights, equality of treatment, and the necessity-for-punishment maxim. And as people through the years contemplated and applied that necessity-for-punishment maxim, the lack of necessity for a punishment was regularly seen as evidence of its cruelty.[185] Indeed, the principle of Montesquieu and his disciple, Cesare Beccaria, was said to apply regardless of the severity of the punishment, even extending, in prior times, to corporal punishments[186] and capital offenses.[187] As one North Carolina newspaper editorialized in 1846, evocatively describing the field on which the public debate over the death penalty was being fought: "Every drop of blood which is shed as a penalty for crime when *no necessity* existed for it, is *wrongfully shed*: every life which is taken under such circumstances, amounts to nothing less than murder—cold blooded and tyrannical murder in the Government itself!"[188] Even in the face of arguments about the purported need for capital or corporal punishments, various commentators vigorously contended that such practices were barbaric or should be abandoned.[189]

In fact, writers who favored capital punishment for particular crimes felt the need to discuss the maxim of Montesquieu and Beccaria about necessity being the appropriate justification for punishment even as they found fault with Beccaria's call for the death penalty's abolition.[190] Even those not wanting to do away with capital punishment entirely emphasized that any "unnecessary cruelty" should be eliminated from the criminal justice system. For example, in 1874, in an article in Cincinnati's *Lancet and Observer* on the subject of capital punishment, it was observed:

> If it be well to make death the penalty of certain crimes, the question comes to medical men, how shall this extreme punishment be inflicted so as to meet the requirements of justice, and yet avoid unnecessary cruelty in its execution. In various countries, death has been secured by hanging—as in this country—by the garrote, by the guillotine, by shooting. Some experiments by Prof. Brown-Sequard would seem to indicate that death by the guillotine is perhaps one of the most cruel of all known modes.... Now, if death shall continue to be a proper penalty for murder, the question for us, as medical men, to consider, is, how shall death be inflicted? Shall we shoot

the culprit, or hang him like a dog, or cut off his head? The displays to morbid appetite in first-class hangings are too notorious to require comment. We respectfully suggest, then, that our professional influence should be exerted to a more rational and decent death penalty.[191]

Equality and Justice: Sentencing Commissions and Necessity Reviews

In the United States of America, it was understood from the country's founding period that power should check power—and that, as a corollary to that idea, the abuse of power would be checked by power. Article I of the U.S. Constitution sets forth legislative powers and prerogatives, while Article II and Article III, respectively, set forth the powers of the executive branch and the judiciary. To avoid what were collectively seen then as outrageous abuses of power (i.e., sentencing people to death without jury trials, convicting and sentencing people for conduct that had not previously been declared unlawful, and allowing people to be unjustly imprisoned), the U.S. Constitution—as originally framed—explicitly outlawed bills of attainders and *ex post facto* laws and guaranteed the right to petition for a writ of habeas corpus. In the subsequently ratified U.S. Bill of Rights, other protections were added. Grand juries were required to be convened for certain types of cases, petit juries were required to be empaneled to adjudicate guilt or innocence, and the press—the Fourth Estate—had its own special role to play in checking the abuses of the three branches of government: legislative, executive, and judicial. America's founders thus recognized the need for multiple layers of checks on governmental power, including in the criminal justice system to ensure justice, fairness, and proportionality. The popular necessity-for-punishment maxim, as a foundational principle, would help ensure—above all else—that liberty would triumph over tyranny.

Liberty, fairness, and equality are part of the American creed, though how those concepts are discussed by American jurists in particular situations has varied from time to time. The United States Sentencing Commission and equivalent state-law sentencing commissions, institutions that were not around in America's founding period (and that were not even conceived of or imagined by America's founders), themselves began as efforts to rationalize and equalize sentencing outcomes.[192] As University of Minnesota law professor Richard Frase writes of the history of such efforts: "Minnesota was the first jurisdiction to implement legally binding sentencing guidelines developed by an independent sentencing commission." Pointing out that those guidelines "have been in effect since 1980 and have evolved considerably while still retaining their original essence," Frase writes that Minnesota's sentencing commission "recognized the twin goals of uniformity in the use of state prison sentences, with particular emphasis on preventing racial, gender, and socioeconomic disparities; and proportionality of prison commitment and duration decisions, relative to offense severity and offender criminal history."[193] A rigorous application of the necessity-for-punishment principle, both by legislators and the courts, would complement such reform-minded efforts and help Americans achieve a more just and equitable criminal justice system with better outcomes and at less cost to taxpayers.[194]

Criminal activity has, and must have, consequences.[195] But punishments must at all times be proportionate and necessary so as not to be excessive. Any punishment that is excessive would be cruel and unusual, with both the Excessive Fines and Excessive Bail Clauses clearly indicating that a major purpose of the Eighth Amendment was to eliminate excessive governmental actions in the criminal justice sphere. In his concurrence in *Furman v. Georgia*, Justice Thurgood Marshall—writing of substantive due process and the Cruel and Unusual Punishments Clause—specifically wrote of only "necessary" punishments being legitimate.[196] As Marshall wrote in that case:

> The concepts of cruel and unusual punishment and substantive due process become so close as to merge when the substantive due process argument is stated in the following manner: because capital punishment deprives an individual of a fundamental right (i.e., the right to life) the State needs a compelling interest to justify it. Thus stated the substantive due process argument reiterates what is essentially the primary purpose of the Cruel and Unusual Punishments Clause of the Eighth Amendment—i.e., punishment may not be more severe than is necessary to serve the legitimate interests of the State.[197]

But what is necessary? That, of course, is the six-million-dollar question—and one on which people are bound to differ. The meaning of "necessary" or "necessity," it turns out, varies according *to the context*. What *necessary* means has been explored before by the U.S. Supreme Court, so an exploration of what punishments are necessary in any given sphere of criminal law is hardly an impossibility or beyond human comprehension. In *McCulloch v. Maryland*,[198] the Supreme Court—in a completely different context than the Eighth Amendment—held that Congress has the power to incorporate a bank. In that case, Chief Justice John Marshall—in interpreting the Constitution's Necessary and Proper Clause—had this to say about the meaning of the word *necessary* and its context in that clause: "In ascertaining the sense in which the word 'necessary' is used in the clause of the constitution, we may derive some aid from that with which it ... is associated. Congress shall have power 'to make all laws which shall be necessary and proper to carry into execution' the powers of the government."[199] In construing the *necessary and proper* language, Marshall observed of the word *necessary*:

> If reference be had to its use in the common affairs of the world or in approved authors, we find that it frequently imports no more than that one thing is convenient, or useful, or essential to another. To employ the means necessary to an end is generally understood as employing any means calculated to produce the end, and not as being confined to those single means without which the end would be entirely unattainable. Such is the character of human language that no word conveys to the mind in all situations one single definite idea, and nothing is more common than to use words in a figurative sense. Almost all compositions contain words which, taken in their rigorous sense, would convey a meaning different from that which is obviously intended. It is essential to just construction that many words which import something excessive should be understood in a more mitigated sense—in that sense which common usage justifies. The word "necessary" is of this description. It has not a fixed character peculiar to itself. It admits

> of all degrees of comparison, and is often connected with other words which increase or diminish the impression the mind receives of the urgency it imports. A thing may be necessary, very necessary, absolutely or indispensably necessary. To no mind would the same idea be conveyed by these several phrases. The comment on the word is well illustrated by the passage cited at the bar from the 10th section of the 1st article of the Constitution. It is, we think, impossible to compare the sentence which prohibits a State from laying "imposts, or duties on imports or exports, except what may be absolutely necessary for executing its inspection laws," with that which authorizes Congress "to make all laws which shall be necessary and proper for carrying into execution" the powers of the General Government without feeling a conviction that the convention understood itself to change materially the meaning of the word "necessary," by prefixing the word "absolutely." This word, then, like others, is used in various senses, and, in its construction, the subject, the context, the intention of the person using them are all to be taken into view.[200]

The question of *what punishments* are necessary is highly context specific. On the question of the power to punish, the Court in *McCulloch* had this to say on the subject:

> So, with respect to the whole penal code of the United States, whence arises the power to punish in cases not prescribed by the Constitution? All admit that the Government may legitimately punish any violation of its laws, and yet this is not among the enumerated powers of Congress. The right to enforce the observance of law by punishing its infraction might be denied with the more plausibility because it is expressly given in some cases.
>
> Congress is empowered "to provide for the punishment of counterfeiting the securities and current coin of the United States," and "to define and punish piracies and felonies committed on the high seas, and offences against the law of nations." The several powers of Congress may exist in a very imperfect State, to be sure, but they may exist and be carried into execution, although no punishment should be inflicted, in cases where the right to punish is not expressly given.
>
> Take, for example, the power "to establish post-offices and post-roads." This power is executed by the single act of making the establishment. But from this has been inferred the power and duty of carrying the mail along the post road from one post office to another. And from this implied power has again been inferred the right to punish those who steal letters from the post office, or rob the mail. It may be said with some plausibility that the right to carry the mail, and to punish those who rob it, is not indispensably necessary to the establishment of a post office and post road. This right is indeed essential to the beneficial exercise of the power, but not indispensably necessary to its existence. So, of the punishment of the crimes of stealing or falsifying a record or process of a Court of the United States, or of perjury in such Court. To punish these offences is certainly conducive to the due ad-

ministration of justice. But Courts may exist, and may decide the causes brought before them, though such crimes escape punishment.

The baneful influence of this narrow construction on all the operations of the Government, and the absolute impracticability of maintaining it without rendering the Government incompetent to its great objects, might be illustrated by numerous examples drawn from the Constitution and from our laws. The good sense of the public has pronounced without hesitation that the power of punishment appertains to sovereignty, and may be exercised, whenever the sovereign has a right to act, as incidental to his Constitutional powers. It is a means for carrying into execution all sovereign powers, and may be used although not indispensably necessary. It is a right incidental to the power, and conducive to its beneficial exercise.

If this limited construction of the word "necessary" must be abandoned in order to punish, whence is derived the rule which would reinstate it when the Government would carry its powers into execution by means not vindictive in their nature? If the word "necessary" means "needful," "requisite," "essential," "conducive to," in order to let in the power of punishment for the infraction of law, why is it not equally comprehensive when required to authorize the use of means which facilitate the execution of the powers of Government, without the infliction of punishment?

In ascertaining the sense in which the word "necessary" is used in this clause of the Constitution, we may derive some aid from that with which it is associated. Congress shall have power "to make all laws which shall be necessary and proper to carry into execution" the powers of the Government. If the word "necessary" was used in that strict and rigorous sense for which the counsel for the State of Maryland contend, it would be an extraordinary departure from the usual course of the human mind, as exhibited in composition, to add a word the only possible effect of which is to qualify that strict and rigorous meaning, to present to the mind the idea of some choice of means of legislation not strained and compressed within the narrow limits for which gentlemen contend.[201]

In interpreting the U.S. Constitution's Necessary and Proper Clause, the Court in *McCulloch* concluded:

The result of the most careful and attentive consideration bestowed upon this clause is that, if it does not enlarge, it cannot be construed to restrain, the powers of Congress, or to impair the right of the legislature to exercise its best judgment in the selection of measures to carry into execution the Constitutional powers of the Government. If no other motive for its insertion can be suggested, a sufficient one is found in the desire to remove all doubts respecting the right to legislate on that vast mass of incidental powers which must be involved in the Constitution if that instrument be not a splendid bauble.

We admit, as all must admit, that the powers of the Government are limited, and that its limits are not to be transcended. But we think the sound construction of the Constitution must allow to the national legislature that discretion

> with respect to the means by which the powers it confers are to be carried into execution which will enable that body to perform the high duties assigned to it in the manner most beneficial to the people. Let the end be legitimate, let it be within the scope of the Constitution, and all means which are appropriate, which are plainly adapted to that end, which are not prohibited, but consist with the letter and spirit of the Constitution, are Constitutional.[202]

Words, of course, must be interpreted in their context. But the U.S. Constitution, through the Eighth Amendment, makes clear that "cruel and unusual punishments" are forbidden. In other words, while Congress has the undisputed *power* to punish, Congress cannot select punishments that are *cruel and unusual* in nature. Modern U.S. Supreme Court decisions, pointing to Chief Justice Marshall's words in *McCulloch v. Maryland*, have found that "[t]he scope of the Necessary and Proper Clause is broad," and that legislatures are vested with considerable discretion.[203] As the Supreme Court emphasized in 2013[204] of what Chief Justice Marshall wrote back in 1819 about the Necessary and Proper Clause: "As we have come to understand these words and the provision they explain, they 'leav[e] to Congress a large discretion as to the means that may be employed in executing a given power.'"[205] "The Clause," the Court found, "allows Congress to 'adopt any means, appearing to it most eligible and appropriate, which are adapted to the end to be accomplished and consistent with the letter and spirit of the Constitution.'"[206] As the Supreme Court further emphasized in *United States v. Kebodeaux*[207] in 2013:

> The Constitution, for example, makes few explicit references to federal criminal law, but the Necessary and Proper Clause nonetheless authorizes Congress, in the implementation of other explicit powers, to create federal crimes, to confine offenders to prison, to hire guards and other prison personnel, to provide prisoners with medical care and educational training, to ensure the safety of those who may come into contact with prisoners, to ensure the public's safety through systems of parole and supervised released, and, where a federal prisoner's mental condition so requires, to confine that prisoner civilly after the expiration of his or her term of imprisonment.[208]

But in the punishment context, the U.S. Constitution's Eighth and Fourteenth Amendments put clear and written constraints on governmental action. American courts are tasked with delineating what those exact constraints are, but in determining whether a particular punishment is legitimate or illegitimate, the courts should, as they read the Constitution, evaluate each and every punishment in light of Beccaria's and Montesquieu's necessity-for-punishment maxim—the one produced by the Enlightenment and that so captivated American and French revolutionaries.[209] Just because legislative bodies and prosecutors have *discretion*—even considerable discretion—to decide how to exercise power and what coercive power of the state is necessary in the first instance, such discretion should—indeed, must—have limits, and it is, in fact, the Constitution that lays down the applicable and fundamental law that sets those constraints. The Eighth and Fourteenth Amendments, among other portions of the U.S. Constitution, are the operating instructions we have that American courts have been given to use, and those provisions must be given effect. The U.S.

Constitution, of course, is unlike an appliance or automobile user's manual, for the Constitution—in addition to explaining how the government is to work—is also about protecting people's liberty and fundamental rights.

When the government decides to take away people's lives or to strip people of their liberty, such government actions should raise immediate red flags and prompt caution lest lives or liberty be needlessly taken away. Indeed, in the death penalty context, because the right to life and the right to be free from cruelty and torture are fundamental rights, the burden should be on the government[210] to demonstrate that the state's ultimate sanction (*i.e.*, capital punishment) is absolutely necessary for the protection of society and is not, itself, an arbitrary, cruel and unusual, or torturous punishment. Such a burden, plainly, the government cannot meet because of the death penalty's inherent and immutable torturous characteristics, the highly arbitrary way the death penalty is actually administered in practice, and the utter lack of proof that the death penalty is necessary for the protection of society. The argument that capital punishment is unnecessary actually dates back to the eighteenth century, to Beccaria's time, and that argument has been made by Europeans, Americans, and others since that time. The modern American death penalty has actually been challenged for decades as an unnecessary, and therefore illegitimate, tool of state power, including within the confines of the Cass Gilbert-designed U.S. Supreme Court building in Washington, D.C.

Way back in the 1960s, U.S. Supreme Justice Arthur Goldberg—in a memo distributed to his fellow justices regarding capital punishment—tried in vain to convince his colleagues of the death penalty's unconstitutionality. In that memo, he wrote: "This Court has never explicitly considered whether, and under what circumstances, the Eighth and Fourteenth Amendments to the United States Constitution proscribes the imposition of the death penalty." "I am convinced that whatever may be said of times past," Goldberg wrote in a section of his memo on the evolving standards of decency, that those evolving standards "now condemn as barbaric and inhuman the deliberate institutionalized taking of human life by the state." "I conclude therefore," Goldberg stressed, "that under the 'evolving standard of decency' test, punishment by death is cruel and unusual."[211] In another section of his memo, titled "Unnecessary and Excessive Punishment," Justice Goldberg further observed:

> Even if it could be said that our "evolving standards of decency" do not yet condemn the death penalty, I suggest nevertheless that this penalty is unconstitutional under the following additional test derived from the *Weems* case: Giving full weight to reasonable legislative findings, a punishment is cruel and unusual if a less severe one can as effectively achieve the permissible ends of punishment.[212]

After discussing the issue of deterrence, a topic framed long before by Beccaria's *On Crimes and Punishments*, Goldberg specifically addressed the burden of proof and necessity-for-punishment issues, writing:

> Thus, the meaningful question—at least at this point in the development of our methods of studying the relationship between punishments and crimes—is not whether capital punishment really deters crime (for we do

> not know the answer to this question); it is: "where [does] the onus of proof [lie] in this matter of the death penalty." If the State must affirmatively show that capital punishment has a unique deterrent impact, then it has failed. If the advocates of abolition must prove that capital punishment lacks a unique deterrent impact, then they have failed.
>
> Whatever standard is generally applicable in passing on legislative findings based on conflicting evidence, the State must, in my opinion, show an overriding necessity before it can take human life. This principle was recognized as long ago as 1794,[213] when the preamble to the Pennsylvania criminal statutes announced that " ... the punishment of death ought never to be inflicted, where it is not *absolutely necessary* to the public safety...." (Emphasis added.) The Court has frequently held that doubts should always be resolved against the application of the death sentence. *See, e.g.*, Andres v. United States, 333 U.S. 740, 752.[214]
>
> I conclude therefore that since there is no persuasive evidence that capital punishment uniquely deters capital crime, and since doubts should be resolved against the death penalty, this penalty runs afoul of the *Weems* test which proscribes punishments unnecessarily severe in relation to the permissible goals of punishment.[215]

In evaluating any punishment, whether capital punishment, prolonged solitary confinement, or any other, the overriding Eighth Amendment concern should always be whether a particular punishment is proportionate and necessary. If a punishment is disproportionate, it is cruel and should be classified as unusual. And if a punishment is unnecessary, it is not only cruel and unusual, it is gratuitous and inhuman. Lawmakers, naturally, may not always agree on what punishments are necessary, or on what kind of punishments best fit the crimes. In most circumstances, it must be acknowledged, disagreements over sentencing policies by lawmakers are legitimate and, when legislatures pass legislation in the criminal law arena, those laws should ordinarily be respected by the courts.[216] But again, the U.S. Constitution and equivalent state constitution provisions set defined limits, with those legal instruments put in place—as history shows—to *check* legislative and executive power. Consequently, independent judges are not only entitled to strike down laws and punishments they find to be *excessive* or *cruel and unusual* (or *cruel* or *cruel or unusual*, as the case may be in particular states), but they are *duty bound* to do so. After all, judges are the only ones entrusted with that power. The U.S. Supreme Court Justices, like lower court judges, were given—and thus possess—the power of judicial review and they take specific oaths to support and defend the Constitution of the United States.[217] Judges must honor those oaths and show fidelity to the U.S. Constitution and its counterparts, the state constitutions. And when they strike down excessive or cruel and unusual punishments that infringe on life or liberty, their actions should be seen as patriotic expressions of that fidelity to the U.S. Constitution, to state constitutions, and to human rights and the rule of law.

In addition, carefully evaluating whether a particular punishment is necessary (in addition to assessing whether it is proportionate) would, at long last, allow American jurists to make Eighth Amendment law internally consistent. Right now, in excessive force cases brought by prisoners, the Eighth Amendment imposes a standard that is less demanding than in the Fourth Amendment context, which governs the use of force in making an arrest.[218] The Fourth Amendment "excessive force" standard is an objective one[219] and seeks to determine whether a reasonable police officer, confronted with the same facts, would have believed that the level of force used was reasonable or necessary.[220] In *Los Angeles County, California v. Rettele*,[221] the U.S. Supreme Court put it this way:

> In executing a search warrant officers may take reasonable action to secure the premises and to ensure their own safety and the efficacy of the search. The test of reasonableness under the Fourth Amendment is an objective one. Unreasonable actions include the use of excessive force or restraints that cause unnecessary pain or are imposed for a prolonged and unnecessary period of time.[222]

On the other hand, the Eighth Amendment is only violated at present when excessive force is used with a malicious and sadistic intent to inflict injury.[223] Not only must inherently torturous punishments such as the death penalty be declared off limits by the courts, but a focus on the objective necessity for punishments or disciplinary actions within prisons would help to cull out needlessly severe punishments and behavior while furthering human rights and human dignity.

Prison guards, like police officers, must make split-second decisions that impact public safety. Accordingly, the decisions they make—as objectively gauged from the perspective of a reasonable police officer or prison guard—should not be viewed through the lens of hindsight. Instead, they should be judged from the perspective of what was known and understood at the time—and in the context of that moment. If evaluated through that lens, however, some punishments—the death penalty and the use of prolonged solitary confinement come readily to mind—utterly fail even that largely deferential test. With respect to the death penalty, there is clearly no necessity for executing someone. After all, at the very moment that the death row inmate is to be put to death, the inmate has likely already been residing on death row *for years, even decades*, so it cannot be plausibly argued that the execution is necessary. And unlike the situation where a police office or a prison guard is called upon to use lethal force to protect himself, herself, or others from death or bodily injury during a moment of crisis (e.g., a police officer being fired upon or a knife-wielding prisoner imminently threatening lives during a prison riot), an inmate tied down on a prison gurney poses no imminent threat in that situation.

The use of prolonged solitary confinement cannot be justified either. While isolating an inmate for a short period of time may be necessary in certain situations, to deprive an inmate of all human contact for a prolonged period of time is simply not necessary to prison security. In fact, the use of that practice probably only serves to make the individuals subjected to that treatment more volatile and more dangerous, whether to themselves or others. Inmates put in solitary confinement for prolonged periods of time, one encyclopedia observes, "are at risk of experiencing severe physical, psychological, and social consequences." The potential physical effects: sensitivity to light, lethargy, joint pain, and the exacerbation of preexisting medical conditions.

The psychological: anxiety, depression, paranoia, and psychosis. And the unintended social consequences: "The deprivation of human contact and social interactions during isolation may create deficiencies in a person's socialization and communication skills." As that encyclopedia entry adds of solitary confinement: "Anger and rage are common emotions in a person who has experienced long-term exposure to isolation. An overload of these emotions may be cause for volatile outbursts, enhanced criminal tendencies, and other negative behaviors that may affect one's adjustment during the reentry process." "These security risks posed to society by those who served time in solitary confinement," the entry concludes, "may be greater than prior to their incarceration due to inadequate coping skills and cognitive deficiencies brought on by long periods of time spent in isolation."[224]

Punishments can be justified on multiple grounds, from those based on a deterrence rationale, to those based or retributive principles, to those seeking to incapacitate a dangerous offender. The government has a duty to keep the public safe from criminals, so criminality—whether directed against people or property—must be punished, albeit with the parsimony and proportionality principles in mind. And in practical terms, that means that certain offenders, including dangerous and repeat offenders, should be incarcerated (as is fully appropriate under the particular circumstances of the case). But if a punishment is not necessary to deter violent crime or other criminal activity, or if a punishment crosses into the realm of revenge and becomes nothing more than the gratuitous infliction of pain or suffering, it is disproportionate, unnecessary, and excessive and should be classified as a "cruel and unusual punishment." Nonviolent offenders, clearly, should not be treated the same way as violent offenders, and prisons should be seen as a last resort for offenders. All too often, as shown by the statistics, American criminal justice systems have used draconian sentences and prisons to routinely incarcerate non-violent offenders,[225] often exacerbating—not solving—difficult social problems such as poverty, drug and alcohol abuse, and mental illness.[226]

The provisions of the U.S. Constitution's Eighth Amendment must be read together. In fact, case law interpreting the Excessive Bail Clause supports the idea that the Cruel and Unusual Punishments Clause should be read to bar any unnecessary punishments. It has been held, for example, that "excessive bail" is that which is "greater than necessary to achieve the purposes for which the bail is imposed."[227] The right to bail is not absolute; it may be refused where a heinous or serious crime is committed and the person poses a danger to society. It may also, for example, be refused "when the defendant presents a threat to the judicial process by intimidating witnesses."[228] But when an accused defendant is entitled to bail, a court—in setting a reasonable amount of bail and other conditions—"must fix them at the least restrictive levels" which ensure the defendant's attendance at all conferences and hearings and at the trial.[229] As one court recently declared: "Excessive bail refers to an amount more than necessary to ensure that a defendant appears for his hearings and trial, as opposed to his ability to pay."[230] Yet another court—one in Texas—put it this way: "Both the federal and state constitutions prohibit 'excessive' bail. Bail is considered excessive if it is 'set in an amount greater than is reasonably necessary to satisfy the government's legitimate interests.'"[231] Just as the amount of bail should not be more than necessary when it comes to governmental justifications for pre-trial detention, punishments should not be more than necessary to satisfy the legitimate rationales for punishment.

The requirement of a reasonable necessity for bail is actually a long-standing one. Back in 1951, in *Stack v. Boyle*,[232] the U.S. Supreme Court itself specifically ruled: "[T]he modern practice of requiring a bail bond or the deposit of a sum of money subject to forfeiture serves as additional assurance of the presence of an accused. Bail set at a figure higher than an amount reasonably calculated to fulfill this purpose is 'excessive' under the Eighth Amendment."[233] In a case of much more recent vintage, a U.S. District Court in New York, citing *Stack* and other cases, wrote: "[T]he relinquishment of constitutionally protected rights, such as the freedom of movement, on conditions that are more than necessary to satisfy legitimate governmental interests would constitute excessive bail in violation of the Eighth Amendment."[234] "Bail conditions are unconstitutionally excessive if they impose restraints that are more than necessary to achieve the government's interest," another federal district court in New York proclaimed in 2010, referring to the government's interests in "preventing the risk of flight and of danger to society or children."[235] Reading the Eighth Amendment's Cruel and Unusual Punishments Clause in line with the Excessive Bail Clause, with a continual focus on the *necessity* concept, is not only logical, it makes good sense as it supplies a unifying Eighth Amendment principle alongside human dignity, proportionality, and excessiveness.

American trial and appellate courts should thus conduct necessity reviews to ensure that criminal sentences are truly necessary to further legitimate penological objectives. On occasion, the U.S. Supreme Court itself has previously ordered that people be resentenced because sentences were deemed to be too harsh. For example, in *Miller v. Alabama* (2012), the Supreme Court held that mandatory sentences of life without the possibility of parole were unconstitutional for juvenile offenders. In the opinion written by Justice Elena Kagan, the Court took up the cases of two 14-year-old offenders who were convicted of murder and sentenced to life imprisonment without the possibility of parole. The Court explicitly held in *Miller* that "mandatory life without parole for those under the age of 18 at the time of their crimes violates the Eighth Amendment's prohibition on 'cruel and unusual punishments.'" While the Court did not consider whether the Eighth Amendment "requires a categorical bar on life without parole for juveniles, at least for those 14 and younger," the Court noted in dicta: "we think appropriate occasions for sentencing juveniles to this harshest possible penalty will be uncommon."

In a later case, *Montgomery v. Louisiana* (2016), the U.S. Supreme Court decided that *Miller* should be applied retroactively, resulting in the reexamination of the treatment of scores of previously sentenced juvenile offenders. "The 'foundation stone' for *Miller*'s analysis was this Court's line of precedent holding certain punishments disproportionate when applied to juveniles," Justice Anthony Kennedy wrote for the Court in *Montgomery*. In the course of his opinion, Justice Kennedy, writing for the Court, emphasized of the substantive nature of the *Miller* decision and that decision's implications: "Before *Miller*, every juvenile convicted of a homicide offense could be sentenced to life without parole. After *Miller*, it will be the rare juvenile offender who can receive that same sentence." "A State may remedy a *Miller* violation by permitting juvenile homicide offenders to be considered for parole, rather than by resentencing them," Justice Kennedy wrote for the majority.[236] "Since the U.S. Supreme Court decision in *Montgomery v. Louisiana*," Riya Saha Shah, a senior supervising attorney at the Juvenile Law Center notes, "most states have rolled back the harsh sentencing practices imposed on youth, offering both opportunities for resentencing and the opportunity for parole."[237]

The reexamination of an array of American criminal justice policies, just like the reexamination of juvenile sentences in the post-*Miller* era, is necessary to remake and recalibrate America's criminal justice system. Indeed, a 2014 report of the National Research Council, which studied that system, concluded that change is necessary—indeed, past due. In that report, "The Growth of Incarceration in the United States: Exploring Causes and Consequences," the report's authors laid out four guiding principles to frame the way forward: (1) proportionality of sentences to the seriousness of the crime committed; (2) parsimony, the idea that punishments should not exceed the minimum needed to achieve their purpose; (3) citizenship, the importance of every individual's status as a member of society; and (4) social justice, the notion that "as public institutions in a democracy, prisons should promote the general well-being of all members of society." As the summary of that report highlighted its importance in guiding future policy and research:

> *The Growth of Incarceration in the United States* recommends changes in sentencing policy, prison policy, and social policy to reduce the nation's reliance on incarceration. The report also identifies important research questions that must be answered to provide a firmer basis for policy. The study assesses the evidence and its implications for public policy to inform an extensive and thoughtful public debate about and reconsideration of policies.[238]

Above all else, greater knowledge of the innermost workings of America's criminal justice system is necessary so that citizens can become more engaged in working to reform the system. That criminal justice system needs to be brought into the twenty-first century, and facts—not assumptions or conjectures—should drive its overhaul as much as possible. More lawmakers and judges need to visit prisons so that they better understand the consequences of their decisions, and more criminal justice research should be done—and then peer-reviewed and disseminated—to evaluate the effectiveness of particular initiatives and approaches. An informed society is indispensible if reforms are to be successfully implemented. "A popular Government, without popular information, or the means of acquiring it," James Madison wrote to a friend in Kentucky, "is but a Prologue to a Farce or a Tragedy; or, perhaps both." "Knowledge will forever govern ignorance," Madison emphasized in 1822 of the importance of education in a self-governing society, adding that "a people who mean to be their own Governors, must arm themselves with the power which knowledge gives."[239] The clear-headed idea from the Enlightenment, Montesquieu's and Beccaria's necessity-for-punishment maxim, provides the underlying intellectual foundation for reform, but real and lasting reform only comes about through the intelligence and hard work of individuals working for the greater good.

Conclusion

The Baron de Montesquieu and the Marquis Beccaria, through *The Spirit of the Laws* and *On Crimes and Punishments*, made an indelible impression on Western civilization. In *Montesquieu and the Despotic Ideas of Europe: An Interpretation of* The Spirit of the Laws, political scientist Vickie Sullivan—in a section of her book titled "Hobbesian Fear and the Tranquility of Montesquieu's Conception of Political Liberty"—explains part of that transformation, writing of how Machiavelli's and Thomas Hobbes' conceptions of society gradually gave way to a more enlightened one. As Sullivan initially observes: "Nowhere are the opposing views of Montesquieu and Hobbes on government more evident than in their divergent treatments of fear. In order to combat the state of war among individuals, governments must be endowed with an immense and fearsome power, Montesquieu, like Hobbes, recognizes." Yet, as Sullivan further notes, Montesquieu "teaches emphatically that when the state wields that power domestically, as necessary as it is, it must be narrowly focused." "Even when states do the necessary work of prosecuting and punishing criminals," Sullivan stresses, "Montesquieu pleads for the gentlest possible punishments." Montesquieu's maxim—that any punishments not derived from necessity are tyrannical—beautifully articulates that core principle of human liberty. "Hobbes's portrait of the Leviathan with sword held aloft is very much akin to Montesquieu's depiction of despotism in *The Spirit of the Laws*," Sullivan concludes, noting the contrasting viewpoints.[1]

Like Montesquieu, the Italian thinker Cesare Beccaria favored liberty over tyranny and despotism, and he applied the same powerful idea—that unnecessary punishments are tyrannical—in *On Crimes and Punishments*. As Beccaria scholar and legal historian John Hostettler writes in *The Politics of Punishment*: "To Beccaria punishments were necessary both to prevent society plunging into chaos and to defend public liberty. But, equally, any punishment which was not absolutely necessary was tyrannical."[2] In *A Treatise on Political Economy*, the prominent French economist Jean-Baptiste Say (1767–1832) once wrote, summarizing Beccaria's impact on the body politic: "The efficacy of the characteristics of punishment has been placed beyond all doubt by Beccaria, in his tract, *Dei delitti e delle pene*."[3] For Beccaria, the *certainty* of punishment was more important than its *severity*. And in that tract, one that argued against torture and for a scale of crimes and a corresponding scale of punishments, Beccaria—building upon Montesquieu's ideas on proportionality and the foundational principle that unnecessary punishments are tyrannical—specifically concluded that an application of Montesquieu's maxim pointed to the lack of necessity for capital punishment. The death penalty, then a long-entrenched punishment regularly used by monarchs, he concluded, was not necessary. Instead, imprisoning someone for life was available—and more than adequate—to protect society from offenders.

The ideas of Montesquieu and Beccaria worked in tandem to shape penal reform around the world. Their ideas had an immediate impact, and those ideas were much talked about for decades to come, not only by America's founders but by scores of lawyers, political theorists, and other intellectuals. While Montesquieu's separation-of-powers principle promised to curtail—and did, in fact, curtail—abuses of power, the necessity-for-punishment maxim Montesquieu articulated (and that Beccaria repeated) reshaped the debate over punishment practices. At a great distance from its inception, William Archibald Dunning, in *A History of Political Theories*, takes note of both men's powerful ideas, writing specifically of "the influential essay of Cesare Beccaria," which focused specifically on the criminal law. As Dunning wrote in 1922 of the Enlightenment:

> Protests against the barbarous practices that were in vogue in both the trial and the punishment of accused persons were a feature of all the programmes of social amelioration at this period. Montesquieu had sketched the ends toward which improvement should be directed. Beccaria filled out the sketch with a force and clarity of presentation that won universal applause. The approval of his plea for rational methods in restraining crime naturally extended to the general principles on which the special plea was based. He became thus an influential promoter of the dogmas that the sole aim of legislation should be the greatest good of the greatest number; that laws (*leggi*) are but the conditions under which men, naturally independent, unite themselves into society; that individual self-interest is the supreme motive of human actions, both before and after entering into social bonds; and that laws and punishments are just, therefore, only so far as they are indispensable to the maintenance of society. From these distinctly Hobbesian principles Beccaria reaches conclusions in favor of a clear, compact and explicit code of criminal law, intelligible to all, shaped by pure reason and secure against the influence of passion or prejudice in its application.[4]

Both Montesquieu and Beccaria's ideas stimulated, guided and swayed the thinking of America's founders and framers. In a telling article, "Cesare Beccaria and the American Founding Fathers," two academics, Janet Funston and Richard Funston, wrote in the year of America's bicentennial about Cesare Beccaria's significant influence on America's founders. "The intellectual origins of the American Revolution and its ultimate realization, the Constitution of the United States," those scholars emphasized in 1976, "were numerous and diffuse." Along with Locke and Montesquieu, they noted, paying tribute to Enlightenment writers more broadly, "[t]he great Italian penological reformer Cesare Bonesana, Marchese di Beccaria, was also read and quoted by Adams, Madison, and Jefferson, and many of his ideas found their way into the Bill of Rights." "In this year of the American Bicentennial," they argued, taking note of Beccaria's substantial impact, including on shaping Jefferson's thought before he drafted the all-important Declaration of Independence, "it is appropriate that we accord Beccaria the recognition which he deserves." Rightfully noting that "Beccaria found in Montesquieu the source for many of his ideas," Janet and Richard Funston aptly observed: "[i]t is no exaggeration to say that Beccaria's famous essay, together with Voltaire's commentary, 'was known in America immediately after its first appearance in France.'"

Indeed, *On Crimes and Punishments* has been called "the small and valuable gift of the immortal Beccaria," with Thomas Jefferson transcribing numerous passages from it into his commonplace book. While Cesare Beccaria's ideas, along with Montesquieu's, laid the intellectual foundation for liberty and the field of criminology, those ideas were put to practical use not long after their first appearance. Jefferson, feeling the magnetic pull of Beccaria's ideas, drafted a lengthy bill to proportion crimes and punishments in Virginia, one James Madison pushed for the adoption of in his home state, though it narrowly failed to pass in the 1780s. Even before that heart-wrenching, single-vote defeat, one that, to both Jefferson and Madison's disappointment and chagrin, left the legacy of England's ruthless Bloody Code in place, Madison had included Beccaria's treatise is a list of books he recommended for the Library of Congress. As demonstrated by the historical record, one reflected by newspapers, periodicals, and speeches, many other early Americans, including penal reformers in Massachusetts, Pennsylvania, Virginia, and elsewhere, looked, as Jefferson and Madison had, to Beccaria's book for guidance.[5]

Cesare Beccaria died in Milan in 1794 while the French Revolution, inspired in part by Montesquieu's and Beccaria's ideas, was still playing out. Shortly after Beccaria's death, Beccaria's passing was publicly grieved in the pages of the *Philadelphia Gazette & Universal Daily Advertiser*. In a 1795 letter to "Mr. Brown," an anonymous letter writer, using the penname "PHILANTROPY," began the letter to the editor as follows:

> WHEN we hear of the death of great and good men, we cannot help lamenting the loss as the common loss of society. The impression of this sentiment was strong upon my mind, when I read an article in your Gazette of Friday last, which mentions the decease of the celebrated Marquis of Beccaria: and I am persuaded that thousands of my fellow-citizens, I may say, the citizens of all countries, who have been so fortunate as to peruse his inestimable Essay on Crimes and Punishments, will feel the same regret. Different nations have admired his theory of an amelioration of penal laws: but it appears that Pennsylvania alone has had sufficient virtue and independence to leave the long-beaten tract, and to attempt to introduce the practice of his mild system.

Taking a measure of Beccaria's importance to Pennsylvanians, as well as Beccaria's proper place in history and, in particular, to the reform of Pennsylvania's laws, "PHILANTROPY" emphasized that "[t]o the honor of human nature, a successful experiment has been made" in Pennsylvania. "[T]he severity of capital punishments," PHILANTROPY wrote, "has been so softened" that while the criminal "suffers the demand of justice for his offences, he benefits both himself and the society he has injured." The shift from executions to hard labor was clearly seen as a progressive step forward.

Early Americans had an affection bordering on reverence for *On Crimes and Punishments*, just as they greatly admired Montesquieu's *The Spirit of the Laws*. "Experiencing the beneficial effects of the measure, we can, with a well-grounded assurance,"

PHILANTROPY's letter to the editor continued, "look forward to a time when the unanimous voice of an enlightened community will explode those cruel, perhaps tyrannical modes of punishment which have so long disgraced the world, and which will always disfigure the page of history." As "PHILANTROPY" ended his 1795 letter, written in the year after Beccaria's death and specifically lauding *On Crimes and Punishments* and the penal reforms that it helped to inspire in Pennsylvania:

> Naturally, therefore, led to the sources of these invaluable blessings, we contemplate Beccaria with an affectionate regard. His heart and his head were devoted to the cause of humanity: by his great exertions he has contributed to lessen and prevent many of the principal evils of life: and his letter bequest to posterity, increasing in estimation, will enrol[l] his name among the benefactors of mankind, and endear his memory to the virtuous, benevolent, and social affections.[6]

In those days, it took time for news to travel across the Atlantic, so it is not surprising that Beccaria's death in Milan in 1794 did not become known in America until the following year. In the Friday, March 27, 1795, edition of *The Philadelphia Gazette & Universal Daily Advertiser*, Andrew Brown, its editor, had run a short item on the death in late November 1794 of "the celebrated Marquis Beccaria, the well-known author of the Work on Crimes and punishments."[7] Educated at Trinity College, Dublin, Andrew Brown (1744–1797) had come to America in 1773 as a British officer, but then resigned his commission and settled in Massachusetts. He fought on the side of American patriots at Lexington and Bunker Hill, and after the Revolutionary War moved to Philadelphia. He became the editor of *The Federal Gazette*, the first to report the debates of Congress, with the *Gazette* (which began issuing editions on October 1, 1788) said to be "the organ of the friends of the Constitution." The name of the paper was changed to the *Philadelphia Gazette* in 1783, with the newspaper's offices burning down on January 27, 1797, less than two years after the death notice of Cesare Beccaria appeared in print. Badly burned in the fire, Andrew Brown died nine days later.[8]

Because Montesquieu and Beccaria's books so shaped the American Revolution and its supporters' fight for liberty, the ideas and lives of the authors of those books were, naturally, of considerable public interest. And the parsimony principle, as first articulated by Montesquieu in the 1740s and then repeated by Beccaria in the 1760s, certainly left an indelible European and American legacy, with the importance of the necessity-for-punishment principle frequently noted by modern thinkers. As Beccaria's views were recently summarized by historian John Cyril Barton: "If, as Montesquieu stated in *The Spirit of Laws* and Beccaria reiterated in *On Crimes and Punishments*, any punishment that was unnecessary was 'tyrannical,' then the death penalty epitomized tyranny." It was a powerful idea, and one that, in effect, catalyzed the shift from the *Ancien Régime* to modernity. In *The Ideas that Made the Modern World*, Beccaria is called "[t]he greatest representative of the Italian Enlightenment," with his *Dei delitti e delle pene*—a work indebted, in part, to Montesquieu—said to have "exerted significant influence on criminal-law reform throughout western Europe" and to be reflected in "[t]he legislation of several American states."

The necessity-for-punishment principle profoundly influenced America's founders, including Dr. Benjamin Rush—a signer of the Declaration of Independence. For that reason alone, it should never be forgotten. While Dr. Rush concluded that death sentences and executions should be abandoned altogether, other founders urged that the death penalty's use be restricted or curtailed—a fact that, itself, represented a break from the world's barbarous past and England's rigid common law tradition—one that, at one time, had viewed death as the appropriate response to pretty much any criminal act. "No less a figure than Thomas Jefferson," historian Louis Masur stresses, "credited Beccaria with awakening the world to the unnecessary severity of capital punishment."[9] If not all of the founders agreed on the *application* of the principle, the principle itself became a rather uncontroversial one. Although originalists and living constitutionalists may not agree on everything when they examine the text of the U.S. Constitution's Eighth Amendment, the widely embraced maxim of Montesquieu and Beccaria is something that both sides of the originalism vs. living constitutionalism debate should be willing to embrace as they talk about the Eighth Amendment's history and purpose.

In the Enlightenment's wake, the concept of cruelty came to be understood by the American public to relate to barbarous or inhuman acts giving *unnecessary* pain or suffering to others, whether that pain or suffering be bodily pain or mental distress. For example, in the first edition of *An American Dictionary of the English Language* (1828), Noah Webster defined "CRUEL" as follows: (1) "Disposed to give pain to others, in body or mind; willing or pleased to torment, vex or afflict; inhuman; destitute of pity, compassion or kindness; fierce; ferocious; savage; barbarous, hardharded; *applied to persons or their dispositions....*"; and (2) "Inhuman; barbarous; savage; causing pain, grief or distress; exerted in tormenting, vexing or afflicting." That dictionary also defined "CRUELLY" as "In a cruel manner; with cruelty, inhumanly; barbarously" and as "Painfully; with severe pain, or torture; as, an instrument may cut the flesh most *cruelly*." The entry for "CRUELTY"—specifically discussing the necessity concept, and associating a lack of necessity with injustice—gave these two complementary definitions: (1) "Inhumanity; a savage or barbarous disposition or temper, which is gratified in giving unnecessary pain or distress to others; barbarity; *applied to persons*; as the *cruelty* of savages; the cruelty and envy of the people."; and (2) "Barbarous deed; any act of a human being which inflicts unnecessary pain; any act intended to torment, vex or afflict, or which actually torments or afflicts, without necessity; wrong; injustice; oppression."[10]

Just as enlightened societies began to embrace religious toleration and a separation of church and state, those societies—including in American jurisdictions—began to recognize the importance of separation of powers and the need for milder punishments. Ironically, the same Roman Catholic Church that *excommunicated* Cesare Beccaria in the 1760s for his rationalistic ideas, including against the death penalty, *embraced* those ideas centuries later. In his *Evangelium Vitae*, known as "The Gospel of Life," issued in 1995, Pope John Paul II articulated the modern-day teachings of the Catholic Church in religious terms, including through the commandant, "You shall not kill." But he also placed the death penalty in a broader context, noting that "there is a growing tendency, both in the Church and in civil society, to demand that it be applied in a very limited way or even that it be abolished completely." "Public authority," Pope John Paul II wrote, "must redress the violation of personal and social rights by imposing on the offender an adequate punishment for the crime, as a condition for the offender to regain the exercise of his or her freedom." "In this way," he observed, "authority also fulfills the purpose of defending public order and ensuring people's safety, while at the same time offering the offender an incentive and help to change his or her behaviour and be rehabilitated." Pope John Paul II then invoked a variation of the parsimony principle in these words: "It is clear that, for these purposes to be achieved, *the nature and extent of the punishment* must be carefully evaluated and decided upon, and ought not go to the extreme of executing the offender except in cases of absolute necessity: in other words, when it would not be possible otherwise to defend society. Today however, as a result of steady improvements in the organization of the penal system, such cases are very rare, if not practically non-existent." More recently, Pope Francis went even further, declaring that "the death penalty is inadmissible because it is an attack on the inviolability and dignity of the person." He vowed that the Roman Catholic Church would work "with determination for its abolition worldwide."[11]

The American Revolution was, from an historical standpoint, about more than battles between British soldiers and American patriots with guns and bayonets; it was also a battle of ideas. In 1776, American revolutionaries—at great risk to their lives and their often vast fortunes and estates—formed a republic, a very different form of government than the English monarchy then in place. In *Crime and Punishment in American History*, an eminent legal historian, Lawrence Friedman, emphasizes that "the Revolution boiled up out of a ferment of new ideas, including ideas about the rights of man, and, not incidentally, about criminal justice." As Friedman writes: "The American leaders were intelligent men who read books and discussed ideas. They were very much men of the Enlightenment." "The Revolution," he observes, "swept away what was left of royal theories of justice." Noting that "the king's name disappeared from legal forms and writs," Friedman stresses that America's founders "read and absorbed the work of Cesare Beccaria, on criminal justice; they knew about Jeremy Bentham, John Howard, and other English writers on crime and criminal justice." "The post-Revolutionary age," Friedman concludes, "was an age of reform in criminal justice."[12]

It was, in fact, in the Age of Montesquieu, and in the post-*On Crimes and Punishments* era, that America's founders adopted the U.S. Constitution's Eighth Amendment. That amendment specifically bars "excessive" bail and fines, language that implicitly recognizes the importance of proportionality and that suggests that bail determinations and impositions of fines be no more than necessary to accomplish their purposes.[13] The Eighth Amendment's additional prohibition against "cruel and unusual punishments," which must be read in the context of the Excessive Bail and Excessive Fines Clauses, can itself be broken down into three concepts: cruelty, unusualness, and punishment. As noted earlier, Samuel Johnson's *A Dictionary of the English Language* gave this concise definition of *cruel*, a word that means basically the same thing today: "Pleased with hurting others; inhuman; hard-hearted; barbarous."[14] That source also lists this definition of *unusual*, one that also still captures the essence of that word's widely accepted meaning in the modern world: "Not common; not frequent; rare."[15] Finishing out the Cruel and Unusual Punishments Clause's trifecta of concepts, Johnson's famed dictionary—the one so popular at the time—defined *punishment* as "[a]ny infliction imposed in vengeance of a crime."[16] "Punish" itself was defined as "[t]o chastise; to afflict with penalties" and "[t]o revenge a fault with pain or death."[17] The state's ultimate sanction, the death penalty, qualifies, of course, as a punishment, one that must be subjected to constitutional scrutiny just like any non-lethal corporal punishment.[18]

Regardless of whether a particular punishment was once authorized or imposed, every modern American lawmaker and jurist has a duty, in his or her own time, to decide whether that punishment must *now*—in this day and age—be adjudged cruel and unusual.[19] It has been clear for more than a century, in fact, that the U.S. Supreme Court has rejected an "originalist" interpretation of the U.S. Constitution. As legal scholar Andrew Novak writes: "The first successful challenge to a form of punishment and its appropriateness for an offense under the Eighth Amendment was in *Weems v. United States* in 1910, a constitutional attack on the punishment of cadena temporal (chaining with hard labor) for the crime of forgery of an official document in American-occupied Philippines."[20] "The Court's decision in *Weems*," Novak observes, "was the first to turn away from an 'originalist' view of the Eighth Amendment and find that even forms of punishment in existence at the time the constitution entered into force could be unconstitutional."[21] "The *Weems* case," two scholars, Matthew Pate and Laurie Gould, note, "serves as the basis for interpreting all Eighth Amendment claims."[22] Since 1910, when *Weems* was handed down, much has changed, of course, in American life and, for that matter, throughout the entire world.

Language matters, especially where the law is concerned. Statutes proscribe conduct, and constitutions guide judicial decision-making and proscribe what legislatures and executive-branch officials (and even judges) can do. In the distant past, various acts—from beatings and whippings to manslaughters and murders—were described as, or were said to have the characteristics of, "cruel"[23] or "cruel and unusual" acts.[24] For example, in *The Magistrate's Criminal Law*, one grade of manslaughter committed "in the heat of passion" (*i.e.*, second-degree manslaughter) was classified as one "[w]hen done in a cruel and unusual manner."[25] Likewise, in 1853, a Mississippi slave was found to have been whipped in a "cruel and unusual manner."[26] Many courts used the "cruel and unusual manner" phraseology even before the Civil War, so that language—indicating that certain acts can be found to be cruel and unusual because of their inherent characteristics—has been employed for a very long time.[27] If a beating or a whipping or a manslaughter or a murder can be carried out in a cruel and unusual manner and classified as such,[28] then surely a death sentence or an execution—one intentionally designed to dehumanize and kill, and thus to strip a person of all rights—might also earn the "cruel and unusual" moniker. Other severe punishments might also fall under the "cruel and unusual punishments" rubric.

The U.S. Supreme Court itself has long recognized that once-common punishments can fall out of favor—and in fact have throughout world and American history. For example, in *District of Columbia v. Clawans*,[29] the Supreme Court noted: "If we look to the standard which prevailed at the time of the adoption of the Constitution, we find that confinement for a period of ninety days or more was not an unusual punishment for petty offenses, tried without jury."[30] Yet, in noting that punishments such as whippings were no longer in use, the Court in that case went on to emphasize in 1937: "Laying aside those for which the punishment was of a type no longer commonly employed, such as whipping, confinement in stocks, and the like, and others, punished by commitment for an indefinite period, we know that there were petty offenses, triable summarily under English statutes, which carried possible sentences of imprisonment for periods from three to twelve months."[31] There, the Court thus suggested that a reading of the U.S. Constitution might evolve to bar whipping or the use of the stocks, just as the public's views about punishments, in general, will naturally evolve.[32] Although terms of imprisonment, clearly, remain a vital and necessary criminal sanction that judges can and do regularly employ, bodily punishments such as whipping are no longer seen as acceptable.

The law sometimes changes slowly, often painfully so. But if an examination of the law since America's founding reveals anything, it is that it does change—and often substantially.[33] Once lawful punishments have become unlawful, once usual punishments have become unusual, and practices such as slavery have been outlawed and given way to legal prohibitions against discrimination.[34] Certainly, the late eighteenth-century Eighth Amendment, which forbade "cruel and unusual punishments" and which was originally directed solely against *federal* action,[35] must now be read in conjunction with the nineteenth-century Fourteenth Amendment's Due Process and Equal Protection Clauses and considered in its twenty-first century context. "It is the genius of the common law to resist innovation," the American revolutionary Patrick Henry offered in 1788 at a speech to Virginia's ratifying convention for the U.S. Constitution.[36] Yet, the common law—like constitutional and statutory law—has materially changed through the centuries, with the Eighth Amendment now plainly applicable to the states as well as the federal government, as held by the U.S. Supreme Court since the 1960s. There is no reason to believe—nor should there be—that the law will ever stop evolving to adjust to modern times and contemporary circumstances.

Change is, and always has been, a natural part of life, and the law inevitably changes with the times (just as societal customs and mores change). Whereas British monarchs once more or less did as they pleased, and whereas the English prohibition against cruel and unusual punishments, once put in place as a constraining principle, was originally directed at reigning in the arbitrary discretion of courts, the American prohibitions against cruel and unusual punishments—whether set forth in the U.S. Constitution or its state-law equivalents—constrain the actions of all three branches of government.[37] The breadth and scope of the legal prohibitions against excessive bail, excessive fines, and cruel and unusual punishments, coupled with the use of the U.S. Supreme Court's long-standing "evolving standards of decency" test, means it is *inevitable* that American courts will, in time, put a halt to certain punishments or the way in which they are administered. "The 'evolving standards of decency' test," as two scholars have stressed, "sees the Eighth Amendment as 'progressive,' recognizing that contemporary society may reject a punishment that was accepted when the Framers wrote the Bill of Rights."[38]

That, in fact, has occurred already in multiple instances, with more changes sure to come. For instance, whereas the death penalty was once the mandatory punishment for a wide array of felonies, mandatory death sentences are now unconstitutional. Death sentences are now handed out in a highly discretionary (and, it must be said, highly inequitable) fashion.[39] While getting rid of mandatory death sentences for a wide array of crimes was a clear step forward, the only constant that runs through the history of the American death penalty, one rife with endless arbitrariness and caprice,[40] is that death sentences and executions have always been parsed or meted out in a torturous, discriminatory, and error-prone manner.[41] While torture, the aggravated form of cruelty, was once thought of as a practice that operated principally *on the body*, it is now clear from the modern-day definition of torture—one found in the Convention Against Torture and other similar legal instruments—that both physical *and* mental torture are strictly prohibited.[42] Consequently, even if a surefire way to carry out executions in a *physically* pain-free way could be found, they should still be categorized under the rubric of torture as it is impossible to eliminate the psychological torment associated with them.

The most severe sentences and punishment practices, of course, are the most likely to be problematic under the parsimony principle. Death sentences and executions—the record shows—invariably inflict particularly cruel and inhuman torment and, in a very unusual manner, what modern-day jurists should classify, at the very least, as *psychological* torture.[43] While torture and capital punishment were seen as completely separate concepts during the Enlightenment, Cesare Beccaria concluded centuries ago that capital punishment was unnecessary.[44] And in the wake of the publication of his book, *Dei delitti e delle pene*, many lawmakers and civic leaders reached the exact same conclusion, if not for all crimes (e.g., treason and murder were almost universally thought of as capital offenses in those days) then at least for some.[45] While Immanuel Kant called Beccaria's advocacy against the death penalty "sophistry and juristic trickery,"[46] the abolitionist movement nonetheless attracted many followers—again, if not for all crimes, then at least for certain offenses (*i.e.*, non-homicide crimes)—in early America.[47]

The writings of the French baron and the Italian marquis, including their respective observations on the necessity-for-punishment maxim, were destined to shape the field of criminology. In late-eighteenth century America, for example, William Bradford explicitly endeavored, using the limited statistical evidence he had available, to try to figure out if the death penalty was truly necessary, examining the data for a wide variety of crimes. His conclusion: the death penalty was generally *not* necessary, though he desired more evidence as regards whether the death penalty was necessary for the crime of premeditated murder.[48] That evidence, he recognized, would take time to gather, and sadly, William Bradford did not live long enough to gather it himself. After successively working for the reformation of Pennsylvania's criminal law in the early 1790s, and after briefly serving as the Attorney General of the United

States from 1794 to 1795, he died on August 23, 1795, in the year after Cesare Beccaria's own death.[49] But before his death, both Montesquieu and Beccaria had shaped his views—and, thus, his own legacy.

Modern studies have shown that the death penalty is not necessary, even for murderers, something numerous studies confirm and that is, in fact, borne out in practice by the abandonment of capital punishment by the vast majority of the world's countries. For instance, in August 2017, the Committees on Capital Punishment of the American Bar Association Section of Civil Rights and Social Justice and of the New York City Bar Association presented "Life After the Death Penalty: Implications for Retentionist States." That gathering, later summarized in a subsequent report, examined the aftermath and outcome of the death penalty's abolition in states such as Connecticut, Illinois, Maryland, New Mexico and New York. One of the speakers, Robert Dunham (the Executive Director of the Washington, D.C.-based Death Penalty Information Center), had, himself, specifically set out to find if there would be a "parade of horribles" following the death penalty's abolition. In particular, he wanted to know the answer to three questions: (1) If murder rates rose in states that, at some point in the twenty-first century, had abolished the death penalty? (2) Did killings of police officers go up in those states? (3) Was there an increase in the number of murders of police officers as a percentage of all homicides? "The short answer to these questions," Dunham reported, "was: 'No.' "[50]

In fact, after examining the evidence and analyzing all the data, the Death Penalty Information Center has found that American death penalty states, on average, have the *highest* murder rates.[51] After comparing murder rates in death penalty and non-death penalty states from 1990 to 2016, the Death Penalty Information Center found that *in every single year* the average murder rate was higher in death penalty states than in non-death penalty states. And the differences were not trivial. For instance, for the 23-year period from 1994 to 2016, the "Percent Difference in Murder Rate Between Death Penalty and Non-Death Penalty States" ranged from 17% to 46% higher in death penalty states. While many factors, including a state's demographics, can obviously affect crime rates, it is telling that *in no year from 1990 to 2016* did death penalty states collectively register a lower murder rate than in non-death penalty states.[52] In actuality, centuries of experience with the death penalty has shown that, if anything, capital punishment has only *brutalized* societies in which it has been put to use. In other words, not only is capital punishment *not necessary*, it is, at best, *brutalizing* and *counterproductive* to law enforcement and crime-fighting efforts.[53]

From Beccaria's time to modern times, many lawyers and non-lawyers alike have vehemently argued over the necessity of capital punishment.[54] For example, many decades ago, Edward Livingston—the prominent American politician and penal reformer—argued, in opposing capital punishment, that "in civilized society, in the usual course of events, we can never suppose it necessary" because "[i]mprisonment is an obvious and effectual alternative."[55] While some countries abolished the death penalty long ago, it is only in the past few decades that the abolitionist movement has galvanized, with abolitionist countries now outnumbering retentionist nations. In his book, *The Contradictions of American Capital Punishment*, scholar Franklin

Zimring thus wrote in 2003 that "[o]nly quite recently has the abolition of capital punishment become more than a trend in government policy." As Zimring explained in that book: "A stand against capital punishment is now an orthodoxy in Europe and most Commonwealth nations, a moral imperative believed necessary to the status of any civilized modern state, and this morality is exported to other nations with missionary vigor."[56] In short, what was once thought necessary (i.e., capital punishment) is now thought necessary to get rid of to ensure a civilized approach to law, to promoting human rights, and to the protection of human decency and human dignity.

Since Cesare Beccaria's *Dei delitti e delle pene* and William Bradford's *Enquiry How Far the Punishment of Death Is Necessary in Pennsylvania*, human societies have had more than two hundred years of experience with capital punishment. And the evidence, when objectively viewed, is now in: not only does the death penalty bear all the indicia and immutable characteristics of torture, but the death penalty—through all those centuries—has not been shown to be a more effective deterrent than the viable alternative of life imprisonment without the possibility of parole.[57] Because the death penalty takes life and deprives individuals of the very right to have rights,[58] the State should bear the heavy burden to show that the death penalty is necessary. Because the State, in light of all the accumulated evidence, cannot meet that high burden, the use of death sentences and executions should be declared unconstitutional as a violation of the U.S. Constitution's Eighth and Fourteenth Amendments. Cesare Beccaria's Enlightenment wisdom and assessment, that capital punishment was unnecessary,[59] has been confirmed by a host of modern-day thinkers, some of whom have seen the death penalty's administration up close. Retired U.S. Supreme Court Justice John Paul Stevens, speaking in May 2015 at the George Washington University Law School, himself observed of the punishment of death: "it's really not necessary because life imprisonment without parole protects the public at least as well as execution does and so the justification for the death penalty is diminished."[60]

Through the centuries, individuals have quarreled mightily over whether the use of executions is necessary in either wartime or peacetime.[61] But experience has shown that the death penalty is *not* necessary in either circumstance. Scores of nations on multiple continents no longer use capital punishment, and perhaps most telling of all, murder rates in death penalty-free Europe are lower than in the United States. A recent Global Study on Homicide, produced by a U.N. agency, shows that Western Europe, Southern Europe, and Northern Europe (sub-regions that make no use of the death penalty) have homicide rates that are considerably lower than in American death penalty states.[62] The evidence has thus borne out the Enlightenment claims of thinkers such as Beccaria and Bentham, both death penalty opponents. As Jeremy Bentham (1748–1832), the famous English philosopher and penal reformer, once presciently offered: "The more we examine the punishment of death, the more we shall be induced to adopt the opinion of Beccaria. This subject is so well discussed in his work that there is scarcely any necessity for further investigation." As Bentham concluded: "Sanguinary laws have a tendency to render men cruel, either by fear, by imitation, or by revenge. But laws dictated by mildness humanize the manners of a nation and the spirit of government."[63]

When it comes to American criminal justice reform, outlawing the death penalty is just one piece of the reform equation. In the Age of Mass Incarceration, when record numbers of people in the United States are locked up behind bars, much more must be done to safeguard life and liberty and to reign in unnecessary punishments and its adjunct, unnecessary torture and cruelty. In deciding what must be done, a look back at the Enlightenment yields the necessity-for-punishment principle, one that has been neglected for far too long by modern American lawmakers, prosecutors and jurists. When Enlightenment thinkers such as Montesquieu and Beccaria wrote about crimes and punishments, they wrote about *liberty* versus *tyranny* and they argued for *proportionality* between crimes and punishments, not merely for punishments that would not be *grossly disproportionate* to crimes.[64] Liberty, Enlightenment thinkers recognized, was dependent on imposing only necessary punishments, and any punishments that exceeded that threshold veered into the realm of tyranny. As historian Peter Gay writes in *The Enlightenment*: "[I]n a radical break with older conceptions and in wholehearted agreement with Montesquieu, Beccaria sees punishment not as a measure of vengeance but as a measure of prevention. 'It is better to prevent crimes than to punish them,' better to educate people and give them greater liberty than to seek conformity by repression." "The only proper test of a penalty," Gay explains, writing of Enlightenment thought, "is a pragmatic one: if it deters crime at minimum expense to all, it is justifiable—all else is tyranny."[65]

In the twenty-first century, the prerogative of American legislatures to set fines and punishments for offenses should generally be respected. After all, legislative bodies are duly elected by the people and legislatures are an excellent place for vigorous, public debate to occur—and for societal decision-making to take place. But at the same time, American lawmakers and executive-branch officials should always carefully consider—and take into account—the parsimony principle in making their judgments. That principle is critical to the protection of American liberty, the very thing that America's founders fought—and sometimes died—for. American courts—bound by law to interpret the U.S. Constitution and state constitutions, and themselves an important check on executive and legislative power—should also be willing to subject the fines and punishments imposed in actual cases to more searching scrutiny. Where fines or punishments are unnecessary to further a legitimate penal objective, or where impositions of bail are found to be unnecessary, independent and impartial courts are needed to protect the liberty interests of those who appear before the bar of justice. After all, the prohibition on "excessive" bail was, itself, designed to safeguard liberty, and punishments themselves should neither be "excessive" nor "cruel and unusual." Instead, judgments about bail, fines and punishments should be consistent with human rights principles, property rights, and human dignity, and they should not be authorized or imposed if they are truly unnecessary. Unnecessary government actions or punishments, simply put, infringe on liberty—the concept that lies at the very heart of America's representative democracy.

A renewed focus on the necessity-for-punishment maxim has broad implications. Societal punishments for *non-violent* offenses, for example, should be subjected to particular scrutiny,[66] as should especially *severe* punishments, such as prolonged solitary confinement and capital punishment, which the evidence has shown to be unnecessary and torturous in nature.[67] The use of prolonged solitary confinement in U.S. prisons has come under rigorous attack in recent years, both domestically and in the international community. For example, a U.N. Special Rapporteur who has addressed both capital punishment and prolonged solitary confinement in his work, has brought the issue—and the effects—of prolonged solitary confinement into greater public consciousness. "After Juan Méndez's 2011 report recognizing a 15-day limit on solitary confinement and encouraging the prohibition of solitary for youth and the mentally disabled," one writer, Cynthia Soohoo, emphasizes, American activists "issued reports documenting the extensive use of solitary confinement in the United States as a human rights issue." "In 2012," that writer observes, "the New York Civil Liberties Union (NYCLU) released *Boxed In*, which focused on the excessive use of solitary confinement in New York prisons." And in February 2015, Soohoo writes, "Méndez testified to a Congressional subcommittee on solitary confinement practices in the United States," and then, in March 2015, "submitted an expert report in litigation challenging the constitutionality of the use of prolonged solitary confinement in California's Pelican Bay State Prison where more than 400 prisoners were held in solitary confinement for more than a decade."[68]

Both lawmakers and jurists alike, as well as American prosecutors and the American people more broadly, need to embrace a new American Enlightenment when it comes to sentencing and the treatment of criminal suspects and offenders. Although dangerous offenders can and should be held without bail, the imposition of excessive bail for those entitled to bail can lead to unintended consequences, such as the loss of a job or housing (or, in certain cases, even false admissions of guilt). Excessive bail can, in fact, lead to an impoverished family's descent into bankruptcy, even homelessness. Criminalizing poverty, it must be said, is hardly the answer to fighting poverty. And punishments that are disproportionate to crimes—that, for example, send non-violent offenders to prison for lengthy, disproportionate periods of time—risk unnecessarily *institutionalizing* such offenders, putting them in prison environments for so long that they, whether by design or not, become long-term wards of the state. Prisons should be designed to rehabilitate offenders, and they should not endeavor to strip offenders of their humanity or to render them effectively incapable of ever being able to function properly in the real world again.

The long-term effects of prison on those who are confined in them is almost self-evident. And the younger the offender, perhaps the greater the long-term consequences. As the skills of people atrophy in prison, they are also publicly stigmatized by virtue of their incarceration, with their long-term prospects of employment thus greatly diminished. As the years go on as they sit in their cells, they become further removed from normal civilian life and the prison—not the outside world—becomes the norm. And as such offenders are daily exposed in prison to other offenders, they are more and more likely to encounter much worse, often violent offenders, and the chances that they will later emerge from prison as productive citizens only diminishes. Instead of reflexively resorting to prisons to address social problems such as poverty, drug and alcohol abuse, and mental illness, more objective, evidence-based assessments of the best way to prevent crime—and to deal with offenders—must be made. Prisons are necessary and they always will be, but reason and logic must not be shelved in the oftentimes highly charged emotional debate over crime and punishment. Prisons should be a last resort, not a first resort, to solving social ills.

In short, there is a need in this day and age—in this, the twenty-first century—for American citizens, policymakers, and judges to pay closer attention to the parsimony principle, the one first articulated in the Enlightenment as necessary to avoid tyrannous punishments. What is necessary, is necessary. If a punishment is needed to protect the public safety or to deter crime, it is worthy of imposition. But what is *unnecessary*—as Beccaria and Montesquieu proclaimed more than 250 years ago—is nothing less than tyrannical, an infringement on liberty that is unworthy of the great republic, the United States of America, founded in 1776 in Philadelphia. That city's iconic Liberty Bell, cast with the inscription "Proclaim LIBERTY Throughout all the Land unto all the Inhabitants Thereof," and then twice recast by two local founders, John Pass and John Stow, after the bell cracked when rung, personifies and represents—like few other pieces of Americana—the ideal of American liberty. And liberty, as America's founders would have readily agreed, is definitely worth fighting for and arguing over, even if modern-day Americans are seeking to preserve liberty in a much different context than George Washington—or Madison and Jefferson—experienced.

Throughout American history, soldiers and civilians have fought, strived, and died for liberty—and to protect our rights and freedoms for future generations. During the Revolutionary War, American patriots, hoisting up flags that read "Don't Tread on Me" or "Liberty," took up arms against the British Empire; during the Civil War, Union soldiers fought to end the scourge of slavery; and American soldiers are still deployed in far-flung places around the world in the defense of liberty.[69] The Stars and Stripes, the alternating red and white stripes with a blue field of thirteen stars "representing a new constellation," itself became, through a 1777 declaration of the Continental Congress, "the flag of the thirteen United States."[70] That flag, as well as the Liberty Bell and the present-day American flag, with its fifty stars that regularly flies above the U.S. Capitol and statehouses, all symbolize the liberty set in motion by America's founders. The Union was perfected, to a degree, by the passage of the U.S. Constitution's Reconstruction Amendments—the ones abolishing slavery and involuntary servitude, guaranteeing equal protection of the laws, and ensuring that minorities would have the right to vote. But it would take the women's suffrage and civil rights movements to ensure voting rights and to secure the passage of anti-discrimination laws, with the 1860s Reconstruction Amendments only setting the stage for the hard-fought social progress that followed in future decades.

Despite America's past and such important historical milestones, it is only through the concrete actions of *modern-day* Americans that powerful *symbols* of American liberty—and the laws themselves—can be translated *into liberty*. The state of the laws matters a great deal, as does the *administration* of those laws and the *interpretation* of those laws by the courts. With the U.S. Constitution as the overarching framework for the Rule of Law, it is only through a renewal of the Enlightenment maxim laid down by Montesquieu and Beccaria in the eighteenth century that Americans can, in truth, discard present-day tyrannical acts and practices and actualize their abstract conceptions of liberty. In 1831, a century before Francis Scott Key's "The Star-Spangled Banner" became the official national anthem of the United States, Samuel Francis Smith wrote "My Country, 'Tis of Thee," the song also popularly known as "America." When Smith wrote that song, he, like every American founder, had liberty on his mind, with the very first verse of his own patriot song beginning, "*My country, 'tis of thee, Sweet land of liberty, Of thee I sing.*"[71] If the liberty Americans so value and so valiantly fought for in the past, is to be preserved and realized, the Enlightenment origins of that liberty must never be forgotten, lest liberty—that watchword of the American Revolution—be substituted for tyranny.

Notes

Introduction

1. *E.g.*, Matthew Sharpe, "What of All the Others? On Recovering the Enlightenment," *in* Geoff Boucher & Henry Martyn Lloyd, eds., Rethinking the Enlightenment: Between History, Philosophy, and Politics 61 (2018):

[T]he Enlightenment, however one looks at it, was unquestionably a period of the highest cultural importance. In the words of the French philosopher, Michel Foucault, this period of European cultural history has largely determined "what we are, what we think, and what we do today." A brief list of the Enlightenment's legacies bears Foucault out. As Jonathan Israel reminds us, this legacy includes: the separation of powers; liberalism; natural rights; feminism; freedom of the press; the secularization of education; opposition to trial without charge; opposition to torture; opposition to capital punishment; and, freedom of religion, conscience, and toleration.

2. William Hague, William Wilberforce: The Life of the Great Anti-Slave Trade Campaigner 129 (2007) (describing Montesquieu's summation of the case against slavery, with Montesquieu writing in 1748: "Slavery in its proper sense is the establishment of a right which makes one man so much the owner of another man that he is the absolute master of his life and of his goods. It is not good by its nature; it is useful neither to the master nor to the slave: not to the slave, because he can do nothing from virtue; not to the master, because he contracts all sorts of bad habits from his slaves, because he imperceptibly grows accustomed to failing in all the moral virtues, because he grows proud, curt, harsh, angry, voluptuous, and cruel."); *see also* id. ("It was not long before other French thinkers, whose work would be fundamental to the upheavals of the subsequent Revolution, would go further, with Rousseau arguing in 1762 in *Le Contrat social* that men were born with the right to be free and equal, and that 'The words *slave* and *right* contradict each other, and are mutually exclusive.' ") (italics in original).

3. 4 Cathal J. Nolan, The Greenwood Encyclopedia of International Relations 1502 (2002) ("Most Scandinavian countries abolished serfdom in the late eighteenth century. In France, Belgium, and the Rhineland, liberation of the peasantry arrived with the *French Revolution*'s confirmation of the independence of peasant farmers, other than in the *Vendée* where recalcitrant *Catholic* peasants were slaughtered, in the name of liberty, from 1794.") (italics in original); *see also* 2A Philippe Aghion & Steven N. Durlauf, eds., Handbook of Economic Growth 482 (2014) ("When Prussian serfdom was abolished in 1807, for instance, the state legislated that each former serf was to be allocated a parcel of land and freed from forced labor services, but was also legally obliged to compensate his landlord for the loss of this land and labor by making a series of redemption payments over a period of decades.") (citations omitted).

4. Steven G. Koven, Responsible Governance: A Case Study Approach 158 (2008) ("Legalized torture came under attack with the rise of the Enlightenment. Many eighteenth-century authors, such as Montesquieu, Voltaire, and Beccaria, argued that torture was a relic of barbarism, superstition, and tyranny.").

5. Clive Emsley, Hard Men: The English and Violence since 1750, at 150 (2005) ("The penal system of eighteenth-century England is commonly referred to as 'the Bloody Code'. There were more than two hundred offences on the statute book that carried the death penalty.").

6. *See generally* J. Neville Figgis, The Theory of Divine Right of Kings (1896).

7. *Compare* Laksiri Fernando, Human Rights, Politics and States: Burma, Cambodia, Sri Lanka 43 (2002) ("The concept of natural rights originated in England in the seventeenth century and spread to North America and Europe. The term 'rights of man' or 'droits de l'homme' was most popular in France in the eighteenth century.") *and* Ellen Frankel Paul, Fred D. Miller, Jr. & Jeffrey Paul, eds., Natural Rights: Liberalism from Locke to Nozick vii (2005) ("In the early modern era, theories of natural rights were advanced by seminal thinkers, including Hugo Grotius, Thomas Hobbes, and Samuel Pufendorf. The most influential of these was the English philosopher John Locke, especially in his *Second Treatise of Government* published in the late seventeenth century. Locke contended that prior to the political state there had existed a state of nature, in which human beings possessed rights to 'life, liberty, and estate.'") *with* A. C. Kapur, Principles of Political Science 229 (1997):

The concept of Natural Rights originated in ancient Rome and came from the discovery that men of all races and countries living under Roman rule seemed to have some common rules of life, some objective standards of right and wrong given to them by the mere fact of their being men with human nature. This body of principles common to all men, the Romans called "Natural Law" and they based on it a considerable part of their legislation.

8. Robert Arp, ed., 1001 Ideas that Changed the Way We Think 442 (2013):

During the "pamphlet wars" of the 1790s (a series of exchanges between reformers and those seeking to resist the application of "French principles" to Britain), two women, Olympe de Gouges (1748–93) in France, and Mary Wollstonecraft (1759–97) in England, published challenges to the view that women were second-class citizens.

9. Jean-Jacques Rousseau, The Social Contract and Discourses xvi (1920).

10. Frederick C. Giffin, ed., Woman as Revolutionary 48 (1973); Joan McMahon Flatt, Powerful Political Women: Stirring Biographies of Some of History's Most Powerful Women 121 (2012).

11. Julia Simon, Beyond Contractual Morality: Ethics, Law, and Literature in Eighteenth-Century France 119 (2000):

In his *Traité sur la tolérance*, Voltaire argues in favor of religious tolerance in the wake of the execution of Jean Calas in Toulouse for the alleged murder of his son, Marc-Antoine. In one of the most infamous cases of religious persecution in France during the eighteenth century, a Protestant father was convicted of murder and condemned to die on the wheel for the hanging of his own son, who supposedly intended to convert to Catholicism in order to set up a legal practice.

12. U.S. Const., preamble.

13. John Algeo & Carmen Acevedo Butcher, The Origins and Development of the English Language 283 (7th ed. 2013).

14. Riitta Jallinoja, Families, Status and Dynasties: 1600–2000, at 93 (2017).

15. Systematic Catalogue of the Public Library of the City of Milwaukee with Alphabetical Author, Title and Subject Indexes vi (1885).

16. U.S. Const., Art. 1, sec. 9, cl. 8; *see also* Richard Grant White, "Nobility and Gentry," 44 The Atlantic Monthly 370, 370–80 (Sept. 1879) (describing noble titles in English society).

17. Declaration of Independence (July 4, 1776).

18. U.S. Const., amend. VIII.

19. *Compare* John D. Bessler, Cruel and Unusual: The American Death Penalty and the Founders' Eighth Amendment (2012) (arguing that the Cruel and Unusual Punishments Clause should be read to prohibit capital punishment) *with* David A. J. Richards, "Constitutional Interpretation, History, and the Death Penalty," *in* Hugo Adam Bedau, ed., The Death Penalty in America: Current Controversies 214 (1997) ("The argument of Raoul Berger's book, *Death Penalties: The Supreme Court's Obstacle Course*, may be easily summarized: the persons who drafted and approved the eighth and fourteenth amendments to the United States Constitution did not intend the former to limit, let alone invalidate, the use of the death penalty by the federal or state governments."); *see also* 1 Joshua Dressler & Alan C. Michaels, Understanding Criminal Procedure § 3.04 n.33 (5th ed. 2010) ("[T]wo Eighth Amendment provisions—the Excessive Fines Clause and the Excessive Bail Clause—have been the subject of dicta, rather than holdings. As to 'excessive fines,' the Court has contradicted its own dicta.").

20. Beau Breslin, John J. P. Howley & Molly Appel, "Evolutionary History: The Changing Purposes for Capital Punishment," *in* Austin Sarat, ed., Is the Death Penalty Dying? 4 (2008) (noting Justice Scalia's view that the death penalty's use "is explicitly contemplated in the Constitution"); *see also* David A. Strauss, The Living Constitution 11 (2010) ("According to originalists..., it follows that the death penalty cannot ever be 'cruel and unusual.' If capital punishment was not understood to violate the Eighth Amendment in 1791, it cannot violate the Eighth Amendment today or at any time in the future.").

21. *E.g.*, Christopher E. Smith, The Supreme Court and the Development of Law: Through the Prism of Prisoners' Rights 62–63 (2016) (citations omitted):

> The divergence between originalist and flexible interpretations is illuminated well by the disagreements over the meaning of the Eighth Amendment's Cruel and Unusual Punishments Clause. Many originalists regard governmental actions in punishing convicted offenders as violating the Eighth Amendment only when a particular punishment would have been impermissible at the time of the Eighth Amendment's ratification in 1791. Those punishments barred in 1791 are regarded as the ones that the framers and ratifiers of the Eighth Amendment viewed as impermissible. This approach could bar governments from burning offenders at the stake as a form of punishment, but it would not provide protections against inhumane conditions of confinement in prisons because such institutions did not exist as places of long-term incarceration prior to the nineteenth century.
>
> By contrast, Chief Justice Warren's seminal majority opinion in *Trop v. Dulles* (1958) articulated an explicitly flexible text for violations of the Cruel and Unusual Punishments Clause.... In Warren's words, the Clause "must draw its meaning from the evolving standards of decency that mark the progress of a maturing society." Moreover, Warren described the "basic concept" of the Eighth Amendment as "the dignity of man." Clearly, this formulation invites judges to examine punishment contexts and determine according to their own judgments and values whether the punishment conflicts with contemporary societal standards for "decency" and "the dignity of man." Moreover, Warren's statement indicated an open recognition that Eighth Amendment standards for permissible punishments change over time as society changes so that punishments that were acceptable in one era may no longer be acceptable in another era.

22. John Bessler, "Introduction," *in* Stephen Breyer, Against the Death Penalty 16 (John D. Bessler, ed., 2016).

23. Id. at 16–17.

24. Bessler, Cruel and Unusual, *supra* note 19, at 333.

25. Breyer, *supra* note 22, at 17.

26. Christian Jarrett, "How Prison Changes People," BBC, May 1, 2018, http://www.bbc.com/future/story/20180430-the-unexpected-ways-prison-time-changes-people.

27. *See generally* Rob Warden & Daniel Lennard, *Death in America Under Color of Law: Our Long, Inglorious Experience with Capital Punishment*, 13 Nw. J.L. & Soc. Pol'y 194 (2018); Michael L. Radelet, Hugo Adam Bedau & Constance E. Putnam, In Spite of Innocence: Erroneous Convictions in Capital Cases (1992).

28. Jean Casella, James Ridgeway & Sarah Shourd, eds., Hell Is a Very Small Place: Voices from Solitary Confinement 2 (2016).

29. Jennifer McNulty, "Judge Relies Heavily on Haney's Testimony in Case Banning Solitary Confinement," UC Santa Cruz, Jan. 18, 2018, https://news.ucsc.edu/2018/01/haney-canada.html.

30. "Congress Holds First-Ever Hearing on Solitary Confinement," National Juvenile Justice Network, June 28, 2012, http://www.njjn.org/article/congress-holds-first-ever-hearing-on-solitary-confinement.

31. Hilde Wermink, Paul Nieuwbeerta, Anke A. T. Ramakers, Jan W. de Keijser & Anja J. E. Dirkzwager, *Short-Term Effects of Imprisonment Length on Recidivism in the Netherlands*, Crime & Delinquency 1, 23 (2017) ("Our findings suggest that length of imprisonment does not have a significant effect on recidivism in the first 6 months after release, and that this conclusion holds across various measures and types of recorded recidivism, that is, reoffending, reconviction, and reincarceration."), *available at* https://doi.org/10.1177/0011128716687290.

32. "Trends in U.S. Corrections," The Sentencing Project, https://sentencingproject.org/wp-content/uploads/2016/01/Trends-in-US-Corrections.pdf (updated June 2017), p. 3.

33. "Abolitionist and Retentionist Countries (as of March 2018)," Amnesty International, Mar. 5, 2018, https://www.amnesty.org/en/documents/act50/6665/2017/en/ ("More than two-thirds of the countries in the world have now abolished the death penalty in law or practice.").

34. Protocol No. 6 to the Convention for the Protection of Human Rights and Fundamental Freedoms Concerning the Abolition of the Death Penalty, Apr. 28, 1983, 28.IV.1983 (forbidding the death penalty's use in peacetime); Protocol No. 13 to the Convention for the Protection of Human Rights and Fundamental Freedoms, Concerning the Abolition of the Death Penalty in All Circumstances, May 3, 2002, 3.V.2002 (extending the prohibition on the death penalty's use to wartime). For a recent story about executions in Belarus, see Hugo Bachega, "The Secret Executions in Europe's 'Last Dictatorship'," BBC News, May 15, 2018, http://www.bbc.com/news/world-europe-43799280.

35. Convention Against Torture and Other Cruel, Inhuman or Degrading Treatment or Punishment (adopted and opened for signature, ratification and accession by General Assembly resolution 39/46 of 10 December 1984; entry into force 26 June 1986, in accordance with article 27(1)), http://www.ohchr.org/EN/ProfessionalInterest/Pages/CAT.aspx.

36. 2 The Statutes: William & Mary to 10 George III. A.D. 1688—1770, at 11 (rev. ed. 1871).

37. *The Bill of Rights 1689*, The Glorious Revolution, https://www.parliament.uk/about/living-heritage/evolutionofparliament/parliamentaryauthority/revolution/collections1/collections-glorious-revolution/billofrights/; 2 The Statutes: William & Mary to 10 George III. A.D. 1688—1770, at 9 (rev. ed. 1871).

38. John F. Stinneford, *The Original Meaning of "Cruel,"* 105 Geo. L.J. 441 (2016); Joshua L. Shapiro, *And Unusual: Examining the Forgotten Prong of the Eighth Amendment*, 38 U. Mem. L. Rev. 465 (2008); *see also* Meghan J. Ryan, *Does the Eighth Amendment Punishments Clause Prohibit Only Punishments That Are Both Cruel and Unusual?*, 87 Wash. U. L. Rev. 567, 569–70 (2010) ("Although the prohibition on cruel and unusual punishments has been the focus of many a scholarly article, neither the Court nor legal scholars have carefully examined how the cruelty and unusualness components of the Clause relate to each other."); id. at 599 ("[M]ost scholars ... have neglected the role of unusualness in their interpretations and applications of the Eighth Amendment, suggesting that cruelty, alone, is the only relevant factor."); id. at 610 ("'[C]ruel and unusual' cannot be interpreted as simply 'cruel,' because by completely ignoring 'and unusual,' such an interpretation would violate a central principle of construction that every term must be given meaning."). Scholar Meghan Ryan—one of the scholars to focus on the *unusual* terminology—has observed that "[a]lthough 'cruel' and 'unusual' have historically been treated as distinct terms, they are certainly related." Id. at 603.

39. The U.S. Supreme Court itself has only infrequently referred to the notion of "usual punishments." In its 1910 decision in *Weems*, the U.S. Supreme Court, in discussing its prior case of *Wilkerson v. Utah*, 99 U.S. 130 (1878), noted that death was a "usual punishment for murder." *Weems*, 217 U.S. at 369.

40. Evan J. Mandery A Wild Justice: The Death and Resurrection of Capital Punishment in America 180 (2013).

41. Trop v. Dulles, 356 U.S. 86, 101 (1958).

42. John D. Bessler, "The American Death Penalty: A Short (But Long) History," *in* Robert M. Bohm & Gavin Lee, eds., Routledge Handbook on Capital Punishment (2017), ch. 1. The Supreme Court's approach to counting states—and then counting states equally, regardless of population, as part of that nose-counting exercise—has drawn criticism. "Citizens, not states, should count equally in interpreting both the Eighth Amendment word 'unusual' and modern America's lived Constitution more generally," Yale law professor Akhil Amar has written. Akhil Reed Amar, America's Unwritten Constitution: The Precedents and Principles We Live By (2012) (discussing the interpretation of "unusual" in the Eighth Amendment).

43. Bessler, Cruel and Unusual, *supra* note 19, at 17 (discussing *Roper v. Simmons*, 543 U.S. 551 (2005), *overruling* Stanford v. Kentucky, 492 U.S. 361 (1989)).

44. *See, e.g.*, Peterson v. Minidoka Cty. Sch. Dist. No. 331, 118 F.3d 1351, 1359 (9th Cir. 1997) ("The usual rule of interpretation of contracts is to read provisions so that they harmonize with each other, not contradict each other. That task of construction is for the court."). Of course, interpreting a constitution—one that applies to an entire society, one composed of millions of people—is a much more complicated and weighty endeavor than interpreting a private contract between two parties.

Cf. Walter F. Murphy, *Constitutional Interpretation: The Art of the Historian, Magician, or Statesman*, 87 YALE L.J. 1752, 1770 (1978) (reviewing RAOUL BERGER, GOVERNMENT BY JUDICIARY: THE TRANSFORMATION OF THE FOURTEENTH AMENDMENT (1977)) ("Because of the broad and basic political character of a constitution, it is not amenable to the rules of interpretation that apply to private contracts or to statutes. Because of the complex nature of the interlocking arrangements contained in a constitution, an interpreter must look at it as a whole, examine its structure, as Charles Black would say.").

45. G. EDWARD DESEVE, THE PRESIDENTIAL APPOINTEE'S HANDBOOK 129 (2d ed. 2017) ("The men who wrote and signed [the U.S. Constitution] at the 1787 Constitutional Convention—lawyers, merchants, farmers—were students of the Renaissance, the Reformation, and the Enlightenment who learned about the social compact from John Locke and Jean-Jacques Rousseau and wove those principles into the American experiment."); *compare* LOUIS HENKIN, THE AGE OF RIGHTS 93 (1990):

There is a different set of difficulties with treating the United States Constitution as our contemporary social compact. For the Constitution was born without principal ingredients of a social compact, and age has not cured and has even aggravated those defects. A direct and immediate descendant of the Articles of Confederation, "a more perfect union" of the states, the Constitution was declared to be ordained by "We the people" as had been the constitutions of the several states, but the compact implied in that preambular phrase was largely rhetorical and symbolic. The small federal superstructure which the framers projected was not, and was not expected to become, a significant government with significant relations to the people, implicating their rights. The real social compact remained the state constitution, the polity that the people had contracted for was the state polity, the government instituted to secure their rights was the state government; the United States Constitution was only a small "codicil" to state social compacts.

46. The debate over how the U.S. Constitution should be interpreted has generated fierce debate. It was ratified in the eighteenth century and, though amended from time to time, including after the Civil War and in the Progressive Era, it governs twenty-first century citizens—people with very diverse views who were not, themselves, even born either when the original Constitution or, for example, its Reconstruction Amendments, were adopted and ratified. *E.g.*, Christopher J. Peters, *What Lies Beneath: Interpretive Methodology, Constitutional Authority, and the Case of Originalism*, 2013 BYU. L. REV. 1251, 1255 (2014):

We have managed to squeak by for more than two hundred years without a consensus approach to constitutional interpretation. Perhaps our interpretive disagreement even deserves some credit for this: no single approach dominates, so everyone's preferred approach is always in play. Still, it is profoundly strange that we agree so broadly that the Constitution is the supreme law of the land but diverge so widely on how to determine just what that law requires of us.

47. *See generally* RONALD DWORKIN, LIFE'S DOMINION: AN ARGUMENT ABOUT ABORTION, EUTHANASIA, AND INDIVIDUAL FREEDOM (1994).

48. *See generally* JACQUELINE R. KANOVITZ, CONSTITUTIONAL LAW FOR CRIMINAL JUSTICE (14th ed. 2015).

49. *E.g.*, Stephen Macedo, "The Rule of Law, Justice, and the Politics of Moderation," *in* IAN SHAPIRO, ED., THE RULE OF LAW 158 (1994) ("Many debates over the proper nature of constitutional interpretation owe something to the tensions ... between the rule of law and equity: questions about the legitimate grounds and norms of interpretation, questions of constraint and discretion, and questions about the distribution of authority among institutions (founders, legislatures, executives, judges, etc.) and across time."); DWORKIN, *supra* note 47, at 145 ("The Constitution insists that our judges do their best collectively to construct, reinspect, and revise, generation by generation, the skeleton of freedom and equality of concern that its great clauses, in their majestic abstraction, command.").

50. MITCHEL P. ROTH, AN EYE FOR AN EYE: A GLOBAL HISTORY OF CRIME AND PUNISHMENT 77 (2014) ("The term 'Bloody Code' has been used to refer to the English system of criminal law that roughly corresponded with the years 1688–1815, when literally hundreds of felonies carrying the death penalty were added to the criminal statutes.").

51. U.S. CONST. amends. V & XIV.

52. U.S. CONST. amend. XIV.

53. *See generally* JOHN D. BESSLER, THE BIRTH OF AMERICAN LAW: AN ITALIAN PHILOSOPHER AND

the American Revolution (2014) (describing the substantial influence of the Enlightenment—and, in particular, the ideas of the Italian philosopher Cesare Beccaria—on America's founders and framers).

54. Anne M. Cohler, Basia C. Miller & Harold S. Stone, eds. & trans., Montesquieu: *The Spirit of the Laws* xiii (2013).

55. Id. at 316; *see also* John Cyril Barton, Literary Executions: Capital Punishment and American Culture, 1820–1925, at 280 n.18 (2014):

Montesquieu takes up the general question of sovereign authority in relation to civil and criminal laws in volume 1, book 6 of *The Spirit of Laws* (1748; English ed., 1750) He writes specifically about tyranny in book 19, in the course of which he coins the influential phrase: "All punishment which is not derived from necessity is tyrannical." See Baron de Montesquieu, *The Spirit of Laws* (New York: Prometheus Books, 2002), 299.

56. Cohler, Miller & Stone, Montesquieu, *supra* note 54, at 308.

57. Id. at 315.

58. Id. at 309.

59. Id. at 154–57.

60. David J. Bederman, The Classical Foundations of the American Constitution: Prevailing Wisdom 268 n.221 (2008); Kuo-Hsing Hsieh, The Exclusionary Rule of Evidence: Comparative Analysis and Proposals for Reform 84–85 (2016); Jonathan Israel, "The Radical Enlightenment's Critique of the American Revolution," *in* Dustin Gish & Daniel Klinghard, eds., Resistance to Tyrants, Obedience to God: Reason, Religion, and Republicanism at the American Founding 43 (2013).

61. Sean Gorman, "Goodlatte Says U.S. Has the Oldest Working National Constitution," Politifact Virginia, Sept. 22, 2014, http://www.politifact.com/virginia/statements/2014/sep/22/bob-goodlatte/goodlatte-says-us-has-oldest-working-national-cons/.

62. *The Federalist* Number 47, [30 January] 1788," *Founders Online,* National Archives, last modified November 26, 2017, http://founders.archives.gov/documents/Madison/01-10-02-0266. [Original source: *The Papers of James Madison*, vol. 10, *27 May 1787–3 March 1788*, ed. Robert A. Rutland, Charles F. Hobson, William M. E. Rachal, and Frederika J. Teute. Chicago: The University of Chicago Press, 1977, pp. 448–454.] Montesquieu, an opponent of tyranny, himself warned of "How dangerous it is in republics to punish excessively the crime of high treason." "One cannot inflict great [*grandes*] punishments, and consequently, make great changes," Montesquieu wrote, "without putting a great power into the hands of a few citizens." "On the pretext of avenging the republic," Montesquieu asserted, "one would establish the tyranny [*la tyrannie*] of the avengers." Vickie B. Sullivan, Montesquieu and the Despotic Ideas of Europe: An Interpretation of *The Spirit of the Laws* 46–47 (2017); *see also* id. at 61 ("Even when states do the necessary work of prosecuting and punishing criminals, Montesquieu pleads for the gentlest possible punishments.").

63. Christopher Lynch & Jonathan Marks, eds., Principle and Prudence in Western Political Thought 151 (2016).

64. Melvin Richter, The Political Theory of Montesquieu 3 (1977).

65. Henry P. Tappan, A Treatise on the Will 577–88 (1857).

66. Aaron Thomas, ed., Cesare Beccaria, *On Crimes and Punishments* and Other Writings xlv (Aaron Thomas & Jeremy Parzen, trans., 2008). Cesare Beccaria is a foundational figure in the history of the criminal law. As one source notes of Cesare Beccaria's *On Crimes and Punishments*, that book "marked the beginning of modern criminology, and it led to more humane standards in European civilization." Steven C. Hause & William Maltby, Western Civilization: A History of European Society 543 (2004).

67. 1 John Adams, A Defence of the Constitutions of Government of the United States of America 120, 124, 131–32, 153–55, 157, 182, 185, 252, 325 (3d ed. 1797).

68. Thomas, Beccaria, *On Crimes and Punishments* and Other Writings, *supra* note 66, at 11.

69. Id.

70. Bessler, Cruel and Unusual, *supra* note 19, at 31–37, 39, 42, 56, 157, 291.

71. 2 James Paterson, Commentaries on the Liberty of the Subject and the Laws of Eng-

LAND RELATING TO THE SECURITY OF THE PERSON 310–11 (1877).

72. WILLIAM M. FOWLER JR., EMPIRES AT WAR: THE FRENCH AND INDIAN WAR AND THE STRUGGLE FOR NORTH AMERICA, 1754–1763, at xxi–xxv (2005); HERBERT J. REDMAN, FREDERICK THE GREAT AND THE SEVEN YEARS' WAR, 1756–1763, at 1 (2015); JEREMY BLACK, GEORGE III: AMERICA'S LAST KING 43 (2006); JONATHAN MERCANTINI, ED., THE STAMP ACT OF 1765 (2017); FREDERIC KIDDER, HISTORY OF THE BOSTON MASSACRE, MARCH 5, 1770; CONSISTING OF THE NARRATIVE OF THE TOWN, THE TRIAL OF THE SOLDIERS, AND A HISTORICAL INTRODUCTION, CONTAINING UNPUBLISHED DOCUMENTS OF JOHN ADAMS, AND EXPLANATORY NOTES (1870); JIM LAMPOS & MICHAELLE PEARSON, REVOLUTION IN THE LYMES: FROM THE NEW LIGHTS TO THE SONS OF LIBERTY 69 (2016); 1 STEVEN L. DANVER, ED., REVOLTS, PROTESTS, DEMONSTRATIONS, AND REBELLIONS IN AMERICAN HISTORY: AN ENCYCLOPEDIA 202 (2011); WESLEY S. GRISWOLD, THE BOSTON TEA PARTY: 16 DECEMBER 1773, THE NIGHT THE REVOLUTION BEGAN (1973); KEITH L. DOUGHERTY, COLLECTIVE ACTION UNDER THE ARTICLES OF CONFEDERATION 17 (2001); PAULINE MAIER, RATIFICATION: THE PEOPLE DEBATE THE CONSTITUTION, 1787–1788 (2011); PETER MCPHEE, THE FRENCH REVOLUTION, 1789–1799 (2002); T. G. STEWARD, THE HAITIAN REVOLUTION, 1791 TO 1804: OR SIDE LIGHTS ON THE FRENCH REVOLUTION (2d ed. 1914); 17 NEW YORK STATE HISTORICAL ASSOCIATION, PROCEEDINGS OF THE NEW YORK STATE HISTORICAL ASSOCIATION: THE NINETEENTH ANNUAL MEETING, WITH CONSTITUTION, BY-LAWS AND LIST OF MEMBERS 54 (1919); "Editorial Note," *Founders Online*, National Archives, last modified February 1, 2018, http://founders.archives.gov/documents/Adams/05-03-02-0001-0001. [Original source: *The Adams Papers*, Legal Papers of John Adams, vol. 3, *Cases 63 and 64: The Boston Massacre Trials*, ed. L. Kinvin Wroth and Hiller B. Zobel. Cambridge, MA: Harvard University Press, 1965, pp. 1–43.]; "Adams' Argument for the Defense: 3–4 December 1770," *Founders Online*, National Archives, last modified February 1, 2018, http://founders.archives.gov/documents/Adams/05-03-02-0001-0004-0016. [Original source: *The Adams Papers*, Legal Papers of John Adams, vol. 3, *Cases 63 and 64: The Boston Massacre Trials*, ed. L. Kinvin Wroth and Hiller B. Zobel. Cambridge, MA: Harvard University Press, 1965, pp. 242–270.]; *see also* JACQUELINE R. KANOVITZ, CONSTITUTIONAL LAW 7 (13th ed. 2012) ("On September 13, 1788, the Continental Congress passed a resolution putting the new Constitution into effect.").

73. 1 JAMES PATERSON, COMMENTARIES ON THE LIBERTY OF THE SUBJECT AND THE LAWS OF ENGLAND RELATING TO THE SECURITY OF THE PERSON 72–73, 187 n.1 (1877).

74. JEN MANION, LIBERTY'S PRISONERS: CARCERAL CULTURE IN EARLY AMERICA 48 (2015).

75. G. DE BEAUMONT & A. DE TOQUEVILLE, ON THE PENITENTIARY SYSTEM IN THE UNITED STATES, AND ITS APPLICATION IN FRANCE; WITH AN APPENDIX ON PENAL COLONIES, AND ALSO, STATISTICAL NOTES (Francis Lieber, trans. 1833). The translator of this work, Francis Lieber, himself takes notice of Beccaria's influence. Id. at xxxiv.

76. Cesare Beccaria's book, original published in Italian, was quickly translated into English. MANION, *supra* note 70, at 215–16 n.55:

Beccaria's work was first published in 1764 in Italian; early English editions include Cesare Marchese di Beccaria, *Essay on Crimes and Punishments* (London, 1767); *An Essay on Crimes and Punishments, Translated From the Italian; With a Commentary, Attributed to Mons. De Voltaire. Translated from the French* (Charlestown, 1777); *An Essay on Crimes and Punishments. Written by the Marquis Beccaria; of Milan. With a Commentary Attributed to Monsieur de Voltaire* (Philadelphia, 1778); *An Essay on Crimes and Punishments. By the Marquis Beccaria, of Milan. With a Commentary by M De Voltaire* (Philadelphia, 1793).

77. THOMAS, BECCARIA, *ON CRIMES AND PUNISHMENTS* AND OTHER WRITINGS, *supra* note 66, at 52. This quote was frequently reprinted by others. *E.g.*, 2 THE PUNISHMENT OF DEATH: A SELECTION OF ARTICLES FROM *The Morning Herald*, WITH NOTES 243 (1837).

78. THOMAS, BECCARIA, *ON CRIMES AND PUNISHMENTS* AND OTHER WRITINGS, *supra* note 66, at 86.

79. JOHN HOSTETTLER, CESARE BECCARIA: THE GENIUS OF 'ON CRIMES AND PUNISHMENTS' 59–60 (2011):

It is interesting to remember that in 1790 Beccaria sat on a commission appointed to recommend reforms in the penal system of Lombardy. On capital punishment a minority report was presented by Beccaria, Scotti and Risi. It suggested the almost total abolition of the death penalty and its replacement by penal servitude of a severity to be determined by the gravity of the offence. Following Beccaria they argued that the death penalty being unnecessary is not just, that it is not sufficiently deterrent and it is irreparable.

80. Id. at 154.

81. David Luban, Torture, Power, and Law 51 (2014).

82. David Lemmings, Law and Government in England during the Long Eighteenth Century: From Consent to Command 115 (2001) (referencing "disciples of Beccaria like Bentham and Colquhoun"); Bessler, Cruel and Unusual, *supra* note 19, at 48 (noting the influence of Beccaria on William Eden, Voltaire, Robespierre and John Howard). For instance, one source describes the success of Montesquieu's *The Spirit of the Laws* this way:

The vast masterpiece of the Baron de Montesquieu (1689–1755) became extraordinarily influential almost overnight. Its most famous contributions were: a new theory of participatory democracy (which inspired Rousseau among others); a new theory of "despotism" (*l'état despotique*: the term first became current through Montesquieu); a new theory of federalism; a new theory of the decisive influence of climate, geography, and history in shaping human existence; a new theory of the separation of powers (legislative, executive, and judicial); and a new, reformist theory of civil and criminal law to provide greater security for the accused and more reasonable procedures for parties in lawsuits. It was the last two that made Montesquieu *the* authority for the framers of the American Constitution....

Thomas L. Pangle & Timothy W. Burns, The Key Texts of Political Philosophy: An Introduction 307 (2015).

83. *See generally* 1 Charles S. Hyneman & Donald S. Lutz, American Political Writing during the Founding Era 1760–1805 (1983) (containing numerous references to Montesquieu and Beccaria).

84. Bessler, The Birth of American Law, *supra* note 53, at 3, 5, 29, 34–35, 48, 50, 69, 74, 79–80, 136, 147, 164, 166–67, 172, 180, 192, 206, 220, 234, 270, 312, 331, 369–70, 385, 396; John D. Bessler, The Celebrated Marquis: An Italian Noble and the Making of the Modern World 9, 15, 23, 101, 201, 211, 233–35, 246, 259, 269, 272, 284, 286–87, 290, 303–04, 310, 315–16, 322–23 (2018).

85. Bessler, The Celebrated Marquis, *supra* note 84, at 273–74.

86. David Boucher & Paul Kelly, ed., Political Thinkers: From Socrates to the Present 269 (3d ed. 2017) ("*The Spirit of the Laws* was to influence thinkers as diverse as David Hume, Adam Smith, and Adam Ferguson, all key figures in the Scottish Enlightenment, as well as James Madison, one of the authors of *The Federalist* and an architect of the American Constitution."); Michael A. Genovese, Encyclopedia of the American Presidency 346 (rev. ed. 2010) (noting the influence of Montesquieu's *The Spirit of the Laws* on America's founders, including James Madison, Thomas Jefferson and Alexander Hamilton).

87. "Franklin and Hall: Account with Benjamin Franklin, 1750–54," *available at Founders Online*, National Archives, last modified November 26, 2017, http://founders.archives.gov/documents/Franklin/01-04-02-0024. [Original source: *The Papers of Benjamin Franklin*, vol. 4, *July 1, 1750, through June 30, 1753*, ed. Leonard W. Labaree. New Haven: Yale University Press, 1961, pp. 76–77.]

88. "From George Washington to Robert Cary & Company, 6 October 1773," *Founders Online*, National Archives, last modified November 26, 2017, http://founders.archives.gov/documents/Washington/02-09-02-0268. [Original source: *The Papers of George Washington*, Colonial Series, vol. 9, *8 January 1772?–?18 March 1774*, ed. W. W. Abbot and Dorothy Twohig. Charlottesville: University Press of Virginia, 1994, pp. 343–345.]

89. "[Summer 1759.]," *Founders Online*, National Archives, last modified November 26, 2017, http://founders.archives.gov/documents/Adams/01-01-02-0004-0007-0001. [Original source: *The Adams Papers*, Diary and Autobiography of John Adams, vol. 1, *1755–1770*, ed. L. H. Butterfield. Cambridge, MA: Harvard University Press, 1961, pp. 103–123.]; "1760. June 26. Thurdsday.," *Founders Online*, National Archives, last modified November 26, 2017, http://founders.archives.gov/documents/Adams/01-01-02-0005-0002-0022. [Original source: *The Adams Papers*, Diary and Autobiography of John Adams, vol. 1, *1755–1770*, ed. L. H. Butterfield. Cambridge, MA: Harvard University Press, 1961, p. 142.] John Quincy Adams also read Montesquieu's ideas on punishments, writing in February 1787:

The celebrated Montesquieu observes, that the punishment should always derive from the nature of the crime, and consist in the privation of those advantages of which the criminal should have attempted to deprive others. He confesses however, that in many cases, this would not be effected: most frequently the man who robs the property of another, possesses, none himself, and therefore a corporal punishment, must supply the place of confiscation.

"[February 1787]," *Founders Online,* National Archives, last modified November 26, 2017, http://founders.archives.gov/documents/Adams/03-02-02-0002-0002. [Original source: *The Adams Papers,* Diary of John Quincy Adams, vol. 2, *March 1786?–?December 1788,* ed. Robert Taylor J and Marc Friedlaender. Cambridge, MA: Harvard University Press, 1981, pp. 155–167.]

90. "From Thomas Jefferson to Robert Skipwith, with a List of Books for a Private Library, 3 August 1771," *Founders Online,* National Archives, last modified November 26, 2017, http://founders.archives.gov/documents/Jefferson/01-01-02-0056. [Original source: *The Papers of Thomas Jefferson,* vol. 1, *1760–1776,* ed. Julian P. Boyd. Princeton: Princeton University Press, 1950, pp. 76–81.]; "Course of Reading for William G. Munford, [5 December 1798]," *Founders Online,* National Archives, last modified November 26, 2017, http://founders.archives.gov/documents/Jefferson/01-30-02-0405. [Original source: *The Papers of Thomas Jefferson,* vol. 30, *1 January 1798?–?31 January 1799,* ed. Barbara B. Oberg. Princeton: Princeton University Press, 2003, pp. 594–597.]; "A Course of Reading for Joseph C. Cabell, September 1800," *Founders Online,* National Archives, last modified November 26, 2017, http://founders.archives.gov/documents/Jefferson/01-32-02-0110. [Original source: *The Papers of Thomas Jefferson,* vol. 32, *1 June 1800?–?16 February 1801,* ed. Barbara B. Oberg. Princeton: Princeton University Press, 2005, pp. 176–181.]; "*The Farmer Refuted,* &c., [23 February] 1775," *Founders Online,* National Archives, last modified November 26, 2017, http://founders.archives.gov/documents/Hamilton/01-01-02-0057. [Original source: *The Papers of Alexander Hamilton,* vol. 1, *1768–1778,* ed. Harold C. Syrett. New York: Columbia University Press, 1961, pp. 81–165.]; "Remarks on the Quebec Bill: Part One, [15 June 1775]," *Founders Online,* National Archives, last modified November 26, 2017, http://founders.archives.gov/documents/Hamilton/01-01-02-0058. [Original source: *The Papers of Alexander Hamilton,* vol. 1, *1768–1778,* ed. Harold C. Syrett. New York: Columbia University Press, 1961, pp. 165–169.]

91. "Commonplace Book, 1759–1772," *Founders Online,* National Archives, last modified November 26, 2017, http://founders.archives.gov/documents/Madison/01-01-02-0002. [Original source: *The Papers of James Madison,* vol. 1, *16 March 1751?–?16 December 1779,* ed. William T. Hutchinson and William M. E. Rachal. Chicago: The University of Chicago Press, 1962, pp. 4–32.]

92. Bessler, Cruel and Unusual, *supra* note 19, at 56. Madison's 1783 list of books recommended "Montesquieu's work" and "Beccaria's works" right next to each other under the heading of "Politics." "Report on Books for Congress, [23 January] 1783," *Founders Online,* National Archives, last modified November 26, 2017, http://founders.archives.gov/documents/Madison/01-06-02-0031. [Original source: *The Papers of James Madison,* vol. 6, *1 January 1783?–?30 April 1783,* ed. William T. Hutchinson and William M. E. Rachal. Chicago: The University of Chicago Press, 1969, pp. 62–115.]

93. 9 Gaillard Hunt, ed., The Writings of James Madison 300 (1910).

94. 2 Paul Leicester Ford, ed. & comp., The Writings of Thomas Jefferson 17 (1893).

95. Bessler, The Celebrated Marquis, *supra* note 84, at 220.

96. *E.g.*, "From Thomas Jefferson to John Garland Jefferson, 11 June 1790," *Founders Online,* National Archives, last modified November 26, 2017, http://founders.archives.gov/documents/Jefferson/01-16-02-0278. [Original source: *The Papers of Thomas Jefferson,* vol. 16, *30 November 1789–4 July 1790,* ed. Julian P. Boyd. Princeton: Princeton University Press, 1961, pp. 480–482.]

97. Thomas Jefferson to John Norvell, June 11, 1807. Thomas Jefferson was particularly taken with Beccaria's ideas, and unlike most people in that era, appears to have read Beccaria's essay on the criminal law before reading *The Spirit of the Laws.* As one modern sources notes:

Beccaria's *Essay* may have struck Jefferson with peculiar force because he read it before he read, or at least commonplaced, *The Spirit of the Laws.* Moreover, he read it in Italian, and took his notes in that language, although an English edition had appeared in 1767. (The first American edition came in 1777.) What he learned from Montesquieu on the subject of crimes and punishments was therefore supplementary to Beccaria rather than the reverse, which was the normal sequence.

Merrill D. Peterson, "Thomas Jefferson and the Enlightenment: Reflections on Literary Influence," *in* William G. Shade, ed., Revisioning the British Empire in the Eighteenth Century: Essays from Twenty-five Years of the Lawrence Henry Gipson Institute for Eighteenth-Century Studies 133 (1998).

98. 2 The Political Writings of John Dickinson, Esquire, Late President of the State of Delaware, and of the Commonwealth of Pennsylvania (1801) (reprinting "The Address of Congress to the inhabitants of Quebec," dated October 26, 1774, extracted from "the Journals of Congress," and "ascribed to the pen of Mr. Dickinson").

99. Id. at 5, 12; Bessler, Cruel and Unusual, *supra* note 19, at 47.

100. 1 Claude H. Van Tyne, The Causes of the War of Independence 343–44 (1922); 1 John P. Kaminski & Richard Leffler, eds., Federalists and Antifederalists: The Debate over the Ratification of the Constitution 194–95 n.* (2d ed. 1998); Courtney Smith, ed., American History Through Its Greatest Speeches: A Documentary History of the United States 147 (2017); Bessler, Cruel and Unusual, *supra* note 19, at 319; James Alton James & Albert Hart Sanford, American History 157 (1917); J. Kent McGaughy, Richard Henry Lee of Virginia: A Portrait of an American Revolutionary 117 (2004).

101. Sydney George Fisher, The True History of the American Revolution 93 (1902) (noting that revolutionary pamphlets contain "frequent reference" to the ideas of Beccaria, Montesquieu, and others); Merrill D. Peterson, ed., The Portable Thomas Jefferson (1977), intro. ("From his early exposure to English and Scottish rationalists, Jefferson turned to the Continental representatives of the Enlightenment—Montesquieu, Voltaire, Diderot, Holbach, Beccaria, and others—and later, when he went to France, became something of a *philosophe* himself."). In the eighteenth century, Montesquieu and Beccaria's names were often invoked side-by-side. *E.g.*, "Enclosure II: James Wilson to William Bingham, 24 August 1791," *Founders Online*, National Archives, last modified November 26, 2017, http://founders.archives.gov/documents/Washington/05-09-02-0223-0003. [Original source: *The Papers of George Washington*, Presidential Series, vol. 9, *23 September 1791?–?29 February 1792*, ed. Mark A. Mastromarino. Charlottesville: University Press of Virginia, 2000, pp. 351–356.]; "William Duane to Thomas Jefferson, 5 July 1811," *Founders Online*, National Archives, last modified November 26, 2017, http://founders.archives.gov/documents/Jefferson/03-04-02-0025. [Original source: *The Papers of Thomas Jefferson*, Retirement Series, vol. 4, *18 June 1811 to 30 April 1812*, ed. J. Jefferson Looney. Princeton: Princeton University Press, 2007, pp. 25–26.] (forwarding "a single copy of the Review of Montesquieu" and noting: "I have ventured to place two short paragraphs from Hobbes & Beccaria, as mottoes to the title page"). In 1816, Thomas Jefferson, writing from Monticello, sent the Marquis de Lafayette two copies of "the Anonymous Review of Montesquieu," a work written by the French aristocrat Destutt de Tracy in 1807. The Philadelphia publisher, William Duane, published that review of Montesquieu's *Spirit of Laws* in 1811, choosing this quote from Beccaria for the beginning of the work: "The most certain means of rendering a people free and happy, is to establish a perfect method of education." A Commentary and Review of Montesquieu's "Spirit of Laws" (1811), http://www.econlib.org/library/Tracy/ddtMSL0.html; "Nicolas G. Dufief to Thomas Jefferson, 6 September 1816," *Founders Online*, National Archives, last modified November 26, 2017, http://founders.archives.gov/documents/Jefferson/03-10-02-0258. [Original source: *The Papers of Thomas Jefferson*, Retirement Series, vol. 10, *May 1816 to 18 January 1817*, ed. J. Jefferson Looney. Princeton: Princeton University Press, 2013, pp. 370–373.] Jefferson later saw to it that Tracy's *Commentary on Montesquieu* and his *Traité de la volonté* were translated into English. Jefferson translated the latter work into English as *A Treatise on Political Economy*. Thomas Jefferson, ed., A Treatise on Political Economy by The Count Destutt Tracy xi (1817) (reprinted in 1970 by Augustus M. Kelley Publishers).

102. A. Esmein, A History of Continental Criminal Procedure with Special Reference to France 362–65 (John Simpson, trans. 1913); Arthur Shuster, Punishment and the History of Political Philosophy: From Classical Republicanism to the Crisis of Modern Criminal Justice 75–76 (2016).

103. 1 Zephaniah Swift, A System of the Laws of the State of Connecticut 295 (1795).

104. "The Father of Prison Reform," The Literary World, July 8, 1881, p. 1.

105. *See generally* William Edward Hartpole Lecky, The American Revolution, 1763–1783: Being the Chapters and Passages Relating to America from the Author's History of England in the Eighteenth Century (James Albert Woodburn, ed., 1922); *see also* Herbert Aptheker,

The American Revolution, 1763–1783, at 22–29 (1960) (discussing the origins of the American Revolution).

106. *E.g.*, Moses Coit Tyler, The Literary History of the American Revolution, 1763–1783, at 12 (1897) (noting that Samuel Adams devoted "his days and nights ... to Hooker, Coke, Grotius, Locke, Sidney, Vattel, Montesquieu, Blackstone, and Hume"); Sydney George Fisher, The True History of the American Revolution 94–95 (1902):

Beccaria ... also exercised great influence on the colonists. His famous book, "Crimes and Punishments", was also a short, concise, but very eloquent volume. It caused a great stir in the world. The translation circulated in America had added to it a characteristic commentary by Voltaire. Beccaria, though not writing directly on the subject of liberty, necessarily included that subject, because he dealt with the administration of the criminal law. His plea for more humane and just punishments, and for punishments more in proportion to the offence, found a ready sympathy among the Americans, who had already revolted in disgust from the brutality and extravagant cruelty of the English criminal code.

But Beccaria also stated most beautifully and clearly the essential principles of liberty. His foundation doctrine, that "every act of authority of one man over another for which there is not absolute necessity in tyrannical," made a most profound impression in America. He laid down also the principle that "in every human society there is an effort continually tending to confer on one part the highest power and happiness, and to reduce the other to the extreme of weakness and misery." That sentence became the life long guide of many Americans. It became a constituent part of the minds of Jefferson and Hamilton. It can be seen as the foundation, the connecting strand, running all through the essays of the Federalist. It was the inspiration of the "checks and balances" in the national Constitution. It can be traced in American thought and legislation down to the present time.

107. Brice Dickson, The European Convention on Human Rights and the Conflict in Northern Ireland 139 n.1 (2010) ("The French Declaration of the Rights of Man of 1789 prohibits punishments that are not strictly and obviously necessary (cl 8) and states that 'if arrest shall be deemed indispensable, all harshness not essential to the securing of the prisoner's person shall be severely repressed by law' (cl 9).").

108. Mitchell Cohen & Nicole Fermon, eds., Princeton Readings in Political Thought: Essential Texts since Plato 347–48 (1996).

109. Ana María Prieto del Pino, "The Proportionality Principle in a Broad Sense and Its Content of Rationality: The Principle of Subsidiarity," *in* Adán Nieto Martín & Marta Muñoz de Morales Romero, eds., Towards a Rational Legislative Evaluation in Criminal Law 282–83 (2016).

110. 18 U.S.C. §3553(a).

111. Farmer v. Brennan, 511 U.S. 825, 838 (1994) ("the deliberate indifference standard applies to all prison-conditions claims"); *see also* Pitre v. Cain, 131 S. Ct. 8, 9 (2010) (Sotomayor, J., dissenting from denial of cert.) ("To determine whether prison officials' conduct violates the Eighth Amendment in the context of prison conditions, we ask whether 'the officials involved acted with 'deliberate indifference' to the inmates' health or safety.' ").

112. Estelle v. Gamble, 429 U.S. 97, 104 (1976) ("deliberate indifference to serious medical needs of prisoners constitutes the 'unnecessary and wanton infliction of pain' proscribed by the Eighth Amendment") (citation omitted); Helling v. McKinney, 509 U.S. 25, 32 (1993) ("In *Estelle*, we concluded that although accidental or inadvertent failure to provide adequate medical care to a prisoner would not violate the Eighth Amendment, 'deliberate indifference to serious medical needs of prisoners' violates the Amendment because it constitutes the unnecessary and wanton infliction of pain contrary to contemporary standards of decency.") (citing *Estelle*).

113. Wilkins v. Gaddy, 559 U.S. 34, 37 (2010) ("The 'core judicial inquiry,' we held, was not whether a certain quantum of injury was sustained, but rather 'whether force was applied in a good-faith effort to maintain or restore discipline, or maliciously and sadistically to cause harm.' ") (quoting Hudson v. McMillian, 503 U.S. 1, 7 (1992)); Whitley v. Albers, 475 U.S. 312, 320–21 (1986) ("Where a prison security measure is undertaken to resolve a disturbance, such as occurred in this case, that indisputably poses significant risks to the safety of inmates and prison staff, we think the question whether the measure taken inflicted unnecessary and wanton pain and suffering ultimately turns on 'whether force was applied in a good faith effort to main or restore discipline or maliciously and sadistically for the very purpose of causing harm.' ") (quoting Johnson v. Glick, 481 F.2d 1028, 1033

(2d Cir.) (Friendly, J.), *cert. denied sub nom.* John v. Johnson, 414 U.S. 1033 (1973)).

114. *E.g.*, Edward C. Carter III, Criminal Law and Procedure for the Paralegal 562 (2016) (noting that while, in non-capital cases, the Cruel and Unusual Punishments Clause "does not require strict proportionality between the crime and the sentence and forbids only extreme sentences that are 'grossly disproportionate' to the crime," but that in capital cases "the courts engage in a detailed proportionality analysis and apply the proportionality rule much more strictly than in non-capital cases").

115. *See, e.g.*, Gregg v. Georgia, 428 U.S. 153, 173 (1976) (citations omitted):

[O]ur cases also make clear that public perceptions of standards of decency with respect to criminal sanctions are not conclusive. A penalty also must accord with "the dignity of man," which is the "basic concept underlying the Eighth Amendment." This means, at least, that the punishment not be "excessive." When a form of punishment in the abstract (in this case, whether capital punishment may ever be imposed as a sanction for murder) rather than in the particular (the propriety of death as a penalty to be applied to a specific defendant for a specific crime) is under consideration, the inquiry into "excessiveness" has two aspects. First, the punishment must not involve the unnecessary and wanton infliction of pain. Second, the punishment must not be grossly out of proportion to the severity of the crime.

See also Coker v. Georgia, 433 U.S. 584, 592 (1997):

Under *Gregg*, a punishment is 'excessive' and unconstitutional if it (1) makes no measureable contribution to accepted goals of punishment and hence is nothing more than the purposeless and needless imposition of pain and suffering; and (2) is grossly out of proportion to the severity of the crime. A punishment might fail the test on either ground.

116. Estelle v. Gamble, 429 U.S. 97, 102 (1976) ("[W]e have held repugnant to the Eighth Amendment punishments which are incompatible with 'the evolving standards of decency that mark the progress of a maturing society.'") (quoting *Trop v. Dulles*); *see also* Hutto v. Finney, 437 U.S. 678, 685 (1978) (noting that the Eighth Amendment prohibits penalties "that transgress today's "'broad and idealistic concepts of dignity, civilized standards, humanity, and decency.'"").

117. Allison Steele, "Once a Prison, Soon to be Waterfront Park in South Jersey," The Inquirer, Mar. 16, 2017, http://www.philly.com/philly/news/new_jersey/Camden-prison-waterfront-park-development.html.

118. *See generally* Jonathan Simon, Mass Incarceration on Trial: A Remarkable Court Decision and the Future of Prisons in America (2014).

119. Estelle v. Gamble, 429 U.S. 97, 102–03 (1976) ("we have held repugnant to the Eighth Amendment punishments … which 'involve the unnecessary and wanton infliction of pain'") (citations omitted).

120. *Estelle*, 429 U.S. at 103 n.7 ("The [Eighth] Amendment also proscribes punishments grossly disproportionate to the severity of the crime.") (citing Gregg v. Georgia, 428 U.S. 153, 173 (1976) (joint opinion); Weems v. United States, 217 U.S. 349, 367 (1910)); Hutto v. Finney, 437 U.S. 678, 685 (1978) (noting that the Eighth Amendment "prohibits penalties that are grossly disproportionate to the offense"); *see also* Coker v. Georgia, 433 U.S. 584, 592 (1977) ("We have concluded that a sentence of death is grossly disproportionate and excessive punishment for the crime of rape and is therefore forbidden by the Eighth Amendment as cruel and unusual punishment.").

121. *E.g.*, Enmund v. Florida, 458 U.S. 782, 788 (1982) ("The Cruel and Unusual Punishments Clause of the Eighth Amendment is directed, in part, "'against all punishments which by their excessive length or severity are greatly disproportioned to the offenses charged.'"") (quoting Weems v. United States, 217 U.S. 349, 371 (1910), quoting O'Neil v. Vermont, 144 U.S. 323, 339–40 (1892) (Field, J., dissenting)). The Eighth Amendment also "imposes substantive limits on what can be made criminal and punished." *Estelle*, 429 U.S. at 103 n.7 (citing Robinson v. California, 370 U.S. 660 (1962)). In *Ingraham v. Wright*, 430 U.S. 651 (1977), the Supreme Court recognized that the Cruel and Unusual Punishments Clause "circumscribes the criminal process in three ways": (1) "it limits the kinds of punishments that can be imposed on those convicted of crimes"; (2) "it proscribes punishment grossly disproportionate to the severity of the crime"; and (3) "it imposes substantive limits on what can be made criminal and punished as such." Id. at 667. "We have recognized the last limitation as one to be applied sparingly," the Court stressed in 1977. Id.

122. Glossip v. Gross, 576 U.S. ___ (2015) (Scalia, J., concurring).

123. *E.g.*, GILLIAN BROWN, THE CONSENT OF THE GOVERNED: THE LOCKEAN LEGACY IN EARLY AMERICAN CULTURE 3 (2001):

When the founding fathers invoked Locke's *Second Treatise of Government* (1690), in which he presented the theory that government emanated from the people, they were marshalling an idea long familiar to Americans. In ratifying a new government based on Locke's principle that no one can be "subjected to the Political Power of another without his own Consent," Americans were legislating their childhood convictions.

124. *E.g.*, 1 MONTESQUIEU, THE COMPLETE WORKS OF M. DE MONTESQUIEU 397 (1777) ("All punishment which is not derived from necessity is tyrannical. The law is not a mere act of power; things in their own nature indifferent are not within its province."); 1 BARON DE MONTESQUIEU, THE SPIRIT OF THE LAWS 132 (Mr. Nugent, ed., 1752) ("[T]he use of the rack against criminals cannot be defended on a like plea of necessity."); W. F. REDDAWAY, ED., DOCUMENTS OF CATHERINE THE GREAT: THE CORRESPONDENCE WITH VOLTAIRE AND THE *INSTRUCTION* OF 1767 IN THE ENGLISH TEXT OF 1768, at 222 (1931) ("In a Word, every Punishment, which is not inflicted through Necessity, is tyrannical."); *see also* id. at 248 ("All Severity *exceeding* these Bounds is *useless*, and consequently *tyrannical*.") (italics in original); id. at 248–49 (italics in original):

209. Q. 6. *Whether the Punishment of* Death *is really useful and necessary in a Community, for the Preservation of Peace and good Order?*

210. Proofs from Fact demonstrate to us, that the frequent Use of capital Punishment never mended the Morals of a People. Therefore, if *I* prove the *Death* of a Citizen to be neither *useful* nor *necessary to Society in general, I* shall confute *those* who *rise up against* Humanity. *I* repeat here, *to Society in general*; because the Death of a Citizen can *only* be useful and necessary in *one* Case; which is, when, though he be *deprived* of Liberty, yet he has *such Power* by his *Connections*, as may *enable* him to raise Disturbances dangerous to the publick Peace. This Case can happen only, when a People either loses, or recovers their Liberty; or in a Time of Anarchy, when the *Disorders* themselves hold the *Place* of Laws. But in a Reign of Peace and Tranquillity, under a Government established with the united Wishes of a whole People; in a State well fortified against external Enemies, and protected within by strong Supports; that is, by its own internal Strength and virtuous Sentiments rooted in the Minds of the Citizens; and where the whole Power is lodged in the Hands of a Monarch; in such a State, there can be *no* Necessity for *taking away the Life* of a Citizen. The twenty Years Reign of the Empress *ELIZABETH PETROVNA* gives the Fathers of the People a more illustrious Example for Imitation than a Reign of the most shining Conquests.

Accord 38 THE GENTLEMAN'S MAGAZINE, AND HISTORICAL CHRONICLE 574–75 (1768) (discussing the Grand Instructions to the Commissioners appointed to frame a new Code of Laws for the Russian Empire, composed by Catherine II, and listing, among them, "Every punishment not inflicted by necessity is tyrannical. Right and not power is the source of law." and "All *useless* punishment is *unjust*.").

125. J.M. BERNSTEIN, TORTURE AND DIGNITY: AN ESSAY ON MORAL INJURY 49 (2015); BENJAMIN BOWLING, VIOLENT RACISM: VICTIMIZATION, POLICING AND SOCIAL CONTEXT 306 (rev. ed. 1998). This principle was being articulated long after Montesquieu's and Beccaria's time. THEODORE PARKER, A SERMON OF THE DANGEROUS CLASSES IN SOCIETY 44 (1847) ("We shall one day remember that the offender is a man, and so his good also is to be consulted. He may be a bad man, voluntarily bad if you will. Still we are to be economical even of his suffering—for the least possible punishment is the best.").

126. West Virginia State Board of Education v. Barnette, 319 U.S. 624, 638 (1943).

127. PAUL HYLAND, ED. (WITH OLGA GOMEZ & FRANCESCA GREENSIDES), THE ENLIGHTENMENT: A SOURCEBOOK AND READER 212 (2003) ("In *The Spirit of the Laws* ... Montesquieu had emphasized how important it was to the liberty of all individuals in society, that they were protected by a small number of strictly defined laws and an independent judiciary.... Moreover, the scope of the criminal law should be clearly limited, and the penalties imposed for breaches of the law should not be excessively harsh or cruel."); KYLE SCOTT, THE FEDERALIST PAPERS: A READER'S GUIDE 141 (2013) ("One cannot deny the influence of Montesquieu and William Blackstone on the thinking of the American founders, particularly when it comes to the development of the separation of powers and an independent judiciary. These two men were cited more than any other Enlightenment thinkers."); Henry J. Abraham,

"The Pillars and Politics of Judicial Independence in the United States," *in* Peter H. Russell & David M. O'Brien, eds., Judicial Independence in the Age of Democracy: Critical Perspectives from Around the World 25 (2001) ("There is no doubt that the founding fathers considered an independent judiciary to be the cornerstone of a free society and the rule of law. Hence, they created Article 3 of the Constitution as a pillar of the separation of powers designed to provide genuine judicial independence.").

128. U.S. Const., Art. III, sec. 1.

129. Marbury v. Madison, 5 U.S. (1 Cranch) 137 (1803); *see also* Sue Davis: Corwin and Peltason's Understanding the Constitution 44 (17th ed. 2008):

One of the major criticisms of judicial review that has continued to persist through the years—known as the countermajoritarian difficulty—holds that there is an inherent tension between judicial review and democratic government. The argument is that because the Court contravenes majority will when it invalidates a policy enacted by elected officials, it should exercise that power only on the rarest of occasions when a challenged policy is incontrovertibly in violation of the Constitution. Critics of judicial review who espouse such a view emphasized the democratic character of the American political system. If one stresses constitutionalism instead, however, judicial review can be seen as consistent with—indeed, necessary to—maintaining limits on majority rule in order to protect the fundamental rights and values that the Constitution guarantees.

130. Thomas Jefferson to James Madison, Sept. 6, 1789, *available at* www.founders.archives.gov. Writing from Monticello, Jefferson repeated this idea to others many years later. Thomas Jefferson to John Wayles Eppes, June 24, 1813, *available at* www.founders.archives.gov ("the earth belongs to the living, not to the dead"; "the will & the power of man expires with his life, by Nature's law"; "each generation has the usufruct of the earth during the period of it's continuance. when it ceases to exist, the usufruct passes on to the succeeding generation, free and unimcumbered, and so on successively from one generation to another for ever"); Thomas Jefferson to William Plumer, July 21, 1816, *available at* www.founders.archives.gov ("[T]he idea that institutions established for the use of the nation, cannot be touched or modified, even to make them answer their end ... may perhaps be a salutary provision against the abuses of a monarch, but is most absurd against the nation itself.").

131. Frank B. Cross, The Failed Promise of Originalism 8 (2013) ("Originalism appears to exalt, in some cases, the ideas of those who died hundreds of years ago over current individuals (the 'dead hand' problem)."); *see also* Bernard E. Harcourt, "Beccaria's *On Crimes and Punishments*: A Mirror on the History of the Foundations of Modern Criminal Law," *in* Markus D. Dubber, ed., Foundational Texts in Modern Criminal Law 53 (2014) ("Richard Posner traces his intellectual genealogy, in the area of criminal law, specifically to Beccaria.").

132. U.S. Const., art. V.

133. Holly J. McCammon & Lee Ann Banaszak, 100 Years of the Nineteenth Amendment: An Appraisal of Women's Political Activism (2018); David A. J. Richards, Conscience and the Constitution: History, Theory, and Law of the Reconstruction Amendments (1993).

134. "Letters of Helvidius," No. 1, *in* 6 Gaillard Hunt, ed., The Writings of James Madison: Comprising His Public Papers and His Private Correspondence, including Numerous Letters and Documents Now for the First Time Printed 138, 144 (1906).

135. J. Kent McGaughy, Richard Henry Lee of Virginia: A Portrait of an American Revolutionary 117 (2004); Bessler, Cruel and Unusual, *supra* note 19, at 27, 96, 165–6; Joseph M. Bessette, ed., Toward a More Perfect Union: Writings of Herbert J. Storing 124–25 (1995); Michael J. Sandel, Democracy's Discontent: America in Search of a Public Philosophy 36 (1996); Richard Vetterli & Gary Bryner, In Search of the Republic: Public Virtue and the Roots of American Government 243 (rev. ed. 1996).

136. In two recent books, I argue that America's death penalty should be declared a cruel and unusual—indeed, a torturous—punishment. *See generally* Bessler, Cruel and Unusual, *supra* note 19; John D. Bessler, The Death Penalty as Torture: From the Dark Ages to Abolition (2017).

137. There are currently less than 3,000 death row inmates in American prisons. "Facts about the Death Penalty," Death Penalty Info. Ctr., Feb. 2, 2018, https://deathpenaltyinfo.org/documents/FactSheet.pdf. By comparison, at year-end 2015, an estimated 6,741,400 persons were supervised by U.S. adult correctional systems. Danielle Kaeble & Lauren E. Glaze, Bureau of Justice Statistics, Dec.

29, 2016, https://www.bjs.gov/index.cfm?ty=pbdetail&iid=5870. Many of those people are in prisons or jails. As one recent source puts it: "The United States in the world's leader in incarceration with 2.2 million people currently in the nation's prisons and jails—a 500% increase over the last forty years." "Trends in U.S. Corrections," The Sentencing Project, https://sentencingproject.org/wp-content/uploads/2016/01/Trends-in-US-Corrections.pdf.

138. Outlawing the death penalty would put a stop to a barbaric practice with roots in the Dark Ages. *See generally* John D. Bessler, *The Abolitionist Movement Comes of Age: From Capital Punishment as a Lawful Sanction to a Peremptory, International Law Norm Barring Executions*, 79 Mont. L. Rev. 7 (2018); John D. Bessler, *What I Think About When I Think About the Death Penalty*, 62 St. Louis U. L.J. 781 (2018). Taking that step would also help usher in a new era of American criminal justice reform. *See, e.g.*, Brandon L. Garrett, End of Its Rope: How Killing the Death Penalty Can Revive Criminal Justice (2017).

139. Travis C. Pratt, Addicted to Incarceration: Corrections Policy and the Politics of Misinformation in the United States xiii (2009).

140. "Americans' Confidence in Institutions Stays Law," Gallup, June 13, 2016, https://news.gallup.com/poll/192581/americans-confidence-institutions-stays-low.aspx?g_source=Politics&g_medium=newsfeed&g_campaign=tiles.

Chapter 1

1. John J. Anderson, C. A. Bloss, Ancient History, Illustrated by Colored Maps, and a Chronological Chart, for the Use of Families and Schools 114 (1875); Richard Dargie, Crime and Punishment 7 (2007); *see also* James A. Harrison, The Story of Greece 204 (1893) ("[D]eath was Draco's favorite mode of punishment, not only for great crimes, but for idleness even, or for stealing an apple or a cabbage.").

2. 1 J. N. Larned & Donald E. Smith, eds., The New Larned History for Ready Reference Reading and Research: The Actual Words of the World's Best Historians, Biographers and Specialists 591 (1922).

3. Lynn Hunt, Inventing Human Rights: A History 80 (2007); Joel F. Harrington, The Faithful Executioner: Life and Death, Honor and Shame in the Turbulent Sixteenth Century 4, 38 41–42, 74–75, 171 (2013); Larissa Tracy, ed., Flaying in the Pre-Modern World: Practice and Representation 71 (2017).

4. Julius R. Ruff, Violence in Early Modern Europe, 1500–1800, at 103 (2001).

5. John Hostettler, A History of Criminal Justice in England and Wales 183 (2009); Stephanie Clarke, Down, Dirty and Divine: A Spiritual Ride Through London's Underground 132 (2012).

6. 3 Jean W. Sedlar, East Central Europe in the Middle Ages, 1000–1500, at 324 (1994).

7. Jennifer Lawler, Encyclopedia of Women in the Middle Ages 49 (2012).

8. David Garland, "Modes of Capital Punishment: The Death Penalty in Historical Perspective," *in* David Garland, Randall McGowen & Michael Meranze, eds., America's Death Penalty: Between Past and Present 38 (2011).

9. Michael Tonry, "Mandatory Penalties," *in* Michael Tonry, ed., The Oxford Handbook of Crime and Criminal Justice 734 (2011).

10. Jo Turner, Paul Taylor, Karen Corteen & Sharon Morley, eds., A Companion to the History of Crime and Criminal Justice 15 (2017).

11. Quentin Skinner & Russell Price, eds., Machiavelli, The Prince 58–59 (1988).

12. Niccolò Machiavelli, Discourses on Livy 210–11 (Harvey C. Mansfield & Nathan Tarcov, trans. 1996); Stuart Hampshire, Innocence and Experience 162–63 (1989).

13. 1 Michael Grossberg & Christopher Tomlins, eds., The Cambridge History of Law in America: Early America (1580–1815), at 193 (2008); George Edward Ellis, The Puritan Age and Rule in the Colony of the Massachusetts Bay 1629–1685, at 197 (2010) (1888).

14. Mark F. Rooker, The Ten Commandments: Ethics for the Twenty-First Century 132 (2010).

15. Dale S. Recinella, The Biblical Truth about America's Death Penalty 48, 66 (2004).

16. Rebecca Stefoff, *Furman v. Georgia*: Debating the Death Penalty 32 (2008).

17. Jeannine Marie DeLombard, In the Shadow of the Gallows: Race, Crime, and American Civic Identity 16 (2012).

18. Id.

19. Thomas Alcock, The Law Not Made for a Righteous Man: An Assise Sermon Preached in the Cathedral-Church of St. Peter, Exon, on Tuesday, March 19, 1754, at 1 (1754) (italics in original).

20. Id. at 3 (italics in original).

21. Id. at 6.

22. Joseph Priestley, The Doctrine of Philosophical Necessity Illustrated; Being an Appendix to the Disquisitions Relating to Matter and Spirit 75–76, 139 (2d ed. 1782) (italics in original).

23. Book IV of William Blackstone's *Commentaries on the Laws of England*, published in 1769, dealt with the topic "Of Public Wrongs." 4 William Blackstone, Commentaries on the Laws of England: A Facsimile of the First Edition of 1765–1769 (1979). In the very first chapter of Book IV, Blackstone wrote that "[t]he knowledge of this branch of jurisprudence, which teaches the nature, extent, and degrees of every crime, and adjusts to it it's adequate and necessary penalty, is of the utmost importance to every individual in the state." Id. at 2. In that chapter, titled "Of the Nature of Crimes; and Their Punishment," Blackstone specifically noted that "Baron Montesquieu" and "marquis Beccaria" were "ingenious writers" who had pointed out "the inhumanity and mistaken policy" of "the criminal law." Id. at 3.

24. Alcock, The Law Not Made for a Righteous Man, *supra* note 19, at 19–20.

25. For example, Gilbert Burnet—a seventeenth-century bishop from Salisbury—made this argument about the need for the death penalty to spur repentance and salvation:

[N]othing is so likely a means to bring the criminal to repent of his sins, and to fit him to die as a Christian, as to condemn him to die for his crimes. If anything can awaken his conscience, and strike terror in him, that will do it. Therefore as capital punishments are necessary to human society, so they are often real blessings to those on whom they fall.

Davison M. Douglas, *God and the Executioner: The Influence of Western Religion on the Death Penalty*, 9 Wm. & Mary Bill Rts. J. 137, 154 (2000) (citation omitted).

26. Jay Paul Gates & Nicole Marafioti, eds., Capital and Corporal Punishment in Anglo-Saxon England 16 (2014). The frequency of capital punishment and the infliction of corporal punishments varied over time, though at some point they became "the exception, not the rule." Id.

27. Niccolò Machiavelli, The Prince 5, 17, 30, 48, 51 (David Wootton, ed. & trans. 1995).

28. Lawrence B. Goodheart, The Solemn Sentence of Death: Capital Punishment in Connecticut 69–70 (2011).

29. The New-Haven Gazette, Vol. II, No. 88, Jan. 12, 1786, pp. 3–4 (italics and capitalization in original); Jeremy Belknap to Isaac Beers, Nov. 15, 1793, *in* 4 Collections of the Massachusetts Historical Society 565 n.* (1891).

30. William Montgomery Meigs, Life of Josiah Meigs 16–17, 44–45 (1887); Andrea Wulf, Founding Gardeners: The Revolutionary Generation, Nature, and the Shaping of the American Nation 63 (2011); Dustin Gish & Daniel Klinghard, Thomas Jefferson and the Science of Republican Government: A Political Biography of *Notes on the State of Virginia* 2 (2017).

31. Daniel Bowen, A History of Philadelphia, with a Notice of Villages, in the Vicinity, Embellished with Engravings, Designed as a Guide to Citizens and Strangers, Containing a Correct Account of the City Improvements Up to the Year 1839, at 180 (1839); 1 William Richard Cutter & William Frederick Adams, Genealogical and Personal Memoirs Relating to the Families of the State of Massachusetts 389 (1910); Charles Angoff, ed., The Humanities in the Age of Science 78 (1968); Mitchel P. Roth, Prisons and Prison Systems: A Global Encyclopedia 222 (2006); 1 Mark G. Spencer, ed., The Bloomsbury Encyclopedia of the American Enlightenment 308 (2015). With Cesare Beccaria described as "a disciple of Montesquieu," one source emphasizes that Beccaria also exerted a great deal of influence in continental Europe, with Beccaria said to be "the first to formulate precisely the criticisms of the old system and

to propose a plan of reform." *Dei delitti e delle pene*, Carl Ludwig von Bar wrote in *A History of Continental Criminal Law* (1916), was the famous "little book" that "was read in almost every European language," that was "so influential" in its day, and that produced "the classical school of criminal law in the 1800s." 6 CARL LUDWIG VON BAR, THE CONTINENTAL LEGAL HISTORY SERIES (A HISTORY OF CONTINENTAL CRIMINAL LAW) 311, 317 & n.7, 413–14 (Thomas S. Bell, trans. 1916). In a section of *A History of Continental Criminal Law* on "The Principle of Parsimony in Punishment," Ludwig von Bar made these observations:

The aspect of criminal law from the viewpoint of national economy is important. In former times human unhappiness and pain were squandered lavishly. Beccaria is entitled to credit for having first brought to attention comprehensively the principle of the greatest possible parsimony with penalties and the superfluity of many punishments. Where other means are effective for the realization of the law the use of punishment is inexcusable, since, as correctly stated by Von Ihering, it recoils upon society.

....

Punishments which do not possess a certain connection with tradition are somewhat odious, even when emanating from the spirit of well-intended moral reform. This is quite natural, as the people regard punishment as merely an echo of their own disapproval. Such acts appear to be merely acts of despotism and undermine the effectiveness of criminal justice in other cases. Too many punishments create indifference. One must not imagine that every coarse or vulgar act, every little violation of right, may demand suppression by punishment. The State, like the individual, must learn to endure many minor iniquities; it must remember that the world will not immediately come to an end and that Nature has guarded against the trees growing up to the sky, and it must have confidence in the firmness of its own position and in the natural effective power of moral opinions. Where there is a progressive increase of penal statutes, or where upon every occasion the public raises a general cry to help something by penal statutes or to increase the severity of the penal statutes, it is not well for freedom. For every penal statute is really one more in-road upon freedom. And the ultimate results may well be felt most keenly by those who have been the most noisy in demanding it. One may well ponder the maxim of Tactius: "Pessima res-publica, plurimæ leges."

Id. at 519–51.

32. LOUIS P. MASUR, RITES OF EXECUTION: CAPITAL PUNISHMENT AND THE TRANSFORMATION OF AMERICAN CULTURE, 1776–1865, at 52 (1989); ANDREW DICKSON WHITE, AN ADDRESS DELIVERED AT THE UNVEILING OF THE STATUE OF BENJAMIN SILLIMAN AT YALE COLLEGE, JUNE 24, 1884, at 18 (1885); *Silliman College*, https://silliman.yalecollege.yale.edu/about-silliman/history.

33. "From an Essay on Crimes and Punishments," THE TELESCOPE: OR, AMERICAN HERALD (Leominster, Mass.), Mar. 13, 1800, p. 4. Beccaria's work was invoked in other contexts, too. John De Witt, "To the Free Citizens of the Commonwealth of Massachusetts," AMERICAN HERALD (Boston, Mass.), Dec. 3, 1787, p. 2.

34. "*To the Legislatures of the Respective States*—LETTER FIFTH," THE DEMOCRAT (Boston, Mass.), Sept. 29, 1804, pp. 1–2.

35. "Gentlemen of the Grand Jury," PENNSYLVANIA CORRESPONDENT, AND FARMERS' ADVERTISER (Doylestown, Penn.), Jan. 8, 1805, p. 2.

36. J. THOMAS SCHARF, HISTORY OF MARYLAND: FROM THE EARLIEST PERIOD TO THE PRESENT DAY 41–42 & n.1 (1879); *see also* id. at 41 (calling the stocks, the pillory, the whipping-post and "the gallows, the ugliest spectacles"—"the active employment" of which occurred "[a]bout the central date of 1770"—"cruel punishments," but noting that "[t]he stocks, the pillory and the gibbet did not pass out of vogue in Maryland, in fact, until about 1810, when, following the impulse given to the science of punishment by Bentham and his school, we adopted the penitentiary system and thus began to build the Maryland penitentiary"). "Previous to the construction of that building, and after the War of Independence had necessarily done away with the sale of white convicts into labor," J. Thomas Scharf wrote in *History of Maryland* of the construction of that state's penitentiary, "the usual punishment of convicts, after the preliminary whipping and pillorying was done, consisted in putting them in the chain-gang to work on the public roads, or, as it was popularly called, 'sending them to the wheelbarrow.'" Id.

37. BRYAN F. LE BEAU, THE STORY OF THE SALEM WITCH TRIALS: "WE WALKED IN CLOUDS AND

Could Not See Our Way" ix (2d ed. 2010).

38. Maurene J. Hinds, Witchcraft on Trial: From the Salem Witch Hunts to *The Crucible* 11 (2009); Sabrina Crewe & Michael V. Uschan, The Salem Witch Trials 17 (2005).

39. John R. Vile, Founding Documents of America: Documents Decoded 33 (2015).

40. Frederick Rosen, "Utilitarianism and the Reform of the Criminal Law," *in* Mark Goldie & Robert Wokler, eds., The Cambridge History of Eighteenth-Century Political Thought 551 (2006).

41. Peter France, ed., The Oxford Guide to Literature in English 271 (2000); A. Owen Aldridge, Thomas Paine's American Ideology 147 (1984); *see also* id. ("The printed catalog of the Library Company of Philadelphia, 1764, for example, reveals that this institution possessed a copy of the second edition (1752) of an English translation of Thomas Nugent."); Cesare Beccaria, On Crimes and Punishments xvii (David Young, trans. 1986); Rosamaria Loretelli, *The First English Translation of Cesare Beccaria's* On Crimes and Punishments*: Uncovering the Editorial and Political Contexts*, Diciottesimo Secolo, anno II, 2017, pp. 1–22.

42. James Raven, London Booksellers and American Customers: Transatlantic Literary Community and the Charleston Library Society, 1748–1811, at 154, 158, 188, 214, 264, 266, 456 (2002); Micheline R. Ishay, The History of Human Rights: From Ancient Times to the Globalization Era 81, 94, 358 (2008).

43. Morris L. Cohen, comp., Bibliography of Early American Law 969–72 (1998); Marcello Maestro, Cesare Beccaria and the Origins of Penal Reform 43 (1973); Cesare Beccaria, An Essay on Crimes and Punishments 6 (1992) (introduction by Adolph Caso); 1 Catalog of the Hampton L. Carson Collection Illustrative of the Growth of the Common Law in The Free Library of Philadelphia 63–64 (1962); *compare* The Johns Hopkins Studies in Romance Literature and Languages (1941), Vol. XXXIX, p. 12 ("According to Evans's *American Bibliography*, James Rivington was supposed to have published in 1773 an edition of Beccaria's *Essay on Crimes and Punishments* with Voltaire's *Commentary*. As yet, no copies have been located and its listing by Evans is probably based on an advertisement inserted by Rivington in his *New York Gazetteer* for October 28, 1773....").

44. 5 Myles Cooper, The Patriots of North-America: A Sketch 26 (1775).

45. This information was obtained through a search of the WorldCat database and from a dictionary of English, Scottish and Irish printers and booksellers. The Bibliographical Society at the Oxford University Press, *A Dictionary of the Printers and Booksellers Who Were at Work in England, Scotland and Ireland from 1726 to 1775* (Oxford: Oxford University Press, 1932). William Creech (1745–1815) was a bookseller and publisher in Edinburgh who was educated at the Edinburgh University who, as a young man, had spent time in London, Paris and Holland and who had toured continental Europe. He became the original publisher of the works of Adam Ferguson and other famous writers. Id. at 296–97. William Gordon was a bookseller in Edinburgh. Id. at 312.

46. James N. Green, "English Books and Printing in the Age of Franklin," *in* 1 Hugh Amory & David D. Hall, eds., A History of the Book in America: The Colonial Book in the Atlantic World 289 (2009).

47. Michael Widener & Mark S. Weiner, *Law's Picture Books: The Yale Law Library Collection* (Clark, NJ: Talbot Publishing, 2017), pp. 1, 9, 122. As Widener and Weiner write of that Italian edition—and of its famous frontispiece—published in London: "The frontispiece image ... was engraved on Beccaria's detailed instructions, and it was frequently reproduced and copied by eighteenth-century publishers. Lady Justice recoils from an executioner's offering of three decapitated heads and instead gazes approvingly at various instruments of labor, measurement, and detention." Id. at 122.

48. 17 Ronald Hamowy, ed., The Constitution of Liberty: The Definitive Edition 288–89 (2011) ("The Collected Works of F. A. Hayek"); Marian Duggan and Vicky Heap, Administrating Victimization: The Politics of Anti-Social Behaviour and Hate Crime Policy 16 (2014).

49. The Bibliographical Society at the Oxford University Press, *A Dictionary of the Printers and Booksellers Who Were at Work in England, Scotland and Ireland from 1726 to 1775*, *supra* note 45, at 178–79.

50. Id. at 362; Richard J. Jones, Tobias Smollett in the Enlightenment: Travels Through

France, Italy, and Scotland 6 (2011).

51. The Bibliographical Society at the Oxford University Press, *A Dictionary of the Printers and Booksellers Who Were at Work in England, Scotland and Ireland from 1726 to 1775*, *supra* note 45, at 383; M. Pollard, A Dictionary of Members of the Dublin Book Trade 1550–1800 Based on the Records of the Guild of St Luke the Evangelist 190 (2000).

52. Richard B. Sher, The Enlightenment and the Book: Scottish Authors and Their Publishers in Eighteenth-Century Britain, Ireland and America 274, 325, 381–82, 388, 453, 703, 762 (2006).

53. Id. at 703; The Bibliographical Society at the Oxford University Press, *A Dictionary of the Printers and Booksellers Who Were at Work in England, Scotland and Ireland from 1726 to 1775*, *supra* note 45, at 77–78.

54. The Annual Register, or a View of the History, Politicks, and Literature, for the Year 1767, at 316–17 (1768).

55. John D. Bessler, The Celebrated Marquis: An Italian Noble and the Making of the Modern World 50–55 (2018).

56. Lucy Morrison & Staci Stone, A Mary Shelley Encyclopedia 470 (2003).

57. Naomi Zack, The Handy Philosophy Answer Book 187 (2010); N. Jayapalan, Historiography 74 (2008); Voltaire, *Candide* and Related Texts viii (David Wootton, trans. 2000); 3 Graham Oppy & N. N. Trakakis, Early Modern Philosophy of Religion: The History of Western Philosophy of Religion 197 (2014); *see also* David Williams, ed., Voltaire: Political Writings xxv (David Williams, trans. 1994):

In 1762, on the basis of weak evidence and strong religious prejudice, a jury in Toulouse had found the head of a Protestant family, Jean Calas, guilty of the murder of his son, rumoured to be about to convert to Catholicism, and sentenced Calas to be broken on the wheel and strangled. The event had a profound impact on Voltaire, who fought the subsequent case for the rehabilitation of the Calas family without respite until the name of Calas and the iniquities of the French judicial system were the talk of Europe. The verdict was quashed in 1765.

See also Lynn Hunt, The French Revolution and Human Rights: A Brief History with Documents 7 (2d ed. 2016) ("In a punishment all too typical of eighteenth-century penal methods, the executioner first broke Calas's bones with an iron rode and then completed the destruction by pulling his limbs apart on a wheel.").

58. David Williams, ed., Voltaire: Political Writings 87, 98–99 (David Williams, trans. 1994).

59. Id. at xxv.

60. John D. Bessler, The Birth of American Law: An Italian Philosopher and the American Revolution 59, 146 (2014).

61. Id. at 61.

62. Alfred Owen Aldridge, Voltaire and the Century of Light 341 (1975); Florian Schui, Early Debates about Industry: Voltaire and His Contemporaries 152 (2005).

63. Nicholas Cronk, ed., The Cambridge Companion to Voltaire 43 (2009).

64. Ishay, The History of Human Rights, *supra* note 42, at 87, 89.

65. An Essay on Crimes and Punishments, Translated from the Italian of Cæsar Bonesana, Marquis Beccaria 59 (1819).

66. Voltaire, A Commentary on the Book of Crimes and Punishments i, *reprinted in* An Essay on Crimes and Punishments, Translated from the Italian; with Commentary Attributed to Mons. De Voltaire, Translated from the French (4th ed. 1775) ("Printed for F. Newbery, at the Corner of St. Paul's Church-Yard").

67. Bessler, The Birth of American Law, *supra* note 60, at 59, 95, 146–47; Henry Kamen, The Spanish Inquisition: A Historical Revision 372 (4th ed. 2014); Brian P. Levac, ed., The Oxford Handbook of Witchcraft in Early Modern Europe and Colonial America 430 (2013).

68. Voltaire, A Commentary on the Book of Crimes and Punishments, *supra* note 66, at iv–v, xviii–xx, xxxi–xxxii, xxxvi–xxxvii.

69. Charles Pastoor & Galen K. Johnson, The A to Z of the Puritans 52 (2009).

70. Harmelin v. Michigan, 501 U.S. 957, 967–68 (1991); Charles Pastoor & Galen K. Johnson,

Historical Dictionary of the Puritans 52 (2007).

71. Virginia Salima Moorhead, "The Trial of Lady Alice Lisle," Alexander Campbell King Law Library, University of Georgia, http://libguides.law.uga.edu/c.php?g=177206&p=1164821.

72. Ronald H. Fritze & William B. Robison, eds., Historical Dictionary of Stuart England, 1603–1689, at 48 (1996); Gwenda Morgan & Peter Rushton, Banishment in the Early Atlantic World: Convicts, Rebels and Slaves 76 (2013); The Panoplist, or The Christian's Armory 341–42 (1850).

73. Nicholas Cronk, Voltaire: A Very Short Introduction 97 (2017); Voltaire, A Commentary on the Book of Crimes and Punishments, *supra* note 66, at xxxvii–xxxix, xl–xliii, xlvi, xlviii, lxi–lxii. In a section titled "Of false Money," Voltaire wrote of the punishment of counterfeiters, then commonly punishable by death: "Yet death is a severe punishment. I knew a lawyer who was of opinion, that such a criminal should be condemned, as a useful hand, to work in the royal mint, with irons to his legs." Id. at lxi.

74. Bessler, The Celebrated Marquis, *supra* note 55, at 81–82; Tighe Hopkins, The Dungeons of Old Paris: Being the Story and Romance of the Most Celebrated Prisons of the Monarchy and the Revolution 10, 209 (1897); 1 Richard Mowery Andrews, Law, Magistracy, and Crime in Old Regime Paris, 1735–1789: The System of Criminal Justice 448 (1994).

75. Nicholas Cronk, "Introduction," *in* Voltaire, A Pocket Philosophical Dictionary vii–viii, xiii, xxiv, xxvi (John Fletcher, trans. 2011).

76. Montesquieu, Persian Letters 110 (Margaret Mauldon, trans. 2008) (quoting from Letter 78: "*Usbek to Rhedi, in Venice*"); The Persian Letters: with Introduction and Notes, Now Completely Done into English, from the Original 151–52 (1897); *see also* Montesquieu, The Persian Letters: with Introduction and Notes, Now Completely Done into English, from the Original 152 (1901) ("Be assured, my dear Rhedi, that the fact of the penalties in a state being more or less cruel does not make the laws the better obeyed. In countries where the punishments are moderate, they are as much dreaded as in those where they are tyrannical and frightful."); Rebecca Kingston, Montesquieu and the Parlement of Bordeaux 12 (1996) ("Montesquieu worked as a magistrate in the Bordeaux *Parlement* from 1714 to 1726, that is from the age of twenty-five to thirty-seven, a significant period in his intellectual development."); F. C. Montague, ed., Jeremy Bentham, A Fragment on Government 23 (1776) (2001); "Baron de Montesquieu, Charles-Louis de Secondat," Stanford Encyclopedia of Philosophy (first published July 18, 2003; revised April 2, 2014), https://plato.stanford.edu/entries/montesquieu/.

77. Louis P. Masur, Rites of Execution: Capital Punishment and the Transformation of American Culture, 1776–1865, at 51 (1989):

It was Montesquieu who set the standard for an Enlightenment critique of the criminal law. In his *Persian Letters* (1721) and especially *The Spirit of Laws* (1748), Montesquieu argued against the severity of punishments. Extreme terror, he thought, violated the liberty of citizens. Since such severity characterized despotic governments, he thought excessive punishments especially unsuitable for republics. To Montesquieu, the distinction between crimes and their corresponding punishments should be "drawn from nature." He argued that to punish a thief as one would a murderer was to destroy any just proportion between crimes and punishments and encourage commission of the greater rather than less offense.

78. Anne M. Cohler, Basia C. Miller & Harold S. Stone, eds. & trans., Montesquieu: *The Spirit of the Laws* 72 (2013) (the title of Book 6 of Montesquieu's *The Spirit of the Laws*: "Consequences of the principles of the various governments in relation to the simplicity of civil and criminal laws, the forms of judgments, and the establishment of penalties").

79. Mark H. Waddicor, Montesquieu and the Philosophy of Natural Law 138 (2012).

80. Cohler, Miller & Stone, Montesquieu, *supra* note 78, at 316. In *The Spirit of Laws*, Montesquieu also stressed that "[t]he right ... of war is derived from necessity and strict justice." 1 Baron de Montesquieu, The Spirit of Laws 166 (1751) (translated from the French and printed for G. and A. Ewing and G. Faulkner in Dublin); *see also* id. at 292 ("It is false that killing in war is lawful, unless in a case of absolute necessity....").

81. Cohler, Miller & Stone, Montesquieu, *supra* note 78, at 74–75.

82. Id. at 82. In Book 6, chapter 10, Montesquieu wrote "*On the old French laws*":

In the old French laws one surely finds the spirit of monarchy. In cases involving pecuniary penalties, non-nobles are punished less than nobles. It is quite the contrary for crimes; the noble loses his honor and his voice at court while the villein, who has no honor, is punished corporally.

Id. at 83.

83. Id. at 85.

84. Id. at 91–92. In another section of Book 6, titled "*On the law of retaliation*," Montesquieu wrote:

Despotic states, which prefer simple laws, make much use of the law of retaliation; moderate states sometimes accept it. But the difference is that the former have it exercised strictly, while the others almost always temper it.

The law of the Twelve Tables admitted both; it sentenced in terms of retaliation only when the pleader could not be appeased. After sentencing, one could pay damage and interest, and the corporal penalty would be converted into a pecuniary penalty.

Id. at 93–94.

85. Id. at 92–93.

86. Mark H. Waddicor, Montesquieu and the Philosophy of Natural Law 138–39 (2012).

87. Id. at 137 n.7.

88. Brief for the United States, Isbrandtsen-Moller Co., No. 307, 1937 WL 40465 (U.S.) (Appellate Brief) *75 (Jan. 13, 1937) (citing Esprit des Lois (Book 2, Chapter 6)); *see also* Brief for Respondent Harold L. Ickes, as Federal Emergency Administrator of Public Works, Duke Power Co. v. Greenwood County, No. 32, 1936 WL 64961 (U.S.) (Appellate Brief) *135–36 (Nov. 2, 1936) (citing the same principle from Montesquieu's treatise); Brief for the United States, United States v. Certain Lands in the City of Louisville, No. 443, 1935 WL 32991 (U.S.) (Appellate Brief) *116 (October Term) (same).

89. William Michael Treanor, *The Case of the Prisoners and the Origins of Judicial Review*, 143 U. Pa. L. Rev. 491, 523 n.135 (1994).

90. Brent Kelley, James Madison: Father of the Constitution (2013); Thomas J. Cleary, *A Wolf in Sheep's Clothing: The Unilateral Executive and the Separation of Powers*, 6 Pierce L. Rev. 265, 278 (2007); *see also* William Michael Treanor, *The Case of the Prisoners and the Origins of Judicial Review*, 143 U. Pa. L. Rev. 491, 522–23 (1994):

[St. George] Tucker began by invoking the provision of the Virginia Bill of Rights under which "the Executive and Legislative powers of the state should be separate and distinct from the Judiciary" and the parallel provision of the state constitution barring each branch from exercising the powers of another. The relevant question thus became what the judicial function was. Tucker did not, however, treat this subject as one over which people could differ. "Now I hold it to be uncontrovertible," he said, "that the power properly belonging to the Judiciary Department, is, to explain the Laws of the Land as they apply to particular cases." That this power of applying the laws to specific cases was vested exclusively in the judiciary was a necessary restraint on legislative tyranny. He invoked Montesquieu for the proposition that "the same Man or body of men should not enact Laws, or afterwards carry them into execution, for in this case Montesquieu observes arbitrary Laws may first be made and then tyrannically executed, or interpreted." "This," Tucker added, "is also the spirit of our Constitution.... The Judiciary ... are by the Constitution appointed as a counterpoise to the legislature."

91. Tatiana Ryckman, Alexander Hamilton: The First Secretary of the Treasury and an Author of the Federalist Papers (2016); James Thomas Tucker, *Tyranny of the Judiciary: Judicial Dilution of Consent under Section 2 of the Voting Rights Act*, 7 Wm. & Mary Bill Rts. J. 443, 465–67 (1999).

92. 1 Joseph Story, Commentaries on the Constitution of the United States; with a Preliminary Review of the Constitutional History of the Colonies and States, Before the Adoption of the Constitution 455 & n.1 (1833); 2 Joseph Story, Commentaries on the Constitution of the United States; with a Preliminary Review of the Constitutional History of the Colonies and States, Before the Adoption of the Constitution 3, 4 & n.1, 8, 55 n.3, 56 n.1, 58 n.2, 67 n.2, 69 n.3, 70 n.1, 74 n.2, 80 n.2, 189 n.1, 215, 365 n.1 (1833); 3 Joseph Story, Commentaries on the Constitution of the United States; with a Preliminary Review of the Constitutional History of the Colonies and States, Before the Adoption of the Constitution 282, 343–44 & n.1, 346, 426, 457 n.1, 489 n.1, 667, 680, 684, 707, 725 (1833).

93. David W. Carrithers, *Montesquieu's Philosophy of Punishment*, 19 History of Political

Thought 213, 214 & n.3, 215, 218–22, 226 & n.49, 228 & n.59, 229, 235–36 (1998); Leon Radzinowicz, A History of the English Criminal Law and Its Administration from 1750, at 269, 273–74 (1948); *see also* Carrithers, *Montesquieu's Philosophy of Punishment*, *supra*, at 232:

Montesquieu's fourth class of crimes consisted of offences warranting the capital penalty of death. In his judgment, these were crimes of treason, or crimes injurious to life or property. Unlike Beccaria, Montesquieu did not oppose the death penalty, although he recommended drastically restricting its use, as compared to existing practice, by making it apply only to treason, murder, attempted murder, and certain large-scale crimes against property where the offender had no property with which to make restitution. Using explicitly retributive language he opined that: 'A man deserves death (*un citoyen mérite la mort*) when he has violated the security so far as to deprive, or to attempt to deprive another man of his life.' The penalty of death for crimes directly threatening the security of individuals or the state is 'derived from the nature of the thing, founded on reason, and drawn from the very sources of good and evil.' (*puisée dans la raison et dans les sources du bien et du mal*)'.

Compare id. at 234:

Those familiar with Montesquieu's massive treatise, written over the course of some twenty years, are well aware that what he asserts in one text he sometimes appears to take back in another. Thus it will come as no surprise that although he must be read as a proponent of the death penalty for a few heinous crimes, and although he referred explicitly to the law of the *talion* in his justification, he also cast aspersions on blatantly retaliatory punishment schemes, by linking such punishment modes to despotic states.

94. Bessler, The Celebrated Marquis, *supra* note 55, at 17, 33–35, 104, 266, 287, 290; Cesare Beccaria, On Crimes and Punishments lx (Graeme R. Newman & Pietro Marongiu, eds., 5th ed. 2009).

95. According to *A Montesquieu Dictionary*:

[T]he cardinal principle of the necessity that alone confers legitimacy not only on all punishment, but more broadly on "every act of authority from one man to another" ("tout acte d'autorité d'homme à homme", *Delitti*, § II, p. 63), is associated by Beccaria with a passage in *L'Esprit des lois*: "Every punishment that does not derive from necessity is tyrannical" ("Toute peine qui ne dérive pas de la nécessité est tyrannique", *EL*, XIX, 14, t. I, p. 336).

"Beccaria, Cesare," A Montesquieu Dictionary, http://dictionnaire-montesquieu.ens-lyon.fr/en/article/1367159675/en/#themes-article.

96. Åke Frändberg, From Rechtsstaat to Universal Law-State: An Essay in Philosophical Jurisprudence 150 (2014). This passage is often translated into English in slightly different ways, though the substance—or central gist or sentiment—is the same regardless of the translation. *E.g.*, David Williams, ed., The Enlightenment 443 (1999):

Every punishment which is not derived from absolute necessity is tyrannous, says the great Montesquieu, a proposition which may be generalised as follows: every act of authority between one man and another which is not derived from absolute necessity is tyrannous.

Accord Micheline R. Ishay, ed., The Human Rights Reader: Major Political Essays, Speeches, and Documents from the Bible to the Present 119 (1997) (reprinting the same translation of the passage).

97. *E.g.*, 4 Anthologia Hibernica: or Monthly Collections of Science, Belles-Lettres, and History 245 (1794); Vol. XL The Antijacobin Review, and True Churchman's Magazine; or, Monthly, Political, and Literary Censor 180 (1811); Bentham on Liberty: Jeremy Bentham's Idea of Liberty in Relation to His Utilitarianism 28 (1977); *see also* The United Service Journal and Naval and Military Magazine 344 (1833) ("Montesquieu asserts, what any body else might have asserted, that every punishment which does not arise from necessity is tyrannical. But the misapplication of this position must not be permitted to dispossess our judges, magistrates, and officers, of the spirit necessary for executing the duties committed to their charge; for, as hath been said by Beccaria,—"*Crimes are more effectually prevented by the* Certainty *than the severity of punishment.*").

98. Daniel J. Boorstin, The Mysterious Science of the Law: An Essay on Blackstone's *Commentaries* Showing How Blackstone, Employing Eighteenth-Century Ideas of Science, Religion, History, Aesthetics, and Philosophy, Made of the Law at Once a Conservative

AND A MYSTERIOUS SCIENCE 150 (1996).

99. MANASSEH DAWES, AN ESSAY ON CRIMES AND PUNISHMENTS, WITH A VIEW OF, AND COMMENTARY UPON, BECCARIA, ROUSSEAU, VOLTAIRE, MONTESQUIEU, FIELDING, AND BLACKSTONE iii, vii, xii–xiii, xvi, xxi, xxv, 11, 53, 63–64, 75, 117, 121, 123, 143, 207, 217, 221 (1782); *see also* DAINES BARRINGTON, OBSERVATIONS ON THE MORE ANCIENT STATUTES FROM MAGNA CHARTA TO THE TWENTY-FIRST OF JAMES I. CAP. XXVII, at 498 (5th ed. 1796) ("The Marquis *Beccaria*, who seems to have adopted most of *Montesquieu's* ideas, makes use of the following argument against the use of torture....").

100. AARON THOMAS, ED., CESARE BECCARIA, *ON CRIMES AND PUNISHMENTS* AND OTHER WRITINGS 11 (Aaron Thomas & Jeremy Parzen, trans., 2008).

101. CHARLTON T. LEWIS, AN ELEMENTARY LATIN DICTIONARY 531 (1918).

102. 2 THOMAS SHERIDAN, A COMPLETE DICTIONARY OF THE ENGLISH LANGUAGE, BOTH WITH REGARD TO SOUND AND MEANING: ONE MAIN OBJECT OF WHICH IS, TO ESTABLISH A PLAIN AND PERMANENT STANDARD OF PRONUNCIATION (3d ed. 1790) (definition of "NECESSITY"); EDWARD PHILLIPS, COMP., THE NEW WORLD OF WORDS: OR, UNIVERSAL ENGLISH DICTIONARY (6th ed. 1706) (definition of "necessity"); NATHAN BAILEY, AN UNIVERSAL ETYMOLOGICAL ENGLISH DICTIONARY; COMPREHENDING THE DERIVATIONS OF THE GENERALITY OF WORDS IN THE ENGLISH TONGUE, EITHER ANCIENT OR MODERN, FROM THE ANCIENT BRITISH, SAXON, DANISH, NORMAN, AND MODERN FRENCH, TEUTONIC, DUTCH, SPANISH, ITALIAN; AS ALSO FROM THE LATIN, GREEK, AND HEBREW LANGUAGES, EACH IN THEIR PROPER CHARACTERS (definition of "NECESSITY").

103. SAMUEL JOHNSON, A DICTIONARY OF THE ENGLISH LANGUAGE (10th ed. 1792) (definition of "NECESSITY").

104. Id. (definition of "NECESSARY"); *accord* 2 THOMAS SHERIDAN, A COMPLETE DICTIONARY OF THE ENGLISH LANGUAGE, BOTH WITH REGARD TO SOUND AND MEANING: ONE MAIN OBJECT OF WHICH IS, TO ESTABLISH A PLAIN AND PERMANENT STANDARD OF PRONUNCIATION (3d ed. 1790) (definition of "NECESSARY").

105. EDWARD PHILLIPS, COMP., THE NEW WORLD OF WORDS: OR, UNIVERSAL ENGLISH DICTIONARY (6th ed. 1706) (definition of "Necessary"); *accord* NATHAN BAILEY, AN UNIVERSAL ETYMOLOGICAL ENGLISH DICTIONARY; COMPREHENDING THE DERIVATIONS OF THE GENERALITY OF WORDS IN THE ENGLISH TONGUE, EITHER ANCIENT OR MODERN, FROM THE ANCIENT BRITISH, SAXON, DANISH, NORMAN, AND MODERN FRENCH, TEUTONIC, DUTCH, SPANISH, ITALIAN; AS ALSO FROM THE LATIN, GREEK, AND HEBREW LANGUAGES, EACH IN THEIR PROPER CHARACTERS (21st ed. 1770) (defining "NECESSARY" as "needful, unavoidable, indispensable").

106. THOMAS DYCHE & WILLIAM PARDON, A NEW GENERAL ENGLISH DICTIONARY; PECULIARLY CALCULATED FOR THE USE AND IMPROVEMENT OF SUCH AS ARE UNACQUAINTED WITH THE LEARNED LANGUAGES (1760) (definition of "NECESSARY").

107. 1 BASIL MONTAGU, COMP., THE OPINIONS OF DIFFERENT AUTHORS UPON THE PUNISHMENT OF DEATH 20–21 (1809) (quoting Beccaria; italics in original). In *On Crimes and Punishments*, Beccaria—living in Milan, then part of the Habsburg Empire—took the following position:

> The death of a citizen *cannot be necessary, but in one case*. When, though deprived of his liberty, he has such power and connections as may endanger the security of the nation; when his existence may produce a dangerous revolution in the established form of government. But even in this case, it can only be necessary when a nation is on the verge of recovering or losing its liberty; or in times of absolute anarchy, when the disorders themselves hold the place of laws. But in a reign of tranquillity; in a form of government approved by the united wishes of the nation; in a state well fortified from enemies without, and supported by strength within, and opinion, perhaps more efficacious; where all power is lodged in the hands of a true sovereign; where riches can purchase pleasures and not authority, there can be no necessity for taking away the life of a subject.

Id. at 21 (italics in original).

108. Id. at 23.

109. AARON THOMAS, ED., CESARE BECCARIA, *ON CRIMES AND PUNISHMENTS* AND OTHER WRITINGS 40 (Aaron Thomas & Jeremy Parzen, trans., 2008).

110. Id. at 65.

111. Michael J. Zydney Mannheimer, *Not the Crime But the Cover-Up: A Deterrence-Based Rationale*

for the Premeditation-Deliberation Formula, 86 Ind. L.J. 879, 914–15 (2011).

112. Richard Vaux, "The Pennsylvania Prison System" (read before the American Philosophical Society, June 20, 1884), *in* 21 Proceedings of the American Philosophical Society Held at Philadelphia for Promoting Useful Knowledge 651, 662, 664 (1884).

113. 1 The Science of Legislation, from the Italian of Gaetano Filangieri 28, 36, 74, 82, 86–88, 95, 138–39, 141, 149, 177–78, 182–83, 240, 256–57, 261, 265 (1806); John D. Bessler, *The Italian Enlightenment and the American Revolution: Cesare Beccaria's Forgotten Influence on American Law*, 37 Mitchell Hamline J. Pub. Pol'y & Prac. (2016), Iss. 1, Article 1, p. 15.

114. Marcello T. Maestro, Transactions of the American Philosophical Society (1976), Vol. 66, Part 6, p. 31.

115. George Richards Minot, "Oration as Delivered at Boston, March 5, 1782," *in* Orations, Delivered at the Request of the Inhabitants of the Town of Boston, to Commemorate the Evening of the Fifth of March, 1770; When a Number of Citizens Were Killed by a Party of British Troops, Quartered Among Them, in a Time of Peace 163–64, 166–67 (2d ed. 1807); To George Washington from George Richards Minot, Aug. 7, 1788, *available at* www.founders.archives.gov. This maxim was referenced in other places, too, around that time. The Grand Instructions to the Commissioners Appointed to Frame a New Code of Laws for the Russian Empire: Composed by Her Imperial Majesty Catherine II, Empress of all the Russias 81 (Michael Tatischeff, trans. 1768) ("In a Word, every Punishment, which is not inflicted through Necessity, is tyrannical."); *compare* William Godwin, An Enquiry Concerning Political Justice, and Its Influence on General Virtue and Happiness 161 (1793):

Punishment is one of those classes of coercion, the multiplication of which is so much to be deprecated, and which nothing but the most urgent necessity can in any case justify. That necessity is commonly admitted to exist, where a man has proved by his unjust actions the injuriousness of his character, and where the injury, the repetition of which is to be apprehended, is of such a nature as to be committed before we can have sufficient notice to guard ourselves against it.

William Godwin's book made explicit reference to "[t]he humane and benevolent Beccaria." Id. at 256.

116. "Address To the People of South-Carolina" & "Serious Questions Proposed to All Friends to The Rights of Mankind, With Suitable Answers" (Boston, 1787), *in* 1 Charles S. Hyneman & Donald S. Lutz, American Political Writing during the Founding Era 1760–1805, at 20, 22–23, 25, 565, 567–92, 599, 675–76 (1983). In 1787, in Boston, one writer penned a piece called "Serious Questions Proposed to All Friends to The Rights of Mankind, with Suitable Answers." Published on November 19, 1787, in the *Boston Gazette*, that piece began:

As much has been said in favour of the proposed New Constitution,—and as little is allowed to be said against it,—I now send you, for the information and consideration *of your readers, the ideas the people had of a Constitution in the year 1776, contained in a number of serious questions and answers, published in the Pennsylvania Evening Post, at a time when the whole people were contending with a powerful nation for the security of their Liberties and a free Constitution, with a determined resolution to transmit the same to succeeding generations. And as we are now about to establish the free Constitution which they then fought and bled for, shall we not be allowed to examine it?—shall we not be allowed to give our sentiments upon it, with the same manly freedom with which they were inspired while the bayonet was held at their breasts?* We Will.

The various questions—for example, "What is government?" "What ought a society to do to secure a good government?" "Who ought to form a new constitution of government?"—and the respective answers—"Certain powers vested by society in public persons for the security, peace and happiness of its members." "Any thing. The happiness of man, as an inhabitant of this world, depends entirely upon it." "The people"—made clear that the Enlightenment had clearly come to America. Id. at 702–704.

117. Walter J. Baldwin, Punishment without Crime: or, Imprisonment for Debt 169 n.* (1813) ("The wise and benevolent Beccaria, in one of the editions of his Essay on Crimes and Punishments, says on this subject, 'In the former editions of this work, I myself fell into this error, when I said that the honest bankrupt should be kept in custody, as a pledge for his debts, or employed as a slave to work for his Creditors. I am ashamed of having adopted so cruel an opinion. I have been

accused of impiety; I did not deserve it. I have been accused of sedition; I deserved it as little. But I insulted all the rights of humanity, and was never reproached.'"); *see also* id. at 152 n.* (referring to "[t]he profound and philanthropic Beccaria"); id. at 140, 152 (quoting and referencing Montesquieu); *see also* Bruce H. Mann, Republic of Debtors: Bankruptcy in the Age of American Independence 101–105 (2002) (noting that William Keteltas, in *Forlorn Hope*, a newspaper he published within prison during 1800, "reprinted a chapter from Cesare Beccaria, the Italian theorist whose writings shaped American penal reform, in which Beccaria asked 'upon what barbarous pretence' the 'honest bankrupt' was imprisoned and 'ranked with criminals.'").

118. An Enquiry into the Effects of Public Punishments upon Criminals, and Upon Society Read in the Society for Promoting Political Enquiries, Convened at the House of His Excellency Benjamin Franklin, Esquire, in Philadelphia, March 9th, 1787, at 4 (1787); A Dictionary of the Book-Arts and Book Trade in Philadelphia to 1820: Including Painters and Engravers 66 (1949).

119. John D. Bessler, "The Birth of American Law: An Italian Philosopher and the American Revolution," American Constitution Society Book Talk, Sept. 16, 2014, https://www.acslaw.org/acsblog/the-birth-of-american-law-an-italian-philosopher-and-the-american-revolution; Noah Webster, "On Education of Youth in America" (1790), *in* Andrew J. Milson, Chara Haeussler Bohan, Perry L. Glanzer & J. Wesley Null, eds., American Educational Thought: Essays from 1640–1940, at 71, 86 (2010); Robert Coram,"Political Inquiries, to which is Added a Plan for the Establishment of Schools Throughout the United States" (Wilmington, 1791), Joel Barlow, "A Letter to the National Convention of France on the Defects in the Constitution of 1791" (New York, 1792) & Noah Webster, "An Oration on the Anniversary of the Declaration of Independence" (New Haven, 1802), *in* 2 Charles S. Hyneman & Donald S. Lutz, eds., American Political Writing during the Founding Era 1760–1805, at 756, 782, 794, 815, 818, 820, 823, 832–35, 1220, 1226 (1983). Jeremiah Atwater (1773–1835), a graduate of Yale who became the first president of Middlebury College, also choose this quote from Montesquieu to introduce an 1801 sermon: "The natural place of Virtue is near to Liberty; but it is not nearer to extreme liberty than to servitude." Id. at 1170.

Chapter 2

1. Alice Ristroph, *Proportionality as a Principle of Limited Government*, 55 Duke L.J. 263, 263 (2005).

2. Id. at 264–65.

3. Julian V. Roberts, Criminal Justice Processing of Sexual Assault Cases 42 (Canadian Centre for Justice Statistics, Integration and Analysis Program, 1994).

4. Robert Cryer, Håkan Friman, Darryl Robinson & Elizabeth Wilmshurst, An Introduction to International Criminal Law and Procedure 25 (2d ed. 2010).

5. Jesper Ryberg, The Ethics of Proportionate Punishment: A Critical Investigation 13 (2004).

6. Alan Norrie, Crime, Reason and History: A Critical Introduction to Criminal Law 213 (2d ed. 2001).

7. Brief of Appellant Weldon Angelos, *United States v. Angelos*, No. 04-4282, 2005 WL 2367629 (10th Cir.) (Appellate Brief) *16 n.11 (June 16, 2015) (citations omitted); *see also* id. (citing Montesquieu's maxim that "[a]ll punishment which is not derived from necessity is tyrannical" and citing Beccaria's and Bentham's writings on proportionality).

8. Aaron Xavier Fellmeth, *Challenges and Implications of a Systemic Social Effect Theory*, 2006 U. Ill. L. Rev. 691, 746 n.242 (2006) (quoting John Locke, An Essay Concerning the True Origin, Extent and End of Civil Government (Peter Latlett, ed., Cambridge Univ. Press 1967) (1690)).

9. Utrum Horum; or God's Ways of Disposing of Kingdoms: And Some Clergy-Men's Ways of Disposing of Them 55, 57 (1691) (containing the recitals about "Excessive Fines" and "Illegal and cruel Punishments," and reprinting the prohibition on "Excessive Bail," "Excessive Fines," and "cruel and unusual Punishments"); 1 The Twelfth and Last Collection of Papers Relating to the Present Juncture of Affairs in England and Scotland 17–18 (1689) (containing the recitals about "Excessive Fines" and "Illegal and Cruel Punishments," and reprinting the prohibition on "Ex-

cessive Bail," "Excessive Fines," and "cruel and unusual Punishments"); The History of the House of Orange; or, A Brief Relation of the Glorious and Magnanimous Atchievements of His Majesties Renowned Predecessors, and Likewise of His Own Heroick Actions till the Late Wonderful Revolution 140–42 (1693) (containing the recitals about "Excessive Fines" and "illegal and cruel Punishments," and reprinting the prohibition on "Excessive Bail," "Excessive Fines," and "cruel and unusual Punishments"); The History of the Desertion, or An Account of All the Publick Affairs in England, from the Beginning of September 1688 to the Twelfth of February Following 128–29 (1689) (containing the recitals about "Excessive Fines" and "Illegal and cruel Punishments," and reprinting the prohibition on "Excessive Bail," "Excessive Fines," and "cruel and unusual punishments"); *accord* 1 Of the Use and Abuse of Parliaments: In Two Historical Discourses 114 (1744).

10. *See generally* John Pollock, The Popish Plot: A Study in the History of the Reign of Charles II (1944); 1 Mary Maples Dunn & Richard S. Dunn, eds., The Papers of William Penn (1644–1679), at 558 n.2 (1981); An Historical Narrative of the Horrid Plot and Conspiracy of Titus Oates, Called the Popish Plot, in Its Various Branches and Progress, Selected from the Most Authentic Protestant Historians, to Which Are Added Some Cursory Observations on the Test Act 61 (1816); "Proceedings on a Writ of Inquiry of Damages between his Royal Highness James Duke of York, in an Action upon the Statute de Scandalis Magnatum, and Titus Oates, in the King's Bench: 36 Charles II. A.D. 1684," *in* 10 T. B. Howell, comp., A Complete Collection of State Trials and Proceedings for High Treason and Other Crimes and Misdemeanors from the Earliest Period to the Year 1783, with Notes and Other Illustrations 126–48 (1816); 23 The Law Magazine and Review; A Quarterly Review of Jurisprudence and Quarterly Digest of Reported Cases 345 (1898).

11. Caroline Jowett, The History of Newgate Prison 54–55 (2017).

12. 2 Thomas Coventry & Samuel Hughes, An Analytical Digested Index to the Common Law Reports from the Time of Henry III to the Commencement of the Reign of George III 1226 (1832).

13. John D. Bessler, Cruel and Unusual: The American Death Penalty and the Founders' Eighth Amendment 174–75 (2012); Charles E. Little, Cyclopedia of Classified Dates with an Exhaustive Index 897 (1900); 1 Nugent Robinson, comp., A History of the World with All Its Great Sensations Together with Its Mighty and Decisive Battles and the Rise and Fall of Its Nations from the Earliest Times to the Present Day 332 (1897); Gilbert Burnet, Bishop Burnet's History of His Own Time: From the Restoration of King Charles the Second to the Treaty of Peace at Utrecht, in the Reign of Queen Anne 383 (new ed. 1857); Leonard W. Levy, Origins of the Bill of Rights 236 (2001); Oates's Manifesto; or, The Complaint of Titus Oates Against the Doctor of Salamanca; and, The Same Doctor Against Titus Oates: Comprized in a Dialogue Between the Said Parties, on Occasion of Some Inconsistent Evidence Given About the Horrid and Damnable Popish Plot (1683); The Memoires of Titus Oates: Written for Publick Satisfaction A3 (1685) ("The Preface"); The Tryals, Convictions & Sentence of Titus Otes, upon Two Indictments for Willful, Malicious, and Corrupt Perjury: At the Kings-Bench-Barr at Westminster, Before the Right Honourable George Lord Jeffreys, Baron of Wem, Lord Chief Justice of His Majesties Court of Kings-Bench, and the Rest of the Judges of that Court Upon Friday the 8th. and Saturday the 9th. Days of May, Anno Domini, 1685. And in the First Year of the Reign of our Soveraign Lord King James the II. &c. 56–58 (1685) [hereinafter "The Tryals"].

14. The Memoires of Titus Oates: Written for Publick Satisfaction A3 (1685) ("The Preface"); Ronald H. Fritze & William B. Robison, eds., Historical Dictionary of Stuart England, 1603–1689, at 48 (1996); The Tryals, *supra* note 13, at 58–59.

15. *E.g.*, Richard West: The Life and Strange Surprising Adventures of Daniel Defoe 24 (1997) ("The suffering of Oates must have shocked Defoe, who always believed at least part of the story about a Popish plot.").

16. The Tryals, *supra* note 13, at 59–60; Humphrey W. Woolrych, The Life of Judge Jeffreys, Chief Justice of the King's Bench under Charles II, and Lord High Chancellor of England during the Reign of James II, at 131–34 (1852).

17. The Tryals, *supra* note 13, at 60.

18. James Q. Whitman, Harsh Justice: Criminal Punishment and the Widening Divide between America and Europe 156 (2003).

19. During the reign of King James II, the Earl of Devonshire had been fined thirty thousand pounds for striking a man with a cane, and he had been committed to the King's Bench prison until such time as he could pay the fine. (A bond was ultimately posted for the full sum of thirty thousand pounds, which bond was later "found among the papers of King *James* after his abdication," whereupon "it was given up to the Earl by King *William*.") It was contended in 1689 that the fine that had been imposed upon the Earl of Devonshire was excessive and "a great violation of the privileges of the peers of this realm." After a "committee of privileges" was appointed by the House of Lords to examine the harsh sentence, it was demanded that the judges who had rendered the judgment in the Earl of Devonshire's case "should be required to attend at the bar of this House, to answer for the great offence, which they have committed thereby."

Each of the judges "were severally asked what they had to say for themselves in this business," with Mr. Justice Powell offering this explanation and response: "That it was his great misfortune, that he was misguided by some books, which he looked on as authorities, which he found by their Lordships judgment were not so: And he humbly begged their Lordships and the Earl of *Devonshire*'s pardon. As to the fine, he looked upon three thousand pounds to be a fine enough; and that his silence in that business was his greatest fault, for which he also begged pardon." Sir Robert Wright, another of judges, also contended "that as to the breach of privilege, they were misguided by precedents." "As to the fine, which is usually set according to the quality and estate of the person fined," he said, "it came from the puny judge thirty thousand pounds, and so to him last, according to the course of the court; and if he was mistaken, he begged pardon, for he never had the least disrespect to the Earl of *Devonshire*." The final judge, Sir Richard Holloway, had this to say, as it was later reported in *The History of England*: "that he as second Judge pronounced the fine thirty thousand pounds, which was set *nemine contradicente*; and if a lesser fine had been proposed, he should have accepted it, and did not justify the proceedings, but looked on it as an excessive fine, and begged my Lord *Devonshire*'s pardon, and submitted all to their Lordships."

When the Lords asked the three judges if they had discussed the fine before handing it out, Wright denied that had happened, Holloway declared he "had no direction from either the King or Lord Chancellor concerning the said fine," while Powell "appealed to the memory of Sir *Richard Holloway*, that there was a discourse of the fine, five or six days before at the Lord Chancellor's" but Holloway "pretended he did not remember" and Wright "denied that they were there purposely about the said fine." Powell specifically recalled that the Lord Chancellor had "first proposed twenty thousand pounds and afterwards said, it would be better, if thirty thousand pounds, and then the King might abate ten thousand pounds." On May 15, 1689, "the Lords Spiritual and Temporal, upon a full consideration of the several cases and precedents, wherein the privileges of Peers had been concerned," declared:

That the court of King's bench, in over-ruling the Earl of *Devonshire*'s plea of privilege of Parliament, and forcing him to plead over in chief, it being within the usual time of privilege, did thereby commit a manifest breach of privilege; and that the fine of thirty thousand pounds imposed by the court of King's Bench upon the said Earl was excessive and exorbitant, and against *Magna Charta*, the common right of the subject, and the law of the land; and that no peer of this realm, at any time, ought to be committed for non-payment of a fine to the king.

3 Rapin de Thoyras, The History of England 92–93 & n.1 (1744).

20. Samuel Johnson, a chaplain and the "author of several tracts which had given offence to the courts of King *Charles* II. and *James* II.," had been charged and brought before the King's Bench "for making, printing, and publishing a scandalous and seditious libel, intitled, *An humble and hearty address to all the Protestants in King James's army*." After being forced to plead, a jury found him guilty of the offense, and the very same justice who had announced Titus Oates's draconian sentence had ordered Mr. Johnson: (1) "To pay five hundred marks to the King, and to lie in the prison of the *King's Bench* till it be paid"; (2) "To stand in the pillory three days, in three several places, *viz.*, the *Palace-Yard Westminster*, *Temple-Bar*, and the *Old-Change*"; and (3) "To be whipt by the common hangman from *Newgate* to *Tyburn*." Mr. Johnson's sentence, carried out in November 1686, was reportedly "executed with rigour and cruelty, the whipping, being with a whip of nine cords." Id. at 93–94 & n.1.

21. Luke Owen Pike, A History of Crime in England: Illustrating the Changes of the Laws in the Progress of Civilisation Written from the Public Records and Other Contemporary Evidence 232 (1876).

22. *E.g.*, 3 Thomas Babington Macaulay, The History of England from the Accession of James II., at 302 (1898) ("Some living Whigs obtained without difficulty redress for injuries which they had suffered in the late reign. The sentence of Samuel Johnson was taken into consideration by the House of Commons. It was resolved that the scourging which he had undergone was cruel, and that his degradation was of no legal effect."); id. at 303 (noting that William III compensated Mr. Johnson "for the wrongs which the Commons had brought to his notice" by conferring the sum of one thousand pounds along with "a pension of three hundred [pounds] a year for two lives"); id. at 303–04:

While the Commons were considering the case of Johnson, the Lords were scrutinising with severity the proceedings which had, in the late reign, been instituted against one of their own order, the Earl of Devonshire. The judges who had passed sentence on him were strictly interrogated; and a resolution was passed declaring that in his case the privileges of the peerage had been infringed, and that the Court of King's Bench, in punishing a hasty blow by a fine of thirty thousand pounds, had violated common justice and the Great Charter.

23. Associates of Oates were also fined, whipped, and subjected to the pillory. An Historical Narrative of the Horrid Plot and Conspiracy of Titus Oates, Called the Popish Plot, in Its Various Branches and Progress, Selected from the Most Authentic Protestant Historians, to Which Are Added Some Cursory Observations on the Test Act 281 (1816).

24. 3 Rapin de Thoyras, The History of England 94 (1744).

25. Stephen Halliday, Newgate: London's Prototype of Hell (2009) (discussing the case of Titus Oates).

26. "Proceedings in the House of Lords on the Case of the Earl of Devonshire after the Revolution" (extracted from the Journals of the Lords), *in* 11 T. B. Howell, comp., A Complete Collection of State Trials and Proceedings for High Treason and Other Crimes and Misdemeanors from the Earliest Period to the Present Time, with Notes and Other Illustrations 1367–72 (1811).

27. 3 Rapin de Thoyras, The History of England 92–93 & n.1 (1744).

28. Bessler, Cruel and Unusual, *supra* note 13, at 175–76; 3 Thomas Babington Macaulay, The History of England from the Accession of James II., at 304–11 (1898); 2 A Collection of the Parliamentary Debates in England, from the Year M,DC,LXVIII. to the Present Time 455–56, 459–63 (1741); 2 Arthur Trevor, The Life and Times of William the Third, King of England, and Stadholder of Holland 59 (1836). The House of Lords also recommended that William III grant Oates "a Pension of three Pounds a Week for his subsistence." The Life of William III, Late King of England, and Prince of Orange 233 (2d ed. corr. 1703).

29. The Riverside Dictionary of Biography 421 (2005); Doyne C. Bell, Notices of the Historic Persons Buried in the Chapel of St. Peter Ad Vincula, in the Tower of London 279–85 (1877); H. B. Butler & C. R. L. Fletcher, Historical Portraits 1600–1700: The Lives, at 237 (1911); Charles Pastoor & Galen K. Johnson, The A to Z of the Puritans 52 (2009); "Incidents and Reflections—No. 181," The Friend, Vol. 62, No. 52 (1889), pp. 1–2.

30. 3 Francis Hargrave, A Complete Collection of State-Trials, and Proceedings for High-Treason, and Other Crimes and Misdemeanours 165–66 (4th ed. 1776); 2 A Collection of State Tracts, Publish'd During the Reign of King William III, at 1–2 (1706). After the death of Queen Mary II in 1694, "*A Defence of the Archbishop's Sermon on the Death of her late Majesty of blessed Memory*" printed in 1695, the writer spoke of "Liberties that we enjoy as the direct Fruits of the Revolution." "We are now deliver'd from excessive Bails and Fines, and cruel unusual Punishments," the writer stressed, among other things. Id. at 522–52, 525–26.

31. Peter Karl Koritansky, Thomas Aquinas and the Philosophy of Punishment 141–42 (2012).

32. Victor Menaldo & Nora Webb Williams, "Judicial Supremacy: Explaining False Starts and Surprising Successes," *in* Robert Hazell & James Melton, eds., Magna Carta and Its Modern Legacy 185 (2015).

33. John R. Vile, Founding Documents of America: Documents Decoded 5 (2015).

34. Craig S. Lerner, "Magna Carta and Modern Myth-Making: Proportionality in the 'Cruel and Unusual Punishments' Clause," *in* ROBERT HAZELL & JAMES MELTON, EDS., MAGNA CARTA AND ITS MODERN LEGACY 147, 153–53 (2015). Though the influential writings of Montesquieu and Beccaria both explicitly and forthrightly address the principle of proportionality very generally *in the context of the criminal law*, the Magna Carta's provisions dealing with proportionality were—it has been noted—focused on amercements. *Compare* id. at 148 ("My claim is that the articles in Magna Carta that are now cited to stand for the principle that the punishment must fit the crime do no such thing because, at bottom, those articles do not concern criminal activity.") *and* id. at 155 ("Attention to the language of Articles 20 to 22, especially in tandem with other articles, undercuts the claim that these provisions contemplated criminal punishment. We then consider reference to amercement in Glanvill's Treatise (written in the years 1187 to 1189); amercement appears as a non-criminal penalty for an administrative offence or an abuse of the litigation process.") *and* id. at 155–56 (noting that articles 20, 21 and 22 "concern 'amercement'" but that "modern editions of Magna Carta translate *amerciteur* as 'fine'" and that "the authors of Magna Carta were attentive to the difference between fines and amercements" and that "Articles 20 to 22 were not intended to apply to fines"), *with* id. 148–51 (noting that Articles 20 to 22 restrict "amercements" to those "in accordance with the gravity of the offense," writing that an *amercement* was "not regarded as a *criminal* penalty," and arguing that a North Carolina case, *State v. Driver* (1878), a decision pointing to the English Bill of Rights and the Magna and the Magna Carta and that the U.S. Supreme Court later cited in *Weems v. United States* (1910), was "the first American case to hold that the cruel and unusual punishments clause embodied a proportionality principle") *and* id. at 153:

In the years that followed, four more justices argued that Magna Carta's embodiment of a proportionality principle in Article 20, traced through the English Bill of Rights, found expression in the Eighth Amendment. This view emerged in 1983 as the triumphant majority position in *Solem v. Helm*, which overturned a life sentence imposed on a non-violent offender: "The principle that a punishment should be proportionate to the crime is deeply rooted and frequently repeated in common-law jurisprudence. In 1215 three [articles] of Magna Carta were devoted to the rule that 'amercements' may not be excessive."

35. Aniceto Masferrer, "The Liberal State and Criminal Law Reform in Spain," *in* MORTIMER SELLERS & TADEUSZ TOMASZEWSKI, EDS., THE RULE OF LAW IN COMPARATIVE PERSPECTIVE 31 (2010).

36. MONSIEUR DE VATTEL, THE LAW OF NATIONS; OR, PRINCIPLES OF THE LAW OF NATURE, APPLIED TO THE CONDUCT AND AFFAIRS OF NATIONS AND SOVEREIGNS 81, 281–82 (1858) (for a new edition by Joseph Chitty with additional notes and references by Edward D. Ingraham).

37. GROTIUS, THE RIGHTS OF WAR AND PEACE: INCLUDING THE LAW OF NATURE AND OF NATIONS 1, 4, 75, 221–22 (A. C. Campbell, trans. 1901).

38. HUGO GROTIUS, THE RIGHTS OF WAR AND PEACE (Richard Tuck, ed. 2005), Book II (containing Grotius's views on punishment and clemency).

39. GROTIUS, THE RIGHTS OF WAR AND PEACE, *supra* note 37, at 222.

40. Id. at 224–25.

41. CESARE BECCARIA, AN ESSAY ON CRIMES AND PUNISHMENTS, TRANSLATED FROM THE ITALIAN OF CÆSAR BONESANA, MARQUIS BECCARIA, TO WHICH IS ADDED, A COMMENTARY BY M. D. VOLTAIRE, TRANSLATED FROM THE FRENCH 158–59 (2d Am. ed., Edward D. Ingraham, trans. 1819). Beccaria's views on this point were also discussed elsewhere. *See* JOSEPH STORY, COMMENTARIES ON THE CONSTITUTION OF THE UNITED STATES; WITH A PRELIMINARY REVIEW OF THE CONSTITUTIONAL HISTORY OF THE COLONIES AND STATES, BEFORE THE ADOPTION OF THE CONSTITUTION 547–59 (1833) (discussing Beccaria's views on the pardoning power).

42. Others also later referenced Cesare Beccaria's views on pardons. Francis Lieber—a well-known nineteenth-century scholar—had this to say in his book, *On Civil Liberty and Self-Government*:

Although the pardoning power has always existed, and has been abandoned by ultra-despotism for the sake of despotism itself, yet the abuse to which it easily leads, and the apparent incongruity which it involves, have induced many men of deep reflection, in ancient as well as in modern times, to raise their voices against it: of whom we mention Plato and Cicero among the ancients, and Pastoret, Servin, Filangieri, and the benevolent Beccaria among the moderns. The later, the pioneer of penal reform, and one of the benefactors of mankind, has the following remarkable passage....

1 Francis Lieber, On Civil Liberty and Self Government 392–93 (1853).

43. Thomas Jefferson to Edmund Pendleton, Aug. 26, 1776, *available at* www.founders.archives.gov.

44. 64. A Bill for Proportioning Crimes and Punishments in Cases Heretofore Capital, 18 June 1779," *Founders Online*, National Archives, last modified February 1, 2018, http://founders.archives.gov/documents/Jefferson/01-02-02-0132-0004-0064. [Original source: *The Papers of Thomas Jefferson*, vol. 2, *1777?–?18 June 1779*, ed. Julian P. Boyd. Princeton: Princeton University Press, 1950, pp. 492–507.] James Madison attempted to pass Thomas Jefferson's Bill for Proportioning Crimes and Punishments in the 1780s. As an editorial note on the Virginia General Assembly of 1785 observes of Madison's efforts:

The influence of Enlightenment thought is evident in the course JM pursued in the 1785 session. An intent to bring order and reason into his state's government became manifest in his efforts to forward passage of the Revised Code and amendments in the Assize Court and Port bills. JM presented 118 bills in the Revised Code early in the session in the hope of completing the long-unfinished business. The legislature slowly progressed through the bills until conservative, pragmatic Virginians balked at Jefferson's bill on crimes and punishments, which was based on enlightened Beccarian principles. Refusing to accept the liberal and humanitarian experiment in penal reform, the legislators debated and delayed, jeopardizing the whole legal experiment. Finally in mid-December the Committee of the Whole discharged the bill from further consideration.

"The General Assembly Session of October 1785 (Editorial Note)," *Founders Online*, National Archives, last modified February 1, 2018, http://founders.archives.gov/documents/Madison/01-08-02-0204. [Original source: *The Papers of James Madison*, vol. 8, *10 March 1784?–?28 March 1786*, ed. Robert A. Rutland and William M. E. Rachal. Chicago: The University of Chicago Press, 1973, pp. 389–391.]

After Jefferson's death, James Madison wrote to Nicholas Biddle from Montpelier on May 17, 1827, penning these words:

I thank you very sincerely for the copy of your "Eulogium on Thomas Jefferson". I have derived from it the peculiar pleasure which so happy a portraiture could not fail to afford one, who intimately knew and feelingly admired the genius, the learning, the devotion to public liberty, and the many private virtues which characterized the distinguished Original. Ably & eloquently as the subject had been handled, all must see that it had not been exhausted; and you are, I am sure, alone in regretting that what remained for some other hand, fell into yours.

Pardon me for remarking that you have been led into an error, in the notice you take of the "Revised Code", provided for by the first Independent Legislature of Virginia. The Revisors appointed were in number not three, but five, viz Mr. Jefferson, Mr. Pendleton, Mr. Wythe, Col. George Mason, & Col: Thomas L. Lee. The last died, and Col. Mason resigned; but not before they had joined in a consultative meeting. In the distribution of the work among the others, Mr. Wythe was charged with the British Statutes, Mr. Pendleton with the Colonial laws: and Mr. Jefferson with certain parts of the Common Law, and the new laws called for by the new State of the Country.

The portion executed by Mr. Jefferson was perhaps the severest of his many intellectual labours. The entire Report, as a Model of technical precision, and perspicuous brevity, and particularly as comprising samples of the Philosophical spirit which ennobled his legislative policy, may, in spite of its Beccarian Illusions, be worthy of a place among the collections of the Society of which he was once the Presiding Member; & if a copy be not already there, it will be a pleasure to me to furnish one.

In page 9th. of the Eulogium, I observe an erratum with respect to the age of Mr. Jefferson when his summary of American rights was penned, which the Reader however may correct, by recurring to the date of his birth previously mentioned, or adverting to his age afterwards mentioned, when the Declaration of Independence was drawn. I offer you, Sir, assurances of my great & cordial esteem.

9 Gaillard Hunt, ed., The Writings of James Madison: Comprising His Public Papers and His Private Correspondence, Including Numerous Letters and Documents Now for the First Time Printed 288–89 (1910). In his 1820s correspondence, Madison expressed some reservations about Beccarian ideas, though it is unclear what particular aspects of Beccaria's multi-faceted work he then found himself in disagreement with. On January 15, 1828, Madison had written these words to Thomas S. Grimke:

One of the earliest acts of the Virginia Legislature, after the State became Independent, provided for a revisal of the Laws in force, with a view to give it a systematic character accomodated to the Republican form of Govt. and a meliorated spirit of Legislation. The task was committed to five Commissioners, and executed by three of them, Mr. Jefferson, Mr. Wythe & Mr. Pendleton. In a consultative meeting of the whole number, the question was discussed whether the Common Laws at large, or such parts only as were to be changed, should be reduced to a text law. It was decided by a majority that an attempt to embrace the whole was unadvisable; and the work as executed, was accordingly limited to the old British Statutes admitted to be in force, to the Colonial Statutes, to the penal law in such parts as needed reform, and to such new laws as would be favorable to the intellectual & moral condition of the Community. In the changes made in the penal law, the Revisors were unfortunately misled into some of the specious errors of Beccaria, then in the zenith of his fame as a philosophical Legislator.

Id. at 298–300.

45. George Washington to Brigadier General James Mitchell Varnum, Feb. 14, 1779, *available at* www.founders.archives.gov.

46. To James Madison from Edmund Randolph, 12 February 1785," *Founders Online*, National Archives, last modified February 1, 2018, http://founders.archives.gov/documents/Madison/01-08-02-0130. [Original source: *The Papers of James Madison*, vol. 8, *10 March 1784?–?28 March 1786*, ed. Robert A. Rutland and William M. E. Rachal. Chicago: The University of Chicago Press, 1973, pp. 239–240.].

47. Enclosure II: Considerations on a Convention with Spain, 22 March 1792," *Founders Online*, National Archives, last modified February 1, 2018, http://founders.archives.gov/documents/Jefferson/01-23-02-0275. [Original source: *The Papers of Thomas Jefferson*, vol. 23, *1 January–31 May 1792*, ed. Charles T. Cullen. Princeton: Princeton University Press, 1990, pp. 328–332.].

48. John R. Vile, Founding Documents of America: Documents Decoded 203 (2015).

49. 1 Salmon P. Chase, ed., Statutes of Ohio and of the Northwestern Territory, Adopted or Enacted from 1788 to 1833 Inclusive: Together with the Ordinance of 1787; the Constitutions of Ohio and of the United States, and Various Public Instruments and Acts of Congress 66–70 (1833); "An Act to provide for the Government of the Territory Northwest of the river Ohio," First Congress, Aug. 7, 1789, *in* A Century of Lawmaking for a New Nation: U.S. Congressional Documents and Debates, 1774—1875, http://rs6.loc.gov/cgi-bin/ampage?collId=llsl&fileName=001/llsl001.db&recNum=173; *see also* Jeffrey L. Kirchmeier, Imprisoned by the Past: Warren McCleskey and the American Death Penalty 49 (2015) ("The Northwest Ordinance's prohibition of 'cruel or unusual punishments' was arguably broader than the language of Virginia's Declaration of Rights that barred 'cruel and unusual punishments.'").

50. William Prest, William Blackstone: Law and Letters in the Eighteenth Century 1 (2008); John Harrison Watts & Cliff Roberson, Law and Society: An Introduction 42 (2013); C. R. L. Fletcher, Historical Portraits 1700–1850, at 226–27 (1919).

51. Daniel G. Payne & Richard S. Newman, eds., The Palgrave Environmental Reader 7 (2005).

52. Erik S. Root, All Honor to Jefferson? The Virginia Slavery Debates and the Positive Good Thesis 48 (2008).

53. 4 William Blackstone, Commentaries on the Laws of England (Book IV of Public Wrongs) 2 (1769) (2016) (with an Introduction, Notes, and Textual Apparatus by Ruth Paley).

54. Id. at ix.

55. The Grand Instructions to the Commissioners Appointed to Frame a New Code of Laws for the Russian Empire: Composed by Her Imperial Majesty Catherine II, Empress of All the Russias 81 (London: Michael Tatischeff, 1768).

56. Daniel J. Boorstin, The Mysterious Science of the Law: An Essay on Blackstone's *Commentaries* Showing How Blackstone, Employing Eighteenth-Century Ideas of Science, Religion, History, Aesthetics, and Philosophy, Made of the Law at Once a Conservative and a Mysterious Science 150 (1996).

57. Robert Reiner, Crime: The Mystery of the Common-Sense Concept (2016), ch. 2.

58. 4 William Blackstone, Commentaries on the Laws of England (Book IV of Public Wrongs) xiv, 9–11, 112, 165, 211–12, 256 (1769) (2016) (with an Introduction, Notes, and Textual Apparatus by Ruth Paley) (italics in original).

59. Richard Davey, The Tower of London 118 (1910).

60. Lisa Silverman, Tortured Subjects: Pain, Truth, and the Body in Early Modern France 74 (2010).

61. 4 William Blackstone, Commentaries on the Laws of England: A Facsimile of the First Edition of 1765–1769, at 178 (1979) (1769).

62. 4 William Blackstone, Commentaries on the Laws of England (Book IV of Public Wrongs) 11 (Ruth Paley, ed., 2016).

63. 1 William Blackstone, Commentaries on the Laws of England: A Facsimile of the First Edition of 1765–1769, at 121–22 (1979) (1765). In the seventeenth century, the British philosopher John Locke himself wrote of man taking "necessary" actions to preserve mankind. Matthew K. Suess, *Punishment in the State of Nature: John Locke and Criminal Punishment in the United States of America*, 7 Wash. U. Jur. Rev. 367, 379 (2015) ("Locke realized that the threat of continued criminal activity impacted mankind as a whole. Because of this, 'every man ... by the right he hath to preserve mankind in general, may restrain, or, where it is necessary, destroy things noxious to them, and so may bring such evil on any one, who hath transgressed that law.'") (quoting John Locke, Two Treatises of Government 103 (Ian Shapiro, ed., 2003) (1689). John Locke (1632–1704)—as one source reports—"believed that civil governments are necessary to ensure that, when transgressions occur, the punishment should be proportional to the crime." As that source summarized Locke's view: "The victim, in a state of nature without government, will tend to overreact to a wrong, leading to social instability. Impartial government magistrates are needed to ensure fair punishments." Peter J. DiDomenica & Thomas G. Robbins, Journey from Genesis to Genocide: Hate, Empathy, and the Plight of Humanity 147 (2013).

64. 11 William S. Holdsworth, A History of English Law 578 (1966).

65. J. G. Marvin, Legal Bibliography, or A Thesaurus of American, English, Irish, and Scotch Law Books 105 (1847).

66. Joseph A. Melusky & Keith Alan Pesto, The Death Penalty: Documents Decoded 10 (2014).

67. 1 M. De Secondant, Baron de Montesquieu, The Spirit of Laws 427 (London: J. Nourse & P. Vaillant, 1750); 1 M. De Secondant, Baron de Montesquieu, The Spirit of Laws 370 (Dublin: G. and A. Ewing & G. Faulkner, 1751); David Wallace Carrithers, ed., Montesquieu, *The Spirit of Laws*: A Compendium of the First English Edition 480 (1977).

68. *E.g.*, Count De Cataneo, The Source, the Strength, and the True Spirit of Laws in Which the Errors of M. de Montesquieu, and some other Eminent Writers, Are Occasionally Considered (1753). These editions of *The Spirit of the Laws* were identified through a WorldCat database search.

69. 7 George C. Rogers, Jr. & David R. Chesnutt, eds., The Papers of Henry Laurens 3 (1979); South Carolina Imprints, 1731–1800: A Descriptive Bibliography xxxi (1985). A July 31, 1777, notice in a South Carolina publication announced that "An Edition of Beccaria on Crimes and Punishments is published here by Mr. Bruce." Id., p. 117. That edition of *On Crimes and Punishments* also contained the commentary attributed to Voltaire. Id.

70. Erwin C. Surrency, A History of American Law Publishing 23 (1990). Robert Bell was described as a "witty, energetic, skeptical, and imaginative man," and fourteen hundred copies of Blackstone's *Commentaries* were ordered in advance from Robert Bell's print shop. Id., pp. 23–24. Robert Bell, who had been born in Glasgow, had moved to Dublin in 1759 after serving as an apprentice to a Robert Taylor, a bookbinder in Berwick-upon-Tweed who has been described as a "famous piratical printer." Bell himself was "a passionate defender of his right to reprint whatever he pleased, not only copyrighted English books but also books his colleagues in Dublin had already printed or reprinted." "In 1767," one source notes of the same year Bell emigrated from Dublin to Philadelphia, "he reprinted a pamphlet by another notorious pirate, the Scot Alexander Donaldson" and was "apparently driven out of town by Irish booksellers whom he had 'printed upon.'" James N. Green, "English Books and Printing in the Age of Franklin," *in* 1 Hugh Amory & David D. Hall, eds., A History of the Book in America: The Colonial Book in the Atlantic World 284 (2009).

71. 1 Amory & Hall, A History of the Book in America, *supra* note 70, at 285.

72. William Blackstone, Commentaries on the Laws of England (Philadelphia: Robert Bell, 1772), "Book the Fourth" (title page).

73. Lisa Gold, Books the Founders Read: Blackstone's Commentaries on the Laws of England, Apr. 21, 2015, https://www.baumanrarebooks.com/blog/blackstones-commentaries-books-founders-read/.

74. Richard B. Sher, The Enlightenment and the Book: Scottish Authors and Their Publishers in Eighteenth-Century Britain, Ireland and America 512, 528 (2006). It was Dr. Benjamin Rush—a disciple of Beccaria—who suggested the title of Paine's famous political pamphlet, the original proposed title being "Plain Truth." 1 Evert A. Duyckinck & George L. Duyckinck, Cyclopædia of American Literature 198 (1856). David Bruce, the South Carolina printer, also reprinted Thomas Paine's *Common Sense*. 7 George C. Rogers, Jr. & David R. Chesnutt, eds., The Papers of Henry Laurens 3 (1979).

75. Sher, The Enlightenment and the Book, *supra* note 74, at 530. Robert Bell's 1778 edition of *On Crimes and Punishments* contained the commentary attributed to Voltaire. His reprinting of Voltaire's *Miscellanies* was also printed in Philadelphia in 1778. Eve Tavor Bannet, Transatlantic Stories and the History of Reading, 1720–1810: Migrant Fictions 259 (2011); Helmut C. Jacobs, Gegen Folter und Todesstrafe 164 (2007).

76. Newport Historical Society, "Found: A First American Edition of Blackstone's Commentaries," July 22, 2016, http://newporthistory.org/2016/found-a-first-american-edition-of-blackstones-commentaries/.

77. Kenneth G. Wilson, The Columbia Guide to Standard American English 161 (1993).

78. Alexander Hamilton, James Madison and John Jay, The Federalist Papers (2014) (a Dover edition reprinting *The Federalist Papers*); John Witte, Jr. & Joel A. Nichols, Religion and the American Constitutional Experiment 39 (4th ed. 2016).

79. William Blackstone, Commentaries on the Laws of England (Philadelphia: Robert Bell, 1772), "Book the Fourth" (listing "Names of the Subscribers"); Mary Sarah Bilder, *James Madison, Law Student and Demi-Lawyer*, 28 Law & Hist. R. 389, 400 n.59 (2010); 4 Charles Evans, American Bibliography: A Chronological Dictionary of All Books, Pamphlets, and Periodical Publications Printed in the United States of America from the Genesis of Printing in 1639 Down to and Including the Year 1820, at 348 (1907); The Johns Hopkins Studies in Romance Literatures and Languages, Vols. 38–40 (1941), p. 12.

80. William Blackstone, Commentaries on the Laws of England (Philadelphia: Robert Bell, 1772), "Book the Fourth" (listing "Names of the Subscribers").

81. William Blackstone, Commentaries on the Laws of England (Philadelphia: Robert Bell, 1772), "Book the Fourth" (listing "Names of the Subscribers"); John D. Bessler, "The American Enlightenment: Eliminating Capital Punishment in the United States," *in* Lill Scherdin, ed., Capital Punishment: A Hazard to a Sustainable Criminal Justice System? (2016), ch. 4.

82. Allen D. Boyer, Sir Edward Coke and the Elizabethan Age 206 (2003).

83. 11 William S. Holdsworth, A History of English Law 575–77 (1966).

84. 1 DeAlva Stanwood Alexander, A Political History of the State of New York 67 (1906).

85. Henry Fielding, An Enquiry into the Causes of the Late Increase of Robbers, &c. with Some Proposals for Remedying this Growing Evil 1, 101, 183, 185, 187–96, 199 (2d ed. 1751) (italics in original; citing 1 Ed. VI. 13 Rep.); George Watson, *Machiavel and Machiavelli*, 84 The Sewanee Review 630 (Fall 1976); Vickie B. Sullivan, Montesquieu and the Despotic Ideas of Europe: An Interpretation of *The Spirit of the Laws* 46–47 (2017).

86. F. C. Montague, ed., Jeremy Bentham, A Fragment on Government (1776) (2001), pp. 1–3, 5–8.

87. Id. at 10–13; Mary K. Stohr & Anthony Walsh, Corrections: The Essentials 26 (2012); 4 Alexander Taylor Milne, ed., The Correspondence of Jeremy Bentham vi (2017).

88. F. C. Montague, ed., Jeremy Bentham, A Fragment on Government (1776) (2001), pp. 23, 26, 30.

89. Id. at 31–32, 105 n.2; Robert B. Downs, Molders of the Modern Mind: 111 Books that Shaped Western Civilization 123 (1961).

90. Alex Tuckness & John M. Parrish, The Decline of Mercy in Public Life 176–77 (2014) (citations omitted).

91. Calvin J. Larson & Gerald R. Garrett, Crime, Justice, and Society 178 (2d ed. 1996).

92. Jeremy Bentham, The Rationale of Punishment 193 (1830) (italics in original).

93. 2 Étienne Dumont, Bentham's Theory of Legislation: Being Principes de Législation and Traités de Législation, Civile et Pénale 146 (Charles Milner Atkinson, trans. 1914).

94. John Bowring, comp., The Works of Jeremy Bentham, Now First Collected; Under the Superintendence of His Executor, John Bowring 162 (1838).

95. Jeremy Bentham, An Introduction to the Principles of Morals and Legislation 178–79, 182, 183 n.3, 329 n.1 (1879).

96. Bernard Bailyn, The Ideological Origins of the American Revolution 27 (15th ed. 2007).

97. J. L. De Lolme, The Constitution of England, or An Account of the English Government; in which It is Compared with the Republican Form of Government, and Occasionally with the Other Monarchies in Europe 33, 86–88, 159, 235 (4th ed. 1776).

98. John Howard, The State of the Prisons in England and Wales, with Preliminary Observations, and an Account of Some Foreign Prisons 30 (1777) (reprinted in 2013 by Cambridge University Press); John Howard, The State of the Prisons in England and Wales, with Preliminary Observations, and an Account of Some Foreign Prisons and Hospitals 19 (2d ed. 1780); John Howard, The State of the Prisons in England and Wales, with Preliminary Observations, and an Account of the Some Foreign Prisons and Hospitals 15, 42 n.*, 118 (3d ed. 1784); John Howard, Appendix to the State of the Prisons in England and Wales, &c.: Containing a Farther Account of Foreign Prisons and Hospitals, with Additional Remarks on the Prisons of This Country 80 n.‡ (1784).

99. Martin Madan, Thoughts on Executive Justice, with Respect to Our Criminal Laws, Particularly on the Circuits 1, 8, 11–12, 23 n.*, 48 n.*, 63 n.*, 66 n.*, 111, 114–15, 137 * n.*, 138–39, 229, 233 (2d ed. 1785) (italics in original).

100. Samuel L. Knapp, The Life of Thomas Eddy, Comprising an Extensive Correspondence with Many of the Most Distinguished Philosophers and Philanthropists of This and Other Countries 42, 52 (1836).

101. Edwin G. Burrows & Mike Wallace, Gotham: A History of New York City to 1898, at 366 (1999).

102. O. F. Lewis, The Development of American Prisons and Prison Customs, 1776–1845, at 43 (1922).

103. Thomas Eddy, An Account of State Prison or Penitentiary House, in the City of New York 6–7, 9, 15, 64 (1801), title page.

104. Id. at 5.

105. Lawyers Guild Review, Vol. 15, p. 43 (1955); "The Establishment of 'Penitentiary Houses,'" Social Service Review 5, no. 1 (Mar 1931), p. 74; 1 The Complete Works of Edward Livingston on Criminal Jurisprudence; Consisting of Systems of Penal Law for the State of Louisiana and for the United States of America; With the Introductory Reports to the Same 1, 4, 8, 11, 31–32, 36–37, 546 (1873).

106. Carolyn Strange, Discretionary Justice: Pardon and Parole in New York from the Revolution to the Depression 35 (2016).

107. Evan Cornog, The Birth of Empire: DeWitt Clinton and the American Experience, 1769–1828, at 20, 190 n.25 (1998); *see also* Edward A. Fitzpatrick, The Educational Views and Influence of DeWitt Clinton 57–57 (1969) (discussing DeWitt Clinton's views on punishment).

108. Here, the legal commentator, Patrick Colquhoun, cited chapter 6 of Cesare Beccaria's *On Crimes and Punishments*.

109. Patrick Colquhoun, A Treatise on the Police of the Metropolis; Containing a Detail of the Various Crimes and Misdemeanors by which Public and Private Property and Security are, at Present, Injured and Endangered: and Suggesting Remedies for Their Prevention (6th ed. 1800), ch. 2 & n.9.

110. Id., ch. 2, n.13.

111. Patrick Colquhoun, A Treatise on the Police of London; Containing a Detail of the Various Crimes and Misdemeanors by Which Public and Private Property and Security Are, at Present, Injured and Endangered 5, 157, 182, 200 & n.*, 215, 227 (1st Am. ed. 1798) (italics in original).

112. Clive Emsley, Crime, Police, and Penal Policy: European Experiences 1750–1940, at 32 (2007).

113. Colquhoun, A Treatise on the Police of London, *supra* note 111, at 208–214 (italics in original).

114. Oscar (King of Sweden and Norway), On Punishments and Prisons 6, 8 (A. May trans. 1842); *see also* id. at 10 ("A raving madman, who has escaped from confinement, may also be very dangerous to all he meets; yet no one would probably ever think of the necessity of his losing his life, to prevent his committing injuries.").

115. 3 Richard Welford, Men of Mark 'Twixt Tyne and Tweed 220 (1895).

116. William Newton, Total Abolition of the Death Penalty Defended 73–75, 85, 95 (1850) (italics in original); *see also* id. at 90 ("To talk of 'the necessity' of capital punishments, in the face of these unanswerable facts, is utterly absurd and childish.") (quoting the "Eclectic Reviewer"); Edict of the Grand Duke of Tuscany, for the Reform of Criminal Law in His Dominions 28 (1789).

117. Tobias Purrington, Report on Capital Punishment, Made to the Maine Legislature in 1836, at 3, 15 (3d ed. 1852); Patty Seleski, "Domesticity is in the Streets: Eliza Fenning, Public Opinion and the Politics of Private Life," *in* Tim Harris, ed., The Politics of the Excluded, *c.* 1500–1850, at 273 (2001).

118. "Report of the Committee on Capital Punishment," *in* Documents Printed by Order of the Legislature of the State of Maine, During Its Session A. D. 1869, at 11 (1869) (emphasis in original).

119. Id. at 4.

120. Id.

121. Reports on the Abolition of Capital Punishment: Reprinted by Order of the House of Representatives from the Legislative Documents of 1835 and 1836, at 10 (1837) ("If society have the right to take away life in any case, nothing but an absolute necessity can justify the exercise of that right; and such absolute necessity, if clearly made out, would justify capital punishment in any other case, as well as in that of murder."); id. at 24 ("It needed not therefore the authority of Montesquieu, or of Beccaria, to give weight to the maxim, that every punishment which does not arise from absolute necessity—and even every act of authority of one man over another, for which there is not an absolute necessity, is tyrannical."); id. at 87:

[T]here is strong ground to believe, that the vindictive feelings are at the bottom of much of the zeal manifested in favor of "cruel and unusual punishments," among those who do not weigh their opinions so carefully as the members of this House. There can be no need to prove, it suffices to suggest, that revenge is an unholy passion, itself the parent of many crimes, often of the crime of murder, and that it cannot be that the law should gratify and foster in the breasts of men the spirit of demons. The law should be wholly passionless, unbiassed by resentment or partiality, sitting in calm serenity in the temple of just, to mete out penalties by the measure of absolute necessity, and staying the hand of the wrongdoer: thus, and thus only, should it guard the public good, and protect individual rights.

122. Nathaniel Chipman, Principles of Government: A Treatise on Free Institutions, including the Constitution of the United States 2 & n.*, 3–5, 7, 21, 51, 54, 61, 64 & n.*, 65, 155, 197, 210–14, 215 & n.*, 256, 298, 300 (1833). In discussing the U.S. Constitution's Necessary and Proper Clause, Chipman wrote: "The word 'necessary,' is not here to be understood in the sense of that necessity which is usually denominated absolute, intending something without which the end could not be possibly effected, but is to be understood in its more usual and popular sense,—of that which is expedient and convenient, of the degree and urgency of which congress are to judge." "The word 'proper,'" Chipman added, "is intended to qualify the term 'necessary;' the measure proposed must not only be expedient, but proper as it respects the object, and as it respects the nature and end of the government,—the limitations of power on the one hand, and the reservation of rights on the other." Id. at 256.

123. *E.g.*, 2 William Godwin, An Enquiry Concerning Political Justice, and Its Influence on General Virtue and Happiness 615 (1793) ("Punishment is one of those classes of coercion, the multiplication of which is so much to be deprecated, and which noting but the most urgent ne-

cessity can in any case justify."); 29 Abraham Rees, The Cyclopædia; or, Universal Dictionary of Arts, Sciences, and Literature (1819) (entry for "Punishment") ("Every punishment which does not arise from absolute necessity, says the great Montesquieu, is tyrannical; and this proposition is rendered more general by Beccaria, who observes, that every act of authority of one man over another, for which there is not an absolute necessity, is tyrannical."); 1 The British Annals of Education for 1844: Being The Scholastic Quarterly Review 68 (1844) (noting in a book review: "A few brief remarks, by way of summary, must close these observations on the subject of punishments. Let knowledge and love direct all the means of discipline which you employ; and let the necessity, and propriety, of every punishment that you inflict be evident."). An article in the *Stanford Law Review* notes that Beccaria recommended that "punishments be the 'least necessary' to achieve deterrence" and that his ideas "gathered enormous support in Europe" and "found a ready audience in America." Matthew W. Meskell, *The History of Prisons in the United States from 1777 to 1877*, 51 Stan. L. Rev. 839, 844 (1999).

124. *E.g.*, John D. Bessler, *The Italian Enlightenment and the American Revolution: Cesare Beccaria's Forgotten Influence on American Law*, 37 Mitchell Hamline L.J. Pub. Pol'y & Prac. 1, 83–84 & n.230 (2016) (citing an 1802 letter to the editor in New York's *Evening Post*, an 1846 article in the *Raleigh Register and North Carolina Gazette*, and an 1867 article in *The Brooklyn Daily Eagle*); "No. X—Beccaria," *in* 21 The Law Review, and Quarterly Journal of British and Foreign Jurisprudence 285, 290 (1855) ("Every punishment which does not arise from absolute necessity, says Montesquieu, is tyrannical. The right of the State to punish crimes is grounded upon the necessity of defending the public liberty from the usurpation of individuals.") (citing Beccaria).

125. J. P. Thomas, A Legal and Constitutional Argument Against the Alleged Judicial Right of Restraining the Publication of Reports of Judicial Proceedings 97 (1822) ("Beccaria warmly remarks that 'every act of authority of one man over another, for which there is not an absolute necessity, is tyrannical.' In which opinion he appears to agree precisely, with Montesquieu:—'every punishment which does not arise from absolute necessity, is tyrannical.'") (citations omitted).

126. Reports and Addresses of James H. Titus, upon the Subject of Capital Punishment 50 (1848) ("The committee have endeavored to show, by a review of the experience of different nations in their criminal jurisprudence as connected with the suppression of crime and the protection of society, the necessity of the death punishment does not exist...."); id. at 1 (noting that the existence of the New York State Society for the Abolition of Capital Punishment reflected "the increasing conviction, which was manifested through all sections of the State and with all classes of citizens, against the idea of the propriety or necessity of the death penalty"); id. at 36 ("in a state defended against enemies from without, sustained by the firm basis of power and general sanction from within, and where authority is lodged in the hands of the sovereign,—in such a state there can be no necessity for taking away the life of a citizen"); id. at 25 ("the death punishment in most cases operates as an entire defeat of the end proposed to be attained, and as regards the prevention of crimes, before this horrid punishment can be justified, it should be demonstrated beyond a doubt that no other means as effectual can be substituted, and that therefore, as of necessity, justice to society requires of the criminal the sacrifice of his life.").

127. 1 Thomas W. Waterman, A Complete Practical Treatise on Criminal Procedure, Pleading and Evidence, in Indictable Cases xlii (1853) ("Every punishment, says Montesquieu, which does not arise from absolute necessity, is tyrannical. This proposition may be made more general, thus: Every act of authority, of one man over another, for which there is not an absolute necessity, is tyrannical.") (citing "Beccaria on Cr. ch. 2"); *cf.* 1 The Law Review, and Quarterly Journal of British and Foreign Jurisdiction 451 & n.3 (1845) (quoting the principle articulated by Montesquieu and Beccaria and emphasizing: "The right to visit offenders with capital punishment stands solely on the ground of absolute necessity, to prevent greater evil; to act on anything less than absolute necessity is a fearful assumption of authority unwarranted by any divine sanction or any consent which has actually been given or which can be presumed to have been given.").

128. Judge J. W. Henry, "Aid to Discharged Prisoners," Proceedings of the Tenth Annual National Conference of Charities and Corrections, Held at Louisville, Ky., September 24–30, 1883, at 230–38 (1884).

129. Alfred Ellingwood Giles, Societies for the Suppression of Vice: Are They Beneficial

or Injurious? Their Methods and Tendencies Considered, by a Former Vice-President of the Boston Young Men's Christian Association 7 (1883):

"Every punishment that does not arise from absolute necessity," said the great Montesquieu, "is tyrannical." "Every act of authority of one man over another, for which there is not an absolute necessity, is tyrannous," says Beccaria. He insists "that it is upon the necessity of defending the public liberty," which includes the liberty of each and every citizen, "from the usurpations of individuals, that the right to punish is founded." (*Essay on Crime, p.* 7.)

Cf. Henry Christmas, Capital Punishment Unsanctioned by the Gospel, and unnecessary in a Christian State. A Letter to the Rev. Sir John Page Wood (London: Smith, Elder, 1845); *see also* 2 The Punishment of Death: A Selection of Articles from *The Morning Herald*, with Notes 257 (1837) ("The spirit of enquiry which has been awakened of late years, not only in this country, but in several others, touching the effects of capital punishments, has been the means of throwing a great deal of light upon criminal jurisprudence, and has shewn that sacrifices of human life are not only not necessary to deter men from crime, but that they are *less effective* for this purpose than punishments which do not revolt the natural feelings of mankind.") (italics in original).

130. As foreign language sources quoted Montesquieu: "Tout châtiment dont la nécessité n'est pas absolue devient tyranique." Édouard Ducpetiaux, De la peine de morte 14 (1827); G. Tourdes, "Supplices (Médecine Légale)," *in* Extrait du Dictionnaire Encyclopédique des Sciences Médicales Publié sous la Direction du Dr. A. Dechambre 440, 445 (same).

131. Luther Hamilton, ed., Memoirs, Speeches and Writings of Robert Rantoul, Jr. 80, 82 (1854). Other writers also concluded that the death penalty was not necessary. Elias E. Ellmaker, The Revelation of Rights 124 (1841) ("But the truth is, that an *absolute necessity* for inflicting capital punishment in any case, does not exist."); *see also* id. at 123 ("there is no *absolute necessity* for putting the guilty to death") (italics in original); James Gregory, Victorians Against the Gallows: Capital Punishment and the Abolitionist Movement in Nineteenth Century Britain (2012):

The Scottish travel writer Samuel Laing, in *Observations on the Social and Political State of the European People* (in 1850), concluded his discussion of capital punishment with the following proposed wording for the preamble of any abolitionist legislation: "Whereas it is expedient to abolish the punishment of death as unnecessary for the protection of society, inoperative for the prevention of crime or the amendment of criminals, and contrary to the feelings of the humane and pious; and whereas, the said infliction of capital punishment rests solely on certain doctrines of atonement contained in the Scriptures of the Old and New Testament, and no social or moral grounds of necessity or utility; be it therefore enacted that the said punishment of death and doctrine of atonement, as taught by the Christian religion, upon which alone it is founded, shall cease and be abolished from and after the passing of this act."

See also id.:

The Sheffield Young Men's association, following a debate on capital punishment, sent the following resolution to the *People's Journal*: "That it is the opinion of this meeting that capital punishments are cruel and unjust; that they do not protect society by preventing crime; that they have a tendency to brutalise the people, and destroy the sensibility of our nature, and all our ideas of the sacredness and inviolability of human life; that they are the direct violations of the precepts of the gospel of Christ; and that they are unnecessary and ought to be immediately abolished."

132. 11 A. W. Plumstead & William H. Gilman, eds., The Journals and Miscellaneous Notebooks of Ralph Waldo Emerson 251 n.208 (1975).

133. Jeremy Bentham, the famed penal reformer, also embraced the idea that the only legitimate punishments are necessary ones. *E.g.*, Jeremy Bentham, The Rationale of Punishment 63 (1830) ("Punishment ought only to be inflicted of necessity, and with feelings of regret and repugnance."); id. at 302 (when writing about "*collective punishment*," emphasizing: "When this mode of punishment is justifiable, it is only on the score of necessity."); id. at 29 ("Every particle of real punishment that is produced more than what is necessary for the production of the requisite quantity of apparent punishment, is just so much misery run to waste. If hanging a man *in effigy*, would produce the same salutary impression of terror upon the minds of the people, it would be folly or cruelty ever to hang a man *in person*.") (italics in original); id. at 430 ("[I]t must be admitted, that if in any case the suffering of the delinquent is not necessary for the attainment of the ends of punishment, the pun-

ishment ought not to be inflicted."); 10 THE WORKS OF JEREMY BENTHAM, PUBLISHED UNDER THE SUPERINTENDENCE OF HIS EXECUTOR, JOHN BOWRING 283 (1843) (quoting letter from Jeremy Bentham to the Minister of the Interior of the French Republic, responding to 1792 letter, with Bentham writing: "For every punishment that is not needed is really a lawless punishment. . . ."). Bentham distinguished between the "*simple*" and "*afflictive*" administration of capital punishment. As Bentham wrote: "I call it *simple* when, if any bodily pain be produced, no greater degree of it is produced than what is necessary to produce death." "I call it *afflictive*," he observed, "when any degree of pain is produced more than what is necessary for that purpose." BENTHAM, THE RATIONALE OF PUNISHMENT, *supra*, at 168.

134. Francis Lieber, "A Popular Essay on subjects of Penal Law, and on uninterrupted Solitary Confinement at Labor, as contradistinguished to Solitary Confinement at Night and Joint Labor by Day, in a Letter to JOHN BACON, Esquire, President of the Philadelphia Society for alleviating the Miseries of Public Prisons" (Philadelphia: 1838), *in* 6 THE NEW YORK REVIEW 124, 130–31 (1839).

135. Id. at 131.

136. Id. at 124.

137. Id. at 131 n.*.

138. JOHN RIPPON, CAPITAL PUNISHMENT UNLAWFUL AND INEXPEDIENT: AN ESSAY ON THE PUNISHMENT OF DEATH 120 (1853).

139. "Before God." COTTON MATHER, DISCOURSES UPON THE NATURE, THE DESIGN, AND THE SUBJECT OF THE LORDS SUPPER: WITH DEVOUT METHODS OF PREPARING FOR, AND APPROACHING TO THAT BLESSED ORDINANCE 30 (1690).

140. RIPPON, CAPITAL PUNISHMENT UNLAWFUL AND INEXPEDIENT, *supra* note 138, at 120 (quoting "*Eighth Report of the Criminal Law Commissioners*, 1846").

141. James Madison, who once professed to not seeing the injustice of capital punishment "in one case at least," believed that an experiment testing the abolition of capital punishment would be an eminently worthy one. As Madison wrote to G. F. H. Crockett, a Kentucky physician, in 1823: "I should not regret a fair and full trial of the entire abolition of capital punishments by any State willing to make it." JOHN D. BESSLER, THE BIRTH OF AMERICAN LAW: AN ITALIAN PHILOSOPHER AND THE AMERICAN REVOLUTION 208 (2014).

142. RIPPON, CAPITAL PUNISHMENT UNLAWFUL AND INEXPEDIENT, *supra* note 138, at 124–25 (italics in original). Rippon cited both Montesquieu and Beccaria in his essay. Id. at 125 ("'Experience shows,' says Montesquieu, 'that in countries remarkable for the lenity of their laws, the spirit of the inhabitants is as much affected by slight penalties as in other countries by severe punishments.'"); id. at 128:

The case of Tuscany is well known to every one who has made the least research on this subject. . . . [T]he Grand Duke Leopold, at the instance of the Marquis Beccaria, entirely abolished the punishment of death in his dominions, even for murder.

143. Id. at 126.

144. Id. at 133–34 (italic in original).

145. "The Proper Punishment of Criminals": An Address by Hon. M. D. Follett, of Marietta, Delivered Before the State Bar Association of Ohio, at Cincinnati, Dec. 28, 1882, *in* OHIO STATE BAR ASSOCIATION REPORTS, PROCEEDINGS OF THE ASSOCIATION HELD AT THE CITY OF CINCINNATI ON THE 27TH AND 28TH OF DECEMBER 1882, Vol. III (1883), pp. 130–31.

146. 21 OHIO ARCHÆOLOGICAL AND HISTORICAL PUBLICATIONS 331–32 (1912).

147. 4 REVISED RECORD OF THE CONSTITUTIONAL CONVENTION OF THE STATE OF NEW YORK—APRIL SIXTH TO SEPTEMBER TENTH 1915, at 4071, 4076 (1916).

148. HERBERT BROOM, A SELECTION OF LEGAL MAXIMS, CLASSIFIED AND ILLUSTRATED 1, 9, 11–12 (7th Am. ed. 1874). The concept of necessity shows up in a number of legal maxims. *See* GEORGE FREDERICK WHARTON, LEGAL MAXIMS, WITH OBSERVATIONS AND CASES 84, 97–98, 177, 222, 239 (3d ed. 1903). In another book written by Herbert Broom, one finds this extended passage about excessive amercements or fines:

The king, by virtue of his prerogative, was entitled to all fines and amercements and penalties, either wholly or in part, and, to prevent the undue exercise of this perogrative, various statutory restrictions were imposed. Thus, the fourteenth chapter of Henry III.'s Magna Carta declares that "a freeman shall not be amerced for a small fault, but after the manner of the fault—and for a great fault after the greatness thereof—saving to him his 'contenement,' and a merchant likewise—saving to him his merchandize." We must understand this word "contenement" to signify that which is necessary for the support and maintenance of a man in his state or condition of life. And, thus, this well-known chapter of Magna Carta forbids the setting upon any man of an amercement heavier than his circumstances or estate would bear—saving, as Lord Coke says, in his commentary on this passage, to the soldier his armour, to the scholar his books, and to the villein the cart or wainage with which his ignoble service was performed....

Magna Carta, as remarked by Lord Coke, "extends to amercements, and not to fines imposed by an Court of Justice." Within the spirit and equity, however, of this enactment, fines imposed judicially must certainly be brought; such fines ought to be moderate and "within bounds", for "where a court has a power of setting fines, that must be understood of setting reasonable fines": an excessive fine "is against law, and shall not bind, for *excessus in re quâlibet jure reprobatur communi*". And accordingly the counsel for Mr. Hampden, who was convicted of a misdemeanor *anno* 36 Car. II., urges upon the court in mitigation of punishment, that his client was possessed but of a moderate estate, and that according to Magna Carta, "there should be a *salvo contenemento* in all fines." So in O'Connell v. Reg., Lord Campbell refers to Magna Carta as providing that "no fine shall be imposed beyond what the party is able to pay."

On many occasions which the reader of history will call to mind—especially during the seventeenth century—were ruinous fines inflicted in violation of law, as well by the Star Chamber as by the Superior Courts; and hence the declaration in the Bill of Rights that "excessive fines ought not to be imposed", grounded on the averment that such had been the practice in the reign of King James II., who in this and other ways, "by the assistance of divers evil counsellors, judges, and ministers employed by him, did endeavour to subvert and extirpate the laws and liberties of this kingdom".

Herbert Broom & George Denman, Constitutional Law Viewed in Relation to Common Law, and Exemplified by Cases 399–401 (2d ed. 1885) (citations omitted).

149. Franklin E. Zimring, Gordon Hawkins & Sam Kamin, Punishment and Democracy: Three Strikes and You're Out in California 188 (2001).

Chapter 3

1. "Proposals for Printing by Subscription, An American Edition of the Spirit of Laws," Pennsylvania Journal (Philadelphia, PA), Jan. 11, 1775, p. 4; "Proposals for Printing by Subscription, An American Edition of the Spirit of Laws," Pennsylvania Journal (Philadelphia, PA), Feb. 15, 1775, p. 5; "Proposals for Printing by Subscription, An American Edition of the Spirit of Laws," Pennsylvania Journal (Philadelphia, PA), Mar. 1, 1775, p. 6.

2. "From the Baron de Montesquieu Spirit of Laws," Pennsylvania Packet (Philadelphia, PA), Jan. 27, 1780, p. 1; "From the Baron de Montesquieu Spirit of Laws," The Independent Ledger, and the American Advertiser (Boston, MA), Feb. 28, 1780, p. 1; "To the Printer of the Providence Gazette," The Providence Gazette and Country Journal (Providence, R.I.), May 3, 1783, p. 1; "Extract from Montesquieu's Spirit of Laws," The Independent Gazetteer (Philadelphia, PA), July 24, 1784, p. 2; "From the Spirit of Laws by Montesquieu," The Boston Gazette, and the Country Journal (Boston, MA), July 3, 1786, p. 1.

3. Susan Gordon, Montesquieu: The French Philosopher Who Shaped Modern Government 90–91 (2006).

4. Kathryn Preyer, "Cesare Beccaria and the Founding Fathers," *in* Mary Sarah Bilder, Maeva Marcus & R. Kent Newmyer, eds., Blackstone in America: Selected Essays of Kathryn Preyer 239, 241–42 (2009); Kathryn Preyer, "Two Enlightened Reformers of the Criminal Law: Thomas Jefferson of Virginia and Peter Leopold, Grand Duke of Tuscany," *in* Blackstone in America, *supra*, at 259. Thomas Jefferson's extensive transcriptions into his commonplace book from Beccaria's *Dei delitti e delle pene* and Montesequieu's *L'Esprit des Lois* demonstrate their role and importance in shaping Jefferson's thinking. 2 Gilbert Chinard, The Commonplace Book of Thomas Jefferson: A Repertory of His Ideas on Government 7–9, 14, 24–25, 28, 31–39, 63–65, 257–96, 298–316 (1926).

5. "A few COPIES of the following much esteemed modern Work, may be had at BELL's BOOK-STORE, next door to St. Paul's Church, in Third-street, Philadelphia," PENNSYLVANIA PACKET, Sept. 26, 1778, p. 4.

6. "A few COPIES of the following much esteemed modern Work, may be had at BELL's ... next door to St. Paul's Church, in Third-Stree[t], Philadelphia," MARYLAND JOURNAL (Baltimore, Maryland), Oct. 13, 1778, p. 3.

7. "Extract from an essay on crimes and punishments. Written by the Marquis Beccaria," PENNSYLVANIA EVENING HERALD, Feb. 25, 1786, p. 40; *see also* "On the PUNISHMENT of DEATH," WASHINGTON PATROL (Salem, NY), Oct. 28, 1795, p. 1 (reprinting Beccaria's ideas "On the Punishment of Death"). Beccaria's fame made his ideas of considerable interest to American readers. "Robbery and Burglary," SUPPLEMENT TO DUNLAP'S AMERICAN DAILY ADVERTISER, Jan. 14, 1793, p. 2:

It might be sound policy to make a distinction between the punishment of those who commit these offences armed with dangerous and mortal weapons and of those who do not indicate such violent intentions. Such a distinction prevails in the laws of Connecticut and also of those of Milan: and I understand from the nephew of the Marquis Beccaria while he was in America, that beneficial effects had resulted from this discrimination.

8. "London," DAILY ADVERTISER (New York, NY), June 17, 1791, p. 2; "London," PENNSYLVANIA MERCURY, June 21, 1791, p. 3; "London," HERALD OF FREEDOM, June 28, 1791, p. 2.

9. JOHN D. BESSLER, THE BIRTH OF AMERICAN LAW: AN ITALIAN PHILOSOPHER AND THE AMERICAN REVOLUTION (2014); JOHN D. BESSLER, THE CELEBRATED MARQUIS: AN ITALIAN NOBLE AND THE MAKING OF THE MODERN WORLD (2018); A. ESMEIN, A HISTORY OF CONTINENTAL CRIMINAL PROCEDURE WITH SPECIAL REFERENCE TO FRANCE 362–64 (John Simpson, trans. 1913).

10. REBECCA M. MCLENNAN, THE CRISIS OF IMPRISONMENT: PROTEST, POLITICS, AND THE MAKING OF THE AMERICAN PENAL STATE, 1776–1941, at 20–21 (2008); *see also* Markus D. Dubber, "'An Extraordinarily Beautiful Document': Jefferson's 'Bill for Proportioning Crimes and Punishments' and the Challenge of Republican Punishment," *in* MARKUS D. DUBBER & LINDSAY FARMER, EDS., MODERN HISTORIES OF CRIME AND PUNISHMENT 132, 134 (2007).

11. 9 PAUL LEICESTER FORD, ED., THE WORKS OF THOMAS JEFFERSON 145–46 (1905).

12. FRANCIS LIEBER, A POPULAR ESSAY ON SUBJECTS OF PENAL LAW, AND ON UNINTERRUPTED SOLITARY CONFINEMENT AT LABOR, AS CONTRADISTINGUISHED TO SOLITARY CONFINEMENT AT NIGHT AND JOINT LABOR BY DAY, IN A LETTER TO JOHN BACON, ESQUIRE 10 (1838); Williams v. Kaiser, 323 U.S. 471, 476 (1945) ("Prompt and expeditious detection and punishment of crime are necessary for the protection of society. But that may not be done at the expense of the civil rights of the citizen."); *see also* THE OCCASIONAL PAPER: OF ACTS OF GRACE (1718), Vol. II, Numb. VI, p. 13 (referring to "the Absolute Necessity of Punishments to support the Authority and Peace of a Government"); "The Object of Punishment," *in* 1 THE JURIST, OR QUARTERLY JOURNAL OF JURISPRUDENCE AND LEGISLATION 354, 377 (1827):

Of the right to inflict punishment little requires to be said. The existence of such a right in the state is one of the first political axioms: the duty of protection, and the right of repelling external aggression, are not more incontrovertible. The only question is, what are the considerations which are to regulate and govern the exercise of the right? ... No punishment is inflicted because it is just; but it is just because necessary.

See also id. at 377–78 (italics in original):

The offender, by infringing the law, subjects himself to the threatened penalty; nor can he complain, if the evil inflicted upon him be made the means of increasing the general good, or diminishing the general mass of evil. It results, however, from the principles laid down, that every excess of punishment, beyond what is absolutely necessary to the public security, is so much superfluous and irreparable evil—a wanton abuse of the powers of government, or, to use the expression of Hobbes, an *act of hostility*.

13. Shortly after penning the Declaration of Independence, Thomas Jefferson wrote a letter to Edmund Pendleton on August 26, 1776, complaining about the "sanguinary hue of our penal laws." Thomas Jefferson to Edmund Pendleton, Aug. 26, 1776, *reprinted in* 1 PAPERS OF THOMAS JEFFERSON 505 (J. Boyd ed. 1950); *see also* 3 THE WORKS OF THE LEARNED AND REVEREND JOHN SCOTT, D.D.: SOMETIME RECTOR OF ST. GILES'S IN THE FIELDS 449 (new ed. 1826):

The law of mercy also obliges us to inflict no more punishment on offenders, than what is absolutely necessary to the obtaining those good ends we design by it. For he who punishes an offender more than is needful to the natural end of punishment, can design no other end by it but what is cruel and barbarous: and whatsoever is more than needful, either to the vindicating our own right, or the reforming the offender, or the giving fair warning to others, serves to no other purpose but to gratify our own revenge and fury. So far as punishment is needful to these good ends, it is not only lawful, but good: but all beyond what is needful to these is perfect savageness and cruelty. When therefore, for the obtaining these ends, we are necessitated to punish an offender, the law of mercy obliges us first to try lighter and gentler punishments; and if by these we cannot obtain our end, to proceed in our severities by degrees, and not to fly to extreme rigour, till we have found all gentler corrections ineffectual. For if a lighter punishment will do the work, it is cruelty to lay on a heavier....

14. A. John Simmons, "Locke and the Right to Punish," *in* A. John Simmons, Marshall Cohen, Joshua Cohen & Charles R. Beitz, eds., Punishment: A Philosophy and Public Affairs Reader 219 (1995).

15. Centuries ago, writers often spoke of punishment as *an evil*—something to be avoided if at all possible. *E.g.*, 1 Basil Montagu, comp., The Opinions of Different Authors upon the Punishment of Death 134 (1809) (quoting the author of *Observations upon Thoughts on Executive Justice* as follows: "All punishment is an evil, but is yet necessary, to prevent crimes, which are a greater evil. Whenever the legislature therefore appoints for any crime, a punishment more severe than is requisite to prevent the commission of it, it is the author of unnecessary evil. If it do this knowingly, it is chargeable with wanton cruelty and injustice; if from ignorance, and the want of a proper attention to the subject, it is guilty of a very criminal neglect."); Richard S. Frase, "Excessive Relative to What? Defining Constitutional Proportionality Principles," *in* Michael Tonry, ed., Why Punish? How Much?: A Reader on Punishment 267 (2011) ("Cesare Beccaria argued that all punishments should be 'necessary; the least possible in the given case.' Jeremy Bentham similarly held that punishment itself is evil and should be used as sparingly as possible; in particular, a penalty should not be used 'in cases where the same end may be obtained by means more mild.'"); Hans Boutellier, The Safety Utopia: Contemporary Discontent and Desire as to Crime and Punishment 94 (2004) ("Bentham is more aware than anyone that punishment is an evil in itself. 'All punishment is unhappiness: all punishment is an evil in itself. If punishment is permitted at all on the basis of the utility principle, it can only occur to the extent that it makes it possible to exclude an even worse evil.'"); Bernard E. Harcourt, The Illusion of Free Markets: Punishment and the Myth of the Natural Order 58 (2011) ("As in Bentham, the right to punish for Beccaria was a necessary evil: an evil, in that punishment is necessarily tyrannous and thus bad; but necessary, in the sense that it is the only way to restrain men. Consequently, 'any punishment that goes beyond the need to preserve this bond is unjust by its very nature.'").

16. A. John Simmons, "Locke and the Right to Punish," *in* A. John Simmons, Marshall Cohen, Joshua Cohen & Charles R. Beitz, eds., Punishment: A Philosophy and Public Affairs Reader 220 (1995).

17. Keegan Callanan, *Liberal Constitutionalism and Political Particularism in Montesquieu's 'The Spirit of the Laws,'* 67 Political Research Quarterly 589, 592, 594 (2014).

18. Steven H. Jupiter, *Constitution Notwithstanding: The Political Illegitimacy of the Death Penalty in American Democracy*, 23 Fordham Urb. L.J. 437, 476 n.191 (1996) (quoting Thomas Jefferson, Third Draft of the Virginia Constitution (1776), *reprinted in* 1 The Papers of Thomas Jefferson 359 (Julian P. Boyd ed. 1950)):

Just before the signing of the Declaration of Independence, Jefferson drafted three proposals for Virginia's constitution. In each draft, Jefferson proposed that the General Assembly of the state "have no power to pass any law inflicting death for any crime, excepting murder, and those offenses in the military service for which they shall think punishment by death absolutely necessary; and all capital punishments in other cases are hereby abolished....

See also John P. Foley, ed., The Jeffersonian Cyclopedia: A Comprehensive Collection of the Views of Thomas Jefferson 225 (1900) (setting forth Thomas Jefferson's views on the death penalty).

19. Thomas Paine Rights of Man: Being an Answer to Mr. Burke's Attack on the French

Revolution 36, 116, 118 (7th ed. 1791); *see also* Charles A. Cerami, Jefferson's Great Gamble: The Remarkable Story of Jefferson, Napoleon and the Men Behind the Louisiana Purchase 99 (2003) (noting that the French Declaration of the Rights of Man "gained added fame when Thomas Paine published his classic English translation of it"); A. W. Brian Simpson, Human Rights and the End of Empire: Britain and the Genesis of the European Convention 9 (2001) ("The expression 'human rights', it is true, has a long history. Thomas Paine first used it in *The Rights of Man* (1791), translating the *Declaration of the Rights of Man and of the Citizen*, adopted by the French National Assembly on 27 August 1789, and accepted by the King in October: 'The representatives of the people of France, formed into a National Assembly, considering that ignorance, neglect, or contempt of human rights, are the sole causes of public misfortunes and corruptions of Government, have resolved to set forth in a solemn declaration, these natural, imprescriptible and inalienable rights ...' "); Helmut K. Anheier & Stefan Toepler, eds., International Encyclopedia of Civil Society 439 (2010) ("The *Declaration of the Rights of Man and the Citizen* by the National Assembly in Paris was a triumph for Paine's advocacy of democratic politics. He hailed it as a milestone in history: 'truth has given it an establishment; and Time will record it with a name as lasting as its own.' ").

20. 2 Griffith J. McRee, Life and Correspondence of James Iredell, One of the Associate Justices of the Supreme Court of the United States 206–07 (1858); E. H. Scott, ed., The Federalists and Other Contemporary Papers on the Constitution of the United States 907–08 (1894); Paul Leicester Ford, ed., Pamphlets on the Constitution of the United States, Published During Its Discussion by the People 1787–1788, at 32, 359–60 (1888); "James Iredell, Marcus, Answers to Mr. Mason's Objections to the New Constitution," The Founders' Constitution, Amendment VIII, http://press-pubs.uchicago.edu/founders/documents/amendVIIIs11.html.

21. *E.g.*, Edwards v. Edwards, 100 A. 608, 609 (N.J. Ct. Chancery 1917) ("The power to punish for contempt is an arbitrary power, and should be used only when absolutely necessary in the interest of justice, and then with great care and discretion."); 17 C.J.S. *Contempt* § 115 (Dec. 2017 Update) ("Courts are authorized and have the power to find summary contempt and imposed punishment, based upon the absolute necessity of maintaining structured order in the courts."); *see also* United States v. Duane, 25 F. Cas. 920, 921 (Cir. Ct. D. Pa. 1801) ("In order to afford complete security, it is absolutely necessary to restrain and punish offences of this kind in a summary manner, and in a summary manner they have been punished, from the earliest times to the present day."). In contempt cases, however, a court must use the " 'least possible power adequate to the end proposed.' " Spallone v. United States, 493 U.S. 265, 276 (1990) (citation omitted); *see also* S.E.C. v. Yun, 208 F. Supp.2d 1279, 1288 n.23 (M.D. Fla. 2002) ("Incarceration is this Court's 'least possible power.' In light of Yun's alleged financial difficulties, this Court finds incarceration, rather than the imposition of an excessive fine, to be the least coercive sanction necessary to encourage Yun's compliance with this Court's order.").

22. *E.g.*, J. Richard Broughton, *The Death Penalty and Justice Scalia's Lines*, 50 Akron L. Rev. 203, 208 (2016) (noting that "Pope John Paul II's 1995 encyclical, *Evangelicum Vitae*, ... viewed capital punishment as limited to " 'cases of absolute necessity' "); Howard Bromberg, *Pope John Paul II, Vatican II, and Capital Punishment*, 6 Ave Maria L. Rev. 109, 118 n.30 (2007) (quoting that encyclical); Carlos Bernal Pulido, *The Migration of Proportionality Across Europe*, 11 N.Z. J. Pub. & Int'l L. 483, 491 (2013) (noting that Carl Gottlieb von Svarez, in discussing Prussian law, wrote that "the first principle of public law" was that "the state is entitled to restrict private freedom only if it is necessary for rendering compatible liberty and security"); *see also* John Pratt & Anna Eriksson, Contrasts in Punishment: An Explanation of Anglophone Excess and Nordic Exceptionalism 104–105 (2013):

[I]n societies where moderation and restraint were paramount, revenge and the emotions underpinning it should have no place in the administration of punishment. Crown Prince Oscar (1840: 6) thus wrote of the quandary of retaining the death penalty: 'society has undeniably the right, as well as the duty, to punish every action which can interrupt the public order of justice ... But should this right go further than the loss of freedom? Every punishment that reaches outside of this boundary enter the territory of revenge.'

In discussing the Belgian Penal Code of 1867, one source had this to say:

The theory of the Penal Code of 1867, and the principle which inspired its authors were opposed to those which characterized the code of 1810. The authors of the Imperial Code belonged to that school which, under the influence of Bentham, considered the application of punishment justified only by utility and necessity. "It is the necessity of punishing," said Target, "which makes it legitimate."

United States Government Printing Office, United States Congressional Serial Set 126 (1901).

23. The penal reformer Jeremy Bentham, his French translator, Pierre Étienne Louis Dumont, and many others focused on whether a particular punishment was truly necessary. *E.g.*, 1 Basil Montagu, comp., The Opinions of Different Authors upon the Punishment of Death 222 (1809) (Pierre Étienne Louis Dumont, Bentham's translator, articulated the concept in this way: "The punishment ought to be economical; that is, it ought to have only the degree of severity which is absolutely necessary for attaining its object. Every thing which exceeds the necessity is not only so much superfluous evil, but produces a multitude of inconveniences that defeat the ends of justice."); id. at 232 (Bentham put it this way: "If the punishment is necessary, it ought not to be remitted: if it is not necessary, it ought not to be pronounced."); id. at 187 (William Eden emphasized that "[n]othing ... but the evidence result of absolute necessity, can authorize the destruction of mankind by the hand of man"; "The infliction of death is not therefore to be considered, in any instance, as a mode of punishment, but *merely* as our last melancholy resources in the extermination of those from society, whose continuance among their fellow-citizens is become inconsistent with the public safety.") (italics in original).

24. As William Blackstone observed:

[N]otwithstanding all the remonstrances of speculative politicians and moralists, the punishment of theft still continues, throughout the greatest part of Europe, to be capital: and Puffendorf, together with sir Matthew Hale, are of opinion that this must always be referred to the prudence of the legislature; who are to judge, say they, when crimes are become so enormous as to require such sanguinary restrictions. Yet both these writers agree, that such punishment should be cautiously inflicted, and never without the utmost necessity.

4 William Blackstone, Commentaries on the Laws of England: A Facsimile of the First Edition of 1765–1769 (1979); William Blackstone, Commentaries on the Laws of England 191 (1841) (1769) (same).

25. In a section of his *Commentaries* titled "Justifiable homicide is of divers kinds," Blackstone wrote, giving this definition and explanation:

Such as is owing to some unavoidable *necessity*, without any will, intention, or desire, and without any inadvertence or negligence, in the party killing, and therefore without any shadow of blame. As, for instance, by virtue of such an office as obliges one, in the execution of public justice, to put a malefactor to death, who hath forfeited his life by the laws and verdict of his country. This is an act of necessity, and even of civil duty; and therefore not only justifiable, but commendable, where the law requires it. But the law must *require* it, otherwise it is not justifiable: therefore wantonly to kill the greatest of malefactors, a felon or a traitor, attained or outlawed, deliberately, uncompelled, and extrajudicially, is murder.

Id. at 178 (italics in original).

26. "All punishments that go beyond the requirements of public safety are by their very nature unjust"—Beccaria, *Dei delitti e delle pene*, ch. 2. "[July 1786]," *Founders Online*, National Archives, last modified November 26, 2017, http://founders.archives.gov/documents/Adams/01-03-02-0005-0004. [Original source: *The Adams Papers*, Diary and Autobiography of John Adams, vol. 3, *Diary, 1782–1804; Autobiography, Part One to October 1776*, ed. L. H. Butterfield. Cambridge, MA: Harvard University Press, 1961, pp. 191–203.]

27. "[July 1786]," *Founders Online*, National Archives, last modified November 26, 2017, http://founders.archives.gov/documents/Adams/01-03-02-0005-0004. [Original source: *The Adams Papers*, Diary and Autobiography of John Adams, vol. 3, *Diary, 1782–1804; Autobiography, Part One to October 1776*, ed. L. H. Butterfield. Cambridge, MA: Harvard University Press, 1961, pp. 191–203.] According to the editor of John Adams' papers: "This shows that JA used the original and the translation together, but the new Italian edition of 1780 varies markedly in its text from the version on which the earlier translation was based. Both volumes are among JA's books in the Boston Public Library; JA presented the English translation to his son TBA in 1800." Id. John Adams gave the 1775 English translation of

Dei delitti e delle pene to his son, Thomas B. Adams, in 1800. An inscription on the title page reads: "Thomas B. Adams. From his Father 1800." That edition, titled *An Essay on Crimes and Punishments*, was published in London and "Printed for F. Newbery, at the Corner of St. Paul's Church-Yard." Stephen P. Halbrook, A Right to Bear Arms: State and Federal Bills of Rights and Constitutional Guarantees 49 (1989). Montesquieu's had made this assessment on killing in war in his *Spirit of Laws*:

That the law of nations, to prevent prisoners being put to death, has allowed them to be made slaves. * * * The reasons of the civilians are all false. It is false, that killing in war in lawful, unless in case of absolute necessity; but when a man has made another his slave, he cannot be said to be under a necessity of taking away his life, since he actually did not take it away. War gives no other right over prisoners than to disable them from doing any further harm, by securing their persons. All nations concur in detesting the murdering of prisoners in cold blood.

H. Byerley Thomson, The Laws of War, Affecting Commerce and Shipping 32–33 (2d ed. 1854); Ari Helo, Thomas Jefferson's Ethics and the Politics of Human Progress: The Morality of a Slaveholder 242 n.142 (2014).

28. Adolph Caso, We, the People ... : Formative Documents of America's Democracy (2011) ("Adams' Copy of *On Crimes and Punishments*" — "Comments"); An Essay on Crimes and Punishments, Translated from the Italian; with Commentary, Attributed to Mons. De. Voltaire, Translated from the French 7 (4th ed. 1775); John S. Chipman, German Utility Theory: Analysis and Translations 92 (2014).

29. John Hostettler, Cesare Beccaria: The Genius of 'On Crimes and Punishments' xvi (2011).

30. 1 John A. Garraty & Mark C. Carnes, eds., American National Biography 101 (1999); Frederic Kidder, History of the Boston Massacre, March 5, 1770; Consisting of the Narrative of the Town, the Trial of the Soldiers, and a Historical Introduction, Containing Unpublished Documents of John Adams, and Explanatory Notes 232 (1870). At the Boston Massacre trial, the concept of "necessity" was discussed by counsel. As the crown's attorney set out the law for the court and the jury: "The laws of society, gentleman, lay a restraint on the passions of men, that no man shall be the avenger of his own cause, unless through absolute necessity, the law giving a remedy for every wrong; if a man might at any time execute his own revenge, there would be an end of law." Id. at 158, 171 (argument of Samuel Quincy, Esq.); *see also* id. at 14 ("Immaterial who gives the mortal blow where there a number of persons together, all present aiding and abetting are guilty, no man shall be an avenger of his own cause unless from absolute necessity.").

31. "John Adams and the Boston Massacre Trial of 1770," Library of Congress, http://www.loc.gov/law/help/rare-books/john_adams.php; "Boston Massacre Trial," National Park Service, National Historical Park — Massachusetts, https://www.nps.gov/bost/learn/historyculture/massacre-trial.htm.

32. James Jackson — like others of his time — was well versed in Enlightenment writings. William Omer Foster, Sr., James Jackson: Duelist and Militant Statesman 1757–1806, at 35 (2009) ("Jackson's essays, addresses, and letters indicate a wide acquaintanceship with the works of such political scientists as Vattel, Grotius, Beccaria, Locke, Rousseau, Montesquieu, and Blackstone.").

33. 2 Thomas Lloyd, The Congressional Register; or, History of the Proceedings and Debates of the First House of Representatives of the United States of America 325 (1790).

34. Michael A. Genovese, Encyclopedia of the American Presidency 543 (rev. ed. 2010).

35. "A Charge Delivered to the Grand Jury in the Circuit Court of the United States, for the District of Virginia, in May, 1791," http://oll.libertyfund.org/titles/wilson-collected-works-of-james-wilson-vol-1.

36. Id.

37. Id. "So that he may feel himself die." Id. n.7.

38. Jeannine Marie DeLombard, In the Shadow of the Gallows: Race, Crime, and American Civic Identity 77 (2012).

39. Id. (italics in original).

40. Edwin R. Keedy, *History of the Pennsylvania Statute Creating Degrees of Murder*, 97 U. Penn. L. Rev. 759, 767–68 & n.73 (1949).

41. Benjamin Rush, Injustice and Impolicy of Punishing Murder by Death 3 (1792).

42. Id. at 7 (italics in original). Writing in 1792, at a time of slavery, tremendous racial prejudice, and when Native Americans were often referred to as "savages," Dr. Rush expressed himself in this way:

The common sense of all nations is in favour of the commerce and slavery of their fellow creatures. But this does not take away from their immorality. Could it be proved that the Indians punish murder by death, it would not establish the right of man over the life of a fellow creature, for revenge we know in its utmost extent is the universal and darling passion of all savage nations. The practice moreover, (if it exist) must have originated in *necessity*; for a people who have no settled place of residence, and who are averse from all labour, could refrain murder in no other way.

43. Id. at 9.

44. Id.

45. Lewis Cass Aldrich, ed., History of Clearfield County, Pennsylvania: With Illustrations and Biographical Sketches of Some of Its Prominent Men and Pioneers 444 (1887).

46. Benjamin Rush, Injustice and Impolicy of Punishing Murder by Death 11–12 (1792) (italics in original); Dagobert D. Runes, The Selected Writings of Benjamin Rush xi, 36, 41 (1947) (reprinting Dr. Benjamin Rush's 1792 essay, "On Punishing Murder by Death").

47. Runes, The Selected Writings of Benjamin Rush, *supra* note 46, at 41, 43–46 (italics in original; reprinting Dr. Benjamin Rush's reply to "Philochoras").

48. Id. at 50–51.

49. Id. at 52–53 (italics in original).

50. Hazel Burgess, ed. & comp., Thomas Paine: A Collection of Unknown Writings 87 (2010) (quoting material written on April 26, 1791). Thomas Paine was certainly not a fan executions. "When, in countries that are called civilized," he observed, we see age going to the workhouse and youth to the gallows, something must be wrong in the system of government...." Harvey J. Kaye, Thomas Paine: Firebrand of the Revolution 100 (2000); *see also* id. at 23, 110 (noting Paine's abhorrence and opposition to capital punishment). Elsewhere, Paine offered that "as France has been the first of European nations to abolish royalty, let her also be the first to abolish the punishment of death, and to find out a milder and more effectual substitute." The Writings of Thomas Paine 341 (1967)

51. 2 John W. Jordan, ed., Genealogical and Personal History of Beaver County, Pennsylvania 1034 (1914); Doris Devine Fanelli & Karie Diethorn, ed., History of the Portrait Collection: Independence National Historic Park 96 (2001); Ruth L. Woodward & Wesley Frank Craven, Princetonians, 1784–1790: A Biographical Dictionary, at 231, 242 (1991); 3 Benjamin Rush, Medical Inquiries and Observations 437 (2d ed. 1805).

52. Christie L. Maloyed & J. Kelton Williams, "Reverend John Witherspoon's Pedagogy of Leadership," *in* 39 American Educational History Journal 349, 362 (Paul J. Ramsey, ed., 2012) (noting that William Bradford was "Madison's friend from the College of New Jersey"); John Rawls, The Law of Peoples with "The Idea of Public Reason Revisited" 165 n.73 (2002) (taking note of how Madison and Bradford "met at Princeton (College of New Jersey)"); *see also* David Nordquest, "Madison and Philosophy: His Coursework and His Statesmanship," *in* John R. Vile, William D. Pederson & Frank J. Williams, eds., James Madison: Philosopher, Founder, and Statesman 3 (2008):

In coursework and study at the College of New Jersey from 1769 until 1772, James Madison acquired much of the grasp of philosophy that distinguishes his statesmanship. He took with him from Princeton, as well, the ideal of the philosopher-statesman that his good friend and fellow alumnus William Bradford would soon find realized in the work of the Continental Congress. In August 1774, anxious for news of the sessions of Congress then being held in Bradford's Philadelphia, Madison appealed to his friend for reports. Bradford's enthusiastic reply professed confidence that Congress's measures would be "wisely plan'd," because they "debate on them like philosophers." He reported that Congress had chosen a place to meet with ready access to a fine library, and he had learned from a talk with the librarian that the delegates were making constant use of the collection and were talking "Vattel, Barlemaqui[,] Locke & Montesquieu" as "the standar[d]s to which they refer either when settling the rights of the Colonies or when a dispute arises on the Justice or propriety of a measure."

William Bradford had special knowledge of what was happening at the First Contintental Congress. As one source puts it:

Bradford was in an advantageous position to know what went on behind the closed doors of the First Continental Congress. His father, William, and his older brother, Thomas, besides publishing *The Pennsylvania Journal; and the Weekly Advertiser*, were the official printers of the Congress. Following its adjournment on 26 October, the Bradfords at their "London Coffee House" address brought out the first edition of the *Journal of the Proceedings of the Congress held at Philadelphia, September 5, 1774.*

"To James Madison from William Bradford, 17 October 1774," *Founders Online,* National Archives, last modified November 26, 2017, http://founders.archives.gov/documents/Madison/01-01-02-0036. [Original source: *The Papers of James Madison*, vol. 1, *16 March 1751?–?16 December 1779*, ed. William T. Hutchinson and William M. E. Rachal. Chicago: The University of Chicago Press, 1962, pp. 125–128.] (editorial note n.4).

53. William Bradford, An Enquiry How Far the Punishment of Death Is Necessary in Pennsylvania 3 (1793). This legislative report was later cited by Justice Thurgood Marshall in his concurrence in *Furman v. Georgia*, 408 U.S. 238, 336 (1972) (Marshall, J., concurring) ("In 1793, William Bradford, the Attorney General of Pennsylvania and later Attorney General of the United States, conducted 'An Enquiry How Far the Punishment of Death is Necessary in Pennsylvania.' He concluded that it was doubtful whether capital punishment was at all necessary, and that until more information could be obtained, it should be immediately eliminated for all offenses except high treason and murder."); id. at 321 n.19 (Marshall, J., concurring) ("There is also evidence that the general opinion at the time the Eighth Amendment was adopted was that it prohibited every punishment that was not 'evidently necessary.' ") (citing William Bradford, An Enquiry How Far the Punishment of Death is Necessary in Pennsylvania (1793), *reprinted in* 12 Am. J. Legal Hist. 122, 127 (1968)).

54. Section 8 of the French *Déclaration des Droits de L'Homme et du Citoyen* (Declaration of the Rights of Man and of the Citizen), adopted by the French Constituent Assembly on August 26, 1789, read: "*La loi ne doit établir que des peines strictement nécessaires et nul ne pent être puni qu'en vertu d'une loi éstablie et promulguée antérieurement au délit et légalement appliquée.*" Georg Jellinek, The Declaration of the Rights of Man and of Citizens: A Contribution to Modern Constitutional History 1, 27, 34–35 (Max Farrand, trans. 1901). The English translation: "The law shall provide for such punishments only as are strictly and obviously necessary, and no one shall suffer punishment except it be legally inflicted in virtue of a law passed and promulgated before the commission of the offense." "Declaration of the Rights of Man—1789," The Avalon Project, Yale Law School, Lillian Goldman Law Library, http://avalon.law.yale.edu/18th_century/rightsof.asp.

55. Section XVIII of the Bill of Rights of the 1784 Constitution of New Hampshire read in full as follows:

All penalties ought to be proportioned to the nature of the offence. No wise legislature will affix the same punishment to the crimes of theft, forgery and the like, which they do to those of murder and treason; where the same undistinguishing severity is exerted against all offences; the people are led to forget the real distinction in the crimes themselves, and to commit the most flagrant with as little compunction as they do those of the lightest dye: For the same reason a multitude of sanguinary laws is both impolitic and unjust. The true design of all punishments being to reform, not to exterminate, mankind.

N.H. Const. (June 2, 1784), sec. XVIII.

56. Section XXXV of the Vermont Constitution of 1777 provided:

To deter more effectually from the commission of crimes, by continued visible punishment of long duration, and to make sanguinary punishments less necessary; houses ought to be provided for punishing, by hard labor, those who shall be convicted of crimes not capital; wherein the criminal shall be employed for the benefit of the public, or for reparation of injuries done to private persons; and all persons, at proper times, shall be admitted to see the prisoners at their labor.

Vt. Const. (July 8, 1777), sec. XXXV.

57. Sections 38 and 39 of Pennsylvania's 1776 constitution read as follows:

SECT. 38. The penal laws as heretofore used shall be reformed by the legislature of this state, as soon as may be, and punishments made in some cases less sanguinary, and in general more proportionate to the crimes.

SECT. 39. To deter more effectually from the commission of crimes by continued visible punishments of long duration, and to make sanguinary punishments less necessary; houses ought to be provided for punishing by hard labour, those who shall be convicted of crimes not capital; wherein the criminals shall be imployed for the benefit of the public, or for reparation of injuries done to private persons: And all persons at proper times shall be admitted to see the prisoners at their labour.

PA. CONST. (Sept. 28, 1776), §§38–39.

58. The full provision of Maryland's constitution read: "That sanguinary laws ought to be avoided, as far as is Consistent with the safety of the State: and no law, to inflict cruel and unusual pains and penalties, ought to be made in any case, or at any time hereafter." MD. CONST. (Nov. 11, 1776), sec. XIV.

59. BRADFORD, *supra* note 53, at 3–5 (italics in original). As William Bradford's essay continued: "One would think, that, in a nation jealous of its liberty, these important truths would never be overlooked; and, that the infliction of death, the highest act of power that man exercises over man, would seldom be prescribed where its necessity was doubtful." Id. at 5.

60. At one point in his report, Bradford emphasized that severe laws were not suited to places such as Pennsylvania. As Bradford wrote in his *Enquiry*:

We perceive ... that the severity of our criminal law is an exotic plant and not the native growth of Pennsylvania. It has been endured, but, I believe, has never been a favorite. The religious opinions of many of our citizens were in opposition to it: and, as soon as the principles of Beccaria were disseminated, they found a soil that was prepared to received them. During our connection with Great Britain no reform was attempted: but, as soon as we separated from her, the public sentiment disclosed itself, and this benevolent undertaking was enjoined by the constitution. This was one of the first fruits of liberty, and confirms the remark of Montesquieu, "That, as freedom advances, the severity of the penal law decreases."

Id. at 20.

61. Id. at 5.

62. In 1786, legal historian Stuart Banner explains, Pennsylvania abolished capital punishment "for robbery, burglary, sodomy, and buggery." "It is the wish of every good government to reclaim rather than to destroy," the statute's preamble declared. STUART BANNER, THE DEATH PENALTY: AN AMERICAN HISTORY 97 (2002). As Bradford himself put it in his *Enquiry* of the Pennsylvania Assembly's actions: "[T]he Assembly proceeded, in the year 1786, to introduce the punishment of hard labor; and the offences (formerly capital) on which its effects have been tried, are, the crime against nature, robbery and burglary." BRADFORD, *supra* note 53, at 20.

63. BRADFORD, *supra* note 53, at 6.

64. Id.

65. Id. at 6–7 (italics in original).

66. Id. at 20–21. As Montesquieu emphasized after laying out the evidence:

These facts prove, that to punish this crime with death would be a useless severity. They may teach us, like the capital punishments formerly inflicted on adultery and witch-craft, how dangerous it is rashly to adopt the Mosaical institutions. Laws might have been proper for a tribe of ardent barbarians wandering through the sands of Arabia which are wholly unfit for an enlightened people of civilized and gentle manners.

Id. at 21.

67. Id. at 26:

It is evident, from this examination, that the principle of the new system, properly modified, coincides with the public safety as much as with the dictates of humanity. The happy result of this experiment is an encouragement to proceed still further.

68. Id. at 27 ("[T]here does not appear to be any necessity for so violent a remedy. It is probable this crime will be neither frequent nor dangerous.").

69. Id. at 30–31:

William Penn considered imprisonment, stripes and hard labour as a punishment adequate to this crime and sufficient to check the commission of it. The Grand Duke of Tuscany prescribes imprisonment at labor, varied as the circumstances may require. The Legislature of Vermont, so late as the year 1791, has followed the humane example, and in that state death is no longer inflicted on this offence.

If any one, mistaking the end of punishment, and more intent on vengeance than the prevention of the crime, deems this chastisement too light, a visit to the penitentiary house lately erected as part of the goal of Philadelphia, will correct the opinion. When he looks into the narrow cells prepared for the more atrocious offenders—When he realizes what it is to subsist on coarse fare—to languish in the solitude of a prison—to wear out his tedious days and long nights in feverish anxiety—to be cut off from his family—from his friends—from society—from all that makes life dear to the heart—When he realizes this he will no longer think the punishment inadequate to the offense.

70. Here, Bradford footnoted Dr. Benjamin Rush's "Observations on the injustice and impolicy of punishment murder with death." Bradford, *supra* note 53, at 35 n.†. William Bradford and Benjamin Rush were the leading proponents of criminal justice reform in Pennsylvania. As one source puts it:

Pennsylvanians heralded their reforms as what one legislator called a "novel experiment." Serving as leading spokesmen for Pennsylvania's criminal justice system, William Bradford and Benjamin Rush spread its fame across the Atlantic. Visitors from Europe, like the duc de Rochefoucauld-Liancourt, flocked to see the Pennsylvania experiment.

Steven Wilf, Law's Imagined Republic: Popular Politics and Criminal Justice in Revolutionary America 149 (2010).

71. Bradford, *supra* note 53, at 35 (italics in original).

72. Id.; Roger Hood & Carolyn Hoyle, The Death Penalty: A Worldwide Perspective (5th ed. 2015), ch. 1.

73. Bradford, *supra* note 53, at 35 (italics in original).

74. Id. at 36 (italics in original).

75. Bessler, The Celebrated Marquis, *supra* note 9, at 218; Benjamin Rush, An Enquiry into the Effects of Public Punishments upon Criminals, and upon Society: Read in the Society for Promoting Political Enquiries, Convened at the House of His Excellency Benjamin Franklin, Esquire, in Philadelphia, March 9th, 1797 (1787). Dr. Rush used the concept of necessity on multiple occasions in referring to punishments. Id. at 14 ("But where punishments are excessive in degree, or infamous from being public, a pardoning power is absolutely necessary. Remove their severity and public infamy, and a pardoning power ceases to be necessary in a code of criminal jurisprudence."); Benjamin Rush, Essays, Literary, Moral and Philosophical 5 (2d ed. 1806) ("Fewer pillories and whipping posts, and smaller goals, with their usual expenses and taxes, will be necessary when our youth are properly educated, than at present...."); id. at 157 ("But where punishments are excessive in degree, or infamous from being public, a pardoning power is absolutely necessary. Remove their severity and public infamy, and a pardoning power ceases to be necessary in a code of criminal jurisprudence.").

76. Bradford, *supra* note 53, at 43.

77. Id. at 45.

78. Id. at 46.

79. 1 Mary Bosworth, ed., Encyclopedia of Prisons and Correctional Facilities 390 (2005):

Hard labor has played an important role in criminal sentencing history as an alternative to corporal punishment and as a substitute for the death penalty—although, in extreme cases, it was just a sentence of slow death. In America, William Penn's Great Law of 1682 eliminated the death penalty for all cases except premeditated murder, and designated imprisonment with hard labor instead as a means of reforming offenders.

80. Constitution of Pennsylvania (Sept. 28, 1776), §§ 38–39; Samuel Hazard, ed., The Register of Pennsylvania (Oct. 3, 1829), Vol. IV, No. 14, pp. 209–213; "Judge Bryan and the Constitutional Convention of 1776," *in* Burton Alva Konkle, George Bryan and the Constitution of Pennsylvania, 1731–1791, at 111, 117 n.1, 120–21, 128 (1922); Chris Coelho, Timothy Matlack, Scribe of the Declaration of Independence 1, 59–60 (2013); Keedy, *supra* note 40, at 765–66.

81. Jonathan I. Israel, Democratic Enlightenment: Philosophy, Revolution, and Human Rights 1750–1790, at 471 (2011).

82. William Bradford, *An Enquiry How Far the Punishment of Death Is Necessary in Pennsylvania*, 12 Am. J. Legal History 122 (1968) (reprinting William Bradford's essay); William Barton, Memoirs of the Life of David Rittenhouse, LLD.F.R.S. Late President of the American Philosophical

Society, &c. 607–608 (1813); Holger Hoock, Empires of the Imagination: Politics, War, and the Arts in the British World, 1750–1850, at 105 (2010); Robert F. Williams, The Law of American State Constitutions 61 (2009); Jamal Barnes, A Geneaology of the Torture Taboo 39 (2017); Keedy, *supra* note 40, at 764.

83. William Bradford, *An Enquiry How Far the Punishment of Death Is Necessary in Pennsylvania*, 12 Am. J. Legal History 122 (1968); Burton Alva Konkle, George Bryan and the Constitution of Pennsylvania 1731–1791, at 115 (1922); Keedy, *supra* note 40, at 766–70.

84. Samuel Hazard, ed., The Register of Pennsylvania (Sept. 28, 1828), Vol. II, pp. 145, 148 (reprinting "Gov. Mifflin's Message, 1792").

85. William W. Smithers (with George D. Thorn), Treatise on Executive Clemency in Pennsylvania 25–26, 107–108 (1909). The title page of the *Treatise on Executive Clemency in Pennsylvania* included this quotation from Alexander Hamilton out of *The Federalist No. 74*: "Humanity and good policy conspire to dictate that the benign prerogative of pardoning should be as little as possible fettered or embarrassed. The criminal code of every country partakes so much of necessary severity that, without an easy access to exceptions in favor of unfortunate guilt, justice would wear a countenance too sanguinary and cruel." Id., title page.

86. Legislative Reference Bureau, Capital Punishment in Wisconsin and the Nation 1 (1990).

87. "An Act for the better preventing of crimes, and for abolishing the punishment of death in certain cases," Apr. 22, 1794, *reprinted in* John Purdon & George M. Stroud, comp., A Digest of the Laws of Pennsylvania: From the Year One Thousand Seven Hundred to the Thirteenth Day of October, One Thousand Eight Hundred and Forty 786–87 (6th ed. 1841).

88. Joseph A. Melusky & Keith Alan Pesto, Capital Punishment 31 (2011); Francis Wharton, A Treatise on the Law of Homicide in the United States: To Which Is Appended a Series of Leading Cases on Homicide, Now Out of Print, Or Existing Only in Manuscript 354 (1855); 2 Basil Montagu, comp., The Opinions of Different Authors upon the Punishment of Death xv (1812); *see also* Franklin E. Zimring & Gordon Hawkins, Capital Punishment and the American Agenda 78 (1989):

The most common definitions of first- and second-degree murder originated from the Pennsylvania Act of 1794. First-degree murder included: (1) premeditated and deliberate homicide ("All murder which shall be perpetrated by means of poison, or by lying in wait, or by any other kind of willful, deliberate and premeditated killing"); and (2) homicides occurring in the course of or in the attempt to commit certain felonies ("or which shall be committed in the perpetration or attempt to perpetrate any arson, rape, robbery or burglary"). Second-degree murder as in substance all other homicides that would have been murder at common law ("and all other kinds of murder shall be deemed murder in the second degree").

89. Keedy, *supra* note 40, at 773.

90. Id. at 771–73.

91. 5 Laws of the Commonwealth of Pennsylvania (1803); 1 Stephen John Hartnett, Executing Democracy: Capital Punishment and the Making of America, 1683–1807 (2010).

92. "The Origin and Object of the Society for the Diffusion of Knowledge upon the Punishment of Death," 6 The Monthly Repository of Theology and General Literature 385, 390–91 (1811). Many nineteenth- and twentieth century reformers believed that capital punishment should be abolished. *E.g.*, 2 Richard Herne Shepherd, ed. The Prose Works of Percy Bysshe Shelley 167 (1906) (Shelley's "On the Punishment of Death: A Fragment" beings this way: "The first law which it becomes a Reformer to propose and support, at the approach of a period of great political change, is the abolition of the punishment of death.").

93. Ford K. Brown, Fathers of the Victorians: The Age of Wilberforce 349 (1961); V. A. C. Gatrell, The Hanging Tree: Execution and the English People 1770–1868, at 331, 398 (1994).

94. Scott Christianson, With Liberty for Some: 500 Years of Imprisonment in America 94–95 (1998); O. F. Lewis, The Development of American Prisons and Prison Customs, 1776–1845, at 33–34, 42, 52 (1922).

95. Matthew W. Meskell, *An American Resolution: The History of Prisons in the United States from 1777 to 1877*, 51 Stan. L. Rev. 839, 840, 843–45, 847–50, 853–54 (1999).

96. William Sneed, A Report on the History and Mode of Management of the Kentucky Penitentiary, from Its Origin, in 1798, to March 1, 1860, at 6 n.*, 10–13 (1860).

97. John D. Bessler, *The Italian Enlightenment and the American Revolution: Cesare Beccaria's Forgotten Influence on American Law*, 37 Mitchell Hamline L. J. Pub. Pol'y & Prac. 1, 159 (2016).

Chapter 4

1. William Eden, Principles of Penal Law 25, 34, 163, 288 (2d ed. 1771).

2. 2 Political Disquisitions: Or, An Enquiry into Public Errors, Defects and Abuses 291 n.a, 392 n.b, 475 (1774).

3. Edmund Gillingwater, An Essay on Parish Work-Houses: Containing Observations on the Present State of English Work-Houses; with Some Regulations Proposed for Their Improvement 4, 42–44 (1786); *compare* John Cartwright, The Legislative Rights of the Commonalty Vindicated; or, Take Your Choice! 95–96 (2d ed. 1777) ("I say, that the moment the necessity ceases the compulsion must cease also."); *see also* id. at 96 ("We all know that necessity supersedes all law: but it doth not overturn the foundations of law. And the most that can be inferred from these supposed cases of necessity, is that the general rule will not hold good in every possible contingency."); id. at 96 n.* ("'The law of necessity is a temporary law; that is, the law of a moment[.]'") (citation omitted).

4. Shahid M. Shahidullah, Crime Policy in America: Laws, Institutions, and Programs 96 (2008); Lynn Adelman, "How Congress, the U.S. Sentencing Commission, and Federal Judges Contribute to Mass Incarceration," 44 Litigation 8, 10 (Fall 2017).

5. United States v. E.L., 188 F. Supp.3d 152, 168 (E.D.N.Y. 2016) ("Pursuant to the 'parsimony clause' in section 3553(a), a court should 'impose a sentence sufficient, but not greater than necessary.' In view of the excessive incarceration rates in the recent past and their unnecessary, deleterious effects on individuals sentenced, their families, society and our economy, frugality in incarceration is prized.") (citations omitted); Sentencing Reform Act of 1984, Pub. L. No. 98–473, §211, 98 Stat. 1987, 1989–90 (1984).

6. United States v. McIntosh, 33 F. Supp.3d 448, 454 (S.D.N.Y. 2014) (citations omitted).

7. United States v. Rosales-Gonzales, 801 F.3d 1177, 1184 (9th Cir. 2015) (citations omitted).

8. *E.g.*, Defendant Juliet Anderson's Memorandum in Aid of Sentencing, *United States v. Anderson*, No. 06-CR-6229CJS, 2009 WL 2041117 (W.D.N.Y.) (Trial Motion, Memorandum and Affidavit) (Feb. 17, 2009):

As Montesquieu stated in 1748, "All punishment which is not derived from necessity is tyrannical." Given the life history of Juliet Anderson and her minimal role in the offense and her history of helping family members (and others in the community) and the fact that Ms. Anderson derived no benefit for her efforts on behalf of defendants Kevin Anderson and Shandrell Dawson, and the fact that Ms. Anderson, at great pain has accepted responsibility for her limited role, the proper application of the parsimony clause of Section 3553(a) strongly indicates that a non incarceration sentence should be imposed.

9. Petitioner's Reply to Government's Response in Opposition to Petitioner's Motion Pursuant to 28 U.S.C. §2255 to Vacate, Set Aside or Correct the Sentence of Federal Prisoner, *Dare v. United States*, No. 06-CR-0429 (LEX), 2009 WL 3027756 (N.D.N.Y.) (Trial Motion, Memorandum and Affidavit) (Jan. 28, 2009).

10. United States v. Ruiz, No. CR13-0049RSL, 2015 WL 6582307 (W.D. Wash.) (June 25, 2015) (Trial Motion, Memorandum and Affidavit) (citing Baron Charles de Montesquieu, The Spirit of the Laws, Bk. XIX 14 (G. Bell & Sons, Ltd. 1914)).

11. Defendant's Sentencing Memorandum, *United States v. Gardner*, No. 4:11-CR-00065-F-1, 2014 WL 2968214 (E.D.N.C.) (Trial Motion, Memorandum and Affidavit) (June 23, 2014) (citations omitted); *see also* Richard Frase, *Punishment Purposes*, 58 Stan. L. Rev. 67, 82–83 (2005) ("Section 3553(a) begins with a statement of the parsimony principle[.] ... [F]ederal trial and appellate courts should interpret section 3553(a) ... subject to the overall requirement of parsimony"); United States v. Jimenez-Beltre, 440 F.3d 514, 525 n.8 (1st Cir. 2006) ("Commentators note that this provision, which was originally part of the House sentencing reform bill and was later added to the Senate res-

olution and adopted in committee, 'is not just another 'factor' to be considered along with others set forth in Section 3553(a)—it sets an independent limit on the sentence a court may impose'") (citations omitted).

12. *E.g.*, Defendant's Sentencing Recommendation, *United States v. Williams*, No. CR07-245RSM, 2007 WL 4626711 (W.D. Wash.) (Trial Motion, Memorandum and Affidavit) (Dec. 11, 2007); Defendant Peter Mahoney's Sentencing Memorandum, *United States v. Mahoney*, No. CR-04-2127-RHW, 2007 WL 2374185 (E.D. Wash.) (Trial Motion, Memorandum and Affidavit) (Mar. 19, 2007); Defendant's Sentencing Memorandum and Recommendation, *United States v. Justice*, No. CR06-067MJP, 2007 WL 4251527 (W.D. Wash.) (Trial Motion, Memorandum and Affidavit) (Jan. 23, 2007); Memorandum in Aid of Sentencing on Behalf of Defendant Robert Goehring, *United States v. Goehring*, No. 05-CR-00209, 2006 WL 5043336 (S.D.N.Y.) (Trial Motion, Memorandum and Affidavit) (Oct. 31, 2006); USA v. Gilliland, No. 3:00CR48-008, 2006 WL 6052359 *n.1 (N.D. Fla.) (Trial Motion, Memorandum and Affidavit) (July 19, 2006).

13. "This Issue in Brief," Federal Probation: A Journal of Correctional Philosophy and Practice (published by the Administrative Office of the United States Courts), Vol. LV, No. 4, p. 1.

14. Kate Stith & José A. Cabranes, Fear of Judging: Sentencing Guidelines in the Federal Courts 38–39 (1998).

15. Id. at 40–41.

16. John B. Oakley & Vikram D. Amar, American Civil Procedure: A Guide to Civil Adjudication in US Courts 45 (2009).

17. Stith & Cabranes, Fear of Judging, *supra* note 14, at 43, 45–49; Congressional Record (1984), p. 29870; Jed S. Rakoff & Jonathan S. Sack, Corporate Sentencing Guidelines: Compliance and Mitigation (2005), § 1.03[5][a], p. 1–17 ("[C]ourts must apply the provisions of Title 18, Section 3553(a) of the United States Code, which provides a framework for imposing a sentence that is 'sufficient but not greater than necessary' to comply with the four purposes of sentencing set forth in Section 3553(a)(2): (1) retribution; (2) deterrence; (3) incapacitation; and (4) rehabilitation.").

18. 18 U.S.C. § 3553(a).

19. Barry Latzer & David McCord, Death Penalty Cases: Leading U.S. Supreme Court Cases on Capital Punishment 239 (3d ed. 2011); 18 U.S.C. § 3553(a)(2); Defendant Lam's Sentencing Memorandum, *United States v. Lam*, No. 09CR05641, 2010 WL 6510309 (W.D. Wash.) (Trial Motion, Memorandum and Affidavit) (Feb. 9, 2010):

The "parsimony clause" is not a new concept. It has deep roots in the 18th Century movement for criminal law reform in England. In 1748, Baron Charles de Montesquieu wrote "all punishment which is not derived from necessity is tyrannical." *The Spirit of the Laws*, B., XIX.14 (G. Bell & Sons, Ltd. 1914). Likewise, less than 40 years later, the English philosopher Jeremy Bentham wrote: "The punishment ought in no case to be more than what is necessary to bring it into conformity with the rules here given." Jeremy Bentham, *An Introduction to the Principles and Morals of Legislation*, Ch. XIV para 13 (1781). These thinkers influenced Jefferson and others during the early days of this country who adopted such principles and incorporated them into our criminal law. The parsimony clause in our own sentencing law derives from these historically-respected thinkers and, rightfully, reminds sentencing courts that the question of just *how much punishment is necessary* must be the primary focus at the time of sentencing.

20. United States v. Booker, 543 U.S. 220, 261 (2005).

21. Id. at 259–68; Rita v. United States, 551 U.S. 338, 341 (2007); *see also* United States v. Browning, 530 Fed. Appx. 864, 865 (11th Cir. 2013):

Applying "deferential" review, we must determine "whether the sentence imposed by the district court fails to achieve the purposes of sentencing as stated in section 3553(a)." *United States v. Talley*, 431 F.3d 784, 788 (11th Cir. 2005). "[W]e will not second guess the weight (or lack thereof) that the [court] accorded to a given factor ... as long as the sentence ultimately imposed is reasonable in light of all the circumstances presented." *United States v. Snipes*, 611 F.3d 855, 872 (11th Cir.2010) (quotation, alteration and emphasis omitted), *cert. denied*, —— U.S. ——, 131 S. Ct. 2962, 180 L.Ed.2d 245 (2011). In other words, we will not reweigh the relevant § 3553(a) factors, and will not remand for resentencing unless the district court committed a clear error of judgment in weighing the § 3553(a) factors by imposing a sentence outside the range of reasonable sentences. *United States v. Langston,* 590 F.3d 1226, 1237 (11th Cir. 2009).

The party challenging the sentence bears the burden to show it is unreasonable. *United States v. Tome,* 611 F.3d 1371, 1378 (11th Cir.), *cert. denied,* — U.S. ——, 131 S. Ct. 674, 178 L.Ed.2d 502 (2010). While we do not automatically presume a sentence falling within the guideline range to be reasonable, we ordinarily expect that sentence to be reasonable. *Talley,* 431 F.3d at 788.

For starters, we are unpersuaded by Browning's argument that the district court violated the "parsimony clause" by sentencing him to a greater sentence than necessary. Indeed, we have criticized the use of the phrase "parsimony principle" when referencing the "sufficient, but not greater than necessary" sentencing requirement of § 3553(a) because the phrase "tends to slant the discussion toward shorter sentences by emphasizing only" the need to avoid sentences that are too long. *See United States v. Irey,* 612 F.3d 1160, 1196–97 (11th Cir.2010) (en banc), *cert. denied,* — U.S. ——, 131 S. Ct. 1813, 179 L.Ed.2d 772 (2011).

22. United States v. Tapia-Vitinio, 463 Fed. Appx. 11 (2d Cir. 2011) (quoting 18 U.S.C. §3553(a), Gall v. United States, 552 U.S. 38, 51 (2007) & United States v. Jones, 531 F.3d 163, 174 (2d Cir. 2008); citing United States v. Williams, 475 F.3d 476–77 (2d Cir. 2007)).

23. Blakely v. Washington, 542 U.S. 296, 300–302, 308, 313–14 (2004) (citing Apprendi v. New Jersey, 530 U.S. 466, 490 (2000); 4 William Blackstone, Commentaries on the Laws of England 343 (1769)).

24. Kimbrough v. United States, 552 U.S. 85, 91 (2007).

25. *About the Commission,* https://www.ussc.gov; *Organization,* https://www.ussc.gov/about/who-we-are/organization.

26. Rita v. United States, 551 U.S. 338, 341, 347–48 (2007) (italics in original).

27. Beckles v. United States, 137 S. Ct. 886, 894 (2017).

28. Pepper v. United States, 562 U.S. 476, 501, 504–505 (2011).

29. Peugh v. United States, 569 U.S. 530, 536 (2013).

30. Andrew von Hirsch, Past or Future Crimes: Deservedness and Dangerousness in the Sentencing of Criminals 6 (1986).

31. Cassia C. Spohn, How Do Judges Decide? The Search for Fairness and Justice in Punishment 4, 10–11, 18, 22–23 (2d ed. 2009).

32. U.S. Const., amend. XIV; John D. Bessler, *The Inequality of America's Death Penalty: A Crossroads for Capital Punishment at the Intersection of the Eighth and Fourteenth Amendments,* 73 Wash. & Lee L. Rev. Online 487, 515, 529, 537–38 (2016); Jana Shortal, "Minnesota Racial Bias Task Force: 25 Years Later, Did It Work?", June 11, 2018, https://www.kare11.com/article/news/minnesota-racial-bias-task-force-25-years-later-did-it-work/89-563375254; *see also* Nora V. Demleitner, Douglas A. Berman, Marc L. Miller & Ronald F. Wright, Sentencing Law and Policy: Cases, Statutes, and Guidelines 249 (3d ed. 2013):

Many observers have noted a tension in the Supreme Court's capital punishment cases decided under the Eighth Amendment. On one hand, cases such as *Furman* and *Gregg* emphasize the importance of guiding or structuring the sentencing jury's discretion through the use of statutory aggravating factors, bifurcated proceedings, appellate review, and other legal controls. On the other hand, cases such as *Woodson* and *Lockett* insist that the decision to impose the death penalty must be individualized, and legal rules must not unduly restrict the information the jury receives about the case or the ability of individual jurors to act on that information.

33. Freeman v. United States, 564 U.S. 522, 529 (2011); *compare* United States v. Soriano, No. 11-5765-cr, 503 Fed. Appx. 4, 2012 WL 5503603 *2 (2d Cir. Nov. 14, 2012) ("Soriano contends that the district court did not adequately address why a shorter period of incarceration would not be sufficient to comply with the purposes of sentencing as provided in the parsimony clause of 18 U.S.C. § 3553(a). We do not require a district court expressly to refer to the parsimony clause to demonstrate satisfaction of its obligations thereunder.") (citing *United States v. Ministro–Tapia,* 470 F.3d 137, 141 (2d Cir. 2006)); Hicks v. United States, 137 S. Ct. 2000, 2000-1 (2017) (Gorsuch, J., concurring) ("A plain legal error infects this judgment—a man was wrongly sentenced to 20 years in prison under a defunct statute. No doubt, too, there's a reasonable probability that cleansing this error will yield a different outcome. Of course, Mr. Hicks's conviction won't be undone, but the sentencing component

of the district court's judgment is likely to change, and change substantially. For experience surely teaches that a defendant entitled to a sentence consistent with 18 U.S.C. § 3553(a)'s parsimony provision, rather than pursuant to the rigors of a statutory mandatory minimum, will often receive a much lower sentence. So there can be little doubt Mr. Hicks's substantial rights are, indeed, implicated.").

34. United States v. Aranda Diaz, 785 F. Supp.2d 1058, 1064-65 (D. N.M. 2011) (citing United States v. Conlan, 500 F.3d 1167, 1169 (10th Cr. 2007) ("[A] district court's job is not to impose a reasonable sentence. Rather, a district court's mandate is to impose a sentence sufficient, but not greater than necessary, to comply with the purposes of section 3553(a)(2).") (citation omitted).

35. Dean v. United States, 137 S. Ct. 1170, 1774-76 (2017).

36. David Debold, ed., Practice Under the Federal Sentencing Guidelines 2016-2 Supplement (5th ed.), § 1.02[D][3], pp. 1-36—1-37; *see also* id. at 1–37 ("Perhaps because its meaning is vague, the statutory command has been perpetually disregarded since *Booker*—a disturbing trend that one of the authors has termed an 'anti-parsimony pandemic.' ").

37. Dillon v. United States, 560 U.S. 817, 819-31 (2010).

38. *Dillon*, 560 U.S. at 831-34, 848 (Stevens, J., dissenting) (citations omitted).

39. Nora V. Demleitner, Douglas A. Berman, Marc L. Miller & Ronald F. Wright, Sentencing Law and Policy: Cases, Statutes, and Guidelines (4th ed. 2018); Todd R. Clear, George F. Cole, Michael D. Reisig & Carolyn Petrosino, American Corrections in Brief 53 (2d ed. 2015).

40. *See, e.g.*, United States v. Arnold, 536 Fed. Appx. 9, 13-14 (2d Cir. 2013):

Arnold submits that his 121–month prison sentence, which represents the low end of his Sentencing Guidelines range, and is one month longer than the statutorily mandated minimum sentence, is substantively unreasonable in that it violates the parsimony clause of 18 U.S.C. § 3553(a) and unspecified provisions of the Constitution. This argument is defeated by precedent. *See United States v. Carter*, 696 F.3d 229, 232–33 (2d Cir.2012) (holding that ten-year mandatory minimum sentence for crack conspiracy does not violate § 3553(a) parsimony clause); *see also United States v. Huerta*, 878 F.2d 89, 91–94 (2d Cir. 1989) (rejecting due process and separation of powers challenges to mandatory minimum sentences). Because this is not one of those "exceptional cases where the trial court's decision cannot be located within the range of permissible [sentences]," his sentence is not substantively unreasonable. *United States v. Cavera*, 550 F.3d 180, 189 (2d Cir. 2008) (*en banc*) (internal quotation marks omitted); *see United States v. Jones*, 531 F.3d 163, 174 (2d Cir. 2008).

Compare *Construction and Application of "Parsimony Clause" of 18 U.S.C.A. § 3553(a), Providing that District Court Shall Impose Sentence Sufficient, but Not Greater Than Necessary, to Comply with § 3553(a)(2)*, 38 A.L.R. Fed.2d 147 (2009):

[T]he courts in a number of cases, in which a challenge was brought against a court-issued sentence on the ground that the "parsimony clause" of 18 U.S.C. § 3553(a) had been violated, in holding that a sentence rendered by the federal district court was "reasonable" with respect to "parsimony clause" principles, referred generally to the mandates of the code provision (§ 4), found the sentence reasonable despite the fact that it was in excess of the recommended United States Sentencing Guidelines (§ 10), and held that the sentence rendered was reasonable in light of the defendant's background factors or criminal record (§ 13). Other courts, however, given the particular circumstances presented, ruled to the contrary in similar factual scenarios (§§ 5, 11, 14).

41. United States v. Almonte, 422 Fed. Appx. 8, 9 (2d Cir. 2011) (citations omitted).

42. United States v. Holloway, 431 Fed. Appx. 233, 234 (4th Cir. 2011).

43. United States v. Mendoza, 414 Fed. Appx. 875, 876 (8th Cir. 2011).

44. Virginia Declaration of Rights, Art. I, § 9; *see also Furman*, 408 U.S. at 319 (Marshall, J., concurring) ("The precise language used in the Eighth Amendment first appeared in America on June 12, 1776, in Virginia's 'Declaration of Rights,' § 9 of which read: 'That excessive bail ought not to be required, nor excessive fines imposed, nor cruel and unusual punishments inflicted.' ").

45. 1 Wm. & Mary, Sess. 2, ch. 2; *see also* Harmelin v. Michigan, 501 U.S. 957, 966 (1991) ("[T]he entire text of the Eighth Amendment is taken almost verbatim from the English Declaration of Rights, which provided '[t]hat excessive Baile ought not to be required nor excessive Fines imposed nor cruell and unusuall Punishments inflicted.' ").

46. Benjamin West Janke & François-Xavier Licari, *Enforcing Punitive Damage Awards in France After* Fountaine Pajot, 60 Am. J. Comp. L. 775, 794 n.76 (2012). The French Declaration of the Rights of Man and of the Citizen was promulgated just weeks after the storming of the Bastille. John Hostettler, Champions of the Rule of Law 74 (2011):

[O]n 14 July 1789 Parisians attacked the Bastille, the feared symbolic institution of the French criminal justice system. Fewer than six weeks later, the French Declaration of the Rights of Man and the Citizen was approved by the French National Assembly on 26 August. The Declaration, which sets out the rule of law, was largely the work of the Marquis de Lafayette after consulting with Thomas Jefferson in Paris where he was then American Minister to France.

See also Lynn Hunt, Inventing Human Rights: A History 136 (2007) ("On October 5, under the pressure of a massive march to Versailles, Louis XVI finally gave his formal approval of the Declaration of the Rights of Man and Citizen."); *see also* Eli Sagan, Citizens and Cannibals: The French Revolution, the Struggle for Modernity, and the Origins of Ideological Terror 55 (2001) ("In 1789, the *question préparatoire*—pretrial torture to obtain a confession—and in 1788, the routinely administered torture of a convicted criminal in order to elicit from him the names of his accomplices (the *question préable*) were abrogated.").

47. Jeff Horn, Economic Development in Early Modern France: The Privilege of Liberty, 1650–1820, at 247 (2015); Clive Emsley, Gendarmes and the State in Nineteenth-Century Europe 33 (1999); *see also* Gilbert Shapiro & John Markoff, Revolutionary Demands: A Content Analysis of the Cahiers de Doléances of 1789 (1998).

48. Alexis de Tocqueville, The Old Regime and the Revolution 308 (John Bonner, trans. 1856); *see also* Sagan, Citizens and Cannibals, *supra* note 46, at 36 ("Tocqueville described the *cahiers* as 'le testament de l'ancienne société française, l'expression suprême de ses désires, le manfestation authentique de ses volontés,' and he devoted himself to the study of them, most especially the *cahiers* of the nobility."); id. ("Some of the noble cahiers, especially those of Paris, demanded the destruction of the Bastille. All forms of corporal punishments of prisoners, including torture, should be done away with...."); Marc Ancel, Social Defence: A Modern Approach to Criminal Problems 34 (J. Wilson, trans. 2001) ("In France, on the eve of the Great Revolution, the *Cahiers de doléances* of the States-General demanded a reformed criminal justice which should show greater respect for the rights of man and would lead, in particular, to an improvement in the prison system."); Beatrice Fry Hyslop, French Nationalism in 1789, According to the General Cahiers 141 (1968) ("A great man cahiers asked that punishment be proportionate to the crime."); id. ("[C]ertain cahiers wished to lighten the punishment of criminals. The assemblies sponsoring such reforms must have been familiar with the works of Voltaire, Beccaria, Dupaty, and others.").

49. Mlada Bukovansky, Legitimacy and Power Politics: The American and French Revolutions in International Political Culture 187 (2002) ("The Declaration of the Rights of Man and Citizen (1789) was based on the marquis de Lafayette's drafts, which in turn were based on the Virginia Declaration of Rights and on the Declaration of Independence. Jefferson himself annotated Lafayette's second draft."). A letter from Lafayette to Jefferson, with the salutation line, "My dear friend," read in part: "To morrow I propose my bill of rights about the middle of the sitting; be pleased to consider it again and make your observations." The initial version of Lafayette's declaration, one endorsed by Jefferson, did not contain the language about "strictly and obviously necessary" punishments. It did, however, contain (as translated into English), the following two provisions, among others: "The rights of man assure his property, liberty, honor, and his life. No limitation to these rights can be introduced except by due process of laws accepted either by him and his representatives and previously promulgated and enforced through a regular tribunal." "Government is divided into three powers: Legislative ... ; Executive ... ; Judiciary, which must be entrusted to tribunals whose only function is to preserve the body of laws and to apply them literally to cases submitted to them, with such an organisation and regime as to insure to the judges their independence, and to the public their impartiality, and to the interested parties means of justification and an easy distribution of justice." The language about "strictly and obviously necessary" punishments appears in the final version of the French Declaration. Gilbert Chinard, comp., The Letters of Lafayette and Jefferson 134–37, 141 (1929).

50. Gordon S. Wood, Friends Divided: John Adams and Thomas Jefferson 224–25 (2017).

51. Id. at 225.

52. George L. Scherger, The Evolution of Modern Liberty 222 (1904).

53. George Athan Billias, American Constitutionalism Heard Round the World, 1776–1989: A Global Perspective 73 (2009).

54. Micheline R. Ishay, The History of Human Rights: From Ancient Times to the Globalization Era 74 (2008),

55. George L. Scherger, The Evolution of Modern Liberty 225 (1904):

On the 27th of July Champion de Cicé, Archbishop of Bordeaux, the reporter for the committee of the constitution, said that the committee had judged it necessary "that the constitution be preceded by a Declaration of the Rights of Man and of the Citizen; not because it was necessary to impress upon these first truths a force they already derived from morals, from reason, and from nature, which had engrafted them in all hearts, but because these ineffaceable principles should be constantly before the eyes and in thought." This Declaration, he said, "would be a constant guarantee against the fear of any disregard of its principles." "If in the course of ages any power should attempt to impose laws upon the people that were not an emanation from these principles, this original and enduring type would instantly denounce crime or error to all citizens." "This noble idea," he proceeded, "conceived in another hemisphere, ought to be, because of its excellence, at once transplanted among us. We have participated in the events that gave to North America her liberty; she has shown us upon what principles the conservation of our own should rest; and it is the new world, whither we had formerly carried only weapons, which to-day teaches us to secure ourselves against the misfortune of betaking thither our persons."

56. Oliver W. Lembcke & Florian Weber, eds., Emmanuel Joseph Sieyès: The Essential Political Writings 35, 118 & n.*a* (2014).

57. Carlson Anyangwe, Criminal Law: The General Part 31 (2015):

[M]ost of Beccaria's ideas were vindicated by the outcome of the French Revolution. Those ideas directly inspired the 1789 Declaration of the Rights of Man and the Citizen, legislation passed by the French revolutionaries in 1791, and the drafting and adoption of the French Penal Code of 1810.

58. Manfred Nowak & Karolina Miriam Januszewski, "Torture: Europe and the Americas," *in* Erik André Andersen & Eva Maria Lassen, eds., Europe and the Americas: Transatlantic Approaches to Human Rights 300–301 (2015); *see also* C. R. Snyman, Criminal Law 37 (1995) ("One of the ideals of the revolution was the abolition of this arbitrary punishment, such could best be done by the codification of the criminal law so that all citizens could know precisely what conduct was punishable. Section 8 of the famous French Declaration of the Rights of Man of 1789 stated that no-one could be punished except in terms of a law that had been passed and promulgated before the act was committed."). Article 8 of the French Declaration of Rights was, along with articles 7 and 9 of that declaration, reportedly "aimed at no imaginary or very distant wrongs" as is said to be "evident from a cursory survey of the administration of the laws of France, and from the protests of French authors." As a history of the First French Republic notes:

Lettres de cachet, arbitrary imprisonments, retroactive laws, and cruelly exaggerated penalties were not uncommon. Mirabeau and Voltaire had both suffered under arbitrary laws and had painted the injustice of such laws in lurid colors. Mirabeau's *Lettres de cachet* and his *Essai sur le despotisme* bristle with protests against the abuses of the old *régime*. The following gruesome picture is a suggestive statement of the way in which justice was administered in France in the eighteenth century:

"The disproportion of crimes and of penalties was flagrant. A house thief was hung in 1733; an ecclesiastic, guilty of having found fault with the expulsion of the Jesuits, was also hung in 1762. The procedure was unjust and inhuman. The accused, assumed to be guilty in advance, ignorant of the crime with which he was charged, without counsellor or advocate, interrogated *à huis clos*, submitted to the preparatory question, was judged secretly. Once condemned, he was tortured before undergoing his punishment. And what punishment! For imprisonment, transportation or hanging was in vogue. The burning at the stake had fallen into desuetude, but the lash, branding with red-hot iron, the galleys, quartering, the rack, still did their savage work."

Protests against these enormities were raised by the philosophers, and later by enlightened magistrates, such as Montesquieu, Servan, Linguet, and Malesherbes. In 1780, the "preparatory question" was abolished.

Horace Mann Conaway, The First French Republic: A Study of the Origin and the Con-

TENTS OF THE DECLARATION OF THE RIGHTS OF MAN, OF THE CONSTITUTION, AND OF THE ADOPTION OF THE REPUBLICAN FORM OF GOVERNMENT IN 1792, at 12–13 (1902).

59. Judgment, Case of Maktouf and Damjanoviæ v. Bosnia and Herzegovina, Grand Chamber, Applications Nos. 2312/08 and 34179/08 (Strasbourg, July 18, 2013) ¶ 2 n.26 (Pinto de Albuquerque, J., concurring) ("Ultimately this principle results from the liberty set out in Article 4: 'Liberty consists in the freedom to do everything which injures no one else; hence the exercise of the natural rights of each man has no limits except those which assure to the other members of the society the enjoyment of the same rights. These limits can only be determined by law.' "); *accord* 2 JOHN BEELER & CHARLES CLARK, SOURCES OF WESTERN SOCIETY: FROM THE AGE OF EXPLORATION TO THE PRESENT 345 (2d ed. 2011); UNA BIRCH, SECRET SOCIETIES: ILLUMINATI, FREEMASONS AND THE FRENCH REVOLUTION 247 (James Wasserman, ed. 2007); JAMES M. ANDERSON, DAILY LIFE DURING THE FRENCH REVOLUTION 244 (2007); THE UNITED STATES DECLARATION OF INDEPENDENCE: ORIGINAL VERSION/MODERN CAPITALIZATION VERSION/FRENCH DECLARATION OF THE RIGHTS OF MAN AND OF THE CITIZEN (WRITTEN BY THE MARQUIS DE LAFAYETTE, WITH HELP FROM HIS FRIEND AND NEIGHBOR, AMERICAN ENVOY TO FRANCE, THOMAS JEFFERSON) 33 (2009). The principle set forth in Article 8 of the Declaration of the Rights of Man and of the Citizen (1789) has been said to result "from the principle of liberty set out in article 4: 'Liberty consists in the freedom to do everything which injuries no one else; hence the exercise of the natural rights of each man has no limits except those which assure to the other members of the society the enjoyment of the same rights. These limits can only be determined by law.' " Judgment, Case of Maktouf and Damjanoviæ v. Bosnia and Herzegovina, Grand Chamber, Applications Nos. 2312/08 and 34179/08 (Strasbourg, July 18, 2013) ¶ 2 n.26

60. Marion Vannier, "A Right to Hope? Life Imprisonment in France," *in* DIRK VAN ZYL SMIT & CATHERINE APPLETON, EDS., LIFE IMPRISONMENT AND HUMAN RIGHTS 203 (2016); *see also* Judgment, Case of G. v. France, Eur. Ct. Hum. Rts., Application No. 15312/89 (Strasbourg), Sept. 27, 1995, ¶ 22 (noting that "Article 8 of the Declaration of the Rights of Man and the Citizen of 1789 ... states that 'the law should impose only such penalties as are absolutely and evidently necessary'."); E. THOMAS SULLIVAN & RICHARD S. FRASE, PROPORTIONALITY PRINCIPLES IN AMERICAN LAW: CONTROLLING EXCESSIVE GOVERNMENT ACTIONS 249 n.153 (2009) (noting that Article 8 of the French Declaration of the Rights of Man (1789) limited punishments to those that are "strictly and evidently necessary"); HELEN MARIA WILLIAMS, LETTERS WRITTEN IN FRANCE 245 (Neil Fraistat & Susan S. Lanser, eds., 2001) (translating Section VIII of the French Declaration as follows: "The law must establish only those punishments that are absolutely and obviously necessary, and no one can be punished except according to a law that is established and promulgated before the offense takes place, and is legally applied."). The principle of *legality* requires that individuals be put on notice of the illegality of an act before being held criminally responsible for it. Sonja Starr, *Extraordinary Crimes and Ordinary Times: International Justice Beyond Crisis Situations*, 101 NW. U. L. REV. 1257, 1306 (2007); *see also* Edward M. Wise, *General Rules of Criminal Law*, 25 DENV. J. INT'L L. & POL'Y 313 (1997) ("the principle of legality has been taken to require that crimes be specifically proscribed by law in advance of the conduct sought to be punished"); Judgment, Case of ?danoka v. Latvia, Eur. Ct. Hum. Rts., Grand Chamber, Application No. 58278/00 (Strasbourg), Mar. 16, 2006 (Zupanèiè, J., dissenting) ("Ever since 1764 when Cesare Beccaria wrote his decisive '*Dei delitti e delle pene*' the retrospective validity of the punitive rule of law has been an integral part of the principle of legality."); Judgment, Case of Streletz, Kessler and Krenz v. Germany, Eur. Ct. Hum. Rts., Grand Chamber, Application Nos. 34044/96, 35532/97 & 44801/98 (Strasbourg, Mar. 22, 2001) (Zupanèiè, J., concurring) ("This tradition of substantive criminal-law protection goes back to at least 1764 and Ce[s]are Beccaria's classic work *Dei delitti e delle pene*, which decisively influenced the whole continental tradition of legality in criminal law.").

61. 9 JEAN BRISSAUD, THE CONTINENTAL LEGAL HISTORY SERIES (History of French Public Law) 542, 544 (James W. Garner, trans. 1915) (noting that "[t]he Principles of 1789 were based on the idea that the nation is sovereign and that all its members are free and of equal rights" and translating Article 8 of the French Declaration as follows: "The law ought to establish only penal ties that are strictly and obviously necessary, and no one can be punished except in virtue of a law established and promulgated prior to the offense and legally applied."); JOHN R. COLE, BETWEEN THE QUEEN AND THE CABBY: OLYMPE DE GOUGES'S RIGHTS OF WOMAN 121–22 (2011) (noting that Gouges's 1791 Declaration, "The Rights of Women and the Female Citizen," as translated, read: "The law may

establish only penalties that are strictly and obviously necessary, and not one may be punished other than by virtue of a Law established and promulgated prior to the offence and legally applied to women."). In her declaration, Gouges thus repeated "the men's Article VIII verbatim, appending only two words, 'to women.'" Id. at 122. *See also* Olympe de Gouges, The Declaration of the Rights of Women: The Original Manifesto for Justice, Equality and Freedom (2018).

62. Cole, *supra* note 61, at 122–26, 128.

63. Wendelin Guentner, ed., Women Art Critics in Nineteenth-Century France: Vanishing Acts 18 (2013).

64. William A. Schabas, The Death Penalty as Cruel Treatment and Torture: Capital Punishment Challenged in the World's Courts 157 (1996); David Williams, Condorcet and Modernity 57–58, 270 (2004); The Wordsworth Dictionary of Phrase and Fable: The Quintessential Guide to Myth, Folklore, Legend and Literature 510 (2001); John Wilson Croker, History of the Guillotine 9 (1853).

65. Condorcet: Foundations of Social Choice and Political Theory 212 (Iain McLean & Fiona Hewitt, trans. & eds., 1994); Ian Hacking, The Taming of Chance 90 (1990); David Williams, Condorcet and Modernity 15, 41 (2004).

66. *See, e.g.*, 10 The Anti-Jacobin Review and Magazine; or, Monthly, Political, and Literary Censor: from January to April, Inclusive 261 (1810):

Much at large does our author expatiate on the severity, and, as he seems to say, the injustice, of the punishment of death; and he quotes most of the well-known writers, who have written on the subject, in support of his own opinions. We so far concur with those who have broached this doctrine, as to admit that all punishment of individuals which is not necessary for the good of the community, is unjust.

67. Thomas Jefferson, a close friend of the Marquis de Lafayette, was appointed to be the Minister for the United States of America in France in 1785. Anthony Arlidge & Igor Judge, Magna Carta Uncovered 163 (2014).

68. Chester Penn Higby, History of Modern Europe: A Survey of the Evolution of European Society from the National Risings Against Napoleon to the Present Day 9 (1932) ("The penal code of 1791 abolished judicial torture, the pillory, branding with a hot iron, and public confession of guilt (*amende honorable*), made the punishment fit the crime, and established liberty of the press in fact though not in law."). The French penal code of 1791 was shaped by the writings of Montesquieu and Beccaria. Jean Pradel, "Criminal Law," in George A. Bermann & Etienne Picard, eds., Introduction to French Law 104 (2008); *see also* "Reviews and Criticisms," *in* 8 Journal of the American Institute of Criminal Law and Criminology 143, 146 ("In France, the writings of Beccaria, Montesquieu and Rousseau, prepared the way for a complete transformation of the criminal law. The Code of 1791 sought to put into effect two principles: prohibition only of acts injurious to society and the impartial infliction of strictly necessary punishments.") (reviewing Carl Ludwig von Bar, A History of Continental Criminal Law (Thomas S. Bell, et al., trans. 1916)). Not only did the writings of Montesquieu and Beccaria find "concrete expression in the French Revolutionary penal code of September 25, 1791," but well-informed Americans were well aware of developments in the law as they unfolded in Europe. Henry Elmer Barnes, *The Historical Origin of the Prison System in America*, 12 J. Crim. L. & Criminology 35, 42 (1922). *See also* Guy Carleton Lee, Historical Jurisprudence: An Introduction to the Systematic Study of the Development of Law 427 (1900):

The demand so persistently made, that the laws should be made uniform throughout France and that the gross injustice in the laws should be removed, found its first definite expression in the decrees of the national Assembly of August 25th and 30th, 1791, as follows:

....

"Art. 21. The Penal Code shall be from time to time amended, so that penalties may be proportionate to offences; care shall be taken that they may be moderate, and sight shall not be lost of the maxim forming part of the Declaration of the Rights of Man, that the laws must inflict punishments only so far as these are strictly and obviously necessary."

69. William A. Schabas, The Death Penalty as Cruel Treatment and Torture: Capital Punishment Challenged in the World's Courts 26 (1996). As Professor Schabas continues in speaking of section 8 of the French Declaration:

This provision of the Déclaration also provoked debate in the National Assembly about the necessity of retaining the death penalty. The French revolutionaries, undoubtedly inspired by the writings of Cesare Beccaria and his followers, including Voltaire, clearly understood that the new human rights principles of the Enlightenment called into question the legitimacy of capital punishment. Initially, Robespierre argued vigorously for the abolition of the death penalty. He failed to convince the majority of the National Assembly, and the death penalty was retained, although in the form proposed by his colleague, Dr. Guillotin. (He was not, however, the inventor of the guillotine, the device having been used for many years as an elite form of punishment reserved for aristocrats. It was introduced generally during the French Revolution to eliminate the suffering involved in executions and to ensure that imposition of the death penalty involved nothing but the extinction of life.) Although discouraged at the National Assembly's refusal to abolish capital punishment altogether, Robespierre later had a change of heart. He called for the execution of Louis XVI, whom he labelled a "criminal envers l'humanité." His American colleague Thomas Paine considered this a betrayal. Robespierre's failure to effect abolition of the death penalty and his subsequent support for it would, of course, have ironic personal consequences.

Id.

70. As one source stresses of section 8 of the French Declaration and what actually transpired in France:

In the event of an arrest and conviction, only "strictly and obviously necessary punishments may be declared by law." The ideals expressed in the declaration were not upheld over the course of the French Revolution. The National Convention, which held power in France from 1792 to 1795, instituted a Reign of Terror characterized by arbitrary arrest and thousands of executions by guillotine.

Carolyn Harris, Magna Carta and Its Gifts to Canada: Democracy, Law, and Human Rights 87 (2015).

71. What became the U.S. Bill of Rights were debated by Congress in 1789 and ratified on December 15, 1791. Patrick T. Conley & John P. Kaminski, eds., The Bill of Rights and the States: The Colonial and Revolutionary Origins of American Liberties 457 (1992); Christine Barbour & Gerald C. Wright, Keeping the Republic: Power and Citizenship in American Politics 139 (6th ed. 2014). In *The Influence of the United States Constitution Abroad*, one author notes of the French Declaration of Rights:

[Lafayette sent a copy of his draft of the Declaration of Rights] to Jefferson in January 1789, and Jefferson immediately sent a copy on to Madison for comment. Gouverneur Morris, who arrived in Paris on February 3, 1789, as a representative of certain American commercial interests, also studied the draft. He recommended a number of changes.... Advice from Jefferson, Madison, and Morris was supplemented by Lafayette's conversations on the subject with Hamilton, Franklin, and Thomas Paine. Thus, while the famous French Declaration of the Rights of Man and of the Citizen of August, 1789, was officially the work of Lafayette, Mirabeau, and Jean Joseph Mounier, it also had claim to American parentage.

Vincent Robert Johnson, *The Declaration of the Rights of Man and of Citizens of 1789, the Reign of Terror, and the Revolutionary Tribunal of Paris*, 13 B.C. Int'l & Comp. L. Rev. 1, 12 (1990).

72. Duncan Wu, ed., Romanticism: An Anthology (4th ed. 2012) (noting in the entry for Thomas Paine (1737–1809) that Paine, the former corset-maker and customs officer, was "one of the foremost political thinkers of his time," emigrated to America at age 37 in 1774, appealed for American independence in his best-selling book, *Common Sense* (1776), and went to France, "where he became an associate of Thomas Jefferson and member of the Lafayette circle").

73. Anthony Arlidge & Igor Judge, Magna Carta Uncovered 163 (2014).

74. Ludwig von Bar, A History of Continental Criminal Law 320 (Thomas S. Bell, trans. 1916) (reprinted in 2007 by The Lawbook Exchange, Ltd.); Thomas Jefferson to Thomas Paine, Sept. 13, 1789, https://founders.archives.gov/documents/Jefferson/01-15-02-0413. The summary description of Ian Davidson's new book, *The French Revolution: From Enlightenment to Tyranny* (2016), captures the essence of what happened with the French Revolution:

The fall of the Bastille on July 14, 1789 has become the commemorative symbol of the French Revolution. But this violent and random act was unrepresentative of the real work of the early revolution, which was taking place ten miles west of Paris, in Versailles. There, the nobles, clergy and commoners of France had just declared themselves a republic, toppling a rotten system of aristocratic privilege and altering the course of history forever. The Revolution was led not by angry mobs, but by the best and brightest of France's growing bourgeoisie: young, educated, ambitious. Their aim was not to destroy, but to build a better state. In just three months they drew up a Declaration of the Rights of Man, which was to become the archetype of all subsequent Declarations worldwide, and they instituted a system of locally elected administration for France which still survives today. They were determined to create an entirely new system of government, based on rights, equality and the rule of law. In the first three years of the Revolution they went a long way toward doing so. Then came Robespierre, the Terror and unspeakable acts of barbarism. In a clear, dispassionate and fast-moving narrative, Ian Davidson shows how and why the Revolutionaries, in just five years, spiralled from the best of the Enlightenment to tyranny and the Terror. The book reminds us that the Revolution was both an inspiration of the finest principles of a new democracy and an awful warning of what can happen when idealism goes wrong.

75. Johnson, *supra* note 71, at 5.

76. Thomas Paine, "Address to the People of France," Thomas Paine National Historical Association, http://thomaspaine.org/essays/french-revolution/address-to-the-people-of-france.html.

77. On July 12, 1789, Thomas Jefferson wrote from Paris to Richard Price to describe how the French had "begun the great work of building up a constitution." In his letter, Jefferson emphasized: "The Declaration of the rights of man, which constitutes the 1st. chapter of this work, was brought in the day before yesterday, and referred to the bureaus. You will observe that these are the outlines of a great work, and be assured that the body engaged in it are equal to a masterly execution of it." "Should this revolution succeed," Jefferson's letter added, "it is the beginning of the reformation of the governments of Europe." "From Thomas Jefferson to Richard Price, 12 July 1789," *Founders Online,* National Archives, last modified November 26, 2017, http://founders.archives.gov/documents/Jefferson/01-15-02-0261. [Original source: *The Papers of Thomas Jefferson*, vol. 15, *27 March 1789?–?30 November 1789*, ed. Julian P. Boyd. Princeton: Princeton University Press, 1958, pp. 271–272.] In July 1789, Jefferson himself had reviewed Lafayette's draft of what became the French Declaration of the Rights of Man. "Lafayette to Thomas Jefferson, 4 July 1812," (editorial note), *Founders Online,* National Archives, last modified November 26, 2017, http://founders.archives.gov/documents/Jefferson/03-05-02-0167. [Original source: *The Papers of Thomas Jefferson*, Retirement Series, vol. 5, *1 May 1812 to 10 March 1813*, ed. J. Jefferson Looney. Princeton: Princeton University Press, 2008, pp. 212–215.]

78. Johnson, *supra* note 71, at 6 n.19 (citations omitted).

79. Alexander A. Reinert, *Reconceptualizing the Eighth Amendment: Slaves, Prisoners, and "Cruel and Unusual" Punishment*, 94 N.C. L. Rev. 817, 832 n.65 (2016) (quoting Declaration of the Rights of Man § 8 (1789)).

80. John D. Bessler, *Revisiting Beccaria's Vision: The Enlightenment, America's Death Penalty, and the Abolition Movement*, 4 NW J. L. & Soc. Pol'y 195 n.122 (2009) (describing Lafayette's opposition to executions).

81. Francis X. Mattingly, *If You Don't Use It, You Lose It: What the U.S. Could Learn from France's Law on Out-of-Commerce Books of the 20th Century*, 27 Ind. Int'l & Comp. L. Rev. 277, 303 (2017); *see also* Aaron Schwabach, *Thomas Jefferson, Slavery, and Slaves*, 33 T. Jefferson L. Rev. 1, 17-18 (2010):

Jefferson left France after the storming of the Bastille but before the executions of Louis XVI and Marie Antoinette. To many of the French revolutionaries, Jefferson was a hero who had overthrown monarchic rule in his own country and created a republic. He worked with Lafayette on the Declaration of the Rights of Man and of the Citizen, Article 1 of which declares in part, "Men are born and remain free and equal in rights."

82. "The New Constitution of France," Medley (published as *The Medley or Newbedford Marine Journal*) (New Bedford, Mass.), Sept. 20, 1793, p. 1. The June 24, 1793 constitution—as a history of France notes—had been "drawn up by the Convention and was submitted to the people." "Although accepted by them," that history observes, "it was never put in operation, being first temporarily suspended and afterwards set aside." Still, that 1793 constitution is of historical importance, as that history notes of it: "It possesses decided interest, nevertheless, since it represents the ideas of the Montagnards as to the best permanent form of government. Article 15 of the 1793 constitution read: "The law ought to impose only penalties that are strictly and obviously necessary: the punishments

ought to be proportionate to the offence and useful to society." FRANK MALOY ANDERSON, THE CONSTITUTIONS AND OTHER SELECT DOCUMENTS ILLUSTRATIVE OF THE HISTORY OF FRANCE 1789–1907, at 171, 173 (2d ed. rev. 1908).

83. *E.g.*, Roger P. Alford, *In Search of a Theory for Constitutional Comparativism*, 53 UCLA L. REV. 639, 656 (2005):

[I]t is curious to say the least that in interpreting the Bill of Rights, an originalist does not take into greater account the influence of the French Declaration of the Rights of Man. That Declaration—drafted in 1788 and 1789 and published on August 27, 1789 (just one month before Congress formally proposed the Bill of Rights on September 25, 1789)—provides a useful prism to understand our own Bill of Rights. While Madison was drafting the Bill of Rights, the French Revolution was in full swing and was greeted in America with great enthusiasm. John Adams expressed the view that "most of the events in the annals of the world are but childish tales compared to it." He hoped the French Revolution would "produce effects in favor of liberty, equity, and humanity as extensive as this whole globe and as lasting as all time." Thomas Jefferson corresponded with Madison in January 1789 informing him that in France "[e]verybody here is trying their hands at forming declarations of rights." Moreover, it is well known that Jefferson read and critiqued Lafayette's June 1789 drafts of the Declaration of the Rights of Man and offered his own version. Jefferson also critiqued the Bill of Rights in light of his experience in France, suggesting that its language mirror provisions of the Declaration.

84. Johnson, *supra* note 71, at 8.

85. Id. at 9. At Benjamin Franklin's instigation, a compilation of American state constitutions was made available in France. As Vincent Robert Johnson recounts:

The young Duc de La Rouchfoucauld was persuaded by Franklin to translate the constitutional texts of all thirteen American states. At the urging of the American minister, the French ministry of foreign affairs officially authorized publication of *Constitutions des Trieze Etats de l'Amerique* in 1783, and thereafter circulated the document throughout France. That same year, by order of Congress, Franklin delivered to each ambassador in Paris two copies of the work, while other copies were distributed throughout Europe. Although prerevolutionary France did not lack for political theoreticians, one author has ventured that some Frenchman looked upon the collection of American state constitutions as a basic "grammar for Liberty."

Id. at 10.

86. EDMUND S. MORGAN, BENJAMIN FRANKLIN 310 (2002).

87. RAYMOND GARFIELD GETTELL, ED. & COMP., READINGS IN POLITICAL SCIENCE 167 (1911); Johnson, *supra* note 71, at 40 n.13. In support of that conclusion, Johnson cites a number of American state constitutions that condemned excessive fines or bail, barred cruel and unusual punishments, and directed that punishments be proportioned to offenses. Id. at 40–41 n.13.

88. SAGAN, CITIZENS AND CANNIBALS, *supra* note 46, at 57.

89. Id.

90. Id. at 57–58.

91. PETER BECKER & RICHARD F. WETZELL, EDS., CRIMINALS AND THEIR SCIENTISTS: THE HISTORY OF CRIMINOLOGY IN INTERNATIONAL PERSPECTIVE 34 (2006).

92. Id.

93. As Catherine Elliott writes in *French Criminal Law* of what led to the 1791 French penal code:

Translated into French in 1766, Beccaria's book was received with enthusiasm by Voltaire and Diderot. Influenced by his and Montesquieu's ideas, the Revolutionary Assemblies made considerable reforms to the criminal law. They passed two Acts dated 19–22 July 1791 and 24 September-6 October 1791, which amounted to a criminal code. Thus, the criminal law moved away from being a custom-based system. The sentences were generally reduced, corporal punishments were abolished and capital punishment was only preserved for a few offences.

CATHERINE ELLIOTT, FRENCH CRIMINAL LAW 7–8 (2011).

94. MORTON S. FREEMAN, A NEW DICTIONARY OF EPONYMS 117 (1997):

Dr. Joseph Ignace Guillotin (1738–1814), a physician during the French Revolution, proposed in a speech on October 10, 1789, to the Constituent Assembly, of which he was a member, a more humanitarian instrument for inflicting capital punishment by decapitation. The device he recommended consisted of a large blade that fell between two upright posts, striking the back of the neck of the victim. Dr. Guillotin informed the amazed assembly: "I can whisk off your head in a twinkling, and you feel no pain."

95. ALBERT GOODWIN, THE FRENCH REVOLUTION 93 (1953).

96. BARRY M. SHAPIRO, REVOLUTIONARY JUSTICE IN PARIS, 1789–1790, at 169 (1993). Decrees issued by France's National Assembly in August 1791 did make a commitment to criminal law reform. As one source translates decrees of the National Assembly, dated August 25 and 30, 1791: "The penal code shall be constantly amended, so that penalties shall be proportioned to offences; care being taken that they be moderate, and that maxim being kept in view which forms part of the Declaration of the Rights of Man, that 'the law can only institute punishments strictly and obviously necessary.'" SHELDON AMOS, THE HISTORY AND PRINCIPLES OF THE CIVIL LAW OF ROME: AN AID TO THE STUDY OF SCIENTIFIC AND COMPARATIVE JURISPRUDENCE 460 (1883).

97. "The French Revolution," in 4 THE ENGLISH HISTORY READERS 177, 181 (1884).

98. Grégoire Chamayou, *The Debate over Severed Heads: Doctors, the Guillotine and the Anatomy of Consciousness in the Wake of the Terror*, 61 REVUE D'HISTOIRE DES SCIENCES 333 (2008).

99. PIU EATWELL, F IS FOR FRANCE: A CURIOUS CABINET OF FRENCH WONDERS 80 (2016); JAMES R. GAINES, FOR LIBERTY AND GLORY: WASHINGTON, LAFAYETTE, AND THEIR REVOLUTIONS 379 (2007).

100. COLIN JONES, THE LONGMAN COMPANION TO THE FRENCH REVOLUTION 192 (1988).

101. 10 JOHN BOWRING, COMP., THE WORKS OF JEREMY BENTHAM 282–83 (1843).

102. 1 BHIKHU PAREKH, ED., JEREMY BENTHAM: CRITICAL ASSESSMENTS 433 (1993).

103. *See* 1 ALEX. FRASER TYTLER, MEMOIRS OF THE LIFE AND WRITINGS OF THE HONOURABLE HENRY HOME OF KAMES, ONE OF THE SENATORS OF THE COLLEGE OF JUSTICE, AND ONE OF THE LORDS COMMISSIONERS OF JUSTICIARY IN SCOTLAND: CONTAINING SKETCHES OF THE PROGRESS OF LITERATURE AND GENERAL IMPROVEMENT IN SCOTLAND DURING THE GREATER PART OF THE EIGHTEENTH CENTURY 73, 101 (1807), Appendix No. X ("*On the* PRINCIPLES *of* CRIMINAL JURISPRUDENCE, *as unfolded in Lord* KAMES'S *Essay on the History of the Criminal Law: with an Examination of the Theory of* MONTESQUIEU *and* BECCARIA, *relative to Crimes and Punishments.*").

104. JOSEPH PRIESTLEY, LECTURES ON HISTORY, AND GENERAL POLICY; TO WHICH IS PREFIXED, AN ESSAY ON A COURSE OF LIBERAL EDUCATION FOR CIVIL AND ACTIVE LIFE 374–78 (J. T. Rutt, ed., 1826) (italics in original); *see also* ROBERT E. SCHOFIELD, THE ENLIGHTENED JOSEPH PRIESTLEY: A STUDY OF HIS LIFE AND WORK FROM 1773 TO 1804, at 256 (2004) ("Lecture 47, 'Of Laws,' referred to John Howard, on prisons, and Cesare Beccaria's *Essay on Crime and Punishment* (English 1767). . . ."). Joseph Priestley was later chided by the editor of his writings for his support for capital punishment. As the editor of his writings wrote in a footnote:

> It is much to be regretted that such a christian philosopher and philanthropist as Dr. Priestley had not more maturely considered this subject. He would, probably, then have been more inclined to recommend the reformation than the destruction of criminals, to which he seems, here, too easily reconciled. *See Selection of Opinions of different Authors upon the Punishment of Death*, by Basil Montague 8vo, 3 vols. 1809 to 1813.—*Ed.*

PRIESTLEY, LECTURES ON HISTORY, AND GENERAL POLICY, *supra*, at 376 n.*.

105. George Washington to the President of Congress, Feb. 3, 1781, *in* 7 JARED SPARKS, ED., WRITINGS OF GEORGE WASHINGTON; BEING HIS CORRESPONDENCE, ADDRESSES, MESSAGES, AND OTHER PAPERS, OFFICIAL AND PRIVATE, SELECTED AND PUBLISHED FROM THE ORIGINAL MANUSCRIPTS 395–96 (1835).

106. "Bills for a Revised State Code of Laws, [31 October] 1785," *Founders Online*, National Archives, last modified February 1, 2018, http://founders.archives.gov/documents/Madison/01-08-02-0205. [Original source: *The Papers of James Madison*, vol. 8, *10 March 1784?–?28 March 1786*, ed. Robert A. Rutland and William M. E. Rachal. Chicago: The University of Chicago Press, 1973, pp. 391–399.]; "From James Madison to Thomas Jefferson, 15 February 1787," *Founders Online*, National Archives, last modified February 1, 2018, http://founders.archives.gov/documents/Madison/01-09-02-0138. [Original source: *The Papers of James Madison*, vol. 9, *9 April 1786?–?24 May 1787 and supplement 1781–1784*, ed. Robert A. Rutland and William M. E. Rachal. Chicago: The University of Chicago Press, 1975, pp. 267–270.]

107. Alexander Hamilton to "Secretary at War," July 29, 1799, *in* 5 JOHN C. HAMILTON, ED., THE

Works of Alexander Hamilton; Comprising His Correspondence, and His Political and Official Writings, Exclusive of The Federalist, Civil and Military 289–90 (1851); James McHenry to Alexander Hamilton, July 25, 1799, *in* 23 Harold C. Syrett, ed. The Papers of Alexander Hamilton 286, 294 (1976).

108. George Mallaby, ed., Wordsworth: Extracts from The Prelude, with Other Poems 116 (1932); William J. Duiker & Jackson J. Spielvogel, The Essential World History 394 (3d ed. 2008); Amy McKenna, ed., The 100 Most Influential World Leaders of All Time 118–20 (2010).

109. Andrew Scott Bibby, Montesquieu's Political Economy 10 (2016); Antoine Louis Claude Destutt de Tracy, A Commentary and Review of Montesquieu's *Spirit of Laws* (1811); The Universalist Union, Devoted to the Doctrine of Universal Benevolence—the Defence of Liberal Principles Generally in Religion, and Miscellaneous Reading of Chaste and Moral Tendency 439 (1842); 1 Louis Blanc, The History of Ten Years, 1830–1840, at 311–12 (1844); Emmanuelle de Champs, Enlightenment and Utility: Bentham in French, Bentham in France 182 (2015).

110. "Thomas Jefferson to Destutt de Tracy, 26 January 1811," *Founders Online*, National Archives, last modified February 1, 2018, http://founders.archives.gov/documents/Jefferson/03-03-02-0258. [Original source: *The Papers of Thomas Jefferson*, Retirement Series, vol. 3, *12 August 1810 to 17 June 1811*, ed. J. Jefferson Looney. Princeton: Princeton University Press, 2006, pp. 334–339.]

111. Count Destutt Tracy, A Treatise on Political Economy; To Which Is Prefixed a Supplement to a Preceding Work on the Understanding, or Elements of Ideology; with an Analytical Table, and an Introduction on the Faculty of the Will (Thomas Jefferson, trans., 1817). In that book, it is noted that "Montesquieu was a very great man," but that "the science" of "political economy" (which Destutt de Tracy said Montesquieu "understood ... very badly") was "quite recent." Id. at 178 & n.*.

112. A Commentary and Review of Montesquieu's *Spirit of Laws* (1811), *available at* http://oll.libertyfund.org/titles/tracy-a-commentary-and-review-of-montesquieus-spirit-of-laws. In his commentary and review of *The Spirit of the Laws*, Destutt Tracy also had this to say on Montesquieu's views on the right of nations to make war:

I am sorry that Montesquieu, in touching the subject of the right of nations to make war, has not explained the fundamental ideas of *the right of war*, which might have afforded much useful information. But we ought to thank him, at least for having rejected the absurdities of all the older writers on this subject, and for having explicitly declared, that the right of making war has no other foundation than that of the necessity of self-defence; that arms should never be taken up to gratify self-love, or ideas of dignity, much less for what has been called the glory or the vanity of a prince.

Id.

113. Marcello Maestro, *Lafayette as a Reformer of Penal Laws*, 39 J. of the History of Ideas 503, 505–509 (1978); *see also* id. at 509:

At the beginning of 1831 the question of the jury came under discussion, and once more Lafayette and Victor de Tracy found themselves on the losing side. The government had asked to confirm the proportion of eight to four as sufficient for a conviction. Lafayette reminded the Chamber that the Constituent Assembly had agreed on a proportion of ten to two, and that Napoleon had changed it to eight to four. Pointing out that he had always favored complete unanimity, as adopted in England and America, Lafayette asked that at least a return to the proportion of ten to two be agreed upon, with a unanimous vote necessary when the death penalty was involved. Lafayette's arguments did not prevail, however, and the Chamber finally voted for proportion of eight to four as sufficient in all cases.

See also 2 B. Sarrans, Memoirs of General Lafayette and of the French Revolution of 1830, at 75–76 (1832) (discussing Lafayette's speech); The United States Declaration of Independence 33 (2009) (reprinting the Declaration of the Rights of Man and of the Citizen); Robert Badinter, Abolition: One Man's Battle Against the Death Penalty (2008) (recounting the battle to abolish the death penalty in France in 1981).

114. 2 B. Sarrans, Memoirs of General Lafayette and of the French Revolution of 1830, at 57–58 (1833).

115. Paul Christian Jones, Against the Gallows: Antebellum American Writers and the Movement to Abolish Capital Punishment 19 (2011); Elon H. Moore, *The Livingston Code*, 19 Am. Inst. Crim. L. & Criminology 344, 347 (1928); Stuart Banner, The Death Penalty: An American History 138 (2002).

Chapter 5

1. Roper v. Simmons, 543 U.S. 551, 577 (2005); Harmelin v. Michigan, 501 U.S. 957, 966 (1991). That protection has been described as a "fundamental principle of the Government of England" intended "to establish mercy, even to convicted offenders." Jean Louis de Lolme, The Constitution of England; or, An Account of the English Government 385 (1789); *see also* J. L. de Lolme, The Constitution of England, or An Account of the English Government (1775) (citing English Bill of Rights, Art. X):

Hence also arose that remarkable forbearance in the English Laws, to use any cruel severity in the punishments which experience shewed it was necessary for the preservation of Society to establish: and the utmost vengeance of those laws, even against the most enormous Offenders, never extends beyond the simple deprivation of life.

Nay, so anxious has the English Legislature been to establish mercy, even to convicted Offenders, as a fundamental principle of the Government of England, that they made it an express article of that great public Compact which was framed at the important æra of the Revolution, that "no cruel and unusual punishments should be used."

2. *See generally* Steve Pincus, 1688: The First Modern Revolution (2009).

3. Abel Boyer, The History of King William the Third 354–56 (1702). That declaration recited that "Excessive Bail hath been requir'd of Persons committed in Criminal Cases," that "Excessive Fines have been impos'd," and that "Illegal and Cruel Punishments inflicted." *Id.*

4. *Id.*; *see also* Meghan J. Ryan, *Does the Eighth Amendment Punishments Clause Prohibit Only Punishments that are Both Cruel and Unusual?*, 87 Wash. U. L. Rev. 567, 575 (2010):

There is no clear evidence as to what Parliament intended to prohibit by the language of Article 10. The preamble of the English Bill of Rights denounces King James II's subversion of English laws and liberties by, among other things, suspending laws without Parliament's consent, prosecuting prelates for petitioning the King, and prosecuting individuals for ecclesiastical offenses. The document also charges that "excessive fines have been imposed; and illegal and cruel punishments inflicted." Historically, scholars have disagreed whether the document prohibited cruel methods of punishment or cruel and illegal punishments, but they seem to agree that, whatever the meaning of the document, it was enacted "to prevent a recurrence of recent events" in England.

5. Stephanie A. Mann, Supremacy and Survival: How Catholics Endured the English Reformation xxxiii, 104, 110 (2007); Toby Barnard, The English Republic 1649–1660, at 3 (2d ed. 1997); Calvin R. Massey, *The Excessive Fines Clause and Punitive Damages: Some Lessons from History*, 40 Vanderbilt L. Rev. 1233, 1246 (1987).

6. 4 Henry B. Wheatley, ed., The Diary of Samuel Pepys 311 (1893); *see also* Anna Keay, The Last Royal Rebel: The Life and Death of James, Duke of Monmouth (2016).

7. Frederick Burwick, Playing to the Crowd: London Popular Theatre, 1780–1830, at 144 (2011); James K. McDonell & Robert B. Campbell, Lords of the North 11 (1997); 2 John Debrett, The Peerage of the United Kingdom of Great Britain and Ireland 616–17 (9th ed. 1814).

8. Harmelin v. Michigan, 501 U.S. 957, 967–68 (1991); Charles Pastoor & Galen K. Johnson, Historical Dictionary of the Puritans 52 (2007).

9. E. Hale, The Fall of the Stuarts and Western Europe from 1678 to 1697, at 82–83 (1876); "The Trial of Robert Frances," *in* 11 T. B. Howell, comp., A Complete Collection of State Trials and Proceedings for High Treason and Other Crimes and Misdemeanors from the Earliest Period to the Year 1783, with Notes and Other Illustrations 503–10 (1816); The History of England from the Accession of James II 332 (1849); 3 George L. Craik & Charles MacFarlane, The Pictorial History of England: Being A History of the People, as Well as a History of the Kingdom 746 (1849).

10. Ruth Tyler Bryan, "George Jeffreys, first Baron Jeffreys of Wem," Alexander Campbell King

Law Library, University of Georgia, http://libguides.law.uga.edu/c.php?g=177206&p=1164803.

11. JOSEPH A. MELUSKY & KEITH ALAN PESTO, CAPITAL PUNISHMENT 21 (2011).

12. Ruth Tyler Bryan, "George Jeffreys, first Baron Jeffreys of Wem," Alexander Campbell King Law Library, University of Georgia, http://libguides.law.uga.edu/c.php?g=177206&p=1164803.

13. JOHN VAN DER KISTE, WILLIAM AND MARY: HEROES OF THE GLORIOUS REVOLUTION (2011), preface.

14. 2 THE STATUES: WILLIAM & MARY TO 10 GEORGE III. A.D. 1688—1770, at 9–10 (rev. ed. 1871).

15. ROLAND ADICKES, THE UNITED STATES CONSTITUTION AND CITIZENS' RIGHTS: THE INTERPRETATION AND MIS-INTERPRETATION OF THE AMERICA CONTRACT FOR GOVERNANCE 132–33 (2001).

16. Anthony F. Granucci, *Nor Cruel and Unusual Punishments Inflicted: The Original Meaning*, 57 CAL. L. REV. 839, 840 (1969).

17. JOSEPH A. MELUSKY & KEITH ALAN PESTO, CAPITAL PUNISHMENT 23 (2011).

18. 4 J. GRANGER, A BIOGRAPHICAL HISTORY OF ENGLAND, FROM EGBERT THE GREAT TO THE REVOLUTION 348 (3d ed. 1779) ("The notorius Titus Oates was, soon after the accession of James, convicted of perjury, upon the evidence of above sixty reputable witnesses, of whom nine were protestants.").

19. AN EXTINCT PEERAGE OF ENGLAND; CONTAINING AN ACCOUNT OF ALL THOSE NOBLE FAMILIES WHOSE TITLES ARE EXTINCT FROM THE EARLIEST ACCOUNTS TO THE PRESENT TIME 219 (1769) (an entry pertaining to "George Jeffries" notes that "his character is too well known to need any recital"); THE BIOGRAPHICAL DICTIONARY; OR, COMPLETE HISTORICAL LIBRARY 409 (1780) (an entry written by "A SOCIETY OF GENTLEMEN" for "JEFFREYS, or JEFFERIES (George)" notes that "[h]e was one of the greatest advisers and promotors of all the oppressive and arbitrary measures carried on in th[e] reign" of James II, and that "his sanguinary and inhuman proceedings against the duke of Monmouth's unfortunate adherents in the West, will ever render his name infamous"); 6 A NEW AND GENERAL BIOGRAPHICAL DICTIONARY; CONTAINING AN HISTORICAL, CRITICAL, AND IMPARTIAL ACCOUNT OF THE LIVES AND WRITINGS OF THE MOST EMINENT PERSONS IN EVERY NATION IN THE WORLD 339 (1795) (noting that, in James II's reign, Jeffreys was "one of the greatest advisers and promotors of all the oppressive and arbitrary measures of that unhappy tyrannical reign: and his sanguinary and inhuman proceedings against Monmouth's miserable adherents in the West will ever render his name infamous").

20. BARBARA BARDES, MACK SHELLEY & STEFFEN SCHMIDT, AMERICAN GOVERNMENT AND POLITICS TODAY: THE ESSENTIALS 31 (2008) ("The conflict between Britain and the American colonies, which ultimately led to the Revolutionary War, began in the 1760s when the British government decided to raise revenues by imposing taxes on the American colonies."). *Compare* 1 ALBERT H. PUTNEY, INTRODUCTION TO THE STUDY OF LAW: LEGAL HISTORY 210 (1908):

The Revolutionary War, in its broadest significance, was not so much between America and England, as one in which the radical forces in both countries were arrayed against the conservative elements in each. William Pitt openly rejoiced that America had resisted, while Fox, in his speeches in the House of Commons habitually referred to Washington's forces as "our army," and even adopted the famous blue and buff of the continental army as the colors of the Whig party. With the mass of the English people the war was so unpopular that the troops for the war mainly had to be hired in Germany. On the other hand, probably at least one-third of the whole population of the colonies were Tories in their sympathies, and this third included the majority (the great majority outside of Massachusetts) of the wealthy and educated classes.

21. The Declaration of Independence, referring to "a long train of abuses and usurpations," "absolute Despotism," and "repeated injuries and usurpations, all having in direct object the establishment of an absolute Tyranny over these States," asserted that it was the "right" and "duty" of the people "to throw off such Government." Among the indictments of George III in the Declaration of Independence: "He has called together legislative bodies at places unusual, uncomfortable, and distant from the depository of their Public Records, for the sole purpose of fatiguing them into compliance with his measures." Declaration of Independence (1776).

22. JOHN D. BESSLER, CRUEL AND UNUSUAL: THE AMERICAN DEATH PENALTY AND THE FOUNDERS' EIGHTH AMENDMENT 20, 155 (2012); *see also* Steven G. Calabresi, Sarah E. Agudo & Kathryn L. Dore, *State Bills of Rights in 1787 and 1791: What Individual Rights are Really Deeply Rooted in American History and Tradition?*, 85 S. CAL. L. REV. 1451, 1518 (2012):

Six states, or 46 percent of the total number of states, comprising 56 percent of the total U.S. population in 1787, had constitutional bans on cruel and/or unusual punishments. These states were Delaware, Maryland, Massachusetts, North Carolina, New Hampshire, and Virginia. Cruel and/or unusual punishment clauses were far more popular in the South....

23. Louis J. Palmer, Jr., The Death Penalty: An American Citizen's Guide to Understanding Federal and State Laws 12 (1998):

A Virginia delegate named George Mason was responsible for taking the tenth clause of the English Bill of Rights and placing it into Virginia's Declaration of Rights. Mason was also a strong advocate at the Constitutional Convention for placing the tenth clause into the Constitution as the Eighth Amendment. His foresight eventually paid off, and in 1791 the tenth clause, with slight modifications, became the Constitution's Eighth Amendment.

24. Va. Declaration of Rights, § IX (June 12, 1776). In America itself, the notion of "usual" punishments—the flip side of "unusual" punishments—can be found in non-legal contexts, too. The Remembrancer; or, Impartial Repository of Public Events, Part III, for the Year 1776 53 (1777) (an entry pertaining to August 21, 1776, in Philadelphia, notes that George Morgan "prevented the usual punishments of the prisoners upon their entry").

25. Bessler, Cruel and Unusual, *supra* note 22, at 178–80. The history of the English prohibition against "cruel and unusual punishments" suggests that seventeenth-century Englishmen may have seen no distinction between "cruel and unusual" or "cruel or unusual" punishments. As one academic has written:

The history of the English Bill of Rights reinforces the conclusion that the phrases "cruel and unusual" and "cruel or unusual" were understood to capture the same meaning. Just months after the House of Lords approved the Bill's prohibition against "cruel and unusual punishments," a group of Lords filed a dissenting [opinion] in the case of Titus Oates. The dissenting Lords concluded that the punishments imposed in Oates's cases violated the Bill of Rights, which they described as providing that neither "cruel nor unusual punishments [be] inflicted." Their mistake suggests that they understood prohibitions of "cruel and unusual" and "cruel or unusual" punishments as equivalents. This history has particular salience because the Cruel and Unusual Punishment Clause was taken virtually verbatim from the English Bill of Rights and because the English Bill of Rights is thought to have been principally a reaction to the punishments in Oates's case.

Tom Stacy, *Cleaning Up the Eighth Amendment Mess*, 14 Wm. & Mary Bill Rts. J. 475, 503–04 (2005); *compare* Michael David Warren Jr., *Constitutional Law*, 56 Wayne L. Rev. 991, 1002–03 (2010) (noting that whereas the U.S. Constitution prohibits "cruel and unusual" punishments, the Michigan Constitution prohibits "cruel or unusual" punishments).

26. Akhil Reed Amar, The Bill of Rights: Creation and Reconstruction 87 (1998). Most notoriously, Chief Justice George Jeffreys of the Kings Bench had presided over the 1685 trial and sentencing of a cleric, Titus Oates (1649–1705), who committed perjury. Oates had fabricated a supposed Catholic conspiracy, a "Popish Plot," to kill King Charles II, with Lord Chief Justice Jeffreys lamenting that death was not a permissible punishment for perjury. As a result of his conduct, which led to the execution of more than a dozen innocent men, Oates was sentenced to be defrocked, to pay a fine of two thousand marks (the equivalent of $10,000), to be whipped from Aldgate to Newgate (a distance of more than a mile) and, two days later, from Newgate to Tyburn (an additional two miles). Oates was then to be imprisoned for life and pilloried four times per year. Leonard W. Levy, Origins of the Bill of Rights 236–37 (2001); Michael J. Zydney Mannheimer, *Cruel and Unusual Federal Punishments*, 98 Iowa L. Rev. 69, 91–94, n.156 (2012); *see also* John F. Stinneford, *Rethinking Proportionality Under the Cruel and Unusual Punishments Clause*, 97 Va. L. Rev. 899, 970 (2011) ("Parliament condemned the punishment inflicted on Titus Oates as "contrary to Law and ancient Practice.").

27. Bessler, Cruel and Unusual, *supra* note 22, at 178–80.

28. *Id.* at 119 (emphasis added); *see also* 2 William Winterbotham, An Historical, Geographical, Commercial, and Philosophical View of the American United States, and of the European Settlements in America and the West-Indies 490 (2d ed. 1799) (reprinting the Northwest Ordinance, providing in Article II that "no cruel or unusual punishment shall be inflicted"). The act providing for the government of the Missouri territory also included a prohibition against

"cruel or unusual punishment." An act providing for the government of the territory of Missouri, § 14 (approved June 4, 1812), *reprinted in* 4 Laws of the United States of America, from the 4th of March, 1789, to the 4th of March, 1815, at 442–43 (1816).

29. Dennis W. Johnson, The Laws that Shaped America: Fifteen Acts of Congress and Their Lasting Impact 9 (2009); Merrill D. Peterson, The Jefferson Image in the American Mind 191 (1998); 3 Albert Bushnell Hart, ed., American History Told by Contemporaries 154–58 (1901); Lawrence Friedman & Lynnea Thody, The Massachusetts State Constitution 91 (2011).

30. Christine Barbour & Gerald C. Wright, Keeping the Republic: Power and Citizenship in American Politics 139 (6th ed. 2014) ("The first ten amendments to the Constitution, known as the Bill of Rights, were passed by Congress on September 25, 1789.").

31. The Eighth Amendment was ratified on December 15, 1791. Richard S. Conley, Historical Dictionary of the U.S. Constitution 74 (2016).

32. U.S. Const. amend. VIII (emphasis added).

33. Steven Harmon Wilson, ed., The U.S. Justice System: An Encyclopedia 568 (2012).

34. John R. Vile, Encyclopedia of Constitutional Amendments, Proposed Amendments, and Amending Issues, 1789–2002 156 (2d ed. 2003) ("Both the Virginia and the North Carolina ratifying conventions called for amendments against cruel and unusual punishments, and James Madison linked this guarantee to the provisions against excessive bail and fines when he presented his proposal for a bill of rights before Congress.").

35. Bessler, Cruel and Unusual, *supra* note 22, at 155.

36. Thomas Wilson, A Complete Christian Dictionary: Wherein the Significations and Several Acceptations of All the Words Mentioned in the Holy Scriptures of the Old and New Testament Are Fully Opened, Expressed, Explained 132 (1661).

37. Guy Miège, A Short Dictionary English and French According to the Present use and Modern Orthography (unpaginated entry for "Cruel") (1684). In other entries, that dictionary also associated "cruel" with words such as "barbarous," "Bloudy," "Hard-hearted," "Incompassionate," "inhumane," "pitiless" and "sanguinary." Id. (unpaginated entries).

38. *E.g.*, Nathaniel Wanley, The Wonders of the Little World: Or, a General History of Man 22, 54–55, 418 (1678).

39. A Continuation of Morning-Exercise Questions and Cases of Conscience, Practically Resolved by Sunday Ministers, in October, 1682, at 109 (Samuel Annesley ed., 1683); Richard Baxter, The Reasons of the Christian Religion 145 (1667); Francis Roberts & Clavis Bibliorum: The Key of the Bible, Unlocking the Richest Treasury of the Holy Scriptures 148, 211 (1675); The Works of the Reverend and Learned John Lightfoot D.D. 797 (George Bright ed., 1684); *see also* Joseph Hall, The Shaking of the Olive-Tree: The Remaining Works of that Incomparable Prelate Joseph Hall, D.D. Late Lord Bishop of Norwich 13 (1660) (referencing "cruell" and "unusuall").

40. Cornelius Nepos, The Lives of Illustrious Men 123 (2d ed. 1685); The Works of Sir William D'avenant 9 (1673).

41. *See generally* Wanley, *supra* note 38.

42. Id. at 55, 89, 116, 149, 152, 157–58, 206, 233, 364, 369, 377–78, 383–84, 401, 438, 458, 609, 620, 629.

43. Id. at 206 (italics in original).

44. Id.

45. Id. at 169; *see also* The Works of Francis Osborne, Esq. 90, 280, 304, 314 (7th ed. 1673) (making reference to "cruel Contention," "cruel death," "*cruel examples*," "cruel Family") (italics in original). The word "cruel" was an especially popular work in the wake of the Glorious Revolution of 1688. *E.g.*, Guy Miège, The New State of England Under Their Majesties K. William and Q. Mary 3 (1691) ("After the *Saxons* came the *Danes*, the next considerable, and the most cruel Actors on the Stage of England.") (italics in original); id. at 10 ("How could he answer the late cruel Burnings and Devastations the French made in Germany, contrary to the Rules of War, and the very Practice of the most barbarous Nations?"); id. ("The Breaking on the Wheel, and other like torturing Deaths, are lookt upon here as too cruel for Christians to use. Neither are the Criminals, who with their Lives

have expiated their Crimes before the World, denied Christian Burial, except in particular Cases."); id. ("All this shews a great deal of Moderation, and averseness from Cruelty."); id. at 40 ("Cock-fighting shews the Courage of their Cocks.... Throwing at Cocks is not only rude, but cruel."); id. at 72 ("The Popish Massacre of the French Protestants in the Reign of Charles IX, as cruel and bloody as it was, was nothing to the late refined Persecution."); id. at 76 ("Men had as good live in a state of Anarchy, as ly at some Princes Mercy, whose unlimited Power serves only to make them furious and outrageous. And where lies the Advantage, when the King proves a cruel Tyrant, to be Robbed or Murdered by a Royal, or a common Robber?"); id. at 125–26 (describing the punishment of "a Traytor"—"to be drawn upon a Hurdle or Sledge to the Gallows, and there to be hanged by the Neck," and to be "cut down alive, his Entrals pulled out of his Belly and burnt before his Face, his Head cut off, and his Body divided into four Parts"—as follows: "This Punishment indeed, considering all its Circumstances, seems cruel to such as do not narrowly consider the nature of the Crime."); id. at 245 ("[A] long and cruel Civil War was ended."); id. at 268 ("[W]ho sometimes proves magget-headed, cruel, or tyrannical.").

46. Nathaniel Wanley, The Wonders of the Little World: Or, a General History of Man in Six Books 2, 15–16, 18, 20–21, 23, 36, 39, 54–57, 91, 106, 112, 165, 214, 239, 240–41, 270, 418, 459–451, 460, 510, 515, 594, 600 (1678).

47. Id. at 59.

48. Richard Phillips, On the Powers and Duties of Juries, and on the Criminal Laws of England 298 (2d ed. 1813) (italics in original). Exile, banishment or transportation were once usual punishments in various locales. *E.g.*, 1 The Oxford Encyclopedia of Ancient Greece and Rome 145 (2010) ("Exile was the usual punishment for murder."); 6 The Polytechnical J. 106 (1842) ("Capital punishment has become exceedingly rare, exile to Siberia being now the usual punishment."); The Secret History of the Court and Cabinet of St. Cloud 112 (4th Am. ed. 1807) ("[T]ransportation was an usual punishment."); Carl Peter Thunberg, Travels in Europe, Africa, and Asia: Performed Between the Years 1770 and 1779, at 138 (1793) ("[T]he usual punishment, which is transportation to Batavia."). Those punishments are no longer used. *See, e.g.*, United States *ex rel.* Klonis v. Davis, 13 F.2d 630, 630 (2d Cir. 1926) ("However heinous his crimes, deportation is to him exile, a dreadful punishment, abandoned by the common consent of all civilized peoples."); *see also* Saad Gul, *Return of the Native? An Assessment of the Citizenship Renunciation Clause in Hamdi's Settlement Agreement in the Light of Citizenship Jurisprudence*, 27 N. Ill. U. L. Rev. 131, 145 (2007) ("[F]ederal courts have held that banishment is prohibited as cruel and unusual punishment."); Michael F. Armstrong, *Banishment: Cruel and Unusual Punishment*, 111 U. Pa. L. Rev. 758 (1963) (arguing that banishment is a cruel and unusual punishment).

49. Richard Phillips, On the Powers and Duties of Juries, and on the Criminal Laws of England 298–99 (2d ed. 1813) (italics in original). The Eighth Amendment's Cruel and Unusual Punishments Clause itself makes no distinction between felonies and misdemeanors. Every punishment is subject to scrutiny under the Eighth Amendment's broad and plain language, and the death penalty's constitutionality—like the constitutionality of non-lethal corporal punishments—must thus be scrutinized by modern American judges.

50. Id. at 299–300 (italics in original); *see also* id. at 317 (an index entry reads: "Banishment for misdemeanours an unusual punishment").

51. Id. at 300–02 (italics in original). Phillips, the ex-sheriff, added:

I know that many persons of the highest influence in the British Government are solicitous for some change in our code of punishments, and that even our heads of the law are no sticklers for many of the present practices. The enormous expence of transportations to Botany Bay, the cruel and crying injustice of sending persons to the Antipodes for terms short of life, the want of moral reform in the hulks, and the barbarity as well as inutility of hanging for so great a variety of offences, are faults of our penal code felt and deplored by many Statesmen; and I am not without hopes that a radical change will be one of the glorious achievements of this enlightened age.

Id. at 302–03.

52. Harmelin v. Michigan, 501 U.S. 957, 972 (1991); *see also* Leonard W. Levy, Origins of the Bill of Rights 236 (2001) (noting that the provision of the English Bill of Rights of 1689 prohibiting cruel and unusual punishments "derived mainly from the reaction to the case of Titus Oates").

53. *Harmelin*, 501 U.S. at 969.

54. Id. at 969–70.

55. Id. at 970.

56. Id.

57. Id.

58. Id. According to a prominent English historian, Thomas Macaulay, "[t]he judges, as they believed, sentenced Oates to be scourged to death." But Oates did not die and four years later petitioned the Parliament to set aside his sentence as illegal. As that historian wrote of the deliberations of the House of Lords: "Not a single peer ventured to affirm that the judgment was legal: but much was said about the odious character of the appellant." 2 T. Macaulay, History of England 204 (1899); *see also* 6 T. Macaulay, History of England 138–41 (1899) (quoted in *Harmelin*, 501 U.S. at 970).

59. Jency Megan Butler, *Shocking the Eighth Amendment's Conscience: Applying a Substantive Due Process Test to the Evolving Cruel and Unusual Punishments Clause*, 48 Hastings Const. L.Q. 861, 864–85 (2016) (italics in original):

In 1689, the English Bill of Rights was created by Parliament, affirming that "cruel and unusual punishments" *ought* not to be inflicted. The Titus Oates case is a famous example of the first application of the English Cruel and Unusual Punishments Clause. Titus Oates, an Anglican cleric, was convicted of lying in court. Oates's lies resulted in the execution of fifteen innocent people. Oates was sentenced to imprisonment, annual pillory, and one day of whipping. What offended the English Members of Parliament was that the pillory would occur annually, and the repetition of pillory made the punishment excessive and disproportionate.

60. The Manuscripts of the House of Lords, 1689–1690, at 83–84 (1889); Granucci, *Nor Cruel and Unusual Punishments Inflicted*, *supra* note 16, at 858. In framing the English Bill of Rights of 1689, the House of Commons later indicated that it had a "particular regard" to Oates's sentence, "amongst others," when the English prohibition against "cruel and unusual punishments" was first made. The House of Commons asserted the "ancient Right of the People of England that they should not be subjected to cruel and unusual Punishments." John F. Stinneford, *The Original Meaning of "Unusual": The Eighth Amendment as a Bar to Cruel Innovation*, 102 Nw. U. L. Rev. 1739, 1762 (2008). William Blackstone, in an apparent reference to the case of Titus Oates, himself indicated that the English prohibition on "cruel and unusual punishments" came about because of "some unprecedented proceedings in the court of king's bench, in the reign of king James the Second." John F. Stinneford, *The Original Meaning of "Cruel"*, 105 Geo. L.J. 441, 478 (2016).

61. *Harmelin*, 501 U.S. at 970.

62. Id. at 971.

63. Id.

64. Id. at 973.

65. 2 The History of King William the Third 101–02 (1702) (printed for "A. Roper"); *see also* id. at 82 (referring to "strange and unusual Cruelties").

66. Leonard W. Levy, Origins of the Bill of Rights 236–37 (2001); Michael J. Zydney Mannheimer, *Cruel and Unusual Federal Punishments*, 98 Iowa L. Rev. 69, 91–94, n.156 (2012); *see also* John F. Stinneford, *Rethinking Proportionality Under the Cruel and Unusual Punishments Clause*, 97 Va. L. Rev. 899, 970 (2011) ("Parliament condemned the punishment inflicted on Titus Oates as "contrary to Law and ancient Practice.").

67. *Harmelin*, 501 U.S. at 973 (quoting 10 Journal of the House of Commons 247 (Aug. 2, 1689)).

68. 1 Lord Macaulay, The History of England: From the Accession of James the Second 238 (1871):

[T]he punishment which was inflicted upon [Oates] cannot be justified. In sentencing him to be stripped of his ecclesiastical habit and imprisoned for life, the judges exceeded their legal power. They were undoubtedly competent to inflict whipping; nor had the law assigned a limit to the number of stripes.... That the law was defective is not a sufficient excuse: for defective laws should be altered by the legislature, and not strained by the tribunals; and least of all should the law be strained for the purpose of inflicting torture and destroying life. That Oates was a bad man is not a sufficient excuse; for the guilty are almost always the first to suffer those hardships which are afterwards used as precedents against the innocent. Thus it was in the present case. Merciless flogging soon became an ordinary punishment for political misdemeanours of no very aggravated kind. Men were sentenced, for words spoken against the government, to pain so excruciating that they, with unfained earnestness, begged to be brought to trial on capital charges, and sent to the gallows. Happily the progress of this great evil was speedily stopped by the Revolution, and by that article of the Bill of Rights which condemns all cruel and unusual punishments.

69. *See generally* Michael Meltsner, Cruel and Unusual: The Supreme Court and Capital Punishment (2011); Carol S. Steiker & Jordan M. Steiker, Courting Death: The Supreme Court and Capital Punishment (2016); *see also* Kenneth P. Miller, Direct Democracy and the Courts 200 (2009) ("In the ferment of the 1960s, the death penalty produced intense debate. Proposals to abolish or restrict capital punishment competed with calls to expand its use.").

70. *Compare* David A. J. Richards, "Constitutional Interpretation, History, and the Death Penalty," *in* Hugo Adam Bedau, ed., The Death Penalty in America: Current Controversies 214 (1997) ("The argument of Raoul Berger's book, *Death Penalties: The Supreme Court's Obstacle Course,* may be easily summarized: the persons who drafted and approved the eighth and fourteenth amendments to the United States Constitution did not intend the former to limit, let alone invalidate, the use of the death penalty by the federal or state governments.") (citing Raoul Berger, Death Penalties: The Supreme Court's Obstacle Course (1982)), *with* Arthur J. Goldberg & Alan M. Dershowitz, *Declaring the Death Penalty Unconstitutional,* 83 Harv. L. Rev. 1773 (1970) (an influential article arguing that the death penalty is unconstitutional); *see also* Jacob Lemon-Strauss, *The States are Right: Arguing for the Continued Use of State Legislators in Forming a National Consensus for the Evolving Standards of Decency,* 47 Am. Crim. L. Rev. 1319, 1319 (2010) ("The Eighth Amendment has spawned a great torrent of scholarship and jurisprudence.").

71. *See, e.g.,* Billy Wayne Sinclair & Jodie Sinclair, Capital Punishment: An Indictment by a Death-Row Survivor (2011) (noting in chapter 10: "In June 2008, the U.S. Supreme Court struck down the death penalty for child rape in *Kennedy v. Louisiana.* The decision caught the attention of then presidential candidates John McCain and Barack Obama, who went on record as disagreeing with it.").

72. Stinneford, *The Original Meaning of "Cruel," supra* note 60.

73. Stinneford, *The Original Meaning of "Unusual", supra* note 60.

74. Stinneford, *The Original Meaning of "Cruel," supra* note 60, at 445.

75. Stinneford, *The Original Meaning of "Unusual", supra* note 60, at 1745; *see also* John F. Stinneford, *Death, Desuetude, and Original Meaning,* 56 Wm. & Mary L. Rev. 531, 536 (2014); John F. Stinneford, *Rethinking Proportionality Under the Cruel and Unusual Punishments Clause,* 97 Va. L. Rev. 899, 901 (2011). *Compare* William C. Heffernan, *Constitutional Historicism: An Examination of the Eighth Amendment Evolving Standards of Decency Test,* 5 Am. U. L. Rev. 1355, 1373 (2005) (discussing the meaning of "unusual" and noting that the U.S. Supreme Court, in *In re Kemmler,* 136 U.S. 436 (1890), "was confronted with the question of whether New York's use of the electric chair, an innovation at the time, was constitutional," and determined that the state's use of the electric chair was constitutional).

76. Stinneford, *The Original Meaning of "Unusual", supra* note 60, at 1767–68.

77. Akhil Reed Amar, *America's Lived Constitution,* 120 Yale L.J. 1734, 1780 n.114 (2011). As Amar writes of the implications of a living constitutionalism approach, using a low-level offense as an example:

Laws exist allowing jaywalkers to be jailed; but being jailed for jaywalking in America is surely "unusual." (Whether it is also "cruel" is another question.) Examining law as actually applied properly brings constitutional institutions other than the legislature into the frame of Eighth Amendment analysis. Criminal laws are often written in overbroad ways precisely because it is understood, and in some respects constitutionally required, that such laws will be softened in practice by merciful discretion exercised by prosecutors, grand juries, criminal trial juries, trial judges, governors, and parole boards. Each of these institutions represents the public, too, and helps define what modern America really does believe and practice when it comes to punishment.

78. *Id.* at 1778. The Supreme Court frequently tallies states that either permit or prohibit a given punishment. *See* Kennedy v. Louisiana, 554 U.S. 407, 426 (2008):

The evidence of a national consensus with respect to the death penalty for child rapists, as with respect to juveniles, mentally retarded offenders, and vicarious felony murderers, shows divided opinion but, on balance, an opinion against it. Thirty-seven jurisdictions—36 States plus the Federal Government—have the death penalty. As mentioned above, only six of those jurisdictions authorize the death penalty for rape of a child. Though our review of national consensus is not confined to tallying the number of States with applicable death penalty legislation, it is of significance that, in 45 jurisdictions, petitioner could not be executed for child rape of any kind. That number surpasses the 30 States in *Atkins* and *Roper* and the 42 States in *Enmund* that prohibited the death penalty under the circumstances those cases considered.

Notably, since *Kennedy v. Louisiana*, additional states have abolished the death penalty altogether. Larry J. Siegel & John L. Worrall, Introduction to Criminal Justice 448 (16th ed. 2018) (noting that Connecticut abolished the death penalty in 2012 and that Maryland abolished the death penalty in 2013).

79. Many U.S. Supreme Court decisions in the Eighth Amendment arena have been decided by five-to-four votes. *See, e.g.*, E. Thomas Sullivan & Richard S. Frase, Proportionality Principles in American Law: Controlling Excessive Government Actions 134 (2009) ("Since 1980 the Supreme Court has decided six cases in which the duration of a prison sentence was attacked on Eighth Amendment grounds. All six cases were 5–4 decisions in form or substance....").

80. *Compare* Mary Welek Atwell, Evolving Standards of Decency: Popular Culture and Capital Punishment 25 (2004) (noting that the U.S. Supreme Court has interpreted the Eighth Amendment in accordance with the "evolving standards of decency that mark the progress of a maturing society," with the Court concluding that the Eighth Amendment "is not static"), *with* Rudolph J. Gerber & John M. Johnson, The Top Ten Death Penalty Myths: The Politics of Crime Control 90 (2007) (discussing Justice Scalia's views of the Eighth Amendment prohibition against "cruel and unusual punishments," with Scalia having expressed the view that because the death penalty "was clearly permitted when the Eighth Amendment was adopted," "it is clearly permitted today").

81. Atkins v. Virginia, 536 U.S. 304, 349 (2002) (Scalia, J., dissenting).

82. Furman v. Georgia, 408 U.S. 238, 309 (1972) (Stewart, J., dissenting).

83. Id. at 242 (Douglas, J., concurring).

84. 501 U.S. 957 (1991).

85. Id. at 976 (quoting Webster's American Dictionary (1828); Webster's Second International Dictionary 2807 (1954)).

86. Trop v. Dulles, 356 U.S. 86, 101 (1958). Several of the U.S. Supreme Court's decisions applying the "evolving standards of decency" test have been in the death penalty arena. *See, e.g.*, Brian W. Varland, *Marking the Progress of a Maturing Society: Reconsidering the Constitutionality of Death Penalty Application in Light of Evolving Standards of Decency*, 28 Hamline L. Rev. 311 (2005).

87. *Trop*, 356 U.S. at 103.

88. 1 George A. Malcolm, The Constitutional Law of the Philippine Islands: Together with Studies in the Field of Comparative Constitutional Law 498–99 (1920).

89. *Trop*, 356 U.S. at 100 n.32 (citations omitted):

Whether the word 'unusual' has any qualitative meaning different from 'cruel' is not clear. On the few occasions this Court has had to consider the meaning of the phrase, precise distinctions between cruelty and unusualness do not seem to have been drawn. These cases indicate that the Court simply examines the particular punishment involved in light of the basic prohibition against inhuman treatment, without regard to any subtleties of meaning that might be latent in the word 'unusual.' If the word 'unusual' is to have any meaning apart from the word 'cruel,' however, the meaning should be the ordinary one, signifying something different from that which is generally done.

90. Id. at 100 (citing Weems v. United States, 217 U.S. 349 (1910)). In *Weems*, the Supreme Court observed: "What constitutes a cruel and unusual punishment has not been exactly decided. It has been said that ordinarily the terms imply something inhuman and barbarous,—torture and the like." 217 U.S. at 368.

91. Malcolm, The Constitutional Law of the Philippine Islands, *supra* note 88, at 498, 500.

92. Denationalization as a punishment was characterized as unusual by the Supreme Court in *Trop*. 356 U.S. at 100 n.32.

93. Bessler, Cruel and Unusual, *supra* note 22, at 196–97; *see also Weems*, 217 U.S. at 378. Even before *Weems*, the U.S. Supreme Court—in a different context—noted that public opinion could shape punishment practices. *See Ex parte* Wilson, 114 U.S. 417, 427–28 (1885):

What punishments shall be considered as infamous may be affected by the changes of public opinion from one age to another. In former times, being put in the stocks was not considered as necessarily infamous. And by the first judiciary act of the United States, whipping was classed with moderate fines and short terms of imprisonment in limiting the criminal jurisdiction of the district courts.... But at the present day either stocks or whipping might be thought an infamous punishment.

94. *Trop*, 356 U.S. at 99.

95. The plurality opinion in *Trop* was authored by Chief Justice Earl Warren and joined by Justices Black, Douglas, and Whittaker. Id. at 87.

96. Id. at 99 (emphasis added). Through the years, the U.S. Supreme Court has distinguished the *dictionary* definition of "cruel" from the concept of cruelty in its *constitutional* sense. Bessler, Cruel and Unusual, *supra* note 22, at 210, 295–96, 331–32. The death penalty today, of course, is no longer "widely accepted." The majority of the world's nations no longer actively make use of executions, and Americans themselves—per public opinion polls—are very divided (as has now long been the case) about the propriety of the punishment. Scott Vollum, Rolando V. del Carmen, Durant Frantzen, Claudia San Miguel & Kelly Cheeseman, The Death Penalty: Constitutional Issues, Commentaries, and Case Briefs 304 (3d ed. 2015) ("The increasing availability of sentences of life without parole (LWOP) has added another dimension to public opinion about the death penalty. Recent data reveal that when given the alternative of LWOP, support for the death penalty drops below 50 percent."); Nathaniel Persily, Jack Citrin & Patrick J. Egan, eds., Public Opinion and Constitutional Controversy 109 (2008) ("In the last hundred years, Americans have directly expressed their views on capital punishment through referendums and public opinion polls. Progressive Era referendums in Ohio, Oregon, and Arizona reveal electorates closely divided on the abolition of the death penalty, with Oregon voters going so far as to affirm the death penalty in 1912, reject it in 1914 by a very narrow margin, and then vote for its restoration in 1920."); Peter Hodgkinson, ed., The International Library of Essays on Capital Punishment: Policy and Governance (2016), Vol. III, Part V:

At the end of the eighteenth century, a movement to abolish, or at least sharply limit, the death penalty emerged in the Western world. Though this abolitionist movement has ebbed and flowed during the past two centuries, it has enjoyed striking success during the past forty years as a majority of the world's nations, including virtually every Western nation except the United States, has abolished capital punishment.

97. John D. Bessler, The Death Penalty as Torture: From the Dark Ages to Abolition 176–78, 183–84 (2017).

98. Lilian Manka Chenwi, Towards the Abolition of the Death Penalty in Africa: A Human Rights Perspective 128 (2007).

99. *See, e.g.*, Atkins v. Virginia, 536 U.S. 304, 312 (2002) (holding that "[p]roportionality review under those evolving standards" should be informed by " 'objective factors to the maximum possible extent,' " and further noting, "[w]e have pinpointed that the 'clearest and most reliable objective evidence of contemporary values is the legislation enacted by the country's legislatures' ") (citations omitted).

100. Marbury v. Madison, 5 U.S. (1 Cranch) 137, 177 (1803) ("It is emphatically the province and duty of the judicial department to say what the law is.").

101. Ian P. Farrell, *Strict Scrutiny Under the Eighth Amendment*, 40 Fla. St. U. L. Rev. 853, 870 (2013) ("While the Court has engaged, on the one hand, in the complex analysis of objective indicia..., it has also insisted that reliance on indicators of public opinion does not amount to the Court abrogating its own responsibility to interpret the Constitution."); *Roper*, 543 U.S. at 575 ("[T]he task of interpreting the Eighth Amendment remains our responsibility."); *Atkins*, 536 U.S. at 312 ("We also acknowledged in *Coker* that the objective evidence, though of great importance, did not 'wholly determine' the controversy, 'for the Constitution contemplates that in the end our own judgment will be brought to bear on the question of the acceptability of the death penalty under the Eighth Amendment.' ") (citing Coker v. Georgia, 433 U.S. 584, 597 (1977)).

102. 543 U.S. 551.

103. Id. at 564.

104. Id.

105. *See, e.g.*, Moore v. Texas, 137 S. Ct. 1039, 1048 (2017) ("Executing intellectually disabled individuals, we concluded in *Atkins*, serves no penological purpose, runs up against a national consensus against the practice, and creates a 'risk that the death penalty will be imposed in spite of factors which may call for a less severe penalty.' ") (citations omitted).

106. Woodson v. North Carolina, 428 U.S. 280, 288 (1976) ("Central to the application of the [Eighth] Amendment is a determination of contemporary standards regarding the infliction of punishment. As discussed in *Gregg v. Georgia*, indicia of societal values identified in prior opinions include history and traditional usage, legislative enactments, and jury determinations.") (citations omitted); Thompson v. Oklahoma, 487 U.S. 815, 822 (1988) ("[W]e first review relevant legislative enactments, then refer to jury determinations."); *see also* Aliza Plener Cover, *The Eighth Amendment's Lost Jurors: Death Qualification and Evolving Standards of Decency*, 92 Ind. L.J. 113, 115 (2016) ("In assessing the constitutionality of the death penalty, the Supreme Court considers aggregate capital trial outcomes as 'objective indicia' of our nation's 'evolving standards of decency.' ") (citations omitted).

107. *See, e.g.*, *Atkins*, 536 U.S. at 316 ("[E]ven in those States that allow the execution of mentally retarded offenders, the practice is uncommon. Some States, for example New Hampshire and New Jersey, continue to authorize executions, but none have been carried out in decades."); *Roper*, 543 U.S. at 564–65 (citations omitted):

Atkins emphasized that even in the 20 States without formal prohibition, the practice of executing the mentally retarded was infrequent. Since *Penry*, only five States had executed offenders known to have an IQ under 70. In the present case, too, even in the 20 States without a formal prohibition on executing juveniles, the practice is infrequent. Since *Stanford*, six States have executed prisoners for crimes committed as juveniles. In the past 10 years, only three have done so: Oklahoma, Texas, and Virginia.

See also Tiffani Darden, *Exploring the Spectrum: How the Law May Advance a Social Movement*, 48 Ariz. St. L.J. 261, 272 (2016) ("When considering the 'objective indicia of consensus,' the Court looks to sentencing statutes and the frequency of their application.").

108. *See, e.g.*, Emily Taft, Moore v. Texas: *Balancing Medical Advancements with Judicial Stability*, 12 Duke J. Const. L. & Pub. Pol'y Sidebar 115, 121 (2017) ("Applying the 'evolving standards of decency' test for the Eighth Amendment, the Court in both *Atkins* and *Hall* found the trends among the states probative to its decisions.") (citations omitted).

109. *Atkins*, 536 U.S. at 315 ("It is not so much the number of these States that is significant, but the consistency of the direction of change.").

110. *Coker*, 433 U.S. 584; *Kennedy*, 554 U.S. 407.

111. Enmund v. Florida, 458 U.S. 782 (1982).

112. *Roper*, 543 U.S. 551.

113. Ford v. Wainwright, 477 U.S. 399 (1986); *see also* Panetti v. Quarterman, 551 U.S. 930, 960 (2007) ("Petitioner's submission is that he suffers from a severe, documented mental illness that is the source of gross delusions preventing him from comprehending the meaning and purpose of the punishment to which he has been sentenced. This argument, we hold, should have been considered.").

114. *Atkins*, 536 U.S. 304; Hall v. Florida, 134 S. Ct. 1986 (2014); *Moore*, 137 S. Ct. 1039.

115. Graham v. Florida, 560 U.S. 48, 74 (2010) ("This Court now holds that for a juvenile offender who did not commit homicide the Eighth Amendment forbids the sentence of life without parole. This clear line is necessary to prevent the possibility that life without parole sentences will be imposed on juvenile nonhomicide offenders who are not sufficiently culpable to merit that punishment."); Miller v. Alabama, 567 U.S. 460, 479 (2012) ("We therefore hold that the Eighth Amendment forbids a sentencing scheme that mandates life in prison without possibility of parole for juvenile offenders."); *see also* Montgomery v. Louisiana, 136 S. Ct. 718, 736 (2016) ("A State may remedy a *Miller* violation by permitting juvenile homicide offenders to be considered for parole, rather than by resentencing them.... Allowing those offenders to be considered for parole ensures that juveniles whose crimes reflected only transient immaturity—and who have since matured—will not be forced to serve a disproportionate sentence in violation of the Eighth Amendment.").

116. Amar, *supra* note 77, at 1778.

117. Id. As Amar writes: "Citizens, not states, should thus count equally in interpreting both the Eighth Amendment word 'unusual' and modern America's lived Constitution more generally." Id.; *see also* id. at 1780 ("Although Justice Scalia has argued that modern Eighth Amendment interpreters should count each state equally regardless of state population, this approach warps the Reconstruction vision."); id. ("Judicial interpreters should be seeking to discover and channel the collective wisdom of the American people, and on certain questions the wisest way to tap that collective wisdom is to survey all Americans and to weight each American equally."); *compare* id. at 1781 ("If the issue is whether a given punishment is genuinely unusual, presumably the punishment may sometimes be upheld even if it is a minority practice. If, say, states accounting for forty-five percent of the nation's population routinely use punishment X, it would be hard to say that X is truly unusual even though it is a minority practice in America.").

118. Id. at 1783 n.118:

In the late 1960s, actual executions dropped to zero in America. In response to this apparent national consensus, the Court in 1972 seemed to hold the death penalty categorially unconstitutional. *See* Furman v. Georgia, 408 U.S. 238 (1972). Over the next four years, both Congress and some thirty-five states representing an overwhelming majority of the American population pushed back against this ruling with a new round of death penalty statutes. In response, the Court reconsidered its position and gave its blessing to the penalty in certain situations where the underlying crime was particularly heinous and where strict procedural safeguards were in place. *See* Gregg v. Georgia, 428 U.S. 153 (1976). Since then the Court has imposed additional substantive and procedural limits on capital punishment with a close eye on evolving American practice. *See, e.g.*, Atkins v. Virginia, 536 U.S. 304 (2002) (overruling, in effect, Penry v. Lynaugh, 492 U.S. 302 (1989)); Roper v. Simmons, 543 U.S. 551 (2005) (overruling Stanford v. Kentucky, 492 U.S. 361 (1989)); Kennedy v. Louisiana, 554 U.S. 407 (2008).

119. U.S. Const., amend. VIII. The Fourteenth Amendment applies these restrictions to the States. Hall v. Florida, 134 S. Ct. 1986, 1992 (2014).

120. Moore v. Texas, 137 S. Ct. 1039, 1048 (2017); Hall v. Florida, 134 S. Ct. 1986, 1992 (2014).

121. Trop v. Dulles, 356 U.S. 86, 100 (1958) (plurality opinion).

122. Hugo Adam Bedau, Killing as Punishment: Reflections on the Death Penalty in America 110 (2004).

123. Id. at 119–20.

124. Aharon Barak, Human Dignity: The Constitutional Value and the Constitutional Right 199 (Daniel Kayros, trans. 2015).

125. Abraham L. Davis & Barbara Luck Graham, The Supreme Court, Race, and Civil Rights 339 (1995).

126. Barak, Human Dignity, *supra* note 124, at 201.

127. *See generally* Stephen Breyer, Against the Death Penalty (John D. Bessler, ed. 2016) (describing the battle between originalists and living constitutionalists in the introduction to Justice Breyer's dissent in *Glossip v. Gross*).

128. 370 U.S. 660 (1962).

129. Id. at 667.

130. Id.

131. 1 Mary Bosworth, ed., Encyclopedia of Prisons and Correctional Facilities 279 (2005) ("By the early 1970s, federal district courts, which had been empowered by the Warren Court to play a key role in evaluating the constitutionality of prison conditions, began to apply the Eighth Amendment to state and federal prisons."); Kenneth Bresler, Constitutional Law for Criminal Justice Professionals and Students: A Plain Language Explanation of Constitutional Law 390 (2014) ("Although not all prison overcrowding violates the Eighth Amendment, overcrowding can be a violation."); David G. Lawrence & Jeff Cummins, California: The Politics of Diversity 185 (9th ed. 2017):

In *Brown v. Plata* (2011), the U.S. Supreme Court ruled that, because of severe overcrowding, the state [of California] had to reduce its prison population by 33,000 inmates. Writing for a 5–4 majority, Justice Anthony M. Kennedy referred to suicidal prisoners being held in "telephone booth-sized cages without toilets," prison gymnasiums filled with bunk beds, and prisoners dying for lack of medical attention.

132. Jonathan Simon, Mass Incarceration on Trial: A Remarkable Court Decision and the Future of Prisons in America 70 (2014).

133. Tom Stacy, *Cleaning Up the Eighth Amendment Mess*, 14 Wm. & Mary Bill Rts. J. 475, 510 (2005).

134. Mary Sigler, *The Political Morality of the Eighth Amendment*, 8 Ohio St. J. Crim. L. 403, 421 (2011).

135. Joseph L. Hoffmann, "The 'Cruel and Unusual Punishment' Clause: A Limit on the Power to Punish or Constitutional Rhetoric?," *in* David J. Bodenhamer & James W. Ely, Jr., eds., The Bill of Rights in Modern America 173 (2008) ("The cruel and unusual punishment clause of the Eighth Amendment today remains a constitutional enigma.").

136. Bessler, Cruel and Unusual, *supra* note 22, at 196.

137. John D. Bessler, *The Anomaly of Executions: The Cruel and Unusual Punishments Clause in the 21st Century*, 2 Brit. J. Am. Legal Stud. 297, 309 (2013).

138. Id. at 304, 428, 450–51; Jackson v. Bishop, 404 F.2d 571, 579 (8th Cir. 1968).

139. Hall v. Florida, 134 S. Ct. 1986, 1992 (2014).

140. M. Cherif Bassiouni, International Extradition: United States Law and Practice 649 (6th ed. 2014) (noting that Protocol No. 6 and Protocol No. 13 to the European Convention on Human Rights abolishes the death penalty during peacetime and wartime, respectively); Lilian Chenwi, Towards the Abolition of the Death Penalty in Africa: A Human Rights Perspective 128 (2007) ("The Constitutional Court of South Africa, in *S v Makwanyane*, had to decide whether the death penalty was cruel, inhuman and degrading within the meaning of section 11(2) of the Interim Constitution Act 200 of 1993. Ten of the 11 judges considered the death penalty as cruel, inhuman and degrading punishment.") (citing *S v Makwanyane* (1995) 3 SA 391 (CC)).

141. Ford v. Wainwright, 477 U.S. 399 (1986).

142. Coker v. Georgia, 433 U.S. 584 (1977); Kennedy v. Louisiana, 554 U.S. 407 (2008).

143. Roper v. Simmons, 543 U.S. 551 (2005).

144. Atkins v. Virginia, 536 U.S. 304 (2002); Hall v. Florida 134 S. Ct. 1986 (2014).

145. Enmund v. Florida, 458 U.S. 782 (1982); *compare* Tison v. Arizona, 481 U.S. 137 (1987) (the death penalty was found to be constitutional when imposed on a felony-murder defendant who was a major participant in the underlying felony and exhibited extreme indifference to human life). To date, a majority of the justices of the U.S. Supreme Court have not read the Eighth Amendment to bar the death penalty *per se*. Glossip v. Gross, 135 S. Ct. 2726 (2015) (upholding the constitutionality of Oklahoma's lethal injection protocol); Baze v. Rees, 553 U.S. 35 (2008) (upholding the constitutionality of Kentucky's lethal injection protocol); Gregg v. Georgia, 428 U.S. 153 (1976) (upholding the constitutionality of Georgia's death penalty). Prior to leaving the Supreme Court, Justices Thurgood Marshall and William Brennan both articulated the view—in dissent after dissent—that the death penalty is unconstitutional per se. *See generally* Michael Mello, Against the Death Penalty: The Relentless Dissents of Justices Brennan and Marshall (1996) (discussing the views of Justices Brennan and Marshall on capital punishment). More recently, Justices Stephen Breyer and Ruth Bader Ginsburg announced in their dissent in *Glossip v. Gross* that it was "highly likely" that the death penalty violates the Eighth Amendment prohibition against cruel and unusual punishment. *Glossip*, 135 S. Ct. at 2755 (Breyer, J., dissenting).

146. Charlie Eastaugh, Unconstitutional Solitude: Solitary Confinement and the US Constitution's Evolving Standards of Decency 72 (2017) ("In addition to its narrowing of the permissible capital crime categories, the Court has also engaged in evolutive interpretation with respect to death-eligible offenders. In so doing, the punishments clause has been expanded to protect juvenile offenders and those affected by intellectual disabilities.").

147. John Boston & Daniel E. Manville, Prisoners' Self-Help Litigation Manual 132 (4th ed. 2010) (citing cases in which Eighth Amendment violations have been found and noting that "[p]risoners need not prove a serious or significant injury to establish excessive force" and that the extent of injury is just one of the factors to be considered).

148. John D. Bessler, "It's Time to Stop Executing People with Severe Mental Illness," National

L.J., June 6, 2018, https://www.law.com/nationallawjournal/2018/06/06/its-time-to-stop-executing-people-with-severe-mental-illness/.

149. 503 U.S. 1 (1992).

150. Id. at. 10 ("[T]he Fifth Circuit found Hudson's claim untenable because his injuries were 'minor.' Yet the blows directed at Hudson, which caused bruises, swelling, loosened teeth, and a cracked dental plate, are not *de minimis* for Eighth Amendment purposes. The extent of Hudson's injuries thus provides no basis for dismissal of his § 1983 claim."); *see also* id. at 13 (Blackmun, J., concurring) ("The Court today appropriately puts to rest a seriously misguided view that pain inflicted by an excessive use of force is actionable under the Eighth Amendment only when coupled with 'significant injury,' e.g., injury that requires medical attention or leaves permanent marks.").

151. Bessler, *The Anomaly of Executions*, *supra* note 137, at 443.

152. Louisiana ex rel. Francis v. Resweber, 329 U.S. 459 (1947); *see also* Austin Sarat & Thomas R. Kearns, eds., The Fate of Law 213 (1993) ("It is difficult to imagine how law's violence could be more painfully present and, ironically, more absent, that is, invisible, than it was in *Francis v. Resweber*, a case in which the United States Supreme Court allowed the State of Louisiana to attempt to execute a convicted murderer twice."); John A. Fliter, Prisoners' Rights: The Supreme Court and Evolving Standards of Decency 63 (2001) ("One month after the Court announced its decision, Francis was executed, this time successfully.").

153. Harmelin v. Michigan, 501 U.S. 957 (1991).

154. Vidar Halvorsen, "Criminal Justice, Sustainability and the Death Penalty," *in* Lill Scherdin, ed., Capital Punishment: A Hazard to a Sustainable Criminal Justice System? 268 (2016).

155. Graham v. Florida, 560 U.S. 48, 60 (2010) (citing Ewing v. California, 538 U.S. 11 (2003)).

156. *Graham*, 560 U.S. at 50 (citing Rummel v. Estelle, 445 U.S. 263 (1980) & Hutto v. Davis, 454 U.S. 370 (1982) (*per curiam*)); *see also* Kara E. Stooksbury, John M. Scheb II & Otis H. Stephens Jr., eds., Encyclopedia of American Civil Rights and Liberties 447 (2017) ("In *Rummel v. Estelle* (1980), the Court upheld a life sentence imposed under a Texas habitual offender statute for three nonviolent theft offenses that totaled $229.11.").

157. Kennedy v. Louisiana, 554 U.S. 407, 419 (2008) (quoting Trop v. Dulles, 356 U.S. 86, 101 (1958) (plurality opinion)).

158. Weems v. United States, 217 U.S. 349, 378 (1910).

159. William J. Chambliss, ed., Juvenile Crime and Justice 78 (2011) (discussing the Supreme Court's use of the national consensus concept).

160. 1 David Schultz, Encyclopedia of the United States Constitution 41 (2009) (discussing the Supreme Court's ruling in *Atkins v. Virginia*, 536 U.S. 304 (2002)).

161. For example, one legal commentator in Pennsylvania—the Provost of the Law Academy of Philadelphia—noted how the prohibition against "cruel and unusual punishments" was clearly viewed differently in seventeenth-century England than in late eighteenth-century America. Peter S. Du Ponceau, A Dissertation on the Nature and Extent of the Jurisdiction of the Courts of the United States: Being a Valedictory Address Delivered to the Students of the Law Academy of Philadelphia, at the Close of the Academical Year, on the 22d April, 1824 (1824):

> But the 10th amendment of our Constitution has sufficiently provided that "no cruel and unusual punishment shall be inflicted," which word "unusual" evidently refers to the United States, and the time when the Constitution was made, and therefore is not to be confounded with the same clause in the English bill of rights, which referring to another period and to another country, may have been differently construed. The *peine forte and dure*, and burning in the hand in cases of manslaughter are abolished, and milder substitutes provided by our national statutes; corruption of blood, trial by battle, all other modes of trial, but trial by jury in criminal cases are also abolished; in short the common law as modified by our Constitution, by our laws, manners and usages, is as wholesome and as harmless a system, in criminal as well as in civil cases, as any that can be devised.

See also id. (referring to "certain harsh punishments which our modern manners reprove, but which still stain the page of the common law; as for instance the punishment of petty treason in men by drawing and quartering, and in women by burning); *compare* id.:

> As to offences not capital, cruel and unusual punishments being forbidden by our Constitution, there remains none but fine, imprisonment and, perhaps, whipping and the pillory. I hope I shall

hear nothing of the ducking stool and other obsolete remains of the customs of barbarous ages. The pillory and whipping, I know, are out of use in most of the States, imprisonment at hard labour having been substituted in lieu of them. Yet Congress have thought proper to retain the latter punishment in their penal code, and we have seen it inflicted not long since in our city on an offender against the laws of the United States. It is in the power of the national Legislature to alter or amend the law in this respect, as they shall think proper; but until they do so, I see nothing inhuman in the moderate infliction of either of these penalties, nor any reason why we should reject the common law on their account.

162. For instance, while U.S. prisoners are no longer lashed, whipping was once a common practice—and a common punishment—in colonial America and in eighteenth-century England and the United States. *Compare* CLARE CUSHMAN, ED., THE SUPREME COURT JUSTICES: ILLUSTRATED BIOGRAPHIES, 1789–2012, at 447 (3d ed. 2013) ("[I]n perhaps the first appellate opinion declaring brutal treatment of prisoners to be illegal, [Eighth Circuit judge Harry] Blackmun wrote in *Jackson v. Bishop* (1968) that disciplining prisoners by lashing them was cruel and unusual punishment. Blackmun later expressed pride in the *Jackson* decision and in the role such cases have played in improving conditions in the nation's prisons.") *with* FANNY E. COE, FOUNDERS OF OUR COUNTRY 212 (1912) ("The whipping post was much used in England and was set up very early in New England. Lying, swearing, and sleeping in church were offenses to be punished by whipping."); SARAH SAUNDERS SMITH, THE FOUNDERS OF THE MASSACHUSETTS BAY COLONY 160 (1897) ("The whipping post seems to have been a favorite mode of punishment for the most minor offences."); SIR WALTER BESANT, LONDON IN THE EIGHTEENTH CENTURY 559 (1903) ("Whipping, either in public or in private, was the most common of all punishments. The vagabond was whipped through the town.... It has been mentioned that it was one of the sights of London to visit Bridewell on whipping days, when the women, stripped to the waist, were flogged in the presence of an alderman."); id. ("This whipping of prostitutes was in force all through the eighteenth century."); Michael Meranze, "Penality and the Colonial Project: Crime, Punishment, and the Regulation of Morals in Early America," *in* 1 MICHAEL GROSSBERG & CHRISTOPHER TOMLINS, EDS., THE CAMBRIDGE HISTORY OF LAW IN AMERICA: EARLY AMERICA (1580–1815), at 204 (2008) ("Although the criminal law and slavery had long and separate histories, in the eighteenth century acceptance of the whip and the gallows fused slavery and penal law in new ways."); John P. Conrad, "Discrimination and Justice," *in* ERNEST VAN DEN HAAG & JOHN P. CONRAD, THE DEATH PENALTY: A DEBATE 218 (1983) ("[P]unishment in eighteenth century America was essentially physical. It allowed for the pillory, the ducking stool, the whip, and, sometimes, the cropping of ears and the slitting of nostrils. The culmination of this variety of punishments was the gallows.").

163. Eberhard P. Deutsch, *United States v. Jefferson Davis: Constitutional Issues in the Trial for Treason* 52 AM. BAR. ASS'N J. 139, 144 (1966) ("[O]n June 16, 1866, Congress had adopted, by a vote of more than two thirds of the members of each house, the Fourteenth Amendment and had submitted it to the states for ratification. On July 28, 1868, pursuant to a resolution adopted by Congress and transmitted to the Department of State on July 21, the Secretary of State issued a proclamation declaring that the amendment had been ratified by thirty of the thirty-six states, being more than the necessary three fourths."); CHARLES WALLACE COLLINS, THE FOURTEENTH AMENDMENT AND THE STATES: A STUDY OF THE OPERATION OF THE RESTRAINT CLAUSES OF SECTION ONE OF THE FOURTEENTH AMENDMENT TO THE CONSTITUTION OF THE UNITED STATES 7 (2013) ("the Secretary of State proclaimed the Fourteenth Amendment as a part of the Supreme Law of the Land, on July 28, 1868, having been ratified by the necessary three-fourths of the States of the Union"). The Civil Rights Act of 1866 required that blacks and whites be subjected to "like punishments." WERNER Z. HIRSCH, LAW AND ECONOMICS: AN INTRODUCTORY ANALYSIS 356 (2d ed. 1988).

164. THOMAS R. HENSLEY, THE REHNQUIST COURT: JUSTICES, RULINGS, AND LEGACY 216 (2006).

165. Christopher J. DeClue, *Sugarcoating the Eighth Amendment: The Grossly Disproportionate Test Is Simply the Fourteenth Amendment Rational Basis Test in Disguise*, 41 SW. L. REV. 533, 554 (2012):

According to the United States Supreme Court, the Fourteenth Amendment was intended to prevent the state and federal government "from abusing [its] power, or employing it as a means of oppression." Government conduct may violate the Fourteenth Amendment if it infringes on a fundamental liberty interest or discriminates against a suspect class. However, when a law does not fall into one of these categories, the law is reviewed under the very deferential rational basis test. Under this test, a law is upheld if it is rationally related to any conceivable government interest, and this standard is exceptionally hard to fail. In fact, a court will only invalidate a law under the rational basis test if the court concludes the law is completely "irrational" or arbitrary.

166. Lyman Tower Sargent, ed., Political Thought in the United States: A Documentary History 258 (1997); Lackland H. Bloom, Jr., Do Great Cases Make Bad Law? 219 (2014); *see also* 1 Paul Finkelman, ed., Encyclopedia of American Civil Liberties 514 (2006):

The language of the Fourteenth Amendment clearly reflected earlier language from the Civil Rights Act of 1866. Indeed, many who voted for the Fourteenth Amendment felt that it was necessary in order to constitutionalize the 1866 legislation that hitherto rested solely on Congress's power to enforce the Thirteenth Amendment.

167. United States v. Bajakajian, 524 U.S. 321, 336 (1998).

168. Id. at 336.

169. If the Eighth Amendment were read in a purely historical fashion, it might become just that.

170. Sarah A. Kellogg, *Just Grow Up Already: The Diminished Culpability of Juvenile Gang Members After* Miller v. Alabama, 55 B.C. L. Rev. 265, 271 (2014):

When the Court reviews a challenge to a noncapital sentence, it generally assesses all of the circumstances of the case to determine if the punishment is grossly disproportionate to the underlying offense. This approach compares the gravity of the sentence to the particular circumstances of the defendant's crime. The proportionality test is met as long as the state has a "reasonable basis" to believe that the sentence is supported by penological objectives.

171. Shane Mountjoy, *Marbury v. Madison*: Establishing Supreme Court Power 112 (2007) ("In *Marbury v. Madison*, the Supreme Court ruled 'that an act of the legislature, repugnant to the constitution, is void.'").

172. Sean O. Hogan, ed., The Judicial Branch of State Government: People, Process, and Politics 88 (2006):

Using the doctrine of independent state grounds, state supreme courts have been willing to challenge the rulings of the U.S. Supreme Court. In some cases, state supreme courts have expanded the rights of individuals beyond what the federal courts require.... In 1983 the U.S. Supreme Court intervened to establish rules for when courts may use the doctrine of independent state grounds. In the case of *Michigan v. Long* (1983), the U.S. Supreme Court ruled that if state supreme courts want to rely on independent state grounds to contravene federal precedents, they must use only state legal precedents.

173. Sullivan & Frase, Proportionality Principles in American Law, *supra* note 79, at 154 (2009) ("Ten states have constitutions that either explicitly or by interpretation require proportionate penalties."); id. ("Nineteen state constitutions prohibit cruel *or* unusual penalties....") (italics in original); id. ("Six state constitutions prohibit cruel penalties (omitting the 'unusual' element)...."); id. ("Twenty-two state constitutions prohibit cruel and unusual penalties...."); id. ("At least nine states ... have additional state constitutional provisions related to excessive penalties or treatment."); Barry Latzer, State Constitutions and Criminal Justice (1991), App. F (listing citations for prohibitions in state constitutions that bar "cruel and unusual," "cruel or unusual," or "cruel" punishments).

174. Dan Friedman, *Tracing the Lineage: Textual and Conceptual Similarities in the Revolutionary-Era State Declarations of Rights of Virginia, Maryland, and Delaware*, 33 Rutgers L.J. 929, 968 (2002); *see also* id. at 1018–19 (tracing the origins of provisions in state constitutions against "sanguinary laws").

175. *E.g.*, 1 James A. Gardner, ed., State Expansion of Federal Constitutional Liberties: Individual Rights in a Dual Constitutional System xx (1999) ("[F]ederal standards for protecting individual rights under the Fourteenth Amendment now provide a minimal level of protection—a 'floor.' States remain free, however, to *exceed* the federal floor by providing protections for individual rights and liberties that exceed the federally mandated minima. States, then, may accord as much or more protection for individual rights as does the United States Constitution, but they may not accord less."). The use of too high a standard—of too much deference to legislatures—can lead to excessive punishments that violate the U.S. Constitution and individual rights. *E.g.*, James J. Brennan, *The Supreme Court's Excessive Deference to Legislative Bodies under Eighth Amendment Sentencing Review*, 94 J. Crim. L. & Criminology 551, 578 (2004) ("[T]he whole point of the Constitution is to protect certain rights against majority infringement. If popular will determined what is constitutional, then the Constitution would have no value."); id. at 579 ("The Supreme Court has protected federal rights

against state infringement in the past, such as the right to an attorney and the right to be free of unreasonable searches and seizures. The Supreme Court must also protect a United States citizen's right to be free from disproportionate sentencing.").

176. 463 U.S. 277 (1983).

177. Id. at 289.

178. Id. at 288. At the beginning of the legal analysis section of the majority's opinion, the Court in *Solum* put it somewhat differently, emphasizing that "[t]he final clause" of the Eighth Amendment—the prohibition against "cruel and unusual punishments"—"prohibits not only barbaric punishments, but also sentences that are disproportionate to the crime committed." Id. at 284; *see also* id. at 284–85:

The principle that a punishment should be proportionate to the crime is deeply rooted and frequently repeated in common law jurisprudence. In 1215, three chapters of Magna Carta were devoted to the rule that "amercements" may not be excessive. And the principle was repeated and extended in the First Statute of Westminister, 3 Edw. I, ch. 6 (1275).

These were not hollow guarantees, for the royal courts relied on them to invalidate disproportionate punishments. *See, e.g., Le Gras v. Bailiff of Bishop of Winchester*, Y.B. Mich. 10 Edw. II, pl. 4 (C. P. 1316), reprinted in 52 Selden Society 3 (1934). When prison sentences became the normal criminal sanctions, the common law recognized that these, too, must be proportional. *See, e.g., Hodges v. Humkin*, 2 Bulst. 139, 140, 80 Eng. Rep. 1015, 1016 (K.B. 1615) (Croke, J.) ("imprisonment ought always to be according to the quality of the offence").

179. *Solem*, 463 U.S. at 279–82.

180. Id. at 290.

181. Id. at 290 n.17. The Supreme Court has treated capital cases differently than non-capital cases. *See* Harmelin v. Michigan, 501 U.S. 957, 995 (1991) ("We have held that a capital sentence is cruel and unusual under the Eighth Amendment if it is imposed without an individualized determination that the punishment is 'appropriate'—whether or not the sentence is 'grossly disproportionate.' Petitioner asks us to extend this so-called 'individualized capital-sentencing doctrine' to an 'individualized mandatory life in prison without parole sentencing doctrine.' We refuse to do so.") (citing Woodson v. North Carolina, 428 U.S. 280 (1976), Lockett v. Ohio, 438 U.S. 586 (1978), Eddings v. Oklahoma, 455 U.S. 104 (1982), Hitchcock v. Dugger, 481 U.S. 393 (1987); quoting Sumner v. Shuman, 483 U.S. 66, 73 (1987)).

182. Solem v. Helm, 463 U.S. 277, 289–90, 303 (1983).

183. 429 U.S. 97 (1976).

184. Id. at 104, 106.

185. Id. at 104 (quoting language from *Gregg v. Georgia*).

186. Id.

187. Id. at 105. In that case, medical malpractice was found not to be enough to constitute an Eighth Amendment violation. Id. ("This conclusion does not mean, however, that every claim by a prisoner that he has not received adequate medical treatment states a violation of the Eighth Amendment. An accident, although it may produce added anguish, is not on that basis alone to be characterized as wanton infliction of unnecessary pain."); id. at 105–06 ("[A] complaint that a physician has been negligent in diagnosing or treating a medical condition does not state a valid claim of medical mistreatment under the Eighth Amendment. Medical malpractice does not become a constitutional violation merely because the victim is a prisoner.").

188. 511 U.S. 825 (1994).

189. Id. at 832.

190. 489 U.S. 189 (1989).

191. Id. at 200; *see also* Williams v. Charlotte County Jail, Civil Action No. 7:08-cv-00640, 2008 WL 5427625 *1 (W.D. Va. Dec. 30, 2008) ("The Eighth Amendment protects prisoners from cruel and unusual living conditions.") (citing Rhodes v. Chapman, 452 U.S. 337 (1981)).

192. *Estelle*, 429 U.S. at 102. In that case, the Court in *Estelle* cited two prior cases dealing with methods of execution. *See Wilkerson v. Utah,* 99 U.S. 130, 136 (1879) ("[I]t is safe to affirm that punishments of torture ... and all others in the same line of unnecessary cruelty, are forbidden by that amendment...."); *In re Kemmler,* 136 U.S. 436, 447 (1890) ("Punishments are cruel when they involve

torture or a lingering death.").

193. *Estelle*, 429 U.S. at 102.

194. 404 F.2d 571 (8th Cir. 1968). *Jackson v. Bishop*—authored by then-Eighth Circuit judge Harry Blackmun—declared the lashing of Arkansas prisoners to be unconstitutional. This represented the culmination of a major shift in the treatment of prisoners. *See, e.g.*, Stephen Stanko, Wayne Gillespie & Gordon A. Crews, Living in Prison: A History of the Correctional System with an Insider's View 119–20 (2004):

Until the late 1960s, corporal punishment was frequently used to subdue prisoners and make them comply with the administration. For example, inmates in Kentucky were regularly whipped with a leather strap eighteen inches long, two inches wide, and attached to a wooden handle. The strap was often soaked in water and dragged through sand before it was used. In 1894, a survey of state correctional facilities revealed that Kentucky used lashing 300 times more often than any other state (Kentucky Department of Corrections, 2001). In *Jackson v. Bishop* (1968), a court ruled for the first time that corporal punishment (in this case, whipping a prisoner) constituted cruel and unusual punishment and violated the Eighth Amendment.

195. 356 U.S. 86 (1958).

196. *Estelle*, 429 U.S. at 102 (quoting *Jackson*, 404 F.3d at 579; *Weems*, 356 U.S. at 101).

197. Id. at 103–104.

198. In *Solem v. Helm*, the U.S. Supreme Court observed:

When the Framers of the Eighth Amendment adopted the language of the English Bill of Rights, they also adopted the English principle of proportionality. Indeed, one of the consistent themes of the era was that Americans had all the rights of English subjects. Thus our Bill of Rights was designed in part to ensure that these rights were preserved. Although the Framers may have intended the Eighth Amendment to go beyond the scope of its English counterpart, their use of the language of the English Bill of Rights is convincing proof that they intended to provide at least the same protection—including the right to be free from excessive punishments.

Solem, 463 U.S. at 286 (citations omitted).

199. Id. at 290–91 ("we look to the gravity of the offense and the harshness of the penalty").

200. For an exploration of the U.S. Supreme Court's relationship with public opinion, see Barry Friedman, The Will of the People: How Public Opinion Has Influenced the Supreme Court and Shaped the Meaning of the Constitution (2009).

201. *Solem*, 463 U.S. at 290 ("When sentences are reviewed under the Eighth Amendment, courts should be guided by objective factors that our cases have recognized."); Graham v. Florida, 560 U.S. 48, 60 (2010) ("The Court first considers 'objective indicia of society's standards, as expressed in legislative enactments and state practice' to determine whether there is a national consensus against the sentencing practice at issue.") (quoting Roper v. Simmons, 543 U.S. 551, 572 (2005)); *see also* Coker v. Georgia, 433 U.S. 584, 592 (1997):

Eighth Amendment judgments should not be, or appear to be, merely the subjective views of individual Justices; judgment should be informed by objective factors to the maximum possible extent. To this end, attention must be given to the public attitudes concerning a particular sentence history and precedent, legislative attitudes, and the response of juries reflected in their sentencing decisions are to be consulted.

202. Norman J. Finkel, Commonsense Justice: Jurors' Notions of the Law 39 (1995) (noting that "the Supreme Court has confirmed in its Eighth Amendment jurisprudence" that "jury decisions are one of the accepted 'objective indicia' of community sentiment").

203. *Graham*, 560 U.S. at 61 ("Next, guided by 'the standards elaborated by controlling precedents and by the Court's own understanding and interpretation of the Eighth Amendment's text, history, meaning, and purpose,' the Court must determine in the exercise of its own independent judgment whether the punishment in question violates the Constitution.") (citations omitted).

204. *Solem*, 463 U.S. at 291.

205. Id.

206. Id. at 292; *see also* id. at 292–93 ("nonviolent crimes are less serious than crimes marked by violence or the threat of violence"); id. at 293 ("The absolute magnitude of the crime may be relevant. Stealing a million dollars is viewed as more serious than stealing a hundred dollars...."); id. ("attempts

are less serious than completed crimes"); id. at 294 ("[T]here are generally accepted criteria for comparing the severity of different crimes on a broad scale, despite the difficulties courts face in attempting to draw distinctions between similar crimes.").

207. Graham v. Florida, 560 U.S. 48, 72 (2010).

208. 538 U.S. 63 (2003).

209. Id. at 72.

210. Id. at 76.

211. DeClue, *Sugarcoating the Eighth* Amendment, *supra* note 165, at 539.

212. Evans v. Ercole, No. 07 Civ. 6686(RJS)(DFE), 2010 WL 1506674 *4 (S.D.N.Y. Apr. 13, 2010) (citing Cooper Industries, Inc. v. Leatherman Tool Group, Inc., 532 U.S. 424, 424–25 (2001)).

213. Id. (citing *Cooper Industries*, 532 U.S. at 435); *see also* Whitworth v. Miller, No. CIV-08-1152-M, 2010 WL 1946711 *9 (W.D. Okla. Apr. 12, 2010) ("In determining whether there is 'gross disproportionality,' the Tenth Circuit has weighed 'a variety of factors, including the seriousness of the crime, the fit between the punishment and the crime, and the existence of legislative determinations of an appropriate sentence range.'") (citations omitted). In *Cooper Industries, Inc. v. Leatherman Tool Group, Inc.*, 532 U.S. 424 (2001), the U.S. Supreme Court noted that prior "constitutional violations" of the Eighth Amendment had been "predicated on judicial determinations that the punishments were 'grossly disproportional to the gravity of ... defendant[s'] offense[s].'" Id. at 434. In that case, the Supreme Court wrote:

We have recognized that the relevant constitutional line is "inherently imprecise," rather than one "marked by a simple mathematical formula." But in deciding whether that line has been crossed, we have focused on the same general criteria: the degree of the defendant's reprehensibility or culpability; the relationship between the penalty and the harm to the victim caused by the defendant's actions; and the sanctions imposed in other cases for comparable misconduct.

Id. at 434–35 (citations omitted).

214. United States v. Certain Real Property and Premises Known as 38 Whalers Cove Drive, Babylon, New York, 954 F.2d 29, 38 (2d Cir. 1992).

215. Ark. Code § 16-90-801 (2012); Richard S. Frase, Just Sentencing: Principles and Procedures for a Workable System 162–63 (2013); *see also* id. at 32, 195 (discussing the parsimony principle).

216. *E.g.*, State v. Turk, 210 So.3d 402, 405–406 (La. Ct. App. 2016) (in interpreting section 20 of the Louisiana Constitution, which states that "No law shall subject any person ... to torture, or to cruel, excessive, or unusual punishment," the Court of Appeals of Louisiana held that "[a] sentence is considered grossly disproportionate if, when the crime and punishment are viewed in light of the harm done to society, it shocks the sense of justice"; "[t]o constitute an excessive sentence, a court must find the sentence makes no reasonable contribution to acceptable penal goals").

217. People v. Reyes, 200 Cal. Rptr.3d 584, 603 (Cal. Ct. App., 4th Dist., Div. 1, 2016).

218. Id. (citations omitted); *see also* id. (citation omitted):

A look at the nature of the offense includes a look at the totality of the circumstances, including motive, the way the crime was committed, the extent of the defendant's involvement, and the consequences of defendant's acts. A look at the nature of the offender includes an inquiry into whether "the punishment is grossly disproportionate to the defendant's individual culpability as shown by such factors as his age, prior criminality, personal characteristics, and state of mind."

219. Id. at 603–04.

220. 5 U.S. (1 Cranch) 137 (1803).

221. The U.S. Supreme Court's first application of the Eighth Amendment against the states occurred in *Robinson v. California*, 370 U.S. 660 (1962). *See, e.g.*, Matthew Lippman, Essential Criminal Law (2d ed. 2017):

In *Robinson v. California*, the U.S. Supreme Court was asked to determine whether Robinson could be held criminally liable for his status of being "addicted to narcotics." The Court found the California law unconstitutional because it did not "require possession or use of narcotics, or disorderly behavior resulting from narcotics, but rather imposed liability for the mere status of being addicted." The justices concluded that just as it would be cruel to make it a crime to be mentally ill or a leper or to be afflicted with venereal disease, it was cruel to convict an individual for the "disease of addition" without requiring proof of narcotics possession or antisocial behavior.

222. 536 U.S. 730 (2002).

223. Id. at 733–35, 737.

224. Id. at 737 (quoting Whitley v. Albers, 475 U.S. 312, 319 (1986)). This does not mean that government actors are unreasonably constrained in their actions. "Prison officials," it has been held, "must ... be free to take appropriate action to insure the safety of inmates and staff, and courts will not normally second-guess prison officials on matters involving internal security." Coats v. Farmer, No. 4:12-cv-01073-TMP, 2014 WL 1612700 *4 (N.D. Ala. Apr. 22, 2014). "The factors to be examined in determining whether the use of force was wanton and unnecessary include an evaluation of: 1) the need for the application of the force, 2) the relationship between that need and the amount of force used, 3) the threat reasonably perceived by the responsible officials and 4) any efforts made to temper the severity of the response." Id. (citing Hudson v. McMillian, 503 U.S. 1, 7 (1992)). Where prison officials' actions "could have gone beyond a good faith effort to restore discipline," allegations of excessive force can state a claim under section 1983. *Coats*, 2014 WL 1612700 at *4.

225. *Hope*, 536 U.S. at 737 (quoting Rhodes v. Chapman, 452 U.S. 337, 346 (1981)).

226. Id. at 745.

227. 430 U.S. 651 (1977).

228. Id. at 670.

229. Id. at 662 (citation omitted). In *Ingraham*, the Supreme Court wrote: "All of the circumstances are to be taken into account in determining whether the punishment is reasonable in a particular case. Among the most important considerations are the seriousness of the offense, the attitude and past behavior of the child, the nature and severity of the punishment, the age and strength of the child, and the availability of less severe but equally effective means of discipline." Id. at 662.

230. John D. Bessler, "The American Death Penalty: A Short (But Long) History," *in* Robert M. Bohm & Gavin Lee, eds., Routledge Handbook on Capital Punishment 17 (2017) ("At Benjamin Franklin's house, Dr. Rush specifically invoked Beccaria's name in March 1787 in an address about public punishments. 'The Duke of Tuscany, soon after the publication of the Marquis of Beccaria's excellent treatise upon this subject,' Rush observed, 'abolished death as a punishment for murder.' ").

231. Quincy A. Kuehner, "The Evolution of the Modern Concept of School Discipline," Ph. D. thesis, University of Pennsylvania, 42–44 (1913); *see also* Lawrence M. Friedman, A History of American Law 101 (2d ed. 1985) (noting that "twenty-five of the fifty-six signers of the Declaration of Independence were lawyers" and that "thirty-one of the fifty-five delegates to the Constitutional Convention were lawyers").

232. Benjamin Rush, Essays, Literary, Moral and Philosophical 57, 67 (2d ed. 1806); 4 John Henry Barrow, ed., The Mirror of Parliament for the Second Session of the Tenth Parliament of Great Britain and Ireland, (Commencing 6th December, 1831,) in the Second Year of the Reign of King William IV, at 3337 (1832).

233. *E.g.*, Graham v. Florida, 560 U.S. 48, 60 (2010) ("The controlling opinion in *Harmelin* explained its approach for determining whether a sentence for a term of years is grossly disproportionate for a particular defendant's crime."); Lockyer v. Andrade, 538 U.S. 63, 72 (2003) ("A gross disproportionality principle is applicable to sentences for terms of years."); id. at 76 ("The gross disproportionality principle reserves a constitutional violation for only the extraordinary case."); Ewing v. California, 538 U.S. 11, 23 (2003) (observing that the Eighth Amendment forbids only "extreme sentences" that are "grossly disproportionate" to the crime"); Solem v. Helm, 463 U.S. 277, 288 (1983) ("[T]he Court has continued to recognize that the Eighth Amendment proscribes grossly disproportionate punishments, even when it has not been necessary to rely on the proscription."); *see also* Dillon v. United States, 560 U.S. 817, 832 (2010) (Stevens, J., dissenting) ("[T]he District Court was compelled to mete out a punishment that it believed to be grossly disproportionate to the offense and, therefore, 'greater than necessary' to meet the goals of our criminal justice system.") (citation omitted).

234. 538 U.S. 63 (2003).

235. Id. at 72.

236. 560 U.S. 48 (2010).

237. *Graham*, 560 U.S. at 72.

238. David W. Carrithers, Michael A. Mosher & Paul A. Rahe, eds., Montesquieu's Science

of Politics: Essays on *The Spirit of Laws* 25 (2001).

239. The U.S. Supreme Court's "grossly disproportionate" test is said to have had its origins in *Weems v. United States*, 217 U.S. 349 (1910). *See* Richard D. Nobleman, Wilson v. Seiter: *Prison Conditions and the Eighth Amendment Standard*, 24 Pac. L.J. 275, 286 n.81 (1992) ("The 'grossly disproportionate' test originated in *Weems v. United States* where the court held that a 15-year sentence of hard labor was disproportionate to the offense of falsifying a public record."). While the *Weems* case did not actually use the "grossly disproportionate" language, the Court in *Weems*—citing a dissenting opinion in *O'Neil v. Vermont*, 144 U.S. 323 (1892)—noted that Justice Field, in that 1892 dissenting opinion, had written that the prohibition against cruel and unusual punishments was directed "not only against punishments which inflict torture, 'but against all punishments which, by their excessive length or severity, are greatly disproportioned to the offenses charged.'" *Weems*, 217 U.S. at 550-51 (quoting O'Neil, 144 U.S. at 339-40 (Field, J., dissenting); *see also* DeClue, *Sugarcoating the Eighth Amendment*, *supra* note 165, at 539-40 ("The United States Supreme Court first considered the Eighth Amendment's proportionality principle in 1892. In *O'Neil v. Vermont*, the defendant challenged a sentence of nearly 20,000 days of hard labor for 307 counts of selling liquor without a license. Although the majority did not address the defendant's Eighth Amendment argument, the issue was raised by Justice Field in his dissenting opinion."). The *Weems* case, along with *Trop v. Dulles*, was cited in *Gregg v. Georgia* for the proposition that "the punishment must not be grossly out of proportion to the severity of the crime." Gregg v. Georgia, 428 U.S. 153, 173 (1976) (citing *Trop*, 356 U.S. at 100; *Weems*, 217 U.S. at 367)).

240. Although the Supreme Court in *Weems* referred to "greatly disproportioned" punishments, the first time the words "grossly disproportionate" actually appear in a U.S. Supreme Court case in relation to a punishment was in a dissent in 1958. Green v. United States, 356 U.S. 165, 197 (1958) (Black, J., dissenting) (taking note of "the majority's very approval of the grossly disproportionate sentences imposed on these defendants"). In *Green v. United States*, the defendants were found guilty of criminal contempt and sentenced to three years' imprisonment, and the U.S. Supreme Court rejected the contention that the sentences "were so excessive as to amount to an abuse of discretion." Id. at 188. In particular, the Court in *Green* found that "the contempt here was by any standards a most egregious one"; that "comparing these sentences with those imposed" on others, the sentences "are shorter by a year" than one upheld previously and "no longer than" one inflicted in another case; and that "the sentences were well within" the maximum five-year imprisonment for bail-jumping provided by federal law. Id. "In these circumstances," the Court ruled, "we cannot say that the sentences imposed were beyond the bounds of the reasonable exercise of the District Court's discretion." Id.

241. *See* Kirby Goidel, Craig Freeman & Brian Smentkowski, Misreading the Bill of Rights: Top Ten Myths Concerning Your Rights and Liberties 177 (2015):

Federal challenges to state punishment based on the "cruel and unusual" provisions of the Eighth Amendment began at the turn of the twentieth century. One of the first involved an issue that would have been familiar to the framers of the Bill of Rights. *Graham v. West Virginia* involved an incorrigible horse thief. James H. Graham, also known in Pocahontas County as John H. Ratliff and in Wood County as J. H. Gray, was convicted of stealing a mare valued at $50 in 1898. Three years later, he attempted to steal another horse valued at $100.... Six years later, he was convicted of stealing yet another horse valued at $75. West Virginia Courts imposed a life sentence on Graham under its recidivist statute. He appealed, claiming that the sentence was cruel and unusual. The Supreme Court disagreed, holding that the West Virginia Legislature was best suited to determine the punishment for repeat offenders.

See also Graham v. West Virginia, 224 U.S. 616, 617 (1912) ("The imposition of a heavier penalty for repeated offenses does not amount to inflicting a cruel and unusual punishment.").

242. Peter Gay, The Enlightenment: An Interpretation (The Science of Freedom) 440 (1967) ("[W]hile punishment is an indispensable element in all societies, it must be minimal for the objective it is intended to achieve to achieve. 'Every act of authority of man over man which does not drive from absolute necessity,' Beccaria writes, generalizing a dictum of Montesquieu's, 'is tyrannical'; penalties justify themselves, as it were, to the degree that the sovereign guarantees his subjects liberty and security."); *see also* Frederick Rosen, Classical Utilitarianism from Hume to Mill 148 (2003) ("Beccaria agreed with Montesquieu that every punishment which was not based on the absolute necessity to defend the security of members of society was tyrannical, and this limited power of punishment was the sole,

legitimate use of that liberty which was given up by individuals to the sovereign.").

243. SULLIVAN & FRASE, PROPORTIONALITY PRINCIPLES IN AMERICAN LAW, *supra* note 79, at 164.

244. Richard S. Frase, "Excessive Relative to What? Defining Constitutional Proportionality Principles," *in* MICHAEL TONRY, ED., WHY PUNISH? HOW MUCH? A READER ON PUNISHMENT 264 n.10 & 267 n.20 (2011); *see also* RICHARD S. FRASE, JUST SENTENCING: PRINCIPLES AND PROCEDURES FOR A WORKABLE SYSTEM 83 n.2 (2013):

Parsimony is sometimes referred to as the requirement of necessity, narrow tailoring, or least restrictive means (Europeans consider it a form of proportionality, which I have called alternative means proportionality). The principle was advocated by all of the leading early utilitarian philosophers (Beccaria, Blackstone, Bentham), and has been widely applied in U.S., foreign, and international law (Sullivan and Frase 2009; Frase 2005a, 2008a, 2012).

245. Richard S. Frase, "Limiting Retributivism," *in* MICHAEL TONRY, ED., THE FUTURE OF IMPRISONMENT 88 (2004).

246. The concept of necessity shows up in numerous judicial opinions. *See, e.g.*, United States v. Bailey, 444 U.S. 394, 409-10 (1980):

Common law historically distinguished between the defenses of duress and necessity. Duress was said to excuse criminal conduct where the actor was under an unlawful threat of imminent death or serious bodily injury, which threat caused the actor to engage in conduct violating the literal terms of the criminal law. While the defense of duress covered the situation where the coercion had its source in the actions of other human beings, the defense of necessity, or choice of evils, traditionally covered the situation where physical forces beyond the actor's control rendered illegal conduct the lesser of two evils. Thus, where A destroyed a dike because B threatened to kill him if he did not, A would argue that he acted under duress, whereas if A destroyed the dike in order to protect more valuable property from flooding, A could claim a defense of necessity.

See also United States v. Oakland Cannabis Buyers' Co-op, 532 U.S. 483, 490 (2001) ("A necessity defense 'traditionally covered the situation where physical forces beyond the actor's control rendered illegal conduct the lesser of two evils.'") (quoting *Bailey*, 444 U.S. at 410); id. at 491 ("Under any conception of legal necessity, one principle is clear: The defense cannot succeed when the legislature itself has made a 'determination of values.'") (quoting 1 W. LAFAVE & A. SCOTT, SUBSTANTIVE CRIMINAL LAW § 5.4, p. 629 (1986)).

247. *E.g.*, State v. Williams, Docket No. 44300, 2018 WL 358149 *10 (Idaho Ct. App. Jan. 11, 2018) ("Using restraints on a defendant during trial is reversible error if the trial judge fails to make a finding that the restraints are necessary for physical security, to prevent escape, or to maintain court decorum, unless the State can show the error was harmless.") (citing Deck v. Missouri, 544 U.S. 622, 629 (2005)); Davidson v. Riley, 44 F.3d 1118, 1122 (2d Cir. 1995) ("The principles consistently applied are that the trial court has discretion to order physical restraints on a party or witness when the court has found those restraints to be necessary to maintain safety or security; but the court must impose no greater restraints than are necessary, and it must take steps to minimize the prejudice resulting from the presence of the restraints.").

248. JOHN BOSTON & DANIEL E. MANVILLE, PRISONERS' SELF-HELP LITIGATION MANUAL 137–38, 715 (4th ed. 2010) (quoting Davidson v. Riley, 44 F.3d 1118, 1122 (2d Cir. 1995)).

249. Canterbury v. Commonwealth, 27 S.W.2d 946, 949 (Ky. Ct. App. 1930):

We have often written that the right of a person to take life in self defense arises from his belief in the necessity for it, and from the reasonableness of the grounds of his belief as judged by the danger as it appears to him, and not from the belief of the jury as to the necessity of it, or the belief of any one else as to that necessity.

See also McBride v. State, 109 So. 556, 567 (Ala. Ct. App. 1926) ("The doctrine of self-defense is the law of necessity."); Williams v. Commonwealth, 66 S.W. 401, 402 (Ky. Ct. App. 1902) ("Self-defense is the law of necessity. Whether the defendant at the time believed, and had reasonable ground to believe, he was in danger of losing his life or suffering great bodily harm, is the question the jury is to determine.").

250. Guzman v. Secretary, Dept. of Corrections, No. 2:08-cv-411-FtM-36SPC, 2011 WL 4346564 *11 (M.D. Fla., Sept. 16, 2011).

251. People v. Soto, 415 P.3d 789, 974 (Cal. 2018) (citations omitted). Morris v. State, 242 A.2d

582, 584 (Md. Ct. App. 1968) (citations omitted).

252. *Guzman*, 2011 WL 4346564 at *11 (emphasis added); *compare* McKee v. McKee, 231 S.W. 213, 214 (Ky. Ct. App. 1921) ("We are not prepared to say that one spouse may never inflict corporal punishment upon the other in the absolutely necessary defense of himself or herself or some member of the family; but the testimony should clearly establish the right to do so, which is by no means true in this case. On the contrary, according to the testimony of plaintiff, each of the difficulties and each of the cruel punishments of her by her husband was without excuse....").

Chapter 6

1. Bob Dylan's "The Times They Are A-Changin'" was released in January 1964. Anthony Varesi, The Bob Dylan Albums: A Critical Study 31–32 (2004).

2. Furman v. Georgia, 408 U.S. 238, 262 (1972) (Brennan, J., concurring); Bessler, Cruel and Unusual: The American Death Penalty and the Founders' Eighth Amendment 186, 328 (2012).

3. Anthony F. Granucci, *"Nor Cruel and Unusual Punishments Inflicted:" The Original Meaning*, 57 Cal. L. Rev. 839, 842 (1969).

4. *E.g.*, Ernest W. Pettifer, Punishments of Former Days 95, 108, 115 (1992); William Firestone, Grandeur and Grace in the Ohio Country: Building America from the Ground Up, 1784–1860, at 5 (2009).

5. 14 Abraham Rees, The Cyclopædia; or, Universal Dictionary of Arts, Sciences, and Literature (1819) (noting in the entry for "FIFER": "We cannot let pass this opportunity of expressing our conviction, founded on the best authorities, that corporal punishments are as unnecessary as they are disgraceful; and that it is not only very practicable, but has in many instances been found very effectual, to substitute moderation for severity, and an attack on the pride of an offender, for one on his flesh.").

6. John Scott, The Christian Life, from Its Beginning to Its Consummation in Glory 627–28 (9th ed. 1729).

7. 3 The Works of the Learned and Reverend John Scott, D.D.: Sometime Rector of St. Giles's in the Fields 449 (new ed. 1826).

8. John F. Stinneford, *The Original Meaning of "Unusual": The Eighth Amendment as a Bar to Cruel Innovation*, 102 Nw. U. L. Rev. 1739, 1770 (2008) (noting that "[a]ctions that comported with long usage were often said to be 'usual'" and that "[a]ctions that were contrary to long usage, on the other hand, were described as 'unusual'"; "Americans in the late eighteenth and early nineteenth centuries also used the term 'unusual' to describe actions that were contrary to 'long usage'"); *see also* id. at 1772 (noting that the English jurist Edward Coke "argued that the common law consisted of customary practices that enjoyed 'long' or 'immemorial usage'"); id. at 1805 (discussing Patrick Henry's use of the "unusual punishments" terminology). While the word *unusual* was, naturally, employed in a wide variety of different contexts and writings in America's founding era, Samuel Johnson's famous dictionary defined "unusual" as "Not common; not frequent; rare." A Dictionary of the English Language 250 (1756); *see also* Thomas Sheridan, A Complete Dictionary of the English Language (2d ed. 1789) (defining "Unusual" as "Not common, not frequent, rare").

9. 88 The Annual Register, or a View of the History, Politics, and Literature, for the Year 1777 244 (1788) ("The usual punishments are fine and imprisonment for such offences...."); Pierre-Joseph Dumont, Narrative of Thirty-Four Years' Slavery and Travels in Africa 17, 42 (J. S. Quesne, comp. 1819) (referencing "threats of the usual punishments" and noting that in one locale "the most usual punishment is decapitation"); 3 George Burder, comp., The Works of the Reverend Isaac Watts, D.D. 358 (1810) (noting that "[a] fine of money or cattle to be paid, a cutting off from the people or congregation, scourging or beating at most with forty stripes, the loss of a limb, or the loss of life" were "some of the usual punishments of criminals appointed in the jewish law"); Isaac Watts, A Short View of the Whole Scriptural History 68 (8th ed. 1767) (noting same); 2 Sarah Trimmer, ed., Sacred History, Selected from the Scriptures; with Annotations and Reflections, Particularly Calculated to Facilitate the Study of the Holy Scriptures in Schools and Families 37 (6th ed. 1810) ("The usual punishments of criminals

among the Israelites were, a fine of money or cattle to be paid, or cutting off from the congregation, scourging or beating (not exceeding forty-nine stripes), the loss of a limb, or the forfeiture of life."); 23 The Lady's Magazine or Entertaining Companion for the Fair Sex, Appropriated Solely to Their Use and Amusement 275 (1792) ("The council of finances at Brussels have published an ordinance, prohibiting the vending to or furnishing the French with provisions, ammunition, &c. under pain of the usual punishments."); 8 The Eclectic Review 36 (1812) (noting in a discussion of George Cook, A History of the Reformation in Scotland (1811) that two people "were condemned to the usual punishments").

10. 1 Edward Gibbon, The History of the Decline and Fall of the Roman Empire 357 (1776). Many during the Enlightenment began to question the propriety of capital punishment, then the usual punishment for various offenses. *See* Charles Coote, The History of Europe: From the Peace of Paris, in 1763, to the Treaty Concluded at Amiens in 1802 283–84 (1817) ("Condorcet said, 'Death is the usual punishment of conspirators; but, as such a sentence is repugnant to my principles, I never will concur in it.'").

11. 4 Robert Bissett, The History of the Reign of George III 233 (1811); Edward Baines, History of the Wars of the French Revolution 156 (1817).

12. 2 Charles Rollin, The Roman History from the Foundation of Rome to the Battle of Actium: That is, to the End of the Commonwealth 406 (1739).

13. 11 T. B. Howell, comp., A Complete Collection of State Trials and Proceedings for High Treason and Other Crimes and Misdemeanors from the Earliest Period to the Year 1783, with Notes and Other illustrations 755 (1816).

14. *See* Bessler, Cruel and Unusual, *supra* note 2, at 299–306 (discussing references to "unusual punishments" in America's founding period).

15. Id. at 299.

16. Id. at 299–300.

17. Id. at 301; *see also* 2 The Works of John Sheffield, Earl of Mulgrave, Marquis of Normanby, and Duke of Buckingham 145–46 (2d ed. 1729):

John Kerby a mercer and John Algore a grocer of the city of *London*, in the time of Richard II, had kill'd John Imperial, a publick Minister from the State of *Genoa*; and the Parliament happening to be sitting, pass'd an Act 3 Richard II. that they should be attainted of High Treason in the *King's Bench*; and they were executed accordingly. It was said, that all Judges after this were oblig'd to hold for Treason the killing any foreign Minister in the same manner, notwithstanding it is none of those crimes recited in the Act of 25 Edward III....

.... [I]f a Parliament upon an extraordinary occasion, as that of the *Genoa* Embassador, shall in their great prudence inflict any unusual punishment; by what colour of reason should that be construed, as if they would have all the ordinary Judges hereafter do the same thing, without tarrying for their judgment?

One Parliament's proceeding is the best sort of precedent for another: But that it should be an example for inferiour Courts, is a preposterous and dangerous, as if a Schoolmaster should imitate a General, and instead of whipping a scholar, should put him to death by a general council of schoolboys.

18. The Eighth Amendment's language was approved and ratified in close proximity to the promulgation of the French Declaration of the Rights of Man and of the Citizen (1789), a declaration that Thomas Jefferson assisted the Marquis de Lafayette—the Revolutionary War hero—in drafting. Winston P. Nagan, John A.C. Cartner & Robert J. Munro, Human Rights and Dynamic Humanism 121 (2017) ("Jefferson collaborated with the Marquis de Lafayette in the first draft of the French Declaration of the Rights of Man and of the Citizen. This Declaration adopted by the French National Assembly on August 26, 1789, was a descendant of the American Declaration of Independence."); David Edwin Harrell, Jr., Edwin S. Gaustad, John B. Boles, Sally Foreman Griffith, Randall M. Miller & Randall B. Woods, Unto a Good Land: A History of the American People (Volume 1: To 1900) 218 (2005) ("On September 25, 1789, the Senate approved the twelve amendments that the House had agreed to the day before. By December 15, 1791, three-fourths of the states ... had ratified the ten amendments that, collectively, are known as the American Bill of Rights."). Whereas the Eighth Amendment bars "cruel and unusual punishments," Article 8 of the French Dec-

laration protects against penalties that are not "strictement et évidemment nécessaires," that is, "strictly and obviously necessary." William A. Schabas, The Death Penalty as Cruel Treatment and Torture: Capital Punishment Challenged in the World's Courts 26 (1996).

19. 2 Matthew Poole, ed., Annotations upon the Holy Bible: Wherein the Sacred Text Is Inserted, and Various Readings Annex'd, Together with the Parallel Scriptures, ch. XVI (1700) (noting that "tis' an usual punishment of Lyars, that they are not believed when they speak the truth"); Samuel Chandler, The History of Persecution, in Four Parts 261 (1736) ("But the most usual Punishment of all, is their wearing Crosses upon their penitential Garments. . . ."); 1 Antonio de Ulloa, A Voyage to South-America: Describing at Large the Spanish Cities, Towns, Provinces, &c. on that Extensive Continent 427 (1758) (noting that "[a]n Indian" in South America who failed to go to church on Sundays had, at a priest's direction, received "some lashes, the usual punishment for such delinquents"); R. & J. Dodsley, eds., The Annual Register, or a View of the History, Politicks, and Literature, of the Year 1759 76 (1760) ("Joseph Halfey was tried for the murder of Daniel Davidson on the high seas, about 100 leagues from Cape Finisterre, found guilty, and immediately sentenced to the usual punishment of such crimes."); 9 W. Sands, A. Murray & J. Cochran, eds., The Scots Magazine: Containing, a General View of the Religion, Politicks, Entertainment, &c. in Great Britain 561 (1747) (noting that "in cases where from some extraordinary circumstance the usual punishment might be too severe," it "therefore required a mitigation"); The Natural History and Antiquities of Selborne, in the County of Southhampton 372 (1789) ("[T]he usual punishment is fasting on bread and beer.").

20. *See e.g.*, Stinneford, *The Original Meaning of "Unusual"*, *supra* note 8, at 1805, 1809–11 (discussing the concept of "unusual punishments" by Patrick Henry in America's founding era, contending that the use of the word "unusual" in the Cruel and Unusual Punishments Clause "was meant to be a check on the federal government's ability to innovate in punishment," and discussing early American cases, including *Barker v. People*, *Commonwealth v. Wyatt*, and *People v. Potter*, where state courts rejected arguments that punishments were "unusual"); *see also* Barker v. People, 20 Johns. 457, 459 (N.Y. Sup. Ct. 1823) ("[T]he disfranchisement of a citizen is not an unusual punishment."); Commonwealth v. Wyatt, 27 Va. (6 Rand.) 694, 701 (Va. Gen. Ct. 1828) ("The punishment of offences by stripes in certainly odious, but cannot be said to be unusual"; the discretion to impose whipping under the statute was said to be "of the same character with the discretion always exercised by Common Law Courts to inflict fine and imprisonment, and subject to be restrained by the same considerations."); People v. Potter, 1 Edm. Sel. Cas. 235, 245 (N.Y. Sup. Ct. 1846) ("[T]he governor may grant a pardon on a condition which does not subject the prisoner to an unusual or cruel punishment. Banishment is neither. It is sanctioned by authority, and has been inflicted, in this form, from the foundation of our government.").

21. 12 T. Osborne, A. Millar & J. Osborn, eds., An Universal History, From the Earliest Account of Time 451 (1747) ("Upon the accusation of a slave, *Betucius* and *Æmilia* were condemned to the usual punishment."); The Pro-Slavery Argument, as Maintained by the Most Distinguished Writers of the Southern States: Containing the Several Essays, on the Subject, of Chancellor Harper, Governor Hammond, Dr. Simms, and Professor Dew 158 (1853) ("Now, in the time of Christ, it was usual for masters to put their slaves to death on the slightest provocation. They even killed and cut them up to feed their fishes."); id. at 136 ("'The usual punishment for theft is to place the culprit's head between the legs of one of the biggest boys, and each boy in the pit—sometimes there are twenty—inflicts twelve lashes on the back and rump with a cat.'").

22. 13 T. Osborne, An Universal History: From the Earliest Account of Time 356 (1748).

23. 1 Terence's Comedies, Translated into English Prose, as Near as the Propriety of the Two Languages Will Admit 232 (S. Patrick, trans., 3d ed. 1767) (showing a scene involving Pythias and Parmeno contains this line: "Now he threatens him also with the usual Punishment of Adulterers: a thing I never saw in my Life, nor desire to see"); John Vanderkemp, The Christian Entirely the Property of Christ, in Life and Death: Exhibited in Fifty-Three Sermons on the Heidelbergh Catechism 96 (John M. Van Harlingen, trans. 1810) ("With regard to Isaiah xxviii. 21, we do not read there, that God's work and act of punishing is strange to God, but only that it is strange: and to whom should it be strange? to God? no: but to the transgressors, on whom God would inflict a strange and unusual punishment."); 1 The Works of Philo Judæus, the Con-

temporary of Josephus 288 (C. D. Yonge, trans. 1800) ("[A]ll those who voluntarily and of deliberated purposes have rejected the living God, exceeding even the bounds of wickedness itself, for what other evil of equal weight can possibly be found? Such men should suffer not the usual punishments of evil doers, but something new and extraordinary.").

24. There is some evidence—and at least some suggestion—that the provision of the English Bill of Rights proscribing "cruel and unusual punishments" was designed to prevent "illegal" punishments, though the clause, on its face, does not refer to *illegal* punishments. *See* Laurence Claus, *The Antidiscrimination Eighth Amendment*, 28 Harv. J.L. & Pub. Pol'y 119, 135 (2004) (noting that clause 19 of a draft of the English Bill of Rights presented to the House of Commons on February 2, 1689, read: "The requiring excessive Bail of Persons committed in criminal Cases and imposing excessive Fines, and illegal Punishments, to be prevented"); id. (noting that the final version of the English Bill of Rights recited: "And excessive Fines have been imposed; and illegal and cruel punishments inflicted"); id. at 136:

> In the context of common law punishment for common law crimes, to punish illegally was to punish differently for no morally sufficient reason. The word *unusual* "was appropriate to convey the idea that the punishments were 'uncommon' and 'exceptional,' outside what the law permitted." To punish *cruelly* and unusually was to single out an offender on a morally insufficient basis for *more* punishment than was customarily applied.

25. Thomas Godwyn, Romanæ Historiæ Anthologia Recognita et Aucta: An English Exposition of the Roman Antiquitie 182 (1661); *cf.* id. at 203 ("Thus have we generally and briefly touched the more usual Punishments. But sometimes wrongs done between party and party, were punished with a retaliation of the same kind: according to that, *A tooth for a tooth, and an eye for an eye*. And this kind of punishing was called *Talio*.").

26. Id.

27. Id. at 183. Punishments involving the taking of one's life were "called *Ultimum Supplicium*." Id.; *cf.* id. at 185 ("Those punishments that deprived of life in ordinary use, and of which there is most frequent mention in *Roman* Authors, are these which follow: *Furca, Crux, Carcer, Culeus, Equuleus, de rupe Tarpeia dejectio, Scala, Gemonia, Tunica, Damnatio, in gladium, in ludum, ad bestias*."). A description of those punishments is set forth elsewhere in the book. Id. at 186–88. For example, in a chapter about "*Crux*," it was noted: "Crucifixion hath been a punishment in ancient use among the Romans; it was abrogated by *Constantine*. It was a death that commonly servants were sentence unto, seldom times freeman...." Id. at 188. Godwyn noted that for floggings, the Romans—"to augment the pains"—"did usually in these scourges tye certain huckle-bones, or plummets of Lead at the end of the whip cords, or thongs, and such scourges they termed *Scorpiones*." Id. at 203. "The cruelty of the scourges," he wrote, "was such, that they many times died under them." Id.

28. Id. at 200; *cf.* id. at 201 ("[T]he punishment which *Suetonius* speaketh of, is some strange or unusual punishment: now seeing that Senators themselves were often exiled, it could not seem strange that *Roman* Knights should be banished into forraign lands; but this was a matter unusual, and unheard of that a *Roman* Knight should be imployed in such drudgeries.").

29. Id. at 189. Other pre-1688, English-language sources—that is, those pre-dating the Glorious Revolution—also contain the "usual" or "unusual" punishments verbiage. One book, printed in 1678, recited that a vagabond attempted to kill France's king in 1593. After being "tortured" and sentenced to die, the man was said to have "suffered the usual punishments." H. C. Davila, The History of the Civil Wars of France 627 (1678).

30. Nigette M. Spikes, Dictionary of Torture 129 (2014).

31. The Student's Law-Dictionary; or Compleat English Law-Expositor (1740) (showing in the entry for "Penance," it reads in part as follows: "[I]n the Cases of Adultery, Fornication, &c. for which we are told the usual Punishment is, that the Offender stands in the Church Barefoot and Bareheaded, in a White Sheet, &c"); 1 Joseph Shaw, The Practical Justice of Peace, and Parish and Ward-Officer: or, A Treatise Shewing the Present Power and Authority of these Officers, in All the Branches of Their Duty 114 (1756) (showing in a section on "Bastardy" written by a lawyer of the Middle Temple, it is recorded that "[t]he usual Punishment for these Offenders, is Pillory, publick Whipping, &c"); Joseph Shaw, Guide to Justices of the Peace, Ministers, Churchwardens, Overseers of the Poor, Constables, Surveyors of the Highways, Vestry-

Clerks, and All Others Concern'd in Parish Business 206 (1753) (showing in a paragraph on "Bastards," it notes that "[t]he usual Punishment for these Offenders, is Pillory, publick Whipping, &c"); Sylvanus Urban, The Gentleman's Magazine and Historical Chronicle Vol. 50, at 249 (1780) ("[H]e sentenced the prisoner to 12 months imprisonment in Newgate, which doubles the usual punishment."); 1 Thomas Carte, A General History of England 689 (1747) (referring to "the usual punishment for the murder of laymen"); 3 George Lyttelton, The History of the Life of King Henry the Second, and of the Age in Which He Lived 210 (referring to "the usual punishment for the murder of a layman"); 1 William Russell, The History of Modern Europe: With an Account of the Decline and Fall of the Roman Empire, and a View of the Progress of Society 340 (1789) (noting of English law: "That the murderers of a clergyman should be tried before the judiciary, in the presence of the bishop or his official; and besides the usual punishment for murder, should be subjected to a forfeiture of their estates, and a confiscation of their goods and chattels"); 5 Paul M. Rapin de Thoyras & Nicholas Tindal, The History of England as Well as Ecclesiastical and Civil 120 (1728) ("The Lord *Scroop* suffered the usual Punishment of Traitors.") (italics in original); Charles Bourne & Villiam Isaac Blanchard, The Trial of Lieutenant Charles Bourne, upon the Prosecution of Sir James Wallace, Knt. for an Assault 144 n.† (1783) ("Mr. Bourne must here observe, that he was tried as a citizen for a breach of the common law, as a citizen he was convicted of a common assault upon a fellow citizen, and if the records of the courts are to be believed, many matters of equally serious and important consideration have come before them, though no such cruel and unusual punishment as that under which he suffers, can be shewn since the revolution.").

32. Richard Baker, A Chronicle of the Kings of England 490 (1684) (reporting a proclamation from 1641 containing the following language: "*And if any person were censured to the Pillory, or Whipping, it was for known Perjury, the ordinary and usual punishment in such a case....*"); 2 William Dampier, Voyages and Descriptions in Three Parts 80 (1699) (noting that, in Tonquin, "[t]heir punishment in capital crimes is usually beheading"; also containing the following index entry: "Stocks, an usual Punishment ..."); *see also* 2 Popery Not Founded Scripture: or, The Texts which Papists Cite Out of the Bible, for Proof of the Points of Their Religion, Examin'd, and Shew'd to Be Alledg'd Without Ground 523 (1689) (referring to "Leprosy, the usual Punishment of Pride"); Trifano Bocalini, I Raggvagli di Parnasso: or, Advertisements from Parnassus 156 (Henry Earl, trans., 2d ed. 1669) ("*Apollo*, who was not well pleased ... condemned the Literato to the usual punishment ... that none should excuse his error, none should pity him, and that all men should laugh at him.") (italics in original); id. at 160 ("*Apollo* highly offended at the immensity of such a fault, gave Sentence, That the guilty party should undergo the usual punishment for sale of Justice: which was, That he should be slayed alive."); *accord* Trafano Bocalini, I Raggvagli di Parnasso: or, Advertisements from Parnassus; in Two Centuries with the Politick Touchstone 181, 186 (Henry Earl. Trans. 1656) ("*Apollo* ... condemned the Litterato to the usual punishment of imprudency."; "*Apollo* highly offended at the immensity of such a fault, gave sentence that the guilty party should undergo the usual punishment for sale of Justice.") (italics in original).

33. Pierre Danet, A Complete Dictionary of the Greek and Roman Antiquities (1700).

34. Id. (unpaginated).

35. Id. (unpaginated).

36. Archibald Bruce, Free Thoughts on the Toleration of Popery, Deduced from a Review of Its Principles and History, with Respect to Liberty and the Interests of Princes and Nations 113 (1780).

37. *See, e.g.*, 2 Philip Horneck, The High-German Doctor 86 (1719) (referring to "the usual Punishment inflicted"); Bartholomew Leonardo de Argensoa, The Discovery and Conquest of the Mulucco and Philippine Islands: Containing Their History, Ancient and Modern, Natural and Political 88 (1708) (noting that an "Ensign" was "Strangled, as a Traytor to his King" and that two other soldiers were "Bannish'd" and that "Severity to some of the Company" was "shew'd ... on Account of the same Crime, which, it was believ'd, had not been so fully prov'd upon them, as is requisite for inflicting the usual Punishment").

38. 1 Matthew Hale, The History of the Pleas of the Crown 384, 388, 709–10 (1778) (the

author says he will consider "[w]hat was the usual punishment of heresy here in *England* before the time of *Richard* II. and *Henry* IV."; "As to the penalty of death, *ultimum supplicium*: it should seem the antient imperial constitutions made a difference between heresies in relation to that punishment: it appears by the edict of *Theodofius Codice*, *cap.* 4 the *Manichees* and *Donatists* were punished with death ... many other heretics were under milder sentences, some were punished with exile, some with extermination from the city, some with pecuniary mulcts, and some with confiscation, which, it seems, was the most usual punishment"; "And tho by the imperial law some particular heresies were punishable with death yet it does not appear, that even in the empire heresy in general was punished capitally, till the constitution of *Frederic* II. about the year 1234, which indistinctly adjudges all heretics to the flames: but in *England* the usual punishment seems to have been imprisonment...."') (citations omitted); *see also* FRANCIS DOUGLAS, A GENERAL DESCRIPTION OF THE EAST COAST OF SCOTLAND, FROM EDINBURGH TO CULLEN 24 (1782):

By an act of King James the First's second parliament, it was enacted, "that heretics should be punished according to the law of the haly kirk, and that the secular power assist." Beaton having called to his assistance a few of the clergy, put this act summarily in execution. It is a pity that a law, so repugnant to religion and humanity, should reproach the reign of one of the wisest and best of our princes. The act is very cautiously worded; it does not mention burning, the usual punishment inflicted upon heretics, as the English statute did, but simply refers to the law of the holy kirk; perhaps from a presumption, that the merciful mother would inflict a milder punishment on her children.

39. 1 DAVID HUME, THE HISTORY OF ENGLAND, FROM THE INVASION OF JULIUS CAESAR TO THE REVOLUTION IN 1688, at 495 (1773).

40. 1 JOHN HAWKINS, THE WORKS OF SAMUEL JOHNSON, LL.D. TOGETHER WITH HIS LIFE AND NOTES ON HIS LIVES OF THE POETS 520 (1787).

41. 2 OLIVER GOLDSMITH, THE HISTORY OF ENGLAND, FROM THE EARLIEST TIMES TO THE DEATH OF GEORGE II, at 43 (1771); *see also* 5 TOBIAS GEORGE SMOLLETT & THOMAS FRANCKLIN, EDS., THE WORKS OF M. DE VOLTAIRE: TRANSLATED FROM THE FRENCH WITH NOTES, HISTORICAL AND CRITICAL 262 (1761) (referring to "the usual punishment for traitors" as being to be "sentenced to be hanged" and to have one's "heart cut out" and "thrown" in one's "face").

42. 1 THOMAS SALMON, A COMPLETE COLLECTION OF STATE-TRIALS, AND PROCEEDINGS FROM HIGH TREASON, AND OTHER CRIMES AND MISDEMEANOURS; FROM THE REIGN OF KING RICHARD II TO THE END OF THE REIGN OF KING GEORGE I, at 235 (2d ed. 1730) (in a discussion of the Gunpowder Plot, one finds this reference: "The Conclusion shall be from the admirable Clemency and Moderation of the King, in that howsoever these Traitors have exceeded all others their Predecessors in Mischief....; yet neither will the King exceed the usual Punishment of *Law*, nor invent any new Torture or Torment for them; but is graciously pleased to afford them as well an ordinary Course of Trial, as an ordinary Punishments, much inferior to their Offence."); *see also* id. at 722 (in a section on The Trial of Thomas Earl of Strafford, one finds this reference: "And if any Person were censured to the Pillory or Whipping, it was for known Perjury, the ordinary and usual Punishment in such a case."); THE GUNPOWDER-TREASON: WITH A DISCOURSE OF THE MANNER OF ITS DISCOVERY 120–21 (1679) ("[Y]et neither will the King exceed the usual punishment of Law, nor invent any new torture or torment for them.").

43. 2 GEORGE BUCHANAN, HISTORY OF SCOTLAND 378 (4th ed. 1752).

44. 3 THOMAS C. HANSARD, ED., THE PARLIAMENTARY DEBATES FROM THE YEAR 1803 TO THE PRESENT TIME 857 (1805) (in a debate on March 12, 1805, over the "Mutiny Bill," it is reported: "He did not say, that the usual punishments inflicted were more severe than necessary, for which reason, the clause he should recommend, would, in its effects, rather serve to strengthen the powers of regimental courts martial."); 1 THE PARLIAMENTARY REGISTER: OR, AN IMPARTIAL REPORT OF THE DEBATES THAT HAVE OCCURRED IN THE TWO HOUSES OF PARLIAMENT IN THE COURSE OF THE SIXTH SESSION OF THE FOURTH PARLIAMENT OF THE UNITED KINGDOM OF GREAT BRITAIN AND IRELAND 552 (1812) (in a February 20, debate over "the Local Militia Bill," a "Lord A. Hamilton" remarked that the bill provided that persons belonging to the local militia found guilty of offenses would suffer "the usual punishments inflicted in such cases").

45. 2 JEREMIAH WHITAKER NEWMAN, THE LOUNGER'S COMMON-PLACE BOOK, OR, MISCELLANEOUS ANECDOTES: A BIOGRAPHIC, POLITICAL, LITERARY, AND SATIRICAL COMPILATION 113–14 (1796) (referencing "the massacres of Paris" and "the severities exercised on her sovereign, her nobles, her priests,

and her citizens" and that "their numerous executions are in fact no other than the usual punishments inflicted, at various times, by all new governments on rebellious subjects").

46. 14 T. C. Hansard, ed., The Parliamentary Debates from the Year 1803 to the Present Time 605 (1809) (quoting discussions during the debate of May 18, 1809).

47. Id. at 182.

48. A. P. R. Howatt & H. G. Widdowson, A History of English Language Teaching 57–59 (2d ed. 2004).

49. Guy Miège, The New State of England Under Their Majesties K. William and Q. Mary (1691). This book was printed "for Jonathan Robinson, at the *Golden Lion* in St. *Paul*'s Church-yard." Id. at title page. The dedication page of the book reads: "To the Most Honourable Thomas, Marquess of Caermarthen, Earl of Danby, Viscount Latimer, Baron Osborn of Kiveton, Lord President of His Majesties Most Honourable Privy-Council, And Knight of the most Noble Order of the Garter, This *New State of England* is humbly Dedicated by the Author." Id. at dedication page.

50. Id. at 80–81.

51. Id.

52. Id. at 125.

53. Id. Miège compared the English practice to those of "other Nations," which, he wrote, "have devised such racking Tortures to extort the Confession, as make often the Innocent cry Guilty, and prefer Death to the Rack." Id. In the course of his book, Miège also described how prisoners could demand "the *Benefit of the Clergy*, an ancient Liberty of the Church, which has been confirmed by divers Parliaments." Id. at 88. As Miège described the process for invoking that ancient right:

By vertue whereof one in Orders arraigned of Felony by a Secular Judge, might pray his Clergy, which was as much as if he prayed to be delivered to his Ordinary, to purge himself of the Offence objected. But the ancient Course of the Law in this point of Clergy is much altered, so that Lay-men have been made capable of this Benefit in many Cases; As in Theft of Oxen, Sheep, Mony, and other Things, not forcibly taken to the terrour of the Owner. So favourable is our Law, that for the first Fault the Felon shall be admitted to his Clergy. In order to which the Bishop sends a Clergy-man, with a Commission under his Seal, to be Judge in that matter at every Goal-Delivery. If the Prisoner demands to be admitted to his Book, the Judge commonly gives him a Psalter, and turns to what place he pleases. The Prisoner reads as well as he can, and it happens most times but sadly. Then the Judge asketh of the Bishops Commissary, *Legit ut Clericus?* To which the Commissary must answer *Legit*, or *Non legit*; for these be the formal Words, and our Men of Law are the most precise in their Forms. If he say *Legit*, the Judge proceeds no further to Sentence of Death. But, if he say *Non legit*, the Sentence follows either that Day or the next, in these Words, *Thou A. hast been Indited of* such *a Felony, and therefore Arraigned; Thou hast pleaded* Not Guilty, *and put they self upon* God and thy Country; *They have found thee* Guilty, *and Thou hast nothing to say for thy Self; The Law is, that Thou shalt return to the Place from whence thou camest, and from thence Thou shalt go to the Place of Execution, where Thou shalt Hang by the Neck till Thou be dead.* Whereupon he charges the Sheriff with the Execution. But he that claimeth his Clergy in Cases where it is admitted is in the presence of the Judges burnt in the brawn of his Hand with a hot Iron, marked with the Letter *T.* for a Thief, or *M.* for Manslayer. Then he is delivered to the Bishops Officer, to be kept in the Bishops Prison; from whence, after a certain time, he is delivered by a Jury of Clerks. But, if he be taken and found Guilty again, and his Mark discovered, then 'tis his Lot to be hanged.

Id. at 88–90.

54. Id. at 125. A later edition of Miege's book said much the same thing. Guy Miege, The Present State of Great-Britain and Ireland, in Three Parts 295 (4th ed. 1718) ("The most usual Punishment in *England* for capital Crimes, is *Hanging*.") (italics in original).

55. Guy Miège, The New State of England Under Their Majesties K. William and Q. Mary 127 (1691); *compare* id. at 128 ("*Burning alive* is sometimes used, but only for Witches, and Women convicted of High Treason, or Petty Treason."); id. ("*Pressing to Death* … is a Punishment for those only that being Arraigned either of Petty Treason or Felony, refuse to Answer, or to put themselves upon the ordinary Trial of God and the Country."); id. at 129 ("For *Petty Larceny*, or small Theft, that is under the ancient value of 12 d. the Punishment since Edward III. is by *Whipping*, and in the late Reigns has been often by Transportation into the West-Indies, where they live for some

Years a slavish Life."); id. at 130 ("*Perjury*, whereby Mens Estates, Reputation, and Lives ly at stake, is commonly punished only with the *Pillory*; never with Death, though it has cost the Lives of many."); id. ("*Forgery, Blasphemy, Cheating, Libelling, False Weights and Measures, Forestalling the Market, Offences in Baking and Brewing*, are also punished with standing in the *Pillory*. But sometimes the Offender is Sentenced besides to have one or both Ears nailed to the Pillory and cut off, or his Tongue there bored through with a hot Iron."); id. at 131 ("*Vagabounds*, and the like, who can give no good account of themselves, are punished by setting their Legs in the Stocks for certain hours. And *Scolding Women* (that are always teazing their Neighbors) by being set in a *Cucking Stool* placed over some deep Water and duck'd therein three several times, to cool their heat...."); id. ("Other *Misdemeanours* are commonly punished with *Imprisonment* or *Fines*, and sometimes with both."); id. ("Those are the *Corporal Punishments* commonly used in England for Criminals that happen to fall into the hands of Justice.").

56. The passage in Blackstone's *Commentaries* reads as follows:

The punishment of petit treason, in a man, is to be drawn and hanged, and, in a woman, to be drawn and burned: the idea of which latter punishment seems to have been handed down to us from the laws of the antient Druids, which condemned a woman to be burned for murdering her husband; and it is now the usual punishment for all sorts of treasons committed by those of the female sex.

4 William Blackstone, Commentaries on the Laws of England 204 (1769).

57. 4 The Works of Francis Bacon, Baron of Verulam, Viscount St. Alban, and Lord High Chancellor of England 294 (new ed. 1826).

58. Bessler, Cruel and Unusual, *supra* note 2, at 173.

59. Sometimes the prohibition was expressed as one against "unusual and cruel punishments." *E.g.*, 30 Thomas Jones Howell, comp., A Complete Collection of State Trials and Proceedings for High Treason and Other Crimes and Misdemeanors from the Earliest Period to the Year 1783, with Notes and Other Illustrations 1342 (1822) ("He quoted the declaration of the Bill of Rights against excessive bail, and unusual and cruel punishments...."); A Complete Collection of State-Trials and Proceedings for High-Treason, and Other Crimes and Misdemeanours: From the Reign of King George II, at xi (3d ed. 1742) (referring to "the Illegality of unusual and cruel Punishments"); William Sullivan, Sea Life; or, What May or May Not Be Done, and What Ought To Be Done by Ship-Owners, Ship-Masters, Mates and Seamen 75 (1837) ("Unusual and cruel punishments are forbidden; nor could any law of congress make them lawful."); The Proceedings and Speeches, at the Meeting the Seventeenth November, 1795, at St. Andrew's Hall, Norwich, to Petition Parliament Against Lord Grenville's and Mr. Pitt's Treason and Sedition Bills 13 (1795) ("The 10th clause of the Bill of Rights declares, that unusual and cruel punishments shall not be inflicted...."); 38 The Parliamentary Debates from the Year 1803 to the Present Time 1128 (1818) ("[T]hough the bill declared against all unusual and cruel punishments ... no provisions were made to carry these declarations into effect.").

60. *E.g.*, 1 Thomas Jones Howell, comp., A Complete Collection of State Trials and Proceedings for High Treason and Other Crimes and Misdemeanors from the Earliest Period to the Year 1783, with Notes and Other Illustrations xxxv (1816).

61. Thomas Bayly Howell, ed., Cobbett's Complete Collection of State Trials, and Proceedings for High Treason and Other Crimes and Misdemeanors from the Earliest Period to the Present Time xxii, xxxv (1809) (reprinting "Mr. Emlyn's Preface to the Second Edition of the State Trials, in Six Volumes Folio: Printed in the Year 1730"); Francis Hargrave, A Complete Collection of State-Trials, and Proceedings for High-Treason, and Other Crimes and Misdemeanours xi–xii (4th ed. 1776) (reprinting the preface to the second edition). Sollom Emlyn (1697–1754) was an Irish legal writer who became a member of Lincoln's Inn, was the compiler of the six-volume second edition of state trials and contributed "a lengthy preface critically surveying the condition of English law at the time." 25 The Encyclopædia Britannica: A Dictionary of Arts, Sciences, Literature and General Information 806 (11th ed. 1911); Peter Cane & Joanne Conaghan, ed., The New Oxford Companion to Law 1123 (2008); Louis Hyman, The Jews of Ireland: From Earliest Times to the Year 1910, at 16 (1972); Basil Montagu, The Opinions of Different Authors upon the Punishment of Death ix (1812) (reprinted 2004); *Emlyn, Sollom (DNBoo)*, Wikisource, https://en.wikisource.org/wiki/Emlyn,_Sollom_(DNB00) (last visited Feb.

24, 2018).

62. This Latin maxim, not defined in the original source, may be unfamiliar to a modern reader but it has been translated as follows: "He who has nothing in his purse must pay the penalty with his body." *See* James A. Ballentine, A Law Dictionary of Words, Terms, Abbreviations and Phrases Which Are Peculiar to the Law and of Those Which Have a Peculiar Meaning in the Law 410 (1916); Alexander M. Burrill, A New Law Dictionary and Glossary: Containing Full Definitions of the Principal Terms of the Common and Civil Law, Together with Translations and Explanations of the Various Technical Phrases in Different Languages, Occurring in the Ancient and Modern Reports, and Standard Treatises; Embracing Also All the Principal Common and Civil Law Maxims 854 (1850) (reprinted 1998) (defining "Qui non habet in crumena, luat in corpore" as "He who has not [the means of satisfaction] in his purse, must pay in his body. If a man cannot pay his fine, he must go to prison").

63. This doctrine has been explored in a recent law review article. *See* Nicholas M. McLean, *Livelihood, Ability to Pay, and the Original Meaning of the Excessive Fines Clause*, 40 Hastings Const. L.Q. 834, 835 (2013) (discussing the "largely forgotten principle of English law known as *salvo contenemento suo* (translated as 'saving his contenement,' or livelihood)," a principle "[e]nshrined in the Magna Carta" that "had become firmly established as a fundamental principle at common law by the seventeenth and eighteenth centuries"); *see also* Richard Burn & John Burn, New Law Dictionary: Intended for General Use as Well as for Gentlemen of the Profession 325 (1792) (emphasis in original):

AMERCEMENT is, to be at the king's mercy with regard to the *quantum* of a fine imposed. By *magna charta*, c. 14. no man shall have a larger amercement imposed upon him than his circumstances or personal estate will bear, saving to the landowner his land, to the trader his merchandize, and to the husbandman his team and instruments of husbandry; in order to ascertain which, the great charter also directs, that the amercement, which is always inflicted in general terms, shall be set or reduced to a certainty by the oath of a jury. In the court-leet and court-baron, this is usually done by *affeerors*, or jurors sworn to *affeere*; that is, to tax and moderate the general amercement according to the particular circumstances of the offence and the offender. In limitation of which, in courts superior to these, the ancient practice was, to inquire by a jury, when a fine was imposed upon any many, how much he was able to pay by the year, saving the maintenance of himself, his wife, and children. And since the disuse of such inquest, it is never usual to assess a larger fine than a man is able to pay, without touching the implements of his livelihood, but to inflict corporal punishment, or a stated imprisonment, which is better than an excessive fine, for that amounts to imprisonment for life, and by the bill of rights it is particularly declared, that excessive fines ought not to be imposed.

64. An *amercement* is "[a] pecuniary penalty imposed upon an offender by a judicial tribunal." 1 John Bouvier, A Law Dictionary, Adapted to the Constitution and Laws of the United States of America, and of the Several States of the American Union: with References to the Civil and Other Systems of Foreign Law 155 (1892); *see also id.* ("As distinguished from a fine, at the old law an *amercement* was for a lesser offence, might be imposed by a court not of record, and was for an uncertain amount...."); *see also* Herbert Broom & George Denman, Constitutional Law Viewed in Relation to Common Law, and Exemplified by Cases 399–401 (2d ed. 1885) (citations omitted):

The king, by virtue of his prerogative, was entitled to all fines and amercements and penalties, either wholly or in part, and, to prevent the undue exercise of this perogrative, various statutory restrictions were imposed. Thus, the fourteenth chapter of Henry III.'s Magna Carta declares that "a freeman shall not be amerced for a small fault, but after the manner of the fault—and for a great fault after the greatness thereof—saving to him his 'contenement,' and a merchant likewise—saving to him his merchandize." We must understand this word "contenement" to signify that which is necessary for the support and maintenance of a man in his state or condition of life. And, thus, this well-known chapter of Magna Carta forbids the setting upon any man of an amercement heavier than his circumstances or estate would bear—saving, as Lord Coke says, in his commentary on this passage, to the soldier his armour, to the scholar his books, and to the villein the cart or wainage with which his ignoble service was performed....

Magna Carta, as remarked by Lord Coke, "extends to amercements, and not to fines imposed by an Court of Justice." Within the spirit and equity, however, of this enactment, fines imposed judicially must certainly be brought; such fines ought to be moderate and "within bounds", for "where a court has a power of setting fines, that must be understood of setting reasonable fines": an excessive fine "is against law, and shall not bind, for *excessus in re quâlibet jure reprobatur communi*". And accordingly the counsel for Mr. Hampden, who was convicted of a misdemeanor *anno* 36 Car. II., urges upon the court in mitigation of punishment, that his client was possessed but of a moderate estate, and that according to Magna Carta, "there should be a *salvo contenemento* in all fines." So in O'Connell v. Reg., Lord Campbell refers to Magna Carta as providing that "no fine shall be imposed beyond what the party is able to pay."

On many occasions which the reader of history will call to mind—especially during the seventeenth century—were ruinous fines inflicted in violation of law, as well by the Star Chamber as by the Superior Courts; and hence the declaration in the Bill of Rights that "excessive fines ought not to be imposed", grounded on the averment that such had been the practice in the reign of King James II., who in this and other ways, "by the assistance of divers evil counsellors, judges, and ministers employed by him, did endeavour to subvert and extirpate the laws and liberties of this kingdom".

65. 1 T. B. Howell, A Complete Collection of State Trials and Proceedings for High Treason and Other Crimes and Misdemeanors from the Earliest Period to the Year 1783, with Notes and Other Illustrations xxxv (1816) (citations omitted).

66. 1 The Debates of the Constitutional Convention of the State of Maryland, Assembled at the City of Annapolis, Wednesday, April 27, 1864: Being a Full and Complete Report of the Debates and Proceedings of the Convention, Together with the Old Constitution, the Law under which the Convention Assembled, and the New Constitution 224 (1864).

67. Id. at 224–25.

68. Id. at 225.

69. Id. A Mr. Chambers also objected to Mr. Stockbridge's proposal, saying it would "but save a half-a-dozen words." Id. "As has been said," Chambers argued, referencing the earlier statement of Mr. Miller of Anne Arundel, "if gentlemen will look to the two articles referred to, they will find that they refer to two different departments of the Government, the one being a direction to the Legislature, and the other a direction to the Courts themselves." Id. Mr. Stockbridge, however, declined to withdraw his proposed amendment, repeating that he considered it "more a matter of form than substance." Id. Mr. Stockbridge then stated as follows:

Now the purpose of this bill of rights is to declare the rights of the people, and this section means only that they shall be exempt from all cruel punishments and excessive bail, and nothing more, and that this principle instead of being incorporated in one section is embodied in two sections, one restraining the legislative department, and the other restraining the judiciary, when they could as well have been embraced in one. There would be just as much propriety in adding another section to restrain the executive department, and so on for every other officer of the government. My object was simply to consolidate these two articles, and make one general declaration that the people shall be protected against all unusual and cruel pains and penalties. Neither the one or the other article amount to much, but as it has been thought best to have this principle asserted, for whatever it may be worth, I thought it best to have it all in one article. However, I am not strenuous on the point.

Id. After further debate, the question of Mr. Stockbridge's amendment was taken up by the state convention and—as the record reflects—"it was not agreed to." Id. at 226.

70. Alfred S. Niles, Maryland Constitutional Law 356 (1915) (noting that Article XIV of Maryland's 1776 Declaration of Rights provided: "That sanguinary laws ought to be avoided, as far as is consistent with the safety of the State; and no law, to inflict cruel and unusual pains and penalties, ought to be made in any case, or at any time hereafter.").

71. Id. at 397 (noting that Article 14 of Maryland's 1851 Declaration of Rights provided: "That sanguinary laws ought to be avoided as far as is consistent with the safety of the State; and no law to inflict cruel and unusual pains and penalties ought to be made in any case, or at any time hereafter.").

72. Id. at 431 (noting that Article 16 of Maryland's 1864 Declaration of Rights provided: "That sanguinary laws ought to be avoided as far as it is consistent with the safety of the State; and no law to inflict cruel and unusual pains and penalties ought to be made in any case or at any time hereafter.").

73. Id. at 36, 476 (citing Article 16 of Maryland's Declaration of Rights (1867)).

74. Article XXII of Maryland's Declaration of Rights (1776) provided: "That excessive bail ought not to be required, nor excessive fines imposed, nor cruel or unusual punishments inflicted, by the courts of law." Id. at 357 (citing Article XXII of the Maryland Declaration of Rights (1776)).

75. Id. at 398 (noting that Article 22 of Maryland's 1851 Declaration of Rights provided: "That excessive bail ought not to be required, nor excessive fines imposed, nor cruel or unusual punishment inflicted by the courts of law.").

76. Id. at 432 (noting that Article 25 of Maryland's 1864 Declaration of Rights provided: "That excessive bail ought not to be required, nor excessive fines imposed, nor cruel or unusual punishment inflicted by the courts of law.").

77. Id. at 49, 476 (citing Article 25 of Maryland's Declaration of Rights (1867)). Alfred Niles, a lecturer on constitutional law at the University of Maryland, later reported in his treatise, *Maryland Constitutional Law* (1915), that Article XVI of Maryland's 1867 constitution "ought properly to be considered in connection with the last clause of article XXV," with—as Niles emphasized—"article XVI forbidding the passage of any *law* inflicting unusual pains and penalties and the last clause of article XXV prohibiting the *court* from inflicting cruel and unusual punishments, even though the law might upon its face be unobjectionable." Id. at 36.

78. *E.g.*, Daniel Lombard, A Succinct History of Ancient and Modern Persecutions 123 (1747) (referring to "the usual Punishment for high Treason"); 7 Andrew Reid, ed., The Present State of the Republick of Letters 299 (1731) (noting that when "*Quacks* that practice ... in a fraudulent manner ... are catch'd ... their usual Punishment is to be forc'd to swallow down all the *Aloes*, *Mercury*, and *Pills* that are found in their Houses, &c."); The New Annual Register, or General Repository of History, Politics, and Literature, for the Year 1788, at 156 (1789) ("In the Visitatio Notabilis the usual punishment is fasting on bread and beer; and in cases of repeated delinquency, on bread and water."); Petronius Arbiter, The Works of Petronius Arbiter, Translated by Several Hands 174 (4th ed. 1714) (writing of a soldier "dreading the usual Punishment"); John Howie, Biographia Scoticana: or, a Brief Historical Account of the Lives, Characters, and Memorable Transactions of the Most Eminent Scots Worthies 490 (2d ed. 1781) (noting that a woman "was burnt at Craigfergus; the usual punishment of malefactors in that country"); John Pennington Muncaster, Historical Sketches of the Slave Trade, and its Effects in Africa: Addressed to the People of Great Britain 59 (1792) (discussing that after a writer referenced that a man, "having lain with one of his Majesty's wives," was sentenced by "the King of Dogo or Hindo" to be banished and to have his ears cut off, it was reported that "this was an unusual punishment inflicted on him, and made him be scorned and laughed at by all who saw him"); 1 John Lyon, The History of the Town and Port of Dover, and of Dover Castle; with a Short Account of the Cinque Ports 317 (1813) ("The pilots in the Isle of Thanet were to keep to their own bays, and the North Foreland. The usual punishments were inflicted for their disobedience."); 5 The Works of Nathaniel Lardner, D.D. 261 (1815) ("The usual punishments among the Jews were strangling and stoning....").

79. A General History of the Several Nations of the World, from the Flood, to the Present Times 401 (1751) (printed for D. Browne, J. Shuckburgh, and W. Johnston in London).

80. Id.

81. Jeffrey A. Lockwood, Six-Legged Soldiers: Using Insects as Weapons of War 36 (2009).

82. Le Fèvre de Morsan, The Manners and Customs of the Romans 109 (1740) ("The usual punishment of slaves was the whip...."); *cf.* Jean Louis de Lolme, Memorials of Human Superstition 51 (2d ed. 1784) ("It is not to be doubted, that flagellations had been invented, and were become, in early times, a common method of punishment in the Pagan world. Even before the foundation of Rome, we meet with instances which prove that it was the usual punishment inflicted on Slaves.").

83. 2 William Guthrie, trans., The Orations of Cicero 16 n.*b* (1758) ("[W]e must here observe, that a Sentence of Banishment was seldom or never pronounced against any Roman; there being no Law which punished any Crime with Exile. The usual Punishment was a pecuniary Mulct; they were condemned to pay a Sum of Money, in Proportion to the Greatness of their Crime.").

84. Charles Rollin, The Roman History from the Foundation of Rome to the Battle of

ACTIUM: THAT IS, TO THE END OF THE COMMONWEALTH 355 (1739) ("The Vestal Oppia was convicted of having broken her vow of chastity, and suffered the usual punishment."); TITUS LIVIUS'S ROMAN HISTORY, TRANSLATED INTO ENGLISH, AND ILLUSTRATED WITH NOTES, CRITICAL, HISTORICAL, AND GEOGRAPHICAL: FOR THE USE OF STUDENTS IN HUMANITY 168 (William Gordon trans., 1783) ("[T]he vestal Opia being convicted of incontinence, was condemned, and suffered the usual punishment."); 1 OLIVER GOLDSMITH, THE ROMAN HISTORY FROM THE FOUNDATION OF THE CITY OF ROME, TO THE DESTRUCTION OF THE WESTERN EMPIRE 3 (1789) ("The mother was condemned to be buried alive, the usual punishment for vestals who had violated their chastity, and the twins were ordered to be flung into the river Tyber.").

85. 2 JOHANN JAKOB RAMBACH, MEDITATIONS AND CONTEMPLATIONS ON THE SUFFERINGS OF OUR LORD AND SAVIOUR JESUS CHRIST; IN WHICH THE HISTORY OF THE PASSION, AS GIVEN BY THE FOUR EVANGELISTS, IS CONNECTED, HARMONISED, & EXPLAINED 343 (1811).

86. 8 A GENERAL DICTIONARY, HISTORICAL AND CRITICAL: IN WHICH A NEW AND ACCURATE TRANSLATION OF THAT OF THE CELEBRATED MR. BAYLE, WITH THE CORRECTIONS AND OBSERVATIONS PRINTED IN THE LATE EDITION AT PARIS, IS INCLUDED 588 (John Peter Bernard, Thomas Birch & John Lockman, eds., 1739).

87. LE FÈVRE DE MORSAN, THE MANNERS AND CUSTOMS OF THE ROMANS 129 (1740).

88. THOMAS GODWYN, ROMANÆ HISTORIÆ ANTHOLOGIA RECOGNITA ET AUCTA: AN ENGLISH EXPOSITION OF THE ROMAN ANTIQUITIES 201 (1680).

89. 1 THOMAS SALMON, MODERN HISTORY: OR, THE PRESENT STATE OF ALL NATIONS 441–42 (3d ed. 1744); *see also* JOSEPH RANDALL, A SYSTEM OF GEOGRAPHY; OR, A DISSERTATION ON THE CREATION AND VARIOUS PHÆNOMENA OF THE TERRAQUEOUS GLOBE 316 (1744):

The usual Punishment appropriated to Crimes are as follow: *viz.* A Murderer is beheaded; a Thief strangled; an Apostate burnt; a Traitor is dragg'd at a Horse's Tail, and afterwards impaled; and, if any one maims or wounds another, the like Punishment is inflicted on the Offender, an Eye for an Eye, a Limb for a Limb, according to the *Jewish* Law. For Perjury they are set upon an Ass, with their Faces towards the Tail, which the Criminal holds in his Hand, and thus they are led through the City, and afterwards burnt in the Cheek.

90. MEMOIRS OF PETER HENRY BRUCE, ESQ.: A MILITARY OFFICER, IN THE SERVICES OF PRUSSIA, RUSSIA, AND GREAT BRITAIN 64 (1782) (printed for the author's widow).

91. THOMAS THORNTON, THE PRESENT STATE OF TURKEY; OR A DESCRIPTION OF THE POLITICAL, CIVIL, AND RELIGIOUS CONSTITUTION, GOVERNMENT, AND LAWS, OF THE OTTOMAN EMPIRE 415–16 (1807) ("[I]n instances of greater enormities the guilty person is punished with the loss of his ears, and is sentenced to work in the salt mines for the remainder of his life"; "[t]he punishment of death, though not wholly abolished, is rarely inflicted.").

92. 1 NEW MEMOIRS OF LITERATURE, CONTAINING AN ACCOUNT OF NEW BOOKS PRINTED BOTH AT HOME AND ABROAD 129 (1725) (noting in book printed in London for William and John Innys: "Burning is the usual punishment of the Jews, when they are condemned to death, to make a difference between them, and the Turks, Moors and Christians.").

93. 1 CHARLES ROLLINS, THE ANCIENT HISTORY OF THE EGYPTIANS, CARTHAGINIANS, ASSYRIANS, BABYLONIANS, MEDES AND PERSIANS, MACEDONIANS, AND GRECIANS 190 (5th ed. 1768) ("[A]fter having been long tormented by being kept for ever awake in this dreadful torture, his merciless enemies nailed him to a cross, their usual punishment, and left him to expire on it."); 1 JACOB ROBINSON, THE HISTORY OF THE WORKS OF THE LEARNED, FOR THE YEAR ONE THOUSAND SEVEN HUNDRED AND FORTY 152 (1740) (reciting that a man was "nailed" to "a Cross," with the writing saying that, for "the *Carthaginians*," that was the "usual Punishment among them") (italics in original).

94. 1 SALMON, *supra* note 89, at 300 ("[T]he most usual way of punishing those that are intended to be restored, is by banishing them to some distant village, where they remain confined till they are made sensible of their faults; and sometimes they are forgotten, and it proves an imprisonment for life").

95. 2 THOMAS OSBORNE, A COLLECTION OF VOYAGES AND TRAVELS 72 (1745) ("If the *Chineze* are very liberal in their rewards, they are as severe in the punishments, even of the slightest faults; their punishments are adequate to their demerits. The usual punishment is the bastinado on the back. When they receive but forty or fifty blows, they call this a fatherly correction....") (italics in original);

Eusebius Renaudot, Ancient Accounts of India and China, by Two Mohammedan Travellers (1733) (noting the unpaginated index entry for "Bambooing" describes it as "the usual Punishment inflicted in *China*") (italics in original).

96. Jean de Thévenot, Travels into the Levant 259 (1687) ("The usual Punishments in *Ægypt* are Beheading, which they dexterously perform.... Impaling is also a very ordinary Punishment with them....") (italic in original).

97. 4 Stephen Abel Laval, A Compendious History of the Reformation, and of the Reformed Churches in France 168 (1743) ("He was condemned to the usual Punishment inflicted upon such Traitors.").

98. 3 John Stephen Pütter, An Historical Development of the Present Political Constitution of the Germanic Empire 303 (1790) ("The usual punishment in Germany for capital offenses is beheading with a broad sword. The criminal is obliged to kneel, and the executioner seldom fails to perform his office with a single blow.").

99. 5 Samuel Parker, Bibliotheca Biblica: Being a Commentary upon All the Books of the Old and New Testament (1735) (showing unpaginated index entry for "Adultery" describes "Stoning to Death" as "the usual Punishment" for adultery "among the primitive *Greeks*") (italics in original); *id.* at 575 (containing a reference to "*the most usual Punishments inflicted on Slaves*") (italics in original).

100. The Senator: or, Clarendon's Parliamentary Chronicle: Containing an Impartial Register; Recording, with the Utmost Accuracy, the Proceedings and Debates of the Houses of Lords and Commons, Being the Fifth Session in the Seventeenth Parliament of Great Britain, Held in the Year 1795, at 691 (1795) ("His Lordship said, the history, as far as he had seen, proved that fine and confinement were the usual punishments imposed by absolute Princes in India on their dependents for disobedience and contumacy.").

101. 3 John Pinkerton, ed., A General Collection of the Best and Most Interesting Voyages and Travels in All Parts of the World 819 (1809) ("One of their usual punishments (and by no means the most severe) was taking people out of their beds, carrying them naked in winter on horse-back for some distance, and burying them up to their chin in a hole filled with briars, not forgetting to cut off their ears."); *accord* 49 Tobias George Smollett, ed., The Critical Review: or, Annals of Literature 108 (1780) (containing the same language).

102. 1 Salmon, *supra* note 89, at 45 ("Their usual punishments for great offences are burning, crucifying with the head downwards, tearing them to pieces with horses, and boiling them in oil; and where an offender refuses to come in and submit, he is ordered to be cut in pieces wherever he is found. A gentleman or soldier convicted of any capital crime, has the favour of dying by his own hands; and it is reckoned very ignominious if he waits for the executioner to dispatch him in that case.").

103. 2 Thomas Stamford Raffles, The History of Java ccxxxvii (1830) (Appendix K contains the following sentence: "The usual punishments are death, confinement, and servitude.").

104. 1 Salmon, *supra* note 89, at 56, 191, 348, 352, 441–42 (reciting that in Persia "[t]he usual punishment is a fine, which always goes to the King, or rather to the Governor of the province," but that "the usual punishment for capital offences" is that "the criminal's feet are tied to a camel, and his head hanging down to the ground, his belly is ripped open, so that all his bowels come out and hang over his head" with his body "dragged in this manner through the principal streets of the town, an officer marching before him"; also discussing, as the Persia, "the usual punishment of women who have committed capital crimes" and "the usual punishment" of bakers "for cheating in their weights, and raising provisions to an extravagant price"); Jean de Thévenot, Travels into the Levant 106–07 (1687) ("The usual punishments they inflict upon Malefactors whom they would not put to death, is to pluck out their Eyes; or else to pierce the Nerves of their Ankles, and then hanging them up by the feet, to give them a certain number of blows with a Cudgel, and sometimes also to cut the Nerves short off. When they condemn any to death, the most usual punishment is to rip open the Belly.").

105. 7 S. Richardson, T. Osborne, C. Hitch, A. Millar, John Rivington, S. Crowder, P. Davey, B. Law, T. Longman & C. Ware, eds., The Modern Part of an Universal History, from the Earliest Account of Time 266 (1759) (noting that in the Kingdom of Siam "[t]he usual punishment for robbery is to pay double, and sometimes treble, the value of the goods stolen"); Archibald Bower, ed., Historia Litteraria: or, An Exact and Early Account of the Most Valuable

Books Published in the Several Parts of Europe 393 (1731) ("They punish very severely the smallest Faults: as for instance, if one talks too little they slit his Mouth to his Ears; if too much, they sow it quite up. The usual Punishments for other such minute Offences are to pluck out the Delinquent's Teeth, burn his Arms with a red-hot Iron, drive in sharp-pointed Reeds to the Roots of his Nails, &c.").

106. Jonathan Carver, The New Universal Traveller: Containing a Full and Distinct Account of All the Empires, Kingdoms, and States, in the Known World 41 (1779) ("For murder and adultery, the usual punishment is death, which is not inflicted by a professed executioner, but jointly by every person who happens to be within reach of the criminal; and the common weapon is a crice or dagger.").

107. 2 Jedidiah Morse, The American Universal Geography; or a View of the Present State of all the Kingdoms, States, and Colonies in the Known World 173 (6th ed. 1812) ("The penal laws are mild. Whipping and confinement are the usual punishments."); 2 Aubry de La Motraye, A. de La Motraye's Travel's Through Europe, Asia, and into Part of Africa 361 (1723) (discussing beheading and the work of an executioner, the author wrote: "Note, this is the most usual Punishment in *Sweden*; where, for one that is hang'd, a hundred lose their Heads. Amongst others, I have seen him behead a Husband who had left his Wife, and a Wife who had left her Husband. . . .") (italics in original).

108. 3 The Weekly Entertainer; or Agreeable and Instructive Repository; Containing a Collection of Select Pieces, Both in Prose and Verse; Curious Anecdotes, Instructive Tales, and Ingenious Essays on Different Subjects 185 (1784) (describing "the usual punishment" in the West Indies—that is, for the offender to be "whipped on an ass"—for a violation of the law of "the governor or viceroy" that "no Indian should be employed in carrying the baggage of Europeans"); House of Commons (Great Britain), Abridgment of the Minutes of the Evidence, Taken Before a Committee of the Whole House, to Whom it was Referred to Consider of the Slave-Trade 106 (1789) ("The usual punishments of plantation-slaves according to the nature of their crimes; of a runaway, it is exceedingly severe; four negroes to take hold of each arm and leg, and lay him on the ground, when the chief whipper lays upon their bare back 40, 50, 60, or more lashes, just at the pleasure of the owner or overseer.").

109. 3 Plutarch's Lives, Translated from the Original Greek, with Notes Critical and Historical, and a Life of Plutarch 322 (John Langhorne & William Langhorne, trans., 1801) ("Lucullus, at his return, inflicted on the fugitives the usual punishment. He made them strip to their vests, take off their girdles, and then dig a trench twelve feet long; the rest of the troops all the while standing and looking on.").

110. James Anderson, Royal Genealogies: or, the Genealogical Tables of Emperors, Kings and Princes, from Adam to These Times 61 (1732).

111. 2 The Works of the Learned Joseph Bingham, M.A.: Late Rector of Havant, and Sometime Fellow of University-College in Oxford 628 (1726).

112. Rosemary Ellen Guiley, The Encyclopedia of Witches, Witchcraft and Wicca 379 (3d ed. 2008); James R. Acker, Questioning Capital Punishment: Law, Policy, and Practice 342 (2014); Mark Osler, Jesus on Death Row: The Trial of Jesus and American Capital Punishment 109–12 (2009).

113. 18 Encyclopædia Perthensis; or Universal Dictionary of the Arts, Sciences, Literature, &c. 481 (2d ed. 1816).

114. Id. That dictionary also defines "Privilege" as follows: "in law, some peculiar benefit granted to certain persons or places contrary to the usual course of the law." Id. at 331.

115. Of course, early conceptions of torture were much different than modern ones. *See, e.g.*, Michael Peel & Vincent Iacopino, eds., The Medical Documentation of Torture 3–4 (2002):

The early history and evolution of torture—from Greek and Roman times to the 20th century—is well examined by Peters and Ruthven, among other authors. The key understanding of torture during the greater part of this period is that it was a part of the legal process, embodied in written laws and procedures and not regarded by states with any shame. It was viewed as a legitimate tool of investigation. This contrasts dramatically with the contemporary practice of torture where denial of any illegal acts of torture is routine; at most it may be explained away as the practice of 'rogue elements' in the police or security forces.

116. 2 Quintus Curtius Rufus, The History of the Life and Reign of Alexander the Great 393 (1809) (emphasis added).

117. The New Annual Register, or General Repository of History, Politics, Arts, Sciences, and Literature, for the Year 1824, at 424 (1825).

118. Frederick Rosen, "Utilitarianism and the Reform of the Criminal Law," *in* 1 Mark Goldie & Robert Wokler, eds., The Cambridge History of Eighteenth-Century Political Thought 565 (2006); *compare* Jamal Barnes, A Genealogy of the Torture Taboo (2017), intro.:

It was the excess of pain that led the *philosophes* in the eighteenth century to see torture as dangerous to the social order. Torture undermined justice in the social contract by taking away too much liberty from citizens than was necessary to maintain order. Yet cruel and unusual punishments also transformed citizens into callous brutes and generated fears that one's society would regress to a barbarous age.

119. 1825 WL 1899 (Pa. 1825).

120. In *A Treatise of the Pleas of the Crown*, the Englishmen William Hawkins—under the heading "Cucking Stool"—wrote: "Sometimes called Ducking Stool, the usual punishment for a *common scold*." 1 William Hawkins, A Treatise of the Pleas of the Crown; or, A System of the Principal Matters Relating to that Subject, Digested Under Proper Heads 624 (Thomas Leach, ed., 6th ed. 1777); *see also* id. at 352 n.3 (in another section of his treatise, Hawkins also made reference to a "usual" punishment, writing in that unrelated context: "The usual mode of punishment at present is by pillory, fine, imprisonment, and surety for the good behaviour."). While men were traditionally punished in the stocks, ducking-stools had been used extensively in the sixteenth and seventeenth centuries to punish women. Alfred Creigh, History of Washington County: From its First Settlement to the Present Time, at ch. 1 (1870).

121. *James*, 1825 WL 1899, at *1. A ducking stool was a chair connected to a pulley system where slanderers and women, among others, "were restrained and then repeatedly plunged into a convenient body of water." Matthew W. Meskell, *The History of Prisons in the United States from 1777 to 1877*, 51 Stan. L. Rev. 839, 841–42 (1999).

122. *James*, 1825 WL 1899, at *1. Pennsylvania's 1790 constitution omitted any reference to "unusual," providing "[t]hat excessive bail shall not be required, nor excessive fines imposed, nor cruel punishments inflicted." Pa. Const. art. IX, § XIII (1790).

123. The Fourteenth Amendment was not ratified until 1868. Charles Wallace Collins, The Fourteenth Amendment and the States: A Study of the Operation of the Restraint Clauses of Section One of the Fourteenth Amendment to the Constitution of the United States 7 (1912). And the Eighth Amendment was not held applicable to the states until 1962. *See* Robinson v. California, 370 U.S. 660 (1962).

124. The "selective incorporation" doctrine has gradually applied various guarantees of the U.S. Bill of Rights against the states. Milton R. Konvitz, Fundamental Rights: History of a Constitutional Doctrine 84 (2011) (listing constitutional rights, including the right to be free from cruel and unusual punishment, selectively incorporated against the states via the Fourteenth Amendment).

125. *James*, 1825 WL 1899, at *2. Elsewhere in the *James* decision, it was noted: "*Common scolding* has been recognised as an indictable offence in two of our sister states, New York and Massachusetts; and though it was in both held to be punishable only by fine and imprisonment, that might be under peculiar provisions of their laws or constitutions, which would not affect a decision in Pennsylvania." Id. at *4.

126. Id. at *2.

127. Id.

128. Id.

129. Id. The opinion in *James* describes James' counsel's efforts as follows:

To prove that it was disused, even in England, the counsel referred to the case of Regina v. Foxby, 6 Mod. 11, which occurred a few years after the first settlement of this state. Lord HOLT there makes a jest of the matter, and the defendant was permitted to escape, on promise of future good behavior. Later English writers mention ducking as existing only in the memory of a few superannuated persons, and speak of the mouldering ruins of that formidable engine, the *ducking-stool*, as one of the vestiges of a barbarous antiquity.

But supposing this punishment existed at common law, was in full force in England, at the period of William Penn's emigration, and was introduced by his followers into the new province: still the counsel contended the common law had been altered in this particular by the colonists themselves. The attention of the legislature was early attracted to this matter, and we find several laws on this subject in the first years of the infant colony. In 1682, the first years of the settlement, it was enacted by the 34th section of "the great law," that scolding should be punished by "three days' imprisonment." In 1683, the punishment for this offence was changed to "*gagging,*" or five shillings fine. In 1700, the legislature again altered this punishment to "five days' imprisonment, or gagging, or five shillings fine." It is true, that this last act was repealed by the queen in council; but that revived the act of 1683, which never having been repealed since, is now in force, and therefore, superseded the provisions of the common law upon this subject.

Id.

130. Id. James' counsel also argued his client's sentence was too severe, especially in light of the cold weather. Id. at *3. The record records counsel's argument as follows:

[H]e contended that whatever the law might be, there was no precedent or authority for that part of the sentence, which directed the prisoner to be "plunged *three times* into the water." The sheriff would be liable to an action of trespass, if he did not execute the sentence exactly; and if the old woman should die, in consequence of such severe treatment, at this inclement season, the judges who had pronounced the illegal sentence, might be held responsible for her death.

Id.

131. Id.

132. Id.

133. Id. at *4; *see also* Meghan J. Ryan, *Does the Eighth Amendment Punishments Clause Prohibit Only Punishments that are Both Cruel and Unusual?*, 87 Wash. U. L. Rev. 567, 609 (2010) ("The Pennsylvania Constitution omitted the unusualness component of the Clause altogether, providing '[t]hat excessive bail shall not be required, nor excessive fines imposed, nor cruel punishments inflicted.' ").

134. *James*, 1825 WL 1899, at *4.

135. *E.g.*, 1 T. B. Howell, A Complete Collection of State Trials and Proceedings for High Treason and Other Crimes and Misdemeanors from the Earliest Period to the Year 1783, with Notes and Other Illustrations xxxii (1816) ("There is one thing in our Laws which is very singular, and comes the nearest of any thing to the Tortures used in other countries, *viz. le Peine fort et dure*, or, pressing to death: 'Tis true, this is not used to force the Prisoner to confess, but to plead one way or other; but yet even this seems a needless piece of severity.").

136. Laurence Claus, *The Antidiscrimination Eighth Amendment*, 28 Harv. J.L. & Pub. Pol'y 119, 131 (2004) (noting that, after reciting the "cruel and unusual punishments" language of the Virginia Declaration of Rights, Patrick Henry asked rhetorically: What has distinguished our ancestors?—That they would not admit of tortures, or cruel and barbarous punishment."); id. (noting that when George Nicholas contended that the declaration of rights had not succeeded in preventing torture, George Mason—the drafter of the Virginia Declaration of Rights—refuted that, replying: "Another clause of the bill of rights provided that no cruel and unusual punishments shall be inflicted; therefore, torture was included in the prohibition.").

137. John D. Bessler, The Death Penalty as Torture: From the Dark Ages to Abolition 11, 146–47 (2017).

138. The State of Pennsylvania divided murder into degrees in 1794. *E.g.*, David C. Brody & James R. Acker, Criminal Law 212 (2010):

Initially, no discrimination was made between different kinds of murder, and that crime automatically was punished by death. Pennsylvania legislators thought this approach to be excessively harsh and inflexible. In 1794 they passed an innovative statute dividing murder into first degree, which remained a capital crime, and second degree, which was not punished capitally.

The death penalty, however, remained in use in Pennsylvania. *E.g.*, Mitchel P. Roth, Crime and Punishment: A History of the Criminal Justice System 111 (2010).

139. *James*, 1825 WL 1899, at *4.

140. Id.

141. Id. "These cases," it was reported, "occurred a few years prior to the year 1790, when the assembly, sitting in this city, new-modelled the penal code of the state, and after abolishing many of the common-law punishments, concluded by declaring, that 'every other felony or misdemeanor whatsoever, not specially provided for by that act, may and shall be punished as heretofore.'" Id. The case report continued:

As the offence of "scolding" is *not* specially provided for by the act of 1790, the Attorney-General insisted that this was an express legislative sanction of the common-law punishment, which had been recently and publicly inflicted in the place where the assembly was then sitting. Moreover, as this offence is not punishable by fine or imprisonment at common law, ducking is the only penalty that can be inflicted in the absence of positive enactment.

Id. (italics in original). In reply, counsel for James argued that "none of the judges who pronounced those sentences" for scolding, which had been drawn from the records of the quarter sessions, "were lawyers." Id. "[T]his court," he insisted, "was not bound to receive as law, their crude and ill-digested opinions on this subject." Id.; *compare* William H. Loyd, The Early Courts of Pennsylvania 89 n.1 (1910):

It is a matter of some doubt as to whether the ducking-stool ever was actually used in Philadelphia. In 1769 a woman was sentenced to be ducked at the end of Market street wharf, but we are not informed whether the sentence was carried into execution. In 1779 Ann Mease was sentenced to the same punishment but the council remitted the ducking January 26, 1780. XII Colonial Records, 235. In 1781 there was another conviction but the sentence was not carried out.

142. Peter S. Du Ponceau, A Dissertation on the Nature and Extent of the Jurisdiction of the Courts of the United States, Being a Valedictory Address Delivered to the Students of the Law Academy of Philadelphia, at the Close of the Academic Year, on the 22nd of April, 1824 (1824) (published in Philadelphia by Abraham Small and dedicated "To the Honourable William Tilghman, LL.D., Chief Justice of the Supreme Court of the Commonwealth of Pennsylvania, and Patron of the Law Academy of Philadelphia"). That dissertation itself distinguished the *American* prohibition on cruel and unusual punishments from the earlier one contained in the *English* Bill of Rights. In his dissertation, Peter Du Ponceau wrote of "certain harsh punishments which our modern manners reprove, but which still stain the page of the common law; as for instance the punishment of petty treason in men by drawing and quartering, and in women by burning." Id. at 95. He then wrote this about the difference between American and English law:

But the 10th amendment of our Constitution has sufficiently provided that "no cruel and unusual punishment shall be inflicted," which word "unusual" evidently refers to the United States, and the time when the Constitution was made, and therefore is not to be confounded with the same clause in the English bill of rights, which referring to another period and to another country, may have been differently construed. The *peine forte and dure*, and burning in the hand in cases of manslaughter are abolished, and milder substitutes provided by our national statutes; corruption of blood, trial by battle, all other modes of trial, but trial by jury in criminal cases are also abolished; in short the common law as modified by our Constitution, by our laws, manners and usages, is as wholesome and as harmless a system, in criminal as well as in civil cases, as any that can be devised.

Id. at 95–96. As Du Ponceau's *Dissertation* then continued:

As to offences not capital, cruel and unusual punishments being forbidden by our Constitution, there remains none but fine, imprisonment and, perhaps, whipping and the pillory. I hope I shall hear nothing of the ducking stool and other obsolete remains of the customs of barbarous ages. The pillory and whipping, I know, are out of use in most of the States, imprisonment at hard labour having been substituted in lieu of them. Yet Congress have thought proper to retain the latter punishment in their penal code, and we have seen it inflicted not long since in our city on an offender against the laws of the United States. It is in the power of the national Legislature to alter or amend the law in this respect, as they shall think proper; but until they do so, I see nothing inhuman in the moderate infliction of either of these penalties, nor any reason why we should reject the common law on their account.

It may be said, perhaps, that there is too much left to the discretion of the Judges as to the quantum, and even the nature of the punishment and sometimes also as to deciding what is or what is not an indictable act. As to the quantum of punishment, I know no system of laws in which some discretion at least is not left to the Court according to the greater or lesser magnitude of the offence. It is impossible to avoid this inconvenience by any legislation. The same thing may be said of the authority to choose between two or three mild punishments; there may be cases in which imprisonment would be death to the party, and when a fine may be inflicted upon him with greater effect; others when the reverse may be the case.

Id. at 96–97. The pillory and the whipping post were once usual punishments in colonial and early America. PETER C. HOLLORAN, HISTORICAL DICTIONARY OF NEW ENGLAND 496 (2d ed. 2017) ("Boston last used the pillory in 1803."); HOWARD O. SPROGLE, THE PHILADELPHIA POLICE, PAST AND PRESENT 56 (1887):

Fraud sent men to the pillory and workhouse. The last remembered exhibition of this kind was that of a storekeeper, who, to build up his failing credit, made too free use with other people's names. He was exposed in the pillory, where the populace pelted him with eggs, and, to conclude, had his ears clipped by the sheriff, who held up his ghastly trophies to the gaze and shouts of the populace. Whipping was the usual punishment for larceny and for felonious assaults.

143. *James*, 1825 WL 1899, at *5.

144. Id.

145. Id.

146. Id. That Act declared: "in all cases where a remedy is provided or a duty enjoined, or anything directed to be done by any act or acts of assembly of this commonwealth, the directions of the said acts shall be strictly pursued, and no penalty shall be inflicted or anything done agreeably to the provisions of the common law, in such cases, further than shall be necessary for carrying such act or acts into effect." Id.

147. Id. In response to Du Ponceau's arguments, the record reflects that counsel for the state argued as follows:

The Attorney-General replied, that only part of "the great law," had been agreed upon in England, and that the provision with respect to scolds, among others, was not added until after the arrival in this country; as would be seen, by a reference to the printed copy of the laws agreed upon in England. As to the act of assembly of 1806, it expressly recognises the common law, and depends upon it in cases not otherwise provided for; and the present is one of those cases, for although it may have been regulated by statutes, they are not now in force, and the common law rules must, therefore, prevail. He had already referred to some of the latest English elementary writers, to show that *ducking* is still recognised there, as the punishment for *common scolding*.

Id. (italics in original).

148. 9 THE PAPERS OF THOMAS JEFFERSON, RETIREMENT SERIES 179 (J. Jefferson Looney, ed., 2012); PAPERS OF JOHN ADAMS 411 n.5 (Gregg L. Lint, et al., eds., 2010); FROM *LEX MERCATORIA* TO COMMERCIAL LAW 38 (Vito Piergiovanni, ed. 2005); ROBERT M. RIFFLE, THE MIRACLE OF INDEPENDENCE 197 (2009).

149. THE PAPERS OF THOMAS JEFFERSON, *supra* note 148, at 179; C. H. FORBES–LINDSAY, WASHINGTON: THE CITY AND THE SEAT OF GOVERNMENT 389 (1908); "John Pickering," 45 The Nation 255, 256 (Sept. 29, 1887); GEORGE S. BROOKES, FRIEND ANTHONY BENEZET 385 n.4 (1937).

150. THE PAPERS OF THOMAS JEFFERSON, *supra* note 148, at 179; 1 THE DOCUMENTARY HISTORY OF THE SUPREME COURT OF THE UNITED STATES, 1789–1800, at 189 n.82 (1985).

151. STEPHEN HESS, AMERICA'S POLITICAL DYNASTIES: FROM ADAMS TO CLINTON 86, 103–105, 108, 115–17 (2016); CHARLES HAVENS HUNT, LIFE OF EDWARD LIVINGSTON 157, 179, 222, 236, 287, 289–94 (1864).

152. 7 THE DOCUMENTARY HISTORY OF THE SUPREME COURT OF THE UNITED STATES, 1789–1800, at 20 (Maeva Marcus, ed. 2003); THE PAPERS OF THOMAS JEFFERSON, *supra* note 148, at 179; 5 THE DOCUMENTARY HISTORY OF THE SUPREME COURT OF THE UNITED STATES, 1789–1800, at 483 (Maeva Marcus, ed., 1994); ARTHUR E. PALUMBO, THE AUTHENTIC CONSTITUTION: AN ORIGINALIST VIEW OF AMERICA'S LEGACY 227 & n.1 (2009).

153. PETER S. DU PONCEAU, A BRIEF VIEW OF THE CONSTITUTION OF THE UNITED STATES, ADDRESSED TO LAW ACADEMY OF PHILADELPHIA xi, 51–56, 68–85 (1834).

154. ANTHONY F. C. WALLACE, JEFFERSON AND THE INDIANS: THE TRAGIC FATE OF THE FIRST AMERICANS 319 (1999); DEBRA J. ALLEN, HISTORICAL DICTIONARY OF U.S. DIPLOMACY FROM THE

Revolution to Secession 86 (2012); Philadelphia: A Guide to the Nation's Birthplace 288 (1937) (compiled by the Federal Writers' Project Works Progress Administration for the Commonwealth of Pennsylvania).

155. 2 Joan Leopold, ed., The Prix Volney: Early Nineteenth-Century Contributions to American Indian and General Linguistics: Du Ponceau and Rafinesque 1–2 (2000); *see also* 2 J. Thomas Scharf & Thompson Westcott, History of Philadelphia, 1609–1888, at 1532–33 (1884).

156. *James*, 1825 WL 1899, at *5.

157. Id.

158. Id.

159. *See* 17 Thomas Sergeant & William Rawle, eds., Reports of Cases Adjudged in the Supreme Court of Pennsylvania 459 (3d ed. 1874) (describing Thomas Duncan's legal career).

160. *James*, 1825 WL 1899, at *5 (italics in original). In fact, the use of ducking had a very long history, dating back centuries. *E.g.*, Pettifer, *supra* note 4, at 104 ("The history of the ducking-stool goes back, at least, to Norman times, and one of the duties of the Court Leet was to examine the state of repair of the ducking-stool, the pillory and the stocks, but it is extremely likely that the history goes back to far earlier days."); Stephano Skinner, Etymologicon Linguæ Anglicanæ, Seu Explicatio vocum Anglicarum Etymologica ex propriis fontibus, feil. ex Linguis duodecim (1671) (referencing "Cucking-stool" and "Ducking-stool").

161. *James*, 1825 WL 1899, at *6.

162. Id. "There is a tradition," Justice Duncan offered in his opinion, "that at the publication of Bracton's learned work, in which the dimension of this instrument of correction was first stated, the women of the town in which he lived, seized him and ducked him in a horse-pond." Id. Bracton, a thirteenth-century English jurist, wrote a long treatise, *De legibus et consuetudinibus Angliea* (On the Laws and Customs of England) that attempted to describe the whole of English law. *Bracton Online*, Harv. L. Sch. Libr., bracton.law.harvard.edu (last visited Feb. 26, 2018). In it, Bracton spoke of the "ducking-stool." 2 Henry de Bracton, On the Laws and Customs of England 290, 299, 340 (Samuel E. Thorne, trans., 1968).

163. *James*, 1825 WL 1899, at *5.

164. Id.

165. Black's Law Dictionary 188 (10th ed. 2014) (citing State v. Bosse, 42 S.C.L. (8 Rich.) 276 (1855)).

166. Walter Scott, The Poetical Works of Sir Walter Scott 11 n.* (1868).

167. As Justice Duncan noted:

The punishment of the ducking or cucking-stool, is from the cuckoo, "*qui odiose jurgat et rixatur,* as Lord COKE has it, in 3 Inst. 219; or, as Jacob has it, in his dictionary, the gogen-stool, and by some thought to be corrupted from the choke-stool; and the instrument is called in Stat. 51 Hen. III., a trebucket, a pitfall, and in law, as Lord COKE says, signifies a stool that falls into a pit of water; whereas, the last instrument that was seen in England, as Morgan, an editor of Jacob's Dictionary mentions, consisted of a beam or rafter, moving on a fulcrum, and extending to the centre of a large pond, on which end the stool used to be placed; while, on the other hand, Daines Barrington, a learned antiquarian, in his Observations on the Statutes 40, says, it is a machine anciently used in the siege of towns, and the etymology is from the Celtic, *tre,* that is, *ville,* and our own bucket, and signifies a town-bucket.

James, 1825 WL 1899, at *6.

In *A Law Grammar; or, An Introduction to the Theory and Practice of English Jurisprudence* (1791), the term "Castigatory" was similarly described as "the name of the instrument by which a woman is punished when convicted of being a common scold." "It is also," that source added in its section on terms of law, "called *the trebucket* or *cucking-stool,* which is frequently corrupted into *ducking-stool,* because part of the judgment is, that when the offender is placed in it, she shall be plunged into water." That law grammar did go on to point out that "this mode of punishment has been long disused." As evidence, the book cited to a "Mr. Morgan," the editor of the popular law dictionary originally complied by Giles Jacob, in which it was stated in the entry for "Castigatory for *scolds*" by Mr. Morgan: "Though this punishment is now disused, the editor (*J. M.*) remembers to have seen the remains of one, on the estate of a relation of his in *Warwickshire,* consisting of a long beam, or rafter moving on a fulcrum, and extending to the centre of a large pond, on which end the stool used to be placed." A Law Grammar; or, An Introduction to the Theory and Practice of English Jurisprudence 535 (1791); *compare* Giles Jacob, A New Law-Dictionary: Containing, the Interpretation and Definition of Words and Terms Used in the Law; and Also the Whole Law, and the Practice Thereof, under All the Heads and Titles of the Same (6th ed. 1750) (the unpaginated entry for "Cuckingstool" describes it as "an Engine invented for the Punishment of *Scolds*, and unquiet Women, by Ducking them in Water," called in ancient Time a *Tumbrel*; and sometimes a *Trebucket*"; "it was in Use even in our *Saxons* Times, by whom it was described to be *Cathedra*"; "[s]ome think it is a Corruption from *Duckingstool*") *with* Giles Jacob, comp., A New Law-Dictionary: Containing the Interpretation and Definition of Words and Terms Used in the Law; as Also the Law and Practice, under the Proper Heads and Titles (10th ed. J. Morgan, ed., 1782) (containing unpaginated entries for "Cuckingstool" and "Castigatory for *scolds*" and the editor's notation about the disuse of the punishment).

168. *James*, 1825 WL 1899, at *7.

169. Justice Duncan, in discussing England's experience with the punishment, put it this way:

From the country from which, it is suggested, we have borrowed it, we could obtain no information, nor expect a model, for not a vestige of it is there to be found; unless, perhaps, alongside of the rack (the Duke of Exeter's daughter), which is still shown as a curiosity, by a yeoman of the King's guard, as an instrument of punishment, which, like the trebucket, was once used in England (Barrington 366); for no poor woman, in that country, has suffered under the edge of a law so barbarous, for the last century; like unscoured armor, it is hung up by the wall; like the law of witchcraft, it has remained unused; for no one has suffered under that law, either at the stake or on the gibbet, since the reign of Charles II.; although the law stood unrepealed on the statute book, until 9 Geo. II., as our own law against the same offence, until several years after the revolution; or, like the act against the gypsies, which punished those with death, without the benefit of clergy, who remained one month within the realm; and Lord HALE, in his Pleas of the Crown 671, says, "I have not known these statutes put much in execution, only about twenty years since, at the assizes at Bury, about thirteen were condemned and executed for this offence. On this judgment, BLACKSTONE, 4th vol. 166, remarks, "but to the honor of our national humanity, there are no instances more modern."

Id.

170. Id. Charles I was executed in 1649, and England—during the interregnum (1649–1660)—was then governed by a commonwealth government headed by Oliver Cromwell, a cavalry officer and a Puritan member of the Long Parliament who rose to prominence during the English Civil War (1642–1649). The Restoration (1660–1685) began after Charles II, at age 30, claimed his father's throne after a period of exile following the death of Oliver Cromwell. 1 Thomas F. X. Noble, Barry Strauss, Duane J. Osheim, Kristen B. Neuschel, Elinor A. Accampo, David D. Roberts & William B. Cohen, Western Civilization: Beyond Boundaries 455–58 (6th ed. 2011). William Penn's charter for Pennsylvania came in 1682. *See* Paul E. Doutrich, To Form a More Perfect Union: The Federal Constitution and Pennsylvania 18 (1986) ("From the time of William Penn's Charter of Liberties in 1682, Pennsylvania had developed a philosophical foundation upon which a democratic republic could be established. By the time of independence, the State had become one of the foremost proponents of liberty.").

171. *James*, 1825 WL 1899, at *7.

172. Id. at *8.

173. Id. *Non-user* is defined as "neglect to use" or "[t]he neglect to make use of a thing." Henry Campbell Black, A Law Dictionary 828 (2d ed. 1910); 2 John Bouvier, A Law Dictionary, Adapted to the Constitution and Laws of the United States of America, and of the Several States of the American Union: with References to the Civil and Other Systems of Foreign Law 303 (1891). *See also* id. ("Non-user for a great length of time will have the effect of repealing an old law. But it must be a very strong one which will have that effect."); Richard Burn & John Burn, New Law Dictionary: Intended for General Use as well as for Gentlemen of the Profession 385 (1792) ("Forfeiture may accrue ... by ... *non-user*.... By *non-user*; for if one hath liberties, and doth not use them within memory, they are lost."); O'Hanlan v. Myers, 44 S.C.L. (10 Rich.) 128, 130–31 (1856) (an act may become inoperative through non-user or disuse, such as sitting publicly in the stocks).

174. *James*, 1825 WL 1899, at *8. Duncan's opinion was as follows:

Mr. Woodeson, in his second lecture (vol. 1st, 63) of civil, positive and instituted laws, observes, "that the last consideration is the period of their existence;" they may be repealed either expressly or by implication founded on disuse: he cites this passage from the Digest, " *rectissime illud receptum est—ut magis non solus suffragio legislatorum, sed etiam tacito consensu omnium, per desuetudinem abrogatur.* It certainly requires very strong grounds to presume a law obsolete, yet as the whole community includes as well the legislative power as its subjects, total disuse of any civil institution for ages past, may afford just and rational objections against disrespected and superannuated ordinances. Judge WILSON (2d Wilson's Works 38, 39), observes, "that it is the characteristic of a system of common law, that it may be accommodated to the circumstances, the exigencies and the conveniences of the people by whom it is appointed. Now, as these circumstances, exigencies and conveniences silently change, a proportionate change in time and in degree must take place in the accommodated system. Time silently and gradually introduces; it silently and gradually withdraws its customary laws."

Id.

175. Id.

176. Id. Bills of attainder—once frequently used by legislators to sentence people to death in the absence of judicial proceedings—were outlawed by the U.S. Constitution. As *Black's Law Dictionary* summarizes their prohibition by law:

1. *Archaic.* A special legislative act that imposes a death sentence on a person without a trial. 2. A special legislative act prescribing punishment, without a trial, for a specific purpose or group. • Bills of attainder are prohibited by the U.S. Constitution (art. I, § 9, cl. 3; art. I, § 10, cl. 1).

Bills of attainder, Black's Law Dictionary 198 (10th ed. 2014). "At common law," an attainder was "the act of extinguishing a person's civil rights when that person" was "sentenced to death or declared an outlaw for committing a felony or treason." Id. at 152. " 'The word *attainder* is derived from the Latin term *attinctus*, signifying *stained* or *polluted*, and includes, in its meaning, all those disabilities which flow from a capital sentence. On the attainder, the defendant is disqualified to be a witness in any court; he can bring no action, nor perform any of the legal functions which before he was admitted to discharge; he is, in short regarded as dead in law.' " Id. (quoting 1 Joseph Chitty, A Practical Treatise on the Criminal Law 725 (2d ed. 1826)).

177. *James*, 1825 WL 1899, at *8.

178. Id. Such judicial reasoning calls to mind Thomas Jefferson's own words: "laws and institutions must go hand in hand with the progress of the human mind" so that such institutions "keep pace with the times." *Letter to Samuel Kercheval*, TeachingAmericanHistory.org, http://teachingamericanhistory.org/library/document/letter-to-samuel-kercheval/ (last visited Feb. 26, 2018). As Jefferson wrote in his 1816 letter: "We might as well require a man to wear still the coat which fitted him when a boy, as civilized society to remain ever under the regimen of their barbarous ancestors." Id.

179. The opinion in *James* stated as follows:

Lambarde, who first published his Treatise on the Office of Justice of the Peace, in 1581, lib. i. ch. 12, states that corporal punishments are either *capital*, or not *capital*; that capital are inflicted "sundrie ways; as by hanging, burning, boiling, pressing: not capital, are of divers sorts, as cutting off the hand or ear, burning or branding the hand, face, shoulders, whipping, imprisonment, stocking, sitting in the pillory, or on the cucking-stool." Of this kind of punishment our old laws had more sorts than we now have; as pulling out the tongue for false rumors, cutting off the nose, and for adultery, taking away the privy parts. So they had more sorts of punishments, when Lambarde wrote, than we now have. Blessed be GOD! I feel a conviction (and I have examined every book upon which I could lay my hands), that there is no judicial record, certainly no report, of this punishment being inflicted for more than one hundred years. The case in 2 Strange 849, The King v. Taylor, was quashed generally; it was not against her as *communis vexatrix*, but as *calumniatrix et communis perturbatrix;* and in The King v. Margaret Cooper, *Id.* 1246, the judgment was not rendered as for a common scold; and the last of them was as long ago as 19 Geo. II., nearly eighty years ago.

James, 1825 WL 1899, at *8.

180. Id. at *9:

In the Queen v. Foxby, 6 Mod. 11, in the second of Anne, the judgment was likewise arrested for mistake in the indictment. The note of the reporter is, the punishment of a scold is ducking, but the counsel for the prisoner said, "he knew no law for ducking of scolds." Lord HOLT did not give any opinion as to the judgment; he only mentioned that it was indictable in the *Leet, "and that it was better ducking in a Trinity* than a *Michaelmas* term;" better in warm than in cold weather. But it was too much even for the gravity of the grave and learned Chief Justice of the King's Bench, to treat the subject with any solemnity. In page 178, she was brought up again (for the sheriff had let her go at large), and the court let her run again until the next term. HOLT could not conceal his contempt for this farce of ducking; he sneered at the trebucket, declaring that ducking would only harden the criminal; and, if she were once ducked, she would scold all the days of her life. I think, that the trebucket then made its final exit, or afterwards was only heard of in the courts of justice, as John Doe and Richard Roe, pledges of prosecution; a mere nominal thing.

181. Id.:

Judge WILSON, certainly a learned and eminent person, to whom the state committed the revision of her laws, in his third volume, page 311, treats the trebucket with the same contempt with which Lord HOLT had done before him. After giving the judgment against a common scold, in a public lecture, he sneeringly says—"so she shall be plunged into the water, by way of punishment and prevention;" and thus scornfully winds up the trebucket—"our modern men of gallantry would not surely decline the honor of her company; I therefore humbly propose, that in future, the cucking-stool shall be made to hold double." And those only who knew that great man, can form an idea what that look of scorn was. This cucking-stool was a species of the *tumbrellum;* Lord COKE laments that there was no good *Latin* word for the dung-cart, and says, that the pillory and the trebucket were of the dung-cart family.

182. 1 Bird Wilson, ed., The Works of the Honourable James Wilson, L. L. D.: Late One of the Associate Justices of the Supreme Court of the United States, and Professor of Law in the College of Philadelphia xi (1804).

183. *James*, 1825 WL 1899, at *10. Duncan noted that a "cucking-stool" had been defined as "an engine, invented for the punishment of scolding and unquiet women." *Id.* He then proceeded to explain the rationale in earlier years for this instrument of punishment:

Very possibly, as both men and women were, in those days, rude and disorderly, the women were put in the trebucket and the men in the pillory, for disturbing or making a noise in this great court; and Lord COKE, 3 Inst. 219, says, "*furea, pillore et tumbrel appendant al view de frank-pledge,* and every one who hath a leet or market, ought to have a pillory and trebucket to punish offenders; for want whereof, the lord may be fined, or his liberty seized.

Id.

184. In support of this proposition, Duncan gave the following recitation of authorities:

Barrington says, it was a punishment formerly used in this country, for female offenders, and not confined to the offence of scolding; and Jacob says, the punishment is disused. Mr. Morgan, one of his editors, informs us, that he saw the remains of one, on a private estate, in Warwickshire; and Mr. Tomlins, in his last edition of this work, mentions there had been one, which had lately been removed, at Banbury, in Oxfordshire, but that was not a machine for legal punishment, but was used to make sport for the mob, in ducking common women; for this usage, this propensity to ducking women, was pretty inveterate. Old women were generally ducked by the common people, by way of primary or experimental trial, before they were delivered over to the civil magistrate to be hanged as witches; many of the accused died under the experiment. This does not depend on a work of fiction (many of which, in the present day, present the real manners and habits of the times in which they lay the scenes), but on authentic history.

Id.

185. Id. In 1828, Noah Webster, citing Blackstone, defined "DUCKING-STOOL" as "[a] stool or chair in which common scolds were formerly tied and plunged into water." 1 Noah Webster, An American Dictionary of the English Language (1828); *see also Ducking stool,* Dictionary of Sociology 99 (Henry Pratt Fairchild, ed., 2014):

A stool or chair in which common scolds were formerly tied and plunged into water. It is mentioned in the Doomsday Book, and was extensively used throughout Great Britain from the 15th to the beginning of the 18th century. The last recorded instance of it was in England in 1809.

38 Abraham Rees, The Cyclopædia; or, Universal Dictionary of Arts, Sciences, and Literature (1819) (noting in the entry for "WOOTTON-BASSET" that in a "town-hall" there was lately preserved "a machine, called a 'cucking or ducking-stool,' formerly used for the punishment of female scolds"); Pettifer, *supra* note 4, at 104, at 106:

There seems to be some conflict as to when the ducking-stool was last used in England. Horsfall Turner says he cannot find any record in Yorkshire after 1745: another writer thinks its used persisted until 1770, but William Andrews gives two instances in the nineteenth century, at Plymouth in 1808, and in 1809 at Leominster. In 1817, a woman was sentenced to be ducked at Leominster, and was wheeled round the town in the chair, but was not ducked, as the water, luckily for her, was too low.

186. *James*, 1825 WL 1899, at *10 (italics in original). James Wilson, the American founder, spoke in his law lectures of the varied language used to describe the devices used to punish common scolds, even using a little satire in discussing the very idea of the punishment. 3 Bird Wilson, ed., The Works of the Honourable James Wilson, L. L. D.: Late One of the Associate Justices of the Supreme Court of the United States, and Professor of Law in the College of Philadelphia 110–11 (1804):

A common scold, says the law, is a publick nuisance to her neighbourhood: as such she may be indicted, and, if convicted, shall be placed in a certain engine of correction, called the trebucket, castigatory, or *cucking* stool; which, in the Saxon language, signifies the scolding stool; though now it is frequently corrupted into *ducking* stool; because the residue of the sentence against her is, that when she is thus placed, she shall be plunged in the water—for the purpose of prevention, it is presumed, as well as of punishment.

Our modern man of gallantry would not surely decline the honour of her company. I therefore propose humbly, that, in future, the cucking stools shall be made to hold double.

The language Wilson used to describe the ducking stool came in part from Sir William Blackstone.

187. *James*, 1825 WL 1899, at *10. The practice of ducking had a long history, though it eventually passed from the scene. As one English source notes, the ducking-stool "was in use in the parish and town of Liverpool" "[a]s recently as the beginning of the eighteenth century." John Harland & T. T. Wilkinson, Lancashire Legends, Traditions, Pageants, Sports, &c. with an Appendix Containing a Rare Tract on the Lancashire Witches, &c. &c. 167 (1873); *see also id.* at 169 ("The ducking-stool, according to Mr Richard Brooks' 'Liverpool from 1775 to 1800,' was in use in 1779, by the authority of the magistrates, in the House of Correction, which formerly stood upon Mount Pleasant, in that town.").

188. Act of Apr. 5, 1790, *reprinted in* 3 Laws of the Commonwealth of Pennsylvania 440–54 (1803).

189. Id. §4. Prior to 1790, Pennsylvania law explicitly authorized ear cropping, public whipping, and the pillory. *See, e.g.*, Act of Mar. 21, 1772, *reprinted in* 2 Laws of the Commonwealth of Pennsylvania 55–56 (1803) (any person or persons breaking and entering a house at night "shall stand in the pillory during the space of one hour, have his, her or their ears cut off, and nailed to the pillory, be publicly whipped with thirty-nine lashes on the bare back, well laid on"); Act of Feb. 26, 1773, *reprinted in* 2 Laws of the Commonwealth of Pennsylvania 82–83 (1803) (counterfeiters "shall be sentenced to the pillory, and have both his or her ears cut off, and nailed to the pillory, and be publicly whipped on his or her bare back, with thirty-one lashes, well laid on"); Act of Mar. 10, 1780, *reprinted in* 2 Laws of the Commonwealth of Pennsylvania 255–56 (1803) (any person or persons guilty of stealing a horse "for the first offence, shall stand in the pillory for one hour, and shall be publicly whipped on his, her or their backs with thirty-nine lashes, well laid on, and at the same time shall have his, her or their ears cut off, and nailed to the pillory; and for the second offence shall be whipped and pillored in like manner, and be branded on the forehead, in a plain and visible manner, with the letters H. T."); Act of Mar. 16, 1785, *reprinted in* 3 Laws of the Commonwealth of Pennsylvania 24–25 (1803) (counterfeiters "shall be sentenced to the pillory, and to have both his or her ears cut off, and nailed to the pillory").

190. Justice Duncan noted:

[T]he wisdom, humanity, and policy of our Pennsylvania plan, has crossed the Atlantic. England, attached as she is to her own system, has adopted ours; and very lately, by stat. 56 Geo. III., has abolished pillory in all cases but perjury and subornation of perjury. Long before, to the honor of her humanity, in the case of punishments inflicted for clergyable offences, she had extended the benefit of clergy to women, provided that the whipping should be in private, and in the presence of the female sex alone, 19 Geo. II., ch. 26; and I believe the punishment of whipping, as to females, has been altogether abolished.

James, 1825 WL 1899, at *10.

191. David Nordquest, "Madison and Philosophy: His Coursework and His Statesmanship," *in* John R. Vile, William D. Pederson & Frank J. Williams, eds., James Madison: Philosopher, Founder, and Statesman 3 (2008) (discussing James Madison's studies at the College of New Jersey, now Princeton, and his friendship with William Bradford).

192. Bessler, Cruel and Unusual, *supra* note 2, at 85.

193. Jared Ingersoll served as Pennsylvania's attorney general from 1790 to 1799 and also from 1811 to 1817. Robert J. Lukens, *Jared Ingersoll's Rejection of Appointment as One of the "Midnight Judges" of 1801: Foolhardy or Farsighted?*, 70 Temp. L. Rev. 189, 203–05 (1997). In 1821, Ingersoll became the presiding judge of the District Court for the City and County of Philadelphia, but died a year later. Id.

194. *James*, 1825 WL 1899, at *11.

195. *Id.* Noting the Quaker heritage of Pennsylvania, Justice Duncan added:

The sanguinary code of England could be no favorite with William Penn and his followers, who fled from persecution. Cruel punishments were not likely to be introduced by a society who denied the right to touch the life of man, even for the most atrocious crime. For had they brought with them the whole body of the British criminal law, then we should have had the appeal of death, and the impious spectacle of a trial by battle in a Quaker colony; and it is worthy of remembrance, that the charter of William Penn empowered him with the advice and assent of the freemen, to make laws for their own government, and until this was done, the laws of England, in respect to real and personal property, and as to *felonies* were to continue the same. Thus, as to misdemeanors, the common-law punishments were not brought over by the first settlers.

Id.

196. *See also* Aldridge v. Commonwealth, 4 Va. (2 Va. Cas.) 447, 450 (Va. Gen. Ct. 1824):

When this Bill of Rights was declared ... we knew that the best heads and hearts of the land of our ancestors, had long and loudly declaimed against the wanton cruelty of many of the punishments practised in other countries; and this section in the Bill of Rights, was framed effectively to exclude these, so that no future Legislature, in a moment perhaps of great and general excitement, should be tempted to disgrace our Code by the introduction of any of those odious modes of punishment.

197. *James*, 1825 WL 1899, at *11.

198. Id.

199. Id.

200. Id.

201. Id. "It is not true," Duncan held, "that our ancestors brought with them all the common-law offences; for instance, that of champerty and maintenance, this court decided in *Stoever v. Whitman's Lessee*, 6 Binn. 416, did not exist here." Id. at *12.

202. Id. William Tilghman served as the Chief Justice of the Pennsylvania Supreme Court from 1806 until his death in 1827. Peter Stephen Du Ponceau, Eulogium in Commemoration of the Honourable William Tilghman, LL.D.: Chief Justice of the Supreme Court of Pennsylvania, and President of the American Philosophical Society, Held at Philadelphia, for Promoting Useful Knowledge 23 (1827) ("Mr. Tilghman was appointed to the office of Chief Justice, on the 26th of February, 1806, and held it during the space of 21 years, to the time of his death."); 2 David Hoffman, A Course of Legal Study, Addressed to Students and the Profession Generally 646 (1836) (noting that William Tilghman was born in 1756 and died in 1827).

203. 5 Binn. 554, 558 (Pa. 1813).

204. *James*, 1825 WL 1899, at *12.

205. Id. Jurist Samuel Chase, in *United States v. Worrall*, 2 U.S. (2 Dall.) 384 (1798), on the same subject, expressed himself in this fashion:

When the American colonies were first settled by our ancestors, it was held, as well among the settlers, as by the judges and lawyers of England, that they brought hither, as their birthright and inheritance, so much of the common law as was applicable to their local situation and change of circumstances; but each colony judged for itself what part of the common law was applicable to its new condition, and by various modes—by legislative acts, by judicial decisions, or *by constant usage*—adopted some parts and rejected others.

Id. at 394.

206. 1 Kara E. Stooksbury et al., eds., Encyclopedia of American Civil Rights and Liberties 80 (2d ed. 2017):

The English Bill of Rights of 1689, also called the Declaration of Right, was a product of the Glorious, or Bloodless, Revolution of 1688 and marked a significant development in English constitutional history. William III's acceptance of the declaration and its passage by Parliament officially subjugated the English monarch to parliamentary law. In addition, the declaration contains some provisions protecting individual civil rights. Like the Magna Carta, it remains one of the core documents of the English constitution.

207. Vishnoo Bhagwan & Vidya Bhushan, World Constitutions: A Comparative Study 16 (9th rev. ed. 2009).

208. The Federalist, on The New Constitution, Written in 1788, by Mr. Hamilton, Mr. Madison, and Mr. Jay: with An Appendix, Containing the Letters of Pacificus and Helvidius on the Proclamation of Neutrality of 1793; also, the Original Articles of Confederation, and the Constitution of the United States 223 (1842).

209. *James*, 1825 WL 1899, at *12.

210. Id.

211. Id. As Judge Duncan wrote of the work of the court of quarter sessions and the absence of ducking being inflicted as punishment:

The court of quarter sessions was, when this judgment was given, composed entirely of men who (however high their standing in society, and however intelligent) were unversed in law. Since 1782, until the last case in the mayor's court, forty years ran round, and there has been no instance of this punishment. There has been one of an acquittal; that case, therefore, proves nothing.

Id.

212. Id.

213. Id. Judge Duncan described what he found as follows:

In 1769, eighty years after the settlement of the colony, in The King v. Mary Conway, the indictment was against her as a common scold; she pleaded guilty; the sentence was, that she should be publicly ducked at the end of Market street wharf, in the Delaware; all this passed without debate, and we may presume, without the assistance of counsel for the woman. In 1779, ten years after, there was a trial and conviction (The State v. Ann Maize), and the same sentence. In 1781, there was an indictment for the same offence, against Mary Swann; verdict guilty; continued for advisement; continued from March 1781, to June 1782, when there is this most extraordinary entry: "defendant having demeaned herself peaceably, kept under further advisement; and in the next term, on motion of Mr. Bankson, the defendant was recognised, that she will, within one month, leave the neighborhood and pay the costs."

Id.

214. Id.

215. Id.

216. Id.

217. Id. William Bradford was Pennsylvania's Attorney General from 1780 to 1791, when he was appointed to the Pennsylvania Supreme Court. In 1794, Bradford become the Attorney General of the United States, serving in that position until his death in 1795. *William Bradford (1755–1795)*, U. Pa.: U. Archives & Recs. Ctr., http://www.archives.upenn.edu/people/1700s/bradford_wm.html (last visited Nov. 15, 2011).

218. *James*, 1825 WL 1899, at *13.

219. Id.

220. Id.

221. Id. Writers like William Bradford had, following Beccaria, emphasized that the sole purpose of punishments was to prevent crimes. *See, e.g.*, Sharon M. Harris, Executing Race: Early American Women's Narratives of Race, Society, and the Law 66 (2005):

William Bradford, the conservative Federalist attorney general under President Washington, subscribed to the anti-capital punishment philosophy of Montesquieu and Beccaria. In excerpts from his tract published in *The New-York Magazine* in 1793, he defined the principles of opposition: the sole purpose of punishment was the prevention of crime; any punishment which is not absolutely necessary constitutes "a cruel and tyrannical act"; and penalties must be appropriate to the act. These principles, Bradford asserted, "protect the rights of humanity, and prevent the abuses of government." Though murder was still seen as a capital crime by many opponents, including Bradford and Jefferson, Bradford pondered whether it should be, since he doubted its effectiveness as a deterrent.

222. *James*, 1825 WL 1899, at *13.

223. Id.

224. Id.

225. *See* id. at *14.

226. Id. at *13.

227. Id. Ducking was clearly authorized and in use, at least to some degree, in colonial times. *Compare* Emery E. Childs, A History of the United States in Chronological Order: From the Discovery of America in 1492 to the Year 1885, including Notices of Manufacturers as They Were Introduced; of Other Industries; of Railroads, Canals, Telegraphs, and Other Improvements; of Inventions, Important Events, Etc. 18 (1885) (noting that, in 1692, "[a] whipping-post, pillory, and ducking-stool were established in the city of New York"), *with* Henry Collins Brown, Glimpses of Old New-York 310 (1917) (noting that, in 1691, "[a] ducking stool (for punishment of criminals)" was "erected in front of City Hall"); *see also* Kirsten Fischer, Suspect Relations: Sex, Race, and Resistance in Colonial North Carolina 234 n.12 (2002) ("In 1662 the Virginia legislature allowed that 'brabling women' whose slander involved their husbands in 'vexatious suites' could be ducked in lieu of paying fines."); 2 J. Thomas Scharf, History of Maryland: From the Earliest Period to the Present Day 41 (1879) ("The ducking-stool ... for scolding women, was peculiarly a Puritan punishment. It was probably very seldom resorted to in the colony—at any rate, the Act providing for it was abolished in 1676, chapter XXI., together with a great many other Acts of the Puritan regime."). The ducking stool certainly had a long history in America's mother country. *E.g.*, "Queries," 2 The Historical Magazine 90 (Jan. 1858):

The Ducking Stool.—The singular punishment of women in England for the too free use of the tongue, by immersing them in water through the instrumentality of an apparatus called the "*ducking stool*," was early introduced into this country. Towns were required, in some instances, to provide themselves with this instrument, and women indicted and convicted of being "common scolds," were taken to a neighboring pond or stream, and subjected to that ignominious but legal punishment.

228. *James*, 1825 WL 1899, at *14 (citing Duponceau on Jurisdiction, p. 96). In a "NOTE" that followed the opinion itself, it was added that an act of Henry VIII was once passed for the punishment of a cook who poisoned a bishop's family members. *Id.* As the note stated: "[B]y an *ex post facto* law, this was made treason, and he was ordered to be thrown into boiling water; the idea of which punishment, as Barrington suggests, was because he was a *cook.*" Id. (citation omitted; italics in original). "Such were the barbarous institutions of the age," the note concluded, adding: "This punishment accorded with the savage cruelty of the monarch, and was recommended by its quaintness; *to boil a cook*, was quite a royal joke; as the Duke of Clarence was drowned in a butt of Malmsey, a favor granted him by the King; a whimsical choice, says Hume, which implied that he had an extraordinary passion for that liquor." Id. (italics in original).

229. Jeff Biggers, The United States of Appalachia: How Southern Mountaineers Brought Independence, Culture, and Enlightenment to America 103, 105 (2006) (noting that Anne Royall, "a demure, squat, graying woman in her sixties," was born in 1769 and tried as "a common scold" in 1829); *see also* Elizabeth J. Clapp, A Notorious Woman: Anne Royall in Jacksonian America (2016); Sarah Harvey Porter, The Life and Times of Anne Royall (1909); George Stuyvesant Jackson, Uncommon Scold: The Story of Anne Royall (1937).

230. H.S. Boutell, *United States vs. Ann Royal*, 9 Geo. L.J. 30, 32 (1921).

231. Id. at 33.

232. Boutell, *supra* note 230, at 32–33, 43.

233. *E.g.*, "The Ducking Stool," 8 The Percy Anecdotes: Original and Select 29, 32–33 (1826):

How long the ducking-stool has been in disuse in England, does not appear; but that it was not always effectual, is proved from the records of the King's Bench, where we find, that in the year 1681, Mrs. Finch, a notorious scold, who had been thrice ducked previously, for scolding, was a fourth time convicted for the offence, when the court sentenced her to pay a fine of three marks, and to be imprisoned until it was paid.

In the United States of America, where many English customs, now forgotten in this county, are retained, the ducking-stool is still the punishment inflicted on a common scold, by the law of Baltimore, and some other states of the Union; and in one of the American papers for 1818, there is a mention of one Mary Davis, who had been indicted for the offence, and found guilty by the jury, after a consultation of an hour and a half. She was sentenced to be publicly ducked.

234. Boutell, *supra* note 230, at 34.

235. Id.

236. Id.; Jeff Biggers, The Trials of a Scold: The Incredible True Story of Writer Anne Royall 125 (2017) (noting that Richard Coxe was Royall's appointed defense counsel).

237. Boutell, *supra* note 230, at 35; Biggers, *supra* note 236, at 1, 124–25, 129–30, 159–60, 163–64 (recounting the history of ducking in colonial and early America, and discussing the debate in 1829 over whether 60-year-old Anne Royall, a journalist, should be subjected to the punishment of ducking).

238. Boutell, *supra* note 230, at 36–37.

239. Id. at 37 (quotations and citations omitted).

240. Id.

241. Id. at 40.

242. *Id.*

243. *Id.* at 40–41; *accord* Biggers, *supra* note 236, at 165.

244. Biggers, *supra* note 236, at 166; Boutell, *supra* note 230, at 42.

245. 560 U.S. 48 (2010).

246. 567 U.S. 460 (2012).

247. *Graham*, 560 U.S. at 74–75 (the Eighth Amendment prohibits the imposition of life without parole sentence on juvenile offender who did not commit homicide, and the State must give juvenile non-homicide offender sentenced to life without parole a meaningful opportunity to obtain release); *Miller*, 567 U.S. at 479 (the Eighth Amendment forbids a sentencing regime that mandates life in prison without possibility of parole for juvenile homicide offenders).

248. United States v. United Mine Workers, 330 U.S. 258, 306 (1947) (finding that a $3.5 million file against a union was excessive but that a fine of $700,000 was not).

249. The right to bail was once said to be "never refused but in cases of absolute necessity." Punishment of Death: A Series of Short Articles, to appear occasionally in Numbers designed for General Circulation (No. 1—Speech of the Right Hon. Sir William Meredith, Bart. in the House of Commons, May 13, 1777, in Committee on a Bill Creating a New Capital Felony) 58 (2d ed. 1831) ("Bail ... was not originally regarded as a favor, but as the just right of every subject, and was never refused but in cases of absolute necessity. The sole object to be obtained when an individual is charged with crime, is to ensure his appearance at the day of trial. If this can be secured by any other means than by the custody of his person, a commitment to gaol is unnecessary, and therefore unjust."). In his *Commentaries on the Laws of England*, William Blackstone noted that what was "excessive" under the English Bill of Rights "must be left to the courts, on considering the circumstances of the case, to determine." Alexander A. Reinert, *Reconceptualizing the Eighth Amendment: Slaves, Prisoners, and "Cruel and Unusual" Punishment*, 94 N.C. L. Rev. 817, 832 n.65 (2016) (quoting 4 William Blackstone, Commentaries pp. 296–300).

250. During debate over the Eighth Amendment in the First Congress, Representative Livermore noted the vagueness of the amendment's language but then noted that, ultimately, it would be for the *judicial branch* to decide. As Representative Livermore stated in 1789 before the Eighth Amendment was adopted "by a considerable majority":

The clause seems to express a great deal of humanity, on which account I have no objection to it; but as it seems to have no meaning in it, I do not think it necessary. What is meant by the terms excessive bail? Who are to be the judges? What is understood by excessive fines? It lays with the court to determine. No cruel and unusual punishment is to be inflicted; it is sometimes necessary to hang a man, villains often deserve whipping, and perhaps have their ears cut off; but are we in [the] future to be prevented from inflicting these punishments because they are cruel? If a more lenient mode of correcting vice and deterring others from the commission of it could be invented, it would be very prudent in the legislature to adopt it, but until we have some security that this will be done, we ought not to be restrained from making necessary laws by any declaration of this kind.

Neil H. Cogan, ed., The Complete Bill of Rights: The Drafts, Debates, Sources, and Origins 926 (2d ed. 2015).

251. United States v. Bajakajian, 524 U.S. 321 (1998) (a fine or forfeiture of $357,144 was unconstitutional); *compare* United States v. Perez-Jiminez, 654 F.3d 1136, 1146-47 (10th Cir. 2011) (rejecting an argument that a $2,000 fine was "unnecessary" and "excessive") *with* Salazar v. United States, 236 F. 541, 542 (8th Cir. 1916) (remitting a $500 fine to a $300 fine because "the fine imposed exceeds, by $200, the maximum provided by law in such cases"). The Excessive Fines Clause applies in criminal cases and in civil cases that, in spite of their label, are so punitive in nature as to constitute criminal punishment. The Eighth Amendment's purpose, the U.S. Supreme Court has determined, is "to limit the Government's power to punish." Austin v. United States, 509 U.S. 602, 609 (1993). Two years after *Bajakajian*, Congress codified the "gross disproportionality" standard for *in rem* forfeitures. United States v. One Parcel of Property Located at 35 Ruth Street, Unit 30 Bristol, Connecticut, Civil No. 3:06cv1844 (MRK), 2008 WL 4005299 *2 n.2 (D. Conn. Aug. 25, 2008). That federal statute provides that, in a civil forfeiture proceeding, "[i]f the court finds that the forfeiture is grossly disproportional to the offense it shall reduce or eliminate the forfeiture as necessary to avoid a violation of the Excessive Fines Clause of the Eighth Amendment to the Constitution." 18 U.S.C. §983(g)(4).

252. "The touchstone of the constitutional inquiry under the Excessive Fines Clause," the Supreme Court has held, "is the principle of proportionality." *Bajakajian*, 524 U.S. at 334. "If the amount of the forfeiture is grossly disproportional to the gravity of the defendant's offense, it is unconstitutional." Id. at 337; *see also* id. at 334 ("The amount of the forfeiture must bear some relationship to the gravity of the offense that it is designed to punish."); Stefan D. Cassella, Asset Forfeiture Law in the United States 66 n.139 (2007) (noting that, in *Bajakajian*, "[t]he Court derived the 'grossly disproportional' test for forfeiture cases under the Excessive Fines Clause from the test it had used for criminal cases under the Cruel and Unusual Punishments Clause") (citing Harmelin v. Michigan, 501 U.S. 957, 957-58 (1991) (rejecting the general proportionality test from *Solem v. Helm*, 463 U.S. 277 (1983); *Harmelin*, 501 U.S. at 959 (Kennedy, J., concurring) (Eighth Amendment only prohibits grossly disproportional sentences)); United States v. Approximately 627 Firearms, more or less, 589 F. Supp.2d 1129, 1136 (S.D. Iowa 2008) (setting forth the Eighth Circuit's "gross disproportionality" test for an Excessive Fines Clause analysis).

253. *E.g.*, Graham v. Florida, 580 U.S. 48, 59 (2010).

254. The U.S. Supreme Court has made use of the Eighth Amendment, for example, to remedy prison overcrowding. *E.g.*, Brown v. Plata, 563 U.S. 493, 510 (2011):

Prisoners retain the essence of human dignity inherent in all persons. Respect for that dignity animates the Eighth Amendment prohibition against cruel and unusual punishment. " 'The basic concept underlying the Eighth Amendment is nothing less than the dignity of man.' " *Atkins v. Virginia*, 536 U.S. 304, 311 (2002) (quoting *Trop v. Dulles*, 356 U.S. 86, 1000 (1958) (plurality opinion)).

255. Austin v. United States, 509 U.S. 602, 609 (1993); United States v. Salerno, 481 U.S. 739 (1987).

256. *See, e.g.*, Matter of Firestorm 1991, 916 P.2d 411, 416 (Wash. 1996) (en banc) ("Disqualification of counsel is a drastic remedy that exacts a harsh penalty from the parties as well as punishing counsel; therefore, it should be imposed only when absolutely necessary."); Skramstad v. Golden, No. CV-08-0065-FVS, 2008 WL 11336116 (E.D. Wash. Aug. 22, 2008) (same); State v. Devlin, 561 A.2d 280, 287 (N.J. Superior Ct., App. Div. 1989) ("I am satisfied that a custodial sentence is absolutely necessary. Absolutely necessary and in this case for the purpose of punishment, certainly for the purpose of deterrence and certainly for hopefully for rehabilitative purposes."); *cf.* Long v. Niles Co., Inc., No. 08-ADMS-40036, 2010 WL 1139325 *2 (Mass. App. Div., Dist. Ct. Dep't, S. Dist. Mar. 10, 2010) ("[T]he law seeks to enforce gratuitous undertakings only where absolutely necessary, so as not to punish (and

therefore discourage) those who do good deeds without any obligation to do so."); Martin v. Kazulkina, Civil Action No. 12-cv-14286, 2017 WL 971706 *15 (E.D. Mich. Feb. 21, 2017) ("These cases clearly stand for the proposition that involuntary treatment with psychotropic drugs, where not medically necessary, violates the Eighth Amendment prohibition on cruel and unusual punishment. The Sixth Circuit's holding in *Thompson* that 'subjecting a prisoner to involuntary medication *when it is not absolutely necessary or medically appropriate*' violates the Eighth Amendment tends to confirm this conclusion.") (quoting Thompson v. Bell, 580 F.3d 423, 440 (6th Cir. 2009)).

257. 216 F. Supp.2d 227 (S.D.N.Y. 2002).

258. Id. at 246.

259. 545 N.Y.S.2d 693 (N.Y. Sup. Ct.—App. Div., 1st Dept. 1989).

260. Id. at 702 (citation omitted).

261. 561 A.2d 280 (N.J. Super. Ct.—App. Div. 1989).

262. Id. at 287.

263. C. E. Fanning, comp., Debaters' Handbook Series: Selected Articles on Capital Punishment 98 (3d rev. ed. 1917) ("Now, that capital punishment is not absolutely necessary for the protection of society, in almost any epoch of civilization, is proved by the amplest testimony."); A. C. Thomas, "On Capital Punishment—The Preacher: Sermon No. 17," 1 Evangelical Magazine and Gospel Advocate (Utica, N.Y.), Aug. 21, 1830, at 1:

Punishments to be just must be absolutely necessary. Are capital punishments absolutely necessary? Are they necessary to insure the safety of society from the repetition of a similar offence by the same individual? No—they are not. In the rude state of nature, it might have been necessary to put the murderer to death.... But in the present state of civilization, the case is different.—We have prisons in which to secure the criminal.

264. 107 U.S. 265 (1883).

265. Id. at 266, 288.

266. Id. at 288–89.

267. Id. at 317 (Field, J., dissenting).

268. Id. at 318 (Field, J., dissenting).

269. Id.

270. *See* Ho Ah Kow v. Nunan, 12 F. Ca. 252 (C. C. D. Ca. 1879) (No. 6,546) (Field, Circuit J.) (voiding "cruel and punishment" of Chinese prisoners subjected to a cutting of their hair in a manner designed to disgrace and humiliate them); Jonathan H. X. Lee, ed., Chinese Americans: The History and Culture of a People 440 (2016) (discussing *Ho Ah Kow v. Nunan* (1879)).

271. Jackson v. State, 516 So.2d 726, 738 (Ala. Ct. Crim. App. 1985).

272. *E.g.*, Jan Philipp Reemtsma, Trust and Violence: An Essay on a Modern Relationship 148 (2012) ("The tendency to restrict violence to what is absolutely necessary received additional impetus from the idea of our common humanity."). Executions were once carried out in a manner to inflict the maximum amount of pain and suffering. Stuart Banner, The Death Penalty: An American History 70 (2002) ("When government officials wanted to ensure that death would be slow and painful, and thus all the more frightening to contemplate, they resorted to an alternative method—burning alive. Burning had a long history in English jurisprudence.").

273. 745 N.W.2d 229 (Neb. 2008).

274. Id. at 277. *But see* Jackson v. State, 836 So.2d 915, 962 (Ala. Ct. Crim. App. 1999) (upholding Alabama's use of electrocution as a method of execution and pointing to language in an earlier precedent that "[t]here has been absolutely no showing that the State's method of enforcing a death sentence inflicts any more pain that is absolutely necessary."); Hardy v. State, 804 So.2d 247, 296 (Ala. Ct. Crim. App. 1999) (same).

275. *Mata*, 745 N.W.2d at 261 (citations omitted). The court in *Mata* further ruled: "A method of execution violates the prohibition against cruel and unusual punishment if there is a substantial foreseeable risk, inherent in the method, that a prisoner will suffer unnecessary pain." Id. Statutes prohibiting cruelty to animals were themselves put in place to, in part, curtail the infliction of unnecessary pain or suffering. Robert Malcolm Kerr, The Student's Blackstone: *Commentaries on The Laws of England* 493 (1865) (noting in a section on "Cruelty to Animals" in an abridged adaptation of William Blackstone's *Commentaries on the Laws of England*: "Another offence under this

head is wanton *cruelty to an animal*, either by over-driving, beating or torturing it, or by carrying it or causing it to be carried in such a manner as to create unnecessary pain or suffering.") (italics in original); MASS. GEN. L. ch. 344, § 1 (1869) ("[W]hoever having the charge of custody of any animal, either as owner or otherwise, inflicts unnecessary cruelty upon the same, or unnecessarily fails to provide the same with proper food, drink, shelter or protection from the weather...."); CASS R. SUNSTEIN & MARTHA C. NUSSBAUM, EDS., ANIMAL RIGHTS: CURRENT DEBATES AND NEW DIRECTIONS 7, 113-16, 118, 126, 211, 253 269 (2004) (discussing animal cruelty statutes and the unnecessary suffering of animals).

276. *Mata*, 745 N.W.2d at 278. In a concurrence in *Furman v. Georgia*, 408 U.S. 238 (1972), Justice William Brennan himself wrote that the "essential predicate" is "that a punishment must not by its severity be degrading to human dignity." Id. at 281 (Brennan, J., concurring). In that concurrence, Brennan took aim at severe punishments inflicted in a "wholly arbitrary fashion," those "clearly and totally rejected throughout society" and those that are "patently unnecessary." Id. As Justice Brennan emphasized in that concurrence:

The function of these principles, after all, is simply to provide means by which a court can determine whether a challenged punishment comports with human dignity. They are, therefore, interrelated, and, in most cases, it will be their convergence that will justify the conclusion that a punishment is "cruel and unusual". The test, then, will ordinarily be a cumulative one: if a punishment is unusually severe, if there is a strong probability that it is inflicted arbitrarily, if it is substantially rejected by contemporary society, and if there is no reason to believe that it serves any penal purpose more effectively than some less severe punishment, then the continued infliction of that punishment violates the command of the Clause that the State many not inflict inhuman and uncivilized punishments upon those convicted of crimes.

Id. at 282.

277. *Mata*, 745 N.W.2d at 278.

278. As the court in *Mata* ruled:

Mata's sentence of death is affirmed. But under our system of government, while the Legislature may vote to have the death penalty, it must not create one that offends constitutional rights. We recognize the temptation to make the prisoner suffer, just as the prisoner made an innocent victim suffer. But it is the hallmark of a civilized society that we punish cruelty without practicing it. Condemned prisoners must not be tortured to death, regardless of their crimes.

And the evidence clearly proves that unconsciousness and death are not instantaneous for many condemned prisoners. These prisoners will, when electrocuted, consciously suffer the torture that high voltage electric current inflicts on the human body. The evidence shows that electrocution inflicts intense pain and agonizing suffering. Therefore, electrocution as a method of execution is cruel and unusual punishment in violation of the Nebraska Constitution, article I, § 9. And, without a constitutionally acceptable method of execution, Mata's sentence of death is stayed.

Mata, 745 N.W.2d at 279-80.

279. CYNDI BANKS, PUNISHMENT IN AMERICA: A REFERENCE HANDBOOK 10–11 (2005) (discussing the use of branding); JULIET HAINES MOFFORD, "THE DEVIL MADE ME DO IT!": CRIME AND PUNISHMENT IN EARLY NEW ENGLAND 81–84 (2012) (discussing the use of the scarlet letter).

280. *E.g.*, Daniel E. Williams, "'The Horrors of This Far-Famed Penitentiary': Discipline, Defiance, and Death during Ann Carson's Incarcerations in Philadelphia's Walnut Street Prison," *in* MICHELE LISE TARTER & RICHARD BELL, EDS., BURIED LIVES: INCARCERATED IN EARLY AMERICA 206 (2012):

[T]he Walnut Street Prison was famous. Built originally in 1773 as a traditional holding facility for debtors, vagrants, and those awaiting trial, the prison was at the forefront of a wave of penal reform initiatives that took place during the post-Revolutionary years when it was expanded in 1790. Walnut Street Prison was the first penitentiary in the United States remodeled to include cells for solitary confinement.

281. WILLIAM BRADFORD, AN ENQUIRY HOW FAR THE PUNISHMENT OF DEATH IS NECESSARY IN PENNSYLVANIA, 46 (1793) (emphasis added).

282. Trop v. Dulles, 356 U.S. 86, 101 (1958).

283. Id. at 99. In *Louisiana ex rel. Francis v. Resweber*, 329 U.S. 459 (1947), the Supreme Court

had earlier ruled: "The cruelty against which the Constitution protects a convicted man is cruelty inherent in the method of punishment, not the necessary suffering involved in any method employed to extinguish life humanely." Id. at 464. After initially declaring the death penalty unconstitutional in *Furman v. Georgia*, 408 U.S. 238 (1972), the Supreme Court in *Gregg v. Georgia*, 428 U.S. 153 (1976), also later ruled:

[W]e cannot say that the judgment of the Georgia Legislature that capital punishment may be necessary in some cases is clearly wrong. Considerations of federalism, as well as respect for the ability of a legislature to evaluate, in terms of its particular State, the moral consensus concerning the death penalty and its social utility as a sanction, require us to conclude, in the absence of more convincing evidence, that the infliction of death as a punishment for murder is not without justification and thus is not unconstitutionally severe.

Id. at 186–87. *Compare* id. at 236 (Marshall, J., dissenting) ("The available evidence, I concluded in *Furman*, was convincing that 'capital punishment is not necessary as a deterrent to crime in our society.' ") (citation omitted).

284. Walter John Raymond, Dictionary of Politics: Selected American and Foreign Political and Legal Terms 71 (7th ed. 1992).

285. 1 Rodney P. Carlisle, ed., Handbook to Life in America (The Colonial and Revolutionary Era: Beginnings to 1783) 154 (2009).

286. *See* Michael Meranze, Laboratories of Virtue: Punishment, Revolution, and Authority in Philadelphia, 1760–1835, at 1 (1996).

287. Lisa Hajjar, Torture: A Sociology of Violence and Human Rights 19 (2013).

288. Brief on Behalf of Former Federal Judges as *Amici Curiae* in Support of Petitioners (Aug. 24, 2007), *Boumediene v. Bush*, Nos. 06-1195, 06-1196, pp. 1–3, 14–15, 18, http://www.scotusblog.com/archives/former_federal_judges_amicus.pdf.

289. *E.g.*, Pau Pérez-Sales, Psychological Torture: Definition, Evaluation and Measurement 79 (2017) ("Since the *Estrella v. Uruguay* case (1980) there has been increasing jurisprudence from the Human Rights Committee of United Nations, the European Court of Human Rights, and especially the Inter-American Court, that supports the concept of psychological torture as a defined entity.").

290. *See, e.g.*, Gail H. Miller, Defining Torture, Floersheimer Center Occasional Papers, Floersheimer Center for Constitutional Democracy, Benjamin N. Cardozo School of Law, Yeshiva University, https://cardozo.yu.edu/sites/default/files/Defining%20Torture.pdf, pp. 5–6:

Myriad international declarations, agreements, and conventions, including Article 5 of the Universal Declaration on Human Rights, Article 7 of the International Covenant on Civil and Political Rights, the Convention on the Prevention and Punishment of Genocide, the European Convention on Human Rights, the American Convention on Human Rights, and the Vienna Declaration and Programme of Action, *prohibit* torture but fail to *define* it. On December 10, 1984, the U.N. General Assembly gave meaning to the term by adopting the CAT, which entered into force on June 26, 1987. With over 135 signatories, the CAT contains the most commonly used and widely endorsed definition of torture. Explaining the international acceptance of the CAT, the International Criminal Tribunal for the Former Yugoslavia has stated that the CAT torture definition reflects "a consensus ... representative of customary international law."

291. Graham v. Florida, 580 U.S. 48, 59 (2010) (citing *Hope v. Pelzer*, 536 U.S. 730 (2002); quoting *Wilkerson v. Utah*, 99 U.S. 130 (1879)).

292. U.N. Convention Against Torture and Other Cruel, Inhuman or Degrading Treatment or Punishments, U.N. General Assembly (adopted Dec. 10, 1984; entry into force June 26, 1987).

Chapter 7

1. The Supreme Court has not always used the "grossly disproportionate" language in discussing the Eighth Amendment prohibition against cruel and unusual punishments. For example, in *Howard v. Fleming*, 191 U.S. 126 (1903), it was contended that, in a case involving people convicted of conspiracy to defraud, "the defendants were denied the equal protection of the laws, in that the sentence was more severe than ever before inflicted in North Carolina for a like offense, and was cruel and unusual, in

that two [offenders] were given ten years' and the third [offender] only seven years' imprisonment, and also in that they were sentenced to imprisonment in the penitentiary instead of to hard labor on the public roads." Id. at 135. In that case, which did not employ any language about gross disproportionality, the U.S. Supreme Court made this ruling in upholding the sentences at issue:

That for other offenses, which may be considered by most, if not all, of a more grievous character, less punishments have been inflicted, does not make this sentence cruel. Undue leniency in one case does not transform a reasonable punishment in another case to a cruel one. Swindling by means of a pretended gold brick is no trifling crime, and a conspiracy to defraud by such means does not commend itself to sympathy or leniency. But it is unnecessary to attempt to lay down any rule for determining exactly what is necessary to render a punishment cruel and unusual, or under what circumstances this court will interfere with the decision of a state court in respect thereto. It is enough to refer to *[In] Re Kemmler*, 136 U.S. 436 [1890], in which these questions were discussed, and to say that a sentence of ten years for an offense of the nature disclosed by the testimony, especially after it has been sustained by the supreme court of a state, does not seem to us deserving to be called cruel. If the effect of this sentence is to induce like criminals to avoid its territory, North Carolina is to be congratulated, not condemned. Doubtless there were sufficient reasons for giving to one of the conspirators a less term than the others. At any rate, there is no such inequality as will justify us in setting aside the judgment against the two.

2. Oversight over American punishments involves not only Eighth and Fourteenth Amendment jurisprudence but state constitutional law as well. As one source captures some of the complexity in the criminal law arena:

All sentences imposed in state criminal trials are subject to the Eighth Amendment's Cruel and Unusual Punishments Clause. For non-capital, prison term sentences, the "grossly disproportionate" test is all that is required under the Eighth Amendment. However, some states, though perhaps not a majority, require a sentencing judge and an appellate court in review of a sentence to follow a more detailed proportionality review.

In 10 states the state constitution has explicit mandates to judges to conduct a proportionate sentence review of all sentences. As an example, Article 1, § 9 of the Maine Constitution states that "all penalties and punishments shall be proportionate to the offense."

Thomas J. Gardner & Terry M. Anderson, Criminal Law 208 (13th ed. 2018).

3. Hudson v. United States Bureau of Prisons, No. C-92-1360 MHP, 1994 WL 449023 *4 (N.D. Cal. Aug. 4, 1994) ("Punishment inflicted that is not necessary to maintain order is cruel and unusual and prohibited by the Eighth Amendment.") (citing Rhodes v. Chapman, 452 U.S. 337, 346 (1981). In *Rhodes v. Chapman*, 452 U.S. 337, 347 (1981), the Supreme Court ruled: "Conditions must not involve the wanton and unnecessary infliction of pain, nor may they be grossly disproportionate to the severity of the crime warranting imprisonment."

4. Wilkins v. Gaddy, 559 U.S. 34, 38 (2010) ("An inmate who is gratuitously beaten by guards does not lose his ability to pursc an excessive force claim merely because he has the good fortune to escape without serious injury."); Bowden v. Stokely, No. 3:12-cv-652-J-99MMH-JRK, 2013 WL 4500462 *6 (M.D. Fla. Aug. 22, 2013) ("Gratuitous beatings, without causing serious injury, still violate the Eighth Amendment proscription against cruel and unusual punishments.") (citing Wilkins v. Gaddy, 559 U.S. 34, 38 (2010) (per curiam)); Herrera v. Harrington, Case No. 3:13-cv-00570-SMY-PMF, 2016 WL 759554 (S.D. Ill. Feb. 26, 2016) ("[T]he Court agrees with the plaintiff that his Eighth Amendment right to be free from cruel and unusual punishment includes a right to be free from or protected from a series of gratuitous beatings...."); Watson v. Edelen, 76 F. Supp.3d 1332, 1372 (N.D. Fla. 2015) ("Three applications of chemical agents on a completely non-disruptive and compliant prisoner supports a reliable inference that the use of force was a gratuitous, wanton infliction of pain, which constitutes a violation of the Eighth Amendment's prohibition of the use of excessive force."); Philo v. Reams, No. 4:11-cv-394-SPM-GRJ, 2012 WL 7153878 *4 ("a vicious and gratuitous beating of the type alleged by Plaintiff would ... run afoul of the Eighth Amendment's proscription against cruel and unusual punishments"); *cf.* United States v. Walsh, 194 F.3d 37, 50 (2d Cir. 1997) (force was "wanton" as there was absolutely no perceived need for it); Oliver v. Collins, 914 F.2d 56, 59 (5th Cir. 1990) (testimony that a beating was gratuitous and that no force was necessary supported a finding of malice); Lewis v. Downs, 774 F.2d 711, 714 (6th Cir. 1985) (evidence that an officer

kicked a handcuffed person who was lying on the ground established malicious motivation). In Eighth Amendment excessive force cases, "the 'core judicial inquiry' is 'not whether a certain quantum of injury was sustained, but rather whether force was applied in a good-faith effort to maintain or restore discipline, or maliciously and sadistically to cause harm.'" Bowden v. Stokely, 576 F. App'x 951, 953 (11th Cir. 2014) (quoting Wilkins v. Gaddy, 559 U.S. 34, 37 (2010) (per curiam)).

5. *Cf.* Charron v. Medium Sec. Inst., 730 F. Supp. 987, 994 (E.D. Mo. Apr. 28, 1989) ("The imposition of maximum security confinement of detainees when it is not necessary violates their rights to due process and to be free from cruel and unusual punishment...."); Ahrens v. Thomas, 434 F. Supp. 873, 898 (W.D. Mo. 1977) (same).

6. U.S. Const., amend. XIV.

7. Blake Nelson, *The Minnesota Sentencing Guidelines: The Effects of Determinate Sentencing on Disparities in Sentencing Decisions*, 10 Law & Inequality 217, 250 (1992) ("The primary concern for the application of the law is that similar criminal actions be treated in a like manner.").

8. *E.g.*, Hodgson v. State of Vt., 168 U.S. 262, 272-73 (1897) ("We concede the proposition ... that by the fourteenth amendment it is made the right and the consequent duty of this court, when a case has been duly brought before it, to inquire whether, in the enactment and administration of the criminal laws of a state, it is sought to arbitrarily deprive any person of his life ... or to refuse him the equal protection of the laws"); Jones v. Brim, 165 U.S. 180, 182 (1897) ("the clause of the fourteenth amendment of the constitution referred to was undoubtedly intended to prohibit an arbitrary deprivation of life or liberty, or arbitration spoliation of property"); BMW of North Am., Inc. v. Gore, 517 U.S. 559, 586 (1996) (Breyer, J., concurring) ("The Court's opinion, which I join, explains why we have concluded that this award, in this case, was 'grossly excessive' in relation to legitimate punitive damages objections, and hence an arbitrary deprivation of life, liberty, or property in violation of the Due Process Clause.").

9. 113 U.S. 27 (1884).

10. Id. at 31.

11. Bank Markazi v. Peterson, 136 S. Ct. 1310, 1327 n.27 (2016) ("Laws narrow in scope, including 'class of one' legislation, may violate the Equal Protection Clause if arbitrary or inadequately justified."); *see also* Village of Willowbrook v. Olech, 528 U.S. 562, 564 (2000) (citations omitted):

Our cases have recognized successful equal protection claims brought by a "class of one," where the plaintiff alleges that she has been intentionally treated differently from others similarly situated and that there is no rational basis for the difference in treatment. In doing so, we have explained that "'[t]he purpose of the equal protection clause of the Fourteenth Amendment is to secure every person within the State's jurisdiction against intentional and arbitrary discrimination, whether occasioned by express terms of a statute or by its improper execution through duly constituted agents.'"

12. 402 U.S. 183 (1971).

13. Id. at 208.

14. Charles F. Manski, Public Policy in an Uncertain World: Analysis and Decisions 49 (2013).

15. Louis Fisher & Katy J. Harriger, American Constitutional Law 681 (2009).

16. LeBeau v. State, 337 P.3d 254, 275 (Utah 2014).

17. Woodson v. North Carolina, 428 U.S. 280 (1976); Roberts v. Louisiana, 428 U.S. 325 (1976).

18. David Schultz, Encyclopedia of American Law 205 (2002) ("Guided discretion statutes require juries and judges to consider various aggravating and mitigating circumstances when deciding whether a defendant should receive the death penalty.").

19. *E.g.*, Anthony G. Amsterdam, *Opening Remarks: Race and the Death Penalty Before and After* McCleskey, 39 Colum. Hum. Rts. L. Rev. 34, 38 (2007):

Between 1930, when nationwide official statistics began, and 1972, when the Supreme Court of the United States decided *Furman v. Georgia*, almost exactly half of the persons executed for murder in the United States and about ninety percent of those executed for rape were African-American, although African-Americans never constituted more than eleven percent of the nation's population during this period. Unofficial figures running from 1864 to 1972 paint the same picture.

20. Paul Kaplan, Murder Stories: Ideological Narratives in Capital Punishment 54 n.3 (2012) ("During the contemporary era, the South accounts for 81 percent of executions while the

northeast accounts for 0.05 percent executions."). The region where executions most often occur is the same region where lynchings were once so prominent. MARGARET VANDIVER, LETHAL PUNISHMENT: LYNCHINGS AND LEGAL EXECUTIONS IN THE SOUTH 9 (2005) ("The great majority of mob killings took place in the South; lynchings in the eleven states of the former Confederacy accounted for 74 percent of all lynchings in the United States between 1882 and 1968.").

21. Rebekah Barber, "Challenging the Death Penalty in the South," Facing South, Mar. 24, 2017, https://www.facingsouth.org/2017/03/challenging-death-penalty-south.

22. *E.g.*, Andrea Shapiro, *Unequal Before the Law: Men, Women and the Death Penalty*, 8 AM. U. J. GENDER, SOC. POL'Y & L. 427 (2000); Victor L. Streib, *Rare and Inconsistent: The Death Penalty for Women*, 33 FORDHAM URB. L.J. 609 (2006); Elizabeth Rapaport, *The Death Penalty and Gender Discrimination*, 25 LAW & SOC'Y REV. 367 (1991); Steven F. Shatz & Naomi R. Shatz, *Chivalry is Not Dead: Murder, Gender, and the Death Penalty*, 27 BERKELEY J. GENDER L. & JUST. 64 (2012); Harry Greenlee & Shelia P. Greenlee, *Women and the Death Penalty: Racial Disparities and Differences*, 14 WM. & MARY J. WOMEN & L. 319 (2008); *see also* Elizabeth Rapaport, *Equality of the Damned: The Execution of Women on the Cusp of the 21st Century*, 26 OHIO N.U. L. REV. 581, 588 (2000) ("Throughout American history, from early colonial times until the pre-*Furman* moratorium period during which no executions took place, women have been executed; females account for approximately 3% of all executions, or 556 women, from 1632 until the execution of Elizabeth Duncan in California in 1962.").

23. VICTOR STREIB, SAM KAMIN & JUSTIN MARCEAU, DEATH PENALTY IN A NUTSHELL 19 (5th ed. 2017).

24. *E.g.*, PLAUTUS'S COMEDIES, AMPHITRYON, EPIDICUS, AND RUDENS, MADE ENGLISH: WITH CRITICAL REMARKS UPON EACH PLAY 128 (1694) (referencing "*Rods* being the most usual Punishment for Slaves") (italics in original).

25. SAMUEL MARCH PHILLIPPS, A TREATISE ON THE LAW OF EVIDENCE 23 (2d ed. 1815); *see also* HENRY CAMPBELL BLACK, A LAW DICTIONARY CONTAINING DEFINITIONS OF THE TERMS AND PHRASES OF AMERICAN AND ENGLISH JURISPRUDENCE, ANCIENT AND MODERN AND INCLUDING THE PRINCIPAL TERMS OF INTERNATIONAL, CONSTITUTIONAL, ECCLESIASTICAL AND COMMERCIAL LAW, AND MEDICAL JURISPRUDENCE, WITH A COLLECTION OF LEGAL MAXIMS, NUMEROUS SELECT TITLES FROM THE ROMAN, MODERN CIVIL, SCOTCH, FRENCH, SPANISH, AND MEXICAN LAW, AND OTHER FOREIGN SYSTEMS, AND A TABLE OF ABBREVIATIONS 300 (2d ed. 1910) ("'Infamous,' as used in the fifth amendment to the United States constitution, in reference to crimes, includes those only of the class called 'crimen falsi,' which both involve the charge of falsehood, and may also injuriously affect the public administration of justice by introducing falsehood and fraud.").

26. EDWARD PHILLIPS, COMP., THE NEW WORLD OF WORDS: OR UNIVERSAL ENGLISH DICTIONARY (6th ed. 1706) (unpaginated) (italics in original); 6 THE PENNY MAGAZINE OF THE SOCIETY FOR THE DIFFUSION OF USEFUL KNOWLEDGE 339 (1837) *see also* 2 BULSTRODE WHITLOCKE, A JOURNAL OF THE SWEDISH AMBASSY, IN THE YEARS M.DC.LIII. AND M.DC.LIV. FROM THE COMMONWEALTH OF ENGLAND, SCOTLAND, AND IRELAND 18 (1772) ("Presently after this execution was past, two other offenders, for smaller crimes, were brought to the same place to suffer the punishment of the law, which they call running the gauntlet; a usuall punishment among soldiers."); ABEL BOYER, THE ROYAL DICTIONARY, FRENCH AND ENGLISH AND ENGLISH AND FRENCH 311 (1768) (listing "Gantlop," or "Gantlope," as "an usual punishment among soldiers"); NATHAN BAILEY, AN UNIVERSAL ETYMOLOGICAL ENGLISH DICTIONARY (1731) (showing the combined, unpaginated entry for "Gantlet" and "Gauntlet" references "an Iron Glove" and the next combined entry for "Gantlope" and "Gantlop" reads: "[of *Gant*, a Town in *Flanders*, and Loop, a Race, or loopen, to run, *Belg*., because this Punishment was first invented there] an usual Punishment among Soldiers").

27. HENRI MISSON, MEMOIRS AND OBSERVATIONS IN HIS TRAVELS OVER ENGLAND 359 (Mr. Ozell, trans., 1719) ("To be whipp'd thro' the Streets by the Hands of the Hangman, is the usual Punishment inflicted upon those that have stolen any Thing under the ancient Value of Twelve-Pence. Oftentimes this Punishment is commuted for that of being transported into some of the Plantations in the *Indies*, upon Account of the great Want those new Countries are in of People.").

28. 1 THE COUNTY MAGAZINE, FOR THE YEARS 1786 AND 1787; PARTICULARLY DEDICATED TO THE INHABITANTS OF BERKSHIRE, DORSETSHIRE, HAMPSHIRE, SOMERSETSHIRE, AND WILTSHIRE 80 (1788) (referring to "the usual punishment inflicted on persons convicted of manslaughter, that of being

burnt in the hand").

29. 2 Henry Dagge, Considerations on Criminal Law 23 (2d ed. 1774) ("[T]he usual punishment for Treason consists only of cutting the body of the criminal into several pieces, ripping up his belly, taking out his entrails, and then throwing his carcass into a river or ditch, and this is commonly done to great malefactors.").

30. Samuel Annesley, A Supplement to the Morning-Exercise at Cripple-Gate: or, Several More Cases of Conscience Practically Resolved by Sundry Ministers 337 (1674) (quoting from Sermon 17, "What are the Duties of Parents and Children; and how are they to be managed, according to Scripture?"); *see also* 2 William Young, ed., Quintus Curtius, His History of the Wars of Alexander: To Which is Prefix'd Freinshemius's Supplement 182 (John Digby trans., 3d ed. 1747) ("[P]erceiving those who were charg'd with the prisoners, to be dilatory in their office, he commanded them to drown them in the river bound as they were. Nor did this unusual punishment raise any commotion among the soldiers....").

31. Vimalin Rujivacharakul, et al., eds., Architecturalized Asia: Mapping a Continent through History 89 (2013) (stating that the kingdom of Tonquin, as noted by a Danish geographer in 1804, "once belonged to China"). Tonquin later became part of Vietnam. Catherine Beth Lippert, Eighteenth-Century English Porcelain in the Collection of the Indianapolis Museum of Art 172 (1987).

32. 1 Thomas Salmon, Modern History: or, The Present State of All Nations 56 (3d ed. 1744)

33. Id. at 191; *see also* id. at 348, 352, 441–42 (containing other references to the "usual punishment" for particular conduct).

34. People *ex rel.* Peabody v. Baker, 110 N.Y.S. 848, 852 (1908) ("[T]he usual punishment for the act ... is death or a long term of imprisonment."); State v. Foster, 46 A. 833, 837 (R.I. 1900) ("The usual punishment for the violation of statutes of this general character is a fine or imprisonment, or both; and there is certainly nothing in the punishment here prescribed which strikes one as unusual, oppressive, or cruel."); *Ex parte* Swann, 9 S.W. 10, 12 (Mo. 1888) ("The usual punishment for the violation of such statutes is a fine or imprisonment, or both."); *see also In re* Lacov, 142 F. 960, 962 (1905) (referring to "the usual punishment for contempt"); McClung v. McClung, 40 Mich. 493, 496 (Mich. 1879) (referring to same); Commonwealth v. Silsbee, 9 Mass. 417 (Mass. Sup. Jud. Ct. 1812) (reprinting a lawyer's argument that "the usual punishment applied to the act—that of rejecting the party's vote—is probably all that the government thought necessary or convenient").

35. 55 P. 342, 343 (Kan. 1898).

36. Id.

37. Id.

38. Rogers v. Commonwealth, 5 Serg. & Rawle 463, 465 (Pa. 1819).

39. 1834 WL 460 *3 (N.C. 1834).

40. Id. at *1.

41. Id.

42. Id.

43. Id.

44. Id.

45. Id. at *2.

46. Id. at *5.

47. Id. at *12.

48. Id. at *17. In particular, it was also argued in that case:

If the master has no right, then, to take the life of his slave, except when he *resists him by force*, or when the death takes place while the usual punishment is inflicting, it is conceived, that until the occasion occurs which calls for the exercise of this extreme power—until the necessity actually exists—the master or person representing him has no right to resort to means, or to use weapons likely to produce death, and the very moment he does so, he is guilty of an abuse of his power, and if he slays the slave under these circumstances, he is guilty of murder. While on the other hand, the laws of nature and reason must permit the slave under like circumstances to use and call into action the common instinct of self-preservation, or at least, if he does resort to it, they will not, cannot, esteem him a *murderer*, if he unfortunately slays his oppresser, in obeying the impulse of nature, which is, in this instance, too strong to be repressed by any restraints which the laws of man can impose.

Id.

49. 3 General Report of the Emigration Commissioners 5 (H.M. Stationary Office, 1838) ("The usual punishment for prison offences, is confinement for a few hours in a solitary cell. . . .").

50. Walter Sinnott-Armstrong & Robert Fogelin, Understanding Arguments: An Introduction to Informal Logic 107 (9th ed. 2015).

51. J. Grey Jewell, Among Our Sailors: With an Appendix Containing Extracts from the Laws and Consular Regulations Governing the United States Merchant Service 53, 131–32, 266–67 (1874); Matthew Taylor Raffety, The Republic Afloat: Law, Honor, and Citizenship in Maritime America 45–46 (2013).

52. Joan Petersilia & Kevin R. Reitz, eds., The Oxford Handbook of Sentencing and Corrections 3–5 (2012).

53. Craig Haney, "The Psychological Effects of Imprisonment," *in* Joan Petersilia & Kevin R. Reitz, eds., The Oxford Handbook of Sentencing and Corrections 585–86, 589 (2012).

54. 1 Mary Bosworth, ed., Encyclopedia of Prisons and Correctional Facilities 800, 909 (2005). The Auburn Prison, in New York, had two-person cells and single-person cells. The New York legislature authorized its construction in 1816, and after a riot in 1821, the north cell wing—which was rebuilt and reoccupied in 1821, and which housed the prison's worst inmates—was intended to subdue inmate's "depraved hearts and stubborn spirits." G. Larry Mays & L. Thomas Winfree, Jr., Essentials of Corrections 42 (4th ed. 2009).

55. In re Medley, 134 U.S. 160, 172 (1890).

56. British Columbia Civil Liberties Association v. Canada (Attorney General), 2018 BCSC 62 (Vancouver, B.C., Jan. 17, 2018), http://www.courts.gov.bc.ca/jdb-txt/sc/18/00/2018BCSC0062.htm, ¶¶ 15-22, 50-52; *see also* id., ¶ 54 ("In August 2011, the Special Rapporteur on Torture and Other Cruel, Inhuman or Degrading Treatment or Punishment submitted an interim report to the United Nations General Assembly with respect to solitary confinement, which he defined as the physical and social isolation of individuals who are confined to their cells for 22 to 24 hours a day. Of particular concern to him was prolonged solitary confinement, meaning any period of solitary confinement in excess of 15 days, because at that point, according to the medical literature that he surveyed, some of the harmful psychological effects of isolation can become irreversible."); id., ¶ 57 (noting that "[t]he Special Rapporteur's opinions informed the most recent version of the United Nations' *Standard Minimum Rules for the Treatment of Prisoners* ('SMRs')," with Justice Leask noting that "[i]n December 2015, the UN General Assembly unanimously adopted a revised version of the SMRs, known as 'the Nelson Mandela Rules'"; "Whereas the previous rules provided only that '[c]orporal punishment, punishment by placing in a dark cell, and all cruel, inhuman or degrading punishments shall be completely prohibited as punishments for disciplinary offences' (Rule 31), the Mandela Rules" prohibit "indefinite solitary confinement," "prolonged solitary confinement," and "placement of a prisoner in a dark or constantly lit cell"; in the Mandela Rules, "solitary confinement" means "the confinement of prisoners for 22 hours or more a day without meaningful human contact" while "prolonged solitary confinement" means "solitary confinement for a time period in excess of 15 consecutive days.").

57. Id., ¶¶ 177–89.

58. Id., ¶¶ 192–94.

59. Id., ¶¶ 247–48.

60. Id., ¶ 250.

61. John D. Bessler, *Capital Punishment Law and Practices: History, Trends, and Developments*, *in* America's Experiment with Capital Punishment: Reflections on the Past, Present, and Future of the Ultimate Penal Sanction (James R. Acker et al. eds., 3d ed. 2014); *compare* Alice Morse Earle, Colonial Dames and Good Wives 96 (1895):

One of the last indictments for ducking in our own country was that of Mrs. Anne Royall in Washington, almost in our own day. She was a hated lobbyist, whom Mr. Forney called an itinerant virago, and who became so abusive to congressmen that she was indicted as a common scold before Judge William Cranch. . . . She was, however, released with a fine.

Women curst with a shrewish tongue were often punished in Puritan colonies. In 1647 it was ordered the 'common scoulds' be punished in Rhode Island by ducking, but I find no records of the punishment being given. In 1649 several women were prosecuted in Salem, Mass., for scolding; and on May 15, 1672, the General Court of Massachusetts ordered that scolds and railers should be gagged or "set in a ducking-stool and dipped over head and ears three times," but I do not believe that this law was ever executed in Massachusetts. Nor was it in Maine, though in 1664 a dozen towns were fined forty shillings each for having no "coucking-stool."

62. Gabriele Gottlieb, Theater of Death: Capital Punishment in Early America, 1750–1800, Ph.D. thesis, University of Pittsburgh (2005), p. 4.

63. *See generally* John D. Bessler, The Birth of American Law: An Italian Philosopher and the American Revolution (2014) (describing the profound influence of Cesare Beccaria's *On Crimes and Punishments* on America's founders); *see also* John D. Bessler, The Celebrated Marquis: An Italian Noble and the Making of the Modern World (2018) (describing Cesare Beccaria's global influence, including in colonial and early America); Kathryn Preyer, "Cesare Beccaria and the Founding Fathers," *in* Blackstone in America: Selected Essays of Kathryn Preyer 239–251 (Mary Sarah Bilder, Maeva Marcus & R. Kent Newmyer, eds., 2009) (describing the printing and dissemination of Beccaria's book and his ideas in America).

64. *See generally* John D. Bessler, Death in the Dark: Midnight Executions in America (1997).

65. Id. at 41–67, 81.

66. *See generally* Stuart Banner: The Death Penalty: An American History (2002); John Cyril Barton, Literary Executions: Capital Punishment and American Culture 1820–1925 (2014).

67. Benjamin Rush, Considerations on the Injustice and Impolicy of Punishing Murder by Death (1792).

68. William Bradford, An Enquiry How Far the Punishment of Death is Necessary in Pennsylvania (1793).

69. Alan W. Clarke & Laurelyn Whitt, The Bitter Fruit of American Justice: International and Domestic Resistance to the Death Penalty 78 (2007).

70. Marvin H. Bovee, Christ and the Gallows: or, Reasons for the Abolition of Capital Punishment (1870); Paul Christian Jones, Against the Gallows: Antebellum American Writers and the Movement to Abolish Capital Punishment 95–133 (2011) (the title of Chapter 4 of this book is "Walt Whitman's Anti-Gallows Writing: The Appeal to Christian Sympathy").

71. Marvin H. Bovee, Christ and the Gallows: or, Reasons for the Abolition of Capital Punishment 196–97, 200, 202, 207, 217 (1869); *accord* Marvin H. Bovee, Reasons for Abolishing Capital Punishment 200, 217 (1873).

72. Death Penalty Info. Ctr., Facts About the Death Penalty 1 (2017), https://deathpenaltyinfo.org/documents/FactSheet.pdf.

73. The stories about how some states did away with the punishment of death are reported elsewhere. John F. Galliher, Larry W. Koch, David Patrick Keys & Teresa J. Guess, America Without the Death Penalty: States Leading the Way (2002); Larry W. Koch, Colin Wark & John F. Galliher, The Death of the American Death Penalty: States Still Leading the Way (2012).

74. Frank R. Baumgartner, et al., Deadly Justice: A Statistical Portrait of the Death Penalty (2018) (Table 16.1 shows the declining usage of death sentences and executions).

75. John D. Bessler, "The American Enlightenment: Eliminating Capital Punishment in the United States," *in* Lill Scherdin, ed., Capital Punishment: A Hazard to a Sustainable Criminal Justice System? 93 (2016).

76. Death Penalty Info. Ctr., *supra* note 72, at 3.

77. Id. at 1.

78. 428 U.S. 262 (1976).

79. *No Executions in the 'Capital of Capital Punishment' for First Time in 30 Years,* Death Penalty Info. Ctr., https://deathpenaltyinfo.org/node/6940 (last visited Feb. 26, 2018) (citing Keri Blakinger, *For First Time in More Than 30 Years, No Harris County Death Row Inmates Executed*, Hous. Chron., Dec. 4, 2017; Michael Graczyk, *US Executions Increase Slightly in 2017*, Associated Press, Dec. 2, 2017); *see also* Jordan Smith, "For the First Time in Three Decades, the 'Death Penalty Capital of

America' Goes Without an Execution," The Intercept, Dec. 22, 2017, https://theintercept.com/2017/12/22/death-penalty-harris-county-texas/ ("Indeed, 2017 marked the third year in a row that Harris County did not send any new defendants to death row. Even more dramatic, it was the first year in more than three decades that no one from the county was executed.").

80. Blakinger, *supra* note 79.

81. Id.

82. Lane Nelson & Burk Foster, Death Watch: A Death Penalty Anthology 6 (2001); Brian W. Stolarz, Grace and Justice on Death Row: The Race Against Time and Texas to Free an Innocent Man (2016), ch. 9.

83. Robert J. Smith, *The Geography of the Death Penalty and its Ramifications*, 92 B.U. L. Rev. 227, 227 (2012).

84. Id. at 228.

85. Id. at 230.

86. Id. at 230 & n.6 (citing Charles Ogletree, *Black Man's Burden: Race and the Death Penalty in America*, 81 Or. L. Rev. 15, 19 (2002) (listing states in the Death Belt as Alabama, Florida, Georgia, Louisiana, Mississippi, North Carolina, South Carolina, Texas, and Virginia).

87. *See generally* Richard C. Dieter, Death Penalty Info. Ctr., The 2% Death Penalty: How a Minority of Counties Produce Most Death Cases at Enormous Costs to All (2013), https://deathpenaltyinfo.org/documents/TwoPercentReport.pdf.

88. 135 S. Ct. 2726, 2755 (Breyer, J., dissenting) ("[R]ather than try to patch up the death penalty's wounds one at a time, I would ask for full briefing on a more basic question: whether the death penalty violates the Constitution.").

89. Stephen Breyer, Against the Death Penalty 91–92 (John D. Bessler, ed., 2016). This book, published by Brookings Institution Press, reprints, contextualizes and annotates Justice Breyer's dissent in *Glossip v. Gross.*

90. Id. at 92.

91. Id. According to Justice Breyer's dissent: "That leaves 11 States in which it is fair to say that capital punishment is not 'unusual.' And just three of those States (Texas, Missouri, and Florida) accounted for 80% of the executions nationwide (28 of the 35) in 2014." Id.

92. 18 U.S.C. §3593(a)(1).

93. *E.g.*, Sherod Thaxton, *Disciplining Death: Assessing and Ameliorating Arbitrariness in Capital Charging*, 49 Ariz. St. L.J. 137, 168 (2017):

During the period under investigation (1993–2000), there were 1,238 cases resulting in a murder conviction that were eligible for the death penalty under Georgia's capital statute. Prosecutors filed a notice of intent to seek the death penalty in 400 cases and 54 defendants ultimately received the death penalty. Of the 395 capitally charged cases in which the method of disposition in known, 59% were ultimately resolved by plea and 41% were resolved by trial.

94. " 'Americans' support for the death penalty has dipped to a level not seen in 45 years," a 2017 Gallup poll released on October 26 reported. In Gallup's nationwide survey of 1,028 adults, 55% of survey respondents said that they were "in favor of the death penalty for a person convicted of murder," down from the 60% level reported in October 2016. *Gallup Poll: Support for Death Penalty in U.S. Falls to a 45-Year-Low*, Death Penalty Info. Ctr., https://deathpenaltyinfo.org/Gallup-Support_for_Death_Penalty_Falls_in_2017 (last visited Feb. 26, 2018) (citing Jeffrey M. Jones, *U.S. Death Penalty Support Lowest Since 1972*, Gallup News Serv., Oct. 26, 2017; Jeff Jones & Lydia Saad, *Gallup Poll Social Series: Crime*, Gallup News Serv., Oct. 26, 2017).

95. *E.g.*, Nancy M. Marder, Foster v. Chatman: *A Missed Opportunity for* Batson *and the Peremptory Challenge*, 49 Conn. L. Rev. 1137, 1186 n.316 (2017) (citing Lockhart v. McCree, 476 U.S. 162, 176–78 (1986):

A "death qualified" jury is one in which jurors who are staunchly opposed to the death penalty have been removed for cause. If they say they can consider applying the death penalty, then they can be seated as jurors. If they say they could never apply the death penalty, then they will be removed for cause. The Supreme Court has held that death qualification does not violate the fair cross-section requirement of the Sixth Amendment.

96. 1 Donald K. Freedheim & Irving B. Weiner, eds., Handbook of Psychology 405 (2003).

97. *See* Witherspoon v. Illinois, 391 U.S. 510 (1968); Wainwright v. Witt, 470 U.S. 1039 (1985); Lockhart v. McCree, 476 U.S. 162 (1986); Uttecht v. Brown, 551 U.S. 1 (2007).

98. *E.g.*, Ann M. Eisenberg, *Removal of Women and African Americans in Jury Selection in South Carolina Capital Cases, 1997–2012*, 9 Ne. U. L. Rev. 299, 305 (2017):

[D]eath-qualified juries are more inclined to return convictions and death sentences, undermining defendants' rights to an impartial jury. Processes that siphon women and black venire members of juries undermine juries' fairness and effectiveness in numerous other ways as well: more diverse juries are likelier to "engage in wider-ranging deliberations," to address issues of race in their deliberations, and to counterbalance other jurors' biases.

99. *E.g.*, Miller-El v. Dretke, 545 U.S. 231 (2005); Snyder v. Louisiana, 552 U.S. 472 (2008); Foster v. Chatman, 136 S. Ct. 1737 (2016).

100. 136 S. Ct. 1737 (2016).

101. Eisenberg, *supra* note 98, at 301.

102. 481 U.S. 279 (1987).

103. Samuel Walker, Cassia Spohn & Miriam DeLone, The Color of Justice: Race, Ethnicity, and Crime in America 397 (6th ed. 2016) ("After a series of last-minute appeals, requests for clemency, and requests for commutation were denied, Warren McCleskey was strapped into the electric chair at the state prison in Jacksonville, Georgia. He was pronounced dead at 3:13 a.m., September 26, 1991.").

104. Beyond Repair? America's Death Penalty 123 (Stephen P. Garvey ed., 2003) ("There is no question that the death penalty in this country historically was sought and imposed in a racially discriminatory manner. The 'distorting effects of racial discrimination' in the administration of the death penalty are in truth as old as our Republic.").

105. *E.g.*, Brandon L. Garrett, End of its Rope: How Killing the Death Penalty Can Revive Criminal Justice 83–85 (2017) (discussing the racial disparity in capital sentencing, race-of-the-victim discrimination, the racial bias in the selection of jurors, and the systematic exclusion of blacks from capital juries); *see also* Scott Phillips, *Continued Racial Disparities in the Capital of Capital Punishment: The Rosenthal Era*, 50 Hous. L. Rev. 131 (2012); Scott Phillips, *Racial Disparities in the Capital of Capital Punishment*, 45 Hous. L. Rev. 807 (2008).

106. Roger J. R. Levesque, The Psychology and Law of Criminal Justice Processes 332–33 (2006) (discussing studies).

107. James R. Acker, Questioning Capital Punishment: Law, Policy, and Practice 197 (2014) ("The death penalty in the United States historically has been intertwined with the nation's ignoble legacy of racial discrimination. Capital punishment was employed by Whites in several states as a harsh mechanism for repressing slaves in antebellum America.").

108. The Civil Rights Act of 1866 required that blacks and whites be subjected to "like punishment," and the Fourteenth Amendment was intended to constitutionalize the protections of that landmark legislation. John D. Bessler, *The Inequality of America's Death Penalty: A Crossroads for Capital Punishment at the Intersection of the Eighth and Fourteenth Amendments*, 73 Wash. & Lee L. Rev. Online 487, 515, 525–26 (2016). The American death penalty, from the era of slavery to the modern era, has always been used in a discriminatory manner, and the American death penalty has never been carried out in a non-discriminatory way. Id. at 542–64.

109. Corinna Barrett Lain, "Following Finality: Why Capital Punishment Is Collapsing Under Its Own Weight," *in* Final Judgments: The Death Penalty in American Law and Culture 49 (Austin Sarat ed., 2017) ("In 1972, the Supreme Court invalidated the death penalty because it was arbitrary and capricious as then administered. A sentence of death was like being struck by lightning, Justice Stewart famously lamented—and today that is literally true. In 2016, 20 people were executed; 36 were struck by lightning.").

110. A recent study found widely different success rates for ineffective assistance of counsel claims by circuit. Whereas inmates in the Ninth Circuit had a 52.6% success rate with respect to ineffective assistance of counsel claims in the five years after *Wiggins v. Smith*, 539 U.S. 510 (2003), the success rate in other circuits—Fourth Circuit (0%), Fifth Circuit (3.8%), and Eleventh Circuit (4.5%)—was much lower. Kenneth Williams, Most Deserving of Death?: An Analysis of the Supreme Court's Death Penalty Jurisprudence 29 (2012).

111. *Strickland v. Washington*, 466 U.S. 668, 687, 692 (1984), held that a defendant must show

that his or her attorney performed deficiently—and that the deficient performance was prejudicial—to establish ineffective assistance of counsel. It is also largely men, the poor, and the mentally ill who end up on America's death rows. *See generally* Stephen B. Bright, *The Role of Race, Poverty, Intellectual Disability, and Mental Illness in the Decline of the Death Penalty*, 49 U. RICH. L. REV. 671 (2015); Stephen B. Bright, *Counsel for the Poor: The Death Sentence Not for the Worst Crime but for the Worst Lawyer*, 103 YALE L.J. 1835 (1994).

112. Glossip v. Gross, 135 S. Ct. 2726, 2774 (2015) (Breyer, J., dissenting).

113. Id.

114. Id.

115. Id.

116. Id.

117. BAUMGARTNER ET AL., *supra* note 74, at 4.

118. Id.; *see also* "National Academy of Sciences Reports Four Percent of Death Row Inmates are Innocent," Innocence Project, Apr. 28, 2014, https://www.innocenceproject.org/national-academy-of-sciences-reports-four-percent-of-death-row-inmates-are-innocent/ ("In a study released today, the National Academy of Sciences reports that at least 4.1 percent of defendants sentenced to death in the United States are innocent.").

119. BAUMGARTNER ET AL., *supra* note 74, at 192.

120. The U.S. Supreme Court has now made clear that, under the U.S. Constitution's Sixth Amendment, death penalty determinations are to be made by juries. Hurst v. Florida, 136 S. Ct. 616, 619 (2016).

121. PERSPECTIVES ON HEALTH AND HUMAN RIGHTS 322 n.33 (Sofia Gruskin et al. eds., 2005) ("A recent statistical study that reviewed capital appeals in the United States from 1973 to 1995 found the 'overall Prejudicial error rate in the American capital punishment system was 68%.'") (citing James S. Liebman et al., *A Broken System: Error Rates in Capital Cases, 1973–1995* (Columbia Law Sch. Pub. Law & Legal Theory Working Paper Grp., Paper No. 15, 2000)).

122. *E.g.*, 1 RECORDS OF THE COURT OF ASSISTANTS OF THE COLONY OF THE MASSACHUSETTS BAY 1630–1692, at 320 (1901); A MEMBER OF THE NEW YORK BAR, HANGED BY THE NECK UNTIL YOU BE DEAD: OR WHY THE DEATH SENTENCE SHOULD BE ABOLISHED 20 (1877); JAMES JEFFREY PAUL, NOTHING IS STRANGE WITH YOU: THE LIFE AND CRIMES OF GORDON STEWART NORTHCOTT 225 (2008); HARRY M. WARD, PUBLIC EXECUTIONS IN RICHMOND, VIRGINIA: A HISTORY, 1782–1907, at 178 (2012).

123. WILLIAM S. MCFEELY, PROXIMITY TO DEATH 27, 50, 74, 113 (2000). Sometimes, modern American judges—echoing a phrase commonly used in early America—declare in open court: "May God have mercy on your soul." Id. at 82; *see also* EDWARD BAUMANN, MAY GOD HAVE MERCY ON YOUR SOUL: THE STORY OF THE ROPE AND THE THUNDERBOLT (1993).

124. The harsh conditions on death row have been summarized elsewhere and will not be repeated here. *See, e.g.*, AM. CIVIL LIBERTIES UNION, A DEATH BEFORE DYING: SOLITARY CONFINEMENT ON DEATH ROW (2013), https://www.aclu.org/files/assets/deathbeforedying-report.pdf; HUMAN RIGHTS CLINIC, UNIV. OF TEX. SCH. OF LAW, DESIGNED TO BREAK YOU: HUMAN RIGHTS VIOLATIONS ON TEXAS' DEATH ROW (2017), https://law.utexas.edu/wp-content/uploads/sites/11/2017/04/2017-HRC-DesignedToBreakYou-Report.pdf.

125. In 2016, Justice Stephen Breyer dissented from a denial of certiorari in the case of Henry Sireci, a man "tried, convicted of murder, and first sentenced to death in 1976." Sireci v. Florida, 137 S. Ct. 470, 470 (2016) (Breyer, J., dissenting from denial of certiorari). As Breyer wrote of Sireci: "He has lived in prison under threat of execution for 40 years. When he was first sentenced to death, the Berlin Wall stood firmly in place. Saigon had just fallen." *Id.* Justice Breyer then cited *In re Medley*, 134 U.S. 160, 172 (1890), which, referring to a death row inmate's *four-week* period of uncertainty before execution, held that such uncertainly is "one of the most horrible feelings to which he can be subjected." *Id.*

126. MICHAEL MELLO, THE WRONG MAN: A TRUE STORY OF INNOCENCE ON DEATH ROW 89 (2001).

127. Id.

128. HELEN PREJEAN, DEAD MAN WALKING: AN EYEWITNESS ACCOUNT OF THE DEATH PENALTY IN THE UNITED STATES (1993).

129. Id. at 105.

130. Id.

131. Id.

132. Id. at 101, 105. The death penalty's use, of course, affects more than just death row inmates; its use also impacts the family members of such inmates as well as the family members of the murder victims who must endure the lengthy capital litigation process. *E.g.*, Rachel King, *No Due Process: How the Death Penalty Violates the Constitutional Rights of the Family Members of Death Row Prisoners*, 16 B.U. Pub. Int. L.J. 195 (2007).

133. Lisa Bruce, Reviving the Dead: 10 Keys to Unlock Purpose and Destiny 20 (2011); James Garbarino, Listening to Killers: Lessons Learned from My Twenty Years as a Psychological Expert Witness in Murder Cases 57 (2015).

134. Convention against Torture and Other Cruel, Inhuman or Degrading Treatment or Punishment, art. 1, Dec. 10, 1984, 1465 U.N.T.S. 85 (entry into force June 26, 1987).

135. Id.

136. *E.g.*, Sangmin Bae, When the State No Longer Kills: International Human Rights Norms and Abolition of Capital Punishment 24–28, 53–55 (2007) (discussing the death penalty's abolition in Europe, South Africa and elsewhere); *see also* Thomas S. Mowle, Allies at Odds?: The United States and the European Union 102–07 (2004) (discussing the history of the divergence of approach to the death penalty in Europe versus the United States).

137. *See generally* Garrett, End of Its Rope, *supra* note 105.

138. *See generally* Andrea D. Lyon, The Death Penalty: What's Keeping it Alive (2015).

139. John D. Bessler, The Death Penalty as Torture: From the Dark Ages to Abolition xxiv–xxv, 225–26, 316 (2017).

140. David Weissbrodt & Cheryl Heilman, *Defining Torture and Cruel, Inhuman, and Degrading Treatment*, 29 Law & Ineq. 343, 375 (2011).

141. Bessler, The Death Penalty as Torture, *supra* note 139, at 87, 89, 91, 154, 225.

142. *Ex parte* Deardorff, 6 So.3d 1235, 1240 (Ala. 2008) ("'Psychological torture can be inflicted where the victim is in intense fear and is aware of, but helpless to prevent, impending death. Such torture 'must have been present for an appreciable lapse of time, sufficient enough to cause prolonged or appreciable suffering.'") (quoting Norris v. State, 793 So.2d 847, 861 (Ala. Crim. App. 1999) & *Ex parte* Key, 891 So.2d 384, 390 (Ala. 2004)); Smith v. State, 122 So.3d 224, 241 (Ala. Crim. App. 2011); id. at 242 ("After the initial gunshots rendered Smith helpless to prevent her death she suffered great psychological torture as she listened to her abductors discuss how they were going to kill her and dispose of her body while she begged for medical attention."); State v. Bell, 603 S.E.2d 93, 121 (N.C. 2004) (describing killings involving "psychological torture where the victim is left to her 'last moments aware of but helpless to prevent impending death'") (quoting State v. Hamlet, 321 S.E.2d 837, 846 (N.C. 1984)); State v. Mann, 560 S.E.2d 776, 788 (N.C. 2002) ("An example of psychological torture is when the victim is left 'in [her] last moments aware of but helpless to prevent impending death.'") (quoting *Hamlet*, 321 S.E.2d at 846).

143. Bessler, The Death Penalty as Torture, *supra* note 139, at 217–37.

144. Sarah Joseph & Melissa Castan, The International Covenant on Civil and Political Rights: Cases, Materials, and Commentary 254 (3d ed. 2013).

145. *See, e.g.*, Angela April Sun, *"Killing Time" in the Valley of the Shadow of Death: Why Systematic Preexecution Delays on Death Row are Cruel and Unusual*, 113 Colum. L. Rev. 1585, 1586–89, 1615–18 (2013); *see also* Caycie D. Bradford, *Waiting to Die, Dying to Live: An Account of the Death Row Phenomenon from a Legal Viewpoint*, 5 Interdisc. J. Hum. Rts. L. 77, 93–94 (2011) (noting that death row inmates are subjected to the mental torture of not knowing when their sentences will be carried out, that "[t]he sentencing of individuals to long drawn-out incarcerations under the conditions of death row has been shown to have prolonged psychological effects on the inmates," and that the right to life "does not allow for the psychological implications of the death row phenomenon, which are affecting the inmates' right to life").

146. Cesare Beccaria asserted that the death penalty "is not useful because of the example of cruelty that it gives to men." John D. Bessler, Cruel and Unusual: The American Death Penalty and the Founders' Eighth Amendment 35 (2012). Dr. Benjamin Rush, who opposed the death penalty for any crime, said "[t]he punishment of murder by death, is contrary to reason, and to the

order and happiness of society" and that "[h]umanity" revolts "at the idea of the severity and certainty of a capital punishment." Id. at 53, 70; Dagobert D. Runes, The Selected Writings of Benjamin Rush xi, 35–42 (1947) (reprinting Dr. Benjamin Rush's 1792 essay on the topic of "On Punishing Murder by Death"); *see also* Benjamin Rush, Essays, Literary, Moral and Philosophical 63 (2d ed. 1806) ("In barbarous ages every thing partook of the complexion of the times. Civil, ecclesiastical, military, and domestic punishments were all of a cruel nature. With the progress of reason and Christianity, punishments of all kinds have become less severe.").

147. *See, e.g.*, Jackson J. Spielvogel, Western Civilization: Vol. B 1300–1815, at 518 (10th ed. 2018) (noting that punishments in eighteenth-century societies "were often cruel and even spectacular," that "[p]ublic executions were a basic part of traditional punishment," and that "[t]he death penalty was still commonly used for property crimes as well as for violent crimes").

148. John D. Bessler, *Tinkering Around the Edges: The Supreme Court's Death Penalty Jurisprudence*, 49 Am. Crim. L. Rev. 1913, 1943 (2012).

149. The Universal Declaration of Human Rights was an important step forward for the idea that certain rights, such as the right to be free from cruelty and torture, are *universal* human rights. Universal Declaration of Human Rights, G.A. Res. 217A (III), (Dec. 10, 1948).

150. Peter J. Coleman, Debtors and Creditors in America: Insolvency, Imprisonment for Debt, and Bankruptcy, 1607–1900 91, 152, 172, 182 (1999) (noting the use of the pillory, ear cropping, and mutilation as punishments in the eighteenth century); Kenneth L. Kusmer, Down and Out, on the Road: The Homeless in American History 21 (2002) (noting the use of corporal punishments on convicted vagrants in colonial New York, including "the stockades, pillory, ear-cropping, and branding, in addition to whipping"); Paul M. Fink, Jonesborough: The First Century of Tennessee's First Town 13 (2002) ("Lesser crimes might bring confinement in the pillory or stocks, or the whipping post, with a specified number of lashes 'well laid on.' Women as well as men felt the whip. . . .").

151. Daniel W. Crofts, Lincoln and the Politics of Slavery: The Other Thirteenth Amendment and the Struggle to Save the Union 266 (2016) ("The Fourteenth Amendment, [Garrett] Epps writes, brought about 'by far the most sweeping and complex change ever made in the original Constitution.' Indeed, Epps contends that the 1787 Constitution 'died at Fort Sumter' and that the architects of the new 'second Constitution,' who attempted to repair the flawed work of the Founders, should be considered the 'second founders.' ").

152. John D. Bessler, *The Anomaly of Executions: The Cruel and Unusual Punishments Clause in the 21st Century*, 2 Brit. J. Am. Legal Stud. 297, 430–39 (2013); *compare* S. Meeson Morris, *The Obsolete Punishments of Shropshire*, *in* 8 Transactions of the Shropshire Archæological and Natural History Society 92–93 (1885):

The substitution of imprisonment, fines, and similar punishments now in vogue, for the curious contrivances formerly used, has rendered the pillory, ducking stool, and other instruments before referred to, things of the past, but the modes of correction employed by our forefathers, in what are familiarly termed "the good old days," must always prove of considerable interest, serving, as they undoubtedly do, to remind us of the comparative improvement effected in the infliction of punishments during the present age of progress and advancement. Many alterations and amendments remain to be made before perfection can be nearly attained, but anyone looking back at what our system of punishment once was cannot fail to observe the many steps in this direction that have already been taken.

153. 404 F.2d 571 (8th Cir. 1968).

154. *Id.* at 579:

[W]e have no difficulty in reaching the conclusion that the use of the strap in the penitentiaries of Arkansas is punishment which, in this last third of the 20th century, runs afoul of the Eighth Amendment; that the strap's use, irrespective of any precautionary conditions which may be imposed, offends contemporary concepts of decency and human dignity and precepts of civilization which we profess to possess. . . .

155. 536 U.S. 730 (2002).

156. *Id.* at 738.

157. Elizabeth T. Gershoff, Kelly M. Purtell & Igor Holas, Corporal Punishment in U.S.

Schools: Legal Precedents, Current Practices, and Future Policy 61 (2015).

158. Glossip v. Gross, 135 S. Ct. 2726, 2780–81 (2015) (Sotomayor, J., dissenting):

The State plans to execute petitioners using three drugs: midazolam, rocuronium bromide, and potassium chloride. The latter two drugs are intended to paralyze the inmate and stop his heart. But they do so in a torturous manner, causing burning, searing pain.... [I]t leaves petitioners exposed to what may well be the chemical equivalent of being burned at the stake.

159. 408 U.S. 238.

160. *See* Michael S. Green & Scott L. Stabler, Ideas and Movements and Shaped America: From the Bill of Rights to "Occupy Wall Street" 175 (2015) (discussing the ruling in *Furman v. Georgia*, 408 U.S. 238 (1972)).

161. *Furman*, 408 U.S. at 291 (Brennan, J., concurring) ("The outstanding characteristic of our present practice of punishing criminals by death is the infrequency with which we resort to it. The evidence is conclusive that death is not the ordinary punishment for any crime."); id. at 309 (Stewart, J., concurring) ("[T]he Eighth and Fourteenth Amendments cannot tolerate the infliction of a sentence of death under legal systems that permit this unique penalty to be so wantonly and so freakishly imposed."); id. at 313 (White, J., concurring) ("[T]he death penalty is exacted with great infrequency even for the most atrocious crimes and ... there is no meaningful basis for distinguishing the few cases in which it is imposed from the many cases in which it is not.").

162. 428 U.S. 153 (1976).

163. Proffitt v. Florida, 428 U.S. 242 (1976); Jurek v. Texas, 428 U.S. 262 (1976).

164. The first execution after *Gregg v. Georgia*, 428 U.S. 153 (1976), was that of Gary Gilmore in 1977. Mikal Gilmore, Shot in the Heart 349 (1994).

165. 554 U.S. 407.

166. Id. at 420.

167. James E. White, Contemporary Moral Problems 228 (8th ed. 2006).

168. 428 U.S. 227, 231 (1976) (Marshall, J., dissenting).

169. Id. at 237 (citation omitted); *see also* id. at 241 (Marshall, J., dissenting) ("The death penalty, unnecessary to promote the goal of deterrence or to further any legitimate notion of retribution, is an excessive penalty forbidden by the Eighth and Fourteenth Amendments. I respectfully dissent from the Court's judgment upholding the sentences of death imposed upon the petitioners in these cases.").

170. *See generally* Glossip v. Gross, 135 S. Ct. 2726, 2782 (2015) (Sotomayor, J., dissenting).

171. Baze v. Rees, 553 U.S. 35, 113 (2008) (Breyer, J., concurring) ("The upshot is that I cannot find, either in the record or in the readily available literature that I have seen, sufficient grounds to believe that Kentucky's method of lethal injection creates a significant risk of unnecessary suffering.").

172. 471 U.S. 1080 (1985) (Brennan, J., dissenting from denial of cert.).

173. Id. at 1084 (citations omitted).

174. Furman v. Georgia, 408 U.S. 238, 375, 391 (1972) (Burger, C.J., dissenting).

175. 99 U.S. 130 (1878).

176. Id. at 135–36.

177. 329 U.S. 459 (1947).

178. Id. at 463.

179. *Furman*, 408 U.S. at 392 (Burger, C.J., dissenting).

180. Id.

181. Id. at 392–93.

182. Id. at 393.

183. Id. at 393–96 (citations omitted).

184. Richard C. Dieter, *The Future of the Death Penalty in the United States*, 49 U. Rich. L. Rev. 921, 928 (2015).

185. *See generally* Bessler, *The Anomaly of Executions*, *supra* note 152, at 297; Bessler, The Death Penalty as Torture, *supra* note 139.

186. Daniel S. Nagin & John V. Pepper, eds., Deterrence and the Death Penalty (2012) (a publication of the National Research Council of the National Academies). That reports bottom line conclusion and recommendation:

The committee concludes that research to date on the effect of capital punishment on homicide is not informative about whether capital punishment decreases, increases, or has no effect on homicide rates. Therefore, the committee recommends that these studies not be used to inform deliberations requiring judgments about the effect of the death penalty on homicide. Consequently, claims that research demonstrates the capital punishment decreases or increases the homicide rate by a specified amount or has no effect on the homicide rate should not influence policy judgments about capital punishment.

187. Clarke E. Cochran, Lawrence C. Mayer, T.R. Carr, N. Joseph Cayer, Mark J. McKenzie & Laura R. Peck, American Public Policy: An Introduction 159 (11th ed. 2015) (comparing murder rates in death penalty states to those in non-death penalty states and noting that "death penalty states in fact had slightly higher mean homicide rates than did the abolitionist states").

188. Aida Y. Hass, Chris Moloney & William J. Chambliss, Criminology: Connecting Theory, Research and Practice 274 (2d ed. 2017).

189. Unless later exonerated or the recipient of executive clemency, offenders who receive LWOP sentences will spend the rest of their lives in prison. Michael L. Radelet, *The Incremental Retributive Impact of a Death Sentence Over Life Without Parole*, 49 Univ. Mich. J. L. Reform 795, 805–806 (2016); *see also* id. at 800 ("Virtually all contemporary studies on the death penalty, whether completed by legislative bodies, state supreme courts, journalists or academics, have found that the costs of the death penalty far exceed the costs of LWOP.").

190. *Furman*, 408 U.S. at 342 (Marshall, J., concurring).

191. Id. at 353.

192. Ian Marsh (with Gaynor Melville, Keith Morgan, Gareth Norris & John Cochrane), Crime and Criminal Justice 297 (2011); Michelle Ann Abate, Bloody Murder: The Homicide Tradition in Children's Literature 64–65 (2013).

193. Killing as Punishment: Reflections on the Death Penalty in America 7 (2004).

194. Hugo Adam Bedau, "An Abolitionist's Survey of the Death Penalty in America Today," *in* Hugo Bedau & Paul Cassell, eds., Debating the Death Penalty: Should America Have Capital Punishment? 18 (2004).

195. Woodson v. North Carolina, 428 U.S. 280, 293 (1976).

196. Lockett v. Ohio, 438 U.S. 586, 604 (1978) (italics in original):

[W]e conclude that the Eighth and Fourteenth Amendments require that the sentence, in all but the rarest kind of capital case, not be precluded from considering, *as a mitigating factor*, any aspect of a defendant's character or record and any of the circumstances of the offense that the defendant proffers as a basis for a sentence less than death.

197. *Lockett*, 438 U.S. at 613–14 (Blackmun, J., concurring):

It might be that to inflict the death penalty in some such situations would skirt the limits of the Eighth Amendment proscription, incorporated in the Fourteenth Amendment, against gross disproportionality, but I doubt that the Court, in regard to murder, could easily define a convincing bright-line rule such as was used in regard to rape, *Coker v. Georgia*, 433 U.S. 584 (1977), to make workable a disproportionality approach.

198. Notably, Justice Harry Blackmun changed his judicial perspective on the death penalty, ultimately concluding that it should be declared unconstitutional. As Justice Blackmun wrote in 1994 in a famous dissent: "From this day forward, I shall no longer tinker with the machinery of death." Linda Greenhouse, Becoming Justice Blackmun: Harry Blackmun's Supreme Court Journey 178, 197 (2005). Justices Stephen Breyer and Ruth Bader Ginsburg have also recently concluded that it is "highly likely" that capital punishment is unconstitutional. Glossip v. Gross, 135 S. Ct. 2726, 2776-77 (2015) (Breyer, J., dissenting).

199. *See generally* John D. Bessler, *The Abolitionist Movement Comes of Age: From Capital Punishment as a Lawful Sanction to a Peremptory International Law Norm Barring Executions*, 79 Mont. L. Rev. 202 (2018) (describing the trend away from the death penalty as a lawful sanction and toward the recognition of an international law norm barring executions); Garrett, End of Its Rope, *supra* note 105, at 1 ("The death penalty in the United States is at the end of its rope.").

200. 217 U.S. 349 (1910).

201. Id. at 367. The Court in *Weems* found that *cadena temporal*, imprisonment with hard labor in chains and that carried with it permanent civil disabilities, violated the Eighth Amendment because

the sentence was "cruel" as an excessive punishment. Id. at 372–73, 377.

202. Gregg v. Georgia, 428 U.S. 153, 188 (1976) ("the penalty of death is different in kind from any other punishment imposed under our system of criminal justice").

203. *E.g.*, Gary B. Melton, John Petrila, Norman G. Poythress, Christopher Slobogin, Randy K. Otto, Douglas Mossman & Lois O. Condie, Psychological Evaluations for the Courts: A Handbook for Mental Health Professionals and Lawyers 34, 279 (4th ed. 2018) (noting that juveniles and people with intellectual disabilities or who are incompetent are exempt from the death penalty). To date, the Supreme Court has not declared a *per se* bar on executions but has held that capital punishment must be limited to offenders who commit "a narrow category of the most serious crimes" and whose extreme culpability makes them "the most deserving of execution." Donald E. Lively & D. Scott Broyles, Contemporary Supreme Court Cases: Landmark Decisions since *Roe v. Wade* 595 (2d ed. 2016).

204. *Solem*, 463 U.S. at 288 (citing Enmund v. Florida, 458 U.S. 782 (1982) & Coker v. Georgia, 433 U.S. 584, 433 U.S. 592 (1977) (plurality opinion)).

205. *Solem*, 463 U.S. at 292.

206. Darius Rejali, Torture and Democracy 148 (2007).

207. *See* Glossip v. Gross, 135 S. Ct. 2726, 2759 (2015) (Breyer, J., dissenting) ("The arbitrary imposition of punishment is the antithesis of the rule of law.").

208. *E.g.*, David P. Keys & R. J. Maratea, eds., Race and the Death Penalty: The Legacy of *McCleskey v. Kemp* (2015) (discussing the racial prejudice and disparities associated with capital punishment).

209. *E.g.*, Frank R. Baumgartner, Woody Gram, Kaneesha R. Johnson, Arvind Krishnamurthy & Colin P. Wilson, *The Geographic Distribution of US Executions*, 2 Duke J. Const. L. & Pub. Pol'y 1, 2 (2016) ("A small number of jurisdictions in the US generate most of the executions. This high level of geographic concentration is not explained by the number or the rate of homicides."); id. ("The extreme concentration of jurisdictions using the death penalty can be seen whether we compare the 50 states, over 3,000 counties across the country, counties within states, or even the countries of the world.").

210. Cassia Spohn & Pauline K. Brennan, "Sentencing and Punishment," *in* Claire M. Renzetti, Susan L. Miller & Angela R. Gover, Routledge International Handbook of Crime and Gender Studies 219–23 (2013) (describing the gender disparities associated with the capital sentencing process).

211. There is a *jus cogens* norm of international law barring torture. *E.g.*, Hirsh v. State of Israel, 962 F. Supp. 377, 381 (S.D.N.Y. 1997) (citations omitted):

Jus cogens norms "proscribe a limited set of activities so universally condemned by the international community that they cannot be undertaken under any circumstances." A foreign state violates *jus cogens* when it participates in such blatant violations of fundamental human rights as "genocide, slavery, murder, torture, prolonged arbitrary detention, and racial discrimination."

212. Baze v. Rees, 553 U.S. 35, 48 (2008) ("[T]he *Wilkerson* Court simply noted that 'it is safe to affirm that punishments of torture, … and all others in the same line of unnecessary cruelty, are forbidden' by the Eighth Amendment.") (quoting Wilkerson v. Utah, 99 U.S. 130, 136 (1879)); *see also* Gregg v. Georgia, 428 U.S. 153, 169–70 (1976) ("The American draftsmen, who adopted the English phrasing in drafting the Eighth Amendment, were primarily concerned … with proscribing 'tortures' and other 'barbarous' methods of punishment.'") (citation omitted); Furman v. Georgia, 408 U.S. 238 (1972) (Marshall, J., concurring) ("Whether the English Bill of Rights prohibition against cruel and unusual punishments is properly read as a response to excessive or illegal punishments, as a reaction to barbaric and objectionable modes of punishment, or as both, there is no doubt whatever that, in borrowing the language and in including it in the Eighth Amendment, our Founding Fathers intended to outlaw torture and other cruel punishments.").

213. Kennedy v. Louisiana, 554 U.S. 407, 420 (2008).

214. Fred E. Foldvary, The Soul of Liberty: The Universal Ethic of Freedom and Human Rights 115 (1980):

If torture constitutes excessive punishment, even as a deterrent, then so does capital punishment, which is final, and would be an irreversible punishment in the case of a wrongful or mistaken conviction. Some types of harm are never justified, even for the most despicable criminals. The ethical state must defend the nobility and dignity of justice. It must refrain from inflicting punishment just to satisfy vengeful and sadistic desires, for this exceeds what is needed to protect society.

215. Rhodes v. Chapman, 452 U.S. 337, 347 (1981); *see also* Brown v. Plata, 563 U.S. 493, 500 (2011) ("A prison's failure to provide sustenance for inmates 'may actually produce physical 'torture or a lingering death.' ") (quoting Estelle v. Gamble, 429 U.S. 97, 103 (1976) (quoting In re Kemmler, 136 U.S. 436, 447 (1890)); McKune v. Lile, 536 U.S. 24, 41 (2002) ("Courts must decide whether the consequences of an inmate's choice to remain silent are closer to the physical torture against which the Constitution clearly protects or the *de minimis* harms against which it does not."); Lisenba v. People of State of California, 314 U.S. 219, 237 (1941) ("To extort testimony from a defendant by physical torture in the very presence of the trial tribunal is not due process."); Irvine v. People of California, 347 U.S. 128, 141 (1954) (Black, J. dissenting) ("The Fifth Amendment forbids the Federal Government and the agents through which it acts—courts, grand juries, prosecutors, marshals or other officers—to use physical torture, psychological pressure, threats of fines, imprisonment or prosecution, or other governmental pressure to force a person to testify against himself.").

216. *E.g.*, Thompson v. McNeil, 556 U.S. 1114 (2009) (Stevens, J., statement respecting the denial of cert.); Lackey v. Texas, 514 U.S. 1045 (1995) (Stevens, J., memo. respecting denial of cert.).

217. Irvine v. People of California, 347 U.S. 128, 141 (1954); United States v. Carignan, 342 U.S. 36, 41 (1951); Upshaw v. United States, 335 U.S. 410, 413 (1948); Culombe v. Connecticut, 367 U.S. 568, 599 (1961); United States v. Mitchell, 322 U.S. 65, 68 (1968); *see also* Ashcraft v. State of Tennessee, 322 U.S. 143, 155 (1944):

The Constitution of the United States stands as a bar against the conviction of any individual in an American court by means of a coerced confession. There have been, and are now, certain foreign nations with governments dedicated to an opposite policy: governments which convict individuals with testimony obtained by police organizations possessed of an unrestrained power to seize persons suspected of crimes against the state, hold them in secret custody, and wring from them confessions by physical or mental torture. So long as the Constitution remains the basic law of our Republic, America will not have that kind of government.

218. 493 P.2d 880 (Cal. 1972).

219. Id. at 894. This language was quoted by Justice William Brennan in his concurrence in *Furman v. Georgia* and by Justice John Paul Stevens in his statement respecting the denial of certiorari in *Thompson v. McNeil* and *Lackey v. Texas*. *Furman*, 408 U.S. at 288 (Brennan, J., concurring); *Thompson*, 556 U.S. at 1114 (Stevens, J., statement respecting the denial of cert.); *Lackey*, 514 U.S. at 1045 n.* (Stevens, J., memo. respecting denial of cert.).

220. "Death Row Phenomenon: The psychological impact of living in the shadow of execution," Reprieve, https://reprieve.org.uk/death-row-phenomenon-psychological-impact-shadow-execution/.

221. David Musick & Kristine Gunsaulus-Musick, American Prisons: Their Past, Present and Future 2 (2017).

222. Nazgol Ghandnoosh, "Can We Wait 75 Years to Cut the Prison Population in Half?", The Sentencing Project (Mar. 2018), pp. 1–2; *see also* id. at 2 (noting that the prison population has declined by 37% in New Jersey since 1999, by 33% in Alaska since 2006, by 31% in New York since 1999, by 29% in Vermont in 2009, by 28% in Connecticut in 2007, and by 25% in California since 2006).

223. Id. at 2.

224. NAACP, Action Alert—"Urge Immediate Passage of Sentencing Reform Legislation to Bring Fairness and Eliminate Racial Disparities in Federal Sentencing," Sept. 27, 2017, http://www.naacp.org/latest/urge-immediate-passage-sentencing-reform-legislation-bring-fairness-eliminate-racial-disparities-federal-sentencing/.

225. NAACP, "Criminal Justice Fact Sheet," http://www.naacp.org/criminal-justice-fact-sheet/.

226. John Gramlich, "The Gap Between the Number of Blacks and Whites in Prison Is Shrinking," Pew Research Center, Jan. 12, 2018, http://www.pewresearch.org/fact-tank/2018/01/12/shrinking-gap-between-number-of-blacks-and-whites-in-prison/.

227. Annual Report 2017, The Sentencing Project (2018), https://www.sentencingproject.org/wp-content/uploads/2015/10/Annual-Report-2017.pdf, pp. 4–5. Ashley Nellis, "Still Life: America's In-

creasing Use of Life and Long-Term Sentences," The Sentencing Project (2017), https://www.sentencingproject.org/wp-content/uploads/2017/05/Still-Life.pdf, p. 5.

228. American Civil Liberties Union, "A Living Death: Life without Parole for Nonviolent Offences" (Nov. 2013), p. 2.

229. www.mnjrc.org.

230. "Mass Incarceration," Equal Justice Initiative, https://eji.org/mass-incarceration (last visiting Feb. 3, 2018).

231. Aida Y. Hass, Chris Moloney & William J. Chambliss, Criminology: Connecting Theory, Research and Practice 230 (2d ed. 2017).

232. Id.; *see also* Michelle Alexander, The New Jim Crow: Mass Incarceration in the Age of Colorblindness 13 (2012) ("The term *mass incarceration* refers not only to the criminal justice system but also to the larger web of laws, rules, policies, and customs that control those labeled criminals both in and out of prison."); Joan Petersilia & Kevin R. Reitz, eds., The Oxford Handbook of Sentencing and Corrections 27–28 (2012) (citations omitted):

The phrase "mass imprisonment" was coined by David Garland in 2000 to describe the distinctive expansion of imprisonment in the United States between 1975 and the late 1990s. To Garland, mass imprisonment constituted a new regime of penality that differed along two dimensions from varying policies of imprisonment in use by modern societies since the end of the eighteenth century. First, U.S. imprisonment rates in the late 1990s marked a substantial departure from historic norms for the scale of imprisonment during the twentieth century by several magnitudes. Second, in contrast to a history of using imprisonment against individuals based on crime and criminal history, contemporary mass imprisonment reflected a "systematic imprisonment of whole groups of the population".

233. *Bryan Stevenson*, https://eji.org/bryan-stevenson.

234. Bryan Stevenson, Just Mercy: A Story of Justice and Redemption 15 (2014).

235. "Prisoners in 2016," Bulletin, U.S. Department of Justice, Office of Justice Programs, Bureau of Justice Statistics, Jan. 2018, p. 1, https://www.bjs.gov/content/pub/pdf/p16.pdf.

236. "Mass Incarceration: The Whole Pie 2017," Prison Policy Initiative, Mar. 14, 2017, https://www.prisonpolicy.org/reports/pie2017.html.

237. Aimee Picchi, "The High Price of Incarceration in America," CBS News, May 8, 2014, https://www.cbsnews.com/news/the-high-price-of-americas-incarceration-80-billion/.

238. "Prisoners in 2016," Bulletin, U.S. Department of Justice, Office of Justice Programs, Bureau of Justice Statistics, Jan. 2018, p. 1, https://www.bjs.gov/content/pub/pdf/p16.pdf.

239. Heather Ahn-Redding, The "Million Dollar Inmate": The Financial and Social Burden of Non-violent Offenders xiii (2007).

240. Id. at 3.

241. "New CASA Report Finds: 65% of All U.S. Inmates Meet Medical Criteria for Substance Abuse Addiction, Only 11% Receive Any Treatment," The National Center on Addiction and Substance Abuse," Feb. 26, 2010, https://www.centeronaddiction.org/newsroom/press-releases/2010-behind-bars-II.

242. Glenn D. Walters, Drugs, Crime, and Their Relationships: Theory, Research, Practice, and Policy 7-10 (2013).

243. German Lopez, "How America's Prisons Are Fueling the Opioid Epidemic," Vox, Mar. 26, 2018, https://www.vox.com/policy-and-politics/2018/3/13/17020002/prison-opioid-epidemic-medications-addiction.

244. Meghamala S. Tavaragi, "Chronic Mental Illness in Prisons: Global Scenario," *in* Barre Vijaya Prasad, ed., Chronic Mental Illness and the Changing Scope of Intervention Strategies, Diagnosis, and Treatment 207 (2017).

245. 1 Gwendolyn Mink & Alice O'Connor, eds., Poverty in the United States : An Encyclopedia of History, Politics and Policy 216 (2004).

246. 1 Jyotsna Sreenivasan, Poverty and the Government in America: A Historical Encyclopedia 193 (2009).

247. Bernadette Rabuy & Daniel Kopf, "Prisons of Poverty: "Uncovering the Pre-Incarceration Incomes of the Imprisoned," Prison Policy Initiative, July 9, 2015, https://www.prisonpolicy.org/reports/income.html.

248. Chris Mai & Ram Subramanian, The Price of Prisons: Examining State Spending Trends,

2010–2015, Vera Institute of Justice (May 2017), https://storage.googleapis.com/vera-web-assets/downloads/Publications/price-of-prisons-2015-state-spending-trends/legacy_downloads/the-price-of-prisons-2015-state-spending-trends.pdf, pp. 6–7. The Vera report, not surprisingly, noted a reduction in costs where state prison populations had declined. In examining the data from 2010 to 2015, the report found that in the thirteen states where prison population had declined since 2010, total prison costs declined by $1.6 billion. Id. at 16.

249. "Prison Time Serviced and Recidivism," Pew, Public Safety Performance Project, Fact Sheet, Oct. 8, 2013, http://www.pewtrusts.org/en/research-and-analysis/fact-sheets/2013/10/08/prison-time-served-and-recidivism.

250. Hilde Wermink, Paul Nieuwbeerta, Anke A. T. Ramakers, Jan W. de Keijser & Anja J. E. Dirkzwager, *Short-Term Effects of Imprisonment Length on Recidivism in the Netherlands*, Crime & Delinquency 1, 3–4, 11–12, 21, 23–24, 27 (2017), *available at* https://doi.org/10.1177/0011128716687290.

251. Jeffrey A. Butts & Vincent Schiraldi, "Recidivism Reconsidered: Preserving the Community Justice Mission of Community Corrections," Harvard Kennedy School, Program in Criminal Justice Policy and Management (March 2018), https://www.hks.harvard.edu/sites/default/files/centers/wiener/programs/pcj/files/recidivism_reconsidered.pdf.

252. Anne M. Cohler, Basia C. Miller & Harold S. Stone, eds. and trans., Montesquieu: The Spirit of the Laws 35–36 (1989).

253. Cesare Beccaria, An Essay on Crimes and Punishments 130 (5th ed. 1777); Ethan Putterman, Rousseau, Law and the Sovereignty of the People 135 (2010).

254. Marc Santora, "City's Annual Cost Per Inmate Is $168,000, Study Finds," N.Y. Times, Aug. 23, 2013.

255. Associated Press, "At $75,560, housing a prisoner in California now costs more than a year at Harvard," June 4, 2017, http://www.latimes.com/local/lanow/la-me-prison-costs-20170604-htmlstory.html.

256. "Average Published Undergraduate Charges by Sector and by Carnegie Classification, 2017–18," College Board, https://trends.collegeboard.org/college-pricing/figures-tables/average-published-undergraduate-charges-sector-2017-18; Farran Powell, "What You Need to Know About College Tuition Costs," U.S. News and World Report, Mar. 28, 2018, https://www.usnews.com/education/best-colleges/paying-for-college/articles/what-you-need-to-know-about-college-tuition-costs.

257. Delano R. Franklin & Samuel W. Zwickel, "Harvard College Enrollment Costs Rise 3 Percent for 2018–2019," The Harvard Crimson, Mar. 26, 2018, http://www.thecrimson.com/article/2018/3/26/harvard-college-costs-rises-three-percent/.

258. Shannon Wheatley Hartman & Roxanne Lynn Doty, "The Privatization of Punishment in the United States," *in* Rita Abrahamsen & Anna Leander, eds., Routledge Handbook of Private Security Studies 198 (2016).

259. https://www.aclu.org/issues/mass-incarceration/privatization-criminal-justice/private-prisons. "U.S. Immigrations and Customs Enforcement," the ACLU further observed of the use of private facilities, "reported that in 2016, private prisons held nearly three-quarters of federal immigration detainees." Id.

260. Julia Bowling, "Do Private Prison Contracts Fuel Mass Incarceration?", Brennan Center for Justice at New York University School of Law, Sept. 20, 2013, https://www.brennancenter.org/blog/do-private-prison-contracts-fuel-mass-incarceration.

261. Lawrence F. Travis III & Bradley D. Edwards, Introduction to Criminal Justice 394–95 (8th ed. 2015).

Chapter 8

1. Stack v. Boyle, 342 U.S. 1, 5 (1951).
2. United States v. Karper, 847 F. Supp.2d 350, 362 (N.D.N.Y. 2011).
3. Id.
4. Id. (citations omitted); *see also* 8 C.J.S. *Bail* § 7 (2018) ("While the Eighth Amendment prohibition against excessive bail does not make an arrestee's right to bail absolute, the relinquishment of constitutionally protected rights, on conditions that are more than necessary to satisfy legitimate gov-

ernmental interests, constitutes excessive bail in violation of the Eighth Amendment."); United States v. Polouizzi, 697 F. Supp.2d 381, 390 (E.D.N.Y. 2010) ("Bail conditions are unconstitutionally excessive if they impose restraints that are more than necessary to achieve the government's interest[,] ... preventing risk of flight and danger to society or children."); State ex rel. Corella v. Miles, 262 S.W. 364, 365 (Mo. 1924) (en banc) ("The purpose of giving bond is to secure the appearance of the defendant at trial, and when the Constitution forbids excessive bail it means that bail shall not be more than necessary to secure that attendance."); Gusick v. Boies, 233 P.2d 446, 447–48 (Ariz. 1951) (concluding that $150,000 bail for defendant constituted "a clear abuse of discretion" and violated state constitutional provisions guaranteeing right to bail and prohibiting excessive bail, with the court observing that "any bail fixed at more than is necessary to secure [the defendant's] appearance is excessive within the meaning of the [Arizona] constitution"); People v. George, Case No. ST-2016-CR-0000085, 2016 WL 5660283 *4 (V.I. Super. Ct., Sept. 27, 2016) ("Excessive bail refers to an amount more than necessary to ensure that a defendant appears for his hearings and trial, as opposed to his ability to pay.").

5. State v. Whitcomb, 413 N.W.2d 839, 842 (Minn. Ct. App. 1987).

6. Galen v. City of L.A., 477 F.3d 652, 661-62 (9th Cir. 2007).

7. Note, *Bail Reform and Risk Assessment: The Cautionary Tale of Federal Sentencing*, 131 Harv. L. Rev. 1125 (2018); David L. Hudson Jr., The Handy Law Answer Book: Understanding the Law, Navigating the Legal System 151 (2010) ("[I]f a crime is serious enough or the defendant is considered to be a flight risk, a judge does not have to provide bail."); Dean J. Champion, Measuring Offender Risk: A Criminal Justice Sourcebook 38 (1994) ("Under the Eighth Amendment, only those entitled to bail may receive it. Bail is not an absolute right under the Constitution. Ordinarily, those not entitled to bail are considered either very dangerous to others or highly likely to flee the jurisdiction to avoid prosecution for their crimes.").

8. Jessica Silver-Greenburg and Shaila Dewan, "When Bail Feels Less Like Freedom, More Like Extortion," N.Y. Times, Mar. 31, 2018, https://www.nytimes.com/2018/03/31/us/bail-bonds-extortion.html; Daniel L. Hatcher, The Poverty Industry: The Exploitation of America's Most Vulnerable Citizens (2016).

9. Constantinos E. Scaros, Understanding the Constitution 307 (2011).

10. F. E. Devine, Commercial Bail Bonding: A Comparison of Common Law Alternatives 5 (1991).

11. 1 David Levinson, ed., Encyclopedia of Crime and Punishment 1373 (2002).

12. Jeffrey Ian Ross, ed., Encyclopedia of Street Crime in America 17 (2013).

13. Stack v. Boyle, 342 U.S. 1, 1-5 (1951) (citing Judiciary Act of 1789, 1 Stat. 73, 91; Fed. R. Crim. P. 46(a)(1); Hudson v. Parker, 156 U.S. 277, 156 U.S. 285 (1985); Ex parte Milburn, 9 Pet. 704, 34 U.S. 710 (1835); United States v. Motlow, 10 F.2d 657 (7th Cir. 1926)).

14. *Stack*, 342 U.S. at 5-7.

15. Nicholas M. McLean, *Livelihood, Ability to Pay, and the Original Meaning of the Excessive Fines Clause*, 40 Hastings Const. L. Q. 833, 835, 855, 857 (2013) (citing Earl of Devonshire's Case, 11 State Trials 1362–63, 1367 (1689)).

16. Press Release, "Mayor Keisha Lance Bottoms Signs Cash Bond Ordinance into Law," City of Atlanta, Ga., Feb. 6, 2018, https://www.atlantaga.gov/Home/Components/News/News/11448/1338?backlist=%2525252F.

17. Ronald Simpson-Bey, "From the Inside Out: A Perspective on Decarceration from a Formerly Incarcerated Individual", John Chisholm & Jeffery Altenburg, "The Prosecutor's Role in Promoting Decarceration: Lessons Learned from Milwaukee County," and Nazgol Ghandnoosh, "Minimizing the Maximum: The Case for Shortening All Prison Sentences," *in* Matthew Epperson & Carrie Pettus-Davis, eds., Smart Decarceration: Achieving Criminal Justice Transformation in the 21st Century 58, 87, 151 (2017); Leon Neyfakh, "How to Stop Overzealous Prosecutors," Slate, Feb. 25, 2015, http://www.slate.com/articles/news_and_politics/crime/2015/02/overzealous_prosecutors_hold_them_accountable_by_defunding_state_prisons.html.

18. Leanne Fiftal Alarid, Paul Cromwell & Rolando V. del Carmen, Community-Based Corrections 28 (7th ed. 2008).

19. John F. Pfaff, Locked In: The True Causes of Mass Incarceration and How to Achieve Real Reform 2, 13–15 (2017); "Incarceration Rates in OECD Countries as of 2018," Statista, https://

www.statista.com/statistics/300986/incarceration-rates-in-oecd-countries/.

20. Linda K. Mancillas, Presidents and Mass Incarceration: Choices at the Top, Repercussions at the Bottom 3 (2018).

21. Todd R. Clear & Natasha A. Frost, The Punishment Imperative: The Rise and Failure of Mass Incarceration in America xvi, xiv, 2 (2014).

22. Michael Tonry, *Remodeling American Sentencing: A Ten-Step Blueprint for Moving Past Mass Incarceration, Criminology & Public Policy*, Vol. 13, Iss. 4, https://doi.org/10.1111/1745-9133.12097.

23. Michael Ollove, "Elderly Inmates Burden State Prisons," Stateline, The Pew Charitable Trusts, Mar. 17, 2016, http://www.pewtrusts.org/en/research-and-analysis/blogs/stateline/2016/03/17/elderly-inmates-burden-state-prisons.

24. https://famm.org/about-us/staff-board/#; Roberta Rampton, "Trump Pushes Drug-Dealer Death Penalty as Opioid Crisis Response," Reuters, Mar. 19, 2018, https://www.reuters.com/article/usa-trump-opioids/trump-pushes-drug-dealer-death-penalty-as-opioid-crisis-response-idUSL1N1R1112.

25. Lauren-Brooke Eisen, Inside Private Prisons: An American Dilemma in the Age of Mass Incarceration (2017), intro.; Lauren Gill, "Trump Administration Giving Boost to Private Prison Campaign Donors, Leaked Memo Shows," Newsweek, Jan. 30, 2018, http://www.newsweek.com/trump-private-prison-campaign-donors-leaked-memo-795681; Amy Brittain & Drew Harwell, "With Business Booming Again under Trump, Private Prison Company Gathers at President's Resort," Wash. Post, Oct. 25, 2017, *available at* http://www.chicagotribune.com/news/nationworld/politics/ct-trump-private-prison-doral-resort-20171025-story.html.

26. Evan McMorris-Santoro, "Justice Department: You Don't Need Mandatory Prison Sentences to Put the Right Drug Criminals in Jail," BuzzFeed News, July 22, 2015, https://www.buzzfeed.com/evanmcsan/the-justice-department-you-dont-need-mandatory-prison-senten?utm_term=.ku4zdl0Z3#.icMX1LDk8.

27. John Schuppe, "Post Bail," NBC News, Aug. 22, 2017, https://www.nbcnews.com/specials/bail-reform.

28. Peter Edelman, Not a Crime to Be Poor: The Criminalization of Poverty in America (2017), intro. "Right now in the United States," Peter Edelman points out, "ten million people—representing two-thirds of all current and former offenders in the country—owe a total of $50 billion in accumulated fines, costs, fees, charges for room and board in jails and prisons, and other impositions." Id.

29. David M. Oshinsky, Worse Than Slavery: Parchman Farm and the Ordeal of Jim Crow Justice 37, 42 57 (1997); Lori Latrice Martin, Kenneth J. Fasching-Varner & Nicholas D. Hartlep, Pay to Play: Race and the Perils of the College Sports Industrial Complex 70 (2017).

30. Maura Ewing, "How Minor Probation Violations Can Lead to Major Jail Time," The Atlantic, June 9, 2017, https://www.theatlantic.com/politics/archive/2017/06/philadelphia-detainer-holds/529758/.

31. Pedro Nicolaci da Costa, "An Alarming Number of Americans Are Worse Off Than Their Parents and We're Not Talking About It Enough," Business Insider, July 17, 2017, http://www.businessinsider.com/social-mobility-is-on-the-decline-and-with-it-american-dream-2017-7; Imran Cronk, "The Transportation Barrier," The Atlantic, Aug. 9, 2015, https://www.theatlantic.com/health/archive/2015/08/the-transportation-barrier/399728/.

32. Liz Wolfe, "The Laws Cities Use to Make Homelessness a Crime," Daily Beast, Apr. 30, 2017, https://www.thedailybeast.com/the-laws-cities-use-to-make-homelessness-a-crime; Karen Kucher, "Crime and the Homeless: 'You Are Never Safe When You Are Out in the Open,'" The San Diego Union-Tribune, Oct. 1, 2017, http://www.sandiegouniontribune.com/news/hepatitis-crisis/sd-me-homeless-crime-20170928-story.html.

33. "SCHR and Allies Win Historic Bail Reform in Atlanta," The Human Rights Report, Southern Center for Human Rights (May 2018), p. 6.

34. 4 U.S.C. § 4.

35. John Hudson Tiner, The Story of the Pledge of Allegiance (2003).

36. Hyman Gross, Crime and Punishment: A Concise Moral Critique 13 (2012); "Poverty's Not a Crime. Don't Throw Debtors in Jail," The Editorial Board, USA Today, June 18, 2018, https://www.usatoday.com/story/opinion/2018/06/18/poverty-not-crime-debtors-prisons-

illegal-editorials-debates/478199002/; Eli Hager, "Debtors' Prisons, Then and New: FAQ," The Marshall Project, Feb. 24, 2015, https://www.themarshallproject.org/2015/02/24/debtors-prisons-then-and-now-faq.

37. John Frederick Schroeder, comp., Maxims of Washington: Political, Social, Moral, and Religious 24–25 (1854). In his time, George Washington saw "*cruel necessity*" or the disagreeable necessity of "*retaliating*" warranted only "as the *only means left* to put a stop" to "inhuman proceedings" in wartime. Id. at 252.

38. Steve Coffman, comp. & ed., Words of the Founding Fathers: Selected Quotations of Franklin, Washington, Adams, Jefferson, Madison and Hamilton, with Sources 10, 19, 24–25, 268, 271 (2012); James Wood, comp., Dictionary of Quotations from Ancient and Modern, English and Foreign Sources 245 (1893); 1 The Political Works of Thomas Paine 16 (1857); Jay Grossman, Reconstituting the American Renaissance: Emerson, Whitman, and the Politics of Representation 30 (2003); Christopher L. Webber, Give Me Liberty: Speakers and Speeches that Have Shaped America (2004), ch. 1; Steve Coffman, ed. & comp., Words of the Founding Fathers: Selected Quotations of Franklin, Washington, Adams, Jefferson, Madison and Hamilton, with Sources 109, 127 (2012).

39. Francis Lieber, A Popular Essay on Subjects of Penal Law, and on Uninterrupted Solitary Confinement at Labor, as Contradistinguished to Solitary Confinement at Night and Joint Labor by Day, in a Letter to John Bacon, Esquire iii, 9-10-35, 93 (1838).

40. Giles Jacob, A New Law-Dictionary: Containing, the Interpretation and Definition of Words and Terms Used in the Law (1750) (entry for "Conspiracy").

41. A General Index to Dodsley's Annual Register, from the Year 1758 to the Year 1780, Both Inclusive (2d ed. 1784) (chapter on the "History of Europe") (unpaginated).

42. D'Blossiers Tovey, Anglia Judaica: or the History and Antiquities of the Jews in England, Collected from all our Historians, Both Printed and Manuscript, as Also from the Records in the Tower, and Other Publick Repositories 198 (1738).

43. 2 Caleb D'Anvers, The Craftsman 10–11 (1731) (noting that a man "received a Sentence somewhat uncommon in this Country; where *Death*, thou knoweth, is the usual Punishment of *such Offenders*; which this Man escaped, more by the Lenity of his *Accusers* and the Indulgence of his *Royal Master*, than his *own Deserts*; being only dismissed from all his *Employments*; and render'd *incapable* of holding any Office for the future; his Goods *confiscated*, and his Person *banish'd* for Life to a little Province on the Confines of *Russia*") (italics in original).

44. The cruelty of a punishment may itself be indicative of its unusualness (just as the unusualness of a punishment may reflect its cruelty). Hugo Adam Bedau, Death is Different: Studies in the Morality, Law, and Politics of Capital Punishment 97 (1987) ("Were we to try to isolate the unusualness of a punishment from its cruelty, we would focus on a property of punishments that has little or nothing to do with moral condemnation."); *see also* id. ("[A] mode of punishment may be unusual today even though it was common in an earlier, less civilized age"; "[i]n such cases describing the punishment as 'unusual' may well imply not only that it is no longer widely used, but that its use is now intolerable."). Punishments that have become "unusual" can be—and have been—judged to be unconstitutional. People v. Anderson, 493 P.2d 880, 883 (Cal. 1972) (noting that "the California Constitution prohibits imposition of the death penalty if, judged by contemporary standards, it is either cruel or has become unusual").

45. J. Thomas Scharf, History of Maryland: From the Earliest Period to the Present Day 41 (1879) (calling the stocks, the pillory, the whipping-post and "the gallows, the ugliest spectacles"—"the active employment" of which occurred "[a]bout the central date of 1770"—"cruel punishments," but noting that "[t]he stocks, the pillory and the gibbet did not pass out of vogue in Maryland, in fact, until about 1810, when, following the impulse given to the science of punishment by Bentham and his school, we adopted the penitentiary system and thus began to build the Maryland penitentiary"). "Previous to the construction of that building, and after the War of Independence had necessarily done away with the sale of white convicts into labor," the historian J. Thomas Scharf wrote of the construction of Maryland's penitentiary, "the usual punishment of convicts, after the preliminary whipping and pillorying was done, consisted in putting them in the chain-gang to work on the public roads, or, as it was popularly called, 'sending them to the wheel-

barrow.' " *Id.*

46. *Peine forte et dure* refers to pressing to death or to what has been called "[t]he strong and hard pain." 2 Political Dictionary; Forming a Work of Universal Reference, both Constitutional and Legal; and Embracing the Terms of Civil Administration, Political Economy and Social Relations, and of All the More Important Statistical Departments of Finance and Commerce 500 (1846) (describing *peine forte et dure* as "[t]he 'strong and hard pain' " and as "a species of torture used by the English law to compel persons to plead, when charged with crimes less than treason, but amounting to felony").

47. Daines Barrington, Observations on the More Ancient Statutes from Magna Charta to the Twenty-First of James I, at 81, 85–86, 88 (5th ed. 1796).

48. Id. at 81.

49. Id. at 87, 92.

50. Id. at 87.

51. Id. at 88. "Torture," Barrington noted, "was used by the ancient Germans, from whom we are supposed to have derived our laws." Id. Barrington also detailed other instances where torture was either used or contemplated. Id. at 92 (referring to "the actual proofs of torture having been formerly, at least in some instances, used in this country"); id. ("King James, in his Works, mentions, that the rack was shewn to Guy Fawkes during his examination."); id. at 92–93 ("Upon the murder of the duke of Buckingham by Felton, the judges were asked whether he could be tortured in order to extort a confession? They answered indeed to their honour in the negative; but their being thus consulted shews, that, in the apprehension of some of the king's counsellors, they might have inflicted this punishment.").

52. Id. at 93. A footnote after Barrington's use of the word "frequent" read in part as follows: "It may likewise perhaps surprize the read to find, by the 39 th Eliz. cap.iv. published at length by Rastal, that the gallies of this realm seem to have been not an unusual punishment; and Lord Coke mentions it in his 3d Inst. cap. 40. without taking notice of its being uncommon." Id.

53. 2 William Page, ed., The Victoria History of the County of Warwick 182 (1908).

54. The account of *peine forte et dure* in that source reads as follows:

When a Felon, punishable with death, takes a resolution not to make any answer to his Judges, after the second calling upon, he is carry'd back to his dungeon, and is put to a sort of rack called *peine forte et dure*. If he speaks, his indictment goes on in the usual forms; if he continues dumb they leave him to die under that punishment. He is stretched out naked upon his back, and his arms and legs drawn out by cords and fasten'd to the four corners of the dungeon; a board or place of iron is laid upon his stomach, and this is heap'd up *with Stones* to a certain weight. The next day they give him at three different times, three little morsels of barly bread, and nothing to drink: the next day three little glasses of water and nothing to eat: and if he continues in his obstinacy, they leave him in that condition 'till he dies. This is practis'd only upon felons, or persons guilty of petty Treason. Criminals of High Treason in the like case, would be condemned to the usual punishment; their silence would condemn them.

3 C. H. Evelyn White, ed., The East Anglian; or, Notes and Queries on Subjects Connected with the Counties of Suffolk, Cambridge, Essex & Norfolk 280 (1889–1890) (quoting *Memoirs and Observations in His Travels through England*, London 1719).

55. Joshua L. Shapiro, *And Unusual: Examining the Forgotten Prong of the Eighth Amendment*, 38 U. Mem. L. Rev. 465, 465–66 (2008).

56. Id. at 466 (citations omitted).

57. Id.

58. Id. at 471.

59. Rummel v. Estelle, 445 U.S. 263, 282 (1980) ("Absent a constitutionally imposed uniformity inimical to traditional notions of federalism, some State will always bear the distinction of treating particular offenders more severely than any other State.").

60. Shapiro, *supra* note 55, at 471–72.

61. *Id.* at 472.

62. *Id.* at 477–78 ("[A]lthough using the number of states that outlaw a punishment must arguably be an objective measure of the 'evolving standards of decency,' the problem is that the Court uses

such statistics in a results-oriented and undisciplined manner without imposed some measurable or quantifiable ceiling, such as the three-fourths rule, to clearly indicate when a given form of punishment actually satisfies evolving decency standards."); *see also* id. at 484 ("The most appropriate numbers is three-fourths of the states, which is the number required to amend the Constitution."); id. ("When at least thirty-eight states remove capital punishment from their sentencing arsenal, only then should that punishment become effectively rare and unusual. That thirty-eight states agree with the Court would give legitimacy to any pronouncement from the bench.").

63. Obviously, the more states that abolish the death penalty through legislative means only makes the country's death penalty *more* unusual. *E.g.*, Meghan J. Ryan, *Judging Cruelty*, 44 U.C. Davis L. Rev. 81, 81 (2010):

Constitutionally, states may be forced to surrender the punishment if it is considered cruel, and, as a result of a large number of states renouncing it, the punishment also becomes unusual. If a punishment is thus found to be both cruel and unusual, it will be proscribed under the Eighth Amendment Punishments Clause of the U.S. Constitution.

64. *Panetti*, 551 U.S. at 957 (referring to the "'fundamental right to life'") (quoting *Ford*, 477 U.S. 399); *see also Furman*, 408 U.S. at 359 n.141 (Marshall, J., concurring) (citations omitted):

The concepts of cruel and unusual punishment and substantive due process become so close as to merge when the substantive due process argument is stated in the following manner: because capital punishment deprives an individual of a fundamental right (*i. e.*, the right to life, the State needs a compelling interest to justify it. Thus stated the substantive due process argument reiterates what is essentially the primary purpose of the Cruel and Unusual Punishments Clause of the Eighth Amendment—*i. e.*, punishment may not be more severe than is necessary to serve the legitimate interests of the State.

65. International Covenant on Civil and Political Rights, 990 UNTS 171, 6 ILM 368 (1966), Art. 6(1) ("Every human being has the inherent right to life. This right shall be protected by law. No one shall be arbitrarily deprived of his life.").

66. Barbier v. Connolly, 113 U.S. 27, 31 (1884):

The fourteenth amendment, in declaring that no state 'shall deprive any person of life, liberty, or property without due process of law, nor deny to any person within its jurisdiction the equal protection of the laws,' undoubtedly intended not only that there should be no arbitrary deprivation of life or liberty, or arbitrary spoliation of property, but that equal protection and security should be given to all under like circumstances in the enjoyment of their personal and civil rights; ... and that in the administration of criminal justice no different or higher punishment should be imposed upon one than such as is prescribed to all for like offenses.

See also Hodgson v. Vermont, 168 U.S. 262, 272–73 (1897) ("We concede the proposition ... that by the fourteenth amendment it is made the right and the consequent duty of this court, when a case has been duly brought before it, to inquire whether, in the enactment and administration of the criminal laws of a state, it is sought to arbitrarily deprive any person of his life ... or to refuse him the equal protection of the laws."); Jones v. Brim, 165 U.S. 180, 182 (1897) ("[T]he clause of the fourteenth amendment of the constitution referred to was undoubtedly intended to prohibit an arbitrary deprivation of life or liberty, or arbitration spoliation of property."); BMW of N. Am., Inc. v. Gore, 517 U.S. 559, 586 (1996) (Breyer, J., concurring) ("The Court's opinion, which I join, explains why we have concluded that this award, in this case, was 'grossly excessive' in relation to legitimate punitive damages objections, and hence an arbitrary deprivation of life, liberty, or property in violation of the Due Process Clause.").

67. Bank Markazi v. Peterson, 136 S. Ct. 1310, 1327 n.27 (2016) ("Laws narrow in scope, including 'class of one' legislation, may violate the Equal Protection Clause if arbitrary or inadequately justified."); *see also* Village of Willowbrook v. Olech, 528 U.S. 562, 564 (2000) (citations omitted):

Our cases have recognized successful equal protection claims brought by a "class of one," where the plaintiff alleges that she has been intentionally treated differently from others similarly situated and that there is no rational basis for the difference in treatment. In doing so, we have explained that "'[t]he purpose of the equal protection clause of the Fourteenth Amendment is to secure every person within the State's jurisdiction against intentional and arbitrary discrimination, whether occasioned by express terms of a statute or by its improper execution through duly constituted agents.'"

68. U.S. CONST. amend. VIII ("Excessive bail shall not be required, nor excessive fines imposed, nor cruel and unusual punishments inflicted."); *see also Ex parte* Wilson, 114 U.S. 417, 426–27 (1885) ("Infamous punishments cannot be limited to those punishments which are cruel or unusual, because ... 'cruel and unusual punishments' are wholly forbidden, and cannot therefore be lawfully inflicted even in cases of convictions upon indictments duly presented by a grand jury.").

69. 356 U.S. 86 (1958).

70. *Id.* at 101.

71. *Id.*

72. *Id.* at 102.

73. Whether a punishment is cruel or unusual, or both, is something that judges may be called upon to adjudicate not just in the Eighth Amendment context, but in other contexts as well. For example, the U.S. Code of Military Justice prohibits the infliction of "cruel or unusual punishment"—a prohibition that, on its face, already encompasses flogging and branding. 10 U.S.C. § 855 Art. 55 ("Punishment by flogging, or by branding, marking, or tattooing on the body, *or any other cruel or unusual punishment*, may not be adjudged by any court-martial or inflicted upon any person subject to this chapter. The use of irons, single or double, except for the purpose of safe custody, is prohibited.") (emphasis added); *see also* Rich Federico, *The Unusual Punishment: A Call for Congress to Abolish the Death Penalty Under the Uniform Code of Military Justice for Unique Military, Non-Homicide Offenses*, 18 BERKELEY J. CRIM. L. 1, 4–5 (2013) ("The last service member executed for a unique military offense was Private Eddie D. Slovik, who was executed by firing squad on January 31, 1945 for desertion during a time of war.").

74. The W. F. Babcock v. The W. F. Babcock, 85 F. 978, 979–80 (2d Cir. 1898).

75. Hall v. Goodson, 32 Ala. 277, 279, 1858 WL 482 *1 (Ala. 1858); *see also* State v. Maner, 2 Hill (SC) 453, 454–55 (S.C. Ct. App. L. & Equity, 1834) (citations omitted):

The *criminal* offence of assault and battery cannot at common law be committed on the person of a slave. For notwithstanding for some purposes a slave a regarded in law as a person, yet generally he is a mere chattel person, and his right of personal protection belongs to his master, who can maintain an action of trespass for the battery of his slave. There can be therefore no offence against the State for a mere beating of a slave, unaccompanied by an circumstances of cruelty or an attempt to kill and murder....

But notwithstanding these may be regarded as common law principles in this State in relation to slaves, yet our statute law has made some important provisions for the punishment of the more aggravated offences against their persons. The Act of 1740 ... makes any unusual and cruel treatment of a slave an indictable offence. It provides that "in case any persons shall wilfully cut out the tongue, put out the eye, castrate or cruelly scald, burn, or deprive any slave of any limb or member, or *shall inflict any other cruel punishment*, other than by whipping or beating with a horsewhip, cowskin, switch, or small stick, or by putting irons on, or confining or imprisoning such slave, every person shall, for every such offence, forfeit the sum of one hundred pounds current money." I think, under this act, the shooting a slave might be indicted as a cruel punishment.

76. Confinement within a prison, even for one's natural life, has long been described as a usual punishment. *E.g.*, Vera v. United States, 288 F.2d 25, 26 (8th Cir. 1961) (describing confinement as a "usual punishment"); *see also* Rummel v. Estelle, 445 U.S. 263, 285 (1980) ("We ... hold that the mandatory life sentence imposed upon this petitioner does not constitute cruel and unusual punishment under the Eighth and Fourteenth Amendments.") (emphasis in original); People v. Williams, No. 241427, 2003 WL 22928768, at *4 (Mich. Ct. App. Dec. 11, 2003) (noting that the Michigan Supreme Court held in *People v. Hall*, 242 N.W.2d 377 (Mich. 1976), that life sentences without the possibility of parole do not constitute cruel and unusual punishments).

77. ASHLEY NELLIS, THE SENTENCING PROJECT, LIFE GOES ON: THE HISTORIC RISE IN LIFE SENTENCES IN AMERICA 1 (2013), https://sentencingproject.org/wp-content/uploads/2015/12/Life-Goes-On.pdf.

78. ASHLEY NELLIS, THE SENTENCING PROJECT, STILL LIFE: AMERICA'S INCREASING USE OF LIFE AND LONG-TERM SENTENCES 1, 5, 9 (2017), *available at* https://www.sentencingproject.org/publications/still-life-americas-increasing-use-life-long-term-sentences/.

79. DEATH PENALTY INFO. CTR., FACTS ABOUT THE DEATH PENALTY (2018), https://

deathpenaltyinfo.org/documents/FactSheet.pdf.

80. Maura Dolan, *Pace of Executions in California May Be Up to Gov. Jerry Brown*, L.A. Times, Nov. 25, 2017 ("Gov. Jerry Brown's administration has yet to finalize an execution protocol, which is necessary to resolve a federal court case that has blocked lethal injection in California for nearly 12 years.").

81. "Facts about the Death Penalty," Death Penalty Information Center, https://deathpenaltyinfo.org/documents/FactSheet.pdf (updated as of May 17, 2018).

82. Ernest van den Haag & John P. Conrad, The Death Penalty: A Debate 218 (1983):

Incarceration became a standard punishment in the nineteenth century. The first American prison was the Walnut Street Jail in Philadelphia, which accepted its first prisoner in 1790. Its example was not generally followed until well into the nineteenth century. Since that time the physical punishments, except for the gallows, have gradually disappeared. They are no longer allowed, even for the discipline of prisoners, and capital punishment has been discarded—with no apparent ill effects—in fourteen states. In those states in which it is still authorized by law, it has certainly become an unusual punishment.

83. Under the Rome Statute, which set up the International Criminal Court, a life sentence is now the maximum punishment for the worst of the worst offenses of international law: genocide, war crimes, and crimes against humanity. William A. Schabas, The International Criminal Court: A Commentary on the Rome Statute 1159 (2d ed. 2016); Andrew S. Thompson, In Defence of Principles: NGOs and Human Rights in Canada 114 (2010).

84. John D. Bessler, The Birth of American Law: An Italian Philosopher and the American Revolution 43, 171–72, 246, 288, 378, 439 (2014); John D. Bessler, The Death Penalty as Torture: From the Dark Ages to Abolition 37, 80–81, 255, 304 (2017).

85. Robinson v. California, 370 U.S. 660, 664-67 (1962).

86. 138 N.W. 1066 (Mich. 1912).

87. Id. at 1067.

88. Id.

89. Id.

90. *See, e.g.*, Jethro K. Lieberman, A Practical Companion to the Constitution: How the Supreme Court has Ruled on Issued from Abortion to Zoning 295 (1999) ("Those who find judicial rejection of legislative enactments problematic point to its anti-majoritarian nature: unelected judges overturn policies of elected legislators and chief executives in apparent contradiction to the sovereignty of the people."); Jesse H. Choper, Judicial Review and the National Political Process: A Functional Reconsideration of the Role of the Supreme Court (2013) (noting in chapter 1 that when U.S. Supreme Court Justices "exercise the power of judicial review to declare unconstitutional legislative, executive, or administrative action—federal, state, or local—they reject the product of the popular will by denying policies formulated by the majority's elected representatives or their appointees").

91. In early American jurisprudence, and especially before the Eighth Amendment was first applied against the states in *Robinson v. California*, 370 U.S. 660 (1962), courts expressed great reluctance to overturn a legislative enactment. *E.g.*, People *ex rel.* Bradley v. Superintendent of Ill. State Reformatory, 36 N.E. 76, 79 (Ill. 1894):

When the legislature has authorized a designated punishment for a specific crime, it must be regarded that its action represents the general moral ideas of the people, and the courts will not hold the punishment so authorized as either cruel and unusual or not proportioned to the nature of the offense, unless it is a cruel or degrading punishment, not known to the common law, or is a degrading punishment which had become obsolete in the state prior to the adoption of its constitution, or is so wholly disproportioned to the offense committed as to shock the moral sense of the community.

92. 5 U.S. (1 Cranch) 137 (1803).

93. Alan Axelrod & Charles Phillips, What Every American Should Know About American History: 225 Events that Shaped the Nation 67 (3d ed. 2008) ("[T]he Founding Fathers had expected the courts to have some control over the executive and legislative branches of government. The decision reached in *Marbury v. Madison*, however, formalized that control, and the high court has exercised that power since 1803.").

94. Harlow Giles Unger, John Marshall: The Chief Justice Who Saved the Nation 293 (2014) ("Together with *Marbury v. Madison*, the decisions from 1819 to 1832 firmly established the Supreme Court of the United States as the third pillar of America's federal government and final arbiter of the nation's legal matters.").

95. The North Briton, Feb. 18, 1769, *reprinted in* The North Briton, from No. I. to No. XLVI. Inclusive 556–77 (1769) ("'We recommend that you exert your utmost endeavours, that the proceedings in the case of libels, and all other criminal matters, may be confined to the rules of law, and not rendered dangerous to the subject by forced constructions, new modes of enquiry, unconstitutional tribunals, or new and unusual punishments, tending to take away or diminish the benefit of trial by juries.'"); id. at 557:

And of new and unusual punishments, it may be sufficient to observe, that the publisher of the North Briton has suffered and is now suffering a very new and unusual kind of punishment; for he has been and is now imprisoned, not in execution for any offence he has committed, but to compel him to subject to a species of inquisition, which, whatever may be the practice of courts, he is credibly informed, is absolutely inconsistent with the laws of the land. In a word, if these arbitrary and despotic modes of proceeding are suffered to continued, the trials by juries, in the case of libels, will be very soon abolished; for it will always be in the power of any time-serving or prostitute set of judges to construe any paper into a libel upon themselves, and then, by exercising the distinct and incompatible provinces of party, accuser, evidence, jury, and judge, they will at once try, condemn, and inflict upon any person whatever punishment they please.

96. Leo Pfeffer, Church, State, and Freedom 143 (rev. ed. 2017); Gerard N. Magliocca, American Founding Son: John Bingham and the Invention of the Fourteenth Amendment 2, 122, 127, 247 n.68, 249 n.104 (2013).

97. U.S. Const. amend. VIII.

98. Evan J. Mandery, A Wild Justice: The Death and Resurrection of Capital Punishment in America 23 (2013) ("If the Eighth Amendment only prohibited punishments already condemned by public opinion, then it would be a 'dead letter,' since these punishments would already have been abolished by the legislature. 'The Eighth Amendment was intended as a counter-majoritarian limitation on government action,' [Justice Arthur] Goldberg wrote.").

99. Christopher J. DeClue, *Sugarcoating the Eighth Amendment: The Grossly Disproportionate Test Is Simply the Fourteenth Amendment Rational-Basis Test in Disguise*, 41 Southwestern L. Rev. 533, 552 (2012); *see also* id. at 552-53 ("Several circuits take this legislative deference even further. According to the Fourth, Sixth, and Eighth Circuits, proportionality review is not required unless the sentence is life-imprisonment without the possibility of parole."); *compare* id. at 553:

Most courts, however, do not accord such outlandish legislative deference, and the mere fact that a sentence is within the statutory limits does not, in and of itself, end the Eighth Amendment inquiry. According to these courts, the availability of parole is merely one factor to consider, and an additional finding is required to uphold the length of a sentence in the face of an Eighth Amendment challenge: the sentence must further a conceivable penological theory. In other words, if a court decides to review the length of a sentence, there is a rebuttable presumption that the sentence is constitutional. This presumption can only be overcome if the court determines the sentence does not further any conceivable penological theory.

100. Delaware Declaration of Rights, Sept. 11, 1776, http://press-pubs.uchicago.edu/founders/documents/bill_of_rightss4.html; Delaware Constitution, https://law.justia.com/constitution/delaware/#art01/; Randy J. Holland, The Delaware State Constitution 82–82 (2d ed. 2017); DeShields v. State, 534 A.2d 630 (1987).

101. John W. Wright, ed., The New York Times Almanac 2002, at 406 (2006); Phil Milford, Delaware Trivia (2001); Patricia A. Martinelli, Haunted Delaware: Ghosts and Strange Phenomena of the First State 85 (2006); Ed Okonowicz, True Crime: Maryland: The State's Most Notorious Criminal Cases 7 (2009); George Miller, A Delaware Album, 1900–1930, at 94 (2011); Matthew Lippman, Criminal Procedure (3d ed. 2017) (citing Delaware v. Cannon, 190 A.2d 514 (Del. 1963)).

102. Crimes Act of 1790, ch. 9, 1 Stat. 112 (making treason, murder, murder or robbery on the high seas, piracy, mutiny, hostilities against the United States, and being an accomplice to

murder, robbery or piracy, counterfeiting, assisting in a prison break anyone "found guilty of treason, murder, or any other capital crime" punishable by death; making larceny, accessory after the fact to larceny, and punishable, among other things, by up to "thirty-nine stripes"; and making perjury and subornation of perjury punishable by, among other things, standing in the pillory for one hour).

103. 69 S.E. 385 (W. Va. 1910).

104. Id. at 387.

105. Id. Due process has both procedural and substantive components. In his 1972 concurrence in *Furman v. Georgia*, Justice Thurgood Marshall emphasized that an analysis under the Eighth Amendment's Cruel and Unusual Punishments Clause "parallels in some ways the analysis used in striking down legislation on the ground that it violates Fourteenth Amendment concepts of substantive due process...." *Furman*, 408 U.S. at 359 n.141 (Marshall, J., concurring).

106. *Woodward*, 69 S.E. at 386.

107. Id.

108. 136 U.S. 436 (1890).

109. *Woodward*, 69 S.E. at 388.

110. Cyndi Banks, Punishment in America: A Reference Handbook 9–12 (2005) (discussing the history of corporal punishments, including flogging, mutilation, branding, the stocks and the pillory, and the use of the ducking stool for "village scolds and gossips").

111. Edmund S. Morgan, American Heroes: Profiles of Men and Women Who Shaped Early America 70 (2009) (noting that, for Puritans, "[t]he usual punishment" for adultery was "a whipping or a fine, or both, and perhaps a branding, combined with a symbolical execution in the form of standing on the gallows for an hour with a rope about the neck"); *see also* Douglas Litowitz, *The Trouble with 'Scarlet Letter' Punishment: Subjecting Criminal to Public Shaming Rituals as a Sentencing Alternative Will Not Work*, 81 Judicature 52, 53 (1997) ("In Colonial days, the courts favored primitive methods of punishment such as the whipping post, the pillory, stocks, branding, banishment, the dunking stool, and a device known as the 'brank,' a metal mask that wrapped around the face of a woman who talked too much.").

112. Rhodes v. Chapman, 452 U.S. 337, 346 (1981) ("No static 'test' can exist by which courts determine whether conditions of confinement are cruel and unusual, for the Eighth Amendment 'must draw its meaning from the evolving standards of decency that mark the progress of a maturing society.'") (quoting *Trop*, 356 U.S. at 101).

113. Farmer v. Brennan, 511 U.S. 825, 833 (1994) (allowing gratuitous beating or rape of one inmate by another is not consistent with the evolving standards of decency).

114. Roper v. Simmons, 543 U.S. 551, 574 (2005) (abrogating Stanford v. Kentucky, 492 U.S. 361 (1989)) (barring the imposition of death sentences for those under age eighteen).

115. Ford v. Wainwright, 477 U.S. 399 (1986).

116. Atkins v. Virginia, 536 U.S. 304, 311–12 (2002) (finding that the Eighth Amendment must draw its meaning from the evolving standards of decency that mark the progress of a maturing society, and barring the execution of intellectually disabled offenders) (abrogating Penry v. Lynaugh, 492 U.S. 302, 314, 321 (1989), which found that the death penalty was not a cruel and unusual punishment for that category of offenders).

117. Austin Sarat & Patricia Ewick, eds., The Handbook of Law and Society 214 (2015):

Before 1868 when the Fourteenth Amendment was drafted, there was no mention of the term equality in the US Constitution. In fact, before the Fourteenth Amendment, the US Constitution explicitly encouraged and perpetuated inequality among people through its pro-slavery provisions, found in several sections of the Constitution. It was not until after the ratification of the Thirteenth, Fourteenth and Fifteenth Amendments that the Constitution established the right of equality regardless of race.

118. The Fourteenth Amendment was specifically designed, in part, to equalize punishments between people of different races. Samuel R. Gross & Robert Mauro, *Patterns of Death: An Analysis of Racial Disparities in Capital Sentencing and Homicide Victimization*, 37 Stan. L. Rev. 27, 111 (1984) (after noting that Fourteenth Amendment prohibits the denial of "equal protection," recounting that "[t]he sponsors of the fourteenth amendment unquestionably intended this language to prohibit un-

equal punishments for defendants of different races"); *see also* Stan Robin Gregory, *Capital Punishment and Equal Protection: Constitutional Problems, Race and the Death Penalty*, 5 St. Thomas L. Rev. 257, 268–69 (1992) ("The framers of the Fourteenth Amendment intended to prohibit unequal punishments for defendants of all races. As the legislative history of the Fourteenth Amendment clearly illuminates, one of their main goals was to 'constitutionalize' the provision of the Civil Rights Acts of 1866, to embrace the requirement that in every state 'inhabitants of every race and color, without regard to any previous condition of slavery or involuntary servitude ... shall be subject to like punishment, pains, and penalties, and no other.'").

119. Michael J. Perry, We the People: The Fourteenth Amendment and the Supreme Court 51 (1999) (discussing the Fourteenth Amendment and how it constitutionalized the Civil Rights Act of 1866, which required that "white citizens" and others be subject to "like punishment"); *see also* Shelley v. Kraemer, 334 U.S. 1, 23 (1948):

> The historical context in which the Fourteenth Amendment became a part of the Constitution should not be forgotten. Whatever else the framers sought to achieve, it is clear that the matter of primary concern was the establishment of equality in the enjoyment of basic civil and political rights and the preservation of those rights from discriminatory action on the part of the States based on considerations of race or color. Seventy-five years ago this Court announced that the provisions of the Amendment are to be construed with this fundamental purpose in mind.

120. *E.g.*, Vest v. Lubbock Cty. Comm'rs Court, 444 F. Supp. 824, 833–34 (N.D. Tex. 1977) (stating procedures in meting out mass punishment to entire cell-blocks, holding inmates in solitary confinement and imposing other forms of punishment without any hearing or impartial determination of a particular inmate's participation in infraction of rules "are contrary to the mandates of the Due Process Clause of the Fourteenth Amendment and the unequal manner in which punishment is imposed among the various classes of prisoners denies equal protection under the Fourteenth Amendment"). Under existing law, an inmate must show that a government official "acted with an intent or purpose to discriminate" to state a claim under 42 U.S.C. § 1983 for a violation of the Fourteenth Amendment's Equal Protection Clause. Barren v. Harrington, 152 F.3d 1193, 1194 (9th Cir. 1998) (citing cases). But even in the absence of a showing of intentional discrimination in a given capital case, the fact that the death penalty has a long, well-documented history of racial prejudice and bias in its administration is certainly a relevant factor that the U.S. Supreme Court can and should consider in making the determination that the death penalty is both cruel and unusual. John D. Bessler, *The Inequality of America's Death Penalty: A Crossroads for Capital Punishment at the Intersection of the Eighth and Fourteenth Amendments*, 73 Wash. & Lee L. Rev. Online 487, 548 (2016)("While the Eighth Amendment forbids 'cruel and unusual punishments,' the Fourteenth Amendment was put in place to end the nineteenth-century scourge of unequal punishments based on race.").

121. Laurence Claus, *The Antidiscrimination Eighth Amendment*, 28 Harv. J.L. & Pub. Pol'y 119, 162 (2004) (emphasis in original):

> The American founders in 1791, like their English predecessors in 1689, believed that the common law could be discovered only through faithful analysis of precedent. The word "unusual" in the Cruel and Unusual Punishments Clause reflected a commitment to the common law method. That method in turn reflected a commitment to the *commonality* of the common law—a commitment to the principle that like cases be treated alike.

See also id. at 122 ("'Unusual' was a synonym for 'illegal' at common law because the common law doctrine of precedent insisted that judicial decisions could succeed in articulating law if and only if they served an underlying principle of moral—and therefore legal—equality among litigants.").

122. O. W. Holmes, Jr., The Common Law 1, 5 (1881).

123. Nora V. Demleitner, Douglas A. Berman, Marc L. Miller & Ronald F. Wright, Sentencing Law and Policy: Cases, Statutes, and Guidelines 445 (4th ed. 2018).

124. John D. Bessler, *Tinkering Around the Edges: The Supreme Court's Death Penalty Jurisprudence*, 49 Am. Crim. L. Rev. 1913, 1932–33 (2012) (citing cases). The U.S. Constitution's Fifth Amendment states that "no person shall ... be deprived of life, liberty, or property, without due process of law." U.S. Const. amend. V. The Fourteenth Amendment also provides in part: "nor shall any State deprive any person of life, liberty, or property, without due process of law." U.S. Const. amend. XIV.

125. The U.S. Supreme Court has held that "death penalty statutes [must] be structured so as to

prevent the penalty from being administered in an arbitrary fashion." California v. Brown, 479 U.S. 538, 541 (1987) (citation omitted). At the same time, the Supreme Court has required that courts consider the "character and record of the individual offender and the circumstances of the particular offense as a constitutionally indispensable part of the process of inflicting the penalty of death." *Woodson*, 428 U.S. at 304 (plurality opinion); Lockett v. Ohio, 438 U.S. 586, 604–05 (1978) (plurality opinion). Despite the Supreme Court's best efforts to ensure that the death penalty is not administered in an arbitrary fashion, the death penalty's administration is as arbitrary as ever. Lindsey S. Vann, *History Repeats Itself: The Post-*Furman *Return to Arbitrariness in Capital Punishment*, 45 U. Rich. L. Rev. 1255 (2011). Capital punishment is, it has been noted, in decline in the United States. *See generally* Brandon L. Garrett, Alexander Jakubow & Ankur Desai, *The American Death Penalty Decline*, 107 J. Crim. L. & Criminology 561 (2017). And although some prosecutors use capital charges to gain plea-bargaining leverage, many prosecutors are no longer even actively seeking capital charges. Richard A. Bierschbach & Stephanos Bibas, *Rationing Criminal Justice*, 116 Mich. L. Rev. 187, 230–31 (2017). In retentionist jurisdictions, the fact that discretionary plea bargaining is used so frequently in the criminal justice system—a practice that often results in pleas to life sentences to avoid the death penalty—actually ensures that the death penalty (already capriciously administered and highly discretionary in nature) will continue to be employed in a very arbitrary fashion. Jed S. Rakoff, *Why Innocent People Plead Guilty*, N.Y. Rev. Books, Nov. 20, 2014 ("[O]ur criminal justice system is almost exclusively a system of plea bargaining, negotiated behind closed doors with no judicial oversight. The outcome is very largely determined by the prosecutor alone.").

126. Daniels v. Williams, 474 U.S. 327, 331 (1986) (referring to "the traditional and commonsense notion that the Due Process Clause, like its forebear in the Magna Carta ... was intended to secure the individual from the arbitrary exercise of the powers of government") (citations omitted); *see also* State Farm Mut. Auto. Ins. Co. v. Campbell, 538 U.S. 408, 416 (2003) ("The Due Process Clause of the Fourteenth Amendment prohibits the imposition of grossly excessive or arbitrary punishments on a tortfeasor."); Philip Morris USA v. Williams, 549 U.S. 346, 352 (2007) ("[W]e have emphasized the need to avoid an arbitrary determination of an award's amount"; "[u]nless a State insists upon proper standards that will cabin the jury's discretionary authority, its punitive damages system may deprive a defendant of 'fair notice ... of the severity of the penalty that a State may impose,' it may threaten 'arbitrary punishments,' *i.e.*, punishments that reflect not an 'application of law' but 'a decisionmaker's caprice.'") (citations omitted).

127. Historical sources equate "long usage" with a prevailing custom. Encyclopædia Britannica: or, A Dictionary of Arts and Sciences, Compiled upon a New Plan 301 (1777) ("Custom is hence, both by lawyers and civilians, defined *lex non scripta*, a law, or right, not written, established by long usage, and the consent of our ancestors: in which sense it stands opposed to the *lex scripta*, or the written law."); The Complete Dictionary of Arts and Sciences, in Which the Whole Circle of Human Learning Is Explained, and the Difficulties Attending the Acquisition of Everty Art, Whether Liberal or Mechanical, are Removed, in the Most Easy and Familiar Manner (entry for "CUSTOM") (defining same); 1 Giles Jacob, comp. & T. E. Tomlins, ed., The Law-dictionary: Explaining the Rise, Progress, and Present State, of the English Law, in Theory and Practice; Defining and Interpreting the Terms or Words of Art; and Comprising Copious Information, Historical, Political, and Commercial, on the Subjects of Our Law, Trade, and Government 171 (1797) (entry for "CUSTOM" begins: "Is a law not written, established by long usage, and the consent of our ancestors. No law can oblige a free people without their consent: so wherever they consent and use a certain rule or method as a law, such rule, &c. gives it the power of a law; and if it is *universal*, then it is *common-law*: if particular to this or that place, then it is *custom*.") (italics in original); Giles Jacob, The Student's Companion: or, The Reason of the Laws of England 112 (1725) ("Custom, which is Law, is what is Established by long Usage,: shewing, the principal reasons and the general Consent motives whereon our laws and Approbation statutes are grounded, in the most essential and capital points, not only in civil but criminal cases; together with the law it self : so as to convey to all students, and others, the fundamental knowledge of the People, by law, necessary in their own Act."); 4 DeWitt C. studies 112 (1725) ("Custom, which is Law, is what is Established by long Usage, and the general Consent and Approbation of the People, by their own Act."); 4 DeWitt C. Blashfield & George F. Longsdorf,

EDS., ABBOTT'S CYCLOPEDIC DIGEST OF ALL THE DECISIONS OF ALL THE COURTS OF NEW YORK FROM THE EARLIEST TIME TO THE YEAR 1900, at 964 (1901) (citing Wilcox v. Wood, 9 Wend. 346 (Sup. 1832)) ("Custom is a law established by long usage. A universal custom becomes common law...."); *see also* THE CHRISTIAN EUCHARIST NO PROPER SACRIFICE, CLEARLY PROVED IN A LETTER TO THE LORD BISHOP OF NORWICH 39 (1714) (stating "according to a long usage, or *prevailing Custome*") (italics in original); 7 HENRY GWILLIM, AN APPENDIX TO BACON'S NEW ABRIDGEMENT OF THE LAW, ALPHABETICALLY DIGESTED UNDER PROPER TITLES 406 (1801) ("Long usage ... ought not to be shaken lightly"; "the right claimed by the plaintiffs ... is supported by long usage."); Alan Watson, "An Approach to Customary Law," *in* 1 ALISON DUNDES RENTELN & ALAN DUNDES, EDS., FOLK LAW: ESSAYS IN THE THEORY AND PRACTICE OF *Lex Non Scripta* 142 (1994) ("The Roman sources clearly indicate that some additional factor is needed to recognize custom as law, even if the nature of this factor is not apparent. For example, the *Epitome Ulpiani* states that '[c]ustom is the tacit consent of the people, deeply rooted through long usage.'"); ANDY WOOD, THE MEMORY OF THE PEOPLE: CUSTOM AND POPULAR SENSES OF THE PAST IN EARLY MODERN ENGLAND 94 (2013) ("In 1612, the Attorney-General for Ireland, Sir John Davies, summarized the customary basis of the common law as follows: 'the Common Law of England is nothing else but the Common Custome of the Realm; and a Custome which hath obtained the force of a Law is always said to be *Jus non scriptum.*").

128. Rachel King, *No Due Process: How the Death Penalty Violates the Constitutional Rights of the Family Members of Death Row Prisoners*, 16 B.U. PUB. INT. L.J. 195, 228 (2007):

The death penalty has, in some sense, become a symbolic punishment. Less than 1% of murders result in a death sentence, but there is no indication that the minority who are actually sentenced to death are the most serious offenders. Professor David McCord examined all death penalty cases in 2004, examining facts about each death-eligible case. He identified a total of 469 defendants who met the "worst-of-the-worst" standard. He found that, of those 469, only thirty percent had been sentenced to death, meaning that the vast majority received a sentence other than death. Moreover, many of the 341 murderers who were spared the death penalty had more serious cases than those who received it. In the two most aggravated cases that year—Oklahoma City bomber Terry Nichols and serial killer Charles Cullen—neither man received the death penalty. Of the eleven serial killers in the group, only five were sentenced to death.

129. "Expanded Homicide Data Table 8—Murder Victims by Weapon, 2011–2015," Crime in the United States, Department of Justice/Federal Bureau of Investigation, https://ucr.fbi.gov/crime-in-the-u.s/2015/crime-in-the-u.s.-2015/tables/expanded_homicide_data_table_8_murder_victims_by_weapon_2011-2015.xls (listing 12,795 murder victims in 2011, 12,888 in 2012, 12,253 in 2013, 12,270 in 2014, and 13,455 in 2015).

130. "Facts about the Death Penalty, Death Penalty Info. Ctr., Feb. 23, 2018 (listing 43 executions in 2011, 43 in 2012, 39 in 2013, 35 in 2014, and 28 in 2015).

131. Mark Earley, "Even Trickling to a Halt, US Death Penalty Executions Are an Embarrassment," The Hill, Dec. 15, 2017, http://thehill.com/opinion/civil-rights/365008-even-trickling-to-a-halt-us-death-penalty-executions-are-an-embarrassment.

132. Bessler, *The Inequality of America's Death Penalty*, *supra* note 120, at 553 (emphasis in original).

133. 481 U.S. 279 (1987).

134. Id. at 291–92.

135. Cassandra Stubbs, "The Dreg Scott of Our Time," ACLU, Apr. 16, 2012, https://www.aclu.org/blog/capital-punishment/dred-scott-our-time.

136. *McCleskey*, 481 U.S. at 292 (emphasis in original).

137. Id. at 305.

138. Id. at 306–07 (emphasis in original). In his opinion, Justice Powell—drawing considerable public criticism—made this statement: "Apparent disparities in sentencing are an inevitable part of our criminal law system." Id. at 312. Asserting that McCleskey's arguments about racial discrimination "are best presented to the legislative bodies." Id. at 319. Justice Powell contended that it was a legislative, not a judicial, responsibility to determine the punishments for particular crimes. Id. "Capital punishment," he wrote, "is now the law in more than two-thirds of our States," though he conceded that "[i]t is the ultimate duty of courts to determine on a case-by-case basis whether these laws are applied

consistently with the Constitution." Id.

139. Id. at 282; *Justice Powell's New Wisdom*, N.Y. Times, June 11, 1994 ("Too late for Warren McCleskey and numerous other executed prisoners, retired Justice Lewis Powell now concedes that he was wrong to cast the deciding fifth Supreme Court vote to uphold Mr. McCleskey's death sentence in a major case.").

140. "Justice Powell's New Wisdom," N.Y. Times, June 11, 1994, https://www.nytimes.com/1994/06/11/opinion/justice-powell-s-new-wisdom.html.

141. *McCleskey*, 481 U.S. at 314.

142. Id. at 315.

143. Id. at 319.

144. 563 U.S. 493 (2011).

145. Id. at 510.

146. Id.

147. Atkins v. Virginia, 536 U.S. 304, 311 (2002) ("The basic concept underlying the Eighth Amendment is nothing less than the dignity of man....") (quoting *Trop*, 356 U.S. at 100 (plurality opinion)).

148. Estelle v. Gamble, 429 U.S. 97, 102 (1976) ("The [Eighth] Amendment embodies 'broad and idealistic concepts of dignity, civilized standards, humanity, and decency...,' against which we must evaluate penal measures.") (quoting Jackson v. Bishop, 404 F.2d 571, 579 (8th Cir. 1968)); *cf.* Laaman v. Helgemoe, 437 F. Supp. 269, 323 (D.N.H. 1977):

Where the cumulative impact of the conditions of incarceration threatens the physical, mental, and emotional health and well-being of the inmates and/or creates a probability of recidivism and future incarceration, a federal court must conclude that imprisonment under such conditions does violence to our societal notions of the intrinsic worth and dignity of human beings and, therefore, contravenes the Eighth Amendment's proscription against cruel and unusual punishment.

149. Michael J. Perry, Constitutional Rights, Moral Controversy, and the Supreme Court 55 (2009).

150. Id. at 55–56.

151. As two scholars have written of Michael Perry's brand of originalism:

Perry endorses a jurisprudence that seeks the " 'objective meaning' to the public at the time the provision was ratified." Perry explains that this inquiry is hypothetical: "it is what the public 'would have' understood that should matter." But his originalism has a unique flavor. It "does not entail ... a small or passive judicial role." Rather, because the Constitution is so textually vague and open-ended, Perry believes that judges can legitimately choose between many plausible original meanings, at varying levels of generality, such that much of the Supreme Court's modern individual rights jurisprudence can (and should) be defended on originalist grounds.

Thomas B. Colby & Peter J. Smith, *Living Originalism*, 59 Duke L.J. 240, 257 (2009).

152. Perry, *supra* note 149, at 56–57.

153. Id. at 57–58. Samuel Johnson's dictionary has been described as "the standard authority at the time when the Constitution was drawn up in 1787." Id. at 57 n.10 (citation omitted).

154. Id. at 80; *see also* id. (describing *cruel and unusual* as "significantly harsher than necessary to serve the legitimate aims of *punishment and evidenced as such by the fact that the punishment is not commonly used*").

155. Id. at 58.

156. Id. at 78. For Perry, the necessity of punishment is an important part of the Eighth Amendment calculus. Id. at 64 ("[C]apital punishment is *not* consistent with the cruel and unusual punishments clause—the clause *as originally understood*—if: 'no matter what the crime and who the criminal, capital punishment is significantly harsher than necessary to serve the legitimate aims of punishment; and as evidence that it is significantly harsher than necessary, capital punishment is not commonly used for any crime.' ").

157. Miller v. Alabama, 567 U.S. 460, 470 (2012) (discussing the Supreme Court's "strands of precedent reflecting" its concern "with proportionate punishment"). The Supreme Court's different approaches to proportionality review in capital versus non-capital cases has drawn particular notice over the years. As scholar Evan Mandery writes in *Capital Punishment in America*:

The Court has neither explained why it has thus limited is disproportionality review in capital cases to the categorical method nor why it has never used this approach in noncapital cases. The reason for this differentiation between approaches in capital and noncapital cases is discernible from the opinions in *Solem v. Helm*. Two strains unite the several opinions in *Helm*. One strain is that disproportionality is a special concern in capital cases. The other strain is a desire to limit the practice of disproportionality review.

Evan Mandery, Capital Punishment in America: A Balanced Review 251 (2d ed. 2012).

158. Heidi Forster & Emily Ramsey, "The Law Meets Reproductive Technology: The Prospect of Human Cloning," *in* Paul Lauritzen, ed., Cloning and the Future of Human Embryo Research 214 (2001) ("The standard that courts use to review the legitimacy of governmental acts that restrict or impinge on fundamental rights is strict scrutiny. Under the strict scrutiny standard, any governmental action restricting such fundamental rights must be necessary to protect a compelling government interest, and the means must be narrowly tailored to achieve that end; thus, there must be no less restrictive means to achieve the governmental goal."); John O. Spengler, Paul M. Anderson, Daniel P. Connaughton & Thomas A. Baker III, Introduction to Sport Law 158 (2d ed. 2016) (noting that, in Equal Protection Clause cases involving the application of strict scrutiny, a court will allow the government action to survive only if it is necessary to achieve a compelling governmental interest; for purposes of the Equal Protection Clause analysis, "*necessary* means that there is no other way to accomplish the government's objective") (italics in original); Steven D. Jamar, Constitutional Law: Power, Liberty, Equality 920 (2017) ("When the government seeks to regulate content, the Court uses the freedom of expression version of strict scrutiny, which it has expressed in various ways, including: 1. The government must demonstrate a compelling governmental interest for the regulation; and 2. The restriction must be narrowly tailored and 'actually necessary' to accomplish that compelling interest.").

159. *E.g.*, Tassaduq Hussein Jillani, "Impunity and the Emerging Patterns of International Justice," *in* Ana María Salinas de Frías, Katja LH Samuel & Nigel D. White, eds., Counter-Terrorism: International Law and Practice 242 (2012):

The US Supreme Court, as early as 1938, introduced the concept of strict scrutiny of executive actions that purport to infringe certain fundamental rights in the case of *United States v Caroline Products Company*, which established both a concept and a test which courts the world over would do well to emulate. The test is three pronged. First, the act must be in furtherance of a compelling governmental interest. Second, the action must be narrowly tailored, not overbroad. Finally, it must be the least restrictive means to achieve the goal. Further to that, one might add that the action must be limited in time and space, meaning it only occurs for a period and extends as far as is necessary to achieve its ends.

160. Ford v. Wainwright, 477 U.S. 399, 409 (1986) ("[W]e may seriously question the retributive value of executing a person who has no comprehension of why he has been singled out and stripped of his fundamental right to life."); Lucas v. Forty-Fourth General Assembly of State of Colo., 377 U.S. 713, 736 (1964) ("'One's right to life, liberty, and property *** and other fundamental rights may not be submitted to vote; they depend on the outcome of no elections.'") (citation omitted); Johnson v. Zerbst, 304 U.S. 458, 462 (1938) ("The Sixth Amendment guarantees that: 'In all criminal prosecutions, the accused shall enjoy the right *** to have the Assistance of Counsel for his defence.' This is one of the safeguards of the Sixth Amendment deemed necessary to insure fundamental human rights of life and liberty.").

161. Foucha v. Louisiana, 504 U.S. 71, 79 (1992) ("Due process requires that the nature of commitment bear some reasonable relation to the purpose for which the individual is committed."); id. at 80 ("Freedom from bodily restraint has always been at the core of the liberty protected by the Due Process Clause from arbitrary governmental action."); id. ("We have always been careful not to 'minimize the importance and fundamental nature' of the individual's right to liberty.") (citation omitted). In *Turner v. Safley*, 482 U.S. 78, 89 (1987), the U.S. Supreme Court set forth factors to be considered when determining whether a policy limited prisoners' rights is reasonable. The first is that there must be a "valid, rational connection" between the prison policy at issue and the legitimate government interest (e.g., prison security, rehabilitation) put forward to justify it.

162. In re Ohio Execution Protocol Litigation, Case No. 2:11-cv-1016, 2017 WL 5020138 *22

(S.D. Ohio Nov. 3, 2017) ("[T]he right to be free from cruel and unusual punishment is a fundamental right protected from state-imposed burdens that treat similarly situated persons differently without proper justification."); Brinson v. Jackson, No. CV412-105, 2013 WL 1180832 *1 (S.D. Ga. Mar. 20, 2013) (referring to the "Eighth Amendment right to be free from cruel and unusual punishment" as "a fundamental constitutional right"); Lee v. McManus, 543 F. Supp. 386, 392 (D. Kan. 1982) ("[T]he denial of a fundamental constitutional right, such as the Eighth Amendment right to be free of cruel and unusual punishment, has been held to be per se irreparable harm.").

163. Estate of Hernandez-Rojas v. United States, No. 11-cv-0522-L(DHB), 2014 WL 3699929 *3 (S.D. Cal. July 24, 2014) ("To put it simply, torture contravenes fundamental rights of the human person. Its illegality does not hinge on any statute or decisional law enacted by a government."); Filartiga v. Pena-Irala, 630 F.2d 876, 884 (2d Cir. 1980) ("[W]e conclude that official torture is not prohibited by the law of nations. The prohibition is clear and unambiguous, and admits of no distinction between treatment of aliens and citizens."); id. at 885 ("[I]nternational law confers fundamental rights upon all people vis-à-vis their own governments. While the ultimate scope of those rights will be a subject of continuing refinement and elaboration, we hold that the right to be free from torture is now among them."); *see also* Taveras-Lopez v. Reno, 127 F. Supp.2d 598, 609 (M.D. Pa. 2000) (referring to "fundamental human rights law prohibiting genocide, slavery, murder, torture, prolonged arbitrary detention, and racial discrimination"); Tel-Oren v. Libyan Arab Republic, 726 F.2d 774, 777 (D.C. Cir. 1984) ("[I]nternational law today places limits on a state's power to torture persons held in custody, and confers 'fundamental rights upon all people' to be free from torture.") (citation omitted).

164. Brown v. Plata, 563 U.S. 493, 510 (2011) ("Prisoners retain the essence of human dignity inherent in all persons. Respect for that dignity animates the Eighth Amendment prohibition against cruel and unusual punishment."); Atkins v. Virginia, 536 U.S. 304, 311 (2002) ("'The basic concept underlying the Eighth Amendment is nothing less than the dignity of man.'") (quoting Trop v. Dulles, 356 U.S. 86, 100 (1958) (plurality opinion); Hope v. Pelzer, 536 U.S. 730, 745 (2002) (labelling cruel and unusual punishment "antithetical to human dignity"); *see also* John W. Palmer, Constitutional Rights of Prisoners 563 (9th ed. 2010) ("'[C]onvicted prisoners do not forfeit all constitutional protections by reason of their conviction and confinement in prison.'") (quoting Bell v. Wolfish, 441 U.S. 520, 545 (1979)); *Erotic Service Provider Legal Education and Research Project v. Gascon*, 880 F.2d 450, 455 (9th Cir. 2018) ("The fundamental rights protected by the Fourteenth Amendment's Due Process Clause extend to certain personal choices central to individual dignity and autonomy...."); Rodriguez Fernandez v. Wilkinson, 505 F. Supp. 787, 796 (D. Kan. 1980) ("One important document by which the United States is bound is the United Nations Charter.... The Charter entered into force on October 24, 1945, and resolves to reaffirm faith in fundamental human rights and in the dignity of the human person."). *Compare* Kevin Barry, *The Death Penalty & the Dignity Clauses*, 102 Iowa L. Rev. 383, 395 (2017) ("[D]ignity is not a constitutional right, but is instead a core value 'underlying, or giving meaning to, existing constitutional rights and guarantees'—'a lens through which to make sense of the [Constitution's] structural and individual rights guarantees.' Like the invisible matter that holds our universe in place, dignity is the foundation for our constellation of rights."); United States v. Windsor, 133 S. Ct. 2675, 2696 (2013) ("The federal statute [DOMA] is invalid, for no legitimate purpose overcomes the purpose and effect to disparage and to injure those whom the State, by its marriage laws, sought to protect in personhood and dignity. By seeking to displace this protection and treating those persons as living in marriages less respected than others, the federal statute is in violation of the Fifth Amendment.") *with* Ammend v. BioPort, Inc., 322 F. Supp.2d 848, 872 (W.D. Mich. 2004) ("American constitutional jurisprudence has never recognized a right to human dignity.").

165. María José Falcón y Tella & Fernando Falcón y Tella, Punishment and Culture: A Right to Punish? 151 (Peter Muckley, trans. 2006). In his own work, Cesare Beccaria paid tribute to his French predecessor. As Alberto Brugio, in introducing a recent translation of Beccaria's *On Crimes and Punishments*, has written about and contextualized Beccaria's own words:

'The immortal President de Montesquieu has dealt cursorily with this subject,' Beccaria writes in the Introduction, and 'indivisible truth has compelled me to follow the shining footsteps of this great man.' This is not simply a ritual homage to an undisputed authority, for whom not even the most hostile critic could fail to show respect. After all, Beccaria is indebted to Montesquieu for the most important principle regarding penal law expressed in *On Crimes and Punishments*, namely, the idea that 'every punishment that does not derive from absolute necessity is tyrannical.'

Alberto Burgio, "Introduction: Between Law and Politics—The Idea of Equality in *On Crimes and Punishments*," *in* Aaron Thomas, ed., Cesare Beccaria, *On Crimes and Punishments* and Other Writings xlv (Aaron Thomas & Jeremy Parzen, trans. 2008).

166. Emer de Vattel, The Law of Nations, or, Principles of the Law of Nature, Applied to the Conduct and Affairs of Nations and Sovereigns 81 (new ed. 1797).

167. Id.

168. Id. at 82.

169. The French Declaration of the Rights of Man (1789) is referenced in the current French constitution's preamble. Constitution of 4 Oct. 1958, preamble ("The French people solemnly proclaim their attachment to the Rights of Man and the principles of national sovereignty as defined by the Declaration of 1789, confirmed and complemented by the Preamble to the Constitutional of 1946, and to the rights and duties as defined in the Charter for the Environment of 2004."), *available at* http://www.conseil-constitutionnel.fr/conseil-constitutionnel/english/constitution/constitution-of-4-october-1958.25742.html; *see also* Benjamin West Janke & François-Xavier Licari, *Enforcing Punitive Damage Awards in France after* Fountaine Pajot, 60 Am. J. Comp. L. 775, 794 n.76 (2012) ("According to the Preamble of the French Constitution, the principles of the *Declaration* have constitutional value.").

170. William J. Stuntz, The Collapse of American Criminal Justice 77–78 (2011).

171. Georges Vedel, "The *Conseil constitutionnel*: Problems of Legitimization and Interpretation," *in* Eivind Smith, ed., Constitutional Justice Under Old Constitutions 356 (1995) ("The necessity of a law is something that is very imprecise from a legal point of view."). France's *Conseil constitutionnel* (Constitutional Council) is the country's highest constitutional authority, and its duty is to ensure that the principles of the constitution are upheld. This power of constitutional review "does not confer upon the Constitutional Council a general power of judgement and of decision-making identical to that of parliament." Alec Stone, The Birth of Judicial Politics in France: The Constitutional Council in Comparative Perspective 148 (1992); *see also* Federico Fabbrini, *Reasonableness as a test for judicial review of legislation in the jurisprudence of the French Constitutional Council*, 4 J. of Comparative L. 39, 52–53 (2009) (italics in original):

The first, implicit, appearance of the standard of the "manifest error of appreciation" in the Council judgments dates to the 1981 *Securité et liberté* decision: in that case, the Council upheld a bill that tightened the punishments provided in the Criminal Code, affirming that it "is not for the Constitutional Council to replace the appreciation of the Parliament with its personal one in what concerns the most appropriate and needed punishment for a criminal offence *as far as no disposition* of the act of Parliament under review *is manifestly contrasting* with the principle set by Article 8 of the 1789 Declaration".

Compare Valérie Malabat & Véronique Wester-Ouisse, "The Quest for Balance Between Tort and Crime in French Law," *in* Matthew Dyson, ed., Comparing Tort and Crime: Learning from Across and Within Legal System 116 (2015):

In 2010, the Cour de Cassation accepted the principle of punitive damages by recognising a punitive damage award granted by an American court. However, the American judgment was held not to be enforceable since the damage award was 'manifestly disproportionate' to the losses and to the breach of contract. There are several indications that punitive damages are in fact a criminal penalty, applied by a civil judge.

The first indication is the court's reference to the principle of proportionality, which arises from Article 8 Declaration of the Rights of Man and of the Citizen 1789, and according to which '[t]he law shall provide for such punishments only as are strictly and obviously necessary'. This is a criminal law principle, but which the Cour de cassation nonetheless referred to in a civil case.

172. Aniceto Masferrer & Anna Taitslin, "The Ill-Fated Union: Constitutional Entrechment of Rights and the Will Theory from Rousseau to Waldron," *in* James R. Silkenat, James E. Hickey Jr. & Peter D. Barenboim, eds., The Legal Doctrines of the Rule of Law and the Legal State (Rechtsstaat) 123 (2014).

173. John R. Vile, Encyclopedia of Constitutional Amendments, Proposed Amendments, and Amending Issues, 1789–2000, at 134 (2d ed. 2003):

The Declaration of Independence was firmly based on a philosophy of natural rights. According to this philosophy, men are created equal and are all entitled to the right to "life, liberty, and the pursuit of happiness." Governments are instituted to secure such rights. Accordingly, "whenever any form of government becomes destructive of these ends, it is the right of the people to alter or abolish it, and to institute new government, laying its foundation on such principles, and organizing its powers in such form, as to them shall seem most likely to effect their safety and happiness."

174. U.S. Const., amend. V:

No person shall be held to answer for a capital, or otherwise infamous crime, unless on a presentment or indictment of a Grand Jury, except in cases arising in the land or naval forces, or in the Militia, when in actual service in time of War or public danger; nor shall any person be subject for the same offence to be twice put in jeopardy of life or limb; nor shall be compelled in any criminal case to be a witness against himself, nor be deprived of life, liberty, or property, without due process of law; nor shall private property be taken for public use, without just compensation.

175. U.S. Const., amend. XIV, § 1:

All persons born or naturalized in the United States and subject to the jurisdiction thereof, are citizens of the United States and of the State wherein they reside. No State shall make or enforce any law which shall abridge the privileges or immunities of citizens of the United States; nor shall any State deprive any person of life, liberty, or property, without due process of law; nor deny to any person within its jurisdiction the equal protection of the laws.

176. *See* Frank August Schubert, Introduction to Law and the Legal System 24 (11th ed. 2015) ("The Fifth Amendment guarantee of due process of law was included in the Bill of Rights in order to place limits on the federal government. It was intended to control the Congress, and prior to the Civil War, it was primarily used to protect property from governmental regulation."); id. ("The addition of the Fourteenth Amendment to the Constitution in 1868 reflected the abolitionists' position. From that point forward, state governments were constitutionally required to provide due process of law and equal protection of the law to all people.").

177. West Virginia State Bd. of Educ. v. Barnette, 319 U.S. 624, 638 (1943):

The very purpose of a Bill of Rights was to withdraw certain subjects from the vicissitudes of political controversy, to place them beyond the reach of majorities and officials and to establish them as legal principles to be applied by the courts. One's right to life, liberty, and property, to free speech, a free press, freedom of worship and assembly, and other fundamental rights may not be submitted to vote; they depend on the outcome of no elections.

Accord Lucas v. Forty-Fourth General Assembly of State of Colo., 377 U.S. 713, 736-37 (1964) ("'One's right to life, liberty and property *** and other fundamental rights may not be submitted to vote; they depend on the outcome of no elections.' A citizen's constitutional rights can hardly be infringed simply because a majority of the people choose that it be."); Woods v. Nierstheimer, 328 U.S. 211, 216 (1946) (referring to "fundamental rights to life and liberty guaranteed by the United States Constitution"); Pope Mfg. Co. v. Gormully, 144 U.S. 224, 234 (1892) ("There are certain fundamental rights which no man can barter away, such, for instance, as his right to life and personal freedom, and, in criminal cases, the right to be tried by a jury of his peers.").

178. 477 U.S. 399 (1986).

179. Id. at 409–10.

180. Id. at 409.

181. 118 U.S. 356 (1886).

182. Id. at 370.

183. Id.

184. Id. at 374.

185. F. B. W., "Punitive Justice," Jan. 14, 1799 (letter addressed to "Sir"), *in* 3 The Universalist's Miscellany; or, Philanthropist's Museum 49, 49–50 (1799):

As punitive justice ought never to proceed upon principles of revenge, every kind of punishment attended with unnecessary severity will be found contrary to the end and design of proper correction. Montesquieu says, "Every punishment which does not arise from absolute necessity is tyrannical." And it may also be said of harsh and cruel means, by which even proper punishment may be attended in its execution, if not absolutely necessary, they are wanton cruelty. The right to punishment is founded upon the social compact, and that being violated by an individual, and the public tranquility disturbed, there is an absolute necessity of punishing the offender, to preserve the peace, and to guard the security of the whole; and by example, as well as precept, to deter others from the commission of acts of like tendency. The immortal Beccaria says, punishments are just, in proportion as the liberty preserved is sacred and valuable.

See also 20 Mr. Hansard, ed., The Parliamentary Debates: Forming a Continuation of the Work Entitled "The Parliamentary History of England, from the Earliest Period to the Year 1803," at 985–86 (1829) (in section on "Mutiny Bill—Corporal Punishments" emphasizing: "Mr. Hume ... had often before pressed upon the attention of the House, for the discontinuance of corporal punishments in the Army" and "he was convinced that, in no case, was such a cruel remedy necessary"); 19 The Spectator: A Weekly Journal of News, Politics, Literature, and Science 754 (1846) (noting that a "Dr. Bowring" pushed for a resolution "that flogging in the Army should be now and for ever abolished" and that "[h]e contended that the punishment is not necessary"); Timothy Walker, Introduction to American Law: Designed as a First Book for Students 575 (10th ed. 1895) ("Neither *cruel* nor *unusual* punishments can be inflicted; that is, there can be no unnecessary torture or barbarity in administering punishment; and no exercise of invention in devising new modes of punishment.") (italics in original).

186. "Motion Respecting Corporal Punishment in the Army," June 21, 1815, *in* 31 T. C. Hansard, ed., The Parliamentary Debates from the Year 1803 to the Present Time: Forming a Continuation of the Work Entitled "The Parliamentary History of England from the Earliest Period to the Year 1803" 918, 924–25 ("With respect to the general system of corporal punishment, every one must feel that nothing but absolute necessity can justified the practice; on the other hand, the necessity of discipline must be admitted, and the only point at issue is, whether other means might not be found to attain the end than those at present objected to.") (quoting Colonel Palmer); James Milner, A Collection of English Exercises, for the Use of Schools and Academies: Containing New Two Thousand Sentences of False Syntax, Improprieties, or Solecisms (1792) (from unpaginated "Advertisement" for "At the Commercial and Mathematical Academy, Scorton, near Catterick, Yorkshire, Young Gentlemen Are genteely Boarded, and Influenced in every Part of Literature, Necessary in a Commercial or Literary Department By the Rev. James Milner and Monsieur Reyroux, a Foreign": "Corporal punishments are never inflicted but in case of absolute necessity; other modes are adopted, more conducive to the advancement of knowledge and virtue."); *see also* Haycraft v. Grigsby, 88 Mo. App. 354, 360, 1901 WL 1655 *3 (St. Louis Ct. App., Mo. 1901):

If excessive flogging or other punishment is inflicted, the teacher, and all who encourage, aid or abet him, are answerable therefor, regardless of whether the motive which prompted him or them was malicious or not.... Persons are not allowed to immoderately beat and injure either children or adults from any motive good or bad; parents have no such right, nor teachers either. Punishment for the most useful and well-intended objects and when absolutely necessary, must always be kept within moderate bounds. The law allows even malefactors that much protection. No individual is ever so disregarded in this land that others may subject him to unmerited suffering.

In re Can-Ah-Couqua, 29 F. 687, 690 (1887) (D.C. Alaska 1887) (ruling that a superintendent of a mission school "shall maintain order, and refrain from inflicting corporal punishment upon Indian children, unless it should become absolutely necessary to the maintenance of discipline, and even then it must be done in moderation only").

187. Basil Montagu, Some Inquiries Respecting the Punishment of Death for Crimes Without Violence 47 (1818), *reprinted in* 12 The Pamphleteer; Respectfully Dedicated to Both Houses of Parliament 333 (1818) (discussing the views of Pastoret):

Absolute necessity alone can justify the punishment of death. If, as Montesquieu affirms, it is "the remedy of a sick society," it is not sufficient that it is efficacious; it must likewise be indispensable. In proposing it as a mean[s] of security, it will not assuredly be denied, that any other mode of punishment which, without taking away the life of the offender, produces the same effect, is highly preferable. Filangieri confesses, that a punishment which is useless is necessarily unjust; and in his judgment, the object of the law is, through the medium of terror, to prevent crimes. If this prevention, then, can be accomplished without death, death is useless, and therefore by his own concession unjust. Nay, Rousseau himself, the ardent advocate of capital punishments, allows that "we have no right to put to death, even for the sake of example, any but those who cannot be permitted to live without danger.

See also MILO M. QUAIFE, ED., THE CONVENTION OF 1846, at 426, 428 (1919) (citing the views of J. Allen Barber, described as "a prosecuting officer" who had been "engaged in the prosecution of offenders" and "in the administration of the law against those guilty of the highest crime—the crime of murder"):

"Every punishment which does not arise from absolute necessity is tyran[n]ical," says Montesquieu. Is there any absolute necessity to take the life of the murderer in order to [maintain] the protection of society? He contended there was no necessity, but that ample protection could be found in the confinement of the offender.

188. JOHN D. BESSLER, THE CELEBRATED MARQUIS: AN ITALIAN NOBLE AND THE MAKING OF THE MODERN WORLD 218 (2017) (italics in original).

189. *E.g.*, LYMAN COBB, THE EVIL TENDENCIES OF CORPORAL PUNISHMENT AS A MEANS OF MORAL DISCIPLINE IN FAMILIES AND SCHOOLS, EXAMINED AND DISCUSSED 68 n.* (1847) (quoting S. S. Randall, Esquire, "the able editor of the District School Journal, in a notice of the new work, recently published on the "THEORY AND PRACTICE OF TEACHING, by D. P. Page, A. M., Principal of the New York State Normal School"):

While the absolute necessity of an *occasional* resort to CORPORAL FLAGELLATIONS, as an *ultimate* remedy, in *extreme* cases, where every *other* means of reclamation have been *faithfully* but unsuccessfully applied, is contended for, and vindicated upon principle, no less than expediency, we do not understand Mr. PAGE as essentially differing, on this point, from the enlightened views of the most eminent of our professional educators at home and abroad. Those views are, in the main, forcibly expressed by the judicious and pious Dr. LANGHORNE in his Life of Plutarch. 'This mode,' says he, 'of punishment in our public schools is *one of the worst remains of barbarism that prevails among us....* '

See also L. S. Everett, "Essays on Education," 5 SOUTHERN PIONEER AND PHILADELPHIA LIBERALIST 210 (1835) ("The only grounds on which the whipping system can be justified are two—viz.—the *necessity* of resorting to corporal punishments—and the expediency, or utility of doing it, with a view of benefiting such children as are subjected to it.") (italics in original); id. ("Corporal punishments in our public schools are not necessary."); THE NEW ANNUAL REGISTER, OR GENERAL REPOSITORY OF HISTORY, POLITICS, ARTS, SCIENCES, AND LITERATURE, FOR THE YEAR 1824, at 424 (1825) ("He knew well that corporal punishment was defended by many able writers; but some of the best and most humane men in the service had declared it to be unnecessary.").

190. *E.g.*, GEORGE DUFFIELD, THE DIVINE ORGANIC LAW, ORDAINED FOR THE HUMAN RACE; OR, CAPITAL PUNISHMENT FOR MURDER AUTHORIZED BY GOD AND SUSTAINED BY REASON 13 (1848):

Those, who, with Beccaria, and his supposed commentator, Voltaire, have contended that government originates in the sacrifice of portions of personal liberty, made by individuals for the purpose of warding off greater evils and enjoying greater security and tranquility, will resolve, the right to punish guilt, and every act of authority of one man over another, into absolute necessity, and pronounce with Montesquieu, all punishments to be tyrannical, which is not thus absolutely nnecessary [sic]. But who is to be the judge of that necessity, and what is the rule or standard by which it is to be estimated? Admitting the principle that human government grows out of the necessity which men feel, and which makes them consent to part with items of personal liberty, to make an aggregate of sovereignty in the civil magistrate, of course it becomes a question, whether it is necessary to punish murder with death, and whether the life of the murderer might not be spared, and his labor be made to subserve the general interest. But in practice it will be found, that differing opinions will ever be entertained among men, about the nature and degree of that necessity, according as they take narrow or more extended views of the interest of human society, and the best means of promoting it, and according as their sympathies are in unison, either with society or with the criminal.

See also EDWARD I. SEARS, ED., THE NATIONAL QUARTERLY REVIEW 378 (1870):

Beccaria is still more opposed to severity than his countryman of the classic times. The former fully agrees with Montesquieu that every punishment which does not arise from absolute necessity is tyrannical. "As for the death penalty," says Beccaria, "it is pernicious to society from the example of barbarity it affords. If the passions, or the necessity of war, have taught men to shed the blood of their fellow-creatures, the laws, which are intended to moderate the ferocity of mankind, should not increase it by examples of barbarity, the more horrible as this punishment is usually attended with formal pageantry." We do not quote Beccaria because we agree with him....

191. "*Capital Punishment*," *in* R. BEVERLY COLE, ED., THE WESTERN LANCET: A MONTHLY JOURNAL

DEVOTED TO MEDICINE, SURGERY AND THE COLLATERAL SCIENCE (1874), Vol. II, p. 373. The English translator's preface to Beccaria's *On Crimes and Punishments* itself made reference to "unnecessary circumstances of cruelty," with the full opening sentence of the translator's preface reading as follows:

PENAL LAWS, so considerable a part of every system of legislation, and of so great importance to the happiness, peace, and security of every member of society, are still so imperfect, and are attended with so many unnecessary circumstances of cruelty in all nations, that an attempt to reduce them to the standard of reason must be interesting to all mankind.

"Preface of the Translator," *in* AN ESSAY ON CRIMES AND PUNISHMENTS, TRANSLATED FROM THE ITALIAN: WITH A COMMENTARY, ATTRIBUTED TO M. DE VOLTAIRE (1809).

192. The United States Sentencing Commission is an independent agency that was established by the Sentencing Reform Act of 1984. UNITED STATES SENTENCING COMMISSION, THE PAST PREDICTS THE FUTURE: CRIMINAL HISTORY AND RECIDIVISM OF FEDERAL OFFENDERS 16 (2017); *see also* LITTLE HOOVER COMMISSION, SOLVING CALIFORNIA'S CORRECTIONS CRISIS: TIME IS RUNNING OUT 39 (2007) ("In 1980, Minnesota pioneered the guideline-setting sentencing commission structure. Minnesota's sentencing commission was tasked by the Legislature with developing sentencing guidelines that would go into effect unless voted down by the Legislature."); KATJA FRANKO AAS, SENTENCING IN THE AGE OF INFORMATION: FROM FAUST TO MACINTOSH 16 (2005) ("Minnesota was at the forefront of the proportionality and just deserts movement, and the first state to implement presumptive numerical guidelines in 1980.").

193. Richard S. Frase, *Sentencing Guidelines in Minnesota, 1978–2003*, 32 CRIME & JUST. 131, 131-32 (2005).

194. The number of prisons in the United States has grown over the last several decades. DAVID MUSICK & KRISTINE GUNSAULUS-MUSICK, AMERICAN PRISONS: THEIR PAST, PRESENT AND FUTURE (2017), intro. ("The number of state and federal prisons increased from around 600 in the mid-1970s to over 1,000 by 2000."). This growth in prisons comes at a great cost, both human and financial. Id. ("The American practice of sweeping social problems into jails and prisons has become expensive, costing at least $60 billion per year. Our appetite for prisons is stifling other social investments. In California, for example, since 1983, 23 new prisons have been built but no new universities.").

195. Borbála Fellegi, "Retribution and/or Restoration? The Purpose of our Justice System through the Lens of Judges and Prosecutors," *in* DAVID CORNWELL, JOHN BLAD & MARTIN WRIGHT, EDS., CIVILISING CRIMINAL JUSTICE: AN INTERNATIONAL RESTORATIVE AGENDA FOR PENAL REFORM 120 (2013) ("[T]he terms *punishment* and *consequence* and often used by professionals as synonyms, but their meaning is not the same at all. For legal practitioners, *punishment* is necessary to make sure that a reprehensible act does have *consequences*.") (italics in original).

196. Throughout the world, whether the death penalty is necessary has animated—and continues to animate—the debate over that punishment. For example, as the "Right Hon. J. A. Lawson" emphasized on March 11, 1865:

My belief is that Capital Punishment is not necessary at all in order to preserve the security of human life; and although it is, of course, a punishment more dreaded than any other, yet I think that the substitution of another punishment, which would be more certain to follow upon the crime, would be equally deterrent with Capital Punishment in the case of murder.

21 REPORTS FROM COMMISSIONERS: CAPITAL PUNISHMENT 382 (1866); *see also* JOHN MCCRAE MOIR, ED., CAPITAL PUNISHMENT, BASED ON PROFESSOR MITTERMAIER'S 'TODESSTRAFE' 124 (1865):

Even during times of excitement, when Death Punishment was re-enacted by the New Code—although one capital sentence was passed for a revolting crime—the culprit was pardoned. The statistical tables show no increase in heinous crimes, and all the reports of the trustworthy officials justify the inference that the re-introduction of Death Punishment is not necessary.

197. Furman v. Georgia, 408 U.S. 238, 359 n.141 (Marshall, J., concurring) (citing Johnson v. Zerbst, 304 U.S. 458, 462 (1938); Note, *The Death Penalty Cases*, 56 U. CALIF. L. REV. 1268, 1324-54 (1968)). In *Johnson v. Zerbst*, the Supreme Court wrote:

The Sixth Amendment guarantees that: 'In all criminal prosecutions, the accused shall enjoy the right *** to have the Assistance of Counsel for his defence.' This is one of the safeguards of the Sixth Amendment deemed necessary to insure fundamental human rights of life and liberty. Omitted from the Constitution as originally adopted, provisions of this and other Amendments were submitted by the first Congress convened under that Constitution as essential barriers against arbitrary or unjust deprivation of human rights.

Johnson, 304 U.S. at 462.

198. 17 U.S. 316 (1819).

199. Id. at 418.

200. Id. at 413–15

201. Id. at 416–19.

202. Id. at 420–21.

203. United States v. Kebodeaux, 133 S. Ct. 2496, 2502 (2013).

204. Id. (quoting *McColloch*, 4 Wheat 316, 421).

205. Id. at 2503 (quoting Lottery Case, 188 U.S. 321, 355 (1903)).

206. Id. (quoting James Everard's Breweries v. Day, 265 U.S. 545, 559 (1924)).

207. 133 S. Ct. 2496 (2013).

208. Id. at 2503 (citing United States v. Comstock, 560 U.S. 126, 136-37 (2010)).

209. Montesquieu and Beccaria were, from an early time, seen as extremely prominent figures of the Enlightenment whose ideas were regularly invoked side-by-side. *E.g.*, 2 JEREMY BENTHAM, THEORY OF LEGISLATION 101 (1840) ("Montesquieu perceived the necessity of a proportion between offences and punishments. Beccaria insists upon its importance.") (translated from the French of Etienne Dumont by R. Hildreth). Jeremy Bentham, who carefully studied the work of both men, also repeatedly references the concept of necessity. *E.g.*, id. at 38 ("The exercise of lawful power implies the necessity of doing evil to repress evil."); id. at 55 ("Punishment, which, if it goes beyond the limit of necessity, is a pure evil, has been scattered with a prodigal hand."); id. at 163 ("How is it possible to justify the severity of the legislator, who, without necessity, takes away from the laboring classes those little enjoyments which soften their hard lot, and who forces them into gloominess or vice, under pretext of religion?"); id. at 265:

But be slow to believe in this necessity for death. By disusing it as a punishment you will prevent it as a crime; for when men are placed between two offences it is desirable to give them a sensible interest not to commit the greater. It is desirable to convert the assassin into a thief; and to give him a reason for preferring a reparable to an irreparable offence.

210. The notion of the burden being on the state to justify capital punishment has roots that reach back far in time. For example, in F. A. Burleigh's 1901 essay titled "Capital Punishment," Burleigh called the death penalty "an unrighteous and wicked thing," and posed this question: "Can it be necessary to inflict a punishment which necessarily involves the brutalizing of the men who inflict it?" F. A. Burleigh, "Capital Punishment," 18 RAILROAD TRAINMEN'S JOURNAL 807, 810 (1901). In the course of that essay, Burleigh argued:

While society is undoubtedly not in danger of a criminal after he is dead, it is not protected against other evils which result from this legal murder; and the burden of proof is with the upholders of capital punishment to show that it accomplishes the desired result and nothing else. If society could be protected only by putting criminals to death then there might be some excuse for it; but criminals can be confined until they are no longer dangerous.

Id. at 807. In his essay, Burleigh quoted from Pennsylvania's 1794 statute reciting that " 'the punishment of death ought never to be inflicted where it is not absolutely necessary to the public safety.' " Id.

211. BERNARD SCHWARTZ, THE UNPUBLISHED OPINIONS OF THE WARREN COURT 395, 401–402, 405 (1985).

212. Id. at 405–406.

213. This principle actually long pre-dates 1794, with both Montesquieu and Beccaria specifically articulating this principle in their writings. Pennsylvania's Act of April 24, 1794, 3 Sm. Laws, 186, was once called "the true basis of the present humane laws of the Commonwealth." Commonwealth v. Brown, 17 Pa. D. 89, 1908 WL 3009 *7 (Court of Oyer and Terminer and General Jail Delivery of Pennsylvania, Philadelphia County, 1908) (Sulzberger, P. J., concurring).

214. In a 1963 dissent from a denial of certiorari in *Rudolph v. Alabama*, 373 U.S. 889 (1963), Justice Goldberg—joined by two other justices, and writing before the death penalty for non-homicidal rape was declared unconstitutional in *Coker v. Georgia*—expressed a desire for the U.S. Supreme Court to take up these related questions: "Can the permissible aims of punishment (e.g., deterrence,

isolation, rehabilitation) be achieved as effectually by punishing rape less severely than by death (e.g., by life imprisonment); if so, does the imposition of the death penalty for rape constitute 'unnecessary cruelty?' " *Rudolph*, 375 U.S. at 891 (Goldberg, J., dissenting from denial of cert.; joined by Douglas, J. and Brennan, J.). In his concurrence in *Andres v. United States*, 333 U.S. 740 (1948), Justice Felix Frankfurter wrote about the nineteenth-century movement against capital punishment. As Justice Frankfurter emphasized: "The movement was impelled both by ethical and humanitarian arguments against capital punishment, as well as by the practical consideration that jurors were reluctant to bring in verdicts which inevitably called for its infliction." Id. at 753 (Frankfurter, J., concurring).

215. Schwartz, The Unpublished Opinions of the Warren Court, *supra* note 211, at 407–08.

216. Legislative bodies must evaluate complex information about crimes and punishments in their quest for appropriate sentencing policies. And—as noted in the text of this book—in most cases, those decisions should be respected, meaning the courts have a circumscribed—but nonetheless very important—role to play as a check on the abuse of power. George C. Thomas III, Double Jeopardy: The History, the Law 68 (1998) ("in the vast majority of cases, the legislature is free to define crimes and authorize penalties as it sees fit"). The approach in France, which has a Constitutional Council, is much the same. *See, e.g.*, Human Rights Committee, Views adopted by the Committee under article 5(4) of the Optional Protocol, concerning communication No. 2229/2012, CCRP/C/116/D/2229/2012 (15 June 2016), tbinternet.ohchr.org/Treaties/CCPR/ ... / CCPR_C_116_D_2229_2012_8115_E.docx, p. 19 n.*g*:

In France, the constitutional jurisprudence is based on article 8 of the Declaration of the Rights of Man and of the Citizen of 26 August 1789 (which is part of the body of constitutional law): "The law shall provide for such punishments only as are strictly and obviously necessary." On that basis, the Constitutional Council has limited powers of review of the necessity of criminal penalties: it considers that the setting of penalties is primarily the prerogative of the legislature but nonetheless reserves the right to ensure that punishment is not obviously out of proportion to the crime. See in particular Decision No. 2007-554 DC of 9 August 2007, on the Act on stronger measures to prevent reoffending by adults and minors, preambular paragraph 8. See also Decision No. 2000-433 DC of 27 July 2000, on the Act amending Act No. 86-1067 of 30 September 1986 on freedom of communication, preambular paragraphs 51 and 52, in which the Council finds that a penalty automatically requiring the broadcasting of a message where a radio or television service fails to comply with its obligations is contrary to article 8 of the Declaration of the Rights of Man and of the Citizen, and states: "Considering ... that such an automatic requirement could, in some circumstances, result in the imposition of a penalty disproportionate to the offence; that consequently, by barring the Broadcasting Authority from tailoring the punishment to the seriousness of the infraction by taking into account the specific circumstances of the case, the legislature has violated the principle of the necessity of penalties, as expressed in article 8 of the Declaration of the Rights of Man and of the Citizen of 1789."

217. "Text of the Oaths of Office for Supreme Court Justices," Information Sheet, Supreme Court of the United States, https://www.supremecourt.gov/about/oath/textoftheoathsofoffice08-10-2009.pdf.

218. Jacqueline R. Kanovitz, Constitutional Law 468 (13th ed. 2012); *see also* County of Los Angeles, Calif. V. Mendez, 137 S. Ct. 1539, 1546 (2017) (citations omitted):

Our case law sets forth a settled and exclusive framework for analyzing whether the force used in making a seizure compiles with the Fourth Amendment. As in other areas of our Fourth Amendment jurisprudence, "[d]etermining whether the force used to effect a particular seizure is 'reasonable' " requires balancing of the individual's Fourth Amendment interests against the relevant government interests. The operative question in excessive force cases is "whether the totality of the circumstances justifie[s] a particular sort of search or seizure."

219. *E.g.*, Graham v. Connor, 490 U.S. 386, 396-97 (1989) (citations omitted):

The "reasonableness" of a particular use of force must be judged from the perspective of a reasonable officer on the scene, rather than with the 20/20 vision of hindsight. The Fourth Amendment is not violated by an arrest based on probable cause, even though the wrong person is arrested, nor by the mistaken execution of a valid search warrant on the wrong premises. With respect to a claim of excessive force, the same standard of reasonableness at the moment applies: "Not every push or shove, even if it may later seem unnecessary in the peace of a judge's chambers," violates the Fourth Amendment. The calculus of reasonableness must embody allowance for the fact that police officers are often forced to make split-second judgments—in circumstances that are tense, uncertain, and rapidly evolving—about the amount of force that is necessary in a particular situation.

As in other Fourth Amendment contexts, however, the "reasonableness" inquiry in an excessive force case is an objective one: the question is whether the officers' actions are "objectively reasonable" in light of the facts and circumstances confronting them, without regard to their underlying intent or motivation. An officer's evil intentions will not make a Fourth Amendment violation out of an objectively reasonable use of force; nor will an officer's good intentions make an objectively unreasonable use of force constitutional.

220. Id. at 153; *see also* id.

There are three legitimate reasons for using force: (1) for self-defense or protection of others from physical harm, (2) to overcome resistance, or (3) to prevent escape. All others are illegitimate. Police, for example, are not justified in using their nightsticks on people who "mouth off" at them. Furthermore, although force may be justified to overcome resistance, once a suspect has been subdued, the force must cease. Striking, hitting, kicking, and tasering suspects after they have been brought under control violates the Fourth Amendment and, in extreme cases, can result in federal criminal prosecution.

221. 550 U.S. 609 (2007).

222. Id. at 614 (citations omitted); *see also* id. ("The orders by the police to the occupants, in the context of this lawful search, were permissible, and perhaps necessary, to protect the safety of the deputies.").

223. Kanovitz, Constitutional Law, *supra* note 218, at 468.

224. Bruce A. Arrigo, ed., The SAGE Encyclopedia of Surveillance, Security, and Privacy 942 (2018).

225. *E.g.*, 1 Bryon Eugene Price & John Charles Morris, eds., Prison Privatization: The Many Facets of a Controversial Industry 44 (2012):

The dramatic escalation of the U.S. prison population can be traced almost exclusively to the war on drugs and the rise of lengthy mandatory minimum prison sentences for drug crimes and other nonviolent felonies. On average, nonviolent offenders now make up more than 70 percent of the U.S. prison population. Nonviolent offenders, who were once supervised in the community via probation, are now imprisoned for lengthy terms, despite evidence that prison is the most expensive and least effective approach for reducing recidivism.

226. *E.g.*, Flora I. Matheson, Amanda Brazil & Pamela Forrester, "After Prison: Managing Re-integration, Mental Health and Desistance from Offending," *in* Rosemary Sheehan & James Ogloff, eds., Working within the Forensic Paradigm: Cross-Discipline Approaches for Policy and Practice 244 (2015) (noting that the dehumanization of the prison experience and the rejection from mainstream society "places someone leaving prison in a very precarious situation with few options to make positive life changes aimed at staying out of prison"); Amy Levad, Redeeming a Prison Society: A Liturgical and Sacramental Response to Mass Incarceration 34 (2014) ("[T]he majority of families with an incarcerated parent will probably experience greater poverty while the parent is in prison, and in all likelihood, after the parent is released as well. About half of parents in prison (52 percent of mothers and 54 percent of fathers) provided the primary financial support for their children prior to incarceration."); San Diego Association of Governments, Criminal Justice Research Division, Crime in the San Diego Region 66 (2002) ("[M]en and women who are sent to prison have usually faced numerous social problems in their lives prior to being arrested, including poverty, drug and alcohol dependence, mental health issues, infectious diseases, unemployment, and illiteracy.").

227. Galen v. County of Los Angeles, 477 F.3d 652, 661 (9th Cir. 2007).

228. United States v. Salerno, 481 U.S. 739, 753 (1987); *see also* Campbell v. Johnson, 586 F.3d 835 (11th Cir. 2009) ("Although the Excessive Bail Clause does not guarantee a right to bail, it does guarantee that any bail imposed "not be 'excessive' in light of the perceived evil."") (quoting *Salerno*, 481 U.S. at 754).

229. People v. George, Case No. ST-2016-CR-0000085, 2016 WL 5660283 *4 (V.I. Super. Ct. Sept. 27, 2016).

230. Id. (citation omitted).

231. Lawhon v. State, No. 03-15-00265-CR, No. 03-15-00277-CR, No. 03-15-00288-CR, 2015 WL 7424763 *1 (Tex. Ct. App.—Austin, Nov. 20, 2015).

232. 342 U.S. 1 (1951).

233. Id. at 3 (citing United States v. Motlow, 10 F.2d 657 (7th Cir. 1926)); *see also* Lopez v. State, 985 N.E.2d 358, 362 (Ind. Ct. App. 2013) ("[B]ond set at $3,000,000 surety plus $250,000 cash is excessive and more than necessary to assure Lopez's presence in court. Accordingly, we conclude that the trial court abused its discretion when it denied Lopez's motion for bond reduction.").

234. United States v. Karper, 847 F. Supp.2d 350, 363 (N.D.N.Y. 2011).

235. United States v. Polouizzi, 697 F. Supp.2d 381, 390 (E.D.N.Y. 2010).

236. Miller v. Alabama, 567 U.S. 460, 479, 465 (2012); Montgomery v. Louisiana, 136 S. Ct. 718 (2016).

237. Kaitlyn Schallhorn, "Cyntoia Brown, Serving Life for Murder, Asks Tennessee Parole Board for Clemency: A Look at Her Case," Fox News, May 23, 2018, http://www.foxnews.com/us/2018/05/23/cyntoia-brown-serving-life-for-murder-asks-tennessee-parole-board-for-clemency-look-at-her-case.html.

238. Lauren-Brooke Eisen, "New Report Examines the Growth of Incarceration in the United States," The Huffington Post, May 9, 2014 (updated July 9, 2014), https://www.huffingtonpost.com/laurenbrooke-eisen/new-report-examining-the_b_5295626.html; The Growth of Incarceration in the United States: Exploring Causes and Consequences (2014), https://www.nap.edu/catalog/18613/the-growth-of-incarceration-in-the-united-states-exploring-causes.

239. Ralph Ketcham, ed., Selected Writings of James Madison 307–308 (2006).

Conclusion

1. Vicki B. Sullivan, Montesquieu and the Despotic Ideas of Europe: An Interpretation of *The Spirit of the Laws* 61 (2017).

2. John Hostettler, The Politics of Punishment 115 (2016).

3. Jean-Baptiste Say, A Treatise on Political Economy; or the Production, Distribution, and Consumption of Wealth (C. R. Prinsep, trans., new Am. ed., Clement C. Biddle, trans. 1851).

4. William Archibald Dunning, A History of Political Theories: From Rousseau to Spencer 71–72 (1922).

5. Janet Funston & Richard Funston, *Cesare Beccaria and the American Founding Fathers*, 3 Italian Americana 72, 73, 75, 80, 85 (1976) (citing Mary-Margaret H. Barr, Voltaire in America, 1744–1800, at 19 (1941); quoting Robert J. Turnbull, A Visit to the Philadelphia Prison, Containing an Account of the Gradual Reformation and Present Improved State of the Penal Laws of Pennsylvania, with Observations on the Impolicy and Injustice of Capital Punishment 6 (1797)).

6. "Mr. Brown," The Philadelphia Gazette & Universal Daily Advertiser, Mar. 31, 1795, p. 2. Other newspapers also took note of Cesare Beccaria's death. *See, e.g.*, The Philadelphia Minerva, Mar. 28, 1795, p. 3 ("On the 29th November, died, at Mayland [Milan], the celebrated Marquis BECCARIA, the well-known author of the work on Crimes and Punishments."); Carlisle Gazette (Carlisle, PA), Apr. 8, 1795, p. 3 ("On the 26th Nov. died at Mayland [Milan], the celebrated Marquis Beccaria, the well known author of the work on crimes and punishments."); The Rutland Herald (Rutland, VT), Apr. 20, 1795, p. 2 ("On the 26th November, died at Mayland [Milan], the celebrated Marquis BECCARIA, the well known author of the work on Crimes and Punishment."); City Gazette & Daily Advertiser (Charleston, S.C.), Apr. 22, 1795, p. 2 ("Died, lately, at Milan in Italy, the Marquis of Beccaria, author of the celebrated treatise 'On Crimes and Punishments.'").

7. Philadelphia Gazette, Mar. 27, 1795, p. 2.

8. 3 J. Thomas Scharf & Thompson Westcott, History of Philadelphia, 1609–1884, at 1977 (1884); 5 John Spencer Bassett & Sidney Bradshaw Fay, eds., Smith College Studies in History 33 (1920).

9. John Cyril Barton, "Antigallows Activism in Antebellum American Literature," *in* Katy Ryan, ed., Demands of the Dead: Executions, Storytelling, and Activism in the United States 145–46 (2012); Encyclopædia Britannica, The Ideas that Made the Modern World: The People, Philosophy, and History of the Enlightenment 34–35 (2008).

10. 1 Noah Webster, An American Dictionary of the English Language (1828) (italics in original); *compare* Noah Webster, The American Spelling Book; Containing the Rudiments of English Language, for the Use of Schools in the United States 158 (rev. ed. 1829):

Q. How does cruelty show its effects?

A. A cruel disposition is usually exercised upon those who are under its power. Cruel rulers make severe laws, which injure the persons and properties of their subjects. Cruel officers execute laws in a severe manner, when it is not necessary for public good. A cruel husband abuses his wife and children. A cruel master acts the tyrant over his apprentices and servants. The effects of cruelty are, hatred, quarrels, tumults and wretchedness.

11. Pope John Paul II, *Evangelium Vitae* (The Gospel of Life), Mar. 25, 1995, ¶ 56; *see also* id. at ¶ 57 ("In any event, the principle set forth in the new *Catechism of the Catholic Church* remains valid: 'If bloodless means are sufficient to defend human lives against an aggressor and to protect public order and the safety of persons, public authority must limit itself to such means, because they better correspond to the concrete conditions of the common good and are more in conformity to the dignity of the human person.'"); Jack Jenkins, "Pope Francis Changes Catechism to Declare Death Penalty Inadmissible," The Oakland Press, Aug. 13, 2018, https://www.theoaklandpress.com/lifestyles/pope-francis-changes-catechism-to-declare-death-penalty-inadmissible/article_f3efdab4-9990-11e8-847a-530d1ad990f3.html (discussing the change to the catechism of the Catholic Church ordered by Pope Francis).

12. Lawrence M. Friedman, Crime and Punishment in American History 62–63 (1993).

13. Hyman Gross, Crime and Punishment: A Concise Moral Critique 179 (2012) ("Whatever the purpose of punishment might be, there is implicit recognition that excessive punishment is the key to its being disproportionate, and being more than necessary to serve its purpose is the key to its being excessive.").

14. Samuel Johnson, A Dictionary of the English Language (3d ed. 1768) (unpaginated entry). That dictionary also makes numerous additional references to *cruel*. The dictionary, among others, makes two separate references to "cruel death"; lists "Cruel; inhuman" as one of the definitions of "Barbarous"; lists "Cruel; murderous" as one of the definitions of "Bloody"; lists "Savage; cruel, inhuman" as one of the definitions of "Brutal"; defines "Butcherly" as "Cruel; bloody; barbarous"; defines "Cut-throat" as "Cruel; inhuman; barbarous"; defines "Doghearted" as "Cruel; pitiless; malicious"; defines "Felon" as "Cruel; traitorous; inhuman"; defines "Inhuman" as "Barbarous; savage; cruel; uncompassionate"; defines "Marblehearted" as "Cruel; insensible; hard-hearted"; lists "Cruel; inhuman; unjustly exactious or severe" as one of the definitions of "Oppressive"; defines "Remorseless" as "Unpitying; cruel; savage"; defines "Sanguinary" as "Cruel; bloody; murtherous"; lists "Untamed; cruel" as one of the definitions of "Savage"; lists "Cruel; inexorable" as one of the definitions of "Severe"; defines "Tyrannical" and "Tyrannick" as "acting like a tyrant; cruel; despotick; imperious"; lists "cruel power" and "Cruel government" as definitions of "Tyranny"; lists "A cruel despotick and severe master" as one of the definitions of "Tyrant"; lists "Cruel; severe; not clement" as one of the definitions of "Unmerciful"; and lists "cruel" among the definitions of "Wrath." Id. (unpaginated entries).

15. Id. (unpaginated entry). "Usual," by contrast, was defined as "Common; frequent; customary." Id. (unpaginated entry); *see also* id. (unpaginated entries) (defining "Usually" as "Commonly; frequently; customarily" and "Unusualness" defined as "Commonness; frequency"). Two of the definitions of "Common" are listed as "Frequent; usual; ordinary" and "Commonly; ordinarily"; one of the definitions of "Ordinary" is listed as "Common; usual"; and "Customary" lists "Usual," "Habitual," and "Conformable to established custom" as dictionary definitions. Id. (unpaginated entries). While "Accustomed" is defined as "[a]ccording to custom; frequent; usual," "Unaccustomed" is defined as "1. Not used; not habituated" and "2. New; not usual." Id. (unpaginated entries).

16. Id. (unpaginated entry); *see also* id. (showing unpaginated entry for "Inflict" provides; "To put in act or impose as a punishment").

17. Id. (unpaginated entry).

18. 18 Encyclopædia Perthensis; or Universal Dictionary of the Arts, Sciences, Literature, &c. 481 (2d ed. 1816) ("Punishment" defined as "[a]ny infliction or pain imposed in vengeance of a crime."); id. ("Punish" defined as "1. To chastise; to afflict with penalties or death for some crime."

and "2. To revenge a fault with pain or death—I will *punish* your offences with the rod. *Bible*.").

19. Andrew Novak, The Global Decline of the Mandatory Death Penalty: Constitutional Jurisprudence and Legislative Reform in Africa, Asia, and the Caribbean 14 (2014):

[I]n the United States after ratification of the Eighth Amendment, one of the first acts of Congress was to enact a law creating offenses punishable by death and by corporal punishment. Yet, the proportionality principle in American criminal sentencing has a long history in the United States and beyond since its articulation in Cesare Beccaria's book *On Crimes and Punishments* in 1764, which was widely read in the early American colonies by such important figures as John Adams, Thomas Jefferson, and George Mason.

20. Id. at 15.

21. Id. Prisoners in early America were sometimes forced to perform hard labor in chains. Randolph Shipley Klein, ed., Science and Society in Early America: Essays in Honor of Whitfield J. Bell, Jr. 228–29 (1986); Michael Sherman & Gordon Hawkins, Imprisonment in America: Choosing the Future 50 (1981).

22. Matthew Pate & Laurie A. Gould, Corporal Punishment Around the World 94 (2012).

23. In English broadsides, murders were frequently described as "cruel." *E.g., An Account of the Cruel and Barbarous Murder of James Heron, Pitman, at Benwell, near Newcastle, on Saturday, Jan. 19, 1811, available at* http://pds.lib.harvard.edu/pds/view/4787459 (June 19, 2012); Robert Bruce, *An Account of the Cruel and Barbarous Murder of Janet Simpson, Between Earsdon and North-Shields, on Saturday Evening, Jan. 12, 1811, available at* http://pds.lib.harvard.edu/pds/view/4788567 (June 19, 2012). A reference to an "unusual Crime" is found in an Old Bailey record from 1677. *The Proceedings of the Old Bailey, London's Central Criminal Court, 1674 to 1913, Ref. No. t16770117-3, available at* http://www.oldbaileyonline.org/images.jsp?doc=16770117006 (June 19, 2012) ("A man was likewise Condemned to die for a kind of unusual Crime, but such as the Law, by reason of its bad example and mischievous tendency, has thought fit to restrain with capital Punishment ... He begg'd heartily for Transportation, but it could not be granted.").

24. *E.g.*, Trial of Thomas O. Selfridge, Attorney at Law, Before the Hon. Isaac Parker, Esquire for Killing Charles Austin, on the Public Exchange, in Boston, August 4th, 1806, at 146 (1806) ("[I]f even upon a sudden provocation one beats another in a cruel and unusual manner, so that he dies, though he did not intend his death, yet is guilty of murder by express malice."); George Custance, A Concise View of the Constitution of England 344 (1808) (stating "[i]t is also murder by express malice, if a master or teacher upon a sudden provocation beat his servant or scholar in a cruel and unusual manner"); *see also* The Trial of the British Soldiers, of the 29th Regiment of Foot, for the Murder of Crispus Attucks, Samuel Gray, Samuel Maverick, James Caldwell, and Patrick Carr, on Monday Evening, March 5, 1770, at 6, 33, 44 (1824) (referencing a killing in a "cruel and inhuman manner" and in a "cruel and unusual manner").

25. Oliver Barbour, The Magistrate's Criminal Law: A Practice Treatise on the Jurisdiction, Duty, and Authority of Justices of the Peace in the State of New-York in Criminal Cases 58, 60, 63 (1841).

26. John D. Bessler, Cruel and Unusual: The American Death Penalty and the Founders' Eighth Amendment 218 (2012).

27. *E.g.*, Dedieu v. People, 8 E.P. Smith 178, 182 (N.Y. Ct. App. 1860) ("In manslaughter, the most usual example is the killing of another in the heat of passion, but in a cruel and unusual manner. This is the offence in the second degree."); Staten v. State, 30 Miss. 619, 621 (Miss. 1856) ("To constitute manslaughter in the second degree, the killing must be done '*in a cruel and unusual manner*.'") (emphasis in original); People v. Pearce, 2 Edm. Sel. Cas. 76, 77–78 (N.Y. Sup. 1849) (stating a killing is manslaughter in the second degree where the death is effected in a cruel and unusual manner; where the defendant struck decedent on the head with a club, knocking him down, and struck him with the club five or six times after he was down, he was guilty of second-degree manslaughter); *cf.* Jacob v. State, 22 Tenn. 493, 508 (Tenn. 1842) (containing the following argument of a lawyer: "What! shall it be said that a man is indictable for beating his horse in a cruel and unusual manner in the street, and yet that he may lawfully and with impunity beat his slave, a human being ... ?.... Thanks to the enlightened, humanized and Christianized age in which we live, that is not the law."); *In re* Kottman, 2 Hill (SC) 363, 363 (20 S.C.L. 2363, 363 (S.C. Ct. App. L. & Eq. 1834) (referencing the argument of a lawyer that

"the father had beaten" his son "in a cruel and unusual manner without any just cause").

28. *E.g.*, People v. Gallagher, 1 Edm. Sel. Cas. 578, 578 (N.Y. Sup. 1848) ("The prisoner was convicted of manslaughter in the second degree, for having caused the death of his mother, in a cruel and unusual manner, by kicking her, and wounded her womb, where she was afflicted with *prolapsus uteri*."); McWhirt v. Com., 3 Gratt. 594, 1846 WL 2405, at *7 (Va. Ga. 1846) ("[W]here, upon a sudden provocation, one beats another in a cruel and unusual matter, so that he dies, though he did not intend his death, yet he is guilty of murder by express malice: that is, by an express evil design, he genuine sense of *malitia*."); United States v. Travers, 28 F. Cas. 204 (D. Mass. 1814) (Story, J., charging jury) ("If, therefore, upon a sudden provocation of a slight nature one beat another in a cruel and unusual manner so that he dies, though he did not intend to kill him, it is murder by express malice."); 12 Encyclopædia Britannica 451 (1797) ("[I]f even upon a sudden provocation one beats another, in a cruel and unusual manner, so that he dies, though he did not intend his death, yet he is guilty of murder by express malice.").

29. 300 U.S. 617 (1937).

30. *Id.* at 626–27.

31. *Id.* at 626. In that case, the Court examined the history of legislative enactments, noting:

At least sixteen statutes, passed prior to the time of the American Revolution by the Colonies, or shortly after by the newly created states, authorized the summary punishment of petty offenses by imprisonment for three months or more. And at least eight others were punishable by imprisonment for six months.

Id. The Supreme Court further stated in that case:

In the face of this history, we find it impossible to say that a ninety-day penalty for a petty offense, meted out upon a trial without a jury, does not conform to standards which prevailed when the Constitution was adopted, or was not then contemplated as appropriate notwithstanding the constitutional guarantee of a jury trial.

Id. at 626–27.

32. As the Court stated, articulating its view in 1937:

We are aware that those standards of action and of policy which finds expression in the common and statute law may vary from generation to generation. Such change has led to the abandonment of the lash and the stocks, and we may assume, for present purposes, that commonly accepted views of the severity of punishment by imprisonment may become so modified that a penalty once thought to be mild may come to be regarded as so harsh as to call for the jury trial, which the Constitution prescribes, in some cases which were triable without a jury when the Constitution was adopted.

Id. at 627.

33. Opinions of the New York State Comptroller 3012 (1982) ("If there is one constant that permeates the field of law, that constant is change. Statutes change, decisional law changes, local law changes and even regulations change."); Christopher Berry Gray, ed., The Philosophy of Law: An Encyclopedia 127 (2012) (noting that "the common law changes and develops primarily as a consequence of judicial decisions"). As James Madison, writing as "Publius" in *The Federalist No. 14*, himself noted: "Is it not the glory of the people of America, that, whilst they have paid a decent regard to the opinions of former times and other nations, they have not suffered a blind veneration for antiquity, for custom, or for names, to overrule the suggestions of their own good sense, the knowledge of their own situation, and the lessons of their own experience?" The Federalist No. 14 (James Madison).

34. Rainer Nickel, Widening the Scope: Anti-Discrimination Law, Social Equality, and the Right to Equal Treatment, *in* Russell A. Miller & Peer Zumbansen, eds., Annual of German and European Law 358 (2004):

U.S. anti-discrimination law can be taken as a good example for a progressive awareness of the social reality of prejudice and its social costs. Historically, the United States was the avant-garde of an active anti-discrimination policy, with roots reaching back even to the nineteenth century—a history that also reflects the long shadow of slavery and the struggles to overcome the legacy of slavery, racism.

35. John A. Fliter, Prisoners' Rights: The Supreme Court and Evolving Standards of Decency 22 (2001) ("It is important to remember that as part of the Bill of the Rights, the Eighth

Amendment was originally directed against federal action alone.").

36. John F. Stinneford, *The Original Meaning of "Unusual": The Eighth Amendment as a Bar to Cruel Innovation*, 102 Nw. U. L. Rev. 1739 (2008) (quoting Patrick Henry, Speech to the Virginia Ratifying Convention for the United States Constitution (June 9, 1788), *in* 3 The Debates in the Several State Conventions, on the Adoption of the Federal Constitution, as Recommended by the General Convention at Philadelphia, in 1787, at 172 (Jonathan Elliot, ed.)).

37. Terry Johnson, Legal Rights 4 (2005) ("[T]he English Bill of Rights is unlike the American Bill of Rights, which limits the power of all branches of the national government—including the U.S. Congress.").

38. Ruth Hargove & Roberta Thyfault, "The Impact of, and Resistance to, the Use of Foreign law on Juvenile Punishment in the United States," *in* Kyriaki Topidi & Lauren Fielder, eds., Transnational Legal Processes and Human Rights 41 (2016).

39. Robert M. Bohm, DeathQuest: An Introduction to the Theory and Practice of Capital Punishment in the United States 11 (5th ed. 2017) ("In 1837, Tennessee became the first state to enact a discretionary death penalty statute for murder; Alabama did the same four years later, followed by Louisiana five years after that. All states before then employed mandatory death penalty statutes that required anyone convicted of a designated capital crime to be sentenced to death."); id. ("This change from mandatory to discretionary death penalty statutes, which introduced unfettered sentencing discretion into the capital-sentencing process, was considered at the time a great reform in the administration of capital punishment.").

40. Evan J. Mandery, Capital Punishment in America: A Balanced Examination 131 (2d ed. 2012):

The death penalty is arbitrary in many different ways: It is geographically arbitrary—defendants in states without the death penalty are treated differently from how defendants in states that do have the death penalty are treated. It is economically arbitrary—rich people have access to better representation. The death penalty is arbitrary by gender because the death penalty is rarely sought and imposed against women. It is arbitrary by race—people who kill whites are more likely to receive the death penalty than are those who murder blacks. Finally, the death penalty is arbitrary in the most basic sense—it is ultimately within the jury's discretion to impose the death penalty or not, and the jurors need not explain the basis of their decision.

41. *See, e.g.*, Samuel R. Gross & Robert Mauro, *Patterns of Death: An Analysis of Racial Disparities in Capital Sentencing and Homicide Victimization*, 37 Stan. L. Rev. 27, 45 (1984) ("[T]here is a considerable body of published research on racial patterns in capital punishment, and most of it indicates that racial factors have been influential in determining who has been sentenced to die and who has been executed."); *see generally* John D. Bessler, *The Inequality of America's Death Penalty: A Crossroads for Capital Punishment at the Intersection of the Eighth and Fourteenth Amendments*, 73 Wash. & Lee L. Rev. Online 487 (2016) (discussing the long history of racial discrimination in capital cases).

42. Michael John Garcia, *U.N. Convention Against Torture (CAT): Overview and Application to Interrogation Techniques*, Congressional Research Service 1 (Jan. 26, 2009), https://fas.org/sgp/crs/intel/RL32438.pdf; Thomas M. Antkowiak & Alejandra Gonza, The American Convention on Human Rights: Essential Rights 108 (2017).

43. People v. Anderson, 493 P.2d 880, 894 (Cal. 1972):

The cruelty of capital punishment lies not only in the execution itself and the pain incident thereto, but also in the dehumanizing effects of the lengthy imprisonment prior to execution during which the judicial and administrative procedures essential to due process of law are carried out. Penologists and medical experts agree that the process of carrying out a verdict of death is often so degrading and brutalizing to the human spirit as to constitute psychological torture.

44. Jon Yorke, ed., The Right to Life and the Value of Life: Orientations in Law, Politics and Ethics 271 (2016) (noting that Beccaria's argument against the death penalty "was that it was unnecessary for the protection of society").

45. John D. Bessler, The Birth of American Law: An Italian Philosopher and the American Revolution 43, 171–72, 246, 288, 378, 439 (2014) (references to punishments being "absolutely necessary"); id. at 38, 54, 131, 156, 185, 246, 265, 329, 343, 345, 422, 439 (references to the "absolute necessity" for punishments); id. at 9, 43–44, 57, 65–66, 104, 131, 148, 157, 167, 171, 209, 227, 236,

246, 265, 343, 345, 372, 384, 530 (references to the necessity for punishments).

46. Aaron Thomas, ed., Cesare Beccaria, *On Crimes and Punishments* and Other Writings 165 n.31 (Aaron Thomas & Jeremy Parzen, trans., 2008); *see also* Mary Gregor, ed. & trans., Immanuel Kant, The Metaphysics of Morals 108 (1996):

In opposition to this the Marchese Beccaria, moved by overly compassionate feelings of an affected humanity (*compassibilitas*), has put forward his assertion that any capital punishment is wrongful because it could not be contained in the original civil contract; for if it were, everyone in a people would have to have consented to lose his life in case he murdered someone else (in the people), whereas it is impossible for anyone to consent to this because no one can dispose of his own life. This is all sophistry and juristic trickery.

47. Bessler, The Birth of American Law, *supra* note 45, at 219–71.

48. Bessler, Cruel and Unusual, *supra* note 26, at 91 ("Bradford wrote that 'the further diffusion of knowledge and melioration of manners, may render capital punishments unnecessary in all cases.'").

49. Cyndi Banks, Punishment in America: A Reference Handbook 224–25 (2005); 1 David N. Camp, ed., The American Year-Book and National Register for 1869, at 62 (1869); 19 Harold C. Syrett, ed., The Papers of Alexander Hamilton 297 n.3 (1973).

50. American Bar Association, Section of Civil Rights and Social Justice, "Life After the Death Penalty: Implications for Retentionist States" (Aug. 14, 2017) [hereinafter "Life After the Death Penalty"], pp. 13–16, *available at* https://www.americanbar.org/content/dam/aba/administrative/crsj/Life-After-Death-Penalty_Transcript.authcheckdam.pdf.

51. *See* "Life After the Death Penalty," *supra* note 50, at 19:

What we found is that virtually every state that had a murder rate above the national average was a death-penalty state for most or all of the study period. The non-death-penalty states were clustered among the states with the lowest murder rates, and all but one of them had a murder rate below the national average. Death penalty states had 12 of the 16 highest murder rates and 21 of the highest 27. Non-death penalty states had 7 of the 11 lowest murder rates.

52. https://deathpenaltyinfo.org/deterrence-states-without-death-penalty-have-had-consistently-lower-murder-rates.

53. The prospect that the death penalty may actually produce more violence than it prevents has come to be known as the "brutalization effect." Larry J. Siegel & John L. Worrall, Essentials of Criminal Justice 234 (11th ed. 2018).

54. As reported in a mid-nineteenth century source, one Unitarian minister—Rev. Jas. F. Clarke—made this assessment:

The time is coming when it will be seen that it is not our duty to hang men, nor necessary to do so for our own security. And when that time comes, and the gallows shall be abolished, we shall look back upon it with the same horror with which we now regard the auto-da-fe, or the trial by torture; and our children will be astonished that such barbarities could have been so long tolerated in Christendom.

Argument of Edward Livingston, Against Capital Punishment 24 (1847); *see also* id. at 23 (quoting E. P. Hurlbut):

"The innocent and the insane have suffered on the gallows; and although this was not intended, yet the best men in society upheld the State in inflicting the punishment of death. It is unfortunate, said they, if any but the guilty suffer; but this punishment is necessary and rightful, and the State must be careful in determining the question of guilt. Now if it should turn out that this mode of punishment is neither necessary nor rightful, then the sooner a State abstains from the murder of its prisoners, and declares by the constitution that it will so abstain, the sooner will it approach the standard of rightful government."

55. Id. at 2. "Societies have," Livingston emphasized of capital punishment, "existed without it." Id. at 5. As Livingston continued:

In those societies, therefore, it was not necessary. Is there anything in the state of ours that makes it so? It has not, as far as I have observed, been even suggested. But, if not absolutely necessary, have its advocates even the poor pretext that it is convenient,—that the crimes for which it is reserved diminish under its operation, in a greater proportion than those which incur a different punishment? The reverse is the melancholy truth.

Id.

56. Franklin E. Zimring, The Contradictions of American Capital Punishment 17 (2003). There is a special stigma attached to wrongful executions, with Franklin Zimring noting that one of the explanations for why, is that while imprisonment "is regarded as a socially necessary form of punishment and control," "the additional deprivation imposed by execution is not regarded as clearly necessary." Id. at 156. As Zimring adds:

If the additional deprivation of execution as a punishment is regarded as possibly gratuitous, then the obvious remedy when the death sentence is wrongful is to cut back the degree of punishment to that which is strictly necessary, that is, to imprisonment. In this view, the special arrogance of executions is the embrace of an awesomely severe punishment that is not strictly necessary.

Id.

57. A 2012 report of the prestigious National Research Council of the National Academies, one based on a review of more than three decades of research, concluded that studies claiming a deterrent effort on murder rates from the death penalty were "fundamentally flawed." As that report observed:

The committee concludes that research to date on the effect of capital punishment on homicide is not informative about whether capital punishment decreases, increases, or has no effect on homicide rates. Therefore, the committee recommends that these studies not be used to inform deliberations requiring judgments about the effect of the death penalty on homicide. Consequently, claims that research demonstrates that capital punishment decreases or increases the homicide rate by a specified amount or has no effect on the homicide rate should not influence policy judgments about capital punishment.

"NRC: Death Penalty Effect Research 'Fundamentally Flawed,'" USA Today, Apr. 18, 2012 (citing Daniel S. Nagin & John V. Pepper, eds., National Research Council, Deterrence and the Death Penalty (2012), https://www.nap.edu/catalog/13363/deterrence-and-the-death-penalty).

58. A. Reis Monteiro, Ethics of Human Rights 274 (2014) ("[T]he death penalty, in addition to be[ing] an objectifying and irrevocable punishment, puts an end not only to the right to life, but to all rights.").

59. Hans Göran Franck, The Barbaric Punishment: Abolishing the Death Penalty 49 (William Schabas, ed. 2003):

The first decisive step towards the abolition of capital punishment was launched by ... Cesare Beccaria (1738–1794).... According to Beccaria, the state does not have the right to deprive an individual of his or her life, because this would breach the social contract. Furthermore, the death penalty is not necessary, since a sentence of life imprisonment has the same deterrent effect.

60. "Justice Stevens Says Death Penalty Unnecessary, Wasteful, and Creates Higher Risk of Error," Death Penalty Info Ctr., https://deathpenaltyinfo.org/node/6150.

61. *Compare* Peter Hodgkinson & William A. Schabas, eds., Capital Punishment: Strategies for Abolition 42 (2004) ("in 2002 the Council of Europe adopted yet another protocol—Protocol No. 13—to the European Convention, abolishing the death penalty in wartime") *with* Antoni Abat i Ninet, Constitutional Violence: Legitimacy, Democracy and Human Rights 123 (2012) (noting that the Second Optional Protocol to the International Covenant on Civil and Political Rights, aiming at the abolition of the death penalty, adopted by the U.N. General Assembly in 1989, provides for the abolition of the death penalty but allows states to retain the death penalty in time of war) *and* Minutes of Evidence Taken Before the Royal Commission on Capital Punishment 631 (1949):

(*Professor Montgomery*): I notice that in your memorandum you say "I am opposed to capital punishment in peace time in any form". Why do you limit your opposition to capital punishment to peace time?—I limit it to peace time because the conditions of war are so altogether abnormal.

62. United Nations Office on Drugs and Crime, Global Study on Homicide 2013: Trends, Contexts, Data, pp. 12, 32, 43; Roger Hood & Carolyn Hoyle, The Death Penalty: A Worldwide Perspective 405 (5th ed. 2015).

63. "To Define the Crime of Murder, Provided Penalty Therefor, and to Abolish the Punishment of Death," Speech of Gen. Newton Martin Curtis, of New York, in the House of Representatives, Thursday, June 9, 1892 (1892), p. 36.

64. The "grossly disproportionate" language has shown up in Canadian as well as American courts. Section 12 of the Canadian Charter of Rights and Freedoms, in language reminiscent of the Eighth

Amendment, provides: "Everyone has the right not to be subjected to any cruel and unusual treatment or punishment." In *R. v. Smith*, [1987] 1 S.C.R. 1045, which struck down a mandatory minimum sentence of seven year's imprisonment for a drug offense, the Supreme Court of Canada found that section 12 of the Charter "governs the quality of the punishment and is concerned with the effect that the punishment may have on the person on whom it is imposed." "The test for review under s. 12 of the *Charter*," Canada's highest court ruled, "is one of gross disproportionality because s. 12 is aimed at punishments more than merely excessive." As that court wrote:

The court in assessing whether a sentence is grossly disproportionate must consider the gravity of the offence, the personal characteristics of the offender, and the particular circumstances of the case to determine what range of sentences would have been appropriate to punish, rehabilitate, deter or protect society from this particular offender. The court must also measure the effect of the sentence, which is not limited to its quantum or duration but includes also its nature and the conditions under which it is applied. The determination of whether the punishment is necessary to achieve a valid penal purpose, whether it is founded on recognized sentencing principles and whether valid alternative punishments exist, are all guidelines, not determinative of themselves, to help assess whether a sentence is grossly disproportionate. Arbitrariness is a minimal factor in determining whether a punishment or treatment is cruel and unusual.

See also R. v. Nur, [2015] 1 SCR 773, 2015 SCC 15 (CanLII), ¶ 39:

This Court has set a high bar for what constitutes "cruel and unusual ... punishment" under s. 12 of the *Charter*. A sentence attacked on this ground must be grossly disproportionate to the punishment that is appropriate, having regard to the nature of the offence and the circumstances of the offender: *R. v. Smith*, 1987 CanLII 64 (SCC), [1987] 1 S.C.R. 1045, at p. 1073. Lamer J. (as he then was) explained at p. 1072 that the test of gross disproportionality "is aimed at punishments that are more than merely excessive". He added, "[w]e should be careful not to stigmatize every disproportionate or excessive sentence as being a constitutional violation". A prescribed sentence may be grossly disproportionate as applied to the offender before the court or because it would have a grossly disproportionate impact on others, rendering the law unconstitutional.

Compare R. v. Lloyd, [2016] 1 SCR 130, 2016 SCC 13 (CanLII) ¶ 24:

This Court has established a high bar for finding that a sentence represents a cruel and unusual punishment. To be "grossly disproportionate" a sentence must be more than merely excessive. It must be "so excessive as to outrage standards of decency" and "abhorrent or intolerable" to society: *Smith*, at p. 1072, citing *Miller v. The Queen*, 1976 CanLII 12 (SCC), [1977] 2 S.C.R. 680, at p. 688; *Morrisey*, at para. 26; *R. v. Ferguson*, 2008 SCC 6 (CanLII), [2008] 1 S.C.R. 96, at para. 14. The wider the range of conduct and circumstances captured by the mandatory minimum, the more likely it is that the mandatory minimum will apply to offenders for whom the sentence would be grossly disproportionate.

R. v. Boutilier, 2017 SCC 64 (CanLII) ¶ 98:

A law violates s. 12 if it mandates a sentence that is "grossly disproportionate to the sentence the conduct would otherwise merit under the sentencing provisions of the *Criminal Code*" (*R. v. Nur*, 2015 SCC 15 (CanLII), [2015] 1 S.C.R. 773, at para. 82). The appropriate sentence, for comparative purposes, is determined in light of the relevant sentencing principles and objectives set out in ss. 718 to 718.2 of the *Criminal Code* (*Nur*, at paras. 40–42). A mere distinction between the sentence imposed by the challenged provision and the appropriate sentence does not suffice to render the provision unconstitutional. The sentence imposed must be "disproportionate to the extent that Canadians 'would find the punishment abhorrent or intolerable'" in order to constitute cruel and unusual punishment (*R. v. Ferguson*, 2008 SCC 6 (CanLII), [2008] 1 S.C.R. 96, at para. 14, quoting *R. v. Wiles*, 2005 SCC 84 (CanLII), [2005] 3 S.C.R. 895, at para. 4). The law violates s. 12 if it imposes a grossly disproportionate sentence on the individual before the court or in reasonably foreseeable cases (*R. v. Lloyd*, 2016 SCC 13 (CanLII), [2016] 1 S.C.R. 130, at paras. 22–23).

65. Peter Gay, The Enlightenment: An Interpretation—The Science of Freedom 443 (1969).

66. Although incarceration is a traditional, long-standing punishment in the arsenal of justice, alternative sentencing options, such as electronic home monitoring with ankle bracelets, are also now available because of technological developments.

67. John D. Bessler, *The Abolitionist Movement Comes of Age: From Capital Punishment as a Lawful Sanction to a Peremptory, International Law Norm Barring Executions*, 79 Mont. L. Rev. 7 (2018); John D. Bessler, *What I Think About When I Think About the Death Penalty*, 62 St. Louis U. L.J. 781 (2018).

68. Cynthia Soohoo, "Human Rights, Solitary Confinement, and Youth Justice in the United States," *in* Austin Sarat, ed., Human Rights and Legal Judgments: The American Story 25, 28 (2017).

69. George Alexander Ross, Old Glory: The Story of Our Country's Flag 31 (1913) ("The Rattlesnake Flags were used perhaps more than others. Some showed the snake coiled, and bore the legend: 'Don't Tread on Me.'"); id. at 32 ("The earliest flag of the South was an ensign of blue with a silver crescent in the upper corner, and the word 'Liberty' written large across the field. This flag was designed by Colonel William Moultrie of South Carolina. On the 28th of June, 1776, it inspired the patriots to hold the fort of Charleston and drive the British out of the harbor.").

70. Douglas M. Rife, The Flag of the United States: A Brief History of the Star Spangled Banner 8 (1998).

71. Louis P. Masur, 1831: Year of Eclipse 160 (2001); *see also* Debra Hess, The Star-Spangled Banner 30 (2004) ("[I]t was not until 1931 that Congress decided to make the 'Star-Spangled Banner' the national anthem of the United States of America.").

INDEX

P